Ravenspur

Tickhill
＊

Louth ●

+ Lincoln

ostone ●

＊ Newark

Boston ●

Nottingham
＊

● Grantham

● Spalding   ● Lynn

Crowland

Walsingham ●
North Walsham ●
St. Benet of Hulme

Norwich

Yarmouth

cester ＊

Stamford ●

Peterborough

Ely

oventry
nilworth

Ramsey

● Mildenhall

Framlingham
＊

Newmarket ●

ck

Northampton

Cambridge ●

Bury St. Edmunds

＊ Bedford

Ipswich ●

● Deddington

Colchester

Oxford
＊

St. Albans

Abingdon

Berkhamsted
＊

Brentwood ●

＊ Wallingford

London
Westminster   Tilbury ●

rough
＊
Newbury

Reading

Windsor

Erith ●

Rochester

Canterbury

Reigate ＊

Maidstone ●
＊

Sandwich ●

rum

Dover
＊

Winchester

Romney ●

Southampton

Lewes   Winchelsea ●
Senlac ✕
Pevensey ＊   Hastings

urch

Po

D1020521

0   20

Miles

SET IN A SILVER SEA

By the same author

MACAULAY

THE NATIONAL CHARACTER

THE LETTERS AND SPEECHES OF CHARLES II (editor)

THE ENGLAND OF CHARLES II

THE AMERICAN IDEAL

The Story of England
MAKERS OF THE REALM B.C.–1272
THE AGE OF CHIVALRY 1272–1381
THE ELIZABETHAN DELIVERANCE
KING CHARLES II 1630–1685
RESTORATION ENGLAND 1660–1702
ENGLISH SAGA 1840–1940

Samuel Pepys
THE MAN IN THE MAKING 1633–1669
THE YEARS OF PERIL 1669–1683
THE SAVIOUR OF THE NAVY 1683–1689
PEPYS AND THE REVOLUTION

The Napoleonic Wars
THE YEARS OF ENDURANCE 1793–1802
YEARS OF VICTORY 1802–1812
THE AGE OF ELEGANCE 1812–1822
NELSON
THE GREAT DUKE

The Alanbrooke Diaries
THE TURN OF THE TIDE 1939–1943
TRIUMPH IN THE WEST 1943–1946

English Social History
THE MEDIEVAL FOUNDATION
PROTESTANT ISLAND

THE FIRE AND THE ROSE

THE LION AND THE UNICORN

JIMMY

JACKETS OF GREEN

A THOUSAND YEARS OF BRITISH MONARCHY

SPIRIT OF ENGLAND

Set in a Silver Sea

A History of Britain and the British People

Arthur Bryant

"Thank Him who isled us here, and roughly set
His Briton in blown seas and storming showers."
Tennyson

"This royal throne of kings, this scepter'd isle . . .
This fortress built by Nature for herself
Against infection and the hand of war . . .
This precious stone set in the silver sea . . .
This blessed plot, this earth, this realm, this England . . .
This land of such dear souls, this dear, dear land."
Shakespeare

WILLIAM MORROW AND COMPANY, INC.
New York

Library of Congress Cataloging in Publication Data

Bryant, Arthur, Sir, 1899–
Set in a silver sea.

Originally published: 1966.
Bibliography: p.
Includes indexes.
1. England—Civilization.   I. Title.
DA110.B89 1984   941   84-4661
ISBN 0-688-03932-4

Printed in the United States of America

First U.S. Edition

1 2 3 4 5 6 7 8 9 10

CONTENTS

List of Illustrations   vii

Introduction to the *History*   xi

HOW THEY BEGAN

Silent Vanished Races   1
The Coming of the English   15
The Faith   24
Alfred and the Danes   32
The Bones of Shire and State   49

HOW THEY EVOLVED

Norman Discipline   59
The Lawyer King   81
Bell, Book and Candle   93
The Holy Blissful Martyr   106
Magna Carta   123
Counsel, Consent and Parliament   139
Wild Wales   169
Scotland the Brave   189
The Grey Goose Feather   217
War's Nemesis   253
Peasants in Revolt   295
Dethronement of an Anointed King   333

HOW THEY LIVED

The Medieval Village   373
Travellers, Towns and Traders   391
Gothic Glory   411
Twilight of Holy Church   425

CONTENTS

A short list of the chief documented and other
works on which this book is based   443

Acknowledgements   447

Subject Index   448

Persons and Places Index   455

ILLUSTRATIONS

The Desborough Mirror   *British Museum*   between pages 22-23
Hadrian's Wall   *Edwin Smith*
Wells Cathedral, capital of peasant with toothache
British Tourist Authority

Great Coxwell, Tithe Barn   *H. F. Kersting*   facing page 134
Tithe Barn, Great Coxwell, interior
National Monuments Record
Caerphilly Castle   *British Tourist Authority*   facing page 135
Wells Cathedral Interior
National Monuments Record   facing page 166
Salisbury Cathedral, Chapter House
British Tourist Authority   facing page 167

Southwell Minster, capital
National Monuments Record   between pages 246-247
Salisbury Cathedral   *A. E Kersting*
Lincoln Cathedral   *British Tourist Authority*

York Minster, the nave   *A. E Kersting*   facing page 358
Westminster Hall   *A. E Kersting*   facing page 359
Beeleigh Abbey   *A. M. Dann*   facing page 390
King's College Chapel, Cambridge
A. E Kersting   facing page 391

To
TOMMY JOY

Introduction

'Dear Country, O how dearly dear
Ought thy remembrance and perpetual band
Be to thy foster child, that from thy hand
Did common breath and nouriture receive?
How brutish is it not to understand
How much to her we owe that all us gave?'

Spenser

'Our England is a garden, and such gardens are not made
By singing:– "Oh, how beautiful", and sitting in the shade,
While better men than we go out and start their working
lives
At grubbing weeds from gravel-paths with broken
dinner-knives . . .

Oh, Adam was a gardener, and God who made him sees
That half a proper gardener's work is done upon his knees,
So when your work is finished, you can wash your hands
and pray
For the Glory of the Garden that it may not pass away!
And the Glory of the Garden it shall never pass away!'

Kipling

A NATION which has forgotten its past, said Churchill, can have no future. At a time when we are confused and divided as to what ours should be, I have written *A History of Britain and the British People* to recall the meaning and greatness of our past.

When I was a boy every educated Briton had a rough general knowledge of the country's history. It may not have been a scholarly or sophisticated one, but at least it was one of which there was reason to feel proud. Whatever her faults Britain had conferred widening benefits on her people and on all who throughout the world enjoyed British citizenship or had shared in the peaceful expansion of her seaborne trade and libertarian ideals. And her history stimulated, in those who read or were taught it, a desire to serve their country and prove themselves worthy of her.

Today such popular awareness of the nation's history has largely been lost and more than one generation has grown up without being taught it. And the teaching of history for the academic minority who alone today study,it, though highly scientific and scholarly, has become so specialised that the great mass of the nation knows nothing of it. In a democratic age when the welfare and safety of society depend on the opinion of the many, the cumulative guidance of the past and its inherited corporate experience is almost totally lacking. For the instinctive wisdom of the ages is a truer guide than the conflicting opinions of individuals, however clever. 'We are afraid,' wrote Burke, 'to put man to live and trade on his own stock of reason, because we suspect that this stock in each man is small, and that individuals would do well to avail themselves of the general bank and capital of nations and of ages.' It is a bank and capital on which as a nation we have ceased to draw.

Though at no time has more history been written by highly trained and conscientious academic historians, researching and clarifying, for the benefit of fellow scholars, every detail of the past, little or nothing of it has contributed to an awareness of the broad sweep of the nation's past – and, therefore, present – in those on whom in a democracy national policy depends. And though there are several excellent modern composite histories of the country, each period contributed by an expert on it, such impersonal works, however skilfully edited, do not today fill the place once taken by widely-read general histories conceived and executed by a single mind – by a Hume, Lecky or Lingard, a J. R. Green or a Trevelyan.

This is due not only to the failure of those responsible for the nation's educational system to provide for the teaching of history in school, but also to a realisation in those who might otherwise read it that the basis of the history offered has been too narrow. For, if it is to reflect reality, history must record more than the doings of rulers, statesmen and politicians. Political history is history in one dimension only. It is a facet of corporate human existence, not human existence itself. Nor, as economic historians tend to suggest, is history only a record of prices, wages and monetary movements, profound though their effect on people's lives. Economic history, like political, is still only history in one dimension.

It is only when history presents a broad universal view of the past that it becomes a complete, and therefore true, vision of man's evolution in time:

> 'the nations,
> Their markets, tillage, courts of jurisdiction, marriages,
> Feasts and assemblies, navies, armies,
> Priests and sabbaths, trades and business, the voice of the bridegroom,
> Musical instruments, the light of candles,
> And the grinding of mills . . .'[1]

It is here that a growing interest in social history has added a new dimension to the study of the past. And in the last half-century a number of highly readable works of scholarship have appeared in which, by employing a technique first used by Macaulay in the famous third chapter of his unfinished *History of England*, social history has been blended with political to make a new kind of historical art. Such, in the hands of genius, were G. M. Trevelyan's *England in the Reign of Queen Anne*, Veronica Wedgwood's *The King's Peace* with its two sequels, and Professor Sir John Plumb's books on Hanoverian England, all attracting, because of their historical insight and brilliant writing, a wide readership. And though none of these covers more than a limited period, and no single historian's life is now long enough to distil and reduce to readable form all the immense, and often conflicting, volume of learning available to write it, 'the best is the enemy of the good', and what, above all, seems needed today is a complete social and political history of the country for readers of all ages, but particularly for the young.

Because so much of my life has been spent writing and helping to pioneer combined social and political history, a conviction has long grown on me that, were I to live long enough, the best use

[1] Thomas Traherne: *Serious and Pathetical Contemplation of the Mercies of God.*

I could make of my last years would be to try to write a complete history of Britain and her people. The idea that I might do so first came to me in 1950 when, after producing during my 'thirties four full-scale biographies and a social history of the later seventeenth century and, in my 'forties, three late eighteenth- and early nineteenth-century political and social histories of our wars against Revolutionary and Napoleonic France, and another on Victorian and Edwardian Britain, I decided to take a busman's holiday and write a short history of England for boys. But, on trying, I soon discovered that, outside these three special periods, I knew little of our history except what I had learnt at-school and university. And in order to answer the many questions I could not answer without further intensive study, I found myself embarking, not on a boy's history of England in one volume, but on an old boy's history in many.

As a result, I have been able to draw on seven closely written and carefully researched and documented period histories, ranging chronologically from the early and medieval *Makers of the Realm* and *Age of Chivalry* to the nineteenth century *Age of Elegance* and *English Saga*, which together constitute a multi-volume, though still incomplete, political and social history of the nation. Incorporating freely from these, as from my other historical books and biographies, I have spent a decade writing, repeatedly rewriting and revising, a shorter, simplified, yet complete and comprehensive *History of Britain and the British People*. Two successful cancer operations in my 78th year by a brilliant surgeon have added a bonus of additional time for this self-imposed task of re-teaching our history to those deprived of it.

In this I am following the steps of my old friend and master, G. M. Trevelyan, who in 1926 published his widely-read political *History of England* and, sixteen years later, a still more popular sequel, *English Social History 1340–1900*. Instead, however, of treating its political and social aspects in two separate volumes as he did, I have blended them; though, having to cover so vast a span of time in it, my publishers and I have abandoned our earlier plan of launching the whole *History* initially in a single volume.

Instead, it is being issued serially in three volumes of normal readable size.

It is, above all, for the young that I have written it in gratitude for the long working years granted me and in memory of the comrades of my youth who gave their lives for England in battle; and as an attempt, however inadequate, to repay the incalculable debt I owe my country for all she has taught and given me,

> 'Her sights and sounds; dreams happy as her day;
> And laughter, learnt of friends; and gentleness
> In hearts at peace, under an English heaven.'

For it is not intended solely for the educated minority who read scholarly history and for whom I have been writing it for more than half a century, but for the younger generations of a new classless society which has grown up in almost total ignorance of their country's history. Because of this I have refrained from cluttering the text with learned references and footnotes, or adding to its length with appendices, glossaries and other customary evidences of scholarship. Those who require proofs of its authenticity will find them at the end of the volume in a short list of the chief documented works, including my own, on which it is based.

For though in the *History*'s preparation, as in that of my larger and earlier volumes from which it is drawn, I was faced, like all historians, by the necessity defined in John Evelyn's sentence that 'it is not to be imagined what labour an historian (that would be exact) is condemned to; he must read all, good and bad, and remove a world of rubbish before he can lay the foundations', in the final form offered the reader I have relied solely on clarity and simplicity of writing to make the narrative, wherever possible, what Sir Philip Sidney called 'a tale to hold children from play and old men from the chimney corner'. And I have told the story, not as seen from our own age in retrospect, but as it seemed to those living at the time. For history is a record of the order in which events happen, that is of cause and effect. Everything which occurs in the world is a direct consequence of something which has occurred before. A historian's first duty is to be an exact, though

balanced, recorder of what actually happened. He must first recreate, and then interpret, the past; he cannot do the second until
he has done the first. The key to the writing and teaching of history
is to make the past seem as real as it was to those experiencing it.

*   *   *

Set in a Silver Sea, the first of my three volumes, covers all but the
most recent five hundred of our ten thousand years of history.
It ends with the building of the last great English medieval
churches at the close of the fifteenth century when voyages of discovery by Genoese and Portuguese navigators to the Americas and
golden East were opening new vistas of opportunity to the European nations of the Atlantic seaboard. It shows how the foundations of our nation were laid and how its people, descendants of
Britain's many invaders, were blended, under the impact and
teaching of Christianity, into the kingdoms of England and Scotland and the principality of Wales. It traces the creation and evolution of the laws, institutions, moral beliefs and attitudes which,
instinctively governing us from the past, still form the basis of our
continuing nationhood.

Like all our history it begins with the Atlantic flood which,
ten thousand years ago, by creating what today are the Straits of
Dover, cut Britain off from the European mainland and made it an
island. Almost completely covered then by dense forest, it was
gradually colonised in the course of thousands of years by a succession of, at first minute, groups of sea-borne invaders.

All of them were seafarers who, to reach Britain, had to navigate
stormy tidal waters, and who all, though constantly fighting one
another, somehow survived, the earlier sheltering from the more
powerful and better armed late-comers in the hilly and rainy west
and north or in pockets of inaccessible fenland or forest. A mixture of many races, in later centuries – after the growth of a
strong national polity had made armed invasion of the island no
longer practicable – Flemings, Dutch, Huguenots, Jews, Poles,
Asiatics, Africans continued the agelong process of infiltration and
racial amalgamation. All ultimately intermarried to produce a
nation of many strains, which may account for the paradox that

a people famed for stolid, patient, practical common-sense – a nation, as Napoleon said, of 'shopkeepers' – has produced more adventurers, explorers and poets than any other known to history.

The most important of all Britain's invaders were those who came armed only with a cross and the faith and courage that cross gave. From western Europe, where, during the dark centuries of barbaric invasion after Rome's fall, Benedictine monks and Roman bishops had kept alive the message and teaching of the obscure Nazarene who, six centuries earlier, had founded the Christian faith from the cross, and from missionary cells in Celtic Ireland and the western Scottish isles, a succession of heroic evangelists, taking their lives in their hands, converted a savage tribal people and their rulers to Christ's gentle creed of love and sacrifice, and to the revolutionary belief, inherent in Christianity, that every individual was a potential soul of equal value in the eyes of God. With those among whom they went, purseless and on foot, they left an image of the Good Shepherd giving his life for his sheep which was to run like a silver thread through the national tradition.

For the most formative part of Britain's long history was that in which the national consciousness of its rival and quarrelling peoples grew out of the Christian faith. History suggests that the normal political state of human society, as it evolved from the family and tribe, was either anarchy or despotism; either the kind of existence in which there is 'continual fear and danger of violent death', or an authority brutally imposed on the weak by the strong. Now out of Christ's teaching arose a higher option for mankind: the creation of law and order and personal freedom through the exercise of Christian love. The central tenet of Christ's teaching was that, through such love, Christians could create a heaven, not only beyond the grave, but in this world as well. The rock on which the Church on earth rested was that love and trust between Christians were capable of creating islands of mutual endeavour and happiness which, Christ taught, could mirror that greater and timeless happiness to be found through faith in the Heaven to come. 'The Kingdom of Heaven,' He said, 'is within you.'

On this belief our civilization was built. Such cumulative works of faith and love made islands of light in the great ocean of barbaric hatred, cruelty and darkness which had swept across western Europe with the disintegration of imperial Rome, itself a cruel and conquering tyranny. Christian civilization in Britain grew out of barbarism because those who preached Christ's gospel of love to its savage tribesmen established centres of example where it could be put into practice and be seen to operate. It was because where monks and missionaries made their settlements they lived and worked together in constructive amity that they were able to achieve advances in agriculture, in the arts of living and, above all, in social and political organisation impossible in societies torn by perpetual strife, fear and mutual destruction. Everything educative and enduring in medieval Britain was the legacy of the Christian Church and its creed of creative love.

For it was Christianity which taught barbarians to base their social relationships on something wider than tribe or kindred. In its quiet monasteries the Church revived the forgotten classical arts of writing and keeping records. It trained men who could show tribal rulers the means of governing peacefully and justly. It gave them clerics or 'clerks' to reduce their chaotic affairs to order, draft laws and reckon accounts and taxes. For the way of life the Church preached called for a law-abiding world – one in which men made and kept promises instead of perpetually resorting to force. 'The King's Peace' was a better basis for Christian relationships than violence and anarchy.

*   *   *

Among the many technical and scientific discoveries of our age, greater even than those of material power – for it may help to save us from the latter's consequences – has been the rediscovery by a succession of great twentieth-century British medievalists of the living reality of the Middle Ages. In a famous passage in his *Tudor History of England*, writing of the dawn of new horizons for western man opened by the maritime discoveries of the fifteenth century, the Victorian historian, J. A. Froude, contrasted the mental and imaginative gap between his nineteenth-century contemporaries and their medieval ancestors:

'The paths trodden by the footsteps of ages were broken up; old things were passing away, and the faith and the life of ten centuries were dissolving like a dream. Chivalry was dying; the abbey and the castle were soon to crumble into ruins; and all the forms, desires, beliefs, convictions of the old world were passing away, never to return. . . . And now it is all gone – like an insubstantial pageant faded; and between us and the old English there lies a gulf of mystery which the prose of the historian will never adequately bridge. They cannot come to us, and our imagination can but feebly penetrate to them. Only among the aisles of the cathedral, only as we gaze upon their silent figures sleeping on their tombs, some faint conceptions float before us of what these men were when they were alive; and perhaps in the sound of church bells, that peculiar creation of the medieval age, which falls upon the ear like the echo of a vanished world.'

Since Froude wrote historians have dispersed the mists and broken down the mental barriers which concealed from nineteenth-century minds the contribution of our medieval forbears to the institutions and, above all, beliefs and attitudes which still inform and govern our polity. What matters most in history is the continuity in the soul of man. For it is there that the values are formed which prevent the material chronicles of earth from remaining a mere tale

'Told by an idiot, full of sound and fury,
Signifying nothing.'

For all their remoteness from us, what we call the Middle Ages have power to strike a chord in minds not entirely obsessed by the material and ephemeral. Most of the beliefs which men then held have long been abandoned or forgotten. Yet some remain, a towering testimony to the strength and permanence of the greatest of all their beliefs, their intense and abiding sense of the grandeur and immutability of God. To this day the vast cathedrals made with their puny tools and child's machinery tower above the cities of modern Britain; there is nothing in twentieth-century Salisbury which compares with the tower and spire that Richard of Farleigh built in the time of the Black Death or with the choir and nave his predecessors raised a century earlier. That is why, named *Set in a*

Silver Sea after the silvery-grey waters immediately surrounding their remote northern isle, my first volume depicts on its cover a stormy and rocky coast-line and, rising out of the heart of the distant and shadowy land beyond, the soaring spire of Salisbury cathedral – symbol of their Christian faith.

*   *   *

After the Norman conquest England acquired, under its new French-speaking rulers, the framework in which a national civilization could develop. About the same time, or a little earlier, Britain's barren northern and Caledonian moorlands became the kingdom of Scotland. During the next three hundred years, building on their realm's Christian peace, a dynasty of strong Norman and Angevin kings implanted in English minds the habit of feeling and acting together in national matters. Making the hereditary leaders of the country's formerly separatist provinces a responsible part of central royal government, they established a common law for the whole country and made respect for law a continuing English characteristic. In those germinating centuries between 1066 and the dethronement of Richard II in 1399 the essentials of our national society took permanent shape – the Church, Monarchy, the Common Law, the beginnings of Parliament and of that libertarian system which our forbears called Counsel and Consent and which was fashioned, evolved and fought for long before the later seventeenth-century constitutional struggles between Crown and Parliament, so much more familiar to Victorian and Edwardian historians and readers.

With its combination of political and social history, *Set in a Silver Sea* ends politically on the threshold of the fifteenth century with the dethronement of Richard II who tried, so disastrously for himself, to rule without counsel and consent. Socially it continues in four further chapters on how people lived – 'The Medieval Village', 'Travellers, Towns and Traders', 'Gothic Glory', and 'Twilight of Holy Church' – until the penultimate decade of the century when a Welsh and Tudor prince of Lancastrian descent assumed the throne left vacant by the death in battle of England's last Plantagenet king. Coming only a few years before the discovery

of America and the sea-route to the Orient, and on the eve of the
Reformation, it marked the first step in a free and voluntary union
with England of the two indomitable little neighbour nations which
had long fought against her and, by their challenge, helped to make
her, just as England's had been the challenge which had helped
to make them. A century later the process was to be completed by
the union of all three under a Scottish crown in the proud name of
Great Britain.

*   *   *

Their union is the subject of my second volume, *Freedom's Own
Island*, to be published in the early autumn of next year and
followed a year later by my third and final volume, *The Search For
Justice. Freedom's Own Island*, or *The British Ocean Expansion*,
describes how a small and hitherto insular people, uniting under
a common crown and reformed religion based on the reading of
the translated Bible, traded, colonised and spread their love and
practice of freedom across every ocean in the course of what, in
his noble *English Reformation*, Professor A. G. Dickens calls 'those
three great centuries during which Britain placed her stamp upon
world history'. Beginning with Chaucer's mirroring in his
Canterbury Tales the emergence of the English individual from
the anonymity of the feudal and ecclesiastical past, and including
the islanders' every decisive victory from the defeat of the Armada
to Trafalgar and from Agincourt to Waterloo, it comprises the
English and Scottish Reformations, the age of Elizabeth, the
Stuarts' quarrel with Parliament and the Civil War, the Restoration, the Revolution of 1688, the Hanoverian Settlement, the loss
of the American colonies, and the great achievements in commerce,
invention, science, literature, art and architecture of the English
and Scottish eighteenth century.

Yet the main theme of *Freedom's Own Island* remains the
maritime and colonial expansion of a united British people,
transforming what, at the start of Elizabeth's reign, had been a
small divided North Sea island on the outer fringe of European
Christendom into the greatest global empire the world had known.
Lying off the western shores of the Eastern Hemisphere and athwart

SET IN A SILVER SEA

the sea channels between northern Europe and the Atlantic, Britain's geographical potential for strategy and commerce were unique. It is epitomised by Drake's three minute ships – after their crews' apocalyptic experience on the barren gallow-haunted shores of what today is southernmost Argentine – battling their way through the Magellan Straits into the forbidden Pacific, one to sink with all hands in its terrifying storms, one to return to England defeated, her mission unaccomplished, and the third, re-christened the *Golden Hind*, to circumnavigate the globe and bring home inconceivable treasure and glory. And the title and theme of my third volume, carrying our national story from the triumphant aftermath in 1815 of Nelson's victories at sea and Wellington's on land, to the present day, is of that recurrent search for justice which has periodically haunted the English, and British, mind. For the opportunities for almost boundless wealth offered by the freedom of the world's trading oceans ensured by the long nineteenth-century Pax Britannica, and eagerly seized upon by those with the initiative and enterprise to exploit the dazzling mechanical inventions of the Industrial Revolution, brought about alternating contrasts and conflicts between the unprecedented prosperity of its Victorian and Edwardian beneficiaries and the social exploitation, degradation and impoverishment of its less fortunate participants or victims, making two Englands where before there had been – or seemed to be – only one. Twice in the present century re-made one by an aggressor's threat to human freedom and to Britain's very existence, the conflict at her heart still remains to be resolved, as perhaps only a fuller understanding by her people of their own past can enable them to do.

*   *   *

Every generation needs its popular history written in a way it can understand. The great classic historians of the eighteenth and nineteenth centuries wrote the history of England for their time. J. R. Green wrote it for our great grandfathers', and G. M. Trevelyan for our fathers'. Trying to write it for mine, I have presented it in a new and different form. For my *History* contains fewer purely political events and Acts of Parliament, but dwells longer on certain deeds and words which have stirred the hearts of the English and British and awoken their imagination. For history, as a modern poet has written,

> 'is a pattern
> of timeless moments.'

Paulinus and Aidan preaching to the Northumbrians; the Saxon thanes dying to the last man at Maldon and the house-carls in the stricken ring at Senlac; Becket towering above his murderers in the darkened cathedral, and the jingling Canterbury pilgrims riding through the Kentish fields 'the holy blissful martyr for to seek'; Robin Hood in the greenwood and the 'grey goose feather' falling like hail at Crécy and Agincourt; the staplers with their wool-packs, and the church towers among the limestone wolds and dales: such were the stuff out of which England's early banner in time was woven. So, in the age of British global expansion, were the circumnavigatory voyages of Drake, Anson and Cook, the missionary journeys of Wesley and the humanitarian crusades of Howard and Wilberforce; and, in the nineteenth century, the fight for social justice of a Shaftesbury and Florence Nightingale, a General Booth and a Keir Hardie.

I have written for both young and old, for those who know a little of the British past and for those who know scarcely anything at all. My aim has been to set down in a small compass all the essential things a child or adult should know who wants to understand our history. And to do so in a book which can be read at school or by the fireside, on a journey or in bed, and leave the reader with a clearer picture of how our institutions, beliefs and ideals came to be what they are.

The most important element in our history has been the continuity of the Christian tradition. Through it Britain developed a polity in which the sanctity of the individual counted for more than that of central authority, and in which power, instead of being concentrated in a few hands, was distributed in those of many. The value set by her people on the freedom of the individual, on justice and fair play, on mercy and tenderness towards the weak, their dislike of lawless violence and their capacity to tolerate, forget and forgive, have been, for all their many past mistakes and faults, and still are, very real factors in their own and mankind's evolution. 'By this sacredness of individuals,' wrote Emerson, 'the English have in seven hundred years evolved the principles of freedom.' From Philip Sidney passing the cup to the dying soldier to Captain Oates walking into the blizzard to save his friends, from Richard Coeur-de-Lion forgiving the archer who shot him to the men of the Forty-third standing motionless on the deck of the sinking *Birkenhead* while the women and children were lowered in the boats, the common denominator of the nation's idealism has remained the same. It was expressed in the fourteenth-century *Piers Plowman*, in the seventeenth-century *A Pilgrim's Progress* and in the nineteenth-century *A Christmas Carol*. Langland, Bunyan and Dickens all spoke with the same voice. Whenever Britain has been false to that voice she has been false to herself. Her people, Disraeli said, have not committed fewer blunders than others but, being free to criticise their rulers according to individual conscience, have shown themselves more sensible of their errors. In the end, history shows, it has usually been they themselves who have made amends for their injuries to others and reformed the abuses they have perpetrated. 'We must choose our friends for the future,' declared General Smuts in 1940: 'I choose the people under whom we suffered forty to fifty years ago, but who, when we were at their mercy, treated us as a Christian people.'

1984   Arthur Bryant

HOW THEY BEGAN

CHAPTER ONE

Silent Vanished Races

'Grey recumbent tombs of the dead in desert places,
Standing stones on the vacant wine-red moor,
Hills of sheep, and the howes of the silent vanished races,
And winds austere and pure.'

R. L. Stevenson

THE STORY OF BRITAIN – of an island alchemy which has changed human history – began ten thousand years ago when the Atlantic broke through an isthmus joining an outlying peninsula to the world's largest land space. To that flood of salt water which created the Dover strait and the British isle has been due the destiny of England, the kingdom which grew up in the island's largest and most fertile region, and of the two smaller rival nations, Scotland and Wales, which, occupying its more mountainous and remote parts, ultimately merged with it while retaining their own strong national identities and characteristics. The history of an adjacent island, Ireland, though geographically part of the British Isles and long politically – and still partially – associated with the United Kingdom, has followed a different course.

The rocks which form the geological bones of Britain belong, not to the European mainland, but to a vanished continent embracing North America and the Atlantic and, submerged under the ocean, called by archaeologists Atlantis. The British island's western mountains were once the eastern peaks of the poets' drowned land of Lyonnesse. For 'Britannia' was first formed millions of years ago in the Atlantic bed. It arose, as the song has it, 'at Heaven's command from out the azure main'.

Few, if any, of Britain's early inhabitants can have been living here when it was cut off from Europe. At that time it was almost completely covered by dense forest, mostly of gloomy conifers grown up since the last Ice Age but, as a result of the milder oceanic winters since the island's separation from the continent, gradually giving place in the south to the green of deciduous oak, elm, ash, hazel, lime and alder. Had we been able to look down on the island we should have seen that the forests, like the jungles of the East today, were swarming with game: wild boar and oxen, elk and deer and, in the hills, wolves, lynx and bears, eagles and ravens. And, if we had looked closely, here and there, sleeping like beasts on the earthen floor of caves and in huts and wind-breaks made of sods and branches, we might have caught an occasional glimpse of a family group of upright, two-legged creatures, with half-naked, skin-clad bodies, living on roots, berries, eggs and shell-fish and by trapping and slaying wild animals with flint-tipped spears and harpoons. Such men, like the beasts, lived for the hour, their one end today's meal, their unsleeping instinct survival, each generation repeating the pattern of that before. There was no progress, for there was no change.

Yet change was on the way: change of immense significance. It was not those who inhabited Britain before it became an island – aborigines sleeping like beasts in caves and pits among the rocks of the Cheddar Gorge or Gower peninsula – who were to set the course of its history. It was adventurers from distant and more civilized lands who, refusing to be daunted by the waves and tides of the encircling seas, had learnt how to navigate them and, putting out across a stormy ocean, to seek new homes in a rain-swept northern island. For if we had turned from the spectacle of a dark forest-clad Britain – glimpsed through Atlantic rain-cloud and mist – and looked southwards and eastwards beyond the Alps and into the Mediterranean sunlight, we should have seen, in bright islands and peninsulas at the eastern end of that inland ocean, human communities living very different lives from those of the sparse animal-like families dotted about the downs and rocks of misty Britain. And far beyond, in the green Nile valley, in Mesopotamia and on the Persian uplands and, still further away, in India and China, men grouped, not merely in families, but in tribes, cities and even nations. For here, in the sunshine, man had made the greatest step in his history. He had mastered the arts of digging, tilling and planting the soil – of sowing in winter and reaping in summer. Assured of tomorrow's food, he had made a home to hand down to his children and had begun to think beyond the span of his own brief life, to make laws for societies outlasting individuals, and to raise memorials to the dead and altars to the gods whom he imagined controlled his existence. He had learnt, too, to write and keep records. History had begun.

For the real ancestors of the British people were invaders: seamen and colonists, pioneer bearers of new beliefs and techniques. The earliest of all were traders in tin and copper from the Mediterranean, adventuring into the Atlantic through the Pillars of Hercules – today the Straits of Gibraltar. Others were tribal families moving up the eastern coasts of Spain and those of south-western France, in search of fresh soil and hunting grounds. Some of these, striking across the Soundings, made landfalls in Cornwall, Pembrokeshire, Anglesey, Ireland and the islands to the west of Scotland. Others, crossing Europe by a more northerly route, entered Britain across the Dover strait. Such pioneers brought with them a knowledge of agriculture; of grain growing and domestic animals, of the hoe, spade and grinding-stone; of weaving clothes and fashioning pots of clay. They brought, too, another art: that of making boats and navigating.

The settlements of these Iberian and Mediterranean colonisers – little, dark men grouped around Britain's western seas – were at first few and far between. Their primitive mattocks and hoes allowed them to break only the lightest soils: those on the hilltops out of reach of the all-pervading forest, on the drier gravel-terraces above the rivers, and on rocky shores and islands along the coast. Yet during the first five hundred years of their occupation – a period as long as that which divides us from the Wars of the Roses – the appearance of the country had already begun to change. Settlements of beehive-shaped huts, covered with branches and surrounded by little fields, hewn or burnt out of the forests, appeared on higher ground; earthwork entrenchments were dug

3

along the chalk and limestone hills to protect the seasonal round-up of flocks and cattle; tangled downland bushes and scrub were nibbled away by generations of sheep, goats and swine. And in chalk galleries beneath the ground – like those of Grimes' Graves at Brandon – men quarried with antler-picks for flint to grind into axes and spear-heads. The foundations of settled life, tillage and pasturage were being laid.

Great stones or 'dolmens' and mysterious hollow mounds and barrows with tunnelled chambers appeared, too, on the western coasts and on the high, inhabited uplands: tribal tombs, where the spirits of the dead were believed to await, like seeds, a day of resurrection and rebirth. For these primitive farmers, having raised themselves above animal existence and learnt to contemplate past and future, were much concerned with the mystery of life and death. Like the river valley folk of the East, they worshipped the dead and the powers of fertility which recreated life in each generation and spring. To propitiate them and secure their help for the tribe, their priests or magic men offered up human and animal sacrifices in sacred places. And when their leaders died, hopeful of rebirth, they were buried with their belongings around them.

* * *

The first invaders were followed by others. There was nothing to stop them but the waves and tides. Some continued to come from the south in search of Ireland's gold and of the tin and copper which the wandering smiths of that land and Cornwall were learning to smelt into a hard durable alloy called bronze. Others came from the east across the shallow straits and North Sea. Among them were men of a fairer, stronger race, moving from eastern Europe through dense forests and the plains of the Low Countries. These Beaker Folk, as archaeologists call them from their buried drinking-vessels, were nomads from the steppes of western Asia who had learnt a new technique of living – breeding and pasturing flocks which they drove from one grazing-ground to another. They had mastered, too, another technique, that of war, which they waged with bows and arrows and sharp axes, first of polished stone

4

and later of bronze. These lordly shepherds had some affinity with the nomadic warrior peoples who overran the ancient city civilizations of the Middle East: the Semitic tribes who founded Babylon, and the shepherd kings who ruled Egypt in the days of Joseph and his brethren. Toughened by their wandering and possessing stronger weapons through their bronze-smiths' skill in metalwork, they were able to impose their will on their lighter-armed, smaller predecessors. They did not annihilate them – for there was still plenty of room for all, even in a little island covered by forest and marsh. But they made them work for them. And they bred from their womenfolk. After a time intermarriage brought a blending of the types; in their burial grounds the bones of the races are mingled.

These newcomers were also concerned with the causes of life and with what happened after death. But, like their fellow pastoralists in the East, they worshipped, not the patient cultivator's earth-mother, but the sun which, as they watched their flocks on the heights, they conceived to be the source of life. At the axis of their radiating sheep-tracks along the bare chalk-downs of the south-west, they and their slaves laboriously dragged and erected huge stones in mysterious clusters, where they sacrificed men and beasts to their flaming god. The stone circles at Avebury and Stonehenge are among the greatest monuments of early man; they seem to have enshrined the religious beliefs and ritual both of the new Beaker and the old Iberian folk.

The men who brought these vast rocks – some, like the blue Pembrokeshire stones of Stonehenge, from hundreds of miles away – and placed them in elaborate patterns based on the movements of the sun and stars must have learnt much, including the practice of subordination to authority. They created something which has lasted for more than thirty centuries and may still stand on the Wiltshire uplands when we and our works are forgotten.

For more than a thousand years the men of the Bronze Age dominated southern Britain. The earthen ditch in the chalk or oolite, the lonely dewpond on the height, the hill-turf nibbled close and enriched by countless generations of sheep are their legacy. Theirs was a society built on the flocks which gave them

5

food and raiment. Their priests tended the sun-temples, their craftsmen made vessels and weapons of bronze from the tin and copper mines of the south-west, their princes wore splendid helmets and rings and bracelets of gold brought by Irish smiths from Wicklow streams. Their traders, travelling the green hill-roads – Icknield Way, Whiteway, Ridgeway – which linked their priestly capital on Salisbury Plain with the uplands of the east and south-west, carried from earthwork fort to fort the bronze weapons, tools and ornaments that were their wealth. Others, more daring, trafficked tin and copper across the Channel or with Carthaginian merchants from North Africa. Irish gold objects of this period have been found as far away as Denmark and the Mediterranean and Aegean cities, where this remote, half-fabulous country at the world's end was known as the Tin Islands.

*   *   *

The Bronze Age men had their hour, giving place in the fullness of time to others. New races were on the march, moving westwards from the great heartland of the human family on the Asian plains. It is doubtful if at any time during the two thousand years which followed the first Neolithic colonisation of Britain such infiltration ever ceased. There was no central government and, save in a few settled places along the coast, no one to oppose a landing. The numbers involved in each invasion must have been very small, for boats were few and minute.

Most of the invaders brought to the island something new, in husbandry, craftsmanship or ways of living. The most important of all was a language which had originated in western Asia and spread, with the movements of the nomadic peoples who spoke it, into India, Persia, the Aegean, Italy and most parts of western Europe. From the basic sounds of this so-called Aryan speech – 'outlines . . . drawn only in sound, in the air, as elusive almost as the call of birds'[1] – are derived certain words, used with variations by successive invaders, which still constitute the foundation of our language and are to be found, in not dissimilar forms, in other countries colonised by tribes of Aryan stock. Among these are

[1] Jacquetta Hawkes, *A Land*, p. 174.

father, mother, daughter, sister, brother, son and *widow*, the first ten numerals, and some of the more important parts of the body, like *knee, foot* and *tooth.* So are *night, wind* and *star,* and the names of domestic animals, *cow, ox, steer* – with their plurality *herd – hound, goat, sow* and *goose, ewe* and *wether* and their product, *wool.* The words *wheel, axle* and *yoke* show the nomadic character of these Aryan ancestors; our modern *wain* or *wagon* is derived from another of their basic sounds. Other words, whose derivations are not to be found in the speech of the Asiatic descendants of the race but are known to its European descendants – *beech, elm* and *hazel, throstle, finch* and *starling* – must have been added in the centuries when the latter were dwelling, in the course of their westward trek, among the forests of central Europe. Similar words were added, too, before the western branch split into Greek, Latin, Celt and Teuton, revealing the substitution of agriculture for nomadic life – *corn* and *ear, furrow, bean* and *meal.*

It was between 1000 BC and 500 BC when an Aryan-speaking race, the Celts or Gaels, first appeared in Britain. They were a tall, blue-eyed, flame-haired folk who had crossed Europe from the east and settled in the country which is now called France and which took their name of Gaul. For as long a time as that which divides us from the Crusades, Celts were moving into Britain and Ireland, first in small bands and families and later in tribal armies, until they had become the dominant racial strain in both islands. The earlier peoples survived, but were mostly driven into the western moors and hills. They figure in Celtic legends as the faeries or little people – the Tylwyth teg – elusive, mysterious and dangerous, who sometimes stole their neighbours' children or provided a bride, dark, shy and inscrutable, for some giant, clumsy, good-humoured Celtic farmer. In such tales a recurrent feature is their dread of iron – the metal whose use the Celtic smiths introduced from the steppes and which, forged into swords and chariots, gave the latter's warriors their long ascendancy. Smelted in charcoal furnaces in the demon-haunted and till now uninhabited lowland forests, it was made also into rotary-lathes to make wheels, and into ploughs which, drawn by oxen, could break virgin soil too stiff for the hand hoes and small wooden ploughs of the past. This brought

7

about a gradual increase in population which, it is estimated, rose during the Celtic occupation to around a quarter of a million – less than a two-hundredth part of its present size. These iron-users were probably the first of Britain's invaders to create permanent fields and villages, mostly on the greensands and light clays of the south-east and south-west. At their zenith they may have occupied a sixth of the country. The rest of it, including the thick forest clays of the Midlands, remained uninhabited.

The island still had no unity; it had not even a name. To visualise it we must think of it as divided into loosely defined and warring tribal areas, rather like South Africa in the days of the Zulu and Kaffir wars. In the south-east were the latest comers, the warlike Belgae, whose territory stretched as far west as Salisbury Plain and the Dorset coast, with their fine blacksmiths and iron chariots and plough-coulters. Their name survives only on the far side of the Channel in the country from which they came, though one of their tribes, the Cantii, gave theirs to Kent and Canterbury. Another tribe, whose name has endured on the continent, were the Parisii – a warlike people from the Seine and Marne valleys who, landing in the Humber, conquered the plain between what is now Yorkshire and Lincolnshire. Others, like the Brigantes of the Pennine dales and the Iceni of Norfolk, dispersed by later invasions, have left little memorial of their sojourn. But in the south-west, where Celtic and pre-Celtic stock has always been predominant, the Dumnonii and the Durotriges have transmitted their names to the Devonians and men of Dorset. And for no very clear reason one group of invaders – the Prythons or Brythons – later gave their name to the whole island.

The hereditary chieftains of these tribes seem to have had a love of beautiful things. They employed craftsmen whose graceful designs surpassed anything yet seen in the barbaric West. When they died their treasures were buried with them – bronze armour and helmets, embossed shields decorated with vivid enamels, like the one found in the Thames at Battersea, golden torques, bracelets and brooches with which to fasten their tartan plaids; amber cups and hand-mirrors engraved with exquisite circular designs, like the Birdlip mirror in the Gloucester Museum. Vanity was a

8

characteristic of the Celts: a Greek traveller of the time describes them as smearing their fair hair with chalk wash to make it still brighter and then drawing it tightly back from the foreheads till they looked like hobgoblins. 'Their nobles let their moustaches grow so long that they hide their mouths and, when they eat, get entangled in their food. . . . They use amazing colours, brightly dyed shirts with flowing patterns, and trousers called breeches. . . . Their appearance is amazing, with voices deep sounding and very harsh.' They were boastful, threatening and braggart, he added, but their intellects were keen, and they were quick to acquire knowledge. 'When they have killed their foes, they cut off their heads. . . . They nail them up on their walls as trophies and preserve those of their chief enemies in boxes.'

These head-hunting tribesmen cannot have been comfortable neighbours. At Salmonsby in Gloucestershire they were still eating their womenfolk about two thousand years ago. Their religion reeked of blood, and travellers from the civilized South, whose own ideas about sacrifice were far from squeamish, brought back horrifying tales of ritual massacres in dark sacred groves by their magicians or druids. And they were incorrigible fighters. They crowned Britain's hilltops, not with burial-barrows and sun-temples, but with vast earthwork castles with concentric ditches and ramparts, like Mai Dun or Maiden Castle in Dorset, Chanctonbury Ring in Sussex, Almondbury in Yorkshire and the great Dun of Downpatrick in Ireland. In the ancient Celtic ballads of Ireland, Wales and the Scottish Highlands – the parts of Britain least affected by later invasions – pride of battle takes precedence over every other emotion. For centuries these fierce, passionate, braggart, though sometimes touchingly noble, tribesmen constantly raided one another's lands for heads, slaves and cattle, but observed the rules and rites of their savage code of honour. The wars of the early Greeks, fought in the Aegean sunlight and sung by Homer, were matched by wars fought under the misty skies and dripping hills of western Britain by men of the same remote ancestry. In Celtic Ireland, as well as in Wales and the Scottish Highlands, this 'heroic' age continued long after it had ceased in Greece and the British lowlands. The flashing swords and flails of the Fianna, and

Finn Mac Cool and Gull Mac Morna setting targe to targe, were the counterparts of 'godlike Achilles and his squire Automedon and Alkimas in battle upgrown'. And the story of how Grainne, daughter of King Cormac, eloped with Diarmuid, echoes the tale of Helen of Troy.

*   *   *

By now a conqueror of a different kind was approaching Britain. With their breast-plated, helmeted, disciplined infantry and their fleets of triple-banked oar-propelled warships, the Romans were the greatest conquerors the world had known. They were a people of high courage and patriotism with an instinctive feeling for order, led by aristocrats of a strong practical bent. Just over two thousand years ago, having overrun Italy and most of the countries fringing the western Mediterranean, they crossed the Alps and invaded Gaul. In three years their great general, Julius Caesar, conquering by dividing, subdued the warlike Celtic tribes of that land and carried the Roman rule to the Channel. Behind his legions came the metalled military roads, the stone-walled cities, the laws and administration which the Romans took with them wherever they went.

Though Caesar made two brief punitive and exploratory expeditions from Gaul to Britain, for nearly another century it remained outside the great union of races welded together by Roman discipline and good sense – a misty, unexplored forest land of squabbling tribesmen on the world's fringe. But in AD 43 the interference with trade caused by tribal war provoked the Roman imperial authorities into a full-scale invasion, followed by annexation. Thereafter for three and a half centuries the southern half of Britain, comprising virtually the whole of what today is England, was a Roman province. It was Rome's policy to tame the native tribal chieftains by making them citizens; the city was the instrument by which, having conquered barbarians, she shaped them to her ends. They were encouraged to transform the old tribal camps and cattle-kraals into towns on the universal Roman model; to vie with one another in raising temples, colonnades, pillars and arches, and to build themselves houses and gardens where, garbed like

Roman patricians, they could live out their lives in luxury under the eyes of authority. Their sons were educated in Roman schools and taught Latin, and their tribal warriors conscripted into the legions or auxiliary regiments and turned into Roman soldiers.

Behind the legions rose the cities on which Roman civilization depended: rustic miniatures of Rome, even in this remote frontier land, with neat chess-board-pattern streets, forums and temples, porticoed town-halls and amphitheatres, public baths, aqueducts and drains. The capital of the Catuvellauni became *Verulamium*, or, in modern English, St Albans; that of the Atrebates of the Thames valley *Calleva Atrebatum* or Silchester; that of the Iceni *Venta Icenorum* or Caistor-next-Norwich; that of the Dumnonii *Isca Dumnoniorum* or Exeter. Even the wild Silures of Wales built *Venta Silures* or Caerwent and boasted of the little garrison-town of Caerleon with its golden roofs and towers. In these minute but elegant tribal capitals traders built shops, and tribesmen brought their crops and cattle to market and assembled at sacred seasons to sacrifice to their local gods. Yet though Rome, true to her universal policy, encouraged the worship of the older native deities, she subordinated it, as she had done that of her own gods, to that of the all-embracing State. For its head, the distant Emperor, sacrifice and tribute were asked of all. It was to express and enforce that authority that the cities arose. More even than markets and dwelling places, they were temples to Caesar and the imperial bureaucracy.

At the height of the Roman occupation there were more than fifty cities in southern Britain. Most of them were very small by continental standards, with between two and five thousand inhabitants. The largest, Londinium, the hub of the country's road and trading system, may have had four or five times as many.[1] Though all these cities later perished, at Bath or Aquae Sulis, the fashionable watering-place in the southern Cotswolds, the old Roman bath and its tutelary god can still be seen, much as they were when the rich provincials of eighteen centuries ago flocked there for health and amusement. Beyond the tribal capitals and

[1] It covered about 350 acres along the north bank of the Thames. The site of its basilica or town hall is now occupied by Leadenhall Market.

close to the untamed northern and western moors lay the garrison cities of York, Chester, Uriconium and Caerleon, and in their rear Lincoln, Colchester and Gloucester – the *coloniae* where soldiers' families were settled on retirement with land and houses to breed more soldiers. There were also the Channel ports of Richborough, Portchester and Chichester, and naval Dover with its lighthouse or *pharos*, guarding the island's communications with the Mediterranean empire of which it was the farthest province.

Linking the towns and camps ran straight Roman roads, paved and cambered on stone causeways, with milestones marking the distances to the imperial capital on the Tiber. Along them passed, not only the marching legionaries who were the guardians of all this order and prosperity, but the native corn, minerals, slaves and hunting-dogs which were exchanged for jewels, statues, wine and oil in jars, perfumes, marbles, mosaics, glass and pottery from the continent. Britain in those years was called the granary of the north. Though the oak forests of the Midland clays still remained untouched and uninhabited, her population, as a result of agricultural improvements, seems to have risen to more than half a million. The chief grain exporters were the Celtic-Roman landowners, living in villas or country houses on sheltered sunny slopes in the southern half of the island. Here, amid mosaics and tessellated pavements, glazed windows, baths and central heating, statues and terraces, they aped the life of the Mediterranean and tried to ignore the northern mists and forests around them. Drawing their culture from a wider civilization, these aristocrats, with their stately Roman manners and Latin speech, introduced into Britain the poultry and geese of her farmyards, the pheasants of her woods, the pears, cherries, figs and mulberries that, planted in their gardens, survived when their gardens and civilization were no more. They worked their great farms with slave labour which they housed in barracks at their gates.

But there was a flaw in the Roman political system. Everything was centralised in the State's officials, yet the succession to the supreme office of all was uncertain. Again and again the Emperor's death was followed by a scramble for power. Sometimes he was assassinated by rivals or his own Praetorian guards, who became the arbiters of the Empire. The Roman world worshipped a ruler who was the guarantor of its peace, and that ruler turned out, as often as not, a parade-ground bully or a crude political intriguer who stopped at nothing to achieve his ambition.

By treating its possessors as divine, Rome deified despotic power. Those in authority were not responsible to the moral feelings and wishes of those they governed; their sway, while it lasted, was uncontrolled. An all-pervading bureaucracy, increasingly wasteful and petty-minded, represented omnipotence at every level. The cost of that immense army of officials plunged society into ever-deeper debt and taxation and, a millstone round the neck of production and trade, destroyed all private independence and sense of initiative. Little by little it reduced the population of every city in the Empire to a mob.

Rome had grown out of greatness of individual character. It became a community in which individual character counted for nothing compared with an abstraction which proved, in the hour of testing, capable of nothing. By sacrificing the individual to the State, the rulers of the Roman world undermined the real virtues which sustained it. They turned active and self-respecting citizens into inert and selfish ones. They discouraged the capitalist from thrift and foresight, the trader from enterprise, the craftsman from his hereditary skill, the husbandman from pride in the soil, the mother from maternity, and the soldier from courage and self-sacrifice. They made the moral shell which protected society so soft that it could protect it no longer. A creeping inertia paralysed everyone and everything. Even before the barbarians broke in, the elegant cities had begun to crumble, trade to die, for want of purchasers, learning, art and even bureaucratic efficiency to disappear for lack of men of ability. The middle class was exterminated. Civilization slowly gave place to barbarism at the Empire's heart.

By the end of the fourth century after Christ, the Roman Empire was disintegrating, both from internal dissension and inertia and from the attacks of barbaric tribes from outside. Already it had broken into two, one half governed from a Greek city on the Bosphorus named Constantinople, the other – itself split

13

between the rival garrisons of Italy, Gaul, Spain and Britain – nominally subject to Rome. On the last night of AD 406, a vast horde of Teutons from the German forests poured across the frozen Rhine into Gaul. Soon every city north of the Alps was in flames. The last legions in Britain were recalled to defend Italy. In 410 a Visigoth host sacked the imperial city of Rome itself.

CHAPTER TWO

The Coming of the English

'Behind the feet of the Legions and before the Normans'
    ire,
Rudely but greatly begat they the bones of state and of
    shire;
Rudely but deeply they laboured, and their labour stands
    till now,
If we trace on our ancient headlands the twist of their
    eight-ox plough.'

Kipling

FIFTEEN HUNDRED YEARS AGO, with the collapse of the Roman Western Empire, the British people were cut off from the civilization to which they had belonged for nearly four centuries. Their appeals for help were unanswered and they were left to defend themselves. At first, freed from the restrictions of an over-centralised bureaucracy, they seem to have organised themselves under local generals or tribal princes, particularly in the north-west, where the old Celtic organisation had survived and resistance to the Picts had kept men hardy and self-reliant. The province's only land-frontier was short, and the northern barbarians of Caledonia beyond it, though fierce, were few in number, with no new races on the march behind them. For perhaps fifty years British-Roman civilization, though fast disintegrating, seems to have survived.

Yet the threat of barbarism came not only from the land. The fishermen and whalers of the desolate marshes along the eastern shores of the North Sea – the 'Saxons' or men of the long knives, as the British called them – had also felt the pressure of Asiatic hordes moving westward through the forests behind them. Even before Rome fell, spurred on by hunger and hope of loot, they had taken to their boats to prey on the rich Roman island beyond the sunset. From Frisia and the mouths of the Rhine, Ems and Weser, from Schleswig and Angle in what is now Holstein and Denmark, they poured up the estuaries and rivers of southern Britain to plunder and slay. The island became a magnet for the boldest of all the barbarians – the men of the sea. On the continent the cities which had been the glory of Roman civilization escaped complete destruction, for the barbarian chieftains, fancying themselves heirs of the emperors before whom they had so long trembled, made them their own. But in Britain the invaders came from remote shores and mud-flats where the fame of Rome had scarcely penetrated. They despised, not only the effete, luxurious owners of the wealth they seized, but the wealth itself. They took the land, the crops and flocks, the slaves and treasures of gold and silver, but destroyed or shunned the cities – the *chesters*, as they called them – leaving only their charred, lonely, ghost-haunted ruins. For they were countrymen who hated towns and regarded their refinements as vices.

*   *   *

During this confused and savage age, which only the most exquisite scholarship has been able to rescue from oblivion, the island, with its dense forests and undrained valleys, was inhabited by three separate peoples. There were the Teuton invaders, with their boar-crested helmets, woollen cloaks and long ash-shafted spears, moving up the rivers in their shallow war boats or tramping the disused Roman roads – rechristened now with Saxon names like Watling Street and Fosse Way – in search of plunder and land. Behind them came their sturdy womenfolk and children, brought across stormy seas in open boats from the Saxon and Angle settlements in Europe. Opposed to them, fighting also in small divided bands and driven ever farther into the west – into what today are Devon, Cornwall, Wales, the Lake District and the south-western corner of Scotland, then called Strathclyde – were the descendants

16

of the British or Celtic-Roman provincials. But though their petty tyrants or princes, forever squabbling with one another, might still wear Roman armour and flowing togas – or plaids, as they later became called – and boast high-sounding Latin names, the few towns left had become little more than squatters' settlements, bereft of trade and the arts of civilized living, and their inhabitants almost as savage as the barbarians who had driven them from their former homes. And, left behind by the receding British tide in squalid, remote villages as the victors' slaves, were the primitive, pre-Celtic peasants who continued to live much as before. They survived in the impenetrable scrub of the Chiltern hills, on the Pennine and northern moors, in the marshy islands of the Fens – now reverting to inland sea with the decay of the Roman dykes – and on the ancient chalk uplands of the south-west. They were not exterminated but surrounded and absorbed. And their womenfolk, and those of the Celts, bore children to the conquerors.

Nor, for all the bloody battles and massacres of that terrible time, did the British tribes of the west perish. They merely ceased to be civilized and Roman, and became pastoral and Welsh. Like their remote ancestors of the Age of Bronze, they reverted to the hills and sheep. For a time, rendered desperate by suffering and schooled by hardship, they fought back so fiercely that the Saxon advance was halted. And they were sustained, like many others in that calamitous age of falling civilization, by a faith called Christianity which had spread across the Empire during its decline and which, hailing from the East, taught men that happiness could be achieved only by sacrifice. Under two successive leaders with Roman names, Ambrosius Aurelianus and Arturius or 'King' Arthur – heroes of whom little is known save the legends handed down by unlettered folk and later enshrined by poets – they won a series of battles culminating in the victory of Arthur and his cavalry or Knights at Mount Badon which ensured the survival in Britain of the Celtic tribes and Christian faith. The Celtic names of streams, rivers and hills, which, outlasting the Teuton flood, mark our maps, and the scattered farms and hamlets of the West Country are, as much as the Arthurian tales, a memorial to this heroic king of legend and the breathing-space he gained for his people. For fifty more years the invaders were confined to the eastern half of the island, the two races – speaking different tongues and holding different beliefs – facing one another in an uneasy, bitter truce across an uncertain frontier.

But in the middle of the sixth century the Saxons and Angles, first in the south and then in the north, resumed their advance. By the end of it the Britons of the south-west, driven into the Devonian-Cornish peninsula, were cut off from their Celtic kinsfolk of the little, quarrelling principalities of Wales – Gwent, Dyfor, Powys, Gwynedd. In the north an Angle or English kingdom called Northumbria, stretching from coast to coast across the Pennine moors, soon afterwards separated the Welsh from their fellow Celts of the Cumbrian mountains and Strathclyde. For in 603 the Northumbrian king defeated the Britons of Strathclyde and their northern Christian neighbours, the Scots of Dalriada or Argyll-shire, in a great battle in Liddesdale. 'From that day,' a Saxon boasted, 'no king of the Scots dared to meet the English nation in battle.' From the North Sea to the Severn and Dee, from the Channel to the Forth, the conquest of Britain was complete. Except for the rocky, rainswept west and far north, it was Britain no longer. It had become England.

*   *   *

What manner of people were these Anglo-Saxons? They were great seamen, fighters and colonisers. Coming from desolate coasts and windswept mud-flats, gale and storm were in their blood. 'The blast of the tempest,' sang one of their poets, 'aids our oars, the bellowing of the heaven, the howling of the thunder hurt us not; the hurricane is our servant and drives us where we wish to go.' They crossed the seas in undecked, mastless, clinker-built boats – 'foam-cresters' – seventy or eighty feet long, with a paddle in the stern for steering and fourteen or sixteen oars a side. If they were without mercy to their foes, they looked for none at the hands of a Nature very different from that of the sunny Mediterranean of Roman civilization. They viewed even shipwreck as a form of practice. Theirs was a world in which there was no place for the weak or craven. One thinks of them, in those days before they found a permanent home, as wild geese, tense on their solitary flight over the waste of waters as they followed the whale, the herring and the seal.

They loved fighting. Their poetry, chanted in the mead-halls of their chieftains as they sat feasting at the long benches, is full of the clash of 'the hammered blades', 'the serried bucklers', 'the shields of linden wood', of 'arrows sleeting like hail'. They loved the symbols of death and carnage: the raven who followed the host with his beak dripping blood, the hungry hawks hovering over the battlefield, the funeral pyre hung with shields and helmets – 'the beacon of the man mighty in battle' – round which the companions of the fallen sang the joys of war and the warrior's virtues.

Yet they had another side. Though to the defeated Britons, to whose homes they had brought fire and sword, they seemed only cruel, boorish savages, they were great farmers: by far the best the island had known. Their first settlements were on the lighter soils, but presently, with their iron axes and deep four- or eight-ox ploughs, they embarked on the titanic task of clearing the forests and heavier clay soils of the eastern Midlands: rich land that Neolithic and Bronze Age men, Celts and Romans alike had left untouched. For barbarians though they were, they were more patient, industrious and methodical than any of the peoples they had conquered. And, on the lowest and working social level, they had more genius for co-operation. They worked together, just as they had rowed and fought together. They shared the same ploughs, helped to cultivate one another's land and followed common rules of tillage and forestry. In this way they were able to make far steadier progress against the cold, stubborn clay and oaken wilderness around them than any of their predecessors. In their homesteads or *tuns* of thatched, tent-shaped huts, sited by streams in the forest clearings, and in their closely-knit communities whose names – Barkings of Barking, Hastings of Hastings, Gellingas of Ealing – still mark our maps, these sturdy colonists, with their fine smiths, carpenters and wrights, cleared virgin ground to support growing numbers of their folk. In doing so they created in the course of time the English countryside, turning marshy valley bottoms into water-meadows, terracing fields on the slopes and

eating ever farther into the forests. As each village became established, the younger and bolder spirits, for whom the cleared land
was insufficient, 'swarmed off' to found, still deeper in the woods,
new settlements which they distinguished from the old by the
addition of prefixes like Upper and Lower, East, West, South and
North, and suffixes like Bottom and End, Bere and Den – pig-
pasture – Ley and Hurst.

For these people loved the soil and the tending of it and its
beasts. They loved it as much as their fathers had loved fighting
and the sea. They left their memorial, not like the Romans in stone
or the Bronze Age men in burial-grounds, but in the imperishable
shape of the earth they tilled; it is writ large across our shires, with
their villages, meadows, farms and ploughlands. And in the work
of their artists that has come down to us, in their carvings in wood
and stone of leaves, trees and animals, we can see their deep feeling
for nature. 'His coat,' runs the old song, 'is of Saxon green', and
it is as a green-clad folk in a green land that we must think of them,
swinging their axes and driving their ploughs through mysterious
forest and dark earth to make the land we love.

Their main settlements were at first near the coast – the East
Saxons of what became Essex, their big-nosed Jutish neighbours
across the Thames in Kent and the Isle of Wight; the flaxen-
haired, blue-eyed, heavy-limbed South Saxons of Sussex; the
West Saxons who, coming from the Wash or up the Thames, settled
on Salisbury Plain or, in smaller numbers, landed near Southampton Water and followed the Avon to the Plain; the Angles of East
Anglia – the North-folk and South-folk – and their kinsmen who,
pushing up the Midland rivers, established the tribal communities
which by the beginning of the seventh century had merged to form
the kingdom of Mercia. Farther north other Angles, over-running
and inter-marrying with the British tribes of Deira and Bernicia
between Humber and Forth, founded the still greater kingdom of
Northumbria in what today is northern England and south-eastern
Scotland. All brought from their diverse starting-points in Europe
different customs and ways of life. And all were separated from
one another by trackless expanses of oak forest, thorn, scrub and
swamp, like the dense Epping and Chiltern woods which hemmed

in London from the north, the eighty-mile wide Andredsweald between the North and South Downs, Selwood in the west, the Midland forests of Bernwood, Arden and Wyre, Cannock Chase, Sherwood and Hatfield.

The population of these pioneer communities in the backwoods was at first very small. In the whole of Mercia – an area today comprising a dozen crowded counties – a century and a half after the first invasion there were only twelve thousand households. Their form of government, though aristocratic, was far simpler and freer than that of Rome. There were no officials, no central ad-ministration, and every village community kept its own peace and justice. No one could write or keep records, and the only checks on a man's conduct were the customary vengeance of his kin and neighbours, or of his lord or the more distant king for breaches of their simple laws.

The pioneer farmer, or *ceorl* as he was called, was the core both of the local community and of the petty kingdom or 'kindred' to which he belonged. He was a freeman, responsible only to his neighbours and to his fighting leader – chief, king or lord: a man, to use the old English phrase, 'moot-worthy, fold-worthy and fyrd-worthy', worthy, that is, of a place in the justice-court, the sheep-fold and the tribal fyrd or militia which turned out at the king's summons in time of war. He was wont to speak his mind out freely in the court of the village or tun, for among this simple people the man who spoke truth fearlessly was an honoured as the man who fought bravely. Though ready to enslave others, the English were great lovers of their own freedom. Their homes, rude and rough though they were, were their castles.

The tribal king was chosen for life by the kinsfolk and chief warriors from the descendants of the hero who had led the war-band or folk during the invasion. He lived in a little earthwork-palisaded fortress called a *burgh* with his thanes or *gesiths* – war-companions – and their servants and slaves. Such kings, some of them ruling kingdoms smaller than a modern county, were little richer than their subjects. They might wear a few ornaments and jewels in their rough, home-spun clothes and own gold or silver-mounted cups, armour of chain-mail and finely made swords, daggers and shields, like those found in the seventh-century royal ship buried in the sands of Sutton Hoo in East Anglia. Yet a king's or lord's hall was merely a gabled log-barn, with stag-horns and rude arms on its unplastered walls, a sunk open hearth in the centre of a rush-strewn earthen floor, and a hole in the roof to let out the smoke. Here on great occasions he and his companions would gorge themselves on meat and hot spiced ale and mead – a fermented spirit of honey and herbs – and, while the harp passed from hand to hand and the minstrels sang their sagas, shout with drunken joy at the remembrance of their forefathers' heroic deeds and battles.

For the gods of these simple forest folk – seamen and warriors turned farmers – were the spirits of Battle, Storm and Nature common to all the Nordic peoples. They honoured only the brave and warlike. It was because of this that, despite their love of independence, they gave such loyalty to their kings and lords, heirs of the warriors who had led them to conquest and who, perhaps, boasted descent from Woden, god of victory and plunder, or Thunor, god of the mountain-thunder, deities whose names, like those of Tiw and Freya, spirits of war and fertility, survive in the days of our week.[1] The greater the king's prowess, the larger his following of thanes and companions. They felt for him as dogs for their hunting masters: 'Happy days,' sang one, 'when I laid head and hands on my lord's knee.' From him they received the meat, bread and salt, the ale and mead on which they feasted in the winter, the bracelets and buckles of gold and silver, the gems and embroidery with which they loved to adorn their shaggy persons, the crested helmets, ringed mail and runed swords, said to be made by Wayland the smith-giant, which they used in battle.

Such men, though they might slaughter man, woman and child in anger or to placate their cruel gods, were not without rough virtues. They were brave, loyal and true to their kin and leaders; there was no shame in their eyes like that of the man who turned his back in fight or betrayed lord or comrade. Those who had eaten a man's salt must die by his side. 'Never shall the steadfast

[1] Also in the names of towns and villages like Wednesbury (Woden's burgh or borough) and Tewesley (Tiw's lea).

men round Stourmere,' cried the Essex thane as his *eorl* fell, 'reproach me that I journey lordless home.'

In this lay the nobility of these far-off ancestors of ours. There was no weak comfort in their harsh creed. They believed that the end of all was death: that no triumph or happiness, however great, could last. 'Now,' sang their bards, 'is the flower of thy strength lasting awhile, yet soon sickness or the sword, fire or flood, the arrow's flight or blinding age shall take away thy might.' They saw in the mystery of life a riddle beyond man's explaining. 'Where,' they asked, 'is the steed? Where the rider? Where the giver of treasure? The bulwarks are dismantled, the banqueting-hall in ruins, the lords lie bereft of joy, and all their proud chivalry is fallen by the wall!' It was not in man's power to control his lot; his virtue lay in his capacity for suffering and endurance. Even the gods, feasting in their paradise of Waelhaell or Valhalla, must fall in the end to the hateful hags, Hel and Weird – the Fates to whose inexorable decree all things bowed. There was no escape, no mercy or tenderness on icy earth or under storm-riven sky.

In the eyes of this brave people there was only one rule: to accept without flinching whatever the Fates had in store. The craven whined; the valiant kept his grief locked in his heart. The worse fortune treated him, the truer he must be to creed and comrade; the craven and traitor could gain only shame by their baseness. It was a rough, masculine creed, without much subtlety or refinement. It judged men, not by what they said or thought, but by their deeds. Yet it bred a sense of duty and responsibility without which no nation can be great or endure. It taught the rank and file to be loyal, and their leaders to sacrifice themselves for the led. 'I have bought with my death a hoard of treasures,' cried Beowulf after his fight with the dragon. 'I give thanks that before my dying day I have won it for my people.' So long afterwards on the battle-field of Maldon the outnumbered English fought on without hope of victory:

'Thought shall be the harder, heart the keener,
Mood shall be the more as our might lessens.'

In the hour of adversity and danger they closed their ranks and were true to one another.

23

CHAPTER THREE

The Faith

'I saw them march from Dover, long ago,
With a silver cross before them, singing low,
Monks of Rome from their home where the blue sea
    breaks in foam,
Augustine with his feet of snow.'

J. E. Flecker

MORE THAN TWO HUNDRED YEARS after the last Roman legions left
Britain, and soon after the completion of the English conquest, a
tall dark stranger stood before the king and chieftains of Northumbria. His name was Paulinus and, like the men who had once
governed Britain, he was a Roman. Yet he bore no arms and stood
there at the mercy of the rough warriors around him.

He had come to Northumbria – the wild northern kingdom
which stretched from the Forth to the Humber – with a Kentish
royal bride for its king. Thirty years earlier, in 597, the Jutish
ruler of Kent, the most civilized of the barbarous English tribal
kingdoms, had invited to his capital a band of Roman monks to
minister to his queen, a Christian princess from Gaul. It proved
the most important of all the invasions of England and the most
peaceful. Marching across the downs from Dover under their
leader Augustine, with banners and a silver cross, they had been
received by King Ethelbert sitting at his tent door lest they should
cast spells on him. He listened to what they had to say, gave them
a ruined Roman church in his capital, Canterbury, and resolved
to embrace their creed. After he was baptised thousands of his
thanes and warriors had followed his example.

The Northumbrians were no friends to Christianity – the mysterious eastern religion which, officially adopted by the Roman Empire in the days of its decline, had survived the latter's collapse on the continent and, though rooted out of southern Britain by the Saxons, had lingered on in the mountains and islands of the Celtic west. Fourteen years before, they had slaughtered hundreds of its priests after a great victory over the Britons of North Wales. The very word *church*, that they used for its houses of worship, was associated in their minds with plunder. They listened, therefore, to the eloquent Italian with suspicion. Yet what he told caused them to do so in silence. For it was a tale of heroism and devotion. Its purport was that behind the forces of Fate was a God who had made men in his own image and, loving them, had given them freedom to choose between good and evil. He had made them, not helpless actors, but partners in the drama of creation. And because men had misused that freedom and God still loved them, He had sent His son as leader and saviour to show them, by revealing His noble nature, how to live and, by sharing their lot and dying on the cross, how to overcome sin and death.

Paulinus's tale cannot have seemed wholly strange to his hearers. He had spoken of a leader who had been brave and true, who offered his followers a freeman's choice between good and evil and a hero's reward for those who were faithful. But in two respects his message was revolutionary. For the virtues Jesus had shown were not merely those the English honoured, but others they had never regarded as virtues at all. Love not hate, gentleness not force, mercy not vengeance had been the armour of this heroic captain. The Northumbrians' own valour in battle was small compared to the cold courage of facing death with only these meek virtues. And, as proof of it, here was this solitary stranger standing unarmed in their midst.

Most startling of all, Paulinus's message offered the English hope beyond the grave. Here was the reply to a problem deep in the human heart which their priests had never answered. When he ended, an old counsellor spoke. 'The life of man, O king,' he said, 'is like a sparrow's flight through a bright hall when one sits at meat in winter with the fire alight on the hearth, and the icy

25

rain-storm without. The sparrow flies in at one door and stays for a moment in the light and heat, and then, flying out of the other, vanishes into the wintry darkness. So stays for a moment the life of man, but what it is before and what after, we know not. If this new teaching can tell us, let us follow it!'

As the Northumbrians crowded round the man who brought them these tidings, their own high priest was the first to cast his spear at the idols their fathers had worshipped. Afterwards they were baptised in thousands, pressing into the Yorkshire streams to receive from Paulinus's hands the cross of water which enrolled a man as Christ's follower and offered him deliverance from the grave. For Christianity had been presented to them as a correction, rather than a denial, of their own heathen beliefs. They were used to thinking of gods as controlling their fate, though gods of terror. They were now told there was one God – of justice, peace and love. They were used to offering sacrifices to appease the wrath of Heaven; they were told of a new and higher form of sacrifice, self-sacrifice. They believed in magic, and learnt of a heavenly king who was born in a manger, gave his life for man on the 'healer's tree', and rose from the grave to sit at God's right hand. They were wont to celebrate the seed sown in winter darkness and the renewal of life in the spring; they were given a midwinter feast to celebrate Christ's birth and a spring one for his resurrection. Their fertility festival to Eastra, a Teuton goddess, purged of its grossness became Easter; their Yuletide junketings around the December log-fires the Christ Mass or Christmas.

Such a conversion was necessarily incomplete. It made heathens Christian, yet it also made Christianity a little heathen. And it suffered from the disadvantage – the reverse of its bloodless character – that it was a conversion from the top. It rested too much on the Germanic principle of lordship. It depended on the changing policies of a court rather than on the hearts of a people.

Yet it was not only from Rome that the faith was brought to England. Two centuries earlier, when the Saxons had first overrun the lowlands, the Roman-Celts among the mountains and moors of Strathclyde, Wales and Cornwall had fallen back on the one creed of a dissolving civilization that gave them courage and hope to endure. And though, in their harsh life of struggle and poverty, they grew almost as barbarous and illiterate and quite as fierce as their foes, the light of Christ's teaching still shone through the war-clouds which overhung their rugged lands. Chapels of wood and wattle with beehive vaulting, and monasteries with tiny enclosed grass lawns or *llans*, appeared in Welsh valleys, and granite wheelhead crosses flowered beside the Atlantic among the Cornish rocks. All round the western seas, from Brittany to the Isle of Man and Clyde, the names of Celtic saints are still commemorated where once, in tiny cells and oratories, they lived their lives of faith and self-denial – Ninian who converted the Picts of Galloway; Dyfrig, Illtyd, Govan, Teilo, Padern and David, the apostles of Wales; Samson of Dol who crossed the seas from stony Caldey to preach to the Bretons; Morwenna, Cleder, Endellion and a score of others who made the name of Christ loved by the lonely fishermen and herdsmen of Cornwall.

The distinguishing trait of these early evangelists was their selflessness in the love of God and their sublime faith that there was nothing they could not dare in their master's name. St Patrick's mission to the heathen Irish in the fifth century is one of the great stories of mankind. By converting them he made Ireland, in the dark centuries after Rome's fall, a Christian haven in a world of storm. The most famous of his disciples was the evangelist Columba, who founded a monastery church on the island of Iona off the coast of Dalriada. Up and down the northern moors, where even the Roman legionaries had never penetrated, Columba's monks made their way, preaching, healing and winning men's hearts. One of them, St Aidan, became the Celtic apostle of northern England, planting the Christian ideal among the Northumbrian tribesmen. The contribution of these Celtic evangelists to England's conversion lay not in doctrine but in example. It was this that won the simple English to Christ. For if the preachers' arguments were sometimes a travesty of their master's, their lives were touchingly like His. Like Him they took no thought for the morrow, of what they should eat or wear; they put their faith in His spirit and, giving themselves to His selfless gospel, lived it. With those among whom they went, purseless and on foot, they left an image of the Good Shepherd giving His life for His sheep which was to run like a silver thread through the English tradition.

So it came about that during the seventh century England became a Christian land. From Canterbury Roman monks carried their missions into Wessex – the kingdom of the West Saxons – making Christians of the warrior farmers who had driven the Britons beyond Exe and Severn. From Northumbria the disciples of Aidan took their message of faith and goodness to the peoples of Mercia. Though they only partly comprehended Christianity's revolutionary creed of love, humility and self-sacrifice, it came to them as a wonderful revelation. It took the darkness out of their sad, fatalistic beliefs and offered them hope and purpose.

In the century which followed the national genius flowered for the first time. During it the earliest English churches were built, like Brixworth in Northamptonshire and Escombe-by-the-Wear, and the tall, beautiful sculptured Celtic crosses, with their runic inscriptions and Gospel figures of men and beasts, before which the Angles of the north worshipped in the open air. It was the age in which the first English books and manuscripts, with their exquisitely interlaced illuminations of birds and dogs, were copied and painted by monks in their cells; in which the stately Wilfred taught Northumbrian choirs to sing double chants, and Aldhelm, a prince of the West Saxons – the reputed builder of the little cruciform church at Bradford-on-Avon, who became abbot of Malmesbury and first bishop of Sherborne – used to stand on Malmesbury bridge singing the songs of his native land until he had gathered a crowd of listeners, and then preach to them the gospel story and the wonders of God's universe. In that dawn of childlike faith when Cuthbert, the shepherd bishop of Lindisfarne, tramped his wide diocese, the moorland peasants came running to him to confess their sins and beg his intercession. The inspiration of this gentle barefoot saint can still be seen in the beautiful Lindisfarne Gospel in the British Museum, written on Holy Island 'for God and St Cuthbert', and in the great cathedral shrine which long afterwards rose on the rocks above the river at Durham to house his bones.

Perhaps the most wonderful of all the achievements of the time was that of the Venerable Bede, the greatest scholar in Christendom. From his monastery cell at Jarrow he poured out a never-ceasing stream of books: history, theology, poetry, grammar and natural science. To him England owes the practice of dating years from the birth of Christ and the first prose written in Latin by an Englishman. His vision of Hell – 'where there is no voice but of weeping, no face but of the tormentors' – expresses the very soul of the dark ages he helped to illumine. The most famous of his works was the *Ecclesiastical History of the English Nation* – the story of the conversion. Lucid, just, immensely learned, it is a monument to his age, his faith and his country. That life of scholarship and labour, with the tireless hand writing amid the intervals of prayer and teaching, sometimes so frozen that it could hardly grip the pen, is one of the proud memories of England. He left his countrymen the earliest version of the Gospel in their own tongue and a tradition, rare in that age, of gentleness, love of truth and scrupulous fairness.

* * *

After the first enthusiasm roused by the barefoot Celtic missionaries, the spread of Christianity among the pagan peasant masses was very gradual. For centuries, in England as on the continent, it remained mainly a religion of the upper classes, drawing its monks, saints and bishops from the well-born. Even for them it was often only a superior kind of magic: a means of buying, by prayers, incantations and pious benefactions, protection from misfortune or foes and, still more important, from the ancient equaliser, death. It was the promise of eternal life which drew most men to Christ's creed. The hope of everlasting heaven and the fear of its dreadful opposite, the eternal Nordic hell, proved a rival to the hope of plunder and the lust for pleasure and power.

Yet, despite the slowness of Christianity's humanising work and the immense obstacles it had to overcome, its survival in such a rude and bloody age is one of the miracles of history. Into a world inherently unequal, where the strong and fortunate ruled without pity, it introduced the conception of the ultimate worthlessness of earthly distinctions in the light of the far more dreadful distinction between Heaven and Hell. By its doctrine that every man had a soul to save during his time on earth, and its insistence that the winning of salvation was no easier for king or lord than for beggar or slave, it gave some meaning to the life of common men. It offered those with no prospect – the poor toiling in the fields, the weak and sick, the slaves and prisoners – the hope of a spiritual and eternal kingdom open to all. For the first time men were made to feel, however dimly, that it was wrong to maltreat those who were in their power but who, in Christ's universal family, were their brothers.

To women, too, Christianity brought a slow but perceptible improvement of status. For the Church taught that, if their bodies were weaker than men's, their souls were of equal importance, and recognised their moral stature by the responsibilities with which it entrusted them. It stressed the sanctity of marriage and the home. It also offered a career, as leaders of religious society, to women who, renouncing the joys of family life, dedicated themselves to Christ's universal family. In these early centuries queens and princesses took vows of chastity and poverty and embraced the conventual life. It was a woman, St Hilda – a Northumbrian princess and head of the great abbey of Streoneshalh[1] – who trained many of the earliest English bishops and set the first Christian poet in England – the poor herdsman Caedmon – to sing the wonders of creation.

Christianity, too, taught men to base their social relationships on something wider than tribe or kindred. It brought the warlike tribes and nations of England into the same communion as other western European peoples and into closer contact with one another. At the time of the conversion there were seven English kingdoms – Northumbria, Mercia, Kent, Wessex, East Anglia, Essex and Sussex. Their princes were almost constantly at war, with their own kinsmen for their crowns and with their neighbours for new territories. There was no sense of nationhood; a man thought of himself as a Kentish man or a Northumbrian, not as an Englishman. Without communications or regular administration no king's authority could reach far. Even that of the strongest died with him.

But with the coming of Christianity, kings were presented with

[1] After the Scandinavian invasions re-named Whitby.

30

the possibility of an instrument of governance more potent in the long run than any army. In its quiet monasteries the Church began to teach men the forgotten arts of writing and keeping records. At Jarrow and Wearmouth, Melrose and Whitby in the north, at Glastonbury, Malmesbury and Pershore in the west, at Canterbury and Minster in the south, it trained men who could show barbarian rulers a means of governing justly. It gave them clerics or clerks who could reduce their chaotic affairs to order, draft laws and reckon accounts and taxes.

For the way of life the Church preached called for a law-abiding world; one in which men made and kept promises instead of perpetually resorting to force. 'The King's Peace' was a better basis for Christian relationships than violence and anarchy. So long as the rulers of society were faithful Christians the Church supported their authority. It bade men, while rendering unto God the things that were God's, to render unto Caesar the things that were Caesar's. It transformed the military institution of Teutonic kingship into a sacred office. In place of the traditional raising of the chosen leader on the warrior's shield by the armed host, the Church crowned him with a sacred diadem and anointed him with holy oil, praying that God would give him the armour of justice to preserve peace and do righteousness. In return, the king – sanctified as the Lord's anointed – guarded the Church's property, made gifts of land and treasure to its monasteries and conferred high office on its clerics, the only men in his realm who could read or write. At least that was the ideal which the Christian Church set before tribal kings and rulers in an age slowly starting to emerge from anarchy and barbarism.

CHAPTER FOUR

Alfred and the Danes

'So long as I have lived I have striven to live
worthily. I desire to leave men who come after me
a remembrance of good works.'

King Alfred

IF ONE COULD HAVE LOOKED DOWN on Europe in the confused and
barbaric centuries following the conversion of England, one would
have seen a continent in whose western half, from the Mediterranean to Scotland, Christianity had become the nominal faith of
its princes and lords. This vast tract of land was divided into many
little principalities, whose uncertain frontiers changed constantly
with the wars and family quarrels of their rulers. Yet one institution transcended tribal frontiers. In a landscape of peasants' huts
and rude wooden hunting-lodges, the monasteries of the Church
were everywhere the largest buildings to be seen. And winding
past squalid villages and little wooden castles, through forests,
fords and mountain passes, ran the grassy tracks, trodden by
horse-hooves and the feet of monks and pilgrims, which led to
Rome, the see of the Pope or 'Holy Father' – the spiritual head of
western Christendom.

Only in the remote Celtic islands of Ireland and western Scotland, and in the south-east, beyond the Balkan mountains, where
the Greek emperors still maintained the ancient pomp of the
Caesars and the Byzantine Patriarch ignored the Pope's claim to
be Christ's vice-regent on earth, were there Christian communities
which refused to acknowledge the spiritual supremacy of Rome.
Yet Christendom was only a world within a world. Europe itself

32

was half heathen. Its eastern plains and forests and mountainous northern peninsulas were still peopled by savages who had never heard of Christ. And all along the southern and eastern shores of the Mediterranean – the earliest cradle of the faith – the patriarchates of Jerusalem, Antioch and Alexandria had been overrun by Moslem tribesmen from the Arabian deserts. At the very time that England was being converted to Christianity the whole Arab world had been set ablaze by a new fanatic religion. The creed of Islam, or 'surrender', and its devotees, the Moslems, or 'self-surrenderers', united the Near East, long subject to the Greek and Roman West, in a holy war against Christians. A sea, long given over to peaceful trade, had become a pirate-haunted frontier between Christendom and Islam, swept by Arab fleets. Constantinople only escaped capture through its superb strategic position. In the East, emulating Alexander a thousand years before, Moslem armies had passed the Oxus and reached the frontiers of India. And early in the eighth century, while Bede was still working in his cell at Jarrow, the Moors had crossed from Africa into Spain and planted the Crescent on the Pyrenees. Thence they had poured through the passes into Gaul and the land of the Franks.

In that dreadful hour it had seemed as though western Christendom was broken. Then in 732 the Franks under Charles Martel – mayor of the palace and chief minister to their titular king – saved the West at Poitiers. Having secured its southern frontier this great soldier, with his tall Frankish swordsmen, turned eastwards against the heathens of central Europe. It was with his help that St Boniface of Crediton – a Wessex thane's son who became the first archbishop of Mainz – converted the German Saxons and advanced Christendom's outposts to the Elbe. Later this English evangelist, with the Pope's blessing, anointed Charles's son, Pepin, king of the Franks in place of the last Merovingian monarch.

Pepin's son, Charlemagne, like all the men of his age, was haunted by memories of the imperial Roman unity of the past. Though four centuries had elapsed since the western Empire had fallen, every attempt to revive civilization led men back to Rome. Though he could scarcely read and was framed by nature for the saddle and battlefield, Charlemagne had a passionate admiration for learning. This blond, barbarian giant, who slept with a slate under his pillow and made an English scholar, Alcuin of York, his chief counsellor and head of his palace school, conceived the tremendous ambition of reuniting the West in a restored Roman imperium. He tried, though in vain, to reconquer Spain from the Moors; the heroic death of his general, Roland, in the Roncesvalles pass inspired Frankish poetry for centuries. And he sought, with greater success, to embody in his empire all his fellow Teutons beyond the Ems and Weser. For thirty years he warred against them, repeatedly defeating them and striving to break their stubborn savagery by enforced mass baptisms.

Yet more than to the eastern forests from which his forebears had come, Charlemagne's spirit was drawn to the Roman south. He saw himself as the head of Christendom and its guardian. Like his father, Pepin, he led a Frankish army across the Alps against the Lombard conquerors of north Italy. And on Christmas Day 800, as he knelt at mass in St Peter's, Rome, his ally, the Pope, crowned him with traditional imperial rites as Emperor of the Romans. To dreamers it appeared as if the hand of time had been set back and the Roman Empire restored. And it was now, it seemed, a *Holy Roman Empire*.

In Britain, too, attempts were made to revive the Roman past. Under the inspiration of Christianity, the Anglo-Saxon kings were groping towards some wider union of society than the tribal gathering and pioneer settlement. Ine, king of the West Saxons – a contemporary of Charles Martel – published a code of written law for his people and made a pilgrimage to Rome. Half a century later Offa, king of Mercia, established an over-lordship over the whole island south of the Humber and assumed the Roman title of *Rex Anglorum*, King of the English. He encouraged trade with the continent, made a commercial treaty with Charlemagne – with whom he corresponded on friendly terms – and minted gold coins, some of which, bearing his name, circulated as far as the Moslem caliphate of Baghdad. And at home he built an earthen dyke, to keep out Welsh raiders, which, running from Dee to Wye, still marks the border between England proper and Wales and Monmouthshire.

Yet neither Charlemagne's vast empire stretching from the Ebro to the Carpathians, nor Offa's smaller English kingdom endured. Barbarian kings, however lofty their aspirations, could not govern large areas. They lacked roads and bridges, trained servants, regular administration and justice. They could not give their peoples the security from which patriotism and the habit of subordinating self to the public interest spring. They thought of their dominions as family possessions which they were free to treat as they pleased. Even when they ruled, like Charlemagne, with a sense of vocation, they could not transmit it to their sons who, by tribal custom, had the right to divide their patrimony. Charlemagne's empire quickly dissolved after his death. Under his grandchildren and their heirs it was broken up into ever smaller kingdoms.

Nor were the methods by which the rulers of that age sought to widen their realms calculated to preserve them. Their Christianity, though strongly felt, was only skin-deep. Enraged by the resistance of the Saxon tribesmen, Charlemagne massacred his prisoners by the thousands; Offa, founder and patron of monasteries, put out the eyes of a Kentish rival. Such actions created, not love and loyalty, but bitter hatred. When the strong hand of their perpetrators was removed, civil war and vengeance overtook the realms they had created. On Offa's death in 796 his English empire fell to pieces. So did the kingdom of Northumbria, whose rulers had tried to unite the northern half of the island by similar means. In less than a century five of its kings were murdered or slain in battle, five more deposed and four forced to abdicate.

The recurring problem of what historians call the Dark Ages – the long blood-stained centuries after the fall of Rome – was that of preventing society from disintegrating because its stronger members could not be subjected to any law but their own passions. What was lacking was a profession of dedicated kingship, pursued by hereditary princes with the power to preserve peace, social continuity and order.

*   *   *

It was in England that such a king appeared and at a time of universal disaster. For two hundred years Europe had been threatened from the south by crusading Moslems. Now a new and more dreadful threat arose in the north. It came from the fiords of Norway and the Jutland flats where the Scandinavian peoples – Norwegians and Danes – were on the move. The soil they tilled could no longer sustain their rising population, nor a pastoral life satisfy their more turbulent members. These were vigorous, picturesque, flamboyant rascals, younger sons of petty *fiord-jarls* for whom there was no place at home, with long flaxen hair, bright burnished spears and two-handed battle-axes. They delighted in silver-bound swords and jewels, golden bracelets and scarlet cloaks with brilliant borders. And, like all their race, they had a passionate love of independence. Around them they gathered bands of bloodthirsty followers, who feasted and drank in their halls in winter, sallying forth each spring 'to play the game of Freyr'. Berserks and wolfcoats they called themselves; wherever they went, they boasted, the ravens followed.

Accustomed to using the sea as a highway – the only communication between their scattered settlements – they were now offered a wonderful prize. Every spring the young pirate seamen of Norway and Denmark – Vikings as they were called from the *viks* or creeks they haunted – set out in fleets of long, narrow, open-decked war-boats, with carved dragon-heads, raven banners and bright striped sails. The very word sail in English derives from their *seil*. Following the mountainous island fringe of the Atlantic southwards from Norway, they plundered in turn the Shetlands, Orkneys, Sutherland and the Hebrides. In 802 – two years after Charlemagne's coronation in Rome – they sacked the Scottish monastery of Iona. Then they fell on Ireland.

*   *   *

During the three centuries since Patrick's mission the Irish had achieved great things. Their monasteries and monastic schools were among the best and most learned in Europe, their illuminated manuscripts, like the lovely Book of Kells – still preserved at Trinity College, Dublin – the flower of western art. In the monk,

36

John Scotus, they produced the first philosopher of the age, while their wandering scholars and poets fashioned verses more subtle than any to be found in that barbarous time. But politically they had changed little. Their titular High King still reigned with his fellow kings over their five sovereign and equal provinces, while a host of tribal chieftains kept their petty state and raided one another for cattle and hostages. Of unity, or capacity to combine against an external foe, there was none.

Thus the raiders' impact was calamitous. No one could make any effective resistance to them. With their shallow-draft boats they swept up the estuaries and rivers, sacking every monastery, farm and building, and carrying off the younger men and women as slaves. Soon they took to wintering on the coast, making permanent forts on island and promontory. The round-towers, whose ruins can still be seen, were built as shelters from their ravages. Ireland's 'golden age' of art and learning faded into the Atlantic mists at the whip of a few thousand arrogant Norsemen who knew how to combine and to use the sea as a highway.

The Vikings now turned their dreadful attentions to England. The ancestors of the English had also harried Britain from the sea. Now their successors bore down from the same savage shores to plunder the wealth they had created. The island's coasts ceased to be a quiet retreat for saints and scholars and became what it was four centuries before, a place of terror. In 835, 'heathen men' landed in the Isle of Sheppey at the mouth of the Thames. Thereafter, every spring, their dragon-prowed boats, glittering with spears and axes, crept up the east-coast rivers. Then securing themselves on some marsh-encircled island, they seized the horses of the neighbouring countryside and rode out to plunder and slay. If the bewildered farmers combined against them, they formed a ring and, with their massed battle-axes swinging over the 'linden wall' of shields, hacked a way back to their ships. Wherever they went they deliberately spread terror. At Peterborough a single Viking killed eighty-four monks with his own hand; another cut the ribs off an English prince, drew out his lungs and threw salt into his wounds. Breaking open tombs and coffins and stoning obdurate Christians, 'these pagans marched forwards into

Cambridgeshire' with wagons full of plunder, and 'with a violent inundation, brake into the kingdom of the East Angles'. When everyone for whom no ransom was forthcoming had been massacred, they moved on to the next district. Those who paid them enough to go away they left alone till another year, when they returned for more.

'From the fury of the Norsemen,' prayed the peasants in their churches, 'good Lord, deliver us!' So systematic were the ravages of these fearful pirates that, from the Humber to the Solent, hardly a vestige remained of a Saxon church within a day's ride of the coast. By the middle of the ninth century the island seemed their own. In 851, three hundred and fifty of their ships anchored in the Thames. That autumn, after their crews had burnt London and Canterbury, they encamped in Thanet. Thenceforward their armies wintered regularly in England. In two decades they systematically destroyed the Christian kingdoms of Northumbria, East Anglia and Mercia. The final collapse came after 865, when the sons of Ragnar Lothbrok – greatest of Vikings – landed on the east coast. The ancient realm of Northumbria, with its famous monasteries and beautiful crosses, crumbled to dust. So did the library of York which had trained the great European scholar, Alcuin, and the Fenland abbeys – Crowland, Peterborough and Ely. In 869 Edmund, last of the East Anglian kings, after defeat and capture, was barbarously slain for refusing to renounce his faith. When three years later the ruler of Mercia fled to the continent, only one English kingdom remained.

*   *   *

Since the beginning of the century Wessex – once a dependency of Offa's Mercia – had been growing in importance. Absorbing both the small English states of the south-east and the Ibero-Celts of Devon, its rustic princes, ruling a people half Saxon, half Celtic, had carried their golden dragon banner to the Dover strait and the Atlantic. But by 870, half encircled by sea, and with all England north of the Thames in the Norseman's grip, Wessex seemed doomed. In that year the Danes entered it in force and, encamping in an impregnable position between Thames and Kennet near the site of modern Reading, started to ravage it as they had done its sister kingdoms of the north and east. Everywhere in Europe the Christian cause was failing. In the Mediterranean Moslem pirates, after conquering Sicily, had devastated the whole of southern Italy and plundered the suburbs of Rome.

At that moment the Danes encountered, in a young prince or *atheling* of the House of Wessex, one of the great men of all time. Alfred, youngest son of King Ethelwulf, was born at Wantage in 849, three hundred years after the Saxons first settled in Wessex. As a child he had been taken by his father on a pilgrimage to Rome. The journey across Europe, the sight of the great city with its noble ruins of the world of learning and order, had stirred his imagination so that all his life he longed to restore learning and order to his fellow men. He had even tried to teach himself to read from one of the beautiful illuminated Latin books which the monks copied by hand and, so the story goes, loved it so much – a strange love in a little Saxon prince – that his mother gave it to him. Then, when still a boy, he had had to lay aside learning to be a soldier and fight beside his brothers and their fellow English kings against the Norsemen, who every year were advancing deeper into England.

Unlike many other princes of the time, though he won the love of the rough warriors around him, Alfred refused to take any part in the dynastic quarrels which divided his imperilled country. His one thought was not of himself but of serving her. Instead of seeking the crown, he loyally supported each of his three brothers who wore it in turn. At the time the Danish host invaded Wessex, he was acting as second-in-command to the last of them.

It was due to the presence of mind of this young man of twenty-one that the sole remaining English army was not surprised and destroyed early in 871 on the Berkshire hills at Ashdown. While his brother, the king, was at his prayers, Alfred acted with lightning decision and led his rustic levies, 'like a wild boar', against the advancing Danes. 'All day long the opposing ranks met in conflict, with great shouting from all men, one side bent on evil, the other fighting for life, their loved ones and native land.' By nightfall thousands of corpses lay round the stunted thorn tree in the centre of the battle-field. Among them were a Danish king and five earls

39

or *jarls*. The remainder of their host fled across the downs to Reading.

Yet Alfred's struggle against the invaders had only begun. Ashdown was one of eight battles fought in that dreadful year. A few weeks later fresh Danish armies poured into Wessex, whose own levies, composed of farmers with homes and fields to tend, began to dissolve. It was this, almost as much as command of the sea, which gave the Danes their advantage. That spring, when his brother died, Alfred was hastily elected to a falling throne, and left, with a few personal retainers, to defend the last Christian kingdom in England. Hopelessly outnumbered, he managed to hold out till the winter. Then, by paying a ransom or *danegeld*, he was able to secure a brief respite for his unhappy people.

He used it well. During the next few years the Danes were so busy partitioning Northumbria and Mercia and setting up states of their own in what today are Yorkshire, Lincolnshire, Nottinghamshire, Derbyshire, Leicestershire and East Anglia, that they had little time to spare for harrying Wessex. Alfred worked incessantly, reorganising the peasant levies of his half-ruined kingdom and laying the first foundations of an English fleet. When everyone else was in despair and Christians all round the coasts of Europe were meekly submitting to the terrible sea-heathens, this modest, gentle, scholarly man refused to give in. He saw the weakness of the Viking leaders – their greed and savage rivalry – and knew that if he could win time and sustain the courage of his people, he would beat them in the end.

In the spring of 876 the expected blow fell. The Great Army, as it was called, broke up its camp at Cambridge and marched at high speed across Wessex, ravaging the countryside as it went. Reaching the south coast at Wareham, where it stockaded itself between the Frome and Trent, it seized the approaches to the wide anchorage of Poole harbour. Here Danish fleet-armies from France, Wales and Ireland joined it. For, seeing in Alfred the one man in western Europe who could withstand them, the Norsemen were resolved to crush him once and for all.

He met the challenge boldly. Assembling his levies, he encamped before Wareham and blockaded the invaders. The latter's

control of the sea enabled them to receive supplies and reinforcements and to raid the coasts in his rear. But after a time, as he
anticipated, they grew weary of their confinement. Uninterrupted
summer plundering was essential to the very existence of a Danish
army; it could not maintain itself or its morale without. Its leaders
therefore asked for a truce and, on payment of a *danegeld*, agreed
to quit Alfred's realm. Yet scarcely had they sworn to do so than
they treacherously attacked his outposts and broke out on their
horses to the west where, with the help of a fleet, they seized Exeter
and proceeded to lay waste Devon. But the stubborn English king
followed them, drove them back to their entrenchments and once
more resumed his blockade. Then a great storm off the Purbeck
cliffs came to his aid and destroyed more than a hundred of their
ships and thousands of men who were on their way to relieve Exeter.
Before winter fell the besieged offered hostages, made their peace
and withdrew to Gloucester across the Mercian border.

But the Danes were not used to defeat. They still believed they
could destroy Alfred as they had destroyed his fellow English
kings. At midwinter 877–8, a few days after the Christmas feast,
their army under King Guthrum again broke into Wessex. Once
more they stockaded themselves in an impregnable position – at
Chippenham in Wiltshire – and began to plunder the countryside.
Simultaneously a Viking fleet swept down on the Devon coast.
This time the attack was so unexpected and its ravages so widespread that the morale of Wessex at last gave way, as that of
Northumbria and Mercia had done. There was a sudden panic and
many of its chief men fled to France. Alfred himself with a handful
of followers was forced to take refuge in the lake isle of Athelney,
where he lay for a time, 'in great sorrow and unrest amid the woods
and marshes of the land of Somerset'.[1]

Yet Alfred was no despairer. Quietly and with unconquerable
courage he set himself to repair the broken breaches of his kingdom.

---

[1] He loved to tell stories of his adventures there, among them – according to
later legend – the tale of the burnt cakes in the cowherd's cottage. More than
eight hundred years later, in 1693, a gold and enamelled jewel bearing his name,
Aelfred Mec Heht Gewyrcan – 'Alfred ordered me to be made' – was found on a
farm at Athelney, and is now in possession of the University of Oxford.

SET IN A SILVER SEA

While he hid among the Parrett marshes his messengers, travelling the ancient hill-roads of Wessex, carried his orders to his countrymen to rally. Shortly before Easter the men of Devon made a sudden sally against the tormentors, routed them and slew their leader. Then, following a plan prepared by the king, contingents from all the western shires, marching through forest and along the grass hill-tracks, began to converge on a secret rendezvous – a lonely landmark and meeting place of ways called Egbert's Stone, on the downs overlooking the vale of Knoyle east of the forest of Selwood. Here, to their unspeakable joy, Alfred joined them.

Without a day's delay the army set out north towards the enemy's camp. On the second day, after halting for the night near Warminster, they encountered the Danish host, hastily assembling in their path on the rolling chalk downs above Bratton and Ethandun, today Edington. Attacking in a single column of packed shields, after many hours' hard fighting they broke its ranks and drove it in confusion towards Chippenham. In the hour of his victory – perhaps the most important ever won on English soil – Alfred showed one of the rarest attributes of a commander. Exhausted though he and his men were, he pursued his foe relentlessly all the way to their camp fourteen miles off, slaying them in thousands and capturing vast quantities of cattle and stores. He then closely besieged it, preventing every attempt to revictual it. After a fortnight, 'terrified by hunger and cold and fear', the Danes laid down their arms.

In victory Alfred's full grandeur became apparent. Undiscouraged by their past treachery, he took pity on his enemies. He fed them and offered them peace. Having shown heroism in adversity, in triumph he practised the greatest of Christian virtues. He made his cruel foes, who had learnt to respect his valour, realise his nobility. The Danish king at his invitation accepted baptism – the first of his race to do so. 'King Alfred,' wrote his friend and scribe, Bishop Asser, 'stood godfather to him and raised him from the holy font.'

Like his victories, Alfred's peace-making at Wedmore marked a turning-point in English history. It made it possible for Danes and Englishmen – the injurers and injured – to live together in a single island, and opened the way to the former's conversion and civilization. The English king had the wisdom to realise that the sword, though powerful to defend, could settle nothing permanently, and that only a conquest of the heart could endure. And though he and his people had suffered terribly from the invaders, he was too magnanimous to seek revenge and too wise to suppose he could expel them altogether. Christianity and the legacy of Roman order might transform Danes as it had transformed Saxons. No greater act of statesmanship was ever performed by an English king.

Nor was Alfred, in his far-sighted magnanimity, under any illusion. He knew that, though he might make friends with the invaders who had already homes in the east and north of England, other Danish armies would again attack her from the sea. This patient, courageous man refused to rest on his laurels. While he offered friendship to the defeated, he prepared for new attacks from their kinsmen. He used the peace he had won to give his kingdom a fighting force capable of withstanding the worst that could befall her. Once more, seeing that the only certain safety was to defeat the invaders before they could land, he began to build ships. Though he could not hope in his lifetime to defeat a massed Danish fleet – for the pirates' mastery of the northern seas had been unchallenged for generations – the war-galleys he laid down, some twice the size of the largest Viking vessel, made small-scale raiding of the Wessex coast too costly to be profitable.

Even more effective was the English king's re-organisation of his army. To overcome the fatal tendency of a militia of peasants to disperse to their farms after a few weeks' campaigning, he divided the national *fyrd*, as it was called, into two halves, each taking it in turn to serve in wartime until relieved by the other. And to stiffen its amateur ranks, he fostered the growth of a fighting aristocracy by encouraging larger freeholders to assume military rank and responsibility. To every churl with five or more hides of land he offered the right of thaneship and its privileges in return for regular military service with helm, mail-shirt, sword and horse. This semi-professional *corps d'élite*, which in wartime was kept permanently embodied, he also divided into sections, every

43

member in peacetime having to serve for a month in arms for every two at home. This gave him a regular mounted field-force capable of opposing assailants who, living by war, had not, like English fyrdmen, to be for ever thinking about their neglected farms and homes.

The most momentous of Alfred's military reforms was his creation of the fortified burgh or town. The Danish armies had supported themselves by seizing carefully-chosen strategic bases which they provisioned from the surrounding countryside and made impregnable with earthworks and stockades. This had made it impossible for the English either to bring them to action or to maintain themselves in their vicinity. Alfred's answer was to forestall them by turning similar sites into permanently garrisoned English strongholds capable of keeping invaders at bay until his field-army could destroy them. This device of his original yet practical mind not only gave Wessex a shield which, copied later by other European rulers, enabled western Christendom to survive the Viking attacks, but laid the foundations of urban life in England. Our oldest towns arose as sentinels to guard the countryside against the Norsemen.

The strength of these burghs lay, not in imposing fortifications, which Alfred's ill-educated and much-plundered subjects had neither the wealth nor skill to make, but in the valour of their defenders. To people them, he used the pick of his kingdom's manhood. Every district had to support its burgh, and every local thane to build a house in it and either live there in person or maintain a fighting man to defend it. In this way the veterans of Alfred's wars became the burghers of England's earliest towns. Some of these, like Rochester, Exeter and Chichester, and his capital, Winchester, were built on the sites, and partly from the stones, of Roman cities; others, like Oxford and Shaftesbury, were new creations. The most important of all was London – formerly inside the Mercian border – which he won and took over, after it had been destroyed by a Danish raiding party, and re-populated with English veterans. It proved an acquisition of immense strategic and political significance. During the last two decades of his reign, overcoming the national prejudice against urban life, Alfred founded some twenty-five towns, or about half the number the Romans had raised during their three and a half centuries of occupation.

When, towards the end of the reign, the Viking Grand Army again attacked southern England, it was completely frustrated by this ingenious system. After four years' spasmodic and profitless raiding it was driven ignominiously from the land. Only one town in Wessex – the little port of Appledore in Kent – was taken by it, and this had never been an established burgh. Exeter, Rochester and Chichester all successfully withstood sieges, and the invaders were repeatedly brought to battle and defeated by the field-army. The heart of the country was scarcely touched. The English king had both saved his kingdom and given new hope to Christendom.

*   *   *

Yet Alfred's true greatness lay not in war but peace. He wanted to leave behind a kingdom not only secure from foes but rich in the arts of civilization. Around him lay, after two generations of warfare, a ruined country – its farms wasted, its monasteries and schools burnt, its people reduced to ignorance and squalor. Its nobility and even its clergy were almost completely illiterate. At the start of the reign there was hardly a clerk in Wessex who could understand the Latin of the services he repeated. Alone in that ravaged land in his passion for education – the fruit of his early journey to Rome – Alfred set himself to teach his people. Nearly half his revenue was devoted to educational ends: to the training of artificers, to the support of the foreign scholars and craftsmen he brought over as teachers from every country in Christendom; to the restoration of ruined monasteries and convents and the foundation of new ones at Athelney and Shaftesbury; to the great school he established for teaching the sons of thanes and freemen to read and write and which in the course of the next generation created something unique in western Europe: a literate lay nobility. 'All the sons of freemen,' he instructed his bishops, 'who have the means to undertake it should be set to learning English letters, and such as are fit for a more advanced education and are intended for high office should be taught Latin also.' Even their astonished fathers were made to take lessons. 'It was a strange sight,' Alfred's biographer and disciple, Bishop Asser, recorded, 'to see the ealdormen, who were almost all illiterate from infancy, and the reeves and other officials learning how to read, preferring this unaccustomed and laborious discipline to losing the exercise of their power.' 'God Almighty be thanked,' Alfred wrote before his death, 'we have now teachers in office!'

It was characteristic of this modest conscientious man that he taught himself before trying to teach others. He worked with his craftsmen, helping to design houses and even inventing a candle clock and a reading-lantern. And he repaired the defects of his neglected childhood and war-riven youth by making himself a master of Latin – the language in which the knowledge of the civilized past was preserved. Even while he was still fighting the Danes he had learned works read aloud to him at every spare moment until he could read them freely for himself. Then, in the intervals of reconstructing and administering a broken realm, he set to work to translate the books which alone could impart to his people the wisdom he wanted them to share. He made no pretence to being a scholar nor thought of himself as a clever man; he sought only to expound the learning of others. But he personally undertook the task – as heroic as any of his feats in battle – of translating into the rough vernacular of his country the most useful works of Christian and classical knowledge. By doing so – for no one had essayed it before – he became the father of English prose.

Among the books Alfred translated were Bede's *Ecclesiastical History*, St Augustine's *Soliloquies*, Boethius's *Consolations of Philosophy*, Gregory's *Pastoral Care*, and Orosius's *History of the World*. Into the latter he inserted chapters of his own, bringing its geographical knowledge up to date and embodying in popular form the information he loved to collect from travellers. Longfellow's poem about 'Alfred the lover of truth' taking down from the lips of the old Norse sea-captain, Othere, the account of his voyage round the North Cape, is based on one of these insertions. For the warrior who showed Christendom how to defeat the Vikings had an ungrudging admiration for their exploits as seamen and explorers. And his reverence for the past made him recognise their kinship. One of his works was a collection of the ancient heroic

46

songs and poems of the north which were the common legacy of Dane and Englishman – a collection that unhappily perished in the dark and troubled age in which this brave man lit so many candles. The same feeling for the past made him initiate the first history of the English people in their own tongue. For the *Anglo-Saxon Chronicle* – that record compiled by monks of the chief events in England since its occupation by the English tribes – was probably Alfred's conception. It continued to be kept for more than two centuries after his death and is by far the most valuable of sources for the early history of England. No other nation in western Europe possesses any record of the time to compare with it.

Underlying all Alfred's work was the depth of his Christian faith. 'Wisdom,' he wrote, 'is of such a kind that no man of this world can conceive of her as she really is, but each strives according to the measure of his wit to understand her if he may, for wisdom is of God.' In the preface to the collection of laws which he published, he reminded his subjects that, while Christ had come into the world to fulfil the Law, He had bade men be merciful and gentle and do unto others as they would be done by. It was this deeply sincere attempt to model both his life and reign on his Master's that made Alfred's achievement so unforgettable. He not only saved a Christian State by his exertions – and its people by his example – but made it worth saving. His legacy to his country and the world was his conception of what a Christian on the throne could be. Long after his death he was remembered by Englishmen as 'England's darling'.

Because of this, his work – and kingdom – endured. He left no bitterness to be avenged after his death. Having saved Wessex, and with it the English nation, he made no attempt to conquer others. He did not, like Charlemagne, massacre his prisoners, or extend his rule of terror like the Greek emperor who sent fifteen thousand blinded Bulgars back to their heathen land to prove the might of civilization. He did as he would be done by. He defeated enemies, not made them. The suzerainty he won outside his own borders was not imposed by the sword, but by character and example. 'All the English people,' Bishop Asser wrote, 'submitted to Alfred except those who were under the power of the Danes.' The destruction of the other kingdoms had left the king of Wessex the natural leader and protector of all Englishmen. He married his eldest daughter to the patriot ealdorman who led the resistance in western Mercia after its king had fled, and granted him several of his new burghs, including London. Such generosity to less fortunate neighbours made Alfred arbiter of all western England as far as the Dee. Even the Welsh, who had warred incessantly against his race, acknowledged his gentle, unenforced supremacy. So, though their kinsfolk returned for a time to plague his realm, did the Danes he had defeated and who had made their homes in eastern England. Eight years after Ethandun they made a treaty with him by which the frontier between the two races was fixed on the line of the Lea and upper Ouse and thence along Watling Street. Under it, arrangements were made for peaceful commercial intercourse between the two nations.

'I suppose,' Alfred wrote in one of his books, comparing seekers after wisdom with royal messengers, 'they would come by very many roads. Some would come from afar and have a road very long, very bad and very difficult; some would have a very long, very direct and very good road; some would have a very short and yet hard and strait and foul one; some would have a short and smooth and good one; and yet they all would come to one and the same Lord.' He himself had had a very long and hard one, in a hard and barren time. He died soon after his fiftieth year – probably in 899 – worn out by his life of struggle and danger. But he left to those who came after him a free land recovering from its wounds, and an ideal of kingship that was not of vain-glory but Christian service. He had created two things which were to survive disaster and conquest – a kingdom to which all Englishmen instinctively felt they belonged and a native literature to enshrine their culture and tradition. More than any other man he was the first maker of England.

CHAPTER FIVE

The Bones of Shire
and State

'See you our stilly woods of oak
And the dread ditch beside?
O that was where the Saxons broke
On the day that Harold died.'

Kipling

DURING THE CENTURY which followed Alfred's defeat of the Danes,
the process of rebuilding Christian society after the attacks of the
Norsemen went on faster in England than in any other country. A
great king had taught his people to defend their island home and
had endowed it with a realm which was not for ever being parti-
tioned among its princes. His descendants, the fair-haired athelings,
of the House of Wessex, produced in little more than half a century
three other great rulers – Alfred's son, Edward the Elder; his
grandson, Athelstan; and his great-grandson Edgar, the first
acknowledged king of all England. It was at Edgar's coronation
in Bath Abbey in 973 that the earliest form of the service still used
at the crowning of England's kings was read by its author, the
mystic saint and musician, Archbishop Dunstan. Behind the
solemn rites – the royal prostration and oath, the archbishop's
consecration and anointing, the anthem, 'Zadok the Priest', linking
the kings of the Angles and Saxons with those of the ancient
Hebrews, the investiture with sword, sceptre and rod of justice,
the shout of recognition by the assembled lords – lay the idea that
an anointed king and his people were a partnership under God.

49

After that sacramental act, loyalty to the Crown became a Christian obligation. The ideal of patriotism first began to take vague shape in men's minds, superseding the older conception of tribal kingship.

It was this which helped to give England in the tenth century institutions stronger than those of any western land. Her system of taxation, of currency and coinage, of local government, of the issue of laws and charters were all in advance of those prevailing in the half-anarchical kingdoms and dukedoms of the former Frankish Empire. As a result, though a country of little account at the known world's edge, her wealth increased rapidly. It was part of her king's policy to establish in every shire at least one town with a market-place and mint where contracts could be witnessed and reliable money coined. By the beginning of the eleventh century there were more than seventy towns in the country. A dozen – Winchester, the royal capital, York, Norwich and Lincoln, Gloucester, Chester, Canterbury, Thetford, Worcester, Oxford, Ipswich and Hereford – had perhaps three or four thousand inhabitants, and one, the self-governing port of London, four or five times as many. Though most of them were ramparted, and a few walled, their real security and the source of their wealth was the King's Peace and the confidence it inspired. The countryside was famous for beef, bacon and wheaten cakes, for ale, mead and perry, and for plentiful butter and cheese; a writer recorded that, while Italians cooked with oil, the English cooked with butter. Almost every village possessed a water-mill, and in the rich eastern counties of Norfolk and Lincoln often more than one. The Danish town of Derby had fourteen. The rivers swarmed with fish, and many places had eel-traps; the little Fenland town of Wisbech paid the abbot of Ely an annual rent of fourteen thousand eels. Chester sent its earldorman a thousand salmon a year, and Petersham in Surrey a thousand lampreys.

The heart of England's culture was no longer Northumbria – now a wasted and depopulated province – but Wessex. Here, too, as in the northern kingdom which had welcomed Aidan and bred Cuthbert, Celtic blood and tradition mingled with Saxon. Even its early kings had borne names which were not Teuton, like

Cerdic, Cynric, Ceawlin, and Celtic place-names were intertwined mysteriously in its western shires with English: Axe and Exe, avon for river, coombe for valley. The greatest Wessex figure of the age was Archbishop Dunstan who, like his earlier countryman, St Aldhelm, had been partly nursed in the tradition of Celtic Christianity. At Glastonbury, where as abbot his earliest work was done, legend went back far beyond the English conquest to the tiny wattle church which Joseph of Arimathaea was supposed to have built among the water-meadows for the conversion of Roman Britain. Dunstan was a mystic, feeling his way to wisdom through visions and trances; he wrestled with fiends and monsters and heard mysterious, heavenly voices.

Wessex was becoming a settled land of villages, farms and fields whose names still figure on our maps. Its main outlines – church and parish boundary, mill, ford and footpath – were already what they were to remain for a thousand years. 'See you our little mill,' wrote a twentieth-century poet,

> 'that clacks
> So busy by the brook?
> She has ground her corn and paid her tax
> Ever since Domesday Book.'

He might have added, earlier. Puttock's End, Cow Common, Crab's Green, Woolard's Ash, Doodle Oak – names of Essex fields and hamlets in the reign of Elizabeth II – were given them when the athelings of Wessex sat on the English throne. So were the boundaries of shire and hundred, and the customs – themselves far older than their new Christian forms – with which men celebrated the changes of the year. Such were Plough Monday, when the village lads, with ribbons and cracking whips, resumed work after the twelve days of Christmas; May Day when they marched to the woods to gather greenery and danced round the May pole; Whitsun when the Morris dancers leapt through the villages with bells, hobby-horses and waving scarves; Lammas when the first bread was blessed; and Harvest Home when the Corn Dolly – effigy of a heathen goddess – was borne to the barns with reapers singing and piping behind. At Christmas the houses were decked with evergreen and the Yule candles lit.

51

With its fine craftsmen and the rule of its strong kings, England was beginning once more to accumulate treasures, to become a land worth plundering as she was before the Danes attacked her. Ivories and jewelled crucifixes, golden and silver candelabra, onyx vases and elaborate wood-carvings, superbly embroidered vestments, stoles and altar cloths adorned the churches and the halls and hunting-lodges of the great. As they sat, in mantles of brightly coloured silks fastened with golden collars and garnet-inlaid brooches, listening to song, harp and minstrelsy, the princes and ealdormen of Wessex were served from polished drinking-horns chased with silver and wooden goblets with gold. The century of Athelstan and Edgar saw a new flowering of Anglo-Saxon art. Archbishop Dunstan himself, Edgar's chief counsellor, was a craftsman and loved to fashion jewellery and cast church-bells. He loved, too, to work in the scriptoria, as he had done as a young monk; in his day the illuminators of the monastic renaissance, with their gorgeous colouring and boldly flowing margins, reached new heights of achievement. So did the sculptors of the Winchester school who carved the angel at Bradford-on-Avon, the Virgin and Child at Englesham, and the wonderful Harrowing of Hell in Bristol cathedral. The richer parish churches helped to house such treasures: small barnlike buildings, with primitive rounded arches, high walls and narrow windows and bell-towers crowned with weather-cocks – an English invention. A few survive, like the log church at Greenstead in Essex, flint and rubble Braemore in the Avon valley, with its Anglo-Saxon text which no living parishioner can read, stone Barnack and broad-towered Earl's Barton in Northamptonshire.

In the depopulated north a simpler polity prevailed. Here Christian missionaries from Viking-harried Ireland were busy turning the Scandinavian settlements along the coasts and dales into Christian parishes. The wheel-head crosses that marked their open-air sites of worship show the transitional nature of the conversion: the carved Odin cross at Kirk Andrea in the Isle of Man with ravens croaking on a heathen god's shoulder, while on the other side Christ looks down in majesty; the Gosforth cross in Cumberland where the resurrected Saviour – Baldur the Beautiful

52

of northern legend reborn – tramples the dragons and demons of Hell: Surt the fire-god, Fenris the wolf and Loki the serpent. The word 'cross', derived from the Latin crux, was introduced by these Irish evangelists, gradually taking the place of the Anglo-Saxon 'rood'. It first appeared in northern names like Crosby and Cross-thwaite. Other Scandinavian words were being woven into the map of northern England; *gate* a street and *thwaite* a clearing, *fell* a hill and *thorpe* a settlement, *foss* a waterfall and *by* a village. Simi-lar Norse names – Swansea, Caldey, Fishguard, Gresholm, Haverford – appeared on the coasts of Anglesey, Pembrokeshire, Gower and Glamorgan.

Like their kinsfolk in the old Danelaw and East Anglia these northern dalesmen – pirates' brood though they were – had a great respect for law so long as they themselves made it. The very word entered England through their speech. So did the divisions or ridings into which they split the southern part of Northumbria, the juries of twelve leading men employed in the administration of their towns and wapentakes, and their habit of majority decision. For it was a rule among these independent-minded men that, save in a boat or on the battlefield, they were all equal.

*   *   *

Yet all this polity and wealth depended in the last resort on the ability of English kings to keep the good order which Alfred had won. Not all the princes of the House of Wessex were great men or able to ride the tides of anarchy in an age still threatened by Viking invasions. Edgar's eldest son, a boy, was murdered at the instiga-tion of his step-mother; the half-brother who succeeded him in 978 was a spoilt, petulant weakling. Under his inconstant impulses, and those of his brutal favourites, England's new-found unity dissolved. The long reign of Aethelred the Redeless – the unready or lacking in counsel – proved one of the most disastrous in English history. Incapable of running straight, his double dealing set the great ealdormen, who ruled the provinces, by the ears, even before he reached manhood.

Once more, scenting weakness as vultures carrion, the Vikings returned. The European mainland was no longer the easy prey it

53

had been; under the challenge of repeated invasion its divided peoples had learnt to defend themselves. Barred out of Europe, the Norsemen fell on England. For a generation they feasted on the carcass of a rich and now leaderless land. Its monasteries again fell into decay, its farms were plundered, the peasants taxed into starvation or sold as slaves. The worst humiliation came in 1012 when invaders pounced on Canterbury and carried off the primate, Alphege, and most of the monks and nuns. When the brave archbishop refused to appeal for a ransom, he was pelted to death with ox-bones by a pack of drunken pirates.

After Aethelred's ignominious flight to the continent in 1013, his son, Edmund 'Ironside', put up a fight worthy of Alfred himself against the Danish invaders, who were now led by the young king of Denmark, Canute. For nearly three years these two great soldiers fought each other among the forests and marshes of southern England. In the end, after five astonishing victories by the English loyalist forces – at Penselwood on the Somerset-Dorset border, at Sherston in Wiltshire, on the western road to London, at Brentford, and at Otford in Kent – Edmund was defeated by Canute at Ashingdon in Essex through the treachery of one of his ealdormen. Though on his father's death earlier that year he had been elected king by the men of London, he died a few months later at Oxford, leaving his Danish rival master of more than half England.

In that midwinter of disaster the great council of the realm, or *Witan*, met and made its terms with the conqueror. Preferring strength on the throne to weakness, and unity to division, it elected as king, not one of Edmund's infant sons, but the young victorious Dane, Canute. It proved a wise choice. For though Canute was almost as ruthless as his father, he ended the long Norse scourge. At a meeting of the Witan at Oxford he swore to govern his realm by the laws of King Edgar. Henceforward he made no distinction between his new countrymen and his old. He followed Alfred.

For if Canute had conquered England, in a wider sense England conquered him. English missionaries, following Boniface's great tradition, had long been at work in Scandinavia; though born a

54

pagan, Canute had been baptised. With his acceptance of a Christian crown the ravaging of Christendom from the north ceased. While in many things still a heathen, revengeful and hard, he became a devout churchman, enforcing tithes, endowing monasteries, and even making a pilgrimage to Rome where he laid English tribute on the altar of St Peter. He rebuilt the shrine at Bury St Edmunds to the king his countrymen had martyred a century and a half before, and made amends to the murdered Alphege by the honours he paid his tomb at Canterbury.

Had this great, harsh man lived longer, the course of European history might have been different. Being king both of England and Denmark, he tried to make the North Sea an Anglo-Danish lake and England the head of a Nordic confederation stretching from Ireland to the Baltic. After his conquest of Norway he became virtual emperor of the North. But fate was against him. The story of his courtiers telling him he could stay the advancing tide at Lambeth may not have been true but, like many legends, it enshrined a truth. He was not more powerful than death. He died at forty in 1035, his work incomplete and most of his mighty projects still a dream. He was buried at Winchester among the English kings, while his half-barbaric sons divided his Scandinavian empire between them.

They did not even found a dynasty. Seven years later, when the last of them died 'as he stood at his drink at Lambeth', the Witan, in 1042, chose as successor the forty-year-old Edward, son of Aethelred the Unready by his second wife, Emma of Normandy. He was a soft, devout, peace-loving man, with a clerk's long tapering fingers, a rosy face and flaxen hair which turned with age to a beautiful silver. Though exile in his mother's country had made him more French than English, his subjects were much impressed by his piety. He was more like an abbot to them than a king, and they called him the Confessor. His greatest interest was the building of a monastery among the river marshes at Thorney, a mile or two to the west of London. Here, that he might watch his abbey rising – the West Minster, at it was called – he made himself a hall on a site which was one day to become the heart of an empire.

Yet Edward exposed his subjects to almost as many dangers as his father had done. He was so devout that he refused to give his wife a child and his realm an heir. Absorbed in works of piety, he left its affairs to the great ealdormen and his Norman favourites. He made immense grants of land to a Sussex thane named Godwin, whom Canute had created earl of the West Saxons, and who induced Edward to marry his sister and to confer on his spoilt, quarrelling sons the earldoms of East Anglia, Gloucester, Hereford, Oxford, Northampton, Huntingdon and northern Northumbria.

Godwin was not the only subject able to defy the Crown. Equally masters in their provincial strongholds were his rivals, Leofric of Mercia – husband of the legendary Lady Godiva, foundress of Coventry abbey – and the giant Dane, Siward of York, who met his death like a Norse warrior standing fully accoutred with breast-plate, helmet and gilded battle-axe. The power of such magnates was not wholly Edward's fault. It was a result of the cumulative alienation of the royal estates, caused by the difficulty of raising revenue to pay for public services, which had been going on for generations and which deprived the monarchy of its chief and almost only source of income. Appointed in the days of Athelstan to lead the *fyrd* and enforce the royal law in a single shire, the ealdorman by the eleventh century, with his accumulation of shires and hereditary claim to office, had grown beyond the control of any ordinary ruler. His was the disintegrating force of power without responsibility. He was neither a chieftain bound by tribal ties nor a consecrated king with obligations to his people.

When on 5 January 1066, a few days after the consecration of his abbey church at Westminster, the gentle Confessor died, the Witan, meeting in the Godwin stronghold of London, elected the dead Godwin's son and heir, Harold Godwinson, Earl of Wessex, to the throne. In doing so, it ignored three other claimants. One was a son of Edmund Ironside; another Harold Hardrada, king of Norway. The third was the dead king's great-nephew, William, Duke of Normandy, to whom Harold, when shipwrecked there some years earlier, had done homage and sworn to assist his claim to the English throne.

HOW THEY EVOLVED

CHAPTER SIX

Norman Discipline

'There shall be one people – it shall serve one Lord –
  (Neither Priest nor Baron shall escape!)
It shall have one speech and law, soul and strength and
  sword. England's being hammered, hammered,
  hammered into shape!'

———

' "My son," said the Norman Baron, "I am dying, and
  you will be heir
To all the broad acres in England that William gave me
  for my share. . . .

'The Saxon is not like us Normans. His manners are not
  so polite,
But he never means anything serious till he talks about
  justice and right.
When he stands like an ox in the furrow with his sullen
  set eyes on your own,
And grumbles, "This isn't fair dealing," my son, leave the
  Saxon alone. . . .'

Kipling

THE DIFFICULTY FACING RULERS in the Dark Ages was to make any
system of government work except naked force. In tribal times a
king could only impose his will when the horde was assembled for
battle. When Clovis, conqueror of Gaul and the first king of the
Franks, wished to preserve a chalice looted from Soissons cathedral, his sole resource was to split open the head of the warrior who
voiced the customary right of veto. The attempt even of a great
ruler like Charlemagne to recreate an international empire based

59

on Roman law had been shattered not only by the Norse raids but by the difficulty of keeping united large areas inhabited by primitive peoples. Without a trained bureaucracy the Roman system of raising revenue could not work; a Frankish king could only levy taxes by farming them out to local magnates.

Feudalism – the protection of the locality from predatory strangers by its stronger members – seemed the only answer until either the old imperialism could be recreated or a national order take its place. The local knight in his castle, with his horse, lance, shield, and chain and leather armour, proved the answer to the invading hordes of Norsemen, Magyars and Moslems from which the West had suffered so long. His elaborate smith-made protection, his mobility and striking-power and his life-long dedication to arms made him despise mere numbers.

Yet, while he helped to save Europe, the feudal knight added to the problem of its government. If he was invulnerable to his country's foes, he was equally so to its rulers and could become a scourge to everyone within reach of his strong arm. He lived for war and by it. His neighbours had to seek his protection or be ruined. The sole restraint on his power was that of the feudal superior from whom he received his lands. The knight's obligation to his overlord was the counterpart of the loyalty to the crown which Alfred had tried to create in England. He did homage to him for his fief, swore *fidelitas* or fealty to him and gave him in war the precise measure of military service – neither more nor less – laid down in the terms of his enfeoffment.

It was the Church which took the lead in trying to discipline feudalism and harness it to constructive ends. It, too, had suffered from the anarchy caused by the invaders. Simony – the sale of sacred benefices – had become widespread; bishops paid kings and feudal lords at their consecration and recouped themselves from those they ordained, while patrons of livings exacted tribute from parish priests who in turn charged their parishioners for the Church's offices. But in the eleventh century, when Edward the Confessor was governing – or rather failing to govern – England, a succession of great Popes or Bishops of Rome set themselves to reform the Church. Their aim was to rescue the Holy See from its dependence on local princes, to end the commerce in sacred benefices by enforcing canonical election, and to make the parish clergy a sacred caste apart by insisting on celibacy and continence. And in re-establishing law and order in ecclesiastical matters, they tried, also, to end the ravages of private feudal war. They set aside days and seasons for a 'truce of God', when war was forbidden on penalty of expulsion from the Church's communion. They sought, too, by an appeal to conscience, to present knightly power as a trust and to make knight errantry a Christian pursuit; to turn the aggressive, acquisitive Frankish freebooter, armed *cap-à-pie*, into a Christian champion, driving back the heathen, defending Holy Church and punishing iniquity. In chivalry, as it became called, the Church offered the military class a code of honour. It devised an elaborate ceremony at which the young knight, before being invested with arms, knelt all night in solitary prayer before the altar, and, like the king at his crowning, took the sacrament, swearing to use the power entrusted to him in righteousness and the defence of the helpless. And, for the sake of society, it invested the oath of fealty with mystery and sanctity. It was an offence against God, the Church taught, for a vassal to be false to his liege-lord.

In one State, in particular – the little warlike duchy of Normandy – the Church succeeded in establishing a working and mutually profitable partnership with the knightly class. A hundred years earlier, when Alfred's successors were creating a united England, a Viking pirate had secured from the ruler of West Francia or France – the most westerly fragment of Charlemagne's disintegrated empire – a grant of conquered lands at the mouth of the Seine. Here, in what became named after them Normandy, intermarrying with the French and adopting their faith and language, a community of Norsemen established a dukedom whose disciplined chivalry of armoured knights evolved a technique of fighting from the saddle and stirrup which made them the arbiters of western Europe. They rode their horses through the waves of battle as their pirate forebears had sailed their ships. They loved fighting with lance and horse so much that, when they were not at war, they were for ever challenging one another in mimic tourneys or tournaments.

They were masters, too, of law and rhetoric. They knew how to govern, just as they knew how to win battles, because they were quite clear what they wanted. Ruthless, almost entirely without sentiment and, though passionate, self-possessed and cool, they had the simplicity of genius. With their round bullet-heads, blue eyes and long aquiline noses, they looked like intelligent birds of prey. Above all, they had energy. They were as restless as they were greedy and calculating. Like their Norse forebears they would go to the world's end for plunder. In the middle of the eleventh century, four hundred of them seized the south of Italy from the Byzantine Greeks. Then they went on to conquer the rich island of Sicily from the Saracens, the lords of the Mediterranean.

They had a genius for absorbing other civilizations. So thoroughly did they absorb that of the Frankish-Gaulish folk among whom they settled that, within a century of their occupation of Normandy, scarcely a word of their old Norse tongue was in use. They became a Romance or Latin-speaking race and, having conquered a Christian land, fervent champions of the Church and the newly reformed papacy. Nowhere was the monastic reforming movement so enthusiastically supported by the laity, so many monasteries built and such learned and pious clerks appointed to well-endowed benefices. It was as though the Norman knights, the most acquisitive in Europe, were trying to offset their martial outrages by the orthodoxy of their ecclesiastical establishments and, while storming their way into their neighbours' lands, to buy an entry to Heaven. They became the greatest church-builders since the days of Charlemagne and even since those of imperial Rome, whose giant buildings they tried to copy. They were not delicate craftsmen like the English; their chief resource was to build immensely thick walls, and several of their grander achievements fell down. But they had infinite ambition and a sense of space and grandeur.

Their buildings expressed their religion. Their patron-saint, standing above their churches with uplifted sword and outstretched wings, was the warrior archangel Michael, guardian of Heaven; their conception of God, a feudal overlord ready to reward those like themselves who kept the letter of His law. With the spirit they troubled themselves little; they were a practical folk who liked clear definitions. They built, not for comfort like the timber-loving Saxons, but in stone to endure. Their serried arches, marching like armies through space, the vast walls and pillars supporting them, the rude, demon-haunted figures gazing down from the capitals, symbolised the crude magnificence and vigour of their half-barbaric minds. With their grim massiveness and twin-towers rising into the sky like swords, such churches seemed designed, as Henry Adams wrote, to force Heaven: 'all of them look as though they had fought at Hastings or stormed Jerusalem.'

After the collapse of Canute's empire in 1042, the Normans had turned their gaze on England. Its wealth, so much superior to that of Normandy, seemed a standing invitation. They viewed its easy-going provincials with a contempt they hardly tried to conceal: the words *pride* and *proud* first entered the English language to describe the arrogance of the Normans to whom the Confessor granted estates and bishoprics. As he had so conveniently re-frained from giving his kingdom an heir, his great-nephew, Wil-liam, Duke of Normandy, formed the idea of claiming it for him-self. He even succeeded in persuading his saintly uncle to promise it him – though it was not by English law his to promise.

The English at that time were the most civilized people in western Europe. Their achievement in vernacular scholarship, poetry and literature was unique; their craftsmanship – in sculp-ture, embroidery, goldsmith's and coiner's work – most skilful and sensitive. They had evolved a union of Church and State for national ends which had no parallel outside the Byzantine Empire; their bishops and ealdormen sat side by side in the Witan and the provincial and shire courts. But to the radically minded Normans, England was a land without discipline; where the enthusiasm of saints and scholars had become lost in a sluggish stream of petty provincial interests; where married canons lived on hereditary endowments, and the very archbishop of Canterbury was a simon-iac and uncanonically appointed; and where boorish nobles, sunk in swinish drunkenness and gluttony, sold sacred benefices while bucolic warriors, too conservative to change, still fought on foot and with battle-axes. She had lost touch with the new world growing up beyond the Channel: with the international Church, with its reforming Popes and disciplined monasteries, with the new ideals of chivalry, and the mailed knights, battle-trained horses, tall moated castles which were now becoming the dominant features of the European landscape. She was living on the memories of the past, static, conservative, unimaginative. She had barred her mind to change; it remained to be seen if she could bar her gates.

*　　　*　　　*

The man who now set himself to conquer England was one of the great men of history. His mother was the unmarried daughter of a Falaise tanner; his great-great-grandfather had been a pirate. Left fatherless as a child, his boyhood had been spent amid the turmoil caused by the violence of his father's feudal barons. The ruin they unloosed had made an indelible impression on him. Far-sighted, patient, prudent, self-controlled, bold but thorough in all he did, and ruthless towards those who stood in his way, Duke William made his little duchy, with its disciplined chivalry of armoured knights and ruddy-faced men-at-arms from the Normandy apple orchards, the most formidable force in Europe. Compelled to wage war in turn against his barons, his jealous neighbours in Maine, Anjou and Brittany, and his feudal overlord, the titular King of France, he defeated them all. He never lost sight of his aims, never over-reached himself, and steadily increased his domains. When in his fortieth year he began to gather ships for the invasion of England, landless knights from every Frankish province flocked to his banners.

All that summer of 1066 two armadas were preparing to invade England, one on the Norman coast, the other in the Norwegian fiords and islands to the north of Scotland where Harold Hardrada, the barbarian King of Norway, was hoping to re-incorporate the British island in a Scandinavian empire. But though Harold Godwinson, concentrating against the nearer of the two, waited all summer in the south, by the autumn his peasant levies began to slip away to their homes and harvests. Only the house-carles of the royal bodyguard remained until, in September, news came that the King of Norway had landed at Ouse, near York.

Harold at once set out on the long march up the straight, grass-grown highroad which the Romans had built a thousand years before. Four years earlier the lightning speed of his marches had broken the power of the Welsh. Now he was resolved that the Viking king who had come to seize his kingdom should meet the same end, promising him six feet of English earth or, as he was tall, seven. On 25 September, after covering thirty miles since dawn, he fell on the Viking host at Stamford Bridge. All afternoon the clangour of axe and sword continued. By dusk Hardrada had fallen, and King Harold – 'a little man sitting proudly in his stir-rups' – had made good his boast that his foe should win nothing in England but a grave.

Two days later, William, who had been waiting for a favouring wind, sailed from the Somme. On 28 September he landed at Pevensey Bay. The news, galloped through the Midland forests, took two days to reach York where Harold was celebrating his victory. Without a moment's hesitation he and his battered house-carles set out again for the south. In six days they covered the one hundred and ninety miles to London. Waiting there a few days for the *fyrd* of the southern shires to join them, they marched on 12 October for Hastings. Uncertain of his kingdom's loyalty and fear-ful lest his jealous earls should play him false, Harold had to turn out the southern wasps' nest quickly, like the northern, or perish.

The battle which was to decide his fate and England's took place on 14 October at Senlac where the Hastings track emerged from the Sussex oak-forest. The English king, who had meant to attack, was forced to remain on the defensive, as only half his troops had arrived. His house-carles, with their double-handed battle-axes, were probably the finest infantry in Europe, but the rest of his army was a rabble of peasant levies, armed with spears, clubs and pitchforks, and no match for Duke William's armoured knights. Fighting continued all day, but by the evening only the house-carles were left holding the ridge against the Norman horse-men. They were so closely packed that the slain had scarcely room to fall. It was almost dark when a band of knights closed in on

Harold who had been wounded in the eye by an arrow and, as he bent bleeding over his shield, hacked him to pieces. 'In the English ranks,' wrote a Norman chronicler, 'the only movement was the dropping of the dead. They were ever ready with their steel, those sons of the old Saxon race, the most dauntless of men.' By nightfall all lay dead round their fallen king and his banner of the Fighting Man.

*   *   *

The kingdom Alfred had made thus became a colony of a foreign dynastic empire – that of the Dukes of Normandy, whose language and culture were French and who had little understanding of English ways. With a few thousand knights and men-at-arms William the Conqueror subjected a nation of more than a million and a half. Duke of Normandy, he now also became King of the English. At first, like Canute, he tried to govern them with the help of the native lords and prelates who accepted his conquest. Many of his earliest officials were English and some of his first writs and charters were issued in their tongue – the last for three hundred years. But he was faced by two inescapable difficulties. One was the need to reward the followers with whom he had won and without whom he could not maintain his throne; the other the obstinacy of the English and their hatred of foreigners, particularly the French.

He began by confiscating only the lands of those who had fought against him at Hastings and whom, in keeping with his claim to be the Confessor's heir, he treated as traitors. But the discontent aroused by the arrogance of his acquisitive barons and their rough knights forced him to carry the process of confiscation further. A widespread rising three years after the Conquest he suppressed with terrifying ruthlessness. During the next generation, seizing on every act of disobedience or rebellion, he transferred the owner-ship of almost every large estate from English hands to Norman. At the end of his twenty years' reign there were only two major English landowners left and one English bishop. Almost every Englishman held his land at the will of some Norman.

In this way William substituted for the old loose aristocratic direction of the State a new and far more efficient one. He resumed the royal rights over the nation's land which his Anglo-Saxon predecessors had improvidently 'booked' away. He kept a fifth for himself and his family, and a quarter for the Church. Of the remainder he redistributed all but an insignificant fraction among his hundred and seventy chief Norman and French followers on strictly defined conditions of military service. Nearly half went to ten men. Having learnt from his harsh life that no State or throne was safe unless organised for instant war, he attached to every grant of land an inescapable martial obligation. In return for their fiefs or 'honours', as they were called, his tenants-in-chief, including bishops and abbots, had to swear to support the Crown with a fixed number of mounted and armoured knights, to pay specified dues at stated times and to attend the royal courts and councils. To meet these commitments they in turn had to farm out their lands on similar terms to professional knights or fighting-men, whom they 'enfeoffed' as their vassals.

Thus every substantial holding of land, whoever its immediate occupier, was made to furnish and maintain an armoured, mounted and battle-trained knight ready to take the field at any moment. As well as giving protection to its peasant cultivators, who had to perform the same manual services for its new owner as its old, it became a knight's fief or fee, itself part of some greater fief. If its feudal holder failed to perform his military services, it reverted to the overlord to whom he had sworn allegiance for it. It could neither be broken up nor sold without the latter's consent, and on its holder's death his heir, after paying a fine and doing homage, had to render the same services.

To a large extent this system had already been established in France and other parts of western Europe. Yet William's was unique – a mark of his creative genius – in its identification of the protection of the fief with that of the realm. It was the absence of this that had so troubled his own early life in Normandy and broken up the old English kingdom. In the Conqueror's new England the holder of every substantial military fief had to do homage for it, not only to his overlord, but to the Crown.

For after William had crushed two rebellions in which disloyal

Norman tenants-in-chief had called out their vassals against him, and at a time when a new rising and a Danish invasion were threatened, he held, at the Christmas feast and council at Gloucester in 1085, 'very deep speech with his wise men'. Next year he summoned a meeting at Salisbury, not only of his tenants-in-chief, but of all principal land-holders in the country. And by making them swear to obey him even against their own overlords, he made them directly responsible to the Crown as in no other State in Europe. By this simple device, he turned feudalism, without weakening its military efficiency, into an instrument of royal power. He became not only, like the King of France, the nominal lord paramount of the realm, but the actual one. He was able to do so because, having conquered England and its land, he started with a clean slate.

Nor did William make his nobles rulers of provinces like their English predecessors or their counterparts in France. Whether by accident or design, he scattered their estates about the country. This not only made it harder for them to rebel, but forced them to think in national as well as regional terms. Abroad the feudal count, like the old Anglo-Saxon earl, thought only of his county or province; in England, like the King himself, he had to think of the country as a whole. Henry de Ferrers, rewarded with 114 manors in Derbyshire, was given 96 in thirteen other counties. A still greater tenant-in-chief, Robert de Mortain, held his 793 manors in twenty different shires. The only exceptions were on the Welsh and Scottish borders, where the local magnates needed vast powers to keep the tribesmen of the Celtic west and north at bay. The prince bishop of Durham, and the earls of Chester, Shrewsbury, and Hereford, ruled what later were called counties palatine. Yet even these were small compared with the independent provinces of France, and the King appointed to them only men he could trust. He watched them very closely. Within half a century of the Conquest only two of these compact, semi-independent jurisdictions remained.

Within these limits – a framework of discipline in which every baron enjoyed his just feudal rights, but no more – William scrupulously respected the 'liberties' of his nobles. They were the instrument by which he ruled. Fewer than two hundred French-speaking barons – closely inter-related and accustomed to working together – and five or six thousand knights became the principal land-holders of England. Having both a duty and incentive to protect the Conquest, they guaranteed its permanence. They formed a new ruling caste; a colonising warrior aristocracy which possessed not only privilege but creative energy. The names they brought from their Norman homes are writ on our maps and across our history – Montgomery and Mandeville, Warenne and Giffard, Baldwin and Mortimer, Mowbray and Beaumont, Neville and Lacy, Bohum and Courcy, Beauchamp and Percy.

Beneath this military superstructure the Conqueror had the sense to leave England much as it was. He kept the Witanagemot which became the Great Council of his tenants-in-chief, lay and ecclesiastical. He kept the elaborate secretarial and financial machinery which the English kings had devised for raising gelds and land-taxes, and for sending out enquiries and orders to their officers in the shires. He kept the old divisions of shire and hundred; the shire-courts where, under the royal sheriff's eye, the freemen interpreted the customary law of the locality, and the hundred-courts where representatives of the villages – priest, reeve and leading peasants – settled their disputes and answered for breaches of the peace. He left unchanged the free communities of the Dane-law and the ancient tenures by which the Kentish cultivators were protected in their holdings. He left, too, with the Norman manor superimposed on it for military and taxing purposes, the midland English village, with its strip-divided fields, its hereditary rights of cattle-pasture and pig-pannage, its communal system of cultivation and wide variety of tenures. He left the Londoners the rights they had always enjoyed under their elected portreeve and burgesses. And he kept the old Anglo-Saxon shire *fyrd* or militia – an invaluable counterpoise to the Norman feudal array.

Wherever an English institution could serve his end, William improved on it. Having got rid of the independent provincial earls who under Aethelred and the Confessor had acquired the un-English right to own and rule land without relation to the service to the Crown for which it had been granted, he used in their place

SET IN A SILVER SEA

the sheriffs or royal officials with whom his predecessors had vainly
tried to check the earls' powers. The Norman sheriff administered
the royal estates in the shire, presided at its court, collected the
taxes and led the shire militia in time of war or rebellion. This
linked the Crown with the forces, so strong in medieval society, of
local patriotism and self-interest and made for national unity. So
did the system – possibly brought from France, but adapted also
from Anglo-Saxon and Danish practice – by which sworn juries
or panels of neighbours were made judges of local questions of fact.
William used these repeatedly to discover the rights of the Crown
against his powerful Norman followers and the taxable value of
their estates.

*   *   *

For most Englishmen all this was a terribly painful process. 'Cold
heart and bloody hand,' wrote a Norse poet, 'now rule the English
land.' William was guilty, in his own dying words, of 'the barbarous
murder of many thousands, both young and old, of that fine race
of people'.[1] To many the Conquest brought bitter tragedy; the
families of those who died in battle, the peasants on the line of
march, the thanes whose lands were seized to provide fiefs for
William's foreign barons and knights. All who made the least
resistance were ruthlessly stripped of their estates in pursuit of the
royal policy. Most of the old English nobles and thanes who survived Hastings and the later rebellions in the west, north and
midlands became mere farmers; at Marsh Gibbon in Buckinghamshire – the Conqueror's great tax-survey records – Aethelric, the
farmer, 'now holds it of William, the son of Ansculf, in heaviness
and misery'.[2] Some fled to Scotland, where they strengthened the
Saxon elements of that wild land, or took service in the Varangian
bodyguard of the Greek emperor at Constantinople. A few brave

[1] 'I have persecuted its native inhabitants beyond all reason. Whether gentle
or simple, I have cruelly oppressed them; many I unjustly disinherited; in-
numerable multitudes, especially in the county of York, perished through me by
famine or the sword.' Ordericus Vitalis, The Ecclesiastical History cit. *English
Historical Documents*, 1, p. 286.
[2] *'Graviter et miserabiliter'* – one of the few human touches in that grim,
invaluable record.

70

men, preferring liberty to life, took to the marshes and forests as outlaws, like Hereward the Wake, a small Lincolnshire land-owner who held out in the Fens till 1071. 'Most,' as William Fuller wrote six centuries later, 'betook themselves to patience which taught many a noble hand to work, foot to travel, tongue to entreat.'

Humbler folk were left in possession of their holdings; Norman and English alike would have starved otherwise. Yet many of them were subjected to the tyranny of the special courts which the Conqueror set up in the forests, still covering more than a quarter of the land, to preserve the red and fallow deer for his hunting. 'He loved the tall stags like a father,' we are told. To guard them, his forest officers put out the eyes of any man found killing hart or hind, and mutilated poor peasants caught in the woods with dogs or arrows. In these sacred precincts even the lopping of a bough was punished. Rich and poor alike murmured at the King's forest laws, but 'he was so sturdy that he recked nought of them'.

William was hard and ruthless: 'so stark a man', an English monk called him. After the second rising of the northern counties in 1070, when five hundred Norman knights were massacred at Durham, he so harried the countryside that along the road from York to Durham not a house remained standing. Even the northern capital and its famous minster were burnt. It took the north generations to recover. Seventeen years later the royal commissioners, surveying the tax capacity of Yorkshire, entered against place after place the grim word, 'Waste'.

Above all, the Conqueror was a merciless taxer. His first act after his coronation was to 'lay on a geld exceeding stiff'. Close-fisted and grasping – a monk complained that, while the Saxon kings gave their courtiers four meals a day, he gave his only one – he had compiled after 1085, mainly that he might tax his realm more closely, a record of all feudal holdings directly or indirectly liable to the Crown. 'So narrowly did he cause the survey to be made,' wrote an English chronicler 'that there was not one single hide nor rood of land, nor – it is shameful to tell, but he thought it no shame to do – was there an ox, cow or swine that was not set down in the writ.' Using commissioners to hold local enquiries or inquests in every shire and hundred, he had recorded, with meticulous efficiency[1], the ownership and taxable value of every manor or village under lordship, both at the Conquest and at the time of the survey. This included the number of its ploughlands or hides[2], of the freemen, villeins, cottars and slaves living on it, of its mills, fish-ponds, and plough-teams, the extent of its woodland, meadow and pasture – everything, in short, that was capable of being taxed. Originally drawn up on long parchment rolls stored in the Treasury at Winchester, the survey was copied into two volumes christened by the English 'Domesday' because there was no appeal against it. It was the most remarkable administrative document of the age; there is nothing like it in the contemporary annals of any other country. It enabled the King to know the landed wealth of his entire realm; 'how it was peopled and with what sort of men', what their rights were, and how much they were worth.

The taxation William imposed fell directly on the rich but, as the rich could pass it on, even more severely on the poor. The peasants' burdens, the labour and boon-services demanded of them by their lords, became heavier. The English thane, who had taken part of the village produce as his due and occasionally summoned its reluctant young men from the plough to serve in the ealdorman's levies, was supplanted by a Norman or Frenchman. There was a new face – and a new tongue spoken – at the manor house. It is never pleasant to have to pay taxes and rent. It is worse to have to pay them to a foreigner. And these foreigners were great sticklers for their rights. They left no one in any doubt that they were the masters of the country and regarded the natives as a conquered race. In those harsh years when Norman knight and English churl were learning uneasily to live together, many an English back must have smarted from the lash of a French man-at-arms. So must many a sullen English heart.

Behind the Norman knight's bailiff, with his bullying ways and grasping demands, was the castle which his master built to house his retainers and overawe the neighbourhood. Everywhere, on

[1] He employed a second body of commissioners to check the findings of the first. F. M. Stenton, *Anglo-Saxon England*, p. 609.
[2] Usually reckoned at about 120 acres, though its size varied in different parts of the country.

strategic hill and vantage point, the castles rose – little islands of foreign power in a subjected countryside: the high, circular, moated mound, raised by English labour and crowned by a wooden, and often later stone, keep or tower; the outer bailey with its earth-work enclosure and barracks, whence knights and men-at-arms rode forth to police and terrorise the countryside; the moat with its drawbridge. Even proud London was overawed by its Tower, begun in wood immediately after the Conquest and in stone a generation later.[1] The heavily armoured Norman retainers – *cnihtas* or knights, as the English called them – who garrisoned these strong-points, had the whip-hand of the countryside. A poor man, if he was to live and till the soil in peace, had to make what terms he could with them. Otherwise he might find his house burnt over his head, his wife and children driven into the woods, and himself thrown into a stinking dungeon.

* * *

Yet the Norman Conquest brought compensations to the underdog. William conquered more than the English. He used the heritage of Alfred to curb his own turbulent nobility. He brought feudalism under royal control. The stark King fastened his English version of the feudal system, with all his Norman thoroughness, on the free-booter barons and knights who had so long kept western Europe in an uproar with their selfish civil wars. It was this which completed the work that Alfred had begun. It made England a disciplined land, disciplined not only at the base but at the summit. A man could cross her, it was said, with his bosom full of gold.

By making England one, William saved her, too, from future conquests. He closed the door on the northern barbarians who had ravaged her for three centuries and who now withdrew into the Scandinavian mists. Twice during his reign the Danes were invited by rebellious subjects to land on the east coast, and twice were driven out with no profit to themselves and disastrous consequences to their sympathisers. Though, with Norsemen settled round her

---

[1] The White Tower, with its fifteen-feet thick walls, is the only surviving part built by the Conqueror. The words *castle* and *tower* both entered the English language at this time.

northern and western shores, Scotland still looked for another generation to the barbarian North, England ceased to be a frontier land between the Viking world and the reviving civilization of western Europe. Henceforth her lot lay with the lands which inherited the memories and traditions of Rome. Having under Canute been part of a Scándinavian empire spanning the North Sea, she became part of a Norman-French empire spanning the Channel.

Her military forces were now far more formidable than they had been even in the days of Athelstan. In open country the Norman knights on their war-horses were the masters of every field. Six years after his conquest of England, William invaded the lowlands of Scotland, whose king, Malcolm Canmore, had married the atheling's sister, Margaret. His mounted armour quickly reached the Tay, where he forced Malcolm to do homage and surrender his eldest son as a hostage. A later punitive force, following a Scottish raid into England, advanced as far as Falkirk and built a fortress on the Tyne called Newcastle to guard northern England.

The Welsh cattle-raiders learnt the same lesson. From the great border 'Marcher' earldoms of Hereford, Chester and Shrewsbury the Norman barons went out to seize strategic positions in every lowland valley, driving the natives into the hills. The kingdom of Gwent became Norman; so did Chepstow and Monmouth, Gower and Cardigan, Radnor and Brecknock, Montgomeryshire and the Vale of Clwyd. In all of them stone castles rose to dominate the countryside. Even in the far west beyond the mountains, the Marcher lords planted their power in the Pembrokeshire plain. Early in the twelfth century they settled it with English and Flemish farmers, so that it became known as 'little England'.

*　　　*　　　*

In a society so warlike and predatory, kingship called for rare qualities. An eleventh-century king had to appoint and dismiss his own officers, preside over councils and law courts, raise and lead armies and, if his realm was not to relapse into anarchy after his

74

death, choose his successor and secure for him the loyalty of his lords. He had to hear and determine lawsuits, give judgments in person, and constantly travel the country both to preserve order and feed his court. An Anglo-Norman king had not only to do so in England but in Normandy, Brittany and Maine. Wherever he went, he was followed by throngs of suitors, seeking favours and redress of grievances. Even the poor English villeins used to surround William on his progresses, holding up their wooden ploughs to draw attention to their woes.

Above all, the King had to overawe the rough, half-barbaric warriors who surrounded him and on whom his power depended. When he wore his crown in public at the great annual Easter, Ascension and Christmas Feasts at Winchester, Westminster and Gloucester – ceremonies attended by the entire baronage – the peace of the realm turned on the majesty with which he spoke and moved. In days before even the greatest could read and write, formal pageantry – coloured, gilded robe, heraldic device on banner, shield and tent, splendid trappings for horse and throne, glittering arms and armour – were the medium through which the might of the State was expressed. So was the King's presence.

It was England's fortune that during the first centuries after the Conquest so many of her rulers possessed kingly qualities. William himself had tremendous presence. 'He was of moderate height,' wrote the historian, William of Malmesbury, 'immense corpulence, going rather bald in front; of such strength of arm . . . that no one could bend the bow which he drew when his horse was at full gallop. His dignity was of the highest, whether sitting or standing, despite the deformity of a protruding stomach.' It was because his able, tough, short-set, second son, William, had character too that the Conqueror on his deathbed in 1087 sent his English crown, sword and sceptre to him instead of to his weak, good-natured, eldest son, Robert of Normandy. 'Rufus', or the Red King, as he was called from his flaming hair, was a bad man – reckless, vicious, illiterate, cruel and blasphemous. But his English subjects, shocked though they were by his life, remembered with gratitude 'the good peace he kept in the land'. 'He was very strong and fierce to his country,' wrote one of them, 'and to all his neigh-

75

bours and very terrible.' He feared, it was said, God little, and man not at all. When the Norman barons, who turned his eldest brother's duchy into an inferno, raised trouble in England, they got short shrift. He had his cousin, who was one of them, whipped in every church in Salisbury and hanged. And when he needed help against his stronger subjects, he did not hesitate to arm his weaker: his 'brave and honourable English', as he called them.

After William II's death in 1100 from a mysterious arrow in the New Forest, it was the English who enabled his successor, the Conqueror's youngest son, Henry, to wrest Normandy from his brother, Duke Robert. At the battle of Tinchebrai, forty years after Hastings, English infantry, fighting side by side with Anglo-Norman knights, overthrew the baronage of the duchy and annexed it to the English crown. They were trained by the King himself, who showed them how to repel cavalry. Though he was as grasping as his father, the English, whose despised tongue he learnt to speak, made a hero of Henry who, unlike his brothers, had been born in their land. His title to the throne being doubtful, he proclaimed his adherence to English law, swore in his coronation oath to maintain justice and mercy, and promised to 'abolish all the evil practices with which the realm was unjustly oppressed'. He claimed that he had been called to the throne in the old electoral way, 'by the common counsel of the barons of the realm'. Soon after his accession he married a daughter of the Scots king, who through her English mother was descended from Edmund Ironside and Alfred. In later years he loved a Welsh princess, Nest, wife of one of his Marcher barons, who helped him – ruler of a realm speaking three different languages – to understand not only his English subjects but his British.

Henry I, 'the Lion of Justice' as he was called, deserved his people's confidence. 'There was great awe of him,' testified the Anglo-Saxon chronicler; 'no man durst misdo against another in his time; he made peace for man and beast.' For thirty-five years this squat, avaricious, smooth-spoken man gave the English that political stability which those who have known anarchy value most. He was a tremendous worker, a man of business who could read Latin, understood the importance of administration, and introduced into government regular habits and routine. His father had given England a taxing system more accurate and honest than any in Europe; building on his foundations, Henry gave it a permanent officialdom. He made it out of the domestic officers of his household – the treasurer; the chamberlain who looked after the bedchamber; the constable of the knights and the marshal of the stables; the steward who presided in the hall where scores of ushers kept order with rods; the reverend Chancellor with his seal and writing-office – an innovation of the Confessor's – where writs were prepared for the sheriffs.

Henry, a particularly parsimonious man, kept these functionaries in the strictest economy. Their wages and 'liveries' of bread, wine and candles were meticulously laid down in the royal accounts. The Chancellor, the most highly paid of all – for he had to maintain a large staff of clerks – received five shillings daily, three loaves, one of the best quality and two less good, two measures of wine, a wax candle and forty candle-ends. He was also allowed two meals a day at the King's table. A humble official like the man who looked after the cloths in the pantry, only got three halfpence a day and his food; the ewerer had an extra penny a day when the King went on a journey – for drying his clothes – and threepence whenever he had a bath. The state baths before the three great feasts of the year, however, had to be provided free.

The greatest of all the royal servants, the Justiciar, who kept order when the King sat in judgment and deputised in his absence, became, in the person of Roger of Salisbury, a poor Norman priest whom Henry made a bishop[1], head of the national administration. He and his fellow officers formed a kind of inner standing court of the Great Council known as the *Curia Regis*, to which both judicial appeals and affairs of State were referred. With their staffs of trained clerks and chambers where suitors could wait on them, they were the first fathers of our civil service. In the great stone hall of Westminster, which Rufus raised over the marble bench where the English kings had done justice in the open air, public business continued even when the Court was travelling. Here twice a year,

[1] Chosen by Henry, it is said, because of the time-saving speed with which he read the offices in chapel.

under the chairmanship of King or Justiciar, officials called barons of the Exchequer sat at a table with counters and a chequered cloth, carefully checking with the sheriffs the taxes, rents, fines and debts due to the Crown. Every penny had to be accounted for. There was nothing else like it at the time in western Europe.

This capacity for organisation, for creating institutions which continued irrespective of great persons, made a deep impression on Henry's subjects. They admired the unhurried regularity and dignity with which he did business: his daily reception before the midday meal of all who came for justice, the sober recreation after it, the carefully planned arrangements for State progresses through his dominions. His influence was felt in every county, where the sheriffs were kept perpetually busy, receiving writs, making records and collecting the revenue under the eyes of the royal officers at Westminster.

*   *   *

After Henry's death in 1135 from a surfeit of hunting and lampreys, Englishmen again had an experience of life under a weak king. His only legitimate son having been drowned crossing the Channel, Henry had nominated as successor his daughter, the Empress Matilda, widow of the German emperor and wife of the Count of Anjou, Geoffrey Plantagenet – so called from the sprig of broom he wore in his helmet. But the Council, deeming a woman unfit to rule and exercising the old English right of election from the royal house, offered the crown instead to his nephew, Stephen of Blois, son of the Conqueror's daughter. This good-natured monarch lacked the qualities for kingship. 'A mild man, soft and good, and did not justice,' an English chronicler wrote of him. He 'began many things, but never finished them'. Though he reigned for nineteen years – 'nineteen long winters', the chronicler called them – he left little behind save a chapel at Westminster bearing his name and an abiding memory of the anarchy unloosed by his weakness. Taking advantage of his indecision, the Welsh descended from their mountains to sack farms on the Dee and Wye, and a savage horde from Scotland marched into England, massacring the inhabitants and driving off the women and girls as slaves, roped naked

78

together. It was only halted by the resolution of the aged archbishop of York – Thurstan, friend of St Bernard and founder of Fountains – who called out the *fyrd* of Yorkshire. Fighting under the banners of the north-country saints and led by a handful of Norman nobles – one of them named Bruce and another Balliol – the Yorkshiremen routed the invaders at the Battle of the Standard near Northallerton.

In 1139 Matilda, too, invaded the country from Anjou. For eight years England was racked by civil war, while local barons, playing their own selfish game, threw in their lot, first with one side, then the other. It was hard indeed for them to avoid doing so with two sovereigns claiming their allegiance. Freed from the control of the officials of the *Curia Regis*, the worst of them built castles from which they plundered their neighbours and indulged in all the licence – so familiar in Europe, but now almost forgotten in southern England – of private war. Some, like King Stephen himself, brought murderous foreign mercenaries into the country who turned royal fortresses of which they were custodians into private strongholds. In the Isle of Ely – the district that suffered most – the terrible Geoffrey de Mandeville – earl of Essex, made life a hell with his savage foreign soldiers. 'They put men in prison for their gold and silver, they hung them up by the feet and smoked them with foul smoke . . . They put knotted strings round their heads and writhed them till they went into the brain. They put them into dungeons crawling with adders and snakes. Men said that Christ and his saints slept.' The fields were untilled, the crops destroyed, the cattle driven away. On the continent such doings were normal. In England, after seventy years of strong rule and royal justice, they were not. The result was to create a universal longing among Englishmen and even among Norman knights and barons for the strong monarchical rule their fathers had enjoyed.

In the end the disorder was resolved by a compromise. It was agreed that Stephen should reign till his death and be succeeded by Matilda's twenty-year-old son, Henry Plantagenet, Count of Anjou. His father – the most powerful of all the independent vassals of the French king – had left Henry ruler, not only of Anjou, Maine and Touraine, but of Normandy, which he had conquered in Matilda's name. Six months after his accession the young count

79

doubled his dominions by marrying the gay divorced runaway queen of Louis of France, Eleanor of Aquitaine. Twelve years his senior and the greatest heiress in Europe, she brought him the fiefs of Gascony, Guienne, Poitou, Saintonge, Limousin, La Marche and Auvergne, and control of more than half France.

In the spring of 1153, Henry came to England to rally his mother's supporters. In a whirlwind campaign he transformed the military situation. That November at Winchester, amid tumultuous rejoicing, he was accepted by Stephen as his 'son' and heir. When, in 1154, on the King's death, he was crowned and invested at Westminster with the regalia of England – golden crown and sceptre, silver-gilt rod and spurs, embroidered sandals and mantle of white silk – every bell in London rang for joy.

CHAPTER SEVEN

The Lawyer King

'The King is under no man,
but he is under God and the Law'

Bracton

AT TWENTY-ONE Henry II was the richest prince in Europe. He was ruler not only of England and his native Anjou, but of Maine, Touraine and Normandy. His marriage with Eleanor of Aquitaine – the divorced wife of the French King and the greatest heiress of the age – had made him master of south-western France. He was well-read, eloquent, courteous, a lover of learned conversation and a good linguist.

Yet he was as at home in the field as at court, indifferent to hardships and never happier than when jesting with rude soldiers round a camp fire. His short, homely cloak and frugal meals were a by-word; when he cut his finger he sewed it up with his own needle. He bore the press of suitors that surrounded a medieval king with cheerful good-humour; even when vexed by importunity, he let the crowd bear him from place to place while he listened patiently to every man's case. With his round head and eager, freckled face, his sandy, close-cropped hair contrasting with the effeminate locks of the nobles and troubadours of his wife's glittering court, his squat, sturdy frame and long boxer's arms, he looked rather like a good-natured lion; affable, modest and open to all.

Beneath these winning attributes lay a steely will, determination to achieve his ends and tireless industry. 'In night-watches and labours,' wrote one of his secretaries, 'he was unremitting.'

81

He never forgot a face or a lesson. He was as businesslike and methodical as his grandfather. And like him he was adamant in reducing his affairs to order. Those who opposed him were met with unrelenting, unscrupulous resolution. Beneath his urbane manner ran the diabolical temper of the Angevins; there were times when he tore off his clothes in rage and gnawed the straw from his mattresses. 'From the devil we come,' boasted one of his sons, 'and to the devil we shall go!' Yet in Henry, as in them all, ferocity and subtlety were deceptively mingled. And in him, both were subjected to a strong commonsense and prudence.

The greatest master of diplomacy of the age, he liked to settle accounts without bloodshed. Swift to strike, unrelenting in pursuit, he was in victory unusually merciful and magnanimous. He preferred mutilation as a punishment to death and a fine to either. For an avaricious man he was even moderate in fining. And, though he gave his heart to none save his undeserving sons, he was seldom cruel or vindictive. He made enemies, as all who reform with passion must; his vitality drove both his wife and children to rebellion.

Yet those who worked with Henry loved him. The praises of his judges and Exchequer officials were founded on more than flattery. For his devotion to their common task – the creation of order in his kingdom's affairs – was the consuming passion of his life.

At the core of his being lay a daemonic energy. He was always moving, always active, and so restless that even in chapel he chattered and scribbled incessantly. He rose before cock-crow, and only sat down to ride or eat. Slaving like his grandfather far into the night over public business, he shared the passion of all the Conqueror's line for the chase; on his journeys he hunted and hawked along every stream. He never brooked or wasted a minute's delay.

As soon as he ascended the throne this restless genius began, with furious energy, to restore his kingdom. He sent away the foreign mercenaries, dismantled the unlicensed castles, and demanded back the filched Crown lands. When the earls his mother and Stephen had created ignored his writs, he marched against them, scaring the Midland magnate, Peverel of the Peak, into a monastery, and making the great Marcher lord, Hugh de Mortimer, yield up his castles of Bridgnorth, Cleobury and Wigmore. Having restored order in England, he turned against the Welsh princes and Scottish king. He chased the former back to their mountains, and made the latter restore the shires of Northumberland, Westmorland and Cumberland taken during the troubles of Stephen's reign, and do homage at Chester. After which, in the autumn of 1158, this tireless man set out for France to apply, from the Vexin to Toulouse, the same treatment to his own and his wife's continental vassals.

Yet Henry was too shrewd to suppose that much could be won by war. Dominion had come to him so early that conquest made little appeal. What he wanted was to consolidate his possessions and make them a reality instead of, as with other medieval empires, a shadow. He was a realist. The campaigns he fought were either to repress rebellion or secure his frontiers. His reduction of Brittany was to safeguard the long, narrow corridor of his French provinces; his chastening of the Welsh and Scots to save the English Marches from raiding and rapine.

Most of all, he sought to make his rule endure. It is this that constitutes his claim to greatness. The supreme object of his crowded, stormy life was to create institutions which could preserve his inheritance after his death from the disintegrating forces threatening it. The chief of these was the power that had made it; military feudalism. In the hands of a ruler like the Conqueror or Henry I, feudalism gave strength and security to a nation. Under a weak one, like Stephen, its dynamic of self-interest could tear the State to pieces. It was not enough, Henry saw, to discipline it during his lifetime. He had to leave the means of doing so to his successors.

Yet feudalism was an inherent part of society. It could only be destroyed by destroying society itself. In England it was the mainstay of the foreign monarchy. Every earl, baron and knight, as well as being a leader and organiser of the local community, was a trained fighting man, dedicated to arms from boyhood and ready for instant war. He had to be able to leap fully armed into the saddle without touching the stirrups, to wield lance, sword and shield, to wear all day without tiring the heavy armour of his caste. This grew ever more elaborate, and the knight's advantage in battle correspondingly greater. By now even his face was completely covered by a ponderous visor, which let down like a castle portcullis and which, after being dented in action, had to be hammered off his head at the nearest smithy.

The members of this warlike caste, who viewed everyone else with contempt, had two interests: fighting and landed property. They thought of them as synonymous, for each sustained the other. They fought for land, not only under their liege-lords on the battlefield, but in the feudal courts of law, where the sole process for determining ownership was trial-by-battle. If a man was not fit to fight for land, the knightly class felt, he was not fit to own it. His only resource was to hire or enfeoff a young knight or champion to fight for him.

The knight's goal – the end of all his prowess – was the fief. The price of a fief was feudal loyalty. And the chief point of honour with most of the hard-bitten men who lived by knighthood was fidelity to the overlord who had enfeoffed them. Every great lord kept his court of armed vassals – 'all his barons and men French and English', as one charter put it – his courtiers and officials, marshal and constable, treasurer, seneschal and chamberlain, dapifer, dispenser and butler. The principal seat of his honour, like Castle Acre in Norfolk with its hundred knights' fees or Pleschey in Essex, was a capital in miniature. At Bridgnorth, Robert de Bellême housed a thousand knights and retainers in the castle; the palatine earls of Chester dispensed open hospitality all the year round, with feasting, sport and minstrelsy. The great feudal lord sat enthroned in his court like a king, with his tenants-in-chief below him, his 'barons' on one side and abbots on the other, ready, like the peers of the realm, to give him aid and counsel, witness his charters and adjudicate disputes.

In France, where his feudatories could evoke against him his own overlord – the French king – Henry was never really able to discipline such magnates. He was one himself. But in England his grandfather and the Conqueror had already curbed their power.

84

They were still what the Norman kings had made them, part of the realm. For all their retainers, imposing armour and battle-horses, they shrank from war against their acknowledged sovereign. Perhaps it was because they knew that the English people, who ploughed their fields and served as infantry in the *fyrd*, were on his side; perhaps there was something unsympathetic to lawlessness and blood-letting in the very air of the island. Even the tournament – that substitute for private war, in which fully-armed knights jousted, often to the death, for horses, armour and ransoms – was regarded with disfavour in this peaceful realm. Compared with the glittering bloody pastime it had become in chivalric France, it was so tame an affair that many young Anglo-Norman knights took service under some continental duke or count who could show them proper sport. Only in a few places did the English civil war degenerate into the ferocious, town-sacking, village-burning slaughter habitual abroad. When Stephen was barred out of his castle of Newbury by his own marshal, instead of hanging the latter's little son, who had been left with him as a hostage, or catapulting him as he was urged to do into the defiant fortress, he had merely paraded him under a tree in view of the battlements and then carried him back to his camp. He had refused even to gouge his eyes out. A few days later he was seen outside his tent playing conkers with the boy.

It was this gentler strain in English feudalism which enabled Henry to disarm his barons so quickly. So long as he respected their just rights and avoided violence, he knew they were unlikely to combine against him. Having got rid of their mercenaries and unlicensed castles, he subjected them, like his grandfather, to fiscal discipline. He recalled to their old work of punishing infringements of royal rights the Exchequer officials whom the latter had trained. At their head he placed his Treasurer, Nigel of Ely – nephew of the great Roger of Salisbury, gratefully remembered as 'that man of prudence, far-sighted in counsel, eloquent in discourse and, by the grace of God, remarkably qualified to deal with great affairs'.

The methods of these watchdogs were described in the *Dialogue of the Exchequer*, written by Nigel's son, Richard FitzNeal.

Its guiding principle – still enshrined in Treasury practice – was 'devotion to the King's interests with a single mind, due regard being paid to equity'. In its pages we can watch the presiding Justiciar, with the Treasurer, Chancellor and barons of the Exchequer, sitting on the covered benches round the black-and-white squared table, as each sheriff presented his accounts, and the official calculator, as in some gigantic chess-match, moved the piles of coins or counters that represented money. We see the humbler officials of the Lower Exchequer – silverer, melter, ushers, chamberlains and tellers – receiving and weighing the cash, and sometimes assaying or 'blanching' it in the furnace, while the tally-cutter notches and splits the wooden tallys which serve for receipts. And we can still read the Latin entries on the sheep-skin pipe-rolls on which were recorded the state of the sheriff's annual account with the Exchequer, the debts due to the Crown, the farms and rents of the royal estates and woods, the legal fines, the escheats of those whose fiefs had become vacant, and the year's feudal reliefs and tallages. Among the latter was a war-tax on knights' fees called scutage or shield-money, initiated earlier to meet the case of ecclesiastical tenants unable to serve in the field and which Henry adapted to give lay tenants, too, an alternative to accompanying him on his foreign campaigns.

For the field in which Henry mastered his barons was not that of arms but law. At the time of his accession there were at least four different systems of jurisdiction in England. There were the great franchises of the baronial honours, and the village manorial courts, both the private property of their lords. There were the old Anglo-Saxon public courts of shire and hundred, presided over by the sheriff – nominally a royal officer, but in practice a local magnate who farmed their profits and taxes of the county and who, during Stephen's lax rule, had often encroached on the Crown's rights and, in some cases, even tried to make his office hereditary. And there was the King himself, who not only sat in his *Curia Regis* as supreme feudal overlord but, as successor of the athelings, was the traditional fount of national justice.

Henry first sought control of the shire and hundred courts. He revived his grandfather's practice of sending out Exchequer

barons on circuit to sit beside the sheriffs and enforce his fiscal
rights. Before long he had made these progresses annual events.
And since there was then little distinction between the profits of
jurisdiction and jurisdiction itself, he empowered his officers, not
only to look into revenue matters but to hear and try local pleas of
the Crown. To these he added offences which had hitherto been
dealt with by the sheriffs. By two assizes or royal councils – one
held at the Wiltshire hunting palace of Clarendon in 1166 and the
other ten years later at Northampton – trials of murder, robbery,
larceny, rape, forgery, arson and harbouring criminals were reserved to the justices *in eyre*. The criminal jurisdiction of the
Crown – formerly confined to *lèse majesté* and breaches of the
King's Peace on the royal domains and highways – was made
nation-wide, and the sheriffs' chief judicial powers transferred to
officers under the sovereign's eye.

These Henry chose carefully for their loyalty and impartiality
and, as he and they gained experience, for knowledge of the law.
At first he had to rely on bishops, Exchequer officials and minor
barons temporarily executing judicial commissions. But by experiment he gradually created a body of trained judges whose business
it was 'to do justice habitually'. Some were clerics, others laymen,
but all were drawn from the lesser Anglo-Norman families whom
he used as a counterpoise to the great feudal magnates. They were
assigned to six, and later four, regular circuits of counties, round
which, escorted by sheriffs and javelin men, they rode on annual
progresses. Others, sitting on the royal bench in Westminster Hall,
formed a permanent judicial tribunal of the *Curia Regis*, which
later grew into the courts of King's Bench and Common Pleas.
One of its members, Ranulf de Glanvill – or, possibly, his clerk,
Hubert Walter, who succeeded him as Justiciar – wrote the
nation's first legal classic, a Latin treatise on the laws and customs
of England and the procedure of the royal courts.

It was through such procedure that Henry traversed the power
of the feudal jurisdictions. One of the commonest sources of disorder during the civil wars of Stephen's reign had been the
baronial habit of forcibly seizing land on some trumped-up excuse.
The victim had two alternatives: to counter-attack with like force,

if he could command it, or to appeal to his overlord's court to the only process recognised there, trial-by-battle. In this, whether fought by the principals or by professional champions, victory almost invariably went to the strongest and richest, the largest purses securing the longest lance.

By adapting the old English principle – enshrined in the coronation oath – that it was the King's duty to see that justice was done and that every freeman had a right of appeal to him, Henry and his judges devised writs or royal commands restoring possession to any freeman forcibly dispossessed of his land. They offered these for sale to all, Norman and English alike, whose tenures were free from servile services: to all, that is 'free to go with their land where they would'. A writ of summons called *praecipe* directed the sheriff to order the overlord of any land seized to restore it immediately or answer for his failure in the royal court. Another called *novel disseisin* commanded him to reinstate any dispossessed freeholder pending trial and summon 'twelve free and lawful men of the neighbourhood' to 'recognise' and declare, under oath before the King's judges, to whom its possession had belonged. A later writ called *mort d'ancestor* similarly protected the peaceful possession of a freeholder's heir against all claimants not able to prove a superior right in the royal courts.

These possessory writs, as they were called, had three effects. They protected a man's right to possession as distinct from his legal ownership – a matter which might otherwise be disputed for ever. They made everyone with a claim to a freehold plead it, not in the court of the feudal overlord, who was powerless against a royal writ, but in the King's. And, through the procedure laid down for investigating such claims, they substituted for the barbarous custom of proof-by-battle a sworn inquest or 'recognition' by 'twelve free and lawful men of the neighbourhood', summoned by the sheriff to 'recognise' with whom the disputed possession lay.

These 'recognitors' or jurymen were not the doomsmen of the old formalistic English law, swearing in support of a neighbour's oath. Nor were they necessarily witnesses to acts that had happened under their eyes. They were men of substance assembled to answer questions of common knowledge put to them under oath by the King's judges. The Conqueror had used such inquisitions for fiscal purposes. His great-grandson used them for judicial. It is immaterial whether they derived, as some think, from a long-disused device of Charlemagne's from that of the twelve thanes of the Anglo–Danish wapentake swearing to accuse no innocent man and conceal no guilty one. What matters is that, imposed by the royal prerogative, they were at once accepted in a country where presentment and judgment by a man's neighbours had been part of popular law from time immemorial. Through the ingenuity and good sense of this strong, subtle-minded and original ruler, the corporate conscience of a group of neighbours, acquainted with the persons and facts involved and sworn to speak the truth, was substituted for the unpredictable arbitrament of battle. It seemed a more sensible way of ascertaining God's will, in other words the truth. And it was certainly a better way – and this may have appealed even more strongly to Henry – of keeping the peace.

The same procedure was extended to actions to determine legal ownership. By a process called the grand assize a freeholder whose title was challenged could decline trial-by-battle in his overlord's court and, opting for a trial in the King's, put himself 'upon the testimony of the country'. In this, twelve knights of the shire declared in the presence of the royal judges which of the litigating parties had the better right. Once determined, such recognition by grand assize was final. 'So effectively does this procedure,' wrote Glanvill, 'preserve the lives and the civil condition of men that every man may now legally retain possession of his freehold and at the same time avoid the doubtful event of the duel.'

Through these writs – 'infinitely diversified for different causes' – Henry achieved a major and peaceful revolution. He did so under the guise of restoring 'the good old laws'. Appealing to native English tradition, he used the prerogative to bring the whole system of freehold tenure under national law. By making the smaller landowner's right to his property dependent on the royal instead of the feudal courts, he struck at the root of the great lord's power over his military tenants. And he dealt a death-blow to trial-by-battle and private war. He did not abolish the feudal courts and their processes; like the lesser, and very active, private manorial courts they survived for centuries. He merely drove them out of such business as imperilled the unity and safety of the State by offering their clients cheaper, surer and quicker justice in the royal courts. His writs attracted to the latter an ever-growing volume of litigation and revenue. 'The convincing proof of our King's strength and justice,' wrote a grateful subject, 'is that whoever has a just cause wants to have it tried before him.'

Henry's enemies – the great and strong – complained that he wore out their patience with his perpetual assizes and cunning legal formulas: his 'mousetraps', as one of them called them. His justification, in Richard Fitzneal's words, was that 'he spared the poor both labour and expense'. Selfish, crafty, unscrupulous, the great lawyer-king wielded the sword of justice 'for the punishment of evil-doers and the maintenance of peace and quiet for honest men'. His judges made his remedies available in every corner of the realm. With the precedents they enshrined in their judgments, they little by little created a common law for all England. Even that of the shire and hundred courts had varied from district to district; Kent, Wessex, Mercia, the Danelaw, London and the Celtic West had all had their separate customs and practices. Henry's judges established the same system for north, south, east and west, for town and country, for Norman and Englishman. They nationalised, as it were, the law.

In doing so they drew from the principles which Italian jurists had recently rediscovered in the great legal codes left behind six centuries before by the Byzantine Emperor Justinian. But, while the continental lawyers who studied Roman jurisprudence in the new universities of Bologna and Paris had little chance of applying it except in the church courts, law in England, thanks to Henry's triumph over the feudal jurisdictions, was no academic study confined to learned doctors and pursued only in palace courts, but a practical, day-to-day business affecting the whole nation. However much they might admire the logical maxims of imperial Rome, Henry's judges had to administer the kind of law to which ordinary Englishmen were accustomed. In their judgments, based on the decisions of their predecessors, they embodied from popular and local custom whatever seemed compatible with a common national system.

The growth of such case-law, as it was called, was a two-way process. It was not merely imposed from above but grew from below. It was, above all, a collaboration between professional judges stating the law and laymen, drawn from different classes of society, deciding questions of fact. The classic example, pregnant with far-reaching consequences for the future of England and the ocean nations which sprang from her, was the use in criminal jurisdiction of the old Anglo-Saxon principle of enlisting local worthies to sift local accusations. The assize of Clarendon directed the itinerant judges to enquire of twelve 'lawful' men from every hundred, and four from every township, whether any of their neighbours were reputed to have committed felony. Only those so presented were to be put upon their trial. So resolved was Henry to stamp out the violence unloosed by civil war and such the weight he attached to the verdicts of these local worthies that, even when those they accused were proved innocent by the customary 'judgement of God' or trial by water, they were banished the realm.

This principle of allowing representatives of the neighbour-hood to decide questions of fact in criminal law was applied to the trials not only of Englishmen but of Normans. So was the rule – unknown to ancient Rome – that every case should be tried in public, as in the presence of the Anglo-Saxon tribe. The secret tribunal, that instrument of imperial tyranny, was never allowed a lodgment in English Common Law.

When, long afterwards, the kings of other lands brought the feudal jurisdictions under their control, the authoritarian maxims of Roman civil and canon law, deeply rooted in the minds of con-tinental royal lawyers, often became instruments of despotism. In England, where law was founded on popular custom and the open participation of the ordinary man in its processes, it proved a bul-wark of public and private liberties.

Henry's achievement was far in advance of his age. No other ruler could offer his people such a system of national justice. By the end of his reign there was no major offence against the public peace which could not bring the offender within range of a royal

SET IN A SILVER SEA

writ. Even the killing and maiming of villains and cottars were punished by his courts. Within five years of his death an ordinance of his greatest disciple, Hubert Walter, the Justiciar, created in every county officials called coroners to hold inquests on all sudden and suspicious deaths.

All this prepared the way for the rule of law which was to become the dominant trait in England's life. Henceforward, whoever gave law to her was to have a machinery by which it could be enforced – against the strong as well as the weak. The professional judges Henry trained, the regular courts in which they sat, the writs they devised to meet popular needs, and the judgments they left behind to guide their successors, helped to ensure that justice should be done even in the royal absence or in the reign of a weak or unjust sovereign. By making the Common Law the permanent embodiment of a righteous King sitting in judgment, the great Angevin established the English habit of obedience to law which was to prove the strongest of all the forces making for the nation's peaceful continuity and progress.

CHAPTER EIGHT

Bell, Book and Candle

'There is no power but of God;
the powers that be are ordained of God.'

St Paul

IN TRYING TO SUBJECT every part of the nation's life to the law the great Plantagenet fell foul of the one power which in that age no prince could safely challenge – the Church with its hold on Christian hearts and imaginations. By doing so he suffered a defeat which impressed his contemporaries more than all his legal triumphs.

For even the proudest kings – born to the purple and gold, riding in glittering armour to the sound of trumpets, feasting and hunting and giving law – were members of Christ's universal Church. '*Non nobis, Domine!*' they heard their priests chant, 'Not unto us, O Lord, but unto Thee the power and the glory!' Behind their crowns and sceptres lay the memory of the 'mocking reed and crown of thorns'. They acknowledged a faith which proclaimed that whoever exalted himself should be humbled, bade the rich give to the poor and men be brothers to one another. When sickness came and death threatened – and death was never far from the filthy disease-haunted towns and villages of the Middle Ages – even the strongest trembled. It was at such times that princes, barons and rich merchants made gifts to the Church – to endow abbeys, schools and hospitals, to teach the young and nurse the sick, to pay monks and priests to offer prayers for their souls and intercede for them. So when the Conqueror lay dying, remembering the rivers of blood he had shed, he 'hastened to make provision for the future welfare of himself and others, ordering all his treasures to be distributed among the churches, the poor and the ministers of God'. Even his vicious, braggart son, Rufus, who 'kept down God's Church' and blasphemed against every hallowed belief, became a craven when death threatened, crying for the saintly monk Anselm whom he had so long refused to install as archbishop in order that he might retain for himself the revenues of Canterbury. For without the Church's intercession, it was believed, there was no escape from the powers of evil and the eternal torments over which they presided. The greatest ruler and poorest peasant thought the air was full of fiends, that the Devil lay in wait to cast men into hell-fire, that the sole hope of salvation lay in the prayers and services of those ordained of God. Into the hands of their supreme head, the Pope or Bishop of Rome, had been given, it was supposed, the keys of Heaven and Hell.

The God in whom half-heathen medieval man believed was an intensely personal God, forever appearing in acts of nature, visions and apparitions, plagues and cures, storms, fires and miracles. And not only God, but the whole hierarchy of Heaven, angels and saints, apostles and martyrs, lay on the frontiers of the visible, tangible world, ready at any moment to reveal themselves. So did the Devil and his fiends, witches and ministers of evil. A flight of crows could seem a swarm of demons come to fetch the soul of a usurer, the howling of the wind the cries of some wicked lord borne through the middle air to Hell. When Henry I granted the abbey of Peterborough to a simoniac – a notorious purchaser of Church preferments – the country folk throughout the Fens believed they heard horns blowing in the night and saw hunters, 'black and big and loathsome', riding in the woods with satanic hounds. At a time when men knew little of the laws of nature or the world outside their village homes, they accepted such tales with no more question than their twentieth-century descendants the latest scientific marvels.

Behind all this superstition lay a conception shared by rich and poor alike, educated and ignorant. It was that the universe, from its greatest to its minutest part, was governed by divine law. Everything that happened in the world – that had happened, was happening, or was going to happen – was part of the same majestic rule, only partly intelligible to man's puny intellect. All that lay within his power was either, at the instigation of the Devil, to neglect or oppose that law or, with Christ's grace and the guidance and intercession of His Holy Church, to further it. The Church existed to explain it, to help man obey it and, through Christ's love and sacrifice, to obtain forgiveness for him when he broke it.

And the Church existed for everyone. Alone in a world of inequalities it opened its doors to all. It was not merely for certain families or tribes, for kings and landowners, for the successful or learned. It was for fools and failures, for the weak and sick, for women and children, for prisoners and paupers, for saints and sinners. Two things bound the whole of Christendom: belief in Christ and membership of His Church.

It was this universal quality which made its appeal so overwhelming. It gave purpose and significance to every life. The priest praying for souls, the king doing justice, the knight fighting the infidel and invader, the peasant working in the fields, the woman rearing children, the artist and craftsman glorifying creation, all were members of one body and in God's eyes equally important. And it was the Church which united the members of this great family, dead, living and unborn, interceded for their sins and helped them to everlasting bliss. Within the wide limits of human frailty – for which the Church made full allowance – medieval man relied on its guidance at every point. There was a place in its creed and ritual for everyone and everything.

Everywhere, in a still half-barbaric and primitive western Europe, man was confronted by the majesty of the Church. He could not read a book that churchmen had not written and copied by hand; unless he was himself a churchman trained by churchmen, he almost certainly could not read at all. When most people lived in huts little bigger or cleaner than pigsties, the Church's buildings towered above the landscape, and blazed within with colours, jewels and vestments. For the Church did not teach only by its prayers and sermons. Through stone and wooden panel, altar-piece and reredos, painting, glass and embroidery, it depicted the Nativity or the Adoration of the Shepherds, St Michael leading the heavenly host or St George slaying the dragon, the Lamb of God or the flowering Tree of Jesse. In a thousand forms it illuminated the lives of saints and apostles, martyrs and prophets; the clash between Virtue and Evil, Truth drawing the tongue of Falsehood or Sobriety dosing Drunkenness over the door of the Chapter House at Salisbury, the devils carting the souls of the damned to Hell in rustic wheelbarrows whose colours still blaze down from the great fifteenth century window of Fairford church in Gloucestershire. So too the lovely and dramatic ritual of its services helped to shape the imagination of every man, rich and poor, in Christendom. On Good Friday, the crucifix was taken from the altar and hidden in a curtained wall called the Easter sepulchre, from which on Easter morning it was borne in triumphant procession before the rejoicing congregation. The poorest peasant took part, as actor and audience, in the never-ceasing pageantry, drama and music with which, in even the remotest village, the Church invested the changing year. His holidays or 'holy days', were its feasts; his daily work was performed against the familiar background of religious intercession and rejoicing, prayer and ceremony.

Everything medieval man did was blessed or cursed, approved or disapproved, explained and solemnised by the Church. He was baptised by it, married by it, buried by it. He went into battle calling on its saints to aid his arms; he sought a cure for all his ills at its martyrs' shrines or in its holy waters and wells; he made his oaths on its sacred relics. Its superstitions, often touchingly beautiful, were part of his daily life. He prayed before the painted images of its saints and angels for help, comfort and forgiveness. The bells rang, and the familiar gargoyles grinned from the village church tower to guard him from demon or storm; he brought his corn to be blessed at its altars and, repeating its hallowed Latin incantations, danced round his apple trees to make them fruitful. The very oxen of the fields, he believed, knelt in the byres on Christmas night in remembrance of the manger birth.

The Church not only controlled men's minds and imaginations. It enjoyed immense wealth. It commanded in every country a host, not of warriors, but of men and women vowed to its service. They ranged from scarlet-robed cardinals and mitred archbishops to humble parish clerks, bell-ringers and church-sweepers – members of the Minor Orders as they were called; from judges, lawyers and physicians to the poor ragged students who begged and sang their way along the roads of Europe to hear the Church's famous doctors lecture on theology and canon law in its cathedral schools and universities. In its heyday in the twelfth and thirteenth centuries, it has been reckoned, one out of every thirty adult males in western Europe was a cleric of some kind.

The flower of this vast army were the 'regulars', the monks and nuns who had forsworn the world and embraced that of God, living in disciplined communities under rules or orders stricter than those of any other existing society, military or civil. In hundreds of monasteries and convents in every land these dedicated men and women followed a life of routine whose end was Christ's worship and the service of His Church. They rose from their pallets in the dormitories an hour or two after midnight to troop down cold corridors to celebrate Matins and Lauds in chapel; assembled in the chapter-house for admonition or punishment and to discuss the business of the day; dined in silence in the refectory, where the officers and their guests sat in state on the dais and the monks at long tables below, as in an Oxford college today, while one of the brethren read aloud a Latin homily; laboured in the monastic fields, gardens and workshops, or copied and illuminated books in the scriptorium, whose desks looked through unglazed arches on to the grass garth of the cloisters; taught the novices and prescribed to the sick until the hour of Vespers recalled them once more to their devotions. From the first moment of the day to the last when Compline was sung before they withdrew at dusk to their dormitories, their lives were ordered by the chapel bell – a sound familiar in every corner of Christendom.

It would be hard to exaggerate the part played by the monastic houses in forming the character of English and European institutions. They were the centres and creators of civilization, and the principal meeting places of learned men. Our schools, universities and charitable foundations have all grown out of their rules and ordered life. The names of their officers still survive in our collegiate bodies: the precentor in charge of the music, services and

97

books, the chamberlain of the clothing and bedding, the sacristan of the church fabric and sacred vessels, the cellarer of the provisioning and the bursar of the finances, the infirmarer of the hospital, the almoner of the charities. In that simple rustic world there was nothing to compare with these establishments; their chapter-houses, dormitories and guest-houses; their libraries, workshops, kitchens, butteries, bakehouses, breweries, laundries and dairies; their granges, barns, fish-ponds, orchards, vineyards and gardens, their water-pipes, drains and filter-tanks. Far in advance of the richest layman they possessed even lavatories with long stone or marble washing-troughs, brass water-cocks and towels. And in their infirmaries, where the monks were periodically bled, bath-houses were provided for bathing the sick and aged and, before the great Christian feasts, the entire chapter.

During the eleventh and twelfth centuries, the wealth of the greater monasteries grew with every generation. In the magnificent services held at their shrines – the chief events of the medieval year – offerings were showered on them by multitudes of deeply moved Christians. Most visitors left donations with the houses which sheltered them; every rich man wished to win prestige on earth and a friend in Heaven by some gift or legacy to the saint or martyr commemorated by the local shrine; blessed Alban or Edmund, Peter or Paul, or the tender, merciful Virgin. In men's minds the monasteries were personally identified with these divine personages. Their jewelled shrines and crosses, golden and silver vessels and candlesticks, silken and embroidered altar-cloths, chasubles and dalmatics, their rare books bound in gold, and the hallowed relics brought from afar by visiting kings and princes were the glory of neighbourhood and kingdom. Their wealth was immense. An abbey like St Albans or Bury St Edmunds might have estates in a dozen counties. Its officers were constantly travelling to collect its rents and dues. Every fortnight Ramsey drew, from the village whose turn had come to supply its kitchens, twelve quarters of flour for the monks' and guests' bread, two thousand loaves for its servants, ten fat pigs, fourteen lambs, one hundred and twenty hens, two thousand eggs, and vast quantities of malt, honey, lard, cheese, butter, beans and horse-fodder.

The abbot of a major monastic house was a prince of the Church, ruler of a famous society, and lord and administrator of a vast property. He sat in the Great Council of the realm, and presided over the feudal court of the abbey's barons, knights and freeholders. He played a leading part in the political, economic and social life of the neighbourhood, and acted as a judge in a wide range of secular affairs. And, like the monastery itself, he had to provide hospitality for a constant succession of travellers, including the King himself. In days when there were no hotels, newspapers or posts, the monasteries, with their international organisation, were the chief means of communicating news, learning, crafts and discoveries. They provided the schools, hospitals and libraries of the age. Most of the larger abbeys maintained a succession of historiographers who compiled elaborate, if somewhat inaccurate, chronicles of their times; William of Malmesbury, Florence of Worcester, Eadmer and Gervase of Canterbury, and the two thirteenth-century chroniclers of St Albans, Roger of Wendover and Matthew Paris, are among the fathers of English history. And from their cloisters the Christian kings, who were slowly creating England and the other infant States of Europe, drew officers trained in regular habits of routine, business and accountancy and, still more important, in ideals of public service. The monastic officers were called 'obedientiaries'; they commanded because they obeyed. Nowhere else could those who had to keep order over large areas find men so fit for their business. For the Church offered a far wider choice of trained servants than the feudal families whose sons were usually taught only to hunt and fight. Through its hierarchy unaccounted men could rise to the proudest posts in Christendom: could become bishops and abbots, justiciars, chancellors and royal ministers. So the great statesman, Suger, who, as minister to two kings, laid the foundations of French monarchial power in the second quarter of the twelfth century, began his career as an acolyte, serving the altar of the monastery for which his father had worked as a serf. His contemporary Adrian IV – the only Englishman ever to become Pope – had begged his boyhood's bread at the gates of St Albans abbey.

The Norman conquest had coincided with a monastic revival

SET IN A SILVER SEA

throughout western Europe. During the next half-century, not only were the older Benedictine houses in southern England revitalised by the French and Italian abbots whom the Conqueror imported from the Cluniac foundations on the continent and the monastic schools of Normandy but, for the first time since the Danish invasions, monasteries had reappeared after a lapse of two hundred years in the ravaged lands beyond the Humber. In the second decade of William's reign a Norman prior and two English monks from the abbeys of Winchcombe and Evesham set out on foot for the north, with a donkey laden with sacred books and vestments, to restore the tradition of Aidan and Bede in ravaged Northumbria. Two great abbeys, St Mary's at York and St Cuthbert's at Durham, sprang from this act of faith.

But the real revival of monastic life in the north had occurred in the reign of Henry I with the coming of the Cistercians. The splendour, wealth and magnificent ritual of the Benedictine houses, even after the Cluniac reforms, left the more austere spirits of the age unsatisfied, and a movement began in France to restore the simplicity and poverty of early monastic rule.

In 1128 the first Cistercian house in England had been founded at Waverley in Surrey. But it was among the desolate Yorkshire hills and the remote valleys of the Welsh Marshes that the Order made its chief settlements. It was part of its Rule that its monks should live far from the haunts of men, in silence and austerity, and support themselves by their own labour. Even their rough homespun woollen tunics and cowls were undyed, giving them their name of white monks in contrast to the black monks of the older Rule. Their simplicity of life and love of solitude and country pursuits made a deep appeal to the English. By the end of Stephen's reign, there were twenty Cistercian monasteries in Yorkshire alone, and forty in the kingdom. Fountains, founded in 1132 on waste ground in Skeldale by a dozen pioneers from St Mary's, York, grew from a few huts under an elm tree into the great abbey of St Mary's. Rievaulx, Jervaux, Byland and Kirkstall, Tintern, Valle Crucis, Neath, Abbey Dore and Margam, raised in the twelfth and rebuilt in the thirteenth and fourteenth centuries, were among the grandest achievements of the Middle Ages. Bare now of ornament, sculpture and painting, their grave, simple outlines have still the power, even in ruin, to stir the heart. Equally impressive were the woods the monks planted round their homes, and the sheep-runs the lay brethern or *conversi* – drawn from the peasant class – made on the bleak northern and western hills. They were the most enlightened landlords and finest farmers of the age, sowing alternate corn and grass leys and transforming scrubby wilderness with flocks that grazed by day on the uplands and folded at night on the barley ploughlands. Theirs was an instinctive genius for blending the works of God and man; in the Great Coxwell barn in Berkshire we can still see the reverence and skill with which they turned nature to human ends while enriching and beautifying it. *Laborare est orare* was their founder's motto: to work is to pray. They built roads and bridges, drained marshes and planted trees, quarried stone, wrought in wood and metal, laid out gardens and vineyards, and bred fine horses, cattle and sheep. To them England owed the noble Lion breed whose golden hoof raised the Cotswold towns and villages. They made her wool as famous as their brother monks of Cîteaux made the vineyards of the stony Côte d'Or. And if the great names of Chambertin and Clos de Vougeot still recall for lovers of wine the skill of the French Cistercians, their brethren in England are commemorated by the homely cheese which the monks of Jervaux made from ewe's milk in lonely Wensleydale.

Nothing gives a clearer idea of the might of the medieval Church than to stand in one of the cathedrals, still towering above the roofs of modern towns, which were first raised as monastic churches. They express the universal sense of the all-importance of religion and the soaring imagination and practical genius of men who had mastered the lost Roman art of vaulting great spaces in stone. Most of them were originally built on the site of smaller Saxon churches by English masons in the massive Norman style under the prelates whom the Conqueror imported from Normandy, and rebuilt in a still more ambitious style under their successors in the later twelfth and early thirteenth centuries. Canterbury, whose choir the Conqueror's Archbishop Lanfranc started to build with Caen stone in 1072; Rochester begun seven years later; Gloucester in 1080; Ely with its magnificent nave in

1083; Worcester in 1084; and the incomparable Durham in 1093, with its ribbed vaulting – the earliest of its kind in Europe – and its still surviving Norman nave and choir; Norwich, Winchester, Coventry, Carlisle and Chester – were all originally made for monks. So were the abbey churches of St Albans – built partly from Roman tiles and stones – Gloucester, Westminster, Peterborough, Chester, Malmesbury, Tewkesbury, Pershore, Sherborne, Romsey and Bury St Edmunds, whose nave, over three hundred feet long, surpassed that of our largest cathedral today.

These vast edifices were miracles of construction. So were the non-monastic cathedrals served by secular canons, which the Normans raised in London, York, Old Sarum, Lichfield, Lincoln and Winchester; for the last a whole royal wood was felled. They were built without any but the most elementary mechanism for moving and lifting large weights, by men whose wealth consisted almost entirely of crops, flocks and herds and whose sole means of transport were wheeled carts drawn by oxen. Their architecture expressed the unity of existence in which their builders so profoundly and passionately believed: the ordered vaulting; the pillars rising out of the earth like trees; the stone walls and arches carved with flowers and leaves, animals and men; the light of heaven flooding in through windows, at first plain but later painted, like the ceilings, in brilliant colours; the arches soaring into the sky, and the whole made one by the idea, implicit in every image and symbol, of God over all and judging all, and Christ and his Mother, the Virgin, pitying and loving all.

*   *   *

It was no wonder that an institution which evoked such devotion and love should possess power. In a still half barbaric world of shifting, warring feudal states the Church alone had unity and permanence. The election in 1073 to St Peter's apostolic throne, under the title of Gregory VII, of a Tuscan peasant of genius named Hildebrand, had marked the beginning of an age of intensive ecclesiastical reform. During it a succession of great Popes sought to carry the austere standards of the Cluniac monasteries into the still half primitive organisation of the diocese and rural parish. It was the aim of Hildebrand and his successors to bring under their direct control the entire international army of those who wore the tonsure – the symbolic shaving of the crown which set the servants of the Church apart from the rest of mankind. A system of canon law, derived from early Christian and Roman practice, was to provide the machinery – meticulous, bureaucratic, authoritative – for enforcing papal control over all clerics, ordained or not. And a hierarchy of graded courts, administered by ecclesiastical lawyers and stretching upwards to the papal Curia in Rome, was to offer immunity from the jurisdiction of secular courts of law to every churchman, however humble, who, by his ability to mumble a Latin text from the Bible, could claim 'benefit of clergy' and so escape subjection to the criminal and civil law of the land. If any servant of the Church – even a poor church-sweeper or wandering ragamuffin student – committed a murder, rape or burglary, the Church claimed the exclusive right to try and to punish him.

Such a claim seemed incompatible with the social order and discipline which more enlightened European rulers like Henry II were trying to impose on their subjects after the anarchy and lawless violence of the Dark Ages. At a time when, through the pious benefactions of past conquerors and rulers, the Church owned something like a quarter of the taxable wealth of every realm in Christendom, the Pope's denial of secular sovereigns' right to control and tax such wealth struck at the very root of government. Having piously endowed Christian sees and abbeys with land, kings and princes not unnaturally claimed the right to tax their ecclesiastical beneficiaries, not as the heirs of Christ's apostles as the Church claimed they were, but as feudal tenants-in-chief. In return for conferring on them the insignia of their holy office – the episcopal staff and ring – and the broad feudal domains bequeathed for its support, they demanded homage and fealty. Yet to the Gregorian reformers, in their zeal for the Church's independence and doctrinal purity, this seemed a blasphemous infringement of spiritual rights. To them the staff and ring symbolised no earthly lordship but the sacred charge Christ had laid on his apostles. That they should be conferred by a layman – even a crowned and consecrated one – was sacrilege. Nor, they contended, should a layman be allowed to choose, let alone consecrate, those who were to exercise such sacred functions. It might be tolerable in a god-fearing king like William the Conqueror who filled sees and abbeys with reformers and loyal churchmen. It was intolerable when the crown was worn by a blasphemous wretch like his son, Rufus, who appointed evil-living favourites to bishoprics.

Against the dream of the vanished Roman Empire which Charlemagne had tried to recreate and in which a Frankish Emperor had been crowned by a Pope as the secular head of western Christendom – one which still lingered on in the shadowy *imperium* of the German or 'Holy Roman' emperors – Gregory VII sought to substitute one of an ecclesiastical empire transcending all frontiers. And because of the simple piety and faith which its early monks and priests had by example and precept taught Christians everywhere, the Church possessed a weapon which, in a deeply superstitious age, no secular ruler could easily withstand.

During the reign of William the Conqueror in England, by using the dread curse with bell, book and candle which excommunicated a man from the Christian communion, the Pope had made the German Emperor an outcast to his own feudatories and subjects. Deriving his authority as Emperor, not from tribal or national ties like other rulers, but solely from his title as Charlemagne's successor and the bearer of the temporal sword of Christendom, his excommunication and deposition by the Holy See destroyed the grounds of his subjects' allegiance. In the winter of 1077 the first prince in Europe stood barefoot in the snow outside the castle of Canossa to implore the Pope's forgiveness for daring to claim feudal rights over his own clergy. It was the only way he could keep his throne.

In England attempts to make the Church independent of the State had proved less effective. It was not that the Church was less respected, but that the Crown, under rulers like William I and the first two Henrys, was more so. For this reason the lay investiture contest between the English Church and Crown had not ended in a Canossa. It had ended in a working compromise. In 1106 that shrewd monarch, Henry I, recognising that the public was behind the Church's demand for independence in purely ecclesiastical affairs, had granted it the monopoly of investing its bishops with the sacred episcopal staff and rod, He also agreed that their cathedral chapters should elect them. But their right to do so was made dependent on his leave to elect, and his own right to nominate, a candidate himself and to veto any other candidate. And before consecration his nominee had to do homage to the Crown for the stewardship of the episcopal lands and castles conferred on him by royal writ. In this eminently practical way the English King retained control of his kingdom's wealth and political power, while acknowledging the Church's right to confer spiritual authority. This sensible compromise was later adopted in other lands, even, after the Concordat of Worms in 1122, in Germany.

Yet at Canossa the Church had tasted blood. Throughout the twelfth century the initiative lay with the canon lawyers who, seeking to organise the Church as a completely self-governing institution, tried to free it from all secular control. Even in England during Stephen's weak rule it had established the right of clerical appeal to Rome and the freedom of papal legates to exercise independent powers within the realm, together with the exemption of clerics from the processes of ordinary criminal law and the Church's exclusive right to try and punish its own. And, as canon law forbade the use of mutilation or death, and the worst that could befall a clerical malefactor, even a murderer, was a fine or brotherly scourging, Henry II, seeking to restore order after the civil wars of Stephen's reign and establish a common law for all Englishmen, was confronted by ecclesiastical privileges incompatible with his object. For the Church's punishments for its erring members were far too light to maintain order in a violent and unpoliced age. During the first few years of Henry's reign more than a hundred murderers escaped death by pleading clerical immunity. And to Henry II's orderly and autocratic mind it seemed intolerable that episcopal tenants-in-chief should have the right to appeal over his head to a foreign court.

CHAPTER NINE

The Holy Blissful Martyr

'From every shire's end
Of Engeland to Canterbury they wend
The holy blissful martyr for to seek.'

Chaucer

IN HIS ATTEMPT to bring the excessive legal powers of the Church
into line with the royal and national law that it was his life's work
to establish, Henry II proceeded with great caution. As in his
attack on the powers of the feudal magnates, he merely claimed
that he was restoring ancient customs which had been infringed
during the civil war of Stephen's reign. And, as with the baronial
franchises, he relied on subtly disguised and harmless-looking
legal devices to bring the ecclesiastical courts under his control
before anyone could realise what was happening. In this he was
assisted by a brilliant ecclesiastical lawyer whom he had made his
Chancellor and who, while serving in that capacity, showed as
small respect as himself for clerical claims which conflicted with
the needs of royal revenue and justice. Seven years after his accession, the death of the Archbishop of Canterbury presented Henry
with what seemed a wonderful opportunity. In the summer of
1162, brushing aside all opposition, he induced the monastery-
chapter of Canterbury to elect to the vacant see his gorgeous
counsellor, favourite and boon-companion, Thomas Becket – one
who, though a cleric, was not even ordained a priest until the day
before his consecration as head of the English Church.

In doing so, however, the King made a grave miscalculation.
For Becket, who received his sacred office with reluctance, had no

sooner accepted it than, at the age of forty-five, he completely changed his way of life. The most resplendently arrayed and attended man in England, who had taken the field at the head of seven hundred of his own knights and worn the long-embroidered sleeves of a baron, now donned the black robes of a Canterbury monk, attended midnight masses, and daily – and with his habitual ostentation – entertained and washed the feet of the filthiest beggars in Canterbury. A shameless pluralist who had collected benefices and prebendal stalls to support his magnificent entertainments, he insisted on resigning the Chancellorship regardless of the entreaties of his sovereign, who had seen in the union of the primacy and the royal chancery a solution to all his problems.

For, with the thoroughness with which he did everything, Becket refused to serve two masters. Having been the most loyal of royal lieutenants, he now transferred his allegiance to a more powerful and divine master. Instead of applying his vast legal and business experience to subject ecclesiastical encroachments to Exchequer scrutiny, he used them to extend the rights and revenues of his see. He revived long-dormant claims, demanded the restoration of estates alienated by his predecessors, and insisted on receiving homage from knights holding church-lands. When a fellow tenant-in-chief usurped an advowson he summarily excommunicated him, thus depriving the Crown of his services, for no one could have dealings with an excommunicated man. Nor would he yield an inch to the King's demands about criminous clerks. He seemed to go out of his way deliberately to enrage his former friend and benefactor.

Thus the King's attempt to bring the Church under the Law was frustrated by the very man who had been his chief assistant and who, as the repository of his secret plans, was ideally situated to defeat them. His love for his brilliant lieutenant turned to bitter hatred. With all his resolution and cunning he set himself to remedy his mistake. At all costs he had to get Becket out of the key position in which he had so injudiciously placed him.

*   *   *

The two men – the one with the strongest throne in Europe, the other representing the international Church – seemed well matched. They had been the complement of one another and now became the antithesis. Each had the same imperious, overbearing will, each was thorough, persistent and electric with restless energy, each had behind him a career of unbroken triumph. And each knew, or thought he knew, his opponent by heart.

Yet within a year the King had completely outmanoeuvred the tall, gaunt, dark archbishop. For, with all his boldness and courage, Becket lacked the virtues in which Henry, the Achilles-heel of his temper apart, was so strong. He had none of his capacity for patient statesmanship and *finesse* in handling political situations. He was a perfectionist rather than a man of the world. During his seven years as Chancellor he had shown himself a tireless organiser and worker, with a wonderful quickness and versatility. He possessed dazzling address and charm; could be all things to all men and, though revealing his heart to none, win from subordinates affection and even devotion. But while he appealed to the multitude by his dramatic genius and emotional power, his equals could not depend on him. He was far too much of an egoist to be a good colleague. He lacked constancy and stability: was a man of extremes who lived on his nerves. He seemed capable of every attitude except moderation.

The King, who had been so well served and delighted by his Chancellor's genius, understood his weaknesses perfectly: his vanity and hypersensitiveness, his inability not to overstate and dramatise his case, his pathological desire – the result of a lonely childhood – to win applause and justify himself. And in their triangular relations with the English bishops and the Pope, both of whose support was essential to Becket's position, he played the brilliant, excitable archbishop like a fish. First he joined issue with him over what was by far the weakest point in the Church's position – the trial of crimous clerks, to which a notorious murder and an equally notorious acquittal had just drawn everyone's attention. It was an issue on which the Church itself was divided and about which doubts were felt even by the Pope. In October 1163 at a Council at Westminster Henry outlined his proposals for dealing with this pressing scandal. He did not challenge the

Church's right to try its members, but demanded only that clerics found guilty by ecclesiastical courts of major crimes should be degraded and handed over to his officers for punishment. Those who could not be restrained from such outrages by the thought of their sacred orders, he pointed out, could scarcely be wronged by the loss of them.

In January 1164 the King called a Council at his hunting-lodge at Clarendon near Salisbury. Here he placed before it sixteen carefully prepared written clauses, known to history as the Constitutions of Clarendon, and demanded from the archbishop, in the presence of the barons and his fellow bishops, a solemn declaration of agreement. Most of them set out, not unfairly, the relationship which had existed between Church and State in the time of Henry I. Others traversed what had become during the anarchy of Stephen's reign the accepted practice of the Church. And they laid down a procedure for dealing with criminous clerks: preliminary investigation before a lay judge, trial in the ecclesiastical courts in the presence of a royal observer and, where guilt was proved, degradation and delivery to the King's officers for sentence and punishment.

The most contentious provisions were that no regal tenant-in-chief should be excommunicated, no cleric leave the realm and no appeal be made to Rome without the King's leave. This was tantamount to making the King supreme ecclesiastical judge in the realm – a principle which, however much it might conform with ancient English practice as Henry contended, ran diametrically counter to the existing canon law of the reformed Roman Church. It struck at the latter's fundamental claim to international ecclesiastical sovereignty and made the Crown, as in Anglo-Saxon times, the constitutional link between the Pope and the English clergy.

Though it was one thing for the King to try to restore the ancient unwritten and peculiarly English relations between Church and State in a tacit agreement with his own bishops, it was another to reduce these to writing and demand from churchmen a public avowal of principles which violated the displinary canons of their Order. And though the emotional Becket continued to play his cards badly, [1] the Pope, while anxious to reach an agreement with Henry, could not publicly repudiate the principles for which Hildebrand and his predecessors had fought. His refusal to underwrite the Constitutions of Clarendon was laid at Becket's door by the angry King who now resolved to ruin and destroy him. Sentencing him for contempt of his royal Court to the loss of all his own and his see's moveable goods, and calling on him to account for the vast sums which had passed through his hands as Chancellor, he summoned him in October 1164 before the Council to receive judgment.

Yet by making him desperate, Henry drove his adversary back on something greater than either himself or the Church. He forced him on to the rock of the inner spirit. Though ill and afraid, the archbishop resolved to compromise no more and to take his stand, not merely on the Church's tenets, but on the cross of suffering and sacrifice it enshrined. By doing so he became the champion of thousands to whom the rights and wrongs of the constitutional principles under dispute meant nothing.

And for the lonely, spectacular role he now chose Becket was superbly equipped. His towering height, his pale, sensitive face, the aquiline nose and restless penetrating eyes, the white feminine hands and quick eager movements made him look what he aspired to be, a saint and martyr. And the very theatricality and emotionalism, which so annoyed high-born men of the world, appealed to the heart of common folk, who only saw him from afar and knew nothing of his weaknesses. Here was a man who even in that age of pageantry and outward symbols made his meaning ten times clearer than anyone else, speaking to them across the immense barriers of power, rank and wealth. Almost alone among the rulers of the time he laid himself out to please the masses – the peasants and craftsmen of a conquered England who were without the rights and liberties of their Norman feudal lords.

Through the King's vindictiveness Becket had reached solid ground. From that moment, despite all the odds against him, he never quitted it. At the Council meeting at Northampton, wearing

[1] A detailed story of Becket's duel with the King is in Chapters 8 and 9 of the author's *Makers of the Realm.*

his archbishop's cope and pallium and bearing his own cross, he faced all day the insistence of armed barons that he should yield to the King's demands and resign. 'This is a fearful day,' murmured one of his followers as angry baron after baron came in with summons and threat. 'Ay,' replied the archbishop, 'but the Day of Judgment will be more fearful!'

As the bishops – even those most opposed to Becket – dared not, in face of his prohibition, join in judgment against him, the King demanded it from his earls and barons alone. But when the magnates made their way to the archbishop's chamber to inform him of the sentence, he rose and refused to hear them. 'You are come to judge me,' he cried. 'It is not your right . . . It is no sentence; I have not been heard. You cannot judge me. I am your spiritual father; you are lords of the Household, lay powers, secular personages. I will not hear your judgment! Under protection of the Apostolic See I depart hence.' Then, rising to his full height and bearing his cross, he swept into the darkening hall and towards the door, while knights and royal servants, rising from the straw-strewn floor and benches where they had dined, shouted, 'Traitor!' 'Perjurer!' Outside in the wet streets the people thronged round him to beg his blessing, so that he could hardly control his horse.

For the next six years, deprived of the revenues of his see, and his office declared forfeit, Becket remained in exile. From the position he had taken up – that ultimate appeals affecting the Church must lie to the Pope and not the King, and that no lay court had the right to lay hands on an anointed priest – nothing could move him. Against the royal forfeiture of his see he retaliated by surrendering it to the Pope, who restored it to him, thus immeasurably strengthening his position. From time to time he emerged from the French monasteries, into which he had retired to a life of the sternest austerity, to hurl anathemas and excommunications at any of his fellow English prelates who dared to compromise with the King.

Henry was equally unappeasable. But he could not govern England without the Church. And in an international age, himself an international ruler, he could not cut the English Church off from the universal Church, and make himself its ruler instead of the Pope. In the end, using the King of France as a mediator, he agreed to restore the archbishop's forfeited estates and end his banishment.

Yet, although the two disputants met in the French king's presence and were apparently reconciled, their quarrel was only patched up, not appeased. And in agreeing to return to England the primate knew the risk he was running from a passionate and injured autocrat of unpredictable moods. But his own safety was the last thing with which he was now concerned. His only thought was a spiritual victory. Nor did he return unarmed. Before setting out, he secured from the Pope letters of suspension and excommunication against his fellow metropolitan of York and two of his own suffragan bishops for their recent part in crowning Henry's heir without his participation. Just as he was about to embark, he learnt that they were on their way to join the King in Normandy to consecrate royal nominees to five vacant English bishoprics. Faced with the prospect of a packed and hostile episcopal bench, Becket at once used the discretionary powers with which the Pope had armed him and launched his sentences of excommunication and suspension against them.

Then, on 1 December 1170, having shown that he was prepared to abate not one tittle of the Church's authority, and avoiding the royal officials who, infuriated by his latest act of war, were waiting at Dover to seize him, he landed at his own cathedral's port of Sandwich. All the way to Canterbury the roads were lined with praying and rejoicing multitudes; it was like a triumphal procession. In the city he was welcomed with trumpets, psalms and organs. As he took his throne in the cathedral his face was transfigured with happiness. 'My lord,' one of his monks whispered to him, 'it matters not now when you depart from the world. Christ has conquered! Christ is now king!'

When Henry in Normandy learnt what had happened he flew into an ungovernable rage. 'What idle and coward knaves have I nourished as vassals,' he shouted, 'that faithless to their oaths, they suffer their lord to be mocked by a low-born priest!' Four of his knights took the King at his word and, without informing anyone of their intention, set out for England. There they made their way to Saltwood Castle in Kent, the home of Becket's bitterest enemy, Sir Ranulf de Broc, the man who during his absence had farmed his see's revenues.

On 29 December the four knights, with a rabble of de Broc's followers, arrived at Canterbury where the archbishop was sitting after dinner in his chamber. Ostentatiously refusing his servants' offer of food, they strode up to his chamber and sat down on the rushes before him, watching him in grim silence. When after a time he addressed them they broke into curses, telling him that they had something to say to him by the King's command and asking if he would have it said in public. Then they told him that, unless he absolved the excommunicated bishops, he must immediately leave the realm. To which the archbishop replied that they should cease from brawling and that, as his trust was in Heaven, no sea should ever again come between him and his church. 'I have not come back to flee again,' he said; 'here shall he who wants me find me.'

They found him that night in the cathedral. The knights were completely covered in armour save for their eyes, and their swords were naked. They all began shouting together, 'Where is Thomas Becket, traitor to the King and realm?' As the clamour increased, Becket, descending the steps from the choir, called out, 'Lo! here I am, no traitor to the King, but a priest. What do you seek from me? I am ready to suffer in His name who redeemed me by His blood.' Whereupon the armed men came shouting and clattering through the darkness to where he stood beside a pillar in the transept. As they closed in on him, apparently intending to carry him off, they again called on him to absolve the excommunicated bishops. Rising above them in his great height, he answered: 'There has been no satisfaction made, and I will *not* absolve them!' 'Then you shall die this instant,' cried one of the knights, 'and receive your deserts.' 'I am ready to die for my Lord; may the Church through my blood obtain peace and liberty!' As he resisted their efforts to drag him away, the knights, fearing a rescue, began to strike furiously at him with their swords. A blow cut off his scalp, while another severed his cross-bearer's arm. Two more blows brought him to his knees, and a fourth scattered his brains on the pavement. Then the murderers burst out of the cathedral to plunder his lodgings and make their escape before the city could be roused.

*   *   *

When that night in the desecrated cathedral the monks bent over the body of the proud, fastidious archbishop and stripped off his bloodstained Cistercian's habit to replace it by his pontifical vestments, they found to their amazement a covering of filthy sackcloth and a horsehair shirt, long-worn and alive with lice. Beneath it they saw the festering weals of repeated self-scourging. Then, through their grief and fears, they rejoiced exceedingly. For they knew that he had been a true monk and a saint of God.

By death the archbishop had triumphed. As the news became known, a thrill of horror ran through Christendom. The King, against whom Becket had contended, collapsed in an agony of lamentation. Exchanging his robes for sackcloth he shut himself in his chamber, where for three days he refused all food, groaning and crying exceedingly, and from time to time falling into a stupor. When he at last calmed down, he threw himself and his realm on the Pope's mercy. If it was not to disintegrate, it was the only thing he could do.

But it was not the great alone who were shaken. The common people left their rulers in no doubt as to their attitude. Within a few hours of the murder, rumours of miracles began to spread outwards from Canterbury. Four times, it was said, the candles round the bloodstained pall had been lit by invisible hands. A monk in the abbey had seen the archbishop in a vision going towards the high altar in episcopal robes; his deep, beautiful voice had joined in the singing of the introit. A blind woman who touched her eyes with a handkerchief dipped in his blood had regained her sight; 'the blind see, the deaf hear, the dumb speak', wrote John of Salisbury, 'the lame walk, the devils are cast out!' Meanwhile the de Brocs, who had threatened to move the body, were besieged in their castle by a furious crowd.

It was easy for twelfth-century kings and lords to ignore the rights of the individual poor. But they could not ignore popular beliefs. Because the common people everywhere were convinced that Becket was a saint, the Pope, who had so often tried to restrain him during his life, was forced within two years of his death to canonise him. His shrine at Canterbury, blazing with jewels and surrounded by the discarded crutches of those he had cured, became the most famous place of pilgrimage in England. For a time the cult of St Thomas almost rivalled that of the Virgin Mary. Churches were dedicated to him and memorials erected in lands as remote as Scandinavia and Iceland.

In his own country, whose fame he had blazoned through Christendom, Becket's name became better known and more honoured than any other of his age. Before the Reformation there can have been few English churches which did not have a retable, wall-painting, window or other treasure depicting some scene in his troubled life. Even today, despite the wholesale destruction by sixteenth- and seventeenth-century iconoclasts, many survive, like the boss in the roof of the Norwich cloisters with its demons standing over the Canterbury murderers, or the panel at Elham in Kent in which the saint defies the royal anger at Northampton. By a strange paradox – for it had been to strengthen the realm that Henry had fought against him – Becket lived on, not merely as a martyr, but as a national hero to a submerged and conquered people. A Norman born in England who had stood up to her foreign rulers and died at their hands, he became, in a modern writer's words, 'one of the people of England as well as one of the saints of God'.

In a constitutional historian's sense the martyrdom achieved comparatively little. It saved for English clerics the right of appeal to Rome in purely clerical matters. It established the immunity of criminous clerks from lay justice. And it brought the English Church, beyond doubt or cavil, into line with the universal practice of the Roman Catholic Church and the canon law, even though that practice conferred on churchmen a greater independence than had been customary in the Anglo-Saxon and early Anglo-Norman state. As a result power in England, as elsewhere in western Europe, continued to be regarded, not as a force to be operated by a single untrammelled will, but as a balance in which rulers were subjected to the check of organised Christian conscience expressed through the Church. When four centuries later the rulers of England repudiated the authority of Rome, the habit of thought remained – a potent check to tyranny.

In everyday administrative practice, after the first shock of the murder had passed, it was the commonsense views of Henry which prevailed rather than the extreme and unrealist claims of the dead archbishop. Of the sixteen Constitutions of Clarendon only those governing the freedom of appeals to Rome and the trial of criminous clerks were abandoned. Subject to certain formalities the Crown continued to control the election of bishops and abbots, and to deny to English prelates the right to excommunicate their fellow tenants-in-chief without royal permission.

Yet Becket's martyrdom created an emotional content which for centuries remained of immense significance in English life and helped to form the enduring values of England. The Canterbury martyr created the *Canterbury Tales* and all the generations of pilgrims riding or tramping through the Kentish countryside 'the holy blissful martyr for to seek'. It was not the worldly ends for which Becket had fought that mattered after his death. It was the spiritual means with which he had fought for them. That a man in high place who had notoriously loved, and to excess, the wealth and fine things of the world and enjoyed them in dazzling splendour, should voluntarily renounce them and live in exile and poverty, should mortify his body and at the end return to his native land to brave and suffer a violent death for the sake of an ideal, was to reveal the power of Christ and enhance the spiritual dignity of man. It is not easy for one who has lived fine to subdue the flesh, to face unarmed the naked swords of brutal warriors, to place himself in the power of insulting foes. Whoever voluntarily chooses these things is, whatever his failings, a great man. In this sense Becket was great – 'great,' as one of his followers put it, 'in truth always and in all places, great in the palace, great at the altar; great both at Court and in the Church; great, when going forth on his pilgrimage, great when returning, and singularly great at his journey's end.' Historians, who condemn him for contending against administrative measures which were in themselves reasonable, sometimes forget this. But his contemporaries, who witnessed his martyrdom or those who heard of it from their fathers and went on pilgrimage to kneel on the steps where he died or touch with trembling fingers the bloodstained hem of his garments, saw it very clearly. For all the world's coarse obsessions and stupidity and blindness, the saints and martyrs have the last word. It is their triumphs over the frailty of the body which causes men to believe in God.

*   *   *

It was a measure of Henry II's greatness that he and his work for England survived the flood of horror and indignation which overwhelmed him when the news of Becket's death became known. His continental dominions were placed under interdict, and for a time it seemed that, with all Christendom against him, he would be excommunicated and his throne declared forfeit. But, his anger against Becket turned to repentance, the great lawyer King's patience and statesmanship reasserted themselves. He let time do what time alone could do.

Leaving the cauldron to simmer, he vanished from his troubled realm and went on crusade. It was characteristic of him that it was one which served his ends as well as those of the Church in whose name it was undertaken. Sixteen years before he had persuaded an English Pope – Adrian IV – to entrust him with a mission: to conquer for the Roman Church the heretical, slave-raiding island of Ireland which St Patrick had converted to Christianity seven centuries before but which, since the Viking invasions, while remaining nominally Christian, had relapsed into its primitive Celtic division and savagery.

Among the Church's many claims to dominion was one to the sovereignty of all islands. It was in pursuance of this pious, if sweeping, aspiration that Henry now embarked with a papal bull authorising him to subdue and rule the island 'for the enlargement of the Church's borders, the restraint of vice, the correction of morals and planting of virtue, the increase of the Christian religion and whatever may tend to God's glory and the well-being

117

of that land'. A few years earlier one of Ireland's ever-warring petty kings – Dermot of Leinster – had sought aid at the English court against his subjects and fellow kings. Unable at the time to help him, in return for his homage Henry had furnished him with letters authorising any of his own feudatories to do so. Such aid Dermot had found among the warlike Norman adventurers or 'Marchers' whose ancestors had conquered and settled south Wales. Among them was the ruined earl of Pembroke, Richard de Clare who, in an attempt to repair his fortunes, promised King Dermot help in return for his daughter's hand. In the late summer of 1170 this great soldier and adventurer, commonly known as Strongbow, with a force of 1200 men stormed, first the Danish port of Waterford, and then Dublin. Six months later, on the death of his father-in-law, he claimed the kingdom of Leinster.

The news caused Henry to act. He could not afford to let his vassals set up an independent feudal power in an island so near England. During the summer after Becket's murder, while Europe waited for the curse of Heaven to fall on him, he assembled a fleet of little ships in Milford Haven. In October he sailed for Ireland with five hundred knights and several thousand archers and men-at-arms.

Against this disciplined force the unarmoured foot-horde of Ireland, armed with stones and javelins, was as impotent as the ancient Britons against the Romans. The kingdoms of Leinster and Meath fell without a blow. That winter Henry spent in a palace of wattle outside Dublin built by his new subjexts. Here he accepted homage from both the Norman–Welsh adventurers who had pre-ceded him and from the native Irish kings and princes. And here, too, he received the submission of the Irish bishops, who swore to conform to the canon law and practices of the Catholic Church, and to acknowledge him and his heirs as kings of Ireland.

Thus, in the winter following Becket's murder and as an in-direct consequence of it, the foundations of English government in Ireland were laid. It was an alien one but better than none at all. Politically the island was much what it had been a thousand years before – a disunity of warring Celtic tribes. Ecclesiastically, it had scarcely progressed beyond the primitive organisation set up by the first evangelists, with colonies of missionary priests living in beehive wattle huts round monastery churches whose abbots wielded episcopal powers. The austerity, scholarship and enthusiasm of three centuries earlier had vanished; most of the monks were married.

By setting up an orderly government at Dublin Henry did what neither the Roman emperors nor the native princes of Ireland had done. Around the east-coast ports which the Vikings had founded, his English 'Pale' became a civilized province, with royal castles and castellans, regularly enforced laws, a Justiciar and justices, and a settled agriculture. To stimulate trade with England and the continent the monopoly of the Scandinavian pirates and slavers was ended, and a colony of Bristol merchants established in Dublin with the same liberties as in their native town. And to provide hereditary warriors, administrators and prelates to maintain order, organise manorial estates and build castle and cathedrals, Irish land was confiscated and granted on the usual feudal terms to members of the ruling Anglo–Norman caste.

It was a realm, however, with little depth and with fluctuating frontiers beyond which, among the bogs and mountains of the west, the kings and clans of Connaught and Munster, admitting only a nominal allegiance, maintained their ancient, savage independence. The work Henry had begun, and which only such a man could perform, was never to be completed. In the spring of 1172, growing daily more anxious for news of England and the continent, he sailed from Wexford, never to return. A few days of his usual rapid travelling carried him from St David's to Portsmouth and thence to Normandy, where the Pope's legates were impatiently awaiting him.

There, at Avranches, the peccant but penitent crusader made his formal submission to the mighty Church, swearing on the Gospels to accept whatever penance the legates might impose. He agreed to allow appeals to Rome, to restore the possessions of Canterbury as they were before his breach with the martyred Archbishop, and to compensate all who had suffered in the latter's cause. Then he turned against the formidable coalition of enemies who were seeking to seize and partition his dominions. They included the kings of France and Scotland and his own wife and sons, the eldest of whom – 'the young King' as he was called – he had had crowned during his fatal duel with Becket to ensure the future allegiance of his subjects.

Yet though the wolf-pack rounded on the old wolf, he met his enemies with his usual resolution and energy. With the speed which made him so formidable a soldier he out-manoeuvred the slow feudal chivalry of France. While he was chasing King Louis back to his own dominions and reducing Norman and Breton castles, rebellion broke out in England. Its higher feudal nobility, long uneasy at encroachments on their jurisdiction, had been particularly alarmed by a purge of sheriffs in the year of Becket's death and their replacement by Exchequer officials. Encouraged by the rebellion of the young King, to whom at Henry's request they had sworn allegiance, the bolder of them took up arms. The earl of Leicester, head of the great Anglo-Norman family of Beaumont, landed in Suffolk with an army of Flemish mercenaries, while Hugh Bigod, the old earl of Norfolk – a veteran of the civil wars of Stephen's reign – tried from his castle of Framlingham to rouse the eastern counties. Simultaneously William the Lion, King of the Scots, laid siege to Carlisle and, with an army of Lothian knights and naked savages from Galloway, swept across Northumberland.

Yet though Henry himself was forced to remain in France, his island realm withstood the shock. Led by the Justiciar, the official nobility of service which he and his grandfather had created out of the lesser baronage proved as strong as the rebellious feudatories. The 'new men' – the de Lacys, Bohuns, Glanvills, de Veres, Trussabuts, Vernons, Balliols and Bruces – counterbalanced the mighty Beaumonts, Mowbrays, Bigods, de Masseys and Tancarvilles. Even the Welsh princes stood by their allegiance. And the English people, who had no love for French-speaking earls, and even less for plundering foreign mercenaries, supported the royal government vigorously. When an army of Fleming weavers landed at Walton, they were met near Bury St Edmunds by 'the host of England' – the *fyrd* or militia of the eastern counties under the Constable, Humphrey de Bohun – and were cut to pieces by Suffolk peasants with forks and flails.

For, having made his peace with the international Church and purged his crime and sacrilege, Henry had by now done so with the common and Christian people of England. After recovering his continental dominions, in the summer of 1174 he returned, a penitent, to the scene of Becket's murder. From Harbledown, a mile out of Canterbury – the village of 'Bob-up-and-down' of Chaucer's *Canterbury Tales* – he made his way on bare feet through the cobbled streets to the cathedral. Here, before a vast crowd, he prostrated himself before the archbishop's tomb while the monks, at his entreaty, scourged him. At dawn, after kneeling all night before the shrine and showering endowments on it, he rode in haste to London.

Here wonderful news reached him. At midnight on 17 July 1174 a travel-stained messenger from the Sheriff of Lancashire arrived at the royal palace of Westminster with a demand for immediate admission. Asked what brought him, he replied that his master, Ranulf de Glanvill, held the King of Scots in chains in his castle of Richmond. Four days before, on the morning after Henry had knelt all night at Becket's shrine, a handful of English knights under Glanvill and the Sheriff of Yorkshire had made a raid from Newcastle into the heart of the Scottish army then ravaging Northumberland. Riding through thick mist, they had surprised the Scottish king outside Alnwick castle. Despite the odds against them they had resolved then and there to carry him off. Such courage met its reward. A day later, his feet tied beneath his horse's belly, William the Lion was carried into Richmond castle and the drawbridge raised behind him. As the news spread, the bells of all the English churches began to peal.

After that miraculous deliverance everything came Henry's way. The Scottish host, deprived of the leader who was the focus both of its own and of Scotland's precarious unity, dissolved into its component parts and, fighting furiously among itself, vanished into the northern mists. The rebel English magnates, despairing of help, surrendered their castles to the King's officials and his loyal English *fyrdmen*. It was the last time that the higher Norman nobility dared to challenge the joint forces of Crown and Law. Henceforward, the greater feudal magnates, like the lesser, accepted the ancient Anglo-Saxon conception of Alfred and Athelstan that power in England could only be exercised within the framework of royal supremacy and law.

CHAPTER TEN

Magna Carta

'To none will we sell, to none will
we deny or delay right or justice.'

Magna Carta

'And still when mob or monarch lays
Too rude a hand on English ways,
The whisper wakes, the shudder plays
    Across the reeds of Runnymede.
And Thames that knows the mood of kings
And crowds and priests and suchlike things
Rolls deep and dreadful as he brings
    The warning down from Runnymede.'

Kipling

BY THE BEGINNING of the thirteenth century a remarkable thing had begun to happen. The people of England – conquered a hundred and fifty years earlier by a foreign aristocracy who had seized their land and despised their language – were becoming increasingly conscious of their unity and nationhood. And though their new kings and lords still spoke French and boasted French descent, even they had begun to think of themselves as English and of their country as England. Within a generation of the Conquest an Italian Archbishop of Canterbury was writing of 'we English' and 'our island'.

For there seemed to be something in the land which naturalised foreigners and, adapting their ways, absorbed them. It was due largely to its being cut off from Europe by sea, so that its diverse inhabitants gradually came to think of themselves, not merely as barons or knights, churchmen, merchants or peasants, but as members of a distinct community that was both part of western Christendom and yet apart from it. Before Frenchmen had come to regard themselves as Frenchmen, Germans as Germans or Italians as Italians, Englishmen, including the Normans settled in England, were thinking of themselves as Englishmen. This sense of separateness was aided by their kings' insistence on the unity of the realm and on a common system of law. And it was stimulated by the difficulty the conquerors – a few thousand warriors speaking a foreign tongue – experienced in ruling so stubborn a race. A hundred years after Hastings there were still Englishmen who persisted in going unshaved as a protest against the Conquest. Living in this misty land of rain and deep clay forests among an alien population, the Norman knights could only exploit their conquest by meeting the natives half, and more than half, way. They needed English men and women to plough their fields, tend their homes, nurse their children and help them in battle. And the English did so – on terms: that their conquerors left them English and became in the end English themselves.

Since their numbers were so small, the conquerors soon became bilingual. They continued to think and converse among themselves in French, but spoke English with their subordinates. They learnt it from their nurses and servants, reeves and ploughmen, and, after the conquest was complete, from their men-at-arms. Abbot Samson of Bury – head of the richest monastery in the land – preached to the common people in the dialect of Norfolk where he had been born and bred. And by the end of the twelfth century even Normans were coming to take a pride in the history and traditions of the island they had won and to treasure the legends of its saints and heroes. The monkish historians, Henry of Huntingdon and William of Malmesbury, collected the ballads and tales of Britain, and Gerald de Barry, a Marcher's son, loved to boast of his Welsh ancestry and the beauties and antiquities of his Pembrokeshire home. It was a Norman – Geoffrey of Monmouth, bishop of St Asaph – who wrote the romantic tale of King Arthur and his British court and made it almost as favourite a theme with the French-speaking ruling-class as the exploits of Charlemagne and the Song of Roland. It helped to make Britain's inhabitants –

Normans, Welsh and English alike, and even southern Scots –
believe they had a common history.

French and English place-names were blended on the map –
English place and Norman owner grown English – Norton Fitzwarren, Pillerton Hersey, Sturminster Marshal, Berry Pomeroy.
And the marriage of Church and State, spiritual and secular, was
consummated, too, in this land where everything ultimately
merged and became part of something else: Abbots Bromley and
Temple Guiting, Toller Monachorum and Salford Priors, White-
ladies Aston and Whitechurch Canonicorum. The great bishop,
Richard le Poore, who built Salisbury cathedral, left his heart to be
buried in the little Dorset village of Tarrant Crawford.

From all this sprang a new force with which kings and barons
and even the Church had to reckon: that of national opinion. Its
chief repositories were the men who were growing up between the
greater feudal barons and the inarticulate peasant mass of the
nation. It was an upper middle class composed mainly of descendants of the Norman knights who had been enfeoffed as owners – or
rather feudal holders – of the soil, and whose fiefs, though originally granted for life, had become, like other property, hereditary.
As their military functions fell into abeyance, they became, instead
of professional soldiers, landed gentlemen with administrative
responsibilities. They served on the new juries of the grand assize
and in the 'oversight' of the royal forests, performed the customary
duties of suit-of-court in the shire and hundred courts, and gave
testimony on oath in the periodical inquests of kings and sheriffs.
They intermingled increasingly with the wealthier Anglo-Saxon
freemen and landholders and with the Anglo-Norman traders of
London and the new towns. Many of our oldest families – Berkeleys
and Nevilles, Lumleys, Leghs and Clavells – sprang from this
twelfth-century knighthood rising into gentility. It found its
natural leaders in the officials and judges whom the Norman and
Angevin kings set up as a counterpoise to the higher feudal aristocracy and ennobled with grants of land. It was employed by the
Crown for an ever-growing host of local administrative and legal
tasks. It provided laymen of trust and character with the time for
public service, and ecclesiastics with sufficient personal status to

make the Church in England rather more independent of foreign control than elsewhere.

The Norman and Angevin kings' establishment of common law and central administration helped to train this new upper or upper-middle class. So did the ancient Anglo-Saxon institutions of local government. The shire and hundred courts, the juries impanelled to pronounce on questions of fact, the larger towns buying rights of self-government from their overlords, all gave men opportunities of learning to act in co-operation, of administering corporate affairs and finance, and of reaching practical decisions after ordered discussion. As the nation grew in wealth and civilization, more and more public business was left to local men of worth, rich enough to take communal responsibility under the Crown yet not strong enough, like the greater feudal lords, to act without it.

*   *   *

The closing years of Henry II's long and germinative reign were embittered by the rebellion of his restless, turbulent sons. The eldest having died before him, he was succeeded on his death in 1189 by the thirty-two year old Richard 'Coeur-de-Lion'. A giant, golden-haired warrior, his one ambition was to join the Third Crusade to recover the Christian kingdom of Jerusalem, the news of whose capture by the Moslem Saracens in the year before his accession had shocked western Europe. This chivalrous romantic young knight, poet and musician, was so eager to raise an army that he was ready to sell anything, even London, to do so.

Though he turned his back on his kingdom and sailed away into the Orient, he proved a magnificent leader. Despite the fiery temper which made enemies of all his fellow sovereigns, he was the hero of the crusade and put new heart into the dispirited, plague-ridden army besieging Acre. The zeal with which, stricken with fever, he pressed home the attack, led to the city's early fall. Two months later, by his great victory at Arsuf, he re-opened the road to Jaffa and Jerusalem. And though the final prize eluded him, and he was forced to return with his work incomplete, he made a treaty with the Saracens which for another half-century secured the beleaguered Christian kingdoms of the Levant and the pilgrims' road to the Holy Places. He made the name of the northern land over which he ruled more honoured than it had ever been before. Even Saladin praised him. And, though hated by crafty and intriguing princes, he was loved by simple fighting men for his lion heart, his constancy to his word and his frank open nature and generosity. His shield of golden lions and scarlet crusader's cross became part of the heritage of England.

Though during Richard's ten years' reign he was almost continuously out of the country, the judges and officials his father had trained continued to enforce justice and order in his absence. But the real test for them and Henry's rule of law came after the succession in 1199 of the latter's youngest son, John. This erratic and moody tyrant, who inherited much of his father's genius but none of his creative capacity, used the legal and administrative machinery he had inherited to subject the landed classes to intolerable and arbitrary taxation. He levied scutage after scutage – the composition which tenants-in-chief and the military vassals had to pay in lieu of the service in the field by which they held their lands – not only after his campaigns but before them, so getting their money whether he incurred the expenses of a war or not. While his father in thirty-five years had levied only eight scutages and his crusading brother two, John in fifteen years imposed eleven, several for service on campaigns which never took place. Hitherto the extent of such service and of composition for it had been limited by feudal custom. John varied it at his pleasure. The rate at which it was assessed was almost double that of his brother's day.

As well as scutage and the customary feudal aids from his tenants-in-chief, John imposed levies on the capital value of all personal and moveable goods – an impost originally instituted for Richard's crusade to recover Jerusalem – and at least seven general tallages on the manors and boroughs of the royal demesne. Some of these, like Worcester, Northampton and Oxford, had to pay three or four times as much as they had paid before. When his tenants' estates, through death or other cause, fell into his custody John stripped them by special tallages of almost their entire realisable capital. He seized men's children as hostages and

127

trafficked the wardships of minors and the marriages of heiresses to the basest agents. He made mercenary captains sheriffs and simultaneously allowed them to hold judicial office, so enabling them to blackmail property-owners with vexatious writs and false accusations. Summonses were issued in order to extract fines for non-attendance, writs were withheld or sold at exorbitant rates, crushing penalties imposed without regard to the nature of the offence or means of the accused, justice delayed or even denied altogether. The elaborate fiscal and legal system of the two Henrys and the great Justiciars was turned into a merciless machine for extortion.

In the light of his son's use of it, Henry II's achievement had presented England with a terrible dilemma. The great Angevin had convinced the nation and even its feudal magnates that, after the disorders of Stephen's reign, security and prosperity for all depended on the supremacy of the Crown. He had created a legal and financial machinery for making that supremacy effective, and a self-renewing school of trained administrators to operate it. But when his son proved a diabolical maniac, who used the royal power to make life intolerable for his subjects and alienated everyone in turn, those whom Henry had made the agents of that power were, little by little, driven into making a choice. They had either to destroy it, and with it the order and unity on which the prosperity of the realm depended, or subject the wearer of the crown himself to it. The first course might have been easy; the second was superlatively hard. It is the supreme measure of Henry II's achievement in educating his greater subjects that the best of them chose the second, and carried their reluctant fellows with them.

Yet the very cunning and ability of his son also impelled men to that wiser choice. Had John been a weakling as well as an impossible king, the monarchical power which had become the expression of England's unity could scarcely have survived the storms raised by his misdeeds. Yet for all his periodic lethargy, when driven into a corner he fought back with a fury that made even the most reckless or arrogant opponent chary of going to extremes. It was no child's play to dash from his hands the sceptre and rod he misused. The alternative of restraining and controlling him – and with him the royal power – was thus kept open.

It was an alternative, too, to which Englishmen now instinctively turned. It was of the Crown that they thought when they used the word England, for without it there would have been no England. Ever since the days of Alfred the monarchy had been implanting in the English the habit of acting together. The great alien princes who had grasped in their strong hands the athelings' sceptre – Canute the Dane, William and Henry the Normans, Henry II the Angevin – had all strengthened it. It had become natural even to Anglo-Norman barons to act with and through the Crown. They still tried to do so when its wearer of the hour became their oppressor and enemy.

Only the barons, with their armour, horses, castles and men-at-arms, had the means to withstand such a tyrant. Even for them it involved intense danger. But they had been driven to desperation. Some were reactionaries who sought to restore the untrammelled rights of provincial feudalism. Others were selfish bullies who wished to free themselves from royal control in order to oppress their weaker neighbours. Most, however, were members of the new aristocracy of office which Henry II had used to discipline the older nobility and fashion the administrative machine which had now been turned into an instrument of irresponsible tyranny. They were strongest in the north, where authority had always been left to the man on the spot and where local magnates were used to defending themselves against Scottish raiders. It was these northerners who, goaded beyond endurance, in the summer of 1213 refused a royal demand for scutage. In this they were acting beyond their rights, for it was part of the feudal law that an overlord could tax his tenants-in-chief to support his wars. But they maintained that such a right could be denied if it was not used justly and within the limits set by custom.

Others felt that their first duty was to the Crown, irrespective of its wearer. The King's majesty had become more important to them than the King himself. The tenure of their lands, their dignities and honours, the functioning of their local institutions and the administration of justice and order were all inextricably bound up with it. The nation was drifting into war, not only between its best elements and its worst, but between the best themselves. Men were appealing from the King to the King's law and taking their stand, in the name of the just laws of the King's father, against the King's government. The perils inherent in the situation were intense.

To resolve it called not only for loyalty and selflessness, but for the most subtle, comprehending statesmanship. And in its primate, Stephen Langton, England found what it needed. Langton was a scholar trained in the close logic of the medieval Church, with a vision which embraced all Christendom. His temper was essentially moderate, conciliatory and unassuming. He had the kind of good sense and quiet, rather whimsical, humour that takes the hysteria out of strained situations. He was always seeking to achieve what men of goodwill, after calmly hearing and debating all the arguments, considered both just and expedient. His aim was reasonableness even more than reason. In this he was most English. So was he in his respect for established custom and dislike of extremes.

It was not Langton's wish to see the Crown overthrown, the law ignored, the realm divided, the barons petty sovereigns as in the days of Stephen. For two years – amongst the most crucial in English history – he struggled, not only with his treacherous and tyrannical sovereign, but with the factious interests and violent passions of those who were trying to use the resentment the latter had aroused to destroy the peace and the unity of the realm. He repeatedly urged them not to carry things to extremes, while reminding the King of his coronation oath and the solemn compacts of his predecessors to govern justly. All that was needed to restore justice and peace to England, he claimed, was to renew such compacts. 'A charter of Henry I has been found,' he told the barons, 'by means of which, if you desire, you may regain your lost liberty.' And he tried unceasingly to induce them to base their demands on its terms.

Langton's wisdom and moderation failed to save England from the civil war he feared – one in which John, after ravaging his own country, met his death in October 1216 after a disastrous march through the flooded Nene. But before war broke out, on 15 June 1215 in a Thames-side meadow called Runnymede, the armed barons, with the archbishop's aid, forced the reluctant monarch to set his seal to a document which became a blue-print for England's future constitutional development. Ostensibly a restatement of ancient law and custom, it promised that the King should not without 'general counsel', that is without the consent of the Great Council, demand any scutage or aid from his tenants-in-chief other than the three regular aids long recognised by feudal custom; that the heirs of earls and barons should be admitted to their inheritances on payment of the customary reliefs; that the estates of heirs-in-ward should not be wasted during their infancy, nor widows robbed of their dowries or forced against their will to marry royal nominees. It laid down that no free man should be imprisoned or dispossessed save by process of law and the just judgments of his equals; that he should not be taxed or fined unreasonably or to his ruin; that his means of livelihood, including the merchant's stock, the craftsman's tools and the peasant's wainage, should be free from amercement; that London and the chartered boroughs should enjoy their ancient liberties; that merchants should come and go safely in time of war; and that the foreign mercenaries should be dismissed. It provided for the regular administration of the judicial system; ordered that the Common Pleas should be held at Westminster and not follow a perambulating court; that none should be made justices, bailiffs or constables who did not know the law of the land; that sheriffs should not sit in judgment in their own shires; that two justices with four knights of the shire should hold assizes in every county every quarter; that royal writs should not be sold at exorbitant prices or withheld from those entitled to them. 'To none,' the King was made to swear, 'will we sell, to none will we deny or delay right or justice.

In all this the Charter, consisting of more than sixty clauses, was a recital of the wrongs suffered by subjects under a tyrannical King. And, as men of property – and, above all, landed property – were the only subjects with rights enforceable in the King's own courts, it confined itself in the main to setting out particulars of the redress granted them. It was a charter of 'liberties', and to the medieval mind a liberty was a right to the enjoyment of a specific property. It was a freedom to do something with one's own without interference by the King or any other man.

Called Magna Carta because of its length, the Charter was not, therefore, a declaration of general principles, let alone of human rights. Medieval men thought of these only in connection with religion. The Charter enunciated no theories; it was nothing if not specific and practical. Yet, though its chief beneficiaries were tenants-in-chief of the Crown, it was a national as well as feudal document. It made no distinction between Norman and English and guaranteed the liberties of small property-owners as well as large. Thirty-two of its sixty-one clauses dealt with the relations of the King and his subjects and not merely his tenants-in-chief. 'We grant,' it declared, 'to all the freemen of our realm, from us and our heirs forever, all the undermentioned liberties to have and to hold for them as our heirs from us and our heirs.' And it established two precedents of immense significance for the future. One was that when an English king broke the feudal compact and gave his vassals the right – universally recognised by feudal law – to renounce their allegiance, it was not necessary to dissolve the bonds of political society and disintegrate the realm. Magna Carta was a substitute for deposition: a legal expedient to enforce customary law which left the King on the throne and the sword of civil war undrawn. Government in England, though exercised by the King, was to be rooted in justice and based on law, or it was not to be accepted as government at all. Magna Carta was the first great political act in the history of the nation-state – itself an institution of which the English had been the pioneers.

The barons' unity in the face of John's injustice, and their decision to act within the law, had created a new phenomenon: a corporate estate of the realm to prevent the unjust exercise of power by the realm's ruler. The taxpayers had combined to control the tax-imposer. Magna Carta was the product not of a rebellion, as it seemed at the time to the King and his more bitter opponents, but of a revolution carried out by process of law. By the provisions for summoning the Great Council before any new aid or scutage could be granted, it made a representative assembly of feudal tenants a preliminary to taxing those tenants. This was something wholly new. And in establishing the principle that the King must conform to the law which he administered, it created a constitutional device for compelling him to do so. In addition to provisions for regulating the summons of lords to the Council – archbishops, earls, bishops and greater barons by individual writ, and lesser barons by collective summons through the sheriffs – the Charter contained a clause by which twenty-five representative barons, chosen by their Order, were to become its guardians. They were to 'observe, keep and cause to be observed, with all their might' the liberties it guaranteed. Should any of them be infringed, and just redress be refused, these twenty-five lords – almost all of whom had served, or were the sons of men who had served, as royal officials – were empowered to take up arms against the King to enforce the Charter. The indignant John was made to admit his subjects' right to restrain the wearer of the Crown whenever he infringed their liberties. 'These barons,' he had to announce on behalf of himself and his heirs, 'with all the commons of the land shall distrain and annoy us by every means in their power; that is, by seizing our castles, lands and possessions, and every other mode, till the wrong shall be repaired to their satisfaction, saving our person, our queen and our children. And when it shall be repaired, they shall obey us as before.'

By this device, though a clumsy and primitive one, the men who had wrung Magna Carta from the King sought to ensure its permanence. It was dictated by fear and the just belief of the barons that the moment their force was dispersed John would try to destroy both them and their settlement. Its dangers were clearly foreseen by Langton who tried, though in vain, to introduce a mediating body between the King and the barons' council. 'They have given me,' declared the furious monarch, 'twenty-five over-kings!' Yet the pattern of constitutional thought thus set out was to be reproduced in a thousand forms in the history of the English – and British – nation. It is still enshrined, after seven centuries, in the words of the national anthem:

> 'May he defend our laws
> And ever give us cause
> To sing with heart and voice,
> God save the King!'

It was a prayer that the best of those who stood by the King's shoulder at Runnymede had tried to answer.

*   *   *

However great the implications of Magna Carta for the future of the country and the world, few of England's then inhabitants can have been affected by, or even aware of, the barons' struggle with the Crown. But in the years immediately preceding John's surrender at Runnymede, the foundation by an Italian, Francis of Assisi, and a Castilian Spaniard named Dominic, of two new religious Orders was to have a profound effect on contemporary English life. Designed to carry Christ's creed and teaching from the cloister and sanctuary, and from the rich and privileged to the poorest and least accounted, unlike the regulars of the monastic houses, both Dominicans and Franciscans abjured the possesion of all property or land. Open to both clerics and laymen, bound by vows of poverty and chastity, and calling themselves brothers or friars – after the French *frères* and Latin *fratres* – they shunned the static, conventual life of the older monastic Orders, taking the world as their parish and the street and market-place as their cloister.

The two Orders, meeting a universal need, spread rapidly, founding missions in every western land. The black-robed Dominicans – the more scholastically inclined of the two Orders – first came to England in 1221, five years after the death of King John and the succession of his child son, Henry III, being welcomed at Canterbury by Stephen Langton himself. But it was the Franciscans who aroused the real enthusiasm of the English. Following the example of their founder, a rich clothier's son who had abandoned a life of wealth and luxury to preach to the lepers and outcasts of the trading towns of northern Italy, the first Franciscans – a band of nine, three of them Englishmen – landed at Dover in 1224, just under a decade after Magna Carta and when the first stones were being laid of Salisbury Cathedral. Penniless, barefoot and bare-headed, in coarse grey gowns and girdles of rope, they made their way to Canterbury and thence to London and Oxford, begging their bread along the highways and preaching

"Hand mirrors engraved with exquisite circular designs."

Celtic Mirror, 1st century A.D., found at Desborough, Northamptonshire.

Overleaf:

"The Province's only land frontier against the northern barbarians of Caledonia."

The Emperor Hadrian's seventy-three mile Wall from the mouth of the Tyne to the Solway, running over hill and dale with watch towers every mile. 2nd century A.D.

"Masons, working high above column and clerestory, fashioned whole legions of tiny figures on the bosses."

Peasant with toothache. Stone capital from the south transept of Wells Cathedral c. 1200–1210.

"An instinctive genius for blending the works of God and man. We can still see the reverence and skill with which they turned native to human ends while enriching and beautifying it."

One of the "great barns of stone and timber."
Great Coxwell, Berkshire.
13th century.

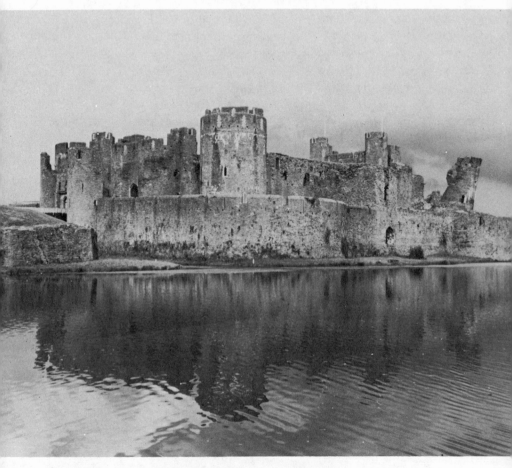

"The Marchers, resolved to prevent further raids from the north, had been building strong castles like the mighty Caerphilly, which Gilbert de Clare, the red earl of Gloucester, raised near Cardiff in Henry III reign."

Caerphilly Castle, 13th century.

"Where dynamics and pure poetry blend and become indistinguishable."
The nave of Wells Cathedral. 13th century.

"The graceful multi-shafted central pillar which bore the vaulted roof."
Chapter House, Salisbury c. 1268–1280.

"Leaves and flowers carved on the capitals; Like Galatea they possess all the qualities of life except movement, though made of stone."

Southwell Minster, c. 1290–1295.

Overleaf:
"Save for its spire and upper tower, added a century later, the only medieval cathedral in England which is all of a piece."

Salisbury Cathedral 1220–1268, and c. 1280–1330.

"Cathedrals still towering above the roofs of modern towns."
Lincoln Cathedral, West front. Early 14th century.

"The pillars of the new nave of York were like the trunk and branches of a beech wood."

York Minster, 14th century.

"Henry Yevele, the King's master mason, earlier supervised by the clerk of the works, the poet Geoffrey Chaucer, reconstructed William Rufus's Hall at Westminster, calling in the royal carpenter, Hugh Herland, to span its 240 foot length and 70 foot width with a hammer-beam roof of Sussex oak – the first of the great hammer-beam roofs which, with the Fan Vault and the Perpendicular style, were England's most original architectural achievements."

Westminster Hall, rebuilt 1393–1400.

"Hearths with chimneys had taken the place in rich men's houses of sooty open fires, Flemish glass had appeared in traceried windows . . . manor houses and fine merchants' dwellings with private bathrooms and plastered walls were rising in place of the old gloomy fortresses where men and beasts slept together on filthy rush-strewn floors in draughty halls, full of smoke and stink."

"14th century additional wing to Beeleigh Abbey, Maldon, Essex, built as a summer homestead for a luxury loving Abbot. Today the home of Christina Foyle and her husband, Ronald Batty, by whose kindness it is illustrated."

"The flowering of the Perpendicular style, England's supreme contribution to the art of architecture."

The chapel of King's College, Cambridge, begun by Henry VI as the companion foundation of his school at Eton, and completed by Henry VII at the end of the 15th century.

to the poorest of the poor. Followed by hundreds of others, both native and foreign, they took for their diocese the lazar-house door, the stews and the stinking hovels along the stagnant ditches outside the town walls; for their pulpit the dung-hill and garbage-pit, the pot-house and brothel. They made their habitation in strongholds of poverty, vice and misery whose very names – the Greyfriars in Stinking Lane, Sheer Hog and Scalding Lane – testify to their lives of dedication.

The all-embracing charity, cheerfulness and courtesy – virtues prescribed by their founder – and the heroic example of these evangelists made a profound impression on the native English. They revived memories of Aidan and the Celtic saints and missionaries of Anglo-Saxon days. Despite the haunts of wretchedness in which they lived and worked, they were so merry that they were known as God's jesters. They seemed to take a special joy in serving outcasts and sinners. They washed the feet of the unclean and kissed their sores. To the rich monks of the conventional houses, they seemed only vulgar sensationalists and interlopers, 'utterly shameless and forgetful of their profession and Order'. To the neglected masses of the city slums, they seemed like heavenly messengers. Their sermons, racy, eloquent, charged with fervent emotion and illustrated by lively, colloquial tales that the simplest could understand, went straight to the hearts of uneducated men and women whose knowledge of the Christian story had been hitherto derived from services conducted in a tongue intelligible only to the learned.

The coming of the friars gave an immense stimulus to works of charity. Till now these had tended to be somewhat spasmodic, like the annual distribution of flour – still made after eight centuries – to the Hampshire villagers of Tichborne. London's two greatest hospitals – St Bartholomew's, first founded by Rufus's courtier, Rahere, in the Smithfield marshes, and the even older St Thomas's in Southwark for sick and needy travellers – had been established by Augustinian canons in the twelfth century. Such 'spitals, as they were called, were very small: St Thomas's, rebuilt after the fire of 1207, had rush beds for forty patients, and a staff of four canons, three nursing sisters and a warden. Following the example of their founder, the Franciscans made a cult of lazar-houses, often establishing their friaries beside them and making their novices undergo a period of training in them. By reminding men that Christ was poor and lived among the poor, they started to deflect Christian alms and legacies from the over-endowed monasteries to institutions which relieved want, sickness and suffering. They introduced into the vernacular speech words of faith like mercy, pity, patience, comfort, conscience and salvation. They were enthusiastic practitioners of medicine – a science recently revived by contact with the Moorish and Jewish scholars of southern Spain[1] – and administered it free to the poor among whom they worked. It was a ministration desperately needed, for the slums of medieval cities, situated mostly by the swampy side of streams outside the walls, were dreadful haunts of disease and wretchedness.

Above all the friars, both Dominicans and Franciscans, were teachers, and played a leading part in the universities which had grown during the previous century out of the cathedral schools. Their eloquence made them the natural leaders of the young students, as penniless and ragged as themselves, who, living in crowded garrets and taverns, flocked to the lectures of the learned doctors of theology, law and grammar in their hired rooms or schools and endeavoured to earn from the chancellor or bishop's representative the Church's licence to teach. These turbulent communities, for all their poverty, were intensely alive – gay, ardent and speculative. Though little accounted by the rich and powerful, it was with them, rather than with the sedentary and devotional monks of the Benedictine and Cistercian houses, that the future of European learning now lay. The friars, in touch with common humanity, had the perception to see this and, through their work in the universities, to mould that future. The famous Dominican house in the Jacobin convent at Paris was for the next half-century the inspiration of Europe's greatest university. It gave her the two most eminent schoolmen of the age: Albert the Great, the Swabian Regent Master, who made the works of Aristotle, rediscovered by Arab commentators, the basis of western scholasticism; and Thomas of Aquinas, 'the big dumb oxe of Sicily' who,

[1] Arabic symbols are still used today by doctors for prescriptions.

136

seeing natural law as 'the mind and will of God', sought to harmonise Christian faith with reason. His vision of the universe was one in which everything was ordered and balanced by the will of God; 'they are called wise,' he wrote, 'who put things in their right order.' His elaborate exposition, through the argumentative method of question and answer, antetype and antithesis, sought to carry men's minds, by a series of stages, to the comprehension of Heaven itself. In the disputations in which they maintained their theses against all comers, these Dominican schoolmen tried to prove God by logic – a heroic feat of mind that in the end, by its failure, proved almost as dangerous to faith as to intellectual freedom.

In no land in Europe was the impact of the friars' teaching greater than in England. It gave a new and European importance to the schools of Oxford – founded in a small stone building in the churchyard of St Mary's after Henry II, during his dispute with Becket, had recalled the English scholars from Paris. Both Dominicans and Franciscans established missions there, and at the new East Anglian university which had arisen at Cambridge, on the site of a 'little waste chester', following a murderous affray in 1208 between town and gown at Oxford. For a time, too, there were nascent universities at Stamford, Northampton and Reading. The exposure to vice and possible heresy of the indisciplined youths who herded together in such places was a challenge to the mendicant friars. The school which the Franciscans built in their friary at Oxford formed the model for the University's earliest halls and colleges. William of Durham's charitable foundation for theological students which grew into University College, Sir John de Balliol's slightly later one that became Balliol, and Merton, founded between 1264 and 1274 by one of Henry III's chancellors 'for the perpetual sustenance of twenty scholars living in the schools', were all inspired by the discipline and communal industry of the friars' house. The lectures and disputations held there drew such crowds that the secular masters were left, we are told, at their desks 'like sparrows alone upon the housetops'. All this, two centuries after the Norman Conquest, tended in a hundred different ways to make the indigenous English majority, particularly in the towns, more politically conscious.

SET IN A SILVER SEA

One of the earliest triumphs of the Franciscans in the universities was to persuade the Master of the Oxford Schools, the great Robert Grosseteste, to become their Lector. Until his election in 1235 as bishop of Lincoln – the diocese in which the university lay – he was the inspirer of a group of young Franciscan scholars, whose experimental approach to the problems of the universe constituted the first serious challenge to the authoritarian ecclesiastical cosmology of the Middle Ages. A Suffolk farmer's son, Grosseteste was a mathematician and physicist, as well as a theologian and grammarian, and was famous for experiments with lenses. His methods, unlike those of most medieval philosophers, were experimental and inductive. The greatest of his pupils, Roger Bacon – 'the marvellous doctor' – a Franciscan from Ilchester in Somerset, carried his practice even further, making an investigation of natural science which brought him at times into conflict with the Church authorities for unorthodoxy and even suspected heresy. His mind, reinforced by his study of Arabic scientific writers, was forever voyaging into the unknown, dreaming of boats without oars, self-propelled carts, and bridges which hung suspended over space. His *Opus Magnus*, written and secretly published at the request of the Pope, is the greatest scientific work of the thirteenth century and possibly of the entire Middle Ages.

CHAPTER ELEVEN

Counsel,
Consent and Parliament

'Let us not be divided from the common
counsel, for . . . if we are divided, we shall
all perish.'

Robert Grosseteste

'The laws of England . . . since they have been
approved by the consent of those who use them,
and have been confirmed by the oath of kings . . .
cannot be changed or destroyed without the
common consent of all those by whose counsel
and consent they were promulgated.'

Bracton

SEVERAL TIMES DURING the fifty-six years' reign of John's son – who
succeeded to the throne in 1216 at the age of nine – the Charter was
re-confirmed. Henry III was a good, weak, obstinate, unreliable
man who got himself and the country into grave financial difficulties
through an ambitious foreign policy which he was incapable of
implementing. In 1255, forty years after Magna Carta, at the
Easter feast at Oxford, he appealed to the assembled magnates –
the country's chief taxpayers with whom he had been quarrelling[1] –
to rescue him and the administration from his almost bottomless
debts. The barons' leaders took counsel of one another and at the
end of April came to the Council armed. They left their swords at

[1] For a fuller account of Henry III's reign, see the author's *Makers of the
Realm*, pp. 311–358.

the door – a custom still enshrined in the ritual of Parliament – but made the King and his eldest son, the young Lord Edward, swear to abide by their advice. It was agreed that a Committee of twenty-four, half chosen by the barons and half by Henry, should draft proposals for a plan of reform to redress the nation's grievances and restore the ancient co-operation between Crown and magnates.

That summer, at a meeting at Oxford of the Great Council, the reforming committee's provisions were announced. They were accepted by the King, who saw in them his only hope of obtaining the aid he needed. They were of a most drastic kind. An *ad hoc* Council of Fifteen was to 'have the power of advising the King in good faith concerning the government of the kingdom . . . in order to amend and redress everything that they shall consider in need of amendment or redress'. If its members failed to agree or were not all present, a decision of the majority was to bind all – a principle of great future significance. It was to have authority over the Justiciar, Treasurer and Chancellor – who was to seal nothing by the King's will alone without the Council's knowledge – to reform the royal household, to place the castles in the hands of native-born custodians, and to appoint sheriffs annually from men of the counties they administered.

Of these measures the most important was that which regulated the meetings of the Great Council of the realm, or Parliament as it was now beginning to be called – the enduring embodiment of the ancient English custom that a King should take counsel of his chief men and have 'deep speech' with them. Parliament was a French word for such deep speech, for talking things over. Magna Carta had indicated the means by which the magnates, earls, barons, bishops and greater abbots were to be summoned to meetings of this body. It was now enacted that Parliament should meet regularly three times a year, at Michaelmas, Candlemas and in June. 'To these three Parliaments,' it was declared, 'the chosen councillors of the King shall come, even if they are not summoned, in order to examine the state of the kingdom and consider its common needs and those of the King.' And to them were to come twelve representatives of the general 'community' – that is, the general body of barons. Their approval of whatever the Council decided was thereafter to bind the community.

The reforming Fifteen acted quickly. While Parliament received and investigated hundreds of judicial petitions, it began with furious energy to reform the kingdom's internal wrongs, appointing four representative knights in every shire to draw up for the consideration of the royal judges lists of grievances and unjust administrative practices. For, with all their limitations, the barons had learnt the lesson Langton had taught them at the beginning of the century. Their attitude was now not only feudal but national; their business, as they saw it, not only to defend their interests, but to champion those of the community as a whole. 'We wish,' their spokesman had declared in the Council as far back as 1234, 'to keep in mind the common welfare of the realm and not to burden the poor.' They had made provision in their periodic meetings for relieving poor suitors from a ruinous attendance on the royal courts by permitting them to plead by attorney, and had sought to protect merchants from royal purveyors, and widows and minors from grasping overlords. Now, at a time of widespread hardship and discontent, when a succession of bad harvests, with famine and pestilence, had brought many to the verge of ruin, they proclaimed their intention of investigating the complaints of the lesser freeholders, even the poorest and most obscure.

Yet in doing so, their movement lost its unity. The zeal of the more ardent reformers outran the disinterestedness of the more conservative. The barons had been united in their resolve to check the King's extravagant foreign adventures, to rid the government of aliens and to take their rightful place in the control of the realm. But when it was proposed that, having reformed the abuses of the royal administration, the Council of Fifteen should investigate those of the baronial courts – in other words, the grievances of their own tenants – many barons, led by the great Marcher earl of Gloucester, Richard de Clare, felt that it was time to call a halt.

Yet, as much as the magnates, the lesser landowners of the shires had been politically awakened by the growing efficiency and extortionate power of the royal officials. They, too, had had to unite to control them or lose their self-respect. And the very use the barons were making of them and the part they already played in the kingdom's administration rendered them a force to be reckoned with. They had been called upon in the past year to elect four of their members in every shire to ensure that the sheriff observed the law and to report his misdemeanours to the Justiciar. They had now been given the duty of electing in the county courts four men from the shire from whom the Exchequer was to choose the sheriff of the year. And they were accustomed, in a humble and attendant capacity, to send representatives or knights of the shire to the King's courts at Westminster, and had occasionally been summoned to meetings of the Great Council or Parliament to answer questions on oath on local matters of taxation or justice.

Had King, barons and prelates – the privileged ruling Orders of the realm – been united, these rustic knights, or bachelors as they were called, would have counted for little. But in the revolutionary situation which now existed they were able to make their voice heard. They did so – in no uncertain fashion – for the first time in English history in the autumn of 1259, when at the royal feast of St Edward held at Westminster before the meeting of Parliament they addressed a corporate protest to the Lord Edward, the King's son and heir. In this document, known as the 'protest of the Community of Bachelors of England', they complained that, while 'the lord King had performed and fulfilled all and singular that the barons had ordained . . . the barons themselves had done nothing of what they had promised for the good of the realm; but only for their own good and to the harm of the King elsewhere'.

The twenty-year-old prince – the future Edward I, whose ardent, noble head as a youth can be seen carved in stone above a capital in the north transept of Westminster Abbey – responded to this tactfully phrased appeal with characteristic frankness. Though devoted to his father, he was in his directness his complete opposite. He had sworn, he declared, a solemn oath at Oxford and, though he had made it reluctantly, 'he was not on this account less prepared to stand by it and to expose himself to death for the community of England and for the advantage of the State'. He therefore informed the barons that unless they fulfilled their oath he would support the 'community' of bachelors and help to enforce it.

As a result, further reforms entitled the Provisions of Westminster – the complement of the earlier Provisions of Oxford – were enacted in Parliament. These laid down among other things that no one except the King and his ministers should levy distraints outside his fief, that no one without a royal writ should compel his free tenants to respond in his court to any matter concerning their free tenements, that none but the King should hear appeals of false judgments, and that no charter of exemption from assize or jury service should exempt a man, however great, from the obligation to testify on oath in the royal courts if his doing so was essential to justice.

The reforms for which the Council of Fifteen had been set up were now complete. A wilful, vain monarch had been taught the lesson that England could only be ruled with the assent of her leading men. And, unlike his father, he had learnt it without bloodshed. Moderate and informed opinion, therefore, began to veer towards the Crown, feeling that the nation should return to the form of government to which it was used.

*   *   *

Yet England had a further lesson to learn and a harsher. Her sovereign's obstinacy had awoken feelings which could not be easily resolved. There was a strange ferment in the air: of vague, vehement talk of justice and treason, not to the King but to the community; of friars preaching apocalyptic sermons in streets and on village greens; of cities arming their men and watching their gates; of war in the Marches where the Prince of Gwynedd, Llywelyn ap Gruffydd, enraged by the encroachments of English officials, was making a new nation of the Welsh and burning the lands and castles of the Marchers.

All this might have come to nothing in that politically immature age but for one circumstance. That circumstance was a great man. Simon de Montfort had come to England from France thirty years earlier to claim the earldom of Leicester and marry the King's sister. He had little liking for the English and never really understood them. But he was obsessed with the belief that power should

143

be exercised as a sacred trust and that it was a Christian noble's duty to enforce justice. It was this conviction, and his dynamic capacity to communicate it to others, which won him the devotion of all whose hopes of a juster society had been quickened by the baronial reforms. He appealed to the discontented, to the hothead young lords and bachelors, to the men outside the Constitution, to the merchants and apprentices of the eastern towns, particularly of London and the Cinque Ports, to the preaching friars who went among the poor, to the ragged scholars and simple craftsmen and artisans who wanted to see God's kingdom made on earth. The son of the crusader who had crushed the Albigensians and won Provence for the French Crown, he invested every policy he championed with a passionate religious earnestness. He was a man, it was said, who watched more often than he slept; 'Sir Simon the Righteous' they called him. The Provisions of Oxford, which he had helped to frame, had become in his eyes divine commandments. 'He stood firm like an immoveable pillar,' wrote a monkish admirer, 'and neither threats, promises, gifts nor flattery could avail to move him . . . to betray the oath which he had taken to reform the kingdom.'

The trouble was that Simon did not attach the same meaning to that oath as either the King, who had subscribed to it, or the ordinary conservative-minded Englishman of his day. He maintained that the Council of Fifteen set up at Oxford was no mere temporary expedient to reform abuses and re-establish government by assent, but a permanent executive Council to rule in the King's name. Yet the throne had always been the medium through which Englishmen had been governed, and it was hard for them to conceive of any other, and still harder to devise a substitute for it. To contrain an English king to rule with the assent of his magnates was one thing, to exercise his functions for him another. De Montfort, in the name of reform, was advocating a form of government wholly foreign to English tradition.

Without this provocative challenge Henry, an ageing man who had learnt his lesson, would almost certainly have acquiesced in the baronial reforms. They had been demanded by the entire nation. But this oligarch, with his haughty claims to subject him to a council of nobles and summon Parliament in his absence, aroused all his obstinacy and petulance and his most treacherous, dangerous mood. And the jealousy and alarm which the proud unbending Frenchman awoke in his associates, and in moderate and conservative men generally, created a party for the King which had not before existed. For Simon's violence and intransigence sooner or later alienated everyone who tried to work with him as an equal. He was incapable of sharing power: he could only give orders and be obeyed. Compromise – the breath of self-government – was alien to him. He wished to establish the rule of righteousness on earth and viewed everyone who opposed him as an agent of unrighteousness.

That winter a final attempt was made to avert disaster by an appeal to the arbitration of the King's brother-in-law, the saintly Louis IX of France. But when his award in Henry's favour was published at Amiens early in 1264, de Montfort refused to accept it. 'Though all should forsake me,' he declared, 'I will stand firm . . . in the just cause to which my faith is pledged.' On 14 May of that year, to the amazement of everyone, his army defeated the royal array on the Lewes downs in Sussex. It was a triumph of youth over numbers, of the towns over the country, of the green-clad archers of the weald – prototypes of the yeoman infantry of England's future – over the glittering but old-fashioned feudal chivalry of the Court. Both Henry and his son were taken prisoners, and de Montfort became virtual dictator.

For a year he ruled England in the King's name, with the help of a nominated council of oligarchs. He proved no more capable than Henry of simultaneously founding the rule of justice on earth and pleasing everyone. His dilemma was that his only legal claim to authority in a land inherently monarchial was either the captive King, in whose name he governed and who could not be permanently constrained by force, or a conception wholly repugnant to a nation which liked law without a sovereign as little as a sovereign without law. Yet, though his triumph at Lewes was ephemeral and the civil war itself unnecessary – since the King had already accepted the principle of government with baronial counsel – the representative conception of Parliament was enlarged through de

Montfort's need to obtain wider support for his rule. In January 1265, he summoned to a Parliament not only the greater barons and prelates by separate writ and two knights elected in the shire court of every county, but two burgesses from each of the larger towns to represent the urban freemen and taxpayers. This was revolutionary, for at law no burgess had any right to refuse consent to a tallage demanded by the Crown. Only a few years earlier such a claim had caused Henry III to imprison some rash London citizens who made it. By this step de Montfort unconsciously placed what, in a precedent-loving nation, was to prove a barrier across an avenue of taxation which might, as commercial wealth grew, have made the Crown independent of a Parliament of land-owners.

The rule of the great champion of oligarchy lasted little more than a year. His difficulties and critics multiplied; the one made the other. In the spring of 1265 he fell out with his chief supporter, the young Marcher earl of Gloucester. At the end of May, Prince Edward – whose political stature had been growing fast – escaped from his captors at Hereford and, joining the Marcher lords with whom he had been secretly negotiating, routed and destroyed de Montfort at Evesham.

Yet, though the royal party had triumphed, there was no going back on the principle for which so many had striven: that the government of England, though primarily and fundamentally monarchial, should be with the counsel and consent of the realm expressed through frequent meetings of its chief men in Parliament. The real victor in the war was the Lord Edward, who was a man of his word and understood England. Unlike his father he was a prince of dominant personality who wished to rule a strong and united people and instinctively saw that the only way to do so was through frequent counsel with their leading representatives. It was this knowledge, learnt from the tragic experience of his father's reign, which made him, when his time came, one of the greatest of English kings. And seeing how bitter and stubborn was the re-sistance of de Montfort's defeated followers, when the first feelings of triumph and bitterness were over, he took a leading part in their reconciliation. In the 'Dictum of Kenilworth' in 1266, he offered the right to the 'disinherited' to buy back their estates at a judicially assessed rate. A year later he was the moving spirit in the great Statute of Marlborough, by which, while subordinating once more and for all time the baronial franchises to the royal, the King in Parliament formally confirmed the Provisions of Oxford and Westminster and made them part of the mainstream of English law.

Nor did de Montfort's influence end with his death. In a sense it became stronger when his over-powerful personality had been removed. Thousands of simple Englishmen sympathised with the disinherited; it was this that had made Edward offer them reconciliation. During this time there seems to have first arisen the popular legend of Robin Hood and merry men, lurking in the greenwood to war against the rich and proud and seize their wealth to help the poor. Sung as ballads and passed from mouth to mouth in hedgerow and ale-house, such tales constituted a new ideal of chivalry: a chivalry so far unknown in feudal Europe, for it glorified the lowly against the great. Simon's own memory was venerated by the poor as that of a saint and martyr. His ideal of the rights of the 'universitas' or 'commonalty', of an imaginary community of the whole realm to which even village craftsmen and petty traders and peasants could appeal in the name of justice, struck deep roots in the English heart.

*　　　　*　　　　*

It was Edward I's supreme achievement – more even than his legal reforms – that he took the nation into a kind of partnership and, by regularly consulting its representatives and seeking their consent, laid the foundations of the greatest of all English institutions: a royal Parliament in which King and subject could meet to treat, co-operate and, if necessary, dispute over matters of common concern. When his father died in 1272 Edward was out of England on a crusade to free the Holy Land. But as soon as he returned, after appointing commissioners to make an exhaustive inquest and report on the grievances of the subject, he called his first Parliament. To it he summoned the magnates, lay and ecclesiastical – the earls and barons, archbishops, bishops and abbots who were his

147

tenants-in-chief – and, through the sheriffs, four elected and representative knights, 'discreet in law', from the shire-court of every county, and four merchants or burgesses from the *burgemote* or borough court of every important town. They were to come without arms and under the King's peace and protection and to be immune from the ordinary processes of law while the court of Parliament was in session. 'And because elections ought to be free,' ran the writ to the sheriffs, 'the King commandeth upon great forfeiture that no man by force of arms nor by malice nor menacing shall disturb or hinder any to make free election.'

For, having learnt through his inquest what was wrong with his realm, Edward had resolved on great changes. For these he needed his subjects' witness and approval. In the Middle Ages there were laws which were seen, not as something that could be changed at will, but as sacred and immutable. However unquestioned a King's right to act, ordain and give judgment, the ancient law of the kingdom was a public inheritance which it was his duty to preserve and enforce. His ordinances might have the force of law but only while he himself could impose them. After his death, if they were contrary to custom, they could be ignored or forgotten. Even in England, where the power of the locality had been far more strictly subordinated to the State than on the continent, the King's word was law only in his lifetime.

If society was to progress, some authority, associated with the Crown yet more enduring than the King's life, was needed to register the nation's acceptance of major changes in the law. In an age of isolated and intensely localised communities the tendency of custom to ossify was a mountain in the path of a reforming King. '*Nolumus leges Angliae mutare*' – 'we do not wish the laws of England to be changed' – Henry III's barons had replied at the Council of Merton to Bishop Grosseteste of Lincoln's plea for a more humane attitude towards children born out of wedlock. Edward could not overcome this traditional inertia merely by devising ingenious legal writs and directives to his judges as his great-grandfather, Henry II, had done. But with his strong practical sense he saw that a royal ordinance or judgment could be given a sanction more than ordinarily binding by having it publicly witnessed and approved in a session of Parliament or the *magnum consilium* – that supreme national Council or court of royal officials and judges, feudal tenants-in-chief, prelates and magnates to which his father in times of need had had resource for 'colloquy and treating' and to which in his later years both he and Edward, as his deputy, had increasingly referred the vast mass of petitions and appeals to the Crown from those unable to obtain justice from the ordinary courts. In the Statute of Marlborough of 1267 Edward himself, in his father's name, had legalised the baronial reforms of the past decade by a solemn public act of the Crown, issued in Parliament under the great seal and enrolled in writing as a permanent national record. By this means he had given to the royal decisions which resolved the controversies of the civil war an enduring validity which, despite his unchallenged right to declare law by ordinance, they could have had in no other way. Henceforward such statutes, as they became called, were cited in pleadings in the royal courts. Like Magna Carta they became part of the continuing life of the nation.

When after their slow, laborious and reluctantly undertaken journeys, the magnates and the representatives of the local communities met the King and his Council at Westminster, they were presented with a document drafted by the royal judges in French – the speech of their knightly class – and read to them by the Chancellor, Robert Burnell. Its object was to define, clarify and, where found necessary, reform the law. 'Because,' ran its preamble, 'our lord the King hath great desire to redress the state of the realm in such things as require amendment for the common profit of holy Church and the realm, and because the state of holy Church hath been evil kept and the people otherwise entreated as they ought to be, and the peace less kept and the laws less used and offenders less punished than they ought to be, the King hath ordained by his Council and the assent of the archbishops, bishops, earls, barons and all the commonalty of the realm the acts under written.'

The fifty-one clauses of this royal enactment of 1275 covered a vast field. They set forth, in easy, almost conversational, speech, a legal remedy for most of the worst abuses the King's commissioners had noted in their winter's visitation. The ideal of securing, by a specific remedy, the just rights of every man according to his status, ran through the whole enactment. Drafted by practising judges, it reflected the preference, always marked in English law, for concrete remedies over abstract principles.

Copies of the Act – the 'new provisions and statutes . . . ordained for the good of the realm and relief of the people', and known as the first Statute of Westminster – were sent, like Magna Carta, to the sheriffs. It was proclaimed in the courts of every county, hundred, city, borough and market-town, and all judges, sheriffs and bailiffs were ordered to enforce it. It was the first of a long succession of parliamentary statutes enacted by Edward in Council in the presence of the assembled magnates and representatives of the nation. Such statutes both changed and became part of the common and customary law. They derived their authority, not from verbally transmitted custom, but from a written document issued under royal seal and preserved in the rolls or records of Parliament which, before the end of his reign, Edward ordered to be kept at Westminster. Copied by pleaders into handbooks which became part of every practising lawyer's equipment, they were cited in the courts and accepted as evidence of law by the judges.

The Parliament which Edward held at Westminster in the spring of 1275 was not only summoned to endorse his proposals for reforming legal procedure. It was called to approve a new kind of tax. With changes in the landed and economic structure of the country; most of the older feudal sources of revenue were drying up and, to support the growing charges of State, the King needed new and extraordinary aids. Sixty years earlier the Great Charter had forbidden the levying of additional aids on land save by consent of the assembled magnates – a thing always hard to obtain. In its search for new revenue the Crown had been forced to turn increasingly to the taxation of moveable or personal wealth, which had not the same sanctity as land in the eyes of the ruling class. Its chief possessors in a taxable form were the merchants of the chartered towns and the flock-masters and wool-exporters who, during the past century, had been creating a new form of national wealth out of the downland sheep.

Legally the King was not obliged to consult merchants before taxing their goods. From time immemorial feudal lords had tallaged the towns and markets of their demesnes; it was for this that they had founded them. But times had changed, and merchants were no longer the helpless, half-emancipated villeins they had been before the crusades had introduced the feudal nobility of Europe to the luxuries of the East. Ever since they had been driven into the rebel ranks by his father's insistence on his right to tax them at will, Edward had wooed the traders of the capital and south-eastern ports, seeing with his realist's eye the power that came from control of cash and credit. He saw that a freely-negotiated agreement under which the merchant community assumed corporate responsibility for its own taxes was likely to prove more valuable to the Crown and, in the elementary administrative conditions of the time, provide a more readily accessible revenue than any forced imposition.

It was this which had caused him to follow de Montfort's revolutionary precedent and to summon to his first Parliament the proctors or representatives of all the cities, boroughs and 'towns of merchants'. He did not call upon them to take part in the discussions about his new land-laws – matters far above them – but to grant him a share of the increased trading profits which his strong rule and wise foreign policy were helping to create. In return for a standing duty of half a mark, or 6s. 8d., on every sack of wool exported and 13s. 4d. on every last of leather, he offered to surrender the royal prerogative of imposing direct taxation on merchandise. This gesture was as far-reaching as it was imaginative and generous. The 'Great and Ancient Custom', as it became called, 'granted at the instance of the merchants' and approved by the magnates, was the beginning of the Crown's permanent customs revenue. Henceforth it took its place, with the older 'tonnage' on wine imports, beside the feudal aids and dues, the rents of the royal estates – now much reduced by the grants of earlier sovereigns – the sheriffs' 'farms' of the shires and the proceeds of justice.

Later that year, in a second Parliament summoned to Westminster at Michaelmas and attended by knights of the shire as well as by the feudal and ecclesiastical magnates, the King obtained

an 'aid' of a fifteenth on all other lay moveables. The idea of representation, of the right of those present to bind the absent, and of
the majority to outvote the minority – a conception which the
friars in their provincial assemblies had first introduced into
England – was beginning to take shape under Edward's guidance.
In his writs to the sheriffs he insisted that elected knights and
burgesses should have full power of attorney to bind their fellows
to 'whatever should be ordained by common counsel'. Needing
his subjects' co-operation, he pursued every means of obtaining it.

*   *   *

After Henry II no king ever did so much to make England law-
conscious and law-abiding as his great-grandson, Edward I. He
took his legal responsibilities very seriously. As a boy he had
studied law under his tutor, Hugh Giffard, one of his father's justices. The hero of his youth had been his uncle, the great French
king, St Louis, who had loved to sit under the oak at Vincennes dis-
pensing justice to his subjects. His ideal and that of his age was of a
delicately poised balance between conflicting claims, one in which
every man's right to his own could be ascertained, weighed and
enforced. For to the medieval mind, haunted by the memory of
dark centuries of barbarism, justice was the highest earthly good,
a mirror of the heavenly state in an imperfect world. It had
nothing to do with equality, a conception then unknown. Its
purpose was expressed by a phrase in a legal treatise called *The
Mirror of Justices* written, it is believed, by a London fishmonger
who had held the office of city chamberlain: that 'folk should keep
themselves from sin and live in quiet and receive right according
to fixed usage and holy judgments'. The goal was a society in
which every man was offered the peaceful means of enjoying his
particular rights. Law was the mechanism provided by the Crown
for ensuring him that opportunity.

Edward's sense of justice was of a narrower, less altruistic
nature than that of St Louis. He was resolved to do justice to all,
but he did not except himself. Lordship to him was the first pre-
requisite of a Christian society – a right to be exercised justly and
firmly and, wherever possible, extended. His duty to God and his

people, he conceived, was to hold fast to his royal prerogative. He was always appealing to his córonation oath against suggestions that he should part with any of his rights, real or imagined; he held them, he said, in trust for his people. While endorsing the dictum of his subject, Andrew Horn, that 'law requires that one should use judgment, not force', he saw it as a contest, like the older trial-by-battle, in which a man was justified in using every technical nicety. He observed the full rigour of the game. Of its hard, intricate rules he showed himself as much a master as of war, seizing every advantage and never yielding a point without the clearest necessity. The courts were his, established to ensure not only that justice was done but that the kingdom was firmly ruled. Though after one or two early attempts he refrained from insisting that his judges should act as his advocates in disputes with the subject, he kept special pleaders or serjeants to 'sue for the King', like William of Gisleham and Gilbert of Thornton, the earliest-known King's Serjeant. They and his attorney, Richard de Bretteville – forerunner of our attorney-general – were kept incessantly busy. 'O Lord,' wrote a clerk at the foot of a membrane recording that officer's many activities, 'have pity on Bretteville!'

Yet Edward abided by his own rules. He used them to further his kingly ends but respected them. His favourite motto was 'Keep troth'. And though he was a strict upholder of his legal rights, his judges were not afraid to take their stand on his law rather than on his will. It was this growing acceptance of law by King and subject that made justice a more realisable commodity in England than in any other land. To offer relief to the subject and strict and impartial justice to all in their degree, to ensure that under the Crown both the obligations and rights of a feudal society were observed, to unify and strengthen the realm, these were Edward's objects, tirelessly pursued. His instruments were the prerogative, the Common Law and royal courts of justice which had grown out of it and the periodic assemblies or Parliaments of magnates, prelates, shire-knights and burgesses that he had taken to summoning whenever he needed common counsel and consent in support of his measures. His three great Statutes of Westminster of 1275, 1285 and 1290 were the crowning heights of his achievement. Each was a comprehensive code framed to amend, clarify and supplement the law and enable him to control the many-sided life of a passionate, turbulent yet conservative people, rooted in ancient ways and divided by regional loyalties, rights and customs.

The summer of 1285 saw the most intensive piece of law-making in medieval history. Drafted by the Chancellor and judges, it bore the impress of the King's authoritative, unifying mind. In accordance with his favourite adage that 'that which touches all should be approved by all', it was submitted to the magnates and representatives of the counties and boroughs at his Whitsun and Michaelmas Parliaments. Like all his reforms of the law, it dealt with things in a severely practical way. It made great changes, yet never for the sake of change, only for clarification and greater working efficiency. Its object was to make the law operate justly and expeditiously.

First place, in that hierarchical age, was given to the grievances of the larger landowners. At a time when revenue from land was almost the sole source of wealth for everyone except a few merchant speculators, its owner had to make provision during his lifetime, not only for his heir, but for his other children and his widow after his death. To prevent them from being left penniless he had to carve out of the family inheritance subsidiary estates to support them and their children and children's children. Yet if his own heirs were not to suffer, he had to ensure that such offshoots from his hereditary estate should revert to it after they had fulfilled the purpose for which they were intended. In his gift to a son when he came of age or a daughter on her marriage, a donor would stipulate that the land should return to him or his heirs if the donee's issue failed within so many generations.

Such settlements were immensely complicated by the rules of feudal enfeoffment. And during the thirteenth century the Common Law lawyers, with their fine and subtle definitions, had adopted the view that, if land had been given 'to X and to the heirs of his body', this must mean to X and his heirs absolutely as soon as an heir of his body was born. By availing himself of this interpretation an unscrupulous person – the husband, say, of a daughter to whom a

154

conditional estate had been given – could dispose of the property as though it was his own fee simple and not a mere life-interest. In this way both the issue of the marriage could be deprived of the gift intended for them, and the donor's estate of the reversion.

Naturally donors and their heirs, unversed in legal subtleties, regarded such alienation as a species of fraud. It particularly outraged the magnates who, as tenants-in-chief of the Crown, had still to find out of their truncated fiefs the feudal services and aids due for the whole. Their plea that the King should redress the wrong that the operation of his own law had made possible was now met in the second Statute of Westminster. This did not seek to establish a perpetually enduring entail – a thing the Common Law regarded as unreasonable and unattainable. Its aim, as stated in the preamble, was to ensure that where a gift had been made on certain conditions to provide what were called estates of curtsey, dower or frank marriage, the rights of both beneficiaries and reversioners should be respected and that 'the will of the donor expressed in the charter of gift should be observed'.

Named after its opening words, *De Donis Conditionalibus* established what was to be the basic principle of English land law for seven centuries. Not only did it protect the reversion to the donor's heirs but, by forbidding alienation by the donee and so safeguarding the rights of his issue, it gave recognition to a new kind of heritable estate, inalienable as long as there was issue-in-tail of the original donee. Within practicable limits it ensured the primogenitary principle in the descent of both the parent estate and its offshoot. Owing to a flaw in one of its clauses, a generation later a loophole was found in the statute which enabled not the donee but his son to alienate the land and so disinherit his issue. But a great judge of Edward II's reign, Chief Justice Bereford, who had known what was in the mind of Edward I and his chief justice, Hengham, when they framed *De Donis*, insisted in a famous judgment on looking to the spirit instead of the letter of the statute and restored the entail in the grandson's favour, so establishing a precedent which was followed by the courts. And though, a century later, lawyers had found other ways of enabling tenants-in-tail to bar the entail, by that time it had become established that the principle of English landed inheritance, in families of modest wealth as well as large, should be primogeniture and not, as was the case in other western kingdoms, partition. Instead of being divided among younger sons, landed property in England was to be transmitted dynastically.

The effect of this on the nation's future can scarcely be exaggerated. It did not render the alienation of entailed estates impossible – for the ingenuity of lawyers proved inexhaustible – but it made it very difficult. At a time when the rigid feudalism of the past was giving place to more elastic forms of tenure, a new land-owning class was encouraged by the Common Law to adopt the feudal military device for preserving landed property intact by transmission through the eldest son. Read aloud in Westminster Hall on 28 June 1285, the second Statute of Westminster subordinated the promptings of personal affection to the long-term interests of the realm. It helped to create landed families whose estates and traditions, preserved from generation to generation, formed a school for training men for public service and the capacity to rule. The heads of such families looked after and enhanced their estates, making England in time to come the wealthiest farming country in the world, while relays of energetic and ambitious younger sons, educated for wealth but not endowed with it, went out from homes rich in transmitted standards of living and behaviour to make their fortunes and serve the State. *De Donis* helped to prevent the landed gentry from becoming, as on the continent, an exclusive caste divorced from responsibility. It made for an elastic as opposed to a rigid system of government, for enterprise and adventure instead of stagnation.

It was from this new landowning class, standing between the greater feudal magnates and the mass of the nation, that Edward created a new local judiciary. In every shire a number of trusted knights and landowners were appointed to act, in an unpaid capacity, as conservators or keepers of the peace. This was an extension of the Plantagenet system of dividing and broadening the exercise of provincial authority, formerly centred in the hands of the sheriff. For, in days of feudal delegation and inadequate communication, it had been found that too much power in a sheriff's hands ended in his becoming an irremoveable and even hereditary official, as ready to defy the Crown as those he was appointed to control. It had, therefore, been the policy of every king since Henry II to entrust every new power of the Crown, not to the sheriffs, but to other officers – to county coroners, justices of assize, commissioners of array and taxes, knights of the shire, and now conservators or, as they became in the next century, justices of the peace. In the reign of Edward's grandson, Edward III, these were to be given power to try felonies and misdemeanours and, in their courts of quarter sessions, to take over much of the criminal jurisdiction hitherto performed by the shire-courts. Working within the traditional unit of local government, with all its binding ties of neighbourhood and regional sentiment, they were subject, not to some provincial satrap whose interest it was to defy the Crown, but to the King's courts and officers at Westminster by whom they were appointed and in whose hands lay the power to dismiss them. The source of their authority was the King, the terms under which they exercised it the Common Law, the link between them and the government the royal judges on their periodic visitations of inquest and gaol-delivery. This interplay of central authority and local representation, of the rule of law and popularly delegated self-government, is the key to much of England's history.

*　　　　*　　　　*

In the century between Henry II's death and Edward I's reign, the legal institutions he had created had continued to grow. It was an age of fertile judicial invention, when a little group of royal justices – sitting on the bench of Common Pleas at Westminster, travelling the country on *eyre* or attending the sovereign's person in the court of King's Bench – were devising and offering the subject an ever-growing number of writs and building up by their judgments a body of law that made England the justest land in Europe. Among them were some very great men – Martin Pattishall, whose tireless industry on assize wore out all his fellow judges; William Raleigh of Devonshire, who became bishop of Norwich and Winchester; and his still more famous pupil, Henry de Bracton – another west-country man who held the rectorships of Coombe-in-Teignhead and Bideford and who lies buried in Exeter cathedral, of which he was chancellor. His text book on litigation, *The Laws and Customs of England*, citing more than five hundred decisions collected from the plea rolls of the royal courts, was the most germinating legal work of the age.

Though case-law was not yet binding on the courts, it was fast becoming so, for the professional judges were the sole interpreters of the 'custom of the King's court' which became through them the Common Law of England. Its strength lay in its popularity with all classes of free Englishmen. It was in the thirteenth century that the words judgment and plea, inquest, assize and heir, acquit and fine first became part of English speech. Even the poorest freeman felt that he could get justice from the royal courts and at a cheaper rate than that offered under any other system of law. For it was a point of honour with the King's judges that, while the sale of writs formed an important source of revenue, a poor litigant should be able to obtain an essential writ for nothing.

In their work of enforcing the law the King's ministers had been faced by a decision – made in 1215 at an international Church Council at Rome – that the clergy should no longer take part in the practice of ascertaining legal guilt by the time-honoured ordeal of fire or water. This sign of growing reliance on human reason, which the Church, through its educational institutions, was slowly if unconsciously creating, robbed the primitive 'judgment by God' of its religious sanction. It presented courts of law throughout Christendom with the problem of finding some alternative method of reaching verdicts when there was a clash of evidence. In southern lands, where there were plenty of clerks trained by the law-schools of Ravenna and Bologna in the rediscovered principles of classical jurisprudence, resort was had to Roman rules of evidence. In England, far removed from the fount of classical learning, a simpler native substitute was found. In 1281, the King's Council issued to itinerant justices a direction that, sooner than keep persons charged with felonies indefinitely in gaol, they should use their discretion. They were to experiment and make use of their experience in ascertaining and estimating local opinion. Just as Henry II's judges had accepted, as proof of a man's right to his lands, a sworn oath from an assize or jury of his neighbours, so his great-grand-son's judges met the Lateran Council's repudiation of trial-by-God by summoning similar, though humbler, juries to resolve the guilt of those accused of felony. Juries of presentment, drawn partly from the knightly class and partly from representatives of the villages, were already presenting suspected criminals to the King's justices. The latter now adopted the idea of using the small freeholders or sokemen assembled by the sheriffs for this purpose to resolve, with a simple yes or no, whether those presented were actually guilty of the crimes of which they had been accused. They took counsel, as the saying was, of the neighbourhood.

Thus for the supposed verdict of God through the elements was gradually substituted the conception – a curiously English one – of a verdict through the inspiration of a dozen decent honest freemen, equipped with local knowledge and sworn under a solemn religious oath to speak the truth in open court. *Vox populi* – not of an anonymous mob but of a group of 'worthy and lawful' men who knew their neighbourhood – was to be accepted as the voice of God. The accused could take his choice of submitting to such a verdict, of putting himself, as it was called, upon the country, or of remaining in gaol. It was a rough and ready way of getting at the truth, but one whose roots lay deep in English history. And in the course of their everyday practice – though it was a process which took centuries to complete – the trained judges of the Crown contrived methods of making evidence available to such petty juries that eventually proved more realistic than all the elaborate rules of Roman Law. The judges expounded and interpreted the law, and the jurymen, who began their long career as corporate witnesses to the opinion of the locality, became in the end judges of fact and assessors of evidence.

*   *   *

The English chain of law was a partnership between Crown and people: between, that is, the hall of justice at Westminster and the local courts, officers and jurymen of the shire, hundred and vill, and the delegated jurisdictions and franchises of the feudal land-owners. These last remained as numerous as ever but now derived their strength not, as in other feudal States, from their separateness but from their participation in the royal machinery of government. The sword and rod of equity with which the King did justice were the earls and barons of the realm, the sheriffs and knights of the shire, the constables of the hundred and vill. And they in their turn depended on the royal authority for the peace, order and growing prosperity of their society.

Behind the royal courts lay 'the community of the realm'. It consisted not only of barons and prelates but of the lesser landowners of the shire, of the petty freeholders of the villages and the burgesses of the free towns. The first, increasingly styled knights of the shire, performed a multitude of duties. They served as sheriffs, escheators and coroners, and as justices on special commissions of gaol-delivery to relieve the overworked royal judges; they sat in judgment in the shire court at its monthly meetings in the county-town, and attended the two great annual assemblies when the lord, knights and freeholders of the shire gathered to meet the justices on *eyre*. They served on the committees which scrutinised the presentments of the hundreds and villages, and carried the record of the shire court to Westminster when summoned there by the King's judges. They acted as jurymen on the grand assize, assessed, as elected representatives of their fellow knights of the shire, any taxes due from each hundred, and investigated and reported on local abuses and grievances. They were constantly being called on for their views in questions put to them on oath by the King's judges and Council. So were the humbler freeholders and sokemen who also, as elected representatives of their neighbours, assessed the village taxes. Even outside the privileged ranks of 'free men', the community of the unfree was represented by the six *villani* or villein-farmers who presented, with the parish priest and reeve, the local malefactors and answered for the village's offences and omissions before the terrible all-enquiring *eyre*.

Co-operation between central officials, paid and trained for their specialist functions, and unpaid and part-time amateurs representing the interests, property and good sense of the local community, was the means by which the Plantagenet kings both ordered and unified their realm. With the growing complexity of legal procedure, the royal justices had become something more than temporary deputies delegated from baronial or episcopal bench to try particular cases in their sovereign's place. They were now permanent royal officials. They still performed a multitude of services, hearing assizes, delivering county gaols on *eyre*, acting as commissioners of array, supervising the collection of subsidies and sitting on the royal Council. Some were in clerical orders like John le Breton or Britton, the bishop of Hereford who is believed to have written a condensation of Bracton's treatise on the laws of England; the much-used Martin of Littleburn; and the Norfolk-born Ralph de Hengham, canon of St Paul's and archdeacon of Worcester, who began his legal career as a clerk to one of Henry III's judges and rose to be Chief Justice both of the Common Pleas and the King's Bench, leaving behind two important tracts on procedure and pleadings. Others were laymen, county knights and local notables or legal specialists who had practised as lawyers in the courts before they became judges. Of the fifteen members of the King's Bench appointed during Edward I's reign seven were clerics and eight laymen, including both the chief justices of his latter years.

Below them were the attorneys, who represented clients, prosecuting their writs and entering their pleas by proxy, and the skilled narrators, pleaders and serjeants-at-law – successors of the professional champions of trial-by-battle – who composed the pleas and narrated and argued the pleadings, so saving suitors from the verbal slips which could so easily unsuit the untrained. For the rules of an action-at-law before the King's judges were most strictly enforced; the very language, a kind of bastard French interlaced with Latin and designed to ensure the utmost precision of meaning, was almost impossible for a layman to understand. Any freeholder who had been dispossessed or kept out of his land could buy from the Chancery clerks a writ addressed to the sheriff of his county directing him to summon the dispossessor to answer the plantiff in an action-at-law. The number of such writs had been steadily increasing in order to cover all conceivable causes of action over freehold-land. Yet, unless the exact one appropriate to the wrong complained of was chosen, the action was bound to fail. The forms of pleading and procedure of the particular remedy sought had to be meticulously observed by both plantiff and defendant, even to the minutest details of wording.

The earliest forms of action, in civil as opposed to criminal law, were all concerned with the ownership or possession of land – the wealth on which the military and political organisation of a feudal State depended. In England, alone among the medieval kingdoms of Christendom, it became established principle that no man need answer for his freehold without a royal writ and that no suit touching the ownership or possession of land could be commenced without one. During the thirteenth century the number of such writs and actions available – *right, praecipe, novel disseisin, mort d'ancestor, aiel, besaiel, cosinage* – steadily increased in order to cover all conceivable disputes over land between freemen. Later they were extended, though with great caution, to cover cases affecting the ownership or possession not only of 'real' property as land was called, but of 'moveable' or 'personal' property. Such was the writ of *replevin* for wrongful distraint of cattle; of *trespass*, ordering the sheriff to compel the defendant to answer a complaint that, 'with force and arms' and against the King's peace, he had carried off the plaintiff's goods or done him some other injury; of *detinue* for wrongful detention of some specific chattel like a plough or horse; and of *debt* to compel the defendant to repay a fixed sum of money of which he was alleged to have 'deforced' the plaintiff; of *account* to make a bailiff, agent or, later, a partner submit an account of moneys received; *covenant* to enforce rights under seal such as leases; and *assumpsit* for certain breaches of general undertakings not under seal; of *case* which was eventually extended by legal fictions to cover all sorts of wrongs for which no redress existed earlier, including slander and libel. But the bounds of each form of action and the remedy provided by it were most narrowly prescribed and only gradually widened, if at all, to cover new wrongs. For many civil injuries, particularly of a contractual kind, no remedy was as yet available in the royal courts, though in some cases it might be so in the mercantile courts of the boroughs, where the international 'law merchant' was adjudicated, or in the ecclesiastical courts administering canon law.

The Exchequer enforced the king's fiscal rights, the King's Bench tried pleas of the Crown and heard appeals from other courts, the Common Pleas sat permanently in Westminster Hall to adjudicate, with the help of local juries from the shires, disputes between the owners of freehold-land. Below them, though also subject to the King's overriding writ, were local courts of an older kind, administering the customary law of the neighbourhood. The most important of these was the shire-court, presided over by the sheriff, which met once a month in the south and every six weeks in the wilder north. Held in some spot hallowed by immemorial usage and dating back to days when the shire had been almost an independent province, it was attended, not only by litigants, but by all, either in person or deputy who, holding freehold-land in the county, owed it suit. For it was the basis of Anglo-Saxon and Danish law – long adopted by England's French-speaking kings and lords – that all freemen should by 'witness of the shire' share responsibility for the administration of justice in the county where their lands lay.

At this great concourse of neighbours and men of substance, held either in the open air or, more often now, in a fine new hall of plea, like the one Edmund of Cornwall built for his duchy at Lostwithiel, royal ordinances and statutes were proclaimed, officers and bailiffs were sworn in, inquests were held into dispute rights, and presentments made on matters relating to pleas of the Crown for trial by the itinerant justices. The suitors of the court also elected those required by the King to 'bear the record of the shire' in the courts at Westminster or in Parliament, and the coroners whose business it was to keep a record, independently of the sheriff, of all crimes and incidents affecting the Crown's rights and to hold inquests on sudden deaths, shipwrecks and discoveries of treasure trove. Sentence of outlawry was passed, too, in the shire-court on anyone who had failed on four successive occasions to answer a summons to a criminal charge. Though its work was being increasingly superseded by the King's courts, it still had cognizance of cases in which the accused elected to be tried by the older methods of compurgation. Sometimes, too, when neither party wanted a jury, a plea of land would remain in the county court to be resolved by two professional champions contending all day with minute horn-tipped pickaxes until one or other yielded as 'craven'.

Below the sheriffs' court was the hundred court, held once every three weeks by a bailiff to whom the sheriff or the owner of the hundred jurisdiction had sublet its profits, but who, as a royal officer, was responsible to the sheriff or, in a few special cases, directly to the Crown. It was usually held in the open air, the suitors of the court – freehold tenants of certain parcels of land – sitting on benches round a table occupied by the bailiff and his clerk. Its business was of a petty kind – claims for services arising out of land, detention of chattels and small debts, complaints about the maiming of beasts, and personal assaults and brawls not amounting to felony. The most common plea was trespass – an elastic offence which it was often easier to bring home to a neighbour in the hundred court than to compass in the rigid limits of a Chancery writ. It is doubtful, for instance, if Robert Kite could have obtained redress at Westminster from Stephen Winter whom he sued in the court of Milton hundred for coming into his garden, breaking down his hedges and carrying off his roses 'against the peace', or John Malkin from Maud-atte-Hythe and her son for beating his pig and egging on their dogs till they bit off its tail. There were other pleas, like verbal contracts and slander, for which the royal courts offered as yet no remedy, but under which rustic litigants could sue one another in those of the hundred.

Twice a year, at Easter and Michaelmas, the sheriff visited every hundred in the shire to hold a tourn or criminal court. Everyone who held freehold-land in the hundred except the greater magnates had to attend or be fined for absence. In the tourn or 'law-hundred', peasants of villein blood as well as freemen played a part. For by Anglo-Saxon law every layman without land that could be forfeited for felony had to belong to a tithing – a group of neighbours responsible for one another's good conduct. Before the sheriff's annual view of *frankpledge*, as it was called, the bailiff checked the tithing lists of every village in his hundred, crossing out the names of those who had died since the last view and swearing in any lad who had reached the age of twelve and so become, in the eyes of the law, a responsible citizen. With his hand on the

Bible the boy had to promise to keep the peace and be neither a thief nor a helper of thieves. 'I will be a lawful man,' he swore, 'and bear loyalty to our lord the King and his heirs, and I will be justiciable to my chief tithing man, so help me God and the saints.' Then he and every other villager paid his tithing-penny, which constituted, with the various court fees and assized rents, the profits of the hundred jurisdiction.

At the sheriff's tourn every village or township was represented by its reeve and four men who answered for any omission in its public duty and for such offences as ploughing up the King's high-way or executing a thief caught red-handed without first securing the official witness of a royal bailiff or coroner. They were respon-sible, too, for the township's payment of fines imposed on it for breaches of the regulations for baking of bread and brewing of ale. They had to report to twelve freeholders called the jury of present-ment all crimes that had been committed within the township. The tourn dealt, also, with nuisances like washing clothes in wells and polluting drinking-water. More serious offences were presented by the jury to the royal justices for trial on their next visit to the shire. When this happened the humble representatives of the village found themselves answering questions put to them under oath by the King's chief legal officers.

*   *   *

If, thanks to her strong line of kings, the law and its subtle complex processes had taken the place of the sword, it was employed, by Crown and subject alike, with the ruthlessness of the battlefield. And it was often grossly abused. In a medieval state without a police force and only a minute administrative service, corruption and maladministration of justice were inevitable. Twice in his reign Edward I was forced to take drastic action against his own officers for abuses of the law. Sheriffs and their servants took bribes, were extortionate, refused writs or sold them at exorbitant prices, and imprisoned men under legal pretences to make them pay for their release. Judges and their clerks let it be known that success in their courts would never attend a suitor who did not fee them. In 1289, on his return to England after three years' absence in his French dominions, Edward I found no less than seven hundred officials guilty of malpractices. Only two of the eight judges of the King's Bench and Common Pleas escaped disgrace, while five justices of *eyre* were found guilty and dismissed.

The most important result of these judicial scandals was a reorganisation of the legal profession. The task was entrusted to the new Chief Justice of the Common Pleas, John de Metyngham – one of the two members of the original bench to escape the purge. In 1292 he and his fellow judges were commissioned to choose from every county a number of the more promising students of law to be officially attached to the courts either as attorneys or as apprentices to the serjeants or *servientes ad legem* who pleaded before the King's judges. They were to enjoy a monopoly and their numbers, fixed at first at a hundred and forty, were to be left to the judges to add to as required. In other words, the profession was to regulate its own recruitment, education and rules of practice.

It was the beginning of a new form of learned education, one outside the Church and independent of it. A century after Henry II had been forced to concede immunity for clerics from lay justice, his great-grandson, Edward I, established secular training for the Common Law as an alternative to the study of civil law which, like every other form of learning, the Church in its universities reserved exclusively for its own members. It was an education based on the practice of the courts, necessitating great precision of thought and speech. It was taught, not by theorists in lecture rooms and libraries, but in crowded courts of law where, under the eye of the King's judges, quick and trained professional wits were pitted against one another, as the masters of forensic science, thinking and arguing on their feet, sought to fit the conflicting facts of their clients' disputes into the sharply defined framework of Common Law writs and procedures.

These tyros or apprentices assisted and devilled for their seniors as they do today, attended their consultations and listened to the thrust and parry of their contests from enclosures called 'cribs' built at the sides of the courts. In the year in which the King entrusted their education to his judges there appeared the first of

COUNSEL, CONSENT AND PARLIAMENT

the Year Books – manuscript notes of cases, pleadings and forensic argument made for young advocates to help them master the intricacies of the law. Written in the legal French of the courts, they set out in staccato jottings the arguments and altercations, exceptions and answers of the great serjeants who dominated the courts at the end of the thirteenth and beginning of the fourteenth century – Lowther, Heyham, Howard, Hertpool, Huntingdon, Spigornel – and the interruptions and often caustic comments of the judges. 'Leave off your noise and deliver yourself from his account,' Chief Justice Hengham interrupts an over-persistent pleader. 'Get to your business,' his successor, Bereford, enjoins. 'You plead one point, they about another, so that neither of you strikes the other.' And when learned counsel tried to gain the day by arguing, 'We have seen damages awarded in similar circumstances,' Bereford replied, 'You will never see them so long as I am here.' 'Where have you seen a guardian vouch on a writ of *dower*?' asked another judge and, when the incautious serjeant answers, 'Sir, in Trinity term last past, and of that I vouch the record,' there came the crushing rejoinder, 'If you find it, I will give you my hat!'

The interest of these early Year Books – and no other nation has anything like them – is the greater because, in those formative years, judges were helping by their judgments and the precedents they created to shape the future course of the law. Some of them, like Hengham, had even drafted it in the King's Council chamber; 'do not gloss the statute,' he remarked on one occasion, 'we know it better than you, for we made it.' For all their insistence on the rigid rules of pleading and procedure, such judges were very conscious of the immense discretionary power to do justice and equity delegated to them by their royal master. 'You wicked rascal,' Saunton, J. interrupted a dishonest attorney who had prayed for a *postea* in defiance of the rules of just dealing, 'you shall not have it! But because you, to delay the woman from her dower, have vouched and not sued a writ to summon your warrantor, this court awards that you go to prison.'[1]

The apprentice pleaders did not only learn together in the courts. They lived together in inns or hospices presided over by

[1] Selden Society XXII, Year Book Series IV, p. 195.

their senior members. In the leafy suburb of Holborn and in the Thames-side meadows between Westminster Hall and London's western walls there sprang up, during the years of expanding litigation which followed Edward I's legislative reforms, a whole colony of such bachelor establishments. Keeping an inn seems to have become a highly profitable source of revenue for leaders of the legal profession, for some of them kept several; a Chancery clerk named John de Tamworth had, in the reign of Edward's grandson, no fewer than four in the neighbourhood of Fetter Lane. Similar inns were kept for the clerks of Chancery. Nearly all were rented from ecclesiastical corporations or dignitaries – Templars, Hospitallers, Black Friars, the priory of St Bartholomew, the convent of Clerkenwell, the abbey of Missenden, the bishop of Ely – who owned most of the land immediately to the west of London. Though never formally incorporated like the Church's residential colleges and halls at Oxford and Cambridge, they helped to create *esprit de corps* and standards of professional conduct among those studying and practising the law.

After Edward I had placed the education of the legal profession under his judges and divorced it from the Church, its wealth and influence grew very rapidly. In an acquisitive and evolving society in which litigation had taken the place of private war, the brethren of the coif – the white silken hood worn by the King's serjeants-at-law and the judges who were chosen from their ranks – constituted a new aristocracy. 'Law,' wrote the poet Langland in the reign of Edward's grandson, 'is grown lord!' By then the judges in their scarlet robes trimmed with white budge or lambskin and the serjeants in their long part-coloured gowns of blue, green and brown, cut almost as great a figure in the realm as the magnates and prelates.

CHAPTER TWELVE

Wild Wales

'Bold immortal country whose hilltops have stood
Stronghold for the high gods when on earth they go,
Terror for fat burghers in far plains below.'

Robert Graves

'Their Lord they shall praise,
Their language they shall keep,
Their land they shall lose
Except wild Wales.'

Taliesin's Prophesy

WHILE USING ROYAL PARLIAMENTS to make and establish new laws
for England – some of which, like his land laws, were to last for
centuries – Edward I longed to give law and lordship to the whole
of Britain, including the barbarous and mountainous west and far
north. For the claim of his remote ancestors to a suzerainty over all
the princes of Britain appealed to him deeply. It was one to which
he attached far more importance than any of his immediate predecessors. For, half Frenchman though he was, he had never shared
his father's and grandfather's dream of regaining their Norman and
Angevin continental patrimony. The only empire he coveted outside Gascony – the inheritance of his great grandmother, Eleanor
of Aquitaine – was that of the British Isles. Nursed in the new
courtly fashion of regarding the legendary King Arthur and his
knights as the champions of Britain and its vanished Roman
imperium, he saw himself as their heir.

169

This, however, was not at all how the real descendants of Arthur's warriors saw him. To the Celts of western Britain Edward was merely a king of the Saxons who had slaughtered and dispossessed their forbears. He was the overlord, too, of the armoured horsemen from France who, while giving the Saxons discipline and leadership, had raised so many outposts of England in the valleys of central and southern Wales. To the fierce tribesmen beyond the Severn the stone castles of the Normans seemed as alien as the Roman legionary camps of a thousand years before.

Divided by tribal and dynastic feuds, the southern and central valleys of Wales had been colonised soon after the Conquest by Norman adventurers who had brought them under the overlordship, though not the direct rule, of the kings of England. From the upper reaches of the Severn in Powys to the ancient princedoms of Deheubarth and Morgannwy along the Bristol Channel, the great Marcher lords – Clares and Mortimers, Bohuns and Fitzalans, Braoses, Chaworths and Giffards – ruled by the sword, the King's licence and their own wits. With their castles and mounted knights they dominated the lowlands, leaving the bare uplands of sheep and heather to the migrant Celtic tribes.

For their penetration was only valley deep. Around them the ancient life of mountain Cambria, half warlike, half pastoral, continued as it had done for a thousand years. Its people lived by raiding and keeping cattle and sheep. In the summer they fed them on the hill-pastures or *hafod*, in the winter on the lowlands or *hendre*. So wild was that sparsely populated countryside that two pilgrimages to St David's were regarded by pious Englishmen as the equal in peril and hardship of one to Jerusalem. Its few minute towns huddled for safety round the Marchers' castles; its very churches, crowning tactical vantage-points, resembled forts. Its petty 'kings' or *brenins* spent their summers in forays on one another and the Saxon, and their winters listening to their bards and harpers nostalgically commemorating the glories of old. With their golden torques and white horses, their bands of young warriors and proud memories of ancient victory, they deemed it 'ignoble to die in bed and an honour to fall on the field of battle'. Every spring the clansmen set out along the cloud-hidden tracks above the valleys to burst in a torrent on some rival tribe or distant English farm. It had been so as long as men could remember.

So long as the Marchers left them to follow this immemorial life the Welsh, preoccupied with tribal and family feuds, made no attempt to combine against them. Only when England was weakly ruled or divided was any concerted effort made to drive the Anglo-Norman lords from the country. For outside their castle walls the latter seldom had the last word against the tribesmen of the hills. Plunder and arson could always be met by plunder and arson and, as their farms offered tempting booty, their presence was accepted philosophically. In their turn the Marchers entered into the life of Wales. They married the native chieftains' daughters and took sides in their tribal affrays. The inconveniences of cattle-raiding and seasonal war were offset for them by the freedom they enjoyed, unknown in judge-ridden England, of living under their own, not the King's law. Theirs was an independence which existed nowhere else in Edward's dominion. No writ ran in their liberties and no appeal lay from their courts. They raised private armies to harry their neighbours' lands and guard their own, as in the far days before a Plantagenet king had made feudalism a political strait-jacket for their warlike class.

In the same way the Cistercian monks and their monasteries became naturalised and part of the life of Wales. Their solitude and austerity recalled to a primitive hill people the lives of their own early evangelists. Despite their Latin affiliations and the splendid churches with which the Marchers and the Welsh princes endowed them, the Cistercian houses in Wales were far more Celtic than Roman, conforming to a traditional pattern in which personal piety and local loyalty counted for more than dogma and the regimentation of an international order. What little Llantwit and Llancarfan had been in the centuries of Rome's eclipse, Margam and Tintern, Abbey Dore and Strata Florida, Aberconway and Valle Crucis became in the new age of Rome's ecclesiastical grandeur. Yet though they formed centres of native learning and culture, they also helped to link Wales to the wider world of Christendom and to render possible her peaceful co-existence with her more orderly neighbour.

Had it not been for one circumstance the absorption of Wales into the Anglo-Norman kingdom might have come about in the end with as little violence as that of Celtic Cornwall. In 1237, with the death of its last hereditary earl, there had lapsed to the Crown the greatest of all the Marcher lordships – the palatine earldom of Chester, whose historic function it was to guard the Cheshire and Shropshire plains from the raiders of the Snowdon hills. Though still remaining a separate legal entity, its administration passed into the hands of royal officials whose orderly minds, schooled in the discipline of the Exchequer and Common Law, abhorred such time-hallowed Cymric customs as cattle-raiding and the blood-feud. And confronting them across a no-man's-land of little wooded hills and uncertain lordships lay the principality of Gwynedd, the last of the old independent 'kingdoms' of Wales and the one place where, guarded by the precipices of Snowdonia, there existed a Welsh royal court, a body of Welsh law administered by native judges and a focus for a sentiment which was not only tribal but national.

A century earlier, after the civil wars of Stephen and Matilda, another semi-independent Welsh principality had flourished on the southern shores of Cardigan Bay under Rhys ap Gruffyd, a prince of the ancient house of Tewdwr or Tudor. Having seized Cardigan castle from the Marcher, Roger de Clare, he had kept it by a shrewd mixture of resistance and subservience to Henry II, whose supremacy he acknowledged and whose vice-regent he claimed to be. In 1176, at his Christmas feast, he had held the first recorded *eisteddfod*, at which entrants from every part of Wales contested for the bardic crowns of music and poetry.

After his death Rhys's dominion had disintegrated, and the primacy among the native chieftains had passed to the heirs of his northern ally, Owen, Prince of Gwynedd. The latter's grandson, Llywelyn ap Ioworth – Llywelyn the Great, as the bards called him – took advantage of King John's difficulties to seize Marcher territory on the upper Dee and Severn and later, by siding with his fellow tenants-in-chief in England, to win concessions from the Crown. Three of the clauses of Magna Carta had been inserted at his instance. At one time he even captured Shrewsbury and, controlling two-thirds of Wales, aroused a surge of national pride in his countrymen. Yet, conscious of their incorrigible separatism, he made no attempt to flaunt his power and, dividing his conquests among the lesser chieftains, chose to reign over his fellow Welshmen's hearts rather than their lands. Recognising the strength of a reunited England, he did homage for Gwynedd to the young king, Henry III, and lived in peace for the rest of his days. [1]

It was this Prince's grandson, Llywelyn ap Gruffydd, who was now, after many vicissitudes, lord of Gwynedd. He, too, had taken advantage of England's troubles under Henry III to impose his suzerainty on the Welsh chieftains of Powys, to seize the Mortimer stronghold of Builth on the upper Wye, and to overrun with his fierce spearmen the Cantrefs of Perfeddwlad, as the Crown fiefs in the disputed coastal borderland between Chester and Gwynedd were called. But by allying himself too closely with de Montfort he had united the royal Earl of Chester, Prince Edward, with the other Marcher lords. After they had overthrown de Montfort they compelled him to make his peace with King Henry who, in return for homage and military service, acknowledged Llywelyn's lordship of Gwynedd and his self-chosen title of Prince or *pendragon* of Wales. Since then the English power had again been rising, and the Marchers, resolved to prevent further raids from the north, had been building new and stronger castles, like the mighty Caerphilly which Gilbert de Clare, the red earl of Gloucester, raised near Cardiff in the closing years of Henry III's reign.

The Prince of Gwynedd and Edward I were thus old rivals. Llywelyn, whose father had been killed trying to escape from the Tower, had tasted triumph over the English when Edward was a raw untried youth. He resented his supremacy and thought of himself as the overlord of all the native chieftains of Wales, whose allegiance he was always trying to deflect to himself. Even more fiercely he resented any legal control from Westminster, Chester or Shrewsbury, not only over, his own rocky acres in Snowdonia and Anglesey – where for geographical

---

[1] He died in 1240 at Aberconway abbey. The village of Beddgelert is said to commemorate the name and grave of a favourite dog who saved his infant son from a wolf.

reasons there had never been any – but over the disputed border-
lands in the Marches.

Edward had no wish to deprive Llywelyn of what was lawfully
his. But he was a feudal king, brought up in the strict tradition of
feudal rights and obligations. He thought of the Prince of Gwynedd
as the Welsh equivalent of an Anglo-Norman earl. By ancient
prescription and a solemn treaty made after the barons' wars,
Llywelyn owed him homage and fealty. And by the English conception of feudalism all lordship under the Crown involved subjection to the Common Law except where a clearly defined liberty
had been granted. What stuck in Edward's gullet was the Welsh
prince's claim, not merely to a feudal liberty like those of his
forbears and the Marchers, but to a completely self-governing
lordship like the Scottish kingdom which, under the kings of
England's nominal suzerainty, had been independent from time
immemorial.

For Llywelyn sought to be ruler, not only of Gwynedd, but of
Wales. Nursed in bardic lore and deeply conscious of his countrymen's right to nationhood, he voiced his claim in a letter to Edward
in 1273, after the royal authorities had refused to allow him to
build an unlicensed castle on land of his own in the Marches near
Montgomery. 'We are sure,' he wrote, 'that the writ was not issued
with your knowledge . . . For you know well that the rights of our
principality are entirely separate from the rights of your kingdom
. . . and that we and our ancestors had the power within our boundaries to build castles and forts and create markets without prohibition by anyone.'

This was the inevitable reaction of a Welsh chieftain to any
scheme of centralised control: one bound to arouse the challenge
of a reforming king with a passion for legal definition. Both unconsciously wanted something new – Llywelyn the sovereignty of
an independent Welsh nation, Edward the legal administration of
the country on the closely-knit pattern of England. It was natural
that, alarmed by the castles which the Marchers were building
against his power, Llywelyn should wish to see not only Gwynedd,
but his new fiefs in the Marches, guarded by castles of his own.
Yet it was by now a principle of English law that a vassal's right

to erect a military fortress could only be granted by royal licence.

Shortly after Edward's coronation, which Llywelyn failed to attend, a new dispute arose. The latter's brother, David, suspected of a plot to dethrone him, fled to England. Instead of handing him back to Llywelyn for punishment, the King's officers, contending that the matter must first be investigated by law, allowed him refuge at Shrewsbury. To Llywelyn this seemed proof that his brother's treachery was being condoned by Edward so that he might plot his death from English soil. Not until he was returned to him, he declared, would he do homage to an overlord who so criminally wronged his own vassal.

According to his lights, the King behaved with considerable restraint. Alone of his tenants-in-chief, Llywelyn had failed to do homage on his accession. By feudal law the price of such contumacy was forfeiture of the fief. After waiting for nearly a year, and after the prince had ignored a further summons to Westminster, Edward invited him to meet him at Chester under safe conduct. To this and the royal journey to the Dee, Llywelyn's only response was to summon a parliament of his own vassals to endorse his refusal. Before he would meet the King, he announced, the latter must surrender as hostages his eldest son, his Chancellor Burnell, and the Marcher earl of Gloucester.

Even this demand did not exhaust Edward's patience. He did not wish to incur the cost of a Welsh campaign or to be deflected from his work of reform in England. Yet he was determined to have his relationship with Llywelyn clarified. Three times he summoned him to do homage: at Westminster in November 1275, at Winchester in the New Year of 1276, and again at Westminster that Easter. It was characteristic of his habit of crossing the t's of his legal claims that the proposed meeting-places were no longer on the Welsh border but in the heart of his own realm.

This made Llywelyn still more indignant. Again he refused, save on conditions to which no overlord could agree. He appealed to the Pope for justice, declaring that the King was harbouring traitors and, as though to underline the breach between them, sent to France for the daughter of Simon de Montfort, with whom ten years earlier, when they were in arms against the English Crown, he had made a treaty of marriage. This was a double offence against feudal law, for not only was Eleanor de Montfort the daughter of a traitor but, as a member of the royal house, she could not marry without the King's consent. By chance the ship bringing her to Wales was intercepted in the Bristol Channel and she was taken prisoner. Henceforward her release became an added condition of Llywelyn's homage.

At the Easter Parliament of 1276 the prelates asked if they might make a last appeal to the stubborn Welshman. A trained canonist was sent as envoy, and the summer passed in fruitless negotiation. When a new Parliament met in November neither its members nor Edward were in a mood for parleying. They agreed that Llywelyn's contumacy must be punished and that the King should 'go upon him as a rebel and disturber of his peace'. The Marches were ordered to be put into a state of war and the feudal host summoned to meet at Worcester at midsummer 1277. A warning was also sent to Llywelyn by the Archbishop of Canterbury – metropolitan of the see in which Wales lay – that unless he submitted he would be excommunicated.

Llywelyn treated the excommunication like the King's summonses. The English had never conquered Gwynedd, neither before nor after their subjection to the Normans, and it was natural for its brave, half barbaric chieftains to regard it as unconquerable. Its ruler was taking no very apparent risk in defying his overlord. He was prince of the mountains and mountain tribes and despised the English host. His forbears had repelled it under Henry II and John and, more lately, under the young Edward himself. He had only to withdraw into the trackless hills to ambush the heavily cumbered invaders in some forest defile or, lying concealed amid mists and precipices, starve them and their horses into retreat. Inspired by the prophesies of the legendary Merlin, he even dreamt of driving them out of Britain altogether and ruling, like his Roman ancestors, over the whole island. For the triumphs won by himself and his grandfather during England's baronial wars suggested to his enthusiastic, mercurial mind that what a few thousand Norman knights had done the Cymri under his leadership might do again.

176

Though they could never refrain from quarrelling with one another the Welsh tribesmen were magnificent fighters. War was their occupation, and training for it their education. Under their laws six weeks of every summer were spent in marauding expeditions and their entire youth was ready for instant service at their chieftains' call. Unlike the English, they were not pinned down by husbandry and harvest; they were used to living hard and travelling light. Able to subsist on the whey of their mountain goats and the cheese of their herds, they needed no commissariat. Some of them, in the hills of the south, had evolved a new and terrifying weapon: the longbow of Gwent, 'made of wild elm, unpolished, rude and uncouth', whose arrows, fired faster than a crossbow's, could pierce the mailed shirt, breeches and saddle of an armoured knight and pin him to his horse's side. Their sudden, swift-footed charge with javelin, sword and war-horn down glen or hillside could break the nerve of all but the hardiest and, though quickly discouraged if withstood, their recovery after defeat had again and again turned the tables on their victors. With their bare, sinewy legs, their squat bodies wrapped in scarlet plaids, their capacity to live out of doors in the depth of winter, they seemed as impervious to weather as the rocks among which they lay in ambush. Their trackless terrain and climate of mist, snow and driving rain made any prolonged campaign against them profitless. Punitive expedition after expedition of English knights had advanced up their mountain valleys only to withdraw, famished, horseless and empty-handed, after a few months in that starve-acre land.

> 'Grevouse est le guerre et dure à l'endurer
> Quand ailleurs est l'été, en Galles est hiver,'

wrote a disgusted Anglo-Norman poet.

Yet Llywelyn had forgotten that times had changed. Under its new ruler England was no longer divided as in the days of de Montfort. Its whole administrative effort was now directed to bringing Gwynedd to heel. Nor was Edward the raw youth who had fought against the Welsh twenty years before. He was a commander of international fame who had led the armies of Christendom and rivalled the fame of his great-uncle Coeur-de-Lion. He was no amateur like his dilettante father.

His preparations for the coming campaign left nothing to chance. During the winter and spring of 1277, while the Marchers took the offensive against Llywelyn's supporters in Powysland and Cardiganshire, Edward was gathering not only the largest English army since the Conquest, but the best-equipped. Agents were sent to France to buy up the huge war-horses that would be needed as remounts for the cavalry of his household guard and, with the help of the feudal levy, nearly a thousand heavily armoured horsemen were assembled in support of the Marchers along the Welsh borderland. But most of the troops Edward raised were infantry. They came from Cheshire, Lancashire and Derbyshire, from Rutland, Shropshire and Worcestershire, from Radnor and Brecon. Some were conscripted by commissioners of array from the *fyrd* or *posse comitatus*, others were veterans who had fought under Edward in the Barons' War or on crusade. In all, over fifteen thousand foot soldiers were brought together, more than half of them Welsh. To these the King added a small force of professional crossbowmen, mostly Gascons, and a contingent of archers from Macclesfield Forest.

It was not an experienced army, for it was twelve years since Evesham, and few young Englishmen outside the March had taken part in a campaign. But their commander was the greatest military organiser of the age, and he knew what was necessary for a campaign in a barren land. He had set himself to do what no one had yet succeeded in doing – not merely to drive the Welsh into the mountains, which was comparatively easy, but to hold them there and wear them down till they yielded. Hitherto it had always been the invaders of Snowdonia who had starved and given up the struggle. This time, by organising a massive commissariat and transport train, Edward meant to see that the defenders did so.

Early in July 1277 the King took command of the host at Worcester. Attended by the hereditary Constable, the Marshal and Llywelyn's brother, Prince David, he marched up the Severn and Dee to Cheshire where, to invoke a blessing on his campaign, he laid the foundation stone of a new Cistercian abbey at Vale Royal.[1]

---

[1] The largest Cistercian church in England, larger even than Fountains. Scarcely a stone now remains.

His plan was to advance by stages along the coast from Chester to Flint, Rhuddlan and the mouth of the Conway, driving clearings through the forests – a bowshot's width – along which his knights and their war-horses and baggage could move in safety. At each point at which the army halted to consolidate before tackling the next stage, he planned to build a castle on or near the coast. For this he employed – impressing where necessary and paying the customary rates of wages – thousands of craftsmen and labourers, drawn from every county of western England, woodmen and carpenters, masons, carters, charcoal-burners, quarrymen, blacksmiths, lime-burners, hodmen, guarding them as they worked by relays of archers.

But the King's trump-card was sea-power. With a fleet to protect his flank and bring up supplies as he moved along the coast, he meant to drive a wedge, not into the high mountains, where the odds would be all in favour of the defenders, but between Gwynedd and the rich isle of Anglesey, the granary on whose crops Llywelyn depended to maintain his tribesmen and their flocks during the winter. Under the terms of their feudal service, the Cinque Ports of Kent and Sussex had to furnish the Crown in time of war with ships and seamen at their own expense for fifteen days. By taking their crews into his pay Edward had secured a weapon which offset all his adversary's geographical advantages.

The advance from Chester began in the middle of July. The King was everywhere, supervising the transport and organising the relays of soldiers and workmen as they drove steadily forward through the densely wooded hills. By the 26th he was at Flint, where a century before his great-grandfather, Henry II, had been ambushed in an attempt to conquer Gwynedd. Three weeks later he moved forward to Rhuddlan, establishing his headquarters there on 20th August. By the 29th he had reached the mouth of the Conway.

The moment had now come for which he had been preparing. Using his fleet to ferry an expeditionary force to Anglesey, he over-ran the island just as the harvest was being got in and robbed Llywelyn of his winter's supplies. By doing so he also threatened a further landing in the rear of the prince's impregnable position on the west bank of the Conway at Penmaenmawr. In two months Edward had completely out-manoeuvred the Welsh.

Llywelyn saw he was checkmated. He did not wait for the end, but surrendered and threw himself on Edward's mercy. By the treaty of Conway on 9 November 1277, he restored the Four Cantrefs of Perfeddwlad, accepted the old frontier of Gwynedd on the Conway and abandoned all claims to suzerainty in the Marches. He also agreed to give hostages for his behaviour, to pay an indemnity for the war and a rent for Anglesey. Next day he swore fealty to the King in his new castle at Rhuddlan.

Edward had won what he sought – the recognition of his lordship and law. He at once remitted the indemnity and rent, and within a year released the hostages. At the Christmas feast at Westminster, where Llywelyn again did homage, he gave him the kiss of peace. Ten months later, satisfied by his peaceful conduct, he permitted his marriage to Eleanor de Montfort and himself presided over their wedding feast.

*   *   *

Yet the Welsh volcano was only slumbering. On the eve of Palm Sunday 1282, without the slightest warning, Edward's former ally, David, fell by night on Hawarden castle, massacred the garrison and carried off the royal Justiciar who had hanged one of his men for an offence unpunishable by Welsh law. Forgetting earlier wrongs at his brother's hands, Llywelyn threw in his lot with him. Everywhere the Welsh rose, laying siege to the hated new castles of Flint and Rhuddlan, storming Llanbadarn – the modern Aberystwyth – and carrying fire and sword to the walls of Chester and through the lands of the Marchers to the Bristol Channel. Everywhere, in that spring of Celtic fury and vengeance, the King's fortresses, except the very strongest, went up in flames.

The rising took Edward completely by surprise. He had showered favours on David, forgiven and befriended Llywelyn, and thought he had done with the barren hills of Wales and its petty princes for ever. The cause of their anger was the English King's denial of Llywelyn's contention that disputes about his lands outside the principality should be governed by the code of of the famous tenth-century Welsh legislator, Hywel Dda or the Good. Yet for more than a hundred years English as well as Welsh law had operated in the Marches. The greatest of all the Cymric chieftains of central Wales – Llywelyn's rebellious vassal, Gruffyd ap Gwenwynwyn, lord of Pool – flatly refused to have his dispute with the Prince of Gwynedd tried by Welsh law, claiming that he should be judged as an English baron. He was prepared, he said, to answer any man according to the Common Law, but in no way according to Welsh Law.

This was too hard a poser for the justices of the March, and the matter was referred to the King. He laid it, as was now his custom with all baronial pleas, before his Council at the next meeting of Parliament. Here it was held that justice could only be done according to the law that Parliament itself administered. The supreme royal court could not give judgment by rules it regarded as unjust, barbarous or unchristian. The Crown, the indignant Welsh Prince was informed, must 'according to God and justice do what the prelates and magnates of the realm shall advise'. Instead of having the matter decided out of hand and by a Welsh judge interpreting a highly elastic local law, Llywelyn was forced to apply for a writ like an English baron and endure the long formalities and delays attendant on a parliamentary suit. The matter was still undecided when, in the spring of 1282, he threw in his lot with his brother.

It was not only Llywelyn and David who felt the irons of subordination to English law. The men of the Four Cantrefs bitterly resented being placed by the Treaty under the jurisdiction of the Justiciar of Chester and the Cheshire shiremoot. It was not like that of the Princes of Gwynedd, or even of their earlier Anglo-Norman rulers, the palatine earls – swift, rough and ready and framed for a warlike society. A nomadic people, who for centuries had viewed cattle-stealing as a branch of agriculture, and war against one another and the Saxon as the poetry of life, did not take kindly to the Common Law. Its slow and elaborate processes seemed to them only tricks for evading justice, its pursuit of truth by the laborious interchange of pieces of parchment an affront to hot-blooded men in search of their rights. They could only respect judgment given instantly and on the spot.

Edward had declared that he would uphold Welsh law and custom in the Four Cantrefs so far as they were not barbarous or at variance with reason and the Ten Commandments. Yet this was just how they seemed to any Englishman trained in the royal courts. The officials of the County Palatine who took over the administration of the conquered borderland had nothing but contempt for Welsh law. To them the code of Hywel Dda seemed as archaic and savage as the laws of their remote Anglo-Saxon forbears. How, they asked, could they be expected to administer a legal system which treated civil war as a legitimate activity, that regarded a judge as a private arbitrator hired by a criminal's kinsmen to compound with his avengers, that punished the murder of a bard with a fine of a hundred-and-twenty-six cows? And how could they keep order in a violent land without a death penalty?

It was hard for the English, with their comparatively law-abiding and stable society, not to regard the Welsh robbers and plunderers as savages. To them, as to the sheriff of Shropshire who offered a shilling for every scalp taken during a Welsh raid on Strattondale, they were wolves' heads outside the law. Unlike the Marchers, with their half Welsh ancestry and love of fighting, the farmers of the Cheshire plain could not appreciate the virtues of a people who burnt homes instead of making them and preferred robbery and idleness to honest husbandry.

This assumption that everything Welsh was beneath contempt aroused deep resentment. During the years immediately after Edward's victory, everyone in the Four Cantrefs who had a suit in the Palatine courts became a passionate nationalist. Every departure from ancient custom, every legal and administrative innovation was seen as an affront. Though far more efficient than any rulers Wales had known, and convinced that they were bringing civilization and justice to a backward people, the bureaucrats of the County Palatine imposed a strait-jacket on the life of an ancient community.

Under the rule of the great athelings and the Norman and Angevin kings the English had mastered political lessons far in advance of the Welsh or even of their most civilized continental neighbours. They had learnt to keep the King's Peace, to pay taxes, to abide by a single law, to take personal part in an administrative

182

and legal hierarchy which stretched from the parish and manorial court to the Council of the realm in Parliament. But their system was far too centralised and complex to be intelligible to a primitive, pastoral race. Everything had to be referred to distant authority or remote precedent. And the rules they imported to the Celtic borderland were too often applied in a narrow, pedantic spirit. When Llywelyn, in full cry after a stag, accidentally crossed the frontier-stream between Gwynedd and the Marches, 'the King's officers came to the huntsmen and immediately called out with horns and cries almost the whole countryside', seizing the hounds and imprisoning the riders.

Nor were the administrators England sent to govern the borderland always honest. The theory of thirteenth-century law was one thing, its practice another. King Edward's judges and bailiffs enforced law and order and did justice as they were trained to do, but they also feathered their own nests. Many subordinate officials took bribes and falsely accused the innocent. In the light of their conduct high-sounding talk about the moral superiority of English law struck the Welsh as nauseating.

Above all, the new rulers of the Four Cantrefs were English, not Welsh. The Welsh did not like Englishmen; they had been accustomed from time immemorial, not to nationhood, but to governing themselves. Most of them preferred to be ruled by an unjust fellow countryman than by an upright foreigner – a thing no Englishman could understand. As the Marchers had always recognised but as the administrators of the borderland had still to learn, only a Welshman could understand Welshmen.

For though Wales had never been a kingdom, and only a handful of her people yet thought of her as a nation, the Welsh loved their country. They loved its land, its traditions, its speech, its faith. 'I am persuaded,' an old Welshman had told Henry II a century before, 'that no other race than this and no other tongue than of Wales, happen what may, will answer in the great day of judgment for this little corner of earth.' Since then, under the two Llywelyns, a growing number of Welshmen, including for a time the inhabitants of the Four Cantrefs, had learnt what it was to live as members, not merely of a Welsh tribe, but of a Welsh State.

With its impenetrable mountain barrier to the east and its rich island-granary of Anglesey, Gwynedd had become something more than a group of loosely-knit tribes. In its prince's wooden hall or *neuydd*, where native bards sang the glories of Wales in the presence of a ruler who claimed the allegiance of all Welshmen, the institutions of a modern national kingdom were beginning to take shape.

It was this that made Llywelyn regard the denial of Welsh law in the Marches as a monstrous injustice and affront. Because as lord of Gwynedd he enjoyed his own law under the titular sovereignty of the imperial Crown, he felt that the law should be equally valid in every part of the land of which he called himself prince. With indignation he brooded over the slights that he and his people suffered. 'Each province,' he wrote to Edward, 'under the *imperium* of the King of England has its own customs and laws according to the mode and use of their respective parts where they are situated, such as the Gascons in Gascony, the Scots in Scotland, the Irish in Ireland and the English in England. I, therefore, seek, being a Prince, that I likewise shall have my Welsh law and proceed according to that law. By common right we ought to have our Welsh law and custom, as the other nations in the King's empire have – and in our own language.'

But, though in Gwynedd no one denied him that right, Llywelyn forgot that, whatever he might call himself, he was not the ruler of Wales as the Scots king was of Scotland and Edward of Gascony. Wales was not, and had never been, like Gwynedd, a single state. Yet though on false ground legally, in a wider, poetic sense Llywelyn was right. Because her people were aware of their separateness, even though politically divided, Wales was already one in spirit. Her bards sang of her now as *Cymru* – the land of all the Cymri – and of Llywelyn as 'the great chieftain of fair Wales'. Those who heard them shared his belief that to be punished by English judges in accordance with English-made law was for Welshmen a kind of servitude. 'All Christians,' wrote one of them, 'have laws and customs in their own lands. The Jews among the English have laws. We and our ancestors in our lands had immutable laws and customs until after the last war the English took them from us.' It was this conviction which made the rising of 1382 such a passionate affair.

It made it, too, a cruel one. The Welsh tribesmen did not spare the English in their path. And in those early weeks of the rising they travelled far. Ruthin castle was captured, the earl of Gloucester ambushed in the hills near Llandeilo Fawr, the valleys as far south as Builth and Cardigan harried. Many perished in cold blood, churches and farms were sacked, atrocious acts done. And these were exaggerated in the telling.

This time the English as well as their King were thoroughly aroused. They were resolved to be done with the Welsh, their raids and broken truces, and to subject them to government.

The strategic problem was the same as in 1277. But it was harder to solve because Llywelyn's successes in the south-west had widened the area of fighting. During July the King worked his way along the coast from Chester to his besieged castles at Flint and Rhuddlan, both of which had held out since the spring against David's attacks. Meanwhile he sent the earl of Surrey to clear his left flank in the vale of Clwyd and to drive David from the Four Cantrefs. His aim was, by encircling Snowdon from the south, to force Llywelyn to abandon his conquests in central and south-western Wales in order to save his principality.

Once again sea-power proved decisive. With forty ships from London and the Cinque Ports, Edward was able to turn the enemy's northern flank. As his army advanced slowly through the wooded defiles to the Conway, a seaborne force under a former seneschal of Gascony, Luke de Tany, landed in Anglesey to knock, in the King's words, the feathers out of Llywelyn's tail. It took a month's fighting to clear the island, for this time the Welsh were expecting the blow. But by the middle of October de Tany had almost completed a bridge of boats across the Menai Strait to enable him, at the decisive moment, to take the Welsh position at Penmaenmawr in the rear. Ruthin and Denbigh had already fallen in the south, and in the centre Edward had reached the Conway.

Faced by this triple threat to Snowdonia, Llywelyn abandoned his southern offensive and hurried back to defend his base. Then, just as an English victory seemed certain, de Tany's impatience precipitated disaster. On 6 November, in disobedience to his orders and without waiting for the concerted attack which had been planned, his lieutenant crossed the Menai Strait at low tide, expecting to surprise the Welsh. Instead he was ambushed near Bangor and overwhelmed, losing his life and his entire force as it tried to escape across the rising waters.

It seemed as though Gwynedd had been saved. Llywelyn was jubilant and, leaving his brother in command in the north, set off on a punitive raid against England's Welsh allies in the Marches. But Edward was never more dangerous than when fortune turned against him. Withdrawing to Rhuddlan he resolved to continue the campaign through the winter. And six weeks after the disaster at Bangor, dramatic news arrived from the headwaters of the Wye. About to plunder the lands of the dead Marcher baron, Roger Mortimer, Llwyelyn had been surprised by Mortimer's sons at Orewin bridge and killed.

With his death the soul went out of the rising. David, who claimed his principality, had been too long in the English camp to take his place in his fellow Welshmen's hearts. For half a year he fought on in the northern mountains while the remorseless ring of Edward's men and the Marchers closed round him. In June 1283, a fugitive in the barren hills round Cader Idris, he was betrayed by his own countrymen and handed over to Edward who refused even to see him. Condemned to a traitor's death by a Parliament called at Shrewsbury to try him, he was dragged to the gallows by horses, disembowelled and quartered and his head set beside his brother's over the Tower.

The rebellion – for it was as such that every Englishman regarded it – ended the last hope of a self-governing Welsh state within the island *imperium*. But, having grown up in the March and absorbed its warlike traditions, Edward had more under-standing of the Welsh than his English subjects. He remained in Wales with his court of King's Bench for nearly eighteen months after his victory and threw himself, with his usual passionate mastery of detail, into the settlement of the country. He did not merge the principality with England but preserved its separate existence under the Crown and royal law. In his Statute of Wales, issued from Rhuddlan castle in March 1284, he divided Gwynedd into three counties on the English model – Caernarvon, Anglesey and Merioneth – and appointed a Justiciar of Snowdon, with a treasury and capital at Caernarvon. At the same time he made a fourth county, Flintshire, out of part of the Four Centrefs, placing it under the Justiciar of Chester. Two other counties, Carmarthen-shire and Cardiganshire, already created out of Llywelyn's former fiefs in the Marches, were provided with the usual English administrative hierarchy of sheriffs, bailiffs and coroners.

The settlement would not have been Edward's without the hard cement of a uniform system of law. It was for this that the war had been fought. Welsh and Anglo-Norman law were now made one. A body of law, half English, half Welsh, and current throughout the six shires, took the place of the old law of Gwynedd and of the many contending laws around its borders. The Welsh were allowed to keep their system of inheritance by which all a man's sons shared his property equally but, in deference to the orthodox Christian view of marriage, the illegitimate were excluded. Civil law remained Welsh, criminal law was anglicised.

For the rest Edward left Wales much as he found it. He left to the Marchers, who had helped him with the war, their feudal jurisdictions and martial lordships. He left the people of the former principality and the Cantrefs as much of their customary law as was compatible with peace and order and of the standards of morality and justice prevailing in Latin Christendom. He left them – the most precious thing of all – their language and, with a few exceptions, their Welsh officers and chieftains to fill the English legal and administrative posts which he imposed on them for their better ordering. He left them, in other words, not a Welsh State, which under provocation he had taken from them, but the wherewithal of Welsh nationhood.

The bards, the repositories of Cymric culture and learning who had shared Llywelyn's dream, bitterly lamented his death. And many Welshmen, who hated all government, including some who had fought on Edward's side, felt the iron of the new law enter into their souls. Twice in the decade after the conquest of the north the Welsh rose, once in 1287 – when Edward was in Gascony –

and again in 1294. Yet such risings could achieve little in the face of the castles which Edward raised after the conquest to hold down the north. Four great fortresses were built – Conway and Caernarvon on strategic promontories on the northern coast, and Criccieth and Harlech on the hills dominating the western coastal corridor round the shores of Cardigan bay. A fifth followed at Beaumaris in Anglesey to control the Menai Strait. Together with the Tower of London and the earl of Gloucester's Caerphilly – both newly rebuilt – they formed the greatest expression of the medieval military engineer's art raised in Britain before that art was superseded.

Edward was very proud of his new principality. For he was not merely King of the English; he was a prince of Christian chivalry. And Celtic Wales, at least in legend, was the most romantic of all the lands of chivalry; the fabled home of Arthur and his Round Table knights, of Gawain and Perceval and Galahad. Four weeks after the proclamation of the Statute of Wales, Queen Eleanor gave birth at Caernarvon to a son who, on his elder brother's unexpected death a few months later, became heir to the English throne. The King, who christened him with his own name, gave the boy a Welsh nurse and attendants and, sixteen years later, the title of Prince of Wales. By such means he hoped to win the Welsh people's hearts as well as their land.

CHAPTER THIRTEEN

Scotland the Brave

'The awful thistle . . . keep it
with a bush of spears.'

Dunbar

'Scots, wha hae wi' Wallace bled,
Scots, wham Bruce has aften led;
Welcome to your gory bed
    Or to victorie . . .
Liberty's in every blow!
Let us do or die!'

Burns

IN THE SUMMER OF 1284, to celebrate his conquest of Wales, Edward, King of England and Ireland, Duke of Aquitaine and rightful heir, as he believed, to the vanished Roman *imperium* or empire of Britain, held a 'round table' tournament at Nevin, the furthest point of his dominion. At it, all the most famous knights in Christendom jousted in his honour. With the last of the Welsh princes gone, there was now no one to challenge his claim to be the representative of the fabled paladins of British antiquity, Arthur and Brutus of Troy. A decade earlier, on his return from the Holy Land, he and his Queen had laid the bones of Arthur and Queen Guinevere – miraculously just rediscovered – before the high altar at Glastonbury. Now, with equal solemnity, he transferred to his royal peculiar of Westminster Abbey the supposed iron crown of King Arthur and the bones of the Emperor

Constantine's British father, together with a fragment of the true cross – the 'rood of St Neot' – which had been found among the vanquished Prince of Gwynedd's relics of the Christian and Roman past.

Wales was not the only part of the British *imperium* to which Edward wished to bring order and law. Four years after his victory over the Welsh princes, when returning from a council meeting at Edinburgh and a stormy March crossing of the Forth, King Alexander III of Scotland, galloping through the night to rejoin his young French bride at Kinghorn, had ridden over a cliff. His death at forty-four, following that of his last surviving child, the Queen of Norway, left her infant daughter sole heir to the Scottish throne.

Alexander's rule and that of his father, Alexander II, had given the Scottish lowlands three quarters of a century of freedom from the perpetual border wars with England which had raged in the days of Henry II and William the Lion of Scotland. Descended from Pictish chieftains and the Irish pirate 'kings' who had given their Scots name to the unconquered peninsula of mountain and moor which the Romans had called Caledonia, a dynasty of able princes, with the help of an Anglo-Norman baronage to which they were kin, had created, in this wild mist-soaked land, the embryo of a feudal kingdom and, with it, a unity it had never known before. In the last fifty years they had forced even the Viking conquerors of Sutherland and the Western Isles to acknowledge their sovereignty. Their rule had brought about an almost complete cessation of the agelong Scottish raids on the farms and monasteries of northern England. For their policy was to be friends with their powerful Plantagenet kinsmen and titular suzerains and, under cover of their benevolent neutrality, to impose some sort of order on the turbulent highlands and islands of the north and west.

With Alexander's death, the prospect of a return to the anarchy of the past appalled the more reasonable Scottish leaders who had sworn to accept the Maid as his heir. In their dilemma they turned to Edward. For by now it had become natural to Scottish nobles and prelates with English estates and affinities to look for support to the more civilized neighbour kingdom. Soon after Alexander's death two friars arrived in London with a message from the

Guardians of Scotland to suggest the possibility of a marriage between their child-queen and the infant son and heir of the English King.

In July 1290, a treaty was sealed at Brigham near Durham by commissioners from both countries. It provided that the rights of neither should be diminished by the proposed marriage and that, if the young couple left no issue to make the union of the two crowns permanent, Scotland should revert to the nearest heirs of its ancient throne, 'free and intact of any subjection to the King of England'. No Parliament was to be held outside Scotland on any matter that concerned it, and no taxes should be exacted from its people except to meet the common expenses of the Crown. It was agreed, too, that until the pair could marry and take the oaths to preserve the customs of the realm, Edward should hold the Scottish royal castles to ensure peace and order.

At the end of the month Edward left Westminster for his usual summer progress to the Midland shrines, while hearing suits and petitions and hunting the great forests of Whittlebury, Rocking-ham and Sherwood. Here, later that autumn, a rumour reached him that, after a stormy voyage from Norway, the Maid had died in the Orkneys and, what was even more ominous, that the Bruces and other Scottish nobles with rival claims to the throne, were gathering arms and forces. Soon still more dire news reached him. His Queen, Eleanor of Castile, had been taken suddenly ill at Harbey in Nottinghamshire. On 20 November she died in his arms.[1] 'My harp is turned to mourning,' he wrote, 'in life I loved her dearly, nor can I cease to love her in death.' She had been his inseparable companion for thirty-six years. For the rest of his life nothing ever went wholly right for him.

[1] She had saved his life by her devoted nursing when he was struck down by an assassin's poisoned dagger at Acre during the crusade. Daughter of the Castilian king who won Cordoba, Seville and Cadiz for the Cross, her memory is preserved by her noble effigy in Westminster Abbey, her favourite residence, Leeds Castle in Kent – the loveliest of all medieval castles – and the Crosses which her stricken husband raised wherever on its journey to Westminster her bier rested. The last of these, the *chere reine* – or Charing Cross – gave its name to the London thoroughfare where Dr Johnson maintained that the full tide of human existence was best encountered.

Death had not only taken from Edward his queen. It had robbed him of a great opportunity. Yet it was not in his nature to despair. The Scottish leaders' request for arbitration revived his hopes. Though he could no longer achieve a single law for Britain by marrying his heir to Scotland's queen, he might still do so as *bretwalda* of the island empire over which he believed King Arthur had ruled and over which his predecessors had claimed suzerainty.

He therefore accepted the regents' invitation. From Amesbury Abbey, where he went after Christmas to visit his dying mother, he asked for extracts from the monastic chronicles to prove his right to Scotland's overlordship. Her last two kings, both of whom had married English princesses, had done homage for their English estates. In accepting such limited fealty Edward had expressly reserved the right to call for a wider. And there had been occasions when it had been rendered. Both William the Lion and Alexander II had paid tribute, the first, after his capture, doing homage to Henry II for his Scottish fief and crown – a vassalage subsequently renounced by Richard Coeur-de-Lion in return for money to finance his crusade. And before the union of the Scottish kingdoms two centuries earlier, homage of a kind had occasionally been rendered to England's Anglo-Saxon rulers by the princes of northern Britain, even though the circumstances were shrouded in the mists of war and antiquity.

Armed with these records of hereditary right, which he had marshalled with his usual thoroughness, Edward summoned the claimants to the vacant throne to meet him at Norham in Northumberland. At the beginning of May 1291, accompanied by judges, monastic chroniclers and a papal notary, he met the representatives of Scotland, announcing through his new chief justice, Roger Brabazon, that out of pity for their plight he had come, 'as the superior and lord paramount of the kingdom of Scotland', to do his lieges justice. Yet he could only do so, Brabazon explained, under the terms of feudal law. Before the King's court could adjudicate, the vacant fief must be surrendered and his right as overlord acknowledged. After which the judge read out the evidences collected by the English chroniclers, reciting all instances of Scottish homage up to the reign of Henry II and ignoring everything that had happened since.

At this point some of the Scots representatives asked if they might consult those who had sent them. In one reply, presented on behalf of 'the community of the good people of Scotland', they argued that, while they did not doubt the king's sincerity, they knew of no right to his overlordship and could not bind their future sovereign to it. Edward thereupon offered them three weeks for consideration. As the only alternative to his adjudication was civil war, in the end none of the competitors refused what he asked. At the beginning of June they all swore to submit to his judgment and abide by his decision.

Having secured his point, in accordance with feudal practice Edward demanded the surrender of the Scottish royal castles while the claims were determined. He reappointed the regents, added an Englishman to their number and proclaimed his peace, promising to govern Scotland according to its ancient laws and customs. Then, pending examination of the claims, he set out on a tour of the country. During July he visited Edinburgh, Stirling, Dunfermline, St Andrews and Perth, installing constables in twenty-three castles and exacting as many oaths of fealty as possible.

The preliminary hearing took place at Berwick at the beginning of September 1291. The full judicial resources of both kingdoms had been mobilised. There were twenty-four English judges or auditors and eight Scottish assessors to advise them on Scottish law. As Edward prided himself on the good justice he offered, the utmost legal nicety was observed. Each of the competitors, who included the King of Norway and the Count of Holland, appeared before him in person or by attorney, and traced his descent from the ancestor from whom he claimed. Those with the strongest claim were the heads of the three Anglo-Scottish baronial families of Balliol, Bruce and Comyn.

By the autumn of 1292, 'the prodigious labours of Brabazon' and his fellow judges were completed. On 17 November he awarded the throne to John Balliol.[1] Two days later Edward ordered his constables to deliver the Scottish castles to him. The magnates did homage to their new king, and the latter did homage

---

[1] His father, a northern English as well as Scottish magnate, had founded an Oxford college for poor students from the north which still bears his name.

to Edward as supreme sovereign lord. The unsuccessful runner-up or 'Competitor' – old Robert Bruce, who had fought by Edward's side at Evesham – avoided acknowledging his rival's claim by relinquishing his rights to his son, the earl of Carrick who, with the same object, made over his Scottish estates to his own son, Robert Bruce, then an eight-year old minor.

Balliol was installed at Scone on St Andrew's Day 1292 on the Stone of Destiny, brought there, it was believed, by the ancient 'kings' of Scots from their native Ireland. He was a quiet un-assertive man, little fitted to serve as a buffer between a turbulent native nobility and a suzerain as zealous for formal law and order as Edward. Trouble began almost immediately.

Almost before Balliol had been crowned, one of his subjects, a Berwick merchant, appealed to the English courts against a decision of the Scottish Justiciars. Edward, whose pride it was never to refuse any man justice, ordered the record to be brought before the King's Bench at Newcastle where he was keeping the Christmas feast. When Balliol reminded him of his undertaking at Brigham that no Scottish subject should be made to plead in any court outside Scotland, Edward replied that he was not bound by a marriage-treaty which had not been carried out.

It was a major political blunder. Edward was one of the greatest definers of law ever to wear a crown. He had received Balliol's homage both as an English baron and as King of Scotland and, as his liege-lord, had pledged himself under the feudal compact to safeguard his rights in both. He had sworn to respect the laws and institutions of Scotland, as he had done to respect those of Gascony, Wales, Ireland and all his other dominions. But as a sovereign lord he was also bound to offer justice, according to the highest stand-ards, to all his subjects alike. If any of them could not obtain it in the court of his immediate lord – even though that lord was a king – he was entitled to appeal to the supreme overlord and seek it in his court. It was the same right which Henry II had given to his English subjects when he had offered them writs entitling them to apply to the royal courts for justice unobtainable in those of their feudal lords. Nor could the King's courts do justice by rules less enlightened than those they habitually administered or by any which conflicted with the principles of natural law.

The same claim to override the primitive codes of a backward people in the name of justice had shipwrecked Edward's plans for a peaceful union with Wales. Once Balliol had renounced his kingdom's rights to the conditions secured at Brigham, he was lost. During the next two years he was repeatedly called to answer appeals in his overlord's court at Westminster as though Scotland were an English barony. Torn between the growing resentment of his turbulent subjects and his English liege-lord's legalistic and feudal demands, he was between the devil and the deep sea. In the end, taking advantage of a similar dispute between Edward and the French king, to whom the latter owed homage for his French dominions, he asserted Scotland's independence by concluding a military alliance with France.

By doing so he precipitated an English invasion of Scotland. In 1296 Edward crossed the Tweed and stormed Berwick, putting its garrison to the sword. A month later John de Warenne, earl of Surrey, routed the Scottish army at Spottsmuir. On July 2nd, Balliol acknowledged himself in mercy. A week later he abdicated in the hall of Brechin castle. Sending him to England under escort Edward continued his northern march. By the end of the month he was on the Moray Firth. No ruler of England had penetrated so far since the Romans.

On the way back he took the Stone of Destiny from Scone abbey – the ancient crowning place of the Scottish kings – and sent it, with Scotland's royal regalia and archives, to Westminster. Then he held a parliament at Berwick. Here, receiving the homage of two thousand Scottish landowners – the entire 'franchise' of the land – he restored their estates in return for sealed submissions, copies of which were sent to Westminster on thirty-five parchment skins known as the Scottish Ragman roll. Scotland itself he treated as non-existent or rather as though it had become a part of England, leaving it to be governed by an English earl, treasurer and Justiciar. 'Now,' wrote a ballad-monger, 'are the two waters come into one and one realm made of two kingdoms. . . . There is no longer any king except King Edward . . . Arthur himself never had it so fully.'

Yet though Scotland's noble, landowning and military classes had submitted to him, within a year Edward was faced by a new

195

kind of unrest in the remoter parts of Scotland. It came from the smaller gentry, farmers and peasants who had hitherto had no share in the government of their wild land. Like the earlier discontent in Wales it had arisen through the tactlessness and corruption of English officials who, contrary to Edward's ideals but in accordance with the general practice of the age, had seized the opportunity to feather their own nests.

The risings, though small affairs, had occurred in widely separated areas, in Galloway and Clydesdale, Ross, Moray and Aberdeenshire. At Lanark the English sheriff and garrison had been overwhelmed and massacred in a sudden night broil by a gang led by a young man of gigantic stature named William le Walyes or Wallace – son of a local knight from Elderslie, a few miles from the little city of Glasgow. Rendered desperate by his bloody exploit and heartened by the enthusiasm it aroused, Wallace had then led his band of fellow outlaws across Scotland and, suddenly descending from the hills, all but captured the royal Justiciar, William de Ormseby, as he was holding his court at Scone.

A new phenomenon, at first unperceived, had appeared in the world to confront the centralising encroachments of great organisers and legalists like Edward. It arose out of the regional loyalties of ordinary men and women and the instinct for personal liberty and dignity which the spread of Christian teaching had implanted in them. It was to become known as patriotism. Five years before, when Edward and his judges had been laboriously selecting the right king for the kingless Scots, the peasants of three remote forest cantons in Alpine Swabia – one of the feudal dukedoms of Germany – had made a league with the neighbouring burghers of Lucerne to resist the unifying attempts of the Emperor Rudolph of Hapsburg to subordinate them to what they regarded as an alien and oppressive vassalage. It was the beginning of the Swiss Confederation which, helped by the wild mountain terrain in which these sturdy hillfolk lived, was to defy every assault of their Hapsburg and Austrian dukes. By his disregard for the feelings of Scottish graziers and crofters, Edward had unconsciously aroused a similar resistance in northern Britain.

*　　　　*　　　　*

What sort of a country was this 'Scotsland' whose humble folk had so unexpectedly defied their English overlord? With a few fertile plains and valleys along its eastern and south-western coasts, it was a narrow, rocky peninsula, tapering away into a remote, misty and inaccessible *ultima Thule* of mountain, lake and island. Across it, cutting off its inhabitants from one another yet forming a series of formidable barriers to any invader from the south, ran a succession of barren mountain ranges and stormy inlets or firths of the sea. Such livelihood as its stony soil afforded could be won only by constant battle with the elements – snow, gale and flood – an existence rendered the more precarious by the lawlessness of its inhabitants. Cattle- and sheep-stealing was the most profitable activity in wide areas – one which united chieftain and laird with their clansmen and tenantry in continual forays and feuds. In such a society human life was held cheap; courage, hardihood and loyalty to the local leader in war honoured above all other virtues.

Partly English or Angle in the south-east and an inter-mixture of Romanised Briton and piratical Irish settler in the wet, wooded south-west, Scotland beyond the Highland line in the sparsely populated mountains and mists of the Gaelic north and west – the old Pictland – afforded its half-million people the same barbaric and pastoral life as their ancestors a thousand years before. Shepherds, graziers, crofters, fishermen, they were as accustomed to violence as to wind and rain and, like the Spartans, were nourished in proud poverty from childhood. They lived in huts of turves and mud, usually of only a single room, with a pile of dung – their chief wealth – on the floor.

Scotland's only contacts with the outer world were her Church, the dual allegiance of her Anglo-Norman lords for their English lands, and a trickle of trade across the North Sea with England, Flanders and northern Europe through the little eastern ports of Berwick, Leith, Kinghorn, Crail, Arbroath, Montrose and Aberdeen. Of these links with European civilization the Church was the greatest. Though Christianity had originally come to Scotland from Ireland and Iona, until the end of the twelfth century the

Scottish Church had been a part, though only a loosely bound and fiercely disputed one, of the province of York and, as such, nominally subordinate to the northern English metropolitan. But after its quarrel with Henry II the papacy had taken the Church in Scotland under its direct control and, though no Scottish arch-bishop had been appointed, its eleven bishops under the primacy of St Andrews had for the past century acknowledged no spiritual superior but the Pope. This had ensured that though, as the champion of civilization and opponent of war, the Church had at first welcomed a union with England through the marriage of the two crowns, its leaders were foremost in rejecting Edward's claim to suppress the nation's separate identity by force.

Since the country was at least a hundred years behind England in civilization, Scottish Christianity was more monastic than episcopal, particularly in the south-east. Here in the first half of the twelfth century David I, inspired by his mother, Queen Mar-garet, had established a chain of priories and monasteries – Augus-tinian at St Andrews, Lochleven, Holyrood, Jedburgh and Cambus-kenneth, Cistercian at Melrose, Newbattle, Kinloss and Dund-rennan. Superseding the hermit communities of the primitive past, they had begun to perform for Lowland Scotland something of the cultural and artistic service that the great Cluniac houses had done for England in the days of St Dunstan and the Anglo-Saxon kings.

In that civilizing mission David himself – greatest of Scotland's royal line – had played a major part. Open to all from the highest to the lowest, a Scottish Alfred from whom, through his mother, he was descended, he had created a small hard core of civilization on either shore of the Forth, which his successors, William the Lion and the two Alexanders, had consolidated and enlarged. It was this Edward had undermined by his attempt to enforce English law and obedience. By doing so he had broken such civilization as Scotland possessed. As a result he found himself confronted by what lay beneath – the stark, savage, native turbulence of a people to whom feuding, violence and vengeance were second nature. Such was the detestation that he and his 'southron' officers and soldiers aroused that, wherever the English penetrated, the Scottish people, for the first time in their history, seemed almost united.

From this rude, tough, resourceful community were drawn the followers of Wallace and his fellow hedge-knights, Andrew de Moray and Sir John Graham – 'the guid Graeme' of the legends. Armed with home-made spears and axes, they wore animal skins and hessian cloaks and carried their rations of oatmeal and dried lentils on their backs or ponies' saddles. Even by the standards of that hardy age they were almost incredibly mobile, traversing vast distances of lonely moor, mountain and forest to waylay and fall on their foes. They were animated by a passionate hatred of the English; Wallace himself, it was said, as a matter of principle slew every 'southron' who started an argument with him. According to the Scottish bard, Blind Harry, when the guerilla chief captured a batch of 'English knaves' he made them drag his loot to his forest lair where he hanged them on trees. Like all partisan warfare in primitive lands, his campaign was waged with merciless ferocity and intimidation. What was most disturbing to the authorities was that it became impossible to collect taxes. 'Not a penny can be raised,' the Treasurer of Scotland, Hugh de Cressingham, reported to his royal master from Roxburgh, 'until my lord the earl of Warenne shall enter in your land and compel the people by force and sentence of law.' For old Surrey, the Warden of the North, resting on his laurels of Spottsmuir, had gone home for the winter to his English estates, leaving Cressingham – a fat cleric of the ledgers – in charge.

However, an army under Surrey, hastily recalled to his charge, was hurrying up the east coast to restore order. With his ragged horde, Wallace was by now besieging Dundee castle. He had no siege-train and could only hope to starve it out. Hearing of Surrey's advance, he broke off the siege and, joining his fellow rebel, Moray, took up a position on the southernmost spur of the Ochils, barring the road from Stirling to the north. Sooner than allow the invaders to penetrate to the liberated lands beyond the Forth, he decided to give battle about a mile from the point where the Stirling road crossed the river, here deep and tidal.

It was a bold decision. The royal forces were far better trained, armed and disciplined. They were particularly strong in mailed cavalry – the dominant arm in war and one in which the Scots, a rabble of low-born, unaccounted men, were almost totally deficient. But Wallace had gained an extraordinary ascendancy over his men and possessed a born soldier's eye for ground. The earl of Surrey was old and infirm, and Cressingham – an Exchequer official of gross girth who had made himself universally hated by his meanness and greed – was notoriously impatient and arrogant. Against the advice of more experienced soldiers, Surrey reluctantly yielded to the importunity of the Treasurer who, in his obsession with financial considerations, viewed every day's delay as a waste of money. On 11 September, in face of a strongly-posted enemy, they committed the army to an advance across a narrow wooden bridge scarcely wide enough for two horsemen and with no room to deploy on the far side.

This was just what Wallace wanted. He had already rejected overtures for an armistice from the Steward of Scotland and the earl of Lennox who, trying to hunt with the hounds and run with the hare, had been offering their services as mediators. 'Tell your people,' he said, 'that we have not come here to gain peace but for battle to avenge and deliver our country. Let them come up when they like and they will find us ready to meet them to their beards.' He ordered his men not to move from their position among the rocks until he blew his horn. He waited till as many of the enemy had crossed as he felt certain he could destroy. Then he gave the signal.

The Scots' charge threw the English armour into confusion while it was trying to deploy in a swampy, congested meadow. A phalanx of Wallace's spearmen reached the bridge, cutting off those who had crossed from their comrades on the other bank. For the next hour Surrey was forced to watch the massacre of his cavalry, with an unfordable river behind them and the only bridge held by the Scots who hacked them to pieces with gusto. Cressingham was slain, and his skin afterwards cut into strips by the victors. Then panic set in, and the rest of the English army fled, not resting till it reached Berwick.

Stirling Bridge restored the independence of Scotland. The Steward and the earl of Lennox threw in their lot with the insurgents, Dundee and Stirling surrendered and by the end of September only the castles of Edinburgh, Dunbar, Roxburgh and Berwick remained in English hands. Wallace himself occupied Berwick town, putting to the sword the few English merchants who had been foolhardy enough to remain.

His triumph, however, was shortlived. In 1298, set on avenging his lieutenant's defeat, Edward invaded Scotland with a huge force of mounted knights and archers, and on 28 July at Falkirk destroyed the flower of the ragged Scots' army, which had rashly defied him in the open field. Yet for a further seven years Wallace continued to hold out in the wilderness, thereby pointing a way to his country's future. For this brave man and his foot kerns had proved that on ground of their own choosing they could defy the proudest chivalry and survive in a war of endurance without giving battle at all. Had he not tried to repeat his earlier success in the field, he might have remained at the head of an undefeated army, while his adversary could have accomplished little in that wild and hungry land save a succession of fruitless marches.

As it was, still fighting, Wallace survived till the summer of 1305. Early that August he was betrayed near Glasgow. Brought south he was paraded through the London streets and tried in Westminster Hall, charged with treason, murder and robbery. Sentenced to be hanged, drawn and quartered, he was dragged for four miles on a hurdle to the Tower and thence to the gallows at Smithfield, where 'he was hung in a noose and afterwards let down half living, his privates cut off and his bowels torn out and burnt'. His severed head was stuck up on London Bridge and his quarters sent to the chief cities of the north – Perth, Berwick, Stirling and Newcastle.

Something went with them, to take root, in Andrew Lang's words

'like a wild flower
All over his dear country.'

Abandoned by the lords and prelates of Scotland and by almost all the members of his knightly class, Wallace's memory lived on in the legends and ballads of the common folk he had led. In the fifteenth century the bard, Blind Harry, enshrined in the vernacular the ineradicable belief of peasant Scotland in his achievement:

'Scotland he freed and brocht it off thirlage
And now in Heaven he has his heritage.'

It was this which, after a summer evening's walk to the Leglen wood in 1793, inspired the greatest of all Scottish peasants to write a song on his hero 'equal to his merits'. Burns's 'Scots wha hae' is still sung wherever Scotsmen honour their native land or men decide to stand or fall for freedom.

*　　　　*　　　　*

With Wallace out of the way Edward issued his ordinance for the administration of Scotland. It was to be ruled, under a royal lieutenant, by an English Chancellor and Chamberlain assisted by an advisory council of eight prelates and fourteen magnates, including the former runner-up claimant, young Robert Bruce, and two Comyns. Judges, coroners and sheriffs were to be appointed on the English model and, though the civil law of Scotland was retained, customary laws, like those of the Celtic Highlands, 'plainly against God and reason' were abolished. Pleased at having set Scotland, as he believed, on the road to civilization and order, the English King graciously suspended the sentences on the remaining exiles.

Yet six months after Wallace's execution terrible news arrived from the north. On 11 February 1306, in a quarrel in the Grey-friars church at Dumfries, Robert Bruce – the thrice pardoned earl of Carrick – had slain his fellow councillor and rival for the forfeit throne, John Comyn the Red – head of the house of Bade-noch. Having committed murder and sacrilege, broken the King's Peace and involved himself in a blood feud with the most powerful family in Scotland, he had then imprisoned the royal judges who were holding an assize in the town and appealed to the cause of national independence, not in the dethroned Balliol's name, but in his own. Hurrying north, he had sought the aid of old Bishop Wishart of Glasgow, who heroically gave him absolution, produced from its hiding-place the royal standard of Scotland and accom-

panied him to the crowning-place of the Scottish kings at Scone.
Here on Palm Sunday, with a golden circlet made by a local
smith and in the presence of Wishart and Bishop Lamberton of
St Andrews and a hundred disaffected lords and knights, mostly
from the Celtic north and west, he was crowned Robert I of
Scotland by the countess of Buchan, wife of Comyn's closest kinsman and sister to the young earl of Fife with whom the hereditary
right of crowning lay.

When the news of the rebellion reached Edward he was in
Hampshire, travelling from hunting-lodge to hunting-lodge and
seeking, in the milder air of the southern counties, relief for his
failing health. He at once ordered the mobilisation of the northern
levies and summoned a Parliament to Westminster.Bruce and all
concerned in the death of Comyn were to be castrated and disembowelled and those who aided him hanged.

Once more in the spring of 1307, the English King assembled a
vast army, vowing that he would not rest till 'the Lord had given
him victory over the crowned traitor and perjured nation'. As soon
as the magnates and knights of the shire and burgesses assembled
in Parliament had voted him taxes for the campaign, too ill to ride
he set out by litter on his northward journey. Already his vanguard
had crossed the Forth. On 20 June Bruce was surprised at Methven
and all but taken, only saving himself, like Wallace after Falkirk,
by vanishing into the heather; as his wife had remarked at their
coronation, he and she were but King and Queen of the May.
Many who had rallied to him in the first flush of enthusiasm were
by now on their way to England in fetters.

For Bruce, throughout that summer of 1306, disaster followed
disaster. In August he was defeated at Dalry by a Scottish force
under John of Argyll, lord of Lorne. Two of his brothers were
hanged, drawn and quartered; his Queen – perhaps to her relief,
for she was more than half English – was taken, while his sister
Mary and the countess of Buchan were imprisoned in cages in the
castles of Roxburgh and Berwick. And the familiar train of deser-
tions, so characteristic till now of Scotland's wars of independence,
began again.

'Bruce durst not to the plainys ga
And all the commons went him fra:
That for their lives were full fain
To pass to the English peace again.'

In October Edward established himself for the winter at Lanercost priory, a few miles east of Carlisle. Most of the insurgents had
by now been caught and hanged and their lands given to Englishmen; Bruce himself had disappeared into the glens and islands of
the far west. No record of his movements during the next few
months exists, but according to one account he spent some time in
the little island of Rathlin off the Irish coast where, sheltering from
his terrible adversary, he is said to have taken heart through watching the efforts of a persistent spider. In February 1307, evading
Edward's searching ships, he reappeared in Arran and in the middle
of the month landed on the Ayrshire coast where he tried to surprise the English garrison of Turnberry castle and captured the
governor's plate. Then he vanished once more into the hills and
heather.

A month later his lieutenant, young James Douglas – a Dumfriesshire knight whose father had died in the Tower – surprised
Castle Douglas while the garrison was at Mass, slew every man and,
leaving their bodies and stores to roast in the blazing keep, disappeared again into the moors. The 'Douglas larder', as it was
called, caused a tremendous sensation. The tall, dark, sallow
young knight, with his lisp, courteous ways and daring imagination,
possessed just the qualities to mystify and terrify the English and
inspire his followers. 'The maist coward,' it was said, 'stouter he
made than a leopard.' In him Bruce possessed what Wallace had
never had: a lieutenant as bold as himself and loyal to the Scottish
cause as the heather.

Edward was eagerly waiting for news of Bruce's capture as he
had waited for Wallace's. In April the English armies closed round
him in the lonely glen of Loch Trool among the Galloway hills.
Yet just when he seemed in the net, Bruce broke the ring of his
pursuers by a sudden charge and again vanished. A month later,
on 10 May, he encountered the viceroy, Pembroke, 'in a fair even
field' at Loudon in the valley of the Ayrshire Avon and defeated

him. Three days later he fell on another searching party under the earl of Gloucester and drove them into Ayr castle. Scotland in arms was once more a reality.

Edward was now sinking fast. But, resolved to put himself at the head of his troops and capture the hated will o' the wisp, he left Carlisle on 3 July, mounting his horse for the first time in a year. The agony proved insupportable. For three days he struggled on, reaching Burgh-on-Sands six miles from his starting point on the 6th. Here on 7 July 1307, within sight of the Scottish border, he died in the arms of his attendants. His last command was that his son should carry his bones at the head of his armies till every Scot had surrendered.

*   *   *

Had Edward lived another year Bruce could not have survived. By Comyn's murder he had aligned against himself England, the papacy and half Scotland, and had alienated not only those of his fellow nobles who were loyal to Edward, but those who had been loyal to Balliol. Now, in place of the greatest soldier of his age, command of the forces of vengeance had passed to an overgrown, self-indulgent youth of twenty-three. For the first time since the Conquest a king sat on the English throne with no feeling for arms.

The first thing Edward II did on his accession was to recall his foreign favourite and foster brother, Piers Gaveston, a handsome but insolent Gascon knight and, by loading him with honours, precipitate a five years' struggle with his English baronage. The second was to abandon the campaign, for he had no love for war and its hardships. Disregarding his father's request that his bones should be borne at the head of his army, he made a brief perfunctory march into south-western Scotland. At the beginning of September he returned to London where, to the unspeakable fury of his nobles, he invested Gaveston with the royal earldom of Cornwall.

The new King's abandonment of the campaign gave Bruce a breathing-space to settle accounts with his Scottish enemies. Leaving Douglas in the Galloway hills, he turned north to harry the lands of the earl of Buchan, head of the house of Comyn. The valleys were swarming with English troops and the principal strongholds were in their hands, while half the Scottish nobles, adherents either of Balliol or the English King, were bitterly opposed to Bruce's claim. But the lesser gentry and common people, smarting under the invaders' injuries, turned instinctively to this God-sent champion whom they saw as Wallace's successor. And though surrounded by enemies and with a price on his head, Bruce himself was already thinking in terms of hunting his hunters.

For weak and divided though she had long been, with all but two or three of her great families in the pay of England, Scotland was now to enjoy real leadership. Bruce had all the traits which the world has learnt to associate with Scottish character, magnified to the point of genius: dogged courage, persistence, unshakeable loyalty to friend and unrelenting enmity to foe, tenderness to women, genial ironic humour, logical uncompromising ruthlessness in pursuit of his purpose. This king in the heather, this mountain-fox with the mist in his beard – 'King Robbe in the mures', as the English contemptuously called him – was one of the great national leaders of all time. Never commanding more than a few thousand men and at first only a few hundred, he evaded every attempt at capture. Whenever his foes thought they had beaten him he reappeared and, in the end, inflicted on them one of the decisive defeats of history.

He and James Douglas, who was waging the same will o' the wisp campaign against the English in the south-west, followed the rules taught by Wallace and improved on them. By mounting their men on moorland ponies they gave them an astonishing mobility. They trained them to disperse after a fight in small companies, to join again and fall on the foe whenever he was momentarily at a disadvantage before vanishing once more into the hills. 'Better,' said the good Sir James, 'to hear the lark sing than the mouse cheep.' And his leader, who knew that certain death awaited him in captivity, shared the same philosophy. Yet when the hour of opportunity came, no man could be swifter or bolder. Nor, in adversity, more wily.

When 1308 began, Bruce was lord of little more than Moray,

with Buchan still in superior force to the east, a hostile Ross to north and west, his enemies of Lorne and the Isles between him and Douglas in the south-west. The English were still in control of every major fortress in Scotland. That February, after bringing home his twelve-year-old bride, the princess Isabella, from France, King Edward II was crowned with every circumstance of pomp at Westminster, Gaveston – 'his brother Peter' – at his side 'so decked out that he more resembled the God Mars than an ordinary mortal'. Scarcely were the celebrations over when Bruce struck at Buchan, routing him at Inverurie. Then, seizing Aberdeen and Forfar, he harried the lands of Buchan, teaching by fire and sword the partisan's unchanging lesson that, in the hour of revolution, no man, however peaceable, can adhere to the powers-that-be with safety. Neither Comyn nor England, Scotsmen discovered that summer, could give protection against Bruce's vengeance. A stark, primitive people, who honoured resolution and hardihood and had no love for the English and little for their own predatory nobles, observed the fact with relish. Bruce's 'harrying of Buchan' became a national legend, establishing his claim to the throne in every Scottish heart.

While the young English King and his lords remained at loggerheads, the run of Scottish successes continued. Bruce's brother, Edward, won a spectacular victory on the Cree; by the summer he and Douglas were in control of the entire south-west except the fortresses of Dumfries, Dalswinton, Caerlaverock and Lochmaben. In August King Robert defeated the men of Lorne and Argyll in the Pass of Brander. In October he received the submission of Ross in the far north. Even in the border country south of Edinburgh, guerilla bands threatened the English convoys as they made their way through moor and forest to revictual the royal castles.

By the end of the year Bruce was *de facto* ruler of almost all Scotland north of the Tay. In 1309 he liberated the major part of Fife and that March held his first parliament in St Andrews. Three of the Scottish earls – Ross, Sutherland and Lennox – now supported him, while the earldoms of Menteith and Caithness, held by infants, were represented in his parliament. After three years of continuous peril and struggle he was a real king at last, enthroned in the hearts of a people resolved to fight to the death for their freedom. 'His mishaps, flights and dangers, hardships, weariness, hunger and thirst, watchings and fastings, nakedness and cold, snares and banishments,' wrote one of them, recalling those years, 'the seizing, imprisonment, slaughter and downfall of his near ones, and – even more – dear ones . . . no one now living, I think, recollects or is equal to rehearsing.' They formed his royal title-deeds.

Meanwhile the English were at sixes and sevens. Edward's childish irresponsibility and dependence on Gaveston infuriated his feudal nobility. For four years they had tried by first one device, then another, to constrain him and his favourite until in 1312, after civil war had broken out, the latter met a brutal death at their hands. Even before he did so Bruce, in the summer of 1311, freed from the threat of an English invasion, had taken the offensive and crossed the Solway to raid the farms of upper Tynedale. A month later he returned and, wasting Coquetdale and Redesdale, penetrated as far as Durham. Scotland, after six years of war, was starving behind him; northern England, he intended, should taste the same medicine. Despairing of help, the men of Northumberland offered him a ransom for their homes and crops. When he recrossed the border it was with £2000 of English money paid for a truce till February.

Next year King Robert, as Bruce had now become to almost every Scotsman, again crossed the border and harried Tynedale, penetrating to the walls of Durham and sacking Hartlepool. Northern England was in a panic, and the Border counties paid £1000 for a truce till spring. With a long trail of hostages and the loot of five towns, Bruce returned to his ravaged poverty-stricken land well content.

During the early months of 1313, under cover of his truce with the northern counties, he struck at the royal garrisons in Scotland. On 8 January, after a seven weeks' siege, he led his men neck-deep through the icy waters of the moat to capture Perth in a midnight escalade. A month later his brother Edward took Dumfries and the Bruce castle of Lochmaben. And at the end of the summer a farmer named Binnock, who was in the habit of supplying the garrison of Linlithgow with hay, blocked the main gate with a wagon, enabling armed men concealed in it to rush the portcullis and capture the fortress.

At this point, Edward Bruce, who lacked his brother's Fabian sense of strategy, brought the long-drawn-out war to a crisis. He made a truce with the governor of Stirling, Sir Thomas Mowbray, by which the latter agreed to surrender the castle if it was not relieved by midsummer. This put both kings in a dilemma. Edward could not ignore the challenge without ignominy, while Robert could only allow Stirling to be relieved at the expense of laying northern Scotland once more open to invasion and jeopardising the successes of the past six years.

During the opening months of 1314 the summons went out to all English fighting men. The greatest army England had ever sent forth was to march to the castle's relief before the day agreed for its surrender. But while Edward was mobilising England's might to crush once and for all 'Robert de Brus who calls himself King of Scotland', the latter was wresting from him his last bases in the north. On the night of Shrove Tuesday Douglas captured the chief fortress of the marches, Roxburgh, while the garrison was keeping the feast in the great hall. A month later Bruce's nephew, Thomas Randolph, to whom he had given the earldom of Moray, secured an even greater prize. Scaling Edinburgh castle from the ravine which today divides the new city from the old, while a frontal attack engaged the garrison, Randolph and his men, wearing darkened armour, reached the ramparts by a track down which one of them in his youth had been wont to visit his lady-love.

Having dismantled the captured castles Bruce withdrew into the Torwood, close to the Roman road to Stirling up which the English would have to march. Here, training his men for the battle which was now inevitable, he awaited the supreme test of his own and his country's life. He had to pit the fighting forces of a nation of less than half a million, desperately impoverished by twenty years of invasion and civil war, against those of a kingdom with more than eight times its population and resources.

For it was an immense array which assembled at Wark on 10

June 1314. There were probably between two thousand and three thousand knights and nearly twenty thousand archers and spearmen. On the 17th they set out, advancing up Lauderdale to Edinburgh and the Forth, while their supplies followed by sea to Leith. This time there was no indecision. The English King meant to make a speedy end of Scotland's defiance. By the evening of 22 June – two days before Stirling had to be relieved – he reached Falkirk, having covered nearly a hundred miles in six days.

That night Bruce's scouts brought news of the invading host – 'so great that it was ferly'. The whole glittering panoply of a rich nation's chivalry was displayed in the summer twilight as the armoured horses and men passed in endless procession through the streets of Falkirk:

> 'Banners right fairly flaming
> And pencels to the wind waving.'

So impressive was the sight that Bruce forbade those who had seen it to speak of it to their comrades. His own force numbered little more than a quarter of the English: some five thousand infantry, mostly spearmen equipped with twelve-foot spears, padded coats, steel helmets and mail gloves, together with a few archers from Ettrick forest and about five hundred lightly armed horse. Another two thousand auxiliaries, 'small folk'· from the neighbouring farms and boroughs, roused by the magnitude of the country's peril, had recently joined him. Save for these, his men were all veterans who had been drilling for many weeks for the battle they would have to fight. And they were defending all they held dear.

Soon after midday on Saturday 23 June, hot and weary from its twenty-mile march from Falkirk, the English army reached the little Bannock burn that, crossing the Roman road to Stirling, serpentined north-eastwards through pools to the Forth. The beleaguered castle, clearly visible on its height, was now only three miles away. The Scots were posted on rising wooded ground barring the road, their front protected by rows of carefully dug pits or *pottis* concealed by turf and branches, with steel calthrops for maiming horses strewn between them. The governor of Stirling had ridden out to warn the King of these. He also pointed out that, as he was within three leagues of the castle, it was already technically 'relieved' and that there was therefore no need for haste.

But, inexperienced in Scottish warfare and believing Bruce's hopelessly outnumbered army to be at their mercy, Edward and the younger English lords would not wait for victory. Despite the long morning's march they decided to attack at once. Throughout the hot afternoon haze the armoured knights under the Constable and earl of Gloucester pressed forward across the burn on their great war-horses without waiting for the rest of the army to deploy.

The Scots were not expecting this move which, after so long a march and so late in the day, seemed contrary to every prudent rule of war. Bruce himself was in front of his outposts, reconnoitring the English positions. At the top of the rise, near the Borestone on the Stirling road, Sir Humphrey Bohun, the earl of Hereford's nephew, suddenly encountered him. Seeing the crown over his helmet and a chance of immortal glory, he put his horse into a gallop and bore down. But Bruce, mounted on a small grey palfrey, was too quick for him. Rising in the stirrups as the English knight thundered past, he cracked open his skull with his battle-axe. Then he galloped back to join his waiting men in the wood.

Here the English cavalry, confronted by the pits and calthrops, were soon in difficulties. The earl of Gloucester himself was thrown and unmounted, and, after some ineffective skirmishing, the exhausted knights and their heavily laden horses fell back in confusion without having penetrated the Scottish position at any point. Meanwhile a smaller contingent of six or seven hundred horse under the lords Clifford and de Beaumont had been feeling its way northwards towards Stirling round the Scots' retracted flank where, immediately below the escarpment, a narrow corridor of firm ground lay unguarded between Bruce's left and the carse that stretched between the Bannock burn and the Forth. Lacking the strength both to hold the road through the wood and bar this alternative approach to the castle, Bruce had deliberately left it open, hoping that, if Edward's troops were to advance along it without first dislodging him, he might, by descending on them while they were still strung out, force them into the carse where their armour would be helpless and unable to manoeuvre.

Confident of being able to drive Bruce from the wood, King Edward had ordered Clifford to take up position between Stirling and the Scots' rear, ready to cut off their retreat and destroy them. Instead of obeying their orders and continuing their march, the English wheeled left and engaged the schiltrons who at once halted, closed and confronted them with the usual impenetrable hedgehogs of spears. Though the riders flung their maces and battle-axes into the Scottish ranks in the hope of breaking them, nothing would make the horses face those steady, glittering circles of steel. In the end the attackers dispersed, some taking refuge in Stirling castle and the remainder galloping back to the English host beyond the Bannock burn, spreading dismay.

A council of war was now held. As no hope remained of driving the Scots from the wood that day, the more prudent urged a halt. But Edward, anxious to obtain water for his horses, fell into the very trap Bruce had baited. Intending next day to attack from the east the position that he had failed to carry from the south, he ordered his entire army to move down into the valley of the Bannock burn and the boggy carse beyond. Here, its morale badly shaken, it passed the night, as one present described it, 'in a deep, wet, evil marsh'. The lights of the Scottish camp-fires could be seen shining through the trees a mile away on the higher ground to the west. Bruce had his enemy at last where he wished him.

Sunday, 24 June, Midsummer Day 1314, was the feast of St John the Baptist. At the first light the Scottish priests, moving from schiltron to schiltron, celebrated mass at the head of each division. Afterwards the men knelt in prayer while the abbot of Inchaffray, armed with sacred relics, blessed them. Meanwhile the trumpets were sounding in the English camp along the burn, and thousands of knights, assisted by their pages, were buckling on their armour and mounting their huge barded horses after their comfortless night among the pools and peat.

But before the ranks could be marshalled the Scots were seen to be on the move. To the amazement of the invaders, instead of awaiting their attack on the higher ground or withdrawing into the forest westwards, the schiltrons were descending the slope towards them in three huge 'battles' of massed spears. Like the great commander he was, rather than wait for the English blow, Bruce had chosen to anticipate it. Using his schiltrons as a slowly moving wall of steel, he sought to compress the vast, unprepared mass of invaders into a steadily diminishing space with the marshes of the carse and the reaches of the Forth behind them. As he brought his right forward and swung his steady footmen northwards along the course of the burn, without the English realising it, he was driving them into the one place where he could destroy them.

Hitherto, in their nine years of trying to bring him to book, the leaders of England's chivalry had encountered only the cautious side of Bruce – the Fabian general who had repeatedly survived by vanishing into his native mists, leaving them to starve amid barren mountain and flood. Now, like their subordinate garrison commanders who had long experienced his sudden lion pounces on lonely moor and midnight escalade, they discovered his other side. For, once he had chosen his moment, no man could be bolder. His chief danger were the English and Welsh archers who, so long as his schiltrons kept their ranks, alone possessed the power to break them. He had only five hundred horse, but knew that the time had come to use them. Most of the enemy's archers were still in the rear of the dense, confused English armour as it struggled to hold back the advancing spears, and their arrows were falling impartially on friend and foe alike. Seeing that they were unprotected by pikesmen, Bruce ordered the Marischal to move his horsemen round their flank and charge.

The move was a brilliant success. In a few minutes the archers had been cut to pieces and the English were without one of their two principal weapons. The other, their armour, unable to deploy and with its horses getting more and more out of control, was by now unusable. Unable either to break or stop the contracting ring of Scottish spears, it was gradually pushed back in confusion into an ever-smaller area of firm ground. Now, King Robert saw, was the moment to throw in his reserve, hidden in the wood to the west of the Stirling highway. Calling on Angus Og, MacDonald of the Isles, in the words still borne on the Clanranald coat-of-arms, 'My hope is constant in thee', he launched the islemen against the receding English flank where, a mile or more to the east of St Ninian's chapel, the Bannock burn narrowed into a small precipitous gorge. Into this the English cavalry were driven as the Scottish officers repeatedly called out, 'Press! Press!', and the pikesmen, keeping their steady ranks, raised the shout of, 'On them! On them! They fail! They fail!'

As the mêlée of falling knights and terror-stricken horses continued in the narrowing space left by the Scottish spears, a further force was seen to be entering the battle. Emerging from the wood on the hill beyond St Ninian's chapel, 'the small folk' and camp followers of Bruce's army moved into the fight to take their share of whatever slaying and plundering there might be. They had made themselves banners of blankets slung on saplings, and the sight filled the by now demoralised invaders with despair.

By this time panic had set in; it was Stirling Brig over again. The English were far from home in a wild hostile land, and their line of retreat was cut by relentless enemies and the bogs of the carse. The only way open was northwards across the narrowing plain to Stirling. The first thought of those immediately about him was to save the King. The tall Plantagenet, his horse stabbed under him, helped to clear a way with his battle-axe, while his entourage hustled him through the milling mob towards the north. But when he reached the walls of Stirling Castle he was reminded by the governor that any stay there would be fatal, since he was obliged to surrender it by the terms of the truce. There was nothing for it but to make a wide detour to the west round the rear of the Scottish army. With five hundred followers the King set out into the unknown, vowing to endow a college of Carmelite friars if he reached England in safety. Riding day and night with Douglas in pursuit, he reached Dunbar castle where he took boat to Berwick.

Other were less fortunate. The Constable, flying towards Carlisle with the earl of Angus and other Balliol supporters, was handed over to his pursuers by the governor of Bothwell castle. Those taken on the field included the Keeper of the Privy Seal, which itself fell into Scottish hands. In all some five hundred men of high rank were made prisoner. Thousands more, including seven hundred knights and many of England's greatest lords, perished

214

in the carse or in the waters of the Forth or were slaughtered by the country folk. Of the magnates who had accompanied the King to Scotland, only Pembroke – flying on foot with a handful of Welsh archers – reached England.

Had Bruce commanded a substantial force of cavalry, it is unlikely that any of the invaders would have got away at all. His booty included the royal wardrobe, a vast haul of jewels and ecclesiastical vestments – brought to celebrate an English victory – and over £200,000 in bullion, worth many millions in modern money. The whole of the royal siege-train and military chest remained in his hands. He treated his prisoners with magnanimity and courtesy like the great gentleman he was. Sir Marmaduke de Twenge, the English hero of the rout of Stirling Brig who, after a night hidden in a bush, surrendered to him personally next day, was sent home without ransom. For nearly a year after the Battle of the Pools, as the English called it, a stream of agents visited Scotland under safe conduct to negotiate the exchange of prisoners.

* * *

After Hastings, Bannockburn was the greatest military disaster in English history. It ended any real hope of reconquering Scotland by arms. For a generation the Scots had suffered invasion. Now, under Douglas and Randolph, they took the offensive. Having expelled the English from every corner of their land save Berwick, they swept across the border. And as the government at Westminster was neither prepared to recognise their independence nor able to oppose them, the people of northern England had to make what terms they could. Cumberland and Durham paid ransom for a truce, and Tynedale did homage to the Scottish King. Such was the terror which Bruce's lieutenant, Douglas, inspired that for generations to come North Country mothers rocked their babies to the refrain,

> 'Hush thee, hush thee, do not fret thee,
> The Black Douglas shall not get thee.'

It was not until 1328, fourteen years after Bannockburn, that the English could be brought to recognise the independence of

Scotland. After a generation of war Bruce had accomplished his work and freed his country. He died a year later, on 7 June 1329, at his favourite hunting palace of Cardross on the Clyde.

CHAPTER FOURTEEN

The Grey Goose Feather

'No warring guns were then in use:
They dreamt of no such thing;
Our Englishmen in fight did use
The gallant grey-goose wing.

And with the gallant grey-goose wing
They shew'd to them such play
That made their horses kick and fling
And down their riders lay.'

Old Ballad

'There are periods at which the history of its wars
is the true history of the people, for they are the
discipline of the national experience.'

Bishop Stubbs

IN 1327, THIRTEEN YEARS after Bannockburn, Bruce's defeated
adversary, Edward II, preceded him to the grave. Undeterred by
the tragic fate of Gaveston and the failure of his earlier attempt to
govern England without 'counsel and consent', Edward had once
more tried – for a time with success – to rule through an all-powerful
and upstart favourite. This time it had cost him his own life as well
as that of the favourite – Hugh Despenser, an intensely ambitious
Marcher[1] who, with his equally avaricious father, led Edward,
'like a cat after a straw'. In 1326, following a spontaneous rising

---

[1] The Despensers were not, by Marcher standards, of the first hereditary
rank, being descended from the household 'dispensers' of the former Palatine
earls of Chester.

and an invasion by his estranged French Queen, Isabella, and her exiled lover, Roger Mortimer – the Despensers' fellow Marcher and bitterest enemy – he was forced to abdicate in favour of his fifteen-year-old son, Edward III. Deposed by an improvised Parliament on the grounds that, through evil advice and refusal to 'hear good counsel', he had 'stripped his realm' of Scotland and his hereditary lands in France and Ireland, the hapless King was incarcerated by the triumphant Mortimer in one vile dungeon after another until, mocked by brutal jailers as a madman in a crown of plaited straw, he suffered an unspeakable death at their hands in Berkeley Castle.

But in overthrowing the Despensers and ridding themselves of an irresponsible sovereign, the English had merely exchanged the rule of one ruthless Marcher lord for another. From this dilemma they were rescued by the courage of the young King, who in 1330, eluding the vigilance of Mortimer's guards, admitted, through a secret passage under the moat of Nottingham Castle, an armed band of his friends at whose head he surprised the hated dictator disrobing in Queen Isabella's apartments. Sent in fetters to the Tower and tried for treason by his fellow peers of Parliament, Mortimer was sentenced, like the Despensers before him, to an ignominious death and, drawn to the common gallows at Smithfield, hanged, disembowelled and quartered.

At eighteen Edward III thus became King in fact as well as in name. Like his grandfather, he meant to rule. Having seen since childhood the fatal consequences of a break between a sovereign and the lords through whom, in an age when a journey from London to York took a week, so much of the administration of a feudal kingdom had to be conducted, he knew there could be no ruling England without the counsel and consent of its nobles. After the struggles of the past generation what was needed was a compromise – a reconciliation between royal authority and the 'liberties' of the magnates. It was the supreme merit of this firm, conciliatory, yet shrewd young King to realise it.

Generous, impulsive, profuse in display, a laggard neither in love nor war, with a boyish charm which won the hearts of warriors and fair women, Edward III was the *beau idéal* of chivalry and of the elaborate code of knightly conduct and manners known as courtesy. To the young English lords, his contemporaries, he seemed a reincarnation of their legendary hero, King Arthur. It was thus that he saw himself – the crowned leader of a brotherhood of Christian knights. Inspired by the long rambling tales of the Arthurian legends, his ambition was to build a Round Tower in Windsor Castle to house a round table at which he and his knights could feast as equals 'in fair fellowship' after their jousts and tournaments.

It was not only with his hereditary magnates that, taught by his father's failure, Edward III achieved a working accord. Resolved to regain the dominions which his father had lost to his feudal overlord, the King of France, and having to go to war to do so, he set himself to woo the non-hereditary and elected representatives of the lesser taxpayers who, throughout his reign, he called to almost every meeting of Parliament. Summoned not by individual name like the lords and prelates, but by general writs addressed to the sheriffs, the seventy-four representative knights of the shire and the two hundred or so burgesses of the chartered towns at first behaved as very humble partners in the *universitas* of the realm. As late as 1348 they declined to advise the King on his conduct of the war as being 'too ignorant and simple to counsel on such important matters'. Yet entrusted, in the traditional words of the royal summons, 'with full and sufficient power for themselves and their respective communities to do and to consent to those things which in our Parliament shall be ordained', so stubbornly did they exercise their right to withhold consent to any new form of taxation which they had not approved – not only direct taxes on moveables but even custom duties in the royal demesnes – that, with a wartime Government's need for additional sources of revenue, they little by little became an indispensable part of the national machinery of 'counsel and consent'. The Crown's demands for money caused the representatives of two very different social groups, the land-owning warrior knights of the shires and the trading burgesses of the towns, to draw together for consultations on finance. In doing so they unwittingly created a single assembly representing the communities of both shire and borough. Thus unique among the rigidly divided class 'estates' which made up the parliaments of European kingdoms, by the end of Edward III's fifty years' reign they had grown into a permanent body, which in the next century became known as the House of Commons. Sitting separately from the Lords in their own chamber – at one time the Painted Chamber of the Palace of Westminster, at another the chapter house of the Abbey – in the course of the fifty or so Parliaments of the reign, they developed a procedure of their own, distinct from the parliamentary procedure of earlier days designed for the convenience of King and Council. This was largely due to the lawyers who, chosen by local communities to represent them because of their professional expertise, brought to the work of an evolving institution their habits of mental precision and insistence on procedure and precedent.

The members of the Commons thus acquired a corporate sense. Their first elected spokesman or Speaker appeared by the end of the reign. Though with their superior social status the knights of the shire led the debates, they constituted, with the burgesses, a single estate – the commonalty or *populus* of the realm as distinct from the Lords, and not, as in continental parliaments, two separate estates of knights and burgesses. They represented, not classes or callings, but localities and, by acting together for the 'common good', made the needs and views of those localities known to the Crown. Their influence and prestige were the greater because, even when, as sometimes happened, they were cadets of baronial families, the knights sat with the burgesses as commoners. More perhaps than any other factor this created a sense of national identity and common interest. It made it easy for Lords and Commons to act together, and hard for any monarch to encroach on the community's liberties by setting class against class. Without this, the tendency to absolutism inherent in the growing power of national monarchy might have become too strong to resist, as it did in almost every other European kingdom between the fourteenth and seventeenth centuries.

*   *   *

By observing the forms of parliamentary consultation and utilising the representative taxing assembly which his grandfather had created out of the Great Council of the realm, Edward III was able to put into the field a professional army better equipped and supported than anything possessed by feudal France with its far greater population and wealth. And in doing so, when the time came, he was able to resort to a novel weapon which, in the hands of his humbler subjects, was to prove a more deadly and accurate instrument of war than anything yet seen on Europe's battlefields. For by Edward I's Statute of Winchester, embodying the old Anglo-Saxon rule under which every free man between the ages of fifteen and sixty was expected to turn out in the shire levy with his personal arms to defend the realm and maintain the peace, the English countryman was trained to arms, unlike his counterpart in the feudal kingdoms of the continent, where fighting was the preserve of heavily armoured mounted nobles and knights and hired professional mercenaries.

The long-bow had first appeared in England at the end of the thirteenth century among the yeoman of Macclesfield and Sherwood forests, who had learnt its use from the Welsh hillmen during the wars of Edward I. Originally in its native Wales made of rough unpolished wild elm, in England it was usually of yew. Drawn not by strength of arm but of the whole frame, it seemed a weapon designed for the Anglo-Saxon Englishman's fine physique. The arrows it fired, a cloth-yard long, were plumed with the feathers of the geese which fed on the village greens:

'Their arrows finely pared, for timber and for feather,
With birch and brazil pierc'd to fly in any weather,
And, shot they with the round, the square or forkèd pile,
The loose gave such a twang, it might be heard a mile.'

By the time of Edward III's accession, after more than half a century of campaigning against the Welsh and Scots, the long-bow had become the popular English weapon *par excellence*. Archery competitions on feast days and holidays were a favourite recreation of the rustic commonalty, and later in the reign, under pressure of war, practice at the butts after Sunday service was enjoined by law. In the popular ballads of Robin Hood – the legendary North Country outlaw who lived with his merry men in the greenwood and robbed the rich but spared the poor – Robin was depicted as an unfailing marksman. 'Bend all your bows,' he bade his men,

> 'and, with the grey goose-wing,
> Such sport now show as you would do
> In the presence of the King.'

Thrice, we are told, at the sheriff's archery competition at Nottingham,

> 'Robin shot about
> And always sliced the wand.'

And when in the ballads he and his followers switched their aim from the butts to the sheriff's men who had tried to apprehend him at the moment of his triumph, the latter had to run for their lives under a hail of arrows.

It was the Scots who first encountered the power of this formidable new national weapon. Nineteen years after Robert Bruce's victory over England's chivalry at Bannockburn, a Scottish army was attempting to relieve Berwick, then besieged by the young English King. When, on 19 July 1333, it came within sight of the town, it found the English barring its path on the northern slopes of Halidon Hill. They were drawn up in a long thin line from which projected four triangular salients formed by archers, one on either flank and two in the centre. The three gradually narrowing funnels formed by these salients were closed at the summit of the hill by three brigades of dismounted armoured knights and men-at-arms, with banners and pennons fluttering above the sheen of their swords and lances. Behind them was a reserve brigade to deal with any attempt to drive in the archers on the wings, while in the rear, encircled by baggage-wagons, were laagers packed with horses awaiting a summons from their riders in the battle-line and guarded by the pages who looked after their masters' steeds and armour.

The trap thus set for the Scots proved as deadly as the Bannockburn bogs and the pits which Bruce had dug on the road to Stirling a generation before. For in the hands of English archers the longbow of Gwent had come of age, and Edward and his lords had found a way to turn it into a tactical arm of startling mobility and killing-power. One of them, the crusader Henry of Grosmont – son

of the King's cousin, the earl of Lancaster – had fought at Bannockburn, and it may have been this brilliant, imaginative commander
who first saw how the long-bow could be used to revolutionise the
art of war. What seems certain is that during those waiting weeks
while the English army was blockading Berwick, the archers, whom
Edward's commissioners of array had gathered from the northern
and midland counties and forests, were trained to manoeuvre and
exercise their art under orders, just as Bruce's pikesmen before
Bannockburn had been trained to fight the battle he had foreseen.
Brigaded with knights and men-at-arms from their native shires
and disciplined by veterans who had learnt war the hard way on
the Welsh and Scottish hills, they were taught to operate, not
merely as individual marksmen, but in massed phalanxes from
which, at the word of command, rhythmic volleys of arrows,
travelling at incredible speed, could be directed first at one part of
an attacking force, then at another, until every living thing in the
target area had been killed or maimed. In their metal helmets and
padded deerskin jackets, these light, active men could manoeuvre
in extended order, enfilade a column from flank or even rear and,
combining fire-power and movement, at a bugle call or other signal,
re-form, under cover of their comrades' volleys, in massed ranks
in which, so long as their ammunition lasted, they were virtually
unassailable.

As the Scottish pikesmen moved forward in dense schiltrons
across the marshy ground at the foot of the hill, they suddenly came
into range of the archers. Though hundreds fell as the showers of
steel-tipped arrows struck home, they pressed stubbornly on.
Lowering their heads against the blinding hail and closing their
ranks they instinctively edged away from the salients of archers on
either side and started to climb. Packed together till they were
almost suffocated, riven and tormented by the massed volleys from
the close formations into which the archers withdrew at every
attempt to attack them, they stumbled up the slope towards the
waiting line of English armour and the one place on the battlefield
where no arrows were falling. When, breathless from the ascent,
the survivors reached that hedge of levelled lances, the knights and
men-at-arms started to hack at them with their swords and battle-

axes, forcing them down the slope where they came once more into that enfilading hail. The Regent of Scotland was mortally wounded, and six of his earls left dead on the field. Altogether seventy Scots lords and five hundred knights and squires fell, and almost the entire infantry. The defenders lost one knight, one man-at-arms and twelve archers.

*   *   *

Four years after Halidon Hill – whose result was little noticed at the time outside the British Isles – England became involved in a long inconclusive war with France, caused by the refusal of King Philip Valois to restore to Edward his father's forfeited fiefs in Ponthieu, Guienne and the Agenais. During the past half-century France had become by far the most powerful state in western Christendom, with a population of over twelve millions, or four times that of England. She was the military, cultural, artistic and even religious leader of western Christendom; the papacy itself had been transferred from Rome to a French enclave on the Rhône where, in their palace at Avignon, a succession of French Popes wielded the authority of their Italian predecessors. While England had been engaged in her long costly attempt to conquer Scotland, Philip the Fair of France, seeking to extend her outer frontiers to the Pyrenees, Rhine and North Sea, had brought under his direct rule Champagne, Brie, Franche-Comté, the Lyonnais, Navarre and part of Lorraine. When he died in the year of Bannockburn, of the great outlying provinces of royal France only Flanders, Brittany and Gascony – the rump of the early Plantagenets' vast duchy of Aquitaine – remained independent fiefs.

To recover his lost feudal territories from his powerful continental neighbour, Edward at first relied on an alliance with the rulers of four small states in the borderland between Germany and France's northern frontiers: Brabant, whose reigning duke was his cousin, and Hainault, Gelderland and Juliers, with all of whom he was allied by his happy marriage to the Count of Hainault's daughter, Philippa. But though, with the forces they put into the field – heavily subsidised through taxes voted by English Parliaments – Edward and his knights 'rode against the tyrant of the

French with banners displayed', ravaging frontier villages and crops in revenge for the burning of English south-coast towns by Norman and Breton privateers, King Philip refused to give battle. Secure behind the fortifications of his northern cities, he merely watched these costly proceedings from the walls of Amiens, ignoring the English King's taunts and challenges. And presently the Hainaulters, Brabanters and Germans tired of the campaign and insisted on returning home for the winter, leaving Edward heavily in debt. 'Our allies,' he wrote in disgust to his son, 'would no longer abide.'

But during the winter of 1339–40 he had an unexpected stroke of fortune. Driven desperate by an embargo on the export of English wool to Flanders, under a rich Ghent merchant, James van Artevelde – a patriot rabble-rouser of the type which had recently risen to power in the Italian city-states – the unemployed workers of the Flemish cloth manufacturing towns rose against their pro-French count and drove him from the country. To save themselves from France's vengeance they then appealed to Edward for help, imploring him to assume the crown of France and so become their suzerain and protector.

It had been the defeat of the French chivalry at Courtrai in 1302 by the burghers and weavers of Bruges and Ghent – the despised 'blue nails' of the clothiers' factories, emulating Wallace at Stirling Bridge and fighting on foot with pikes – which close on half a century earlier had enabled Edward I to recover his Gascon dominions. Regardless of his debts his grandson now promised them arms, the removal of the English wool-staple from Antwerp to Bruges and a subsidy of £140,000. And to legalise their repudiation of homage and protect them from an interdict for their breach of feudal faith, he laid formal claim to the throne of his Capet ancestors. On 24 January 1340 he entered Bruges and was acclaimed by the burghers as king and overlord. Two weeks later, in a proclamation to 'the prelates, peers, dukes, counts, barons, gentle and simple dwelling in the realm of France', he announced that Philip of Valois 'had intruded himself by force' onto his throne while he had been 'of tender years', and that he was now resolved to regain it and 'with unshakeable purpose do justice to all men'.

SET IN A SILVER SEA

Henceforward he and his heirs quartered the fleur-de-lys of France before the leopards of England, bearing them in the semi-position on royal seal and surcoat.

Having secured his alliance Edward hurried home to obtain the wherewithal to finance it. So desperate were his straits that he was forced to leave his Queen and children and the earls of Derby and Salisbury at Antwerp as a pledge for his debts. His expenditure had by now almost drained England of specie. Yet his popularity was still sufficient to rouse the country. Though in the autumn, after being told by the Council that unless they helped him he would have to surrender himself to his foreign creditors, the Commons had asked for time to consult those they represented, they now joined with the magnates in giving him a ninth of every sheaf, fleece and lamb for two years, a ninth from the royal boroughs and a fifteenth from the rest of the community.

Yet they made their grant dependent on his answer to four petitions, one of which, by finally ending the Crown's right to tallage merchandise at will even in the royal demesmes, was a major step on the road to parliamentary control of taxation. In return for allowing Edward to collect the hated *maltote* for another fourteen months they received a promise that it should never be levied again 'except by common consent of the prelates, earls, barons and other lords and commons of the realm'.

Having obtained supplies for a new campaign, Edward prepared to return to the continent where the French were burning the towns and villages of Hainault and threatening Flanders. In his absence a fleet of nearly two hundred French, Genoese and Spanish ships had arrived off Sluys at the mouth of the Zwim to bar his passage and blockade the Flemings. Throughout the past year the position at sea and the raids on England's southern ports had been causing increasing anxiety; in the autumn of 1339 several of the King's own ships had been seized in the North Sea. In its debates, Parliament had stressed the country's maritime weakness and 'how the sea should be guarded against enemies so that they . . . should not enter the kingdom to destroy it'.

As it seemed that the King would have to fight his way back to Flanders, every ship that could be requisitioned was assembled at

Orwell and packed with archers and men-at-arms. Apart from a few royal cogs and galleys specially built for fighting – kept normally at Winchelsea and Portsmouth and administered from the Tower by an officer called the clerk of the King's ships – the fleet consisted of one-masted, single-decked merchant and fishing boats, most of them of under a hundred tons. Impressed by the sheriffs of the maritime countries, they had been adapted for battle by the addition of fighting-tops to the masts and timber superstructures at bow and stern called 'forecastles' and 'aftercastles', from which archers and slingers could shower arrows and stones on the enemy's crews and rigging and from which boarding parties could take off. In honour of the King these were brightly painted and adorned with golden lions. The two largest vessels were the flagship, the cog *Thomas*, and a 240-ton ship called the *Michel*, contributed by the Cinque Port of Rye.

Yet England was only in the second rank in naval force. Her fleet was far inferior to the armada lying off the Flemish coast. To cautious minds it seemed insanity for the King to attempt to break through it to Sluys by ramming and boarding its taller and more heavily manned ships – then the only known method of fighting at sea. Appalled by the shortage of money and reports that the French and Spaniards intended to capture his royal master, the Chancellor, Archbishop Stratford, begged him to abandon the voyage. Both admirals backed the archbishop's request. When the King refused, to his indignation Stratford resigned the seal. 'I will cross in spite of you,' Edward said, 'and those who are afraid where no fear is, may stay at home.'

The fleet sailed on Thursday 22 June 1340, reaching the mouth of the Zwin next day. 'About the hour of noon,' Edward wrote to his son, 'we arrived upon the coast of Flanders before Blankenberghe where we had a sight of the enemy who were all crowded together in the port of Sluys. And seeing that the tide did not serve us to close with them, we lay to all that night. On Saturday, St John's Day, soon after the hour of noon at high tide, in the name of God and confident in our just quarrel, we entered the port upon our enemies who had assembled their ships in very strong array.' There were so many of them, an eye-witness wrote, that 'their masts seemed like a great wood'.

Both sides fought as if on land. The English went in to attack, with wind, sun and tide behind them, in three columns, the King leading the centre in the cog *Thomas*, and each ship manned alternately with men-at-arms and archers. The French and Spanish ships were chained together in four lines across the estuary like the walls of a castle. Built for the Atlantic with high seaboards, they towered above their adversaries, their decks crowded with knights armed with lances and the rigging with stone-throwers and crossbowmen.

It was the English archers who decided the day. As they came into range, they loosed such a storm of arrows that the enemies' decks were strewn with dead before the boarding-parties reached them. So deadly was the marksmanship that many threw themselves into the water. Thousands were killed or drowned; only the Genoese, who had refused to anchor, managed to escape to sea. By morning two-thirds of the allied fleet had been taken or destroyed.

His victory at Sluys sent Edward's prestige soaring. Hitherto he had seemed to his fellow princes only a king of the tournament field and the Scottish moors; now he had proved himself in a major European battle. Though its consequences had still to be realised, he had broken the command of the Channel by the Bay of Biscay seamen. What mattered to him most was the opportunity offered by his victory for an invasion of France. On 18 July he entered van Artevelde's capital, Ghent, as a conquering hero. His Queen was there to greet him with a new-born son, who was to go down to history as John of Ghent or Gaunt.

Together the two men – English King and Flemish clothier – drew up plans for freeing the cities of Artois from the Valois. At the end of July they crossed the French frontier. While Robert of Artois, the exiled claimant to the fief, attacked St Omer, Edward and the German and Netherland princes laid siege to Tournai. But quarrels soon broke out between the allies. When, with the brusque impatience of the self-made, van Artevelde reproached the duke of Brabant for failing to storm the walls, the duke, furious at such low-born insolence, threatened to march his army away. It took all Edward's tact to restrain him. Meanwhile, instead of advancing to the relief of the town, Philip once more refused battle. When Edward challenged him to single combat, Philip merely reminded him of his broken homage.

The final blow to Edward's hopes came when money to pay his allies ran out just as Tournai seemed on the point of surrendering. At that moment the Abbess of Fontenelle – his mother-in-law and a dowager countess of Hainault – appeared in the allied lines with the Church's proposals for a truce. As there was no hope of any more English money, everyone except Edward welcomed her mission with enthusiasm. Such was her immense prestige, the respect felt for the Pope's wishes and the longing of the Netherland princes to return home before the winter, that in his penniless condition Edward was unable to stand out against them. By the truce of Esplechin the combatants agreed to withdraw for a year to their own boundaries, leaving everything as it was before the war, everything, that is, except the English King's and taxpayers' money which had gone beyond recall.

Furious, Edward laid the blame for everything that had happened on the ministers in England who had failed to send him the additional money for want of which the campaign had collapsed. Two summers before, when he first sailed for Brabant, he had issued from Walton in Suffolk a series of administrative ordinances which virtually placed the great permanent offices of state, the Exchequer and Chancery, under the control of the household officers of the Wardrobe and Chamber who accompanied him abroad. The great seal itself had been entrusted to his Keeper of the Privy Seal, William Kilsby. Kilsby was an ambitious and not over-scrupulous cleric who had pleased his master by his ingenuity in raising money. He was on bad terms with the Chancellor, John Stratford – mentor of Edward's early years as King – who since 1333 had also been Archbishop of Canterbury. This dislike was reciprocated by Stratford – the son of a Stratford-on-Avon burgess – who, with his brother, the bishop of Chichester, and his nephew, the bishop of London, formed a powerful family group within the Church and administration. When the archbishop resigned the Chancellorship before Sluys he had been succeeded by his brother and, after the King's return to Flanders, they had been left virtually in charge of England.

There were thus two governments, one at home representing the traditional elements, lay and ecclesiastical, through which the country was normally governed, and the other – in Flanders – composed of courtier-soldiers and the officers of the royal household. But in Edward's eyes the sole function of the first was to keep him supplied with money. Owing to the difficulty of obtaining payment from the overburdened taxpayer and the disappointing results of the wool subsidy, this had now become almost impossible. The growing arrears in the remittances from England and the 'anguish and peril in which the King, Queen and magnates of the host lay for lack of money', made the correspondence between the two branches of government increasingly acrimonious.

By the end of November, getting nothing but excuses in reply to his demands and reproaches, lacking the wherewithal to pay his troops and household, and dunned beyond endurance by his creditors, Edward decided to return, unannounced, to Westminster. Stealing away from Ghent with only eight followers – including Kilsby – he took boat at Sluys and, after a stormy three days' voyage, landed on the night of St Andrew's Day just before cockcrow at the Tower watergate. His temper was not improved by finding the governor absent. He at once ordered his arrest and began a furious investigation into the miscarriages of his ministers. Among those whom he summarily dismissed were the Chancellor, the bishop of Chichester, the Treasurer, the bishop of Coventry, the Chief Justices of the King's Bench and Common Pleas and several other judges, as well as a number of Chancery and Exchequer officials. He also arrested the financiers, William de la Pole and John Pulteney, who had failed to sell the wool he had requisitioned at a sufficiently high price. But his chief anger was reserved for Archbishop Stratford. Accusing him of having counselled him to 'cross the sea without provision of money and horses' and of then withholding supplies, in order to bring about his ruin, he was only with difficulty and, after being reminded of the penalties that would follow such an outrage, prevented from forcibly shipping him and his fellow bishops to Flanders as a pledge for his debts.

As it was, he laid charges against the primate of treason and conversion of public moneys and summoned him to answer at the

Exchequer. In place of the dismissed ministers he appointed a lay Treasurer, Sir Robert Parving, and a lay Chancellor – the first in English history – Sir Robert Bourchier. Both had served as knights of the shire, had held judicial appointments and could be trusted to do his will. Never again, he declared, would he employ anyone as chief minister whom he could not hang if guilty of felony.

Believing, or affecting to believe, that his life was in danger, Stratford took shelter with the monks of Christ Church, Canterbury. On the anniversary of Becket's death he preached a sermon in the cathedral on his martyred predecessor. And on New Year's Day 1341 he addressed a long letter to the King. 'You have had victory of your enemies of Scotland and France,' he told him, 'and at this day are held the most noble prince of Christendom. Consider well your great undertaking and the strong adversary you have, and the great peril of your land . . . Take it not ill, sire, that we send you so largely the truth, for we are moved to do this by the great affection which we have towards you, the safety of your honour and of your land, and, because it belongeth to us, for that we are, all unworthy though we be, primate of all England and your spiritual adviser.'

For while he protested his affection for his royal master, which seems to have been genuine, the archbishop did not shirk from telling him home truths. Though a worldling and a conciliator, he was also a man of courage who in the past had stood up to both Edward II and Queen Isabella and, at the risk of his life, defied the dictator, Mortimer. The veiled menace in his letter was unmistakable. 'Very gentle lord,' he wrote,

> 'may it please you to know that the most sovereign thing which holds kings and princes in due and fitting estate is good counsel. And let it not displease you to remember it in your time, for, by the evil counsel which our lord your father had, he caused to be taken, against the law of the land and the great Charter, the peers and other people of the land and put some to shameful death and of others he caused their goods to be seized . . . And what happened to him for that cause, sire, you know well.'

The archbishop was resolved not to let the underlying constitutional issues be obscured by the royal accusations against his honesty or by his dispute with the household 'intimates' who had poisoned the King's mind. Having been an Oxford doctor of law, a Chancery clerk and dean of the Court of Arches, he knew how to put the issue in its clearest and most compelling form. As in the crisis of 1297 and the days of the Despensers, the principle at stake was whether a King of England, good or bad, could govern without resort to established law and to those who could speak for the nation. 'By evil counsel,' he told the King, 'you begin to seize divers clerks, peers and other folk of the land. You make suit, quite unfitting and against the law of the land, which you are bound by the oath taken at your coronation to keep and maintain, and contrary to the great Charter.' The only place for judging such charges as Edward had brought against his chief subjects was Parliament – the national assembly in which an English King could look into the hearts and minds of his people. 'For the salvation of your enterprise,' he urged, 'be willing to take to you the great and the wise of your land . . . Be willing, sire, if it please you, therefore, to cause them . . . to assemble in a fitting place where we and others may securely come.' The Archbishop had been accused by his master; he was entitled to be judged by his peers in Parliament.

It was a tremendous claim, going to the root of the problem men had been trying to solve since the days of Magna Carta; of how to allow a King the overriding executive power on which the peace and safety of the realm depended and at the same time safeguard the rights and liberties of the subject. And though the angry King denounced Stratford as 'a wily serpent and cunning fox' and, with Kilsby's help, published a venomous attack on him, it soon became clear that the archbishop had judged the issue rightly. Once again, as in 1297 and 1327, magnates, knights of the shire and Londoners came together under the archbishop's lead to protest at a royal attempt to rule by personal will instead of by established law. Stratford's demand to be tried by his peers was a shrewd stroke, for it was a right which every magnate in the land wished to secure for himself.

So it came about that the national crisis set in motion by the King was resolved, as Stratford had proposed, in 'a full Parliament'.

Edward's need for supplies to meet his debts and maintain the Scottish war forced him to yield, and at the end of April the magnates and commons met at Westminster. When Kilsby tried to bar the primate from the House of Lords, John de Warenne, earl of Surrey, doyen of the independent magnates, and his nephew, the earl of Arundel, protested that those who by their rank should be foremost in Parliament were being excluded while others who had no right there were being admitted. 'Lord King,' Warenne is reported to have said, after the manner of his famous grandfather of *quo warranto* fame, 'how goes this Parliament? Things were not wont to be thus. They are all now turned upside down.' And though Stratford never received the trial *in pleno parliamento* which he had been demanding, since the King dropped his charges and, later, even had them annulled as contrary to truth and reason, the principle for which he had contended was triumphantly vindicated. It was Edward who, needing the support of his people, had had to submit to the judgment of Parliament. Seeing that, if he was to have their support in his wars, he must conciliate them, he yielded with grace and good sense.

Before the session ended in May, in reply to petitions from both Lords and Commons the royal assent was given to an Act which not only conceded the right of peers to trial by their fellow magnates in Parliament before suffering imprisonment or forfeiture, but made all ministers and officials of the Crown liable to answer to the same high court for breaches of Magna Carta and the statutes. The Commons also obtained a promise that parliamentary commissioners should audit the moneys voted for the war and that the Lords should share in the appointment of Ministers. Though the magnates later allowed the King to withdraw this last radical concession as unworkable and incompatible with the custom and law of the realm and the royal prerogative, Edward made no further attempt to govern without consultation with the nation's traditional leaders and his customary constitutional advisers.

*   *   *

So far, except for his victory at Sluys, the King's war to recover his French fiefs had been a costly fiasco. Nor, since France came to

Scotland's rescue, had his campaign to reduce the Scots to vassalage fared any better. While Parliament was discussing the royal
charges against the archbishop, Douglas's son, the knight of
Liddesdale, captured Edinburgh castle by the old ruse of blocking
the drawbridge with a supply-wagon. A few weeks later Bruce's
son, King David, now eighteen, returned from France. At the end
of 1341 the truce expired, and Edward took the field against him,
spending Christmas at Melrose abbey and afterwards 'riding'
through Ettrick forest in what the chronicler described as 'a very
ill season'. His foray into that war-wrecked, starving land achieved
nothing. By February 1342 the Scots were once more over the
border, raiding Northumberland where they 'brent much corn and
houses'. And at Easter, Alexander Ramsay of Dalhousie captured
Roxburgh, the last English stronghold in Scotland.

Yet that year, with the death of the duke of Brittany, a new
opportunity opened for England. When his younger brother, John
de Montfort, visited Windsor to obtain the earldom of Richmond
to which, under English law, he was heir, he secured from Edward
a promise of support for his claim to Brittany against the late duke's
son-in-law, Charles of Blois, who was backed by the French King
and French-speaking aristocracy against the Celtic-speaking
peasantry and townsfolk who favoured de Montfort. The crippling
of France's naval strength at Sluys had made the maintenance of
an English base in Brittany possible and, in the spring of 1342, after
a French army had overrun the duchy and captured de Montfort,
a small expedition was despatched to rescue his countess who was
besieged at Hennebont. Arriving just in time, its commander, Sir
Walter Manny, took the offensive. Later in the summer he was
joined by a larger force under the Constable, William Bohun, earl
of Northampton. With him came Edward's French protégé,
Robert of Artois, and his cousin, Henry of Derby – heir to the royal
earldom of Lancaster and the most famous English fighting man
of his day.

In Brittany the English had no longer to wait on their allies as
in Flanders. They were free to fight when they chose. If the enemy
outnumbered them they could apply the tactics which had proved
successful at Halidon Hill – a well-chosen defensive position, the

men-at-arms dismounted in the centre, the horses and baggage wagons in laager in the rear, the archers on either flank behind projecting hedges of stakes, to enfilade the attacking cavalry. Landing near Brest and forcing Charles of Blois to abandon the blockade of that town, Northampton laid siege to Morlaix. Here against a French relieving army seven or eight times as large as his own he won, on 30 September 1342, the first English victory on the continent since the days of Coeur-de-Lion. Fighting with their backs to a wood, his troops were at one time surrounded but, with their incomparable archery, shot their way out and put the French to flight. Morlaix fell almost immediately, while a hundred miles away, by a use of amphibious power, Robert of Artois captured Vannes, the second city of Brittany. A few weeks later this brave French exile, with his handful of Englishmen, was overwhelmed by superior force and died of his wounds.

By this time Edward himself was in Brittany. Having waited for several weeks at Sandwich for the return of Northampton's transports, which were held up by adverse winds, he had marched his troops to Portsmouth and seized enough ships to take them to Brest. Though it was now the end of October he at once took the field. Sweeping across the peninsula in two columns, one under his personal command, he recaptured Vannes and laid siege to Rennes, while a small flying force reached the walls of Nantes on the Loire.

With southern Brittany lost, King Philip was compelled to intervene. Gathering an army at Angers far larger than Edward's sea-borne expedition, he marched to the relief of Nantes and Rennes. The long-awaited test between the rival Kings seemed imminent when two cardinals arrived from papal Avignon to negotiate an armistice. As both armies were now running short of supplies, their mission proved successful. By the three-years' truce of Morbihan it was agreed that both sides should keep what they had won. De Montfort's supporters retained the southern and western parts of the country and those of Charles of Blois the northern and eastern. The truce was also extended to the chief participants' clients, Scotland and Flanders.

Though the war had now gone on for six years Edward had still made no impression on France, while Scotland was almost as free as in the days of Bruce. He had neither recovered his lost lands in Guienne nor unified Britain. Yet his dream of doing so and of winning immortal fame by arms remained. It may have been during his long and stormy voyage home, in which he narrowly escaped shipwreck on the Spanish coast, that he finalised the idea of founding an Order of Christian chivalry to perpetuate the ideals of his hero, King Arthur, and give expression to his desire for knightly glory. Nine months after his return, in January 1344, he held a tournament at Windsor 'for the recreation and solace of men of war who delight in arms'. During it he and nineteen of his bravest knights jousted for three days against all comers.

When Edward of Windsor set his heart on a project no trouble or expense was too great. Within a few weeks workmen were covering the bridges of the castle with sand for the passage of stone and timber to build a round tower crowning the Norman motte. On 16 February letters patent were issued to William of Ramsey, the King's master-mason – designer of the new octagonal lantern at Ely – and the royal carpenter, William of Hurley, empowering them to choose as many masons and carpenters from 'the cities, towns and other places in England' as they might need. Over seven hundred workmen were engaged at wages ranging from 4s. a week for master-masons to 2d. a day for labourers. And within the castle a huge circular table was made to accommodate the companions of the new knightly brotherhood at an annual Whitsuntide feast.

Yet Fate had more in store for England's King than to preside at tournaments. Before the year ended, contending with the same Celtic separatism in Brittany as Edward in Scotland, Philip seized de Montfort's chief supporters and put them to death. Escaping to England, de Montfort did homage to Edward as King of France and appealed to him to avenge the broken truce and recover his duchy. The challenge was accepted. While the Constable, Northampton, returned to Brittany with de Montfort, Edward himself, using his new-found freedom of movement at sea, prepared a triple attack on France from north, west and south. Despatching his cousin Henry of Grosmont, earl of Derby as lieutenant of Aquitaine to rally the loyal forces in Gascony, he sailed in July 1345 for Flanders with the fifteen-year-old Prince of Wales to take counsel with van Artevelde.

Once again the allies on whose aid he had counted failed him. After conferring with Edward on board his flagship at Sluys for a joint invasion of Artois, van Artevelde on his return to Ghent was murdered by a mob of discontented weavers. Though, bound to England by their need for its wool, the Flemish burghers eventually remained loyal to their alliance, Edward was forced to return home with his plans for attacking France from the north still-born.

But at this juncture events in south-western France took a spectacular turn. Landing at Bayonne in June 1345 and marching to Bordeaux, with five hundred men-at-arms and two thousand archers, Derby had been received with immense enthusiasm by the Gascons, who after six years of resisting the French had developed an almost passionate loyalty to their absent English duke. A soldier in the tradition of William the Marshal, simple, pious and courteous,[1] Henry of Derby had fought in every English campaign since Bannockburn and had been a crusader in Cyprus, Prussia and Granada. He was now forty-six – an age at which most men were then considered past fighting. But he had lost none of the fire and speed of youth. Assembling his little force at Libourne he suddenly struck eastwards at Bergerac, fifty miles up the Dordogne, where the French had withdrawn after his landing. Keeping the ramparts under continuous attack by his archers, he stormed the town at the end of August. Then, having regained most of the Agenais, he turned north against Périgord, where he established an outpost at Auberoche, only nine miles from the capital, Périgueux, before returning to Bordeaux with his prisoners and booty.

Derby's six weeks' campaign made an immense impression on southern France. So did his courteous treatment of his prisoners and the civil population. It aroused, too, the French military authorities to action. Early in October they laid siege to Auberoche with seven thousand men. Receiving an urgent appeal from its garrison, Derby at once gathered four hundred men-at-arms and

---

[1] At a time when literacy was only beginning to reach the aristocratic laity Henry was remarkable for writing two works of devotion, in one of which, *Mercy Gramercy*, he set down all the sins he could recall having committed and all the mercies he had received, asking God's forgiveness for the first and giving thanks for the second.

eight hundred archers and, ordering his second-in-command, the earl of Pembroke, to follow, marched at high speed to the relief of the town. Hiding his men in a wood, he waited twenty-four hours for Pembroke, then decided to attack without him rather than fail the garrison. Having made sure that every man knew what to do, he fell on the besiegers as they were cooking their evening meal, his archers spraying them with arrows and his men-at-arms charging out of the wood with shouts of 'A Derby! A Derby!' In the confused fighting which followed, the enemy's superiority in numbers was beginning to tell when the garrison threw themselves on the besieger's rear. By nightfall the French commander and all his lieutenants were prisoners, including eight viscounts and the flower of the Languedoc nobility. "There were many a proper feat of arms done,' wrote Froissart, 'many taken and rescued again . . . If the night had not come on, there had but few escaped. No English man-at-arms but had two or three prisoners.'

Striking once more, Derby turned south to take La Réole in the Garonne valley, thirty miles above Bordeaux. Without a proper siege-train he succeeded after ten weeks, not only in capturing the town – for years a standing threat to the capital – but in bluffing the garrison into the belief that the walls had been undermined, whereas his miners had found them so strongly built as to be impregnable. In this way he made himself master of the strongest fortress on the Garonne.

With Aiguillon, thirty miles up the river, already taken by Lord Stafford, the entire Agenais had been cleared. In four months two provinces and fifty towns and castles had been regained by a few thousand archers and men-at-arms. Derby, who that autumn inherited his father's earldom of Lancaster, had proved that France was no longer invulnerable. For the first time since John's loss of Normandy a French King had been forced to take England's military threats seriously. By the spring of 1346 the whole chivalry of southern France was mobilised at Toulouse under Philip's eldest son, the duke of Normandy, to recover his lost province.

*   *   *

Meanwhile, fired by the success of his soldiers and resolved to share

238

in their glory, Edward himself was preparing to strike. His brilliant cousin had given him the chance for which he had been waiting nine years. While that April the Dauphin laid siege to Aiguillon, and Derby, with only a fraction of his force, watched from La Réole for a chance to relieve the tiny garrison, Edward started to assemble on the Hampshire coast the largest army that had ever sailed from England. He raised it, not by the feudal levy of the past nor even by over-much reliance on the commissions of array which Edward I had adapted to conscript the shire militia for war, but by offering those willing to fight high wages and still more tempting prospects of ransom and plunder.

He was able to do so because he had learnt from experience the value of the representative taxing assembly which his grandfather had created out of the Great Council of the realm. By observing the forms of parliamentary consultation, and ruling with the advice of the great officers of Church and state in whom the taxpayers' representatives reposed their trust, he could now obtain the wherewithal to raise a professional army far superior in quality to anything feudal France could put into the field. Developed during the past half-century in the course of many a bitter tussle between Crown and taxpayer, a system of taxation by consent gave to the English King financial resources unknown to his Valois rival, though the latter ruled a kingdom far richer and more populous.

Having the nation's financial resources behind him, Edward was able to make a royal campaign a national one. He raised his army by indentures made with local leaders with a vocation for war, under which they recruited, at agreed rates of pay, the precise numbers and types of fighting men required. Each indenture specified the number to be raised, the time for which they were to serve and the contribution to be made by the Exchequer. The contingents thus raised were known as 'retinues'. An earl, who was paid eight shillings a day for his services, would contract to raise, say sixty men-at-arms, of whom ten should be knights and a hundred and twenty bowmen, all equipped and with horses, for three months to a year 'at the accustomed wages of war', together with pages called *valets aux armes* who served as apprentices to the knights, cleaned their armour and looked after their horses when dismounted.

The rates of pay were high. At a time when in some places land let for as little as fourpence an acre a year, a mounted archer received sixpence a day if he provided his own horse – or threepence otherwise. Even the Welsh spearmen, the lowest grade of professional fighting men, were paid twopence. The wage of a mounted man-at-arms was a shilling a day, of a knight-bachelor twice as much, of a banneret four shillings a day. Bannerets were knights of proved valour and experience who, distinguished by a rectangular banner, arrayed and directed contingents in the field, commanded castles and acted as staff officers to the commanders-in-chief. Such were Sir John Chandos and Sir Robert Knollys, the Cheshire yeoman who rose to be one of the most famous captains of the age and, through ransom and plunder, one of the richest.

Knights carried a triangular pennon and led the men-at-arms or armoured troopers who, like them, usually provided their own horses and horse-armour. They were armed with a long sword and either a lance or battle-mace, with a dagger for in-fighting. The mail-armour of the past was now giving way to plate-armour; a knight in the 1340s wore a short surcoat marked with his armorial bearings and a baldric or sword-belt over a metal breast-plate, plate-guards for his arms and legs, and on his head a heavy helm crowned with his crest and closed, when in action, with a vizor. There is a picture of one in the Luttrell psalter, bidding farewell to his lady before a tournament, his charger magnificently decked in heraldic trappings.

The archers who, as a result of their spectacular successes, had by now become the largest part of every English army, wore either light steel breast-plates or padded hauberks of boiled leather, rough frieze cloaks and steel caps, not unlike the splinter helmets of modern infantrymen. In addition to their bows and sheaves of goose-quill arrows, they carried short swords, knives and steel-tipped stakes for building protective hedges against cavalry.[1]

[1] There is a contemporary picture of one, the yeoman, in *The Canterbury Tales* of Geoffrey Chaucer, who had served in youth as a page in one of Edward III's military expeditions to France.

'And he was clad in coat and hood of green,
A sheef of peacock arrows bright and keen
Under his belt he bare full thriftily.
Well could he dress his tackle yeomanly;
His arrows droppèd not with feathers low,
And in his hand he bare a mighty bow.'

Though they fought in separate contingents or phalanxes, for purposes of recruitment and discipline they served under the lords or knights who paid them, the army's disciplinary unit being a 'lance'[1] – a professional team, rather like the crew of a modern aircraft, consisting of a knight or man-at-arms, two archers, a swordsman or *courtillier*, and a pair of pages armed with daggers.

The army was also accompanied by auxiliaries: Welsh spearmen and light unarmoured horsemen called *hobelars* – often drawn from Ireland – for reconnaissance and terrorising the country; miners from Durham and the Forest of Dean for siege-operations, smiths, armourers and pavilioners, carpenters for making bridges, *cementarii* for building fortifications, and wagoners for the baggage-train. The King himself was accompanied by a bodyguard of personal knights and archers and a band of minstrels – a dozen trumpeters, a clarioner, fiddler, pipers, a wait or two, a nakerer, a citole and a man playing a shawm. For their services to morale these musicians ranked as archers.[2]

Running through this English army and transcending differences of rank and class was a new-found pride in common nationhood. Two-thirds of those who served in it were yeomen armed with a weapon which, as Morlaix and Auberoche had proved, could match, and more than match, the proud feudal cavalry which had lorded it in Europe for three centuries. Leading them were the representatives of all the great feudal houses – Bohun and Beauchamp, Warenne and Arundel, Mortimer, Despenser, Ufford, Hastings, de Vere – whose ambitions and jealousies in the last generation had all but wrecked the realm, but who, won over by their young King's generosity and magnanimity, were now united behind him and ready to follow him anywhere. Among them were his father's one-time jailers, the lords Berkeley and Maltravers, and the sixteen-year-old grandson of Roger Mortimer, to whom he had restored the fallen traitor's castle of Radnor and other lands.

Such was the force, prepared with all the King's tireless drive and attention to military detail, which with its bright pavilions and

[1] From this our modern rank of lance-corporal derives.
[2] A naker was a kettledrum; a citole a plucked-string instrument, the ancestor of the guitar; and a shawm a wind one, ancestor of the oboe.

banners, encamped that May and June on Southsea common, waiting for a wind to carry it to the continent. Some imagined that its destination was Brittany. Others thought that the King would sail to Flanders where that June the men of Ghent, Bruges and Ypres had agreed to invade Artois and to whose aid he had recently sent six hundred archers. But most supposed the royal host was bound for Gasgony where the earl of Pembroke and Sir Walter Manny were still holding out in Aiguillon against the Dauphin's vast army while Lancaster, with a few thousand archers and men-at-arms at Le Réole, barred the road to Bordeaux.

Yet Edward intended none of these things. When, at long last, on 11 July 1346, the south-westerly winds changed and the great armada of seven hundred vessels sailed from St Helens, sealed orders opened at sea revealed that its destination was the Cotentin peninsula of Normandy, the rich duchy once owned by Edward's Norman ancestors and lost by King John. By ravaging it and threatening Paris he could draw the Dauphin's army from Aiguillon and, linking hands with the Flemings in Artois, strike at France from three sides.

By the secrecy with which he had cloaked his plans, the King had kept the French guessing. Having to guard eight hundred miles of coastline from the Garonne to the Scheldt their fleet was strong nowhere; Edward's, concentrated in one place, was able to put the army ashore on 12 July at St Vaast near La Hogue almost without opposition. Once ashore he wasted no time. On the 18th, after knighting the Prince of Wales and some of his young companions, he began his march on Rouen. Crossing the marshes at the south-eastern foot of the Cotentin peninsula, he reached St Lo on the 22nd. By keeping abreast with the army's left flank the fleet provided a moveable base, while the troops lived on the countryside, avenging the raids of Norman seamen on the English south-coast towns by burning their harbours and ships. The Welsh spearmen and Irish *hobelars* particularly distinguished themselves in this atrocious business – the usual accompaniment of fourteenth-century warfare – though after a few days, the King, as claimant to the French throne, issued an order threatening death to any soldier who should 'set on fire towns or manors, rob churches or holy places, do harm to the aged, the children or women of his realm'.

Edward's new French subjects, however, showed no enthusiasm for their would-be sovereign. The peasants fled in terror from his march and, when on 25 July he summoned Caen, the bishop of Bayeux tore up the summons and imprisoned his messenger. Yet, though a formidable town – larger, a chronicler wrote, than any English city save London – the invaders carried it in a day after the archers had out-shot the crossbowmen defending the Orne crossings, and the fleet, sailing up the river from Ouistreham, had joined in the fight. They took a rich haul of prisoners and a copy of a treaty made eight years before by King Philip with the Norman authorities for an invasion of England, which Edward sent home to be read in Parliament.

On the last day of July the march to the Seine was resumed. On 2 August the army reached Lisieux. But on the same day the French King entered Rouen forty miles ahead, interposing his force between the English and their Flemish allies who, two hundred miles to the north, were just setting out from Ypres. As soon as news had reached him of Edward's landing King Philip had raised the oriflamme at St Denis and, summoning the Dauphin from Aiguillon to join him, had hurried to the Norman capital, gathering troops as he marched. The Seine here was three hundred yards wide and, with the city held in force, the English could not hope to cross.

Instead, on reaching the river at Elboeuf, twelve miles above Rouen, they turned upstream to seek a narrower crossing. By doing so they abandoned their communications with England but threatened Paris. For the next six days the rival armies marched south-westwards along opposite sides of the Seine. Everywhere the English found the bridges demolished or strongly held. But on the 13th, when they were only a dozen miles from the capital, Edward allowed the French to outmarch him and, by a sudden feint, turned back to Poissy, where the bridge, only partially destroyed, was lightly guarded. Crossing by a single sixty-foot beam only a foot wide, Northampton the Constable got a detachment to the far side. For the next two days, while skirmishing parties set fire to St Cloud and other villages under the western walls of Paris to deceive the enemy, the carpenters worked feverishly to repair the bridge. Meanwhile, though by now in far superior strength, King Philip remained in a frenzy of indecision, marching first to one side of his capital and then the other, uncertain whether the English were about to assault it or to move south to relieve Aiguillon.

On 15 August the carpenters finished their work, and during that night and next morning the army and its baggage train crossed the Seine. In the next five days it marched seventy miles due north, hoping to cross the Somme between Amiens and Abbeville and join hands with the Flemings who were besieging Béthune, fifty miles beyond that river. But though he had been temporarily out-witted, when he found that his foe had crossed the Seine, King Philip acted with equal speed. Realising at last Edward's relative weakness, he covered the seventy-three miles from Paris to Amiens in three days, ordering the feudal levies of the north to join him there. With him were the flower of France's chivalry, together with King John of Bohemia and his son, Charles of Moravia – titular King of the Romans.

The position of the English was now grave in the extreme. Between them and their Flemish allies in Artois lay the marshy valley of the Somme, with the French King at Amiens only a day's march away and every bridge over the river in his hands. All contact had been lost with the fleet, whose seamen, with their usual indiscipline, had returned to England in the wake of the ships that had taken home the sick and the spoils of Caen. The army's food supplies were almost exhausted and in the closing stages of their march the troops had been living on unripe fruit. After covering nearly three hundred miles their boots were worn out and the horses dying for lack of forage.

Edward had been far too bold. Yet he showed no sign of his anxiety. On 23 August he started westwards in the hope of finding a crossing above Abbeville but, as the estuary here widened to two miles, the prospect was unpromising. Scarcely had he set out when news arrived that Philip had left Amiens and was moving up the south bank after him, and had almost reached the village where the English had spent the previous night.

Cut off in a strange land and without maps – a military commodity then unknown – the King ordered the prisoners to be brought before him and offered a huge reward for anyone who would reveal a crossing place. A native told him of a submerged causeway across the estuary at Blanchetaque, midway between Abbeville and the sea, where at low tide a man could cross waist-deep. Without hesitation Edward decided to take the risk.

Before dawn on the 24th the English advance-guard reached the ford. The far bank was held by a French force of more than three thousand men. As soon as the tide was low enough for a man to stand without being swept away, the troops started to cross, led by Hugh Despenser, whose father had been hanged on a fifty-foot gallows by Edward's mother.[1] Carrying their bows above their heads to keep them dry, the archers struggled through a mile and a half of water, while the knights followed on horseback. A few hundred yards from the northern bank they came within range of the enemy's cross-bowmen but continued to advance till they were within killing distance. Then, standing ten abreast on the causeway and shooting over one another's heads, they loosed their usual devastating hail. When their arrows were exhausted they stepped into the deeper water on either side and let the mounted armour splash past them into the shallows where, after a brief skirmish, it put the French cavalry to flight. Meanwhile on the south bank Edward's rearguard had been holding off the advance echelons of Philip's host until the baggage-wagons, with their precious load of arrows, had passed through the water now starting to rise. Save for a few stragglers caught by the tide the whole army passed over in safety. Barred by the rising flood, the enemy could only watch in amazement.

That night the English encamped in the forest of Crécy in Edward's confiscated hereditary fief of Ponthieu. Though his troops were still short of rations, their morale was high, for in a deeply religious age the passage of the river had seemed a miracle.

---

[1] He lies in his armour of alabaster, his hands crossed in prayer and a lion at his feet, in the Despenser tomb in Tewkesbury Abbey, whose glorious vaulting posterity owes to his and his wife's munificence. He died in the first Black Death three years after Crécy.

Rather than resume his march to his allies in the north, the King therefore decided to stand and give battle. The odds against him were enormous, but with so cautious an adversary the opportunity might never recur.

All day on Friday the 25th, while the French were crossing the Somme, Edward searched for a defensive position. He found one on a low ridge facing south-west, between the villages of Crécy and Wadicourt. Behind lay forest into which his woodland-trained archers could withdraw in case of need.

On the morning of 26 August 1346, having attended mass, Edward marched his army to its position. He had now about thirteen thousand men, more than two-thirds of them archers, with, at the outside, some three thousand armoured knights and men-at-arms. These he deployed in three divisions or 'battles', two of them a little way down the forward slope of the ridge, which was about a mile long, and the third under his personal command in reserve. He himself took station in a windmill in the centre, with an extensive view of the valley which the French would have to cross. The right-hand division was under the earls of Warwick and Oxford, with the sixteen-year-old Prince of Wales in titular command, and the other under the Constable. As usual, the knights and men-at-arms were dismounted in single line, their horses being taken by the pages to the wagon-leaguer in the rear.

Forming four projecting salients on both flanks of each of the forward divisions were the archers, along whose lines, before they withdrew to the leaguer, the baggage-wagons unloaded a supply of arrows. To protect themselves from cavalry, they hammered in iron-pointed stakes and dug pot-holes as the Scots had taught their predecessors to do. Such a formation, like that at Halidon Hill, was calculated to force the attackers into two narrowing gulleys at the top of which they would have to contend with the armour while raked by arrows from the flanks.

When the troops were all posted, the King rode along the ranks on a small palfrey, carrying a white wand and wearing a crimson surcoat of golden leopards. To each contingent he spoke a few words. Beside him was Sir Guy de Brian, bearing the dragon banner of Wessex – the standard under which the English had fought at Hastings. It was a symbol of the national character Edward had given his army. 'Next to God,' it was said of him, 'he reposed his confidence in the valour of his subjects.' Norman, Angevin, Saxon and Celt, his men all thought of themselves as Englishmen.

After the King's inspection the army dispersed for the midday meal which the cooks had been preparing in the baggage-leaguer, the men-at-arms leaving their helmets to mark their stations and the archers their bows and arrows. It had been arranged that the trumpets should recall them at the first sign of the enemy, who were now believed to be moving up from Abbeville. During the afternoon there was a heavy shower, which brought the archers scurrying back to their lines to guard their bowstrings, each man unstringing his and placing it in a coil under his helmet. Afterwards the sun came out and the men sat down in their lines with their weapons in front of them. There was still no sign of the French, and it was felt that there would be no battle that day.

But a little before four o'clock the trumpets sounded and everyone stood to arms. Coming out of the woods three miles to the south-east along the track still known as *le chemin d'armée* was the French vanguard. For a whole hour the English watched as Philip's immense host moved into view, 'the fresh shining armour, the banners waving in the wind, the companies in good order, riding a soft pace'. According to the lowest estimate that has come down from the fourteenth century, they were forty thousand strong, of whom more than twelve thousand were mounted knights and men-at-arms. They rode in eight successive divisions, so that there seemed no end. The advance-guard was commanded by the blind King John of Bohemia – a romantic figure and world-famous warrior – who was accompanied by the French King's brother, the count of Alençon, and the count of Flanders whom Edward's allies, the burghers of Ghent, had driven from his country.

The King – 'Philip Valois, tyrant of the French', as the English chroniclers called him – followed with the rearguard, together with the German King of the Romans, Charles of Moravia, and the exiled King of Majorca. There were nearly a score of ruling counts, French, German, Luxemburg and Spanish. It was not so much a national army as the embodiment of the international chivalry which for three centuries had dominated the battlefields of the continent, commanded by the greatest monarch in Christendom. Above him waved the oriflamme – the sacred banner flown when no quarter was to be given to France's enemies. For there had been disputes on the previous night about the allocation and ransom of the prisoners, and to prevent quarrelling the King had given orders to slay them all.

In addition to this array of chivalry there marched among the vanguard six or seven thousand Genoese crossbowmen, the best trained troops on the continent and the only professionals in the host. The rest of the army was composed of peasant levies – the 'communes' as they were called – low-spirited serfs considered incapable of standing up to gentlemen, but useful to follow in the wake of their mounted superiors and help crush the foe by sheer weight of numbers. In the French army infantry were despised; it was knights – 'the crested helmets' – who alone counted.

Goliath was pitted against David, but David had a sling. David, too, had discipline, which Goliath lacked. When the French vanguard reached the valley in front of the English position the sun was already starting to sink, and Philip's advisers urged him to halt for the night and deploy for battle in the morning. To this – the only sane course – the King, who had not expected to find the English barring his path, agreed. But his vassals had other views. Seeing the English with their banners on the ridge, the young knights, arrogant and inexperienced, pressed forward, impatiently confident that they were at their mercy. Before even a blow had been struck the French army was out of control and committed to an attack undeployed.

The vanguard, therefore, came straight on, halting only to let the Genoese bowmen open the attack. With trumpets and clarions sounding they started to climb the ridge. The setting sun was in their eyes, and it was hard to focus their target, waiting motionless and ready.

At this point, wrote Froissart, 'when the Genoese began to approach, they made a great leap and cry to abash the Englishmen. But they stood still and stirred not for all that. Then the Genoese

248

again the second time made another leap and a fell cry and stept forward a little, and the English removed not one foot. Thirdly again they leapt and cried and went forward till they came within shot; then they shot fiercely with their crossbows. Then the English archers stept forth one pace and let fly their arrows so wholly together and so thick that it seemed snow.' Firing four or five times faster than the crossbowmen, they shot them out of the field.

As the Genoese broke, the French knights, with a cry of 'Ride down the rascals', charged through their ranks, trampling down the wounded and dying. They rode in a dense, glittering line of solid armour, waving plumes and levelled lances. Everyone expected them to crush the thin, defending line of the Prince of Wales's division before them. But they never reached it. For once again the English archers stepped forward.

As their arrows, aimed at the chargers, struck home, the stately advance dissolved into disorderly heaps and clusters of dead and wounded horses and of dismounted knights weighed down by their armour. Those who went forward on foot, or succeeded in driving their terrified beasts through the hail of arrows, came up against a solid line of English men-at-arms, as steady as the archers who continued shooting down each new batch of attackers as they struggled up the hill through the fading light.

The fight had now become general, with the second French wave assailing the Constable's division. But everywhere the result was the same: the mounted knights struggling to reach and break the line of defenders' armour and the archers continuing to massacre their horses. There was no one to give the attackers orders or co-ordinate the attack. For five hours, though darkness had fallen, the mêlée continued, wave after wave of knights entering the fight only to meet the same fate. At one moment it looked as if the Prince of Wales's slender force would be overwhelmed, and Godfrey de Harcourt hurried across to the nearest unit of the Constable's division to beg its commander to make a flanking attack to relieve the pressure. But when a similar appeal reached the King, he only remarked. 'Let the boy win his spurs', for he knew that the moment to throw in his reserves had not yet come.

When the messenger returned he found the Prince and his commanders leaning quietly on their swords, taking breath as, amid mounds of French corpses, they waited for the next attack.

Soon after midnight, after fifteen or sixteen assaults had failed, the French army began to dissolve. The dead were now piled in walls before the English lines. Among them was the blind King of Bohemia, the reins of his bridle tied to those of the knights with whom he had charged. Two archbishops, the royal count of Alençon, the duke of Lorraine and the counts of Blois and Flanders had all fallen. King Philip himself, his horse shot under him, was led from the field as Edward II had been from Bannockburn. There was no pursuit, for the English King, who had never once lost his grip on the battle, had forbidden his men to break rank.

As the French melted away into the darkness and no more attacks came, the exhausted victors lay down, supperless and waterless, to sleep where they had fought. When, on the misty morrow, they counted the dead, they found the bodies of more than fifteen hundred knights and ten thousand common soldiers. The French army had ceased to exist. Edward himself, with his son, attended the burial of John of Bohemia – a paladin after his own heart who had long predicted that he would die in battle against the bravest knights in the world. His helm-plume of ostrich feathers has ever since graced the arms of the Princes of Wales.

A new phenomenon had appeared in the western world: the military power of England. 'The might of the realm,' wrote the astonished Froissart, 'most standeth upon archers which are not rich men.' The English had shown that on their own ground they could conquer against any odds and almost without cost. Their losses at Crécy were fantastically low; the official figure was forty dead, only three of them men-at-arms.

Edward was now free if he chose, to lay waste the Île-de-France and attack Paris. But he would not be able to reduce the city itself, as he was without catapults and a seige-train. The alternatives were to strike south to join his victorious cousin in Guienne, or resume his interrupted progress towards his Flemish allies. Fifty miles north of Montreuil, where he marched his army after Crécy, lay the port of Calais. Commanding the Dover strait, the haunt of pirates who preyed on the vital trade between London and Flanders, it was the nearest continental harbour to England. If it could be turned into an English settlement the islanders would possess a permanent door into France.

The *annus mirabilis* of 1346 ended with one more victory. Earlier Philip had invoked the Franco-Scottish alliance and called on King David of Scotland to invade England. In the belief that Edward had drained the country of troops, the young Scots King crossed the border. After burning Lanercost abbey he struck eastwards across the moors into the Durham plain. Here, on 17 October, just outside the cathedral city at what became known as Neville's Cross, he encountered an English army under Archbishop de la Zouche of York, the warden of the Marches Lord Percy, and Lord Neville of Raby. Once more the English archers proved irresistible, annihilating every schiltron in turn, as with stubborn courage, the Scots pikesmen in packed ranks faced that hail of driven steel and goose-quill. By nightfall, both King David, wounded in the face by an arrow, and the famous Black Rood of Scotland, were in the victors' hands. Her Constable, the Marshal and two earls were among the dead, and three other earls taken prisoner. Only the Steward escaped.

*   *   *

The next year Edward spent systematically besieging Calais, raising his expeditionary force to more than thirty thousand men and requisitioning more than half the country's ships and fifteen thousand seamen. At the beginning of August 1347, after he had beaten off a last desperate attempt by the French King to relieve it, the city surrendered from starvation. It was then that the famous incident of the Calais burghers occurred, Queen Philippa kneeling before her victorious lord to obtain their pardon as they stood in front of him, bareheaded and barefooted with halters round their necks. Thereafter Edward made Calais what it was to remain for the next two centuries, an English town. He sent those of its inhabitants likely to oppose his rule to the nearest French territory and offered English traders incentives to settle in their stead. He left the town its old franchise, under which magistrates were elected by the leading householders, promised to respect its customs and appointed an English governor. He also transferred the staple there, making it the sole port for the export of wool, tin, lead and cloth to northern Europe. With both sides of the Straits of Dover in his hands he could now claim with some justice to be lord of the narrow seas. On his new gold coin, the noble, issued four years after his victory at Sluys, he appears standing in a ship crowned with sword in hand.

In October 1347, he returned to England. For two dazzling years victory had crowned her every effort: a few thousand of her sons, most of them humble countrymen armed with a weapon which they alone could use with effect, had again and again overcome almost inconceivable odds and laid the chivalry of the first kingdom in Christendom in the dust. Two months after his return from Calais, Edward ordered for himself and the knights of his new Round Table twelve garters of royal blue embroidered with the cross of St George. They wore their insignia for the first time at a tournament at Eltham in January 1348 when nine of the original founders jousted before the King, among them the young Prince of Wales – known from his armour as the Black Prince – and the liberator of Gascony, now earl of Lancaster, who, in three brilliant campaigns against impossible odds, had recovered for the Crown four great provinces, overrun half Poitou, including its capital Poitiers, and carried the English power almost to the gates of Toulouse.

CHAPTER FIFTEEN

War's Nemesis

'There is full many a man that crieth "War,
war", that wot full little what war amounteth.
War at his beginning hath so great an entering
and so large that every wight may enter when him
liketh and lightly find war. But, certes, what end
that shall thereof befall, it is not light to know.'

Chaucer

WHILE THE ENGLISH, after their miraculous victory at Crécy and
their spectacular conquests in southern France, were besieging
Calais, another army two thousand miles away had been blockading
a small Genoese grain port in the Crimea where a band of traders,
operating at the end of the seven-thousand-mile caravan route
from China, had taken refuge from the Tartar horsemen of the
Steppes. Suddenly the besiegers had been struck down by a
pestilence which, spreading everywhere through Tartary and
known as 'the death', had begun, it was believed, in the putre-
faction of unburied multitudes in the wars and earthquakes of
China and Central Asia. Before they raised the siege the Tartars
are said to have catapulted infected corpses into the town.

What is certain is that the disease was carried into Europe at
the end of 1347 or beginning of 1348 by Genoese ships trading
with the Black Sea. No one knew its exact cause or even its nature,
but it is now known to have been bubonic plague – a flea-borne
epidemic of the black rat which had invaded Europe from Asia
at the time of the crusades and with which the wooden trading-
ships of the day were heavily infested. By the time vessels that had

called in the Crimea reached the Bosphorus and Mediterranean the plague was raging among their crews, and every port at which they touched became infected. It struck so suddenly that at first no one had time to escape. The symptoms were a gangrenous inflammation of the lungs, vomiting and spitting blood, vilely infected breath and the appearance, on the second day, of hard black buboes in the arm-pits and groin which were almost always the heralds of death. Few who caught the disease in its first onslaught outlived the third day.

By the end of January 1348 the plague was raging in all the great ports of southern Europe, including Venice, Genoa, Marseilles and Barcelona. In the Mediterranean, ships were found drifting with every member of the crew dead. One after another, despite frantic attempts to isolate themselves, the Italian cities went down before the pestilence. In the spring, having made Venice and Genoa cities of the dead, the plague reached Florence. In the introduction to his *Decameron*, Boccaccio left a first-hand picture of its horrors: the helplessness of the doctors, the stench of the sick, the cautious shutting themselves up in their houses until the infection crept in and the reckless drinking in taverns day and night, the multitude of corpses lying uncovered before every church and the pits into which the dead were packed in layers. The poor perished in the streets or among the crops, the swine rooting in the deserted streets dropped dead as they nosed the bundles of rags stripped from the plague-stricken, and swarms of oxen, sheep and goats – 'and even dogs, those most faithful friends to men' – wandered untended through the fields. The dying were abandoned, the dead were dragged out of the houses and stacked by the roadside, the houses of those who had fled were left open to all, 'the reverend authority of the laws, divine and human, being almost wholly ruined and dissolved'.

All that summer of 1348 the Black Death was drawing nearer to England. In the spring it reached Gascony where it struck down King Edward's youngest daughter, the Princess Jean, who was on her way to Spain to marry the heir of Castile. Soon afterwards it broke out in Paris where vast multitudes died, including the Queens of France and Navarre. By July, creeping north through

Poitou and Brittany and round the coasts, it was in Normandy, where 'it came to such a pass that no one could be found even to carry the corpses to the tomb. People said that the end of the world had come.' All the while clouds and continuous rain poured down on England and, towards the end of the month as men watched the ports, Archbishop de la Zouche of York wrote to his deputy ordering processions and litanies to be held in all parish churches twice a week 'for the stay of pestilence and infection'.

Yet life in England that summer seems to have gone on very much as usual. In days when news travelled only by word of mouth and was carried from village to village along the grass roadways by friars and pedlars, the people of an isolated northern island can have heard little of the fate that had befallen their fellow Christians beyond the Channel. Absorbed in their local affairs, they were more concerned about the weather, the ruin of their crops and the murrain which had broken out among the sheep and cattle. Even the King, who must have been aware of the danger, seemed obsessed with his magnificent building projects for housing the college of his new Order of the Garter. On 6 August, he issued orders for the conversion of St Edward the Confessor's chapel, Windsor, into one 'of befitting splendour' and for the provision of accommodation for the additional canons and twenty-four 'helpless and indigent knights'.

It may have been on that very day that, despite every precaution by the port authorities, the plague crossed the Channel. Some time early that August it broke out in the little Dorset coast town of Melcombe Regis, now Weymouth, 'depriving it almost of inhabitants'. Within a few weeks it reached Bristol, probably by sea, turning it into a mortuary. It treated England as it had treated western Europe, and the English reacted in the same way. At Bristol 'the living were scarce able to bury the dead', and 'the men of Gloucester would not suffer the Bristol men to have access to them'. But no constable's guard could stop the swift-running rats from infecting one another, or their parasites from deserting their putrescent bodies for living men and women. Nor had anyone any idea what caused the mortality: the pallor, the sudden shivering and retching, the dreaded scarlet botches and black boils – 'God's

255

tokens' – the delirium and unbearable agony which came without warning and carried off its victims in a few hours.

During that autumn the plague struck down southern shire after shire. Dorset and its adjoining counties suffered terribly; Poole was so depopulated that it did not recover for more than a century – a hundred years ago a projecting strip of land known as the Baiter was still pointed out as the burial-place of its victims. In some villages, like Bishopstone in Wiltshire, scarcely a soul survived, and when life was renewed after the plague the site was left deserted. The crops rotted in the fields, the church bells were silent, and everywhere corpses were flung, blackened and stinking, into hastily dug pits.

The plague reached London at the beginning of November – 'about the feast of All Hallows'. It took the great financier, Sir Thomas Pulteney – four times mayor and builder of the parish church of Little All Hallows, Thames Street – the Princess Joan of Kent's uncle, Lord Wake of Liddel, four wardens of the Goldsmiths' Company, and the abbot and twenty-six monks of Westminster. The courts of King's Bench and Common Pleas came to a standstill; a Parliament summoned for January was prorogued indefinitely. All though the winter the pestilence raged in the rat-haunted streets and alleys until, having carried off nearly half the population, 'by the intervention of the grace of the Holy Spirit on Whit-Sunday it ceased'. 'The cemeteries,' a chronicler wrote, 'were not big enough and fields had to be set aside for the burying of the dead . . . Men and women bore their own offspring on their shoulders to the church and cast them into the common pit, from which there proceeded so great a stench that hardly anyone dared to cross.' A croft near Smithfield given by the bishop of London for the burial of the dead became known as Pardon Church yard; another just outside the north wall of the city bought by the defender of Aiguillon, Sir Walter Manny, was endowed with a Carthusian cell which was to become the site of the Charterhouse and the great London school which still bears its name.

Owing to the speed with which the plague slew, the worst was over in the south before it struck the midlands and north. By the spring of 1349 it had reached Norfolk. Before the summer ended it had crossed the Humber. In the West Riding the incumbents of nearly half its parishes died; in the East Riding almost as many. The great Cistercian abbey of Meaux in Holderness lost its abbot and all but ten of forty-two monks and seven lay brethren; Fountains was so reduced that one of the twin fireplaces in the calefactorium, where the quarterly bleedings took place, was permanently bricked up. Scotland, protected by a hundred miles of moorland, escaped until the end of the year. At first the Scots ascribed the affliction of their neighbours to English wickedness, swearing 'by the foul death of England' and congratulating themselves on their own immunity. But when they gathered in Selkirk forest to harry the border, 'their joy turned to mourning as the sword of the wrath of God . . . scourged them in fury and suddenness, smiting them not less than the English with abscesses and pustules'. Next year it was the turn of the Welsh mountain valleys, and 'at last, as if sailing thither, the plague reached Ireland, striking down great numbers of the English dwelling there' and wrecking the precarious framework of the manorial system of the Pale. 'It scarcely touched the pure Irish who dwelt in the mountains and upland areas until 1357, when it unexpectedly destroyed them far and wide in terrible fashion.'

Though the Black Death visited every part of England its incidence was uneven. Some villages like Tilgarsley in Oxfordshire and Middle Carlton and Ambion in Leicestershire – site of the future battle of Bosworth Field – were so depopulated that they were never re-occupied. At St Albans the abbot, prior, sub-prior and forty-six monks died; at Christ Church, Canterbury, only four. Those who suffered most were the poor in their over-crowded hovels, and the parish and regular clergy. The nobility, living in comparatively clean and spacious conditions, escaped lightly. Isolating themselves in some retired country place and keeping a strict guard against strangers, they let the pestilence pass them by. A few caught the infection; three Archbishops of Canterbury died in that terrible year, one of them, John Stratford, at the end of August 1348, possibly from natural causes, but the other two of plague. The rest of the episcopal bench, immured in their country manor-houses, escaped, though Gynwell of Lincoln, true to his

257

diocese's great tradition, toured his eight counties throughout the epidemic as usual. Of the parish clergy at least forty per cent died, most of them probably at their posts. The episcopal registers – better preserved and more complete in England than in any other country – suggest that, including monks and friars, nearly half the personnel of the Church was taken.

Of the general public it is impossible to estimate with any certainty the proportion who died; the verdict of modern scholarship is that the first outbreak probably carried off about one in three of the population. What is certain is that, once established in the soil, the plague remained endemic. Dormant for perhaps a dozen years it would suddenly flare up, first in one city, then in another, at least once in a generation. For three hundred years – a period of time as great as that which divides us from the last outbreak in Charles II's reign – the red cross on the stricken door, the cart piled with corpses on its way to the plague-pit, the cry of 'Bring out your dead!' formed a recurrent part of the background of English life. During the three centuries since the Norman Conquest the population of England had probably doubled. The generation born in the middle of Edward III's reign saw it halved.

For anyone who has not experienced it, it is hard to realize the impact of a cataclysm carrying off one in every three, perhaps one in every two, of a civilized community. Its immediate effect, and of the shock and terror that accompanied it, was chaos. In the dirt and squalor of medieval life men were used to epidemic disease, but this was no ordinary epidemic. While it continued, all activity was suspended. The harvest could not be gathered, taxes or rents collected, markets held or justice done. Everywhere there were vacant holdings and uncultivated farms, and for a time it was almost impossible to sell anything.

For most people, it was its impact on labour which constituted the chief post-plague problem. 'So great was the deficiency of workmen of all kinds,' wrote one, 'that more than a third of the land remained uncultivated.' At an inquest on the estate of a Wiltshire landowner who died in June 1349, a jury found three hundred acres of pasture valueless because all the tenants were dead. At another manor near Salisbury only three tenants remained, all the rest having been carried off by the pestilence.

Yet, though even after six years, the Vice-Sheriff of Cumberland complained that the greater part of the manor lands of the royal castle of Carlisle were still lying waste and uncultivated 'by reason of the mortal pestilence lately raging in these parts', the remarkable thing is how quickly the country recovered from its ordeal. Despite a mortality rate higher than that expected today from nuclear war, England showed an astonishing resilience. In the work of the greatest English poet of the age there is only one reference, and that an oblique one, to the Black Death which three times swept across the England of his youth and early manhood. But men were far more used than now to the contemplation of death, and Chaucer grew up as a page in the royal court which largely escaped the fate overwhelming the rest of the community. Even as early as St George's Day 1349, while the plague was still raging in London, the first service of the Order of the Garter was held at Windsor, every knight in plumes and garter-blue robes taking his place in his stall; the great two-handed sword which the King carried on that day still hangs behind the altar of St George's Chapel.

*   *   *

Though both France and England had been denuded of a third of their people, the war had not ceased. While the Black Death was alive, the truce made in 1347 had been extended by mutual consent to the summer of 1350. But that spring, word reached King Edward at Windsor of a French plot to surprise and recapture Calais. A Lombard knight deputising for the governor, who had died of the plague, was bribed to admit a French raiding party into the castle by night. But the plot was betrayed, and it was the raiders who were surprised. For, having secretly crossed the Channel in disguise with a band of picked companions, Edward and the Prince of Wales fell on the intruders as they were being admitted to the castle and took them all captive. Afterwards the royal victor feasted his prisoners and, signalling out a knight who had long resisted him in single combat, crowned him with a chaplet of pearls and set him at liberty.

In August of the same year the King and the Black Prince took part in a more important action, this time at sea. A Castilian fleet, bringing merino wool to Flanders, had taken advantage of the depopulation of the Cinque Ports to plunder English merchantmen in the Channel. To intercept it on its return voyage, a squadron of fifty small vessels and pinnaces was assembled at Sandwich and manned by the flower of England's chivalry. Among them were nearly all the original Knights of the Garter; even the King's ten-year-old son, John of Gaunt, was there. Sailing from Sandwich they sighted the Spanish fleet off Dungeness on the afternoon of 29 August and at once went in to attack. Like Sluys, the battle was a triumph for the English archers who, outshooting the Spaniards' crossbowmen and catapultmen, made their decks a shambles before the knights and men-at-arms swarmed up their sides to complete the slaughter. Though both the King's and the Prince's ships were sunk, the day ended in the capture of seventeen galleons and the flight of the remainder, while crowds cheered the victors from the Winchelsea cliffs. That night the Queen, who had spent the day praying in Battle abbey, was joined by Edward and his sons at Pevensey castle, 'where the lords and ladies passed the night in great revel, speaking of war and love'.

The victory helped to restore England's sea communications with her depleted garrisons in Gascony. For the plague had left the country dangerously short of military man-power. There were not enough seamen to man her ships, or archers and men-at-arms to guard her gains in Guienne and Brittany. A small country suffers more from attrition than a large, and the disproportion between the populations of France and England now mattered far more. With hers reduced to between two and three millions, England was forced to fill her foreign garrisons with Gascons, Bretons, Flemings, Irish and Germans.

In August 1350, a week before Edward's naval victory off Winchelsea, having taken to himself a bride of eighteen Philip of Valois died at the age of fifty-eight. He was succeeded by his son, John II – *le Bon* or 'good fellow'. A devotee, unlike his father, of chivalry and martial glory, he refused to renew the truce. The war, therefore, continued in a rather desultory fashion while both countries recovered from the Black Death. In the south the French gradually built up a large army which, at the beginning of 1353, invaded Saintonge. Henry of Lancaster, crusading in the Baltic with the Teutonic knights, was no longer available to defend his sovereign's southern dominion. But the governor of Calais, Sir John Beauchamp – Lord Warwick's brother – was sent to save the threatened province. Reaching the beleaguered capital, Saintes, just in time, he won with his archers on 7 April another astonishing victory against odds. Two marshals of France were among the captives, the victors making a fortune in ransoms. Afterwards, hurrying back to his post at Calais, Beauchamp defeated the French at Ardres.

In Brittany, with Charles of Blois a prisoner and the de Mont-fort claimant a minor, the attempt of the English to rule the country in their protégé's name was growing increasingly unpopular. For the Bretons had not only to pay for their garrisons but were plundered by them into the bargain. English prestige had suffered a serious blow in 1351 in a chivalric encounter called 'the battle of the Thirty', when thirty Franco-Breton knights defeated thirty Anglo-Breton, Gascon and German ones, killing nine of them. But in 1352, when a French army under Marshal de Nesle invaded the duchy and, after regaining Rennes, advanced towards Brest, it was intercepted on 14 August at Mauron by Sir William Bentley. Bentley, who had succeeded Sir Thomas Dagworth as Keeper of Brittany after the latter's death in an ambush, had been vainly trying to obtain reinforcements from England. But, though he had only a minute force, he drew it up in one of those strong defensive positions on which the English relied, with the men-at-arms dismounted in line and the archers in wedges on the flanks. There were not enough men even to form a reserve. The French attacked at four o'clock on a hot summer's afternoon; those waiting on the ridge long afterwards remembered the droning of the bees in the heather. Though the initial assault forced back the archers on the English right, their comrades on the left wrought the usual execution on the French horses, subsequently attacking their riders with their swords as they struggled to rise. Meanwhile the men-at-arms, falling back up the hill to a belt of trees, put up so staunch a fight that the enemy was halted there too. When Bentley, dangerously wounded, was carried from the field crying, 'Fight on! fight on!'

his lieutenant, Sir Robert Knollys, took command and completed the enemy's rout. Marshal de Nesle was among the dead and more than six hundred knights and nobles were killed or taken prisoner, among them forty-five knights of the Order of the Star – the new Order of chivalry which King John had founded in rivalry of the Order of the Garter.

Mauron left the English masters of Brittany. It brought the little handful who fought there immense wealth. When, two centuries later, Shakespeare wrote of another Plantagenet victory against odds, 'the fewer men the greater share of honour', he might have substituted the word 'ransom' for honour. For the English army in France was raised on the same principle as that of a joint-stock company. The incentive to do or die was the knowledge that the survivors would share the fruits of victory – the booty of every city stormed and, for any man who took a prisoner, two-thirds of the ransom money, the rest being reserved for his commander, who in turn paid a third of his gains to the Crown. That, the use of the longbow and an iron discipline were the secret of the English success. How stern was that discipline was seen after the victory at Mauron when Knollys had thirty archers executed for retreating.

Probably at no time after the Black Death had the English more than ten thousand men in France. Their garrisons were only kept up to strength by recruiting from every western nation. But from earl to archer they were adventurers, with the plunder of the richest country in Europe as the prize for which they staked their lives. Chivalric honour in the higher ranks, loyalty to captain and comrade, even a kind of dawning and arrogant patriotism among the humbler English-speaking men-at-arms and archers, were elements in their courage. But the strongest of all was the gambling spirit and passion for gain which made them ready for any risk.

*   *   *

Though the war brought fortunes to England's fighting men, it was proving a growing strain on the taxpayer. When, having negotiated a year's truce with the war-weary French, the King in 1354 through his Lord Chamberlain asked the assembled Lords and Commons in Parliament whether they desired a permanent peace, they answered with one voice, 'Oeil! oeil!' – forerunner of the 'Aye, aye' with which the House of Commons still signifies its assent. Struggling with the dislocation of her economy by the plague, the country was having to contend not only against France – but also Scotland, with whom, on and off, she had been at war for half a century. That poor, insecure, war-ridden land, her King a captive and her treacherous nobles at constant loggerheads, was still determined not to acknowledge England's overlordship and to fight to the last man to resist it. When, two years before, having secured a provisional recognition of homage from his captive, King David, Edward sent him home on parole, a Scottish parliament unanimously rejected such terms and allowed him to return to captivity.

Edward was no more successful in persuading the French King to abandon claim to his homage than in inducing the Scots to acknowledge his right to theirs. For when in the winter of 1354, through the mediation of a new Pope, he opened peace negotiations with France, his plenipotentiaries on arriving at Avignon found the French, for all their defeats, unwilling to surrender their sovereign's overall right of suzerainty over even the smallest particle of conquered soil. Edward proposed that, in return for renouncing his claim to the French throne, King John should release him from the obligations of homage for Guienne, Ponthieu and the towns he had taken in Brittany and Normandy. He also secretly instructed his ambassadors that he would be prepared to abandon his Norman claims in return for the over-lordship of Flanders. His terms were contemptuously rejected. Despite twenty years of war neither monarch was prepared to abandon his fundamental aim – the English King to full sovereignty over his dominions beyond the Channel, the French to lordship over all France.

The war, therefore, continued. Once more, as ten years before, Edward planned a triple attack, from Gascony, from Calais and, under his personal command, from Normandy, whose largest land-owner, Charles of Navarre, had offered to throw in his lot with him. The disgruntled son-in-law of the French King and a descendant, like Edward himself, of the old Capet line, Charles proposed that they should march on Paris together with the idea of partitioning the Valois inheritance between them. In September 1355, as a preliminary to the combined operations planned for the following summer, the Prince of Wales accordingly sailed for Bordeaux with a force of 3500 men, including a strong contingent of Cheshire and Derbyshire archers. He was received with immense enthusiasm just as Lancaster had been ten years before. His mission was to win back the territories and towns which the count d'Armagnac had recovered in south-western Guienne.

The Black Prince had been brought up in the same school of war as Lancaster and Dagworth. He was now twenty-five and at the height of his powers. His recipe for dealing with superior force was to strike with the utmost audacity and speed. By carrying the war into the rich province of Languedoc and wasting it from end to end, he meant to force d'Armagnac to dance to his tune. Though by the conventions of chivalric war the season for campaigning was over, the Prince set out from Bordeaux on 5 October on a *grande chevauchée* with a mounted Anglo-Gascon force of 5000 men. For a hundred miles he marched south, crossing into French territory on the 11th. Then he turned east towards Toulouse, traversing the country through which Wellington's armies were to march three and a half centuries later. It was lovely weather and the cavalcade presented a brilliant spectacle, each of its captains, as Froissart described Sir John Chandos, riding 'with his banner before him and his company about him, with his coat of arms on him, great and large, beaten with his arms'. Strict discipline was observed, and while buildings, stores and crops were burnt as part of the plan of campaign, churches, monasteries and civilian lives were spared. Yet scarcely a day passed in that luxuriant countryside without some wealthy merchant or local landowner being brought in by the English patrols. Everyone down to the humblest archer was in high spirits, for there was ransom and plunder for all.

The army was equipped with portable pontoons for bridging the broad rivers of southern France, but not with siege-engines for reducing fortified cities. Toulouse was therefore by-passed, while d'Armagnac, not daring to give battle, watched from its walls the smoke of burning villages. Five more days of marching brought the English to Carcassonne, where they fired the lower town. On 8 November they reached Narbonne, only ten miles from the Mediterranean. All southern France was in panic; the Pope at Avignon a hundred miles away barricaded himself in his palace and sent an embassy to the Prince to plead for peace.

By this time two French armies were in the field. The count of Bourbon was advancing south from Limoges to bar the passage of the Garonne while, under the pressure of an angry public opinion, d'Armagnac had at last ventured out from Toulouse. On 10 November therefore, the Prince began his homeward march, intending to fight d'Armagnac before Bourbon's army could join him. But though both were in superior numbers, neither French commander dared give battle, for the memory of Crécy still haunted them. Even when they had joined forces they left the raiders alone.

On 2 December the Prince returned to La Réole, laden with booty, after covering nearly seven hundred miles in nine weeks. Meanwhile his father had been conducting a similar *chevauchée* in northern France. Having waited all the summer for word from Charles of Navarre, who had now composed his quarrel with the French King, he crossed to Calais at the end of October. But nothing would induce King John to leave the shelter of Amiens, and Edward's march through Artois in November rain and mud proved a very different matter from his son's campaign in Languedoc. As winter fell on the Flemish plain he was forced by lack of forage to return to Calais.

Here he was greeted by news that the Scottish Regent, William Douglas, had broken the truce and, with the help of a small French expeditionary force, had laid siege to Berwick castle, capturing the town. As both the warden of the March and the bishop of Durham had withdrawn their troops from the border in order to join him at Calais, Edward was forced to return to England and hurry north. Having secured supplies from Parliament and obtained from his captive, King David, a recognition of his suzerainty, he prepared to teach the Scottish nobles a lesson. In January 1356, in the depth of the winter, he crossed the border to take 'seisin,' as he put it, 'of his kingdom'.

265

With the twin banners of both nations borne before him, Edward reduced to ashes every village and farm along the road to Edinburgh, driving out the inhabitants onto the wintry moors. Yet the 'burnt Candlemas', as it was long called in Scotland, produced nothing except a greater hatred of England. Like Bruce, the Regent Douglas cleared the country of everything edible and vanished into the hills and forests. Campaigning in such a land was an unrewarding business after the rich plains of France, and no one's heart was in it. Storms held up the supply-ships, and by March there was nothing left but to withdraw or starve. The Scots, still evading combat, hung on the flanks of the retreating army and murdered the sick and stragglers, while the English set fire to the beautiful friars' church at Haddington – the 'lantern of Lothian'. Everyone was the loser.

Having safeguarded his northern border, Edward resumed his plans for conquering France. At that moment, back from the crusade in Lithuania where he had taken part in the Battle of Tramassene,[1] Henry of Lancaster was about to sail from Southampton for Brittany whose young duke, now sixteen, was eager to take possession of the duchy. With 500 men-at-arms and 800 mounted archers whom he was taking to reinforce the English garrisons, Lancaster was now deflected to Normandy with orders to relieve three rebel cities – Evreux, Pont Audemer and Breteuil – which the French royal forces were besieging.

Landing at La Hogue on 18 June 1356, the old warrior was joined by a small Norman force and by Robert Knollys of Mauron fame with 300 English men-at-arms and 500 archers. Lancaster, who had been rewarded for his services with a dukedom, was now fifty, but he acted as boldly as ever. With 2500 mounted men he set out on 22 June to relieve the insurgent cities, all of them more than a hundred and thirty miles away and threatened by an army

---

[1] Like the knight commemorated in *The Canterbury Tales*:
    'In fifteen mortal battles had he been
    And foughten for our faith at Tramassene.'
Chaucer, whose first patron was the duke's daughter, wrote *The Canterbury Tales* about the time that his own sister-in-law married Lancaster's widowed son-in-law, John of Gaunt, and may have had Lancaster in his mind when he described his 'very parfit gentil knight'.

which King John has assembled at Dreux to overawe them. Covering sixteen miles on the first day and thirty on the second, he reached Lisieux on 28 June. Next day, after a twenty-three-mile march, he relieved Pont Audemer, surprising and capturing the besiegers' siege-train. Having revictualled the town and strengthened the garrison with some English men-at-arms and archers, he set out again on 2 July and, by the morning of the 4th, after covering a further fifty miles and storming the castle of Conches, had relieved Breteuil.

As Evreux had by now fallen, the duke completed his mission by striking on the same day at Verneuil, the second city of Normandy. Using the siege equipment taken at Pont Audemer, he carried the walls that night, all but one tower which held out till the 6th. Then, on 7 July, with much booty and many prisoners, he set out for home. For with John's huge army only a dozen miles away he was in grave danger. With 2000 fighting men heavily encumbered with booty and prisoners, even Lancaster could not hope to defeat an army of 20,000. That night, in silence, the wily old duke vanished, leaving only a minute rearguard to deceive the French as they deployed next morning for battle. By nightfall he was thirty-five miles away at Argentan. On the 9th he covered a further fifty-two miles and by the 10th was across the Vire and safely back in the Cotentin, having marched three hundred and thirty miles in fifteen days. At his base camp he found that Robert Knollys, with a handful of men-at-arms, had routed a force of local militia men who had tried to ambush him, slaying them all except three rich landowners whom he had kept for ransom.

Leaving the French King to resume the siege of the revictualled insurgent Norman cities, Lancaster now marched south into Maine; while, three hundred miles away at Bergerac, the Prince of Wales set off north towards him. Between them the two English commanders hoped to pinch off a quarter of the French kingdom and, joining hands on the Loire, regain the Angevin inheritance which their ancestor, King John, had lost a century and a half before.

Since his *grande chevauchée* the Black Prince had taken some fifty towns and castles on the northern and eastern borders of

Guienne regained by the French during the years when the English garrisons had been depleted by the Black Death. By the middle of the summer of 1356, having established the English rule as far north as Périgueux, he was ready to strike. On 4 August, while Lancaster was laying siege to Domfront preparatory to marching on Angers, he crossed the Dordogne with 6000 men. Advancing at the rate of about ten miles a day, he passed the old Aquitaine border into France at the end of the month and began to ravage the towns and villages of Touraine.

After covering three hundred and twenty miles in just over a month, the Prince reached the Loire at Amboise in the first week of September, hoping to make contact with Lancaster. Finding all the bridges held or down, he turned downstream towards Tours, before which he encamped for several days while his foraging parties reduced the neighbouring castles. The weather had turned wet and the river was in flood. Meanwhile the French King, making a hasty composition with his Norman rebels, hurried south to oppose the intruders. From Chartres he started during the second week of September to send advance parties across the Loire.

On 10 September, when John was about to march on Blois, the Black Prince gave orders to retreat. His supplies were running short and there was no sign of Lancaster. Without a bridgehead a crossing of the river was out of the question, and his little force was far from home and laden with plunder. During the next four days both armies raced south on parallel courses, the French gathering reinforcements and trying to cut off the English from their base. Yet even now the Prince had not abandoned hope of a junction with Lancaster. On 15 September, disregarding the risk, he halted for two days at Chatellerault on the Vienne, waiting for tidings from the north, while the French King continued to march ahead of him towards Poitiers which he reached on the 17th.

That evening there was a skirmish between the Prince's scouts and King John's rearguard on the Chauvigny-Poitiers road, the English capturing two French counts and the steward of the household. But they were short not only of food but water, and their two days' wait for Lancaster – who, though he had now taken Domfront, was held up before Rennes – had placed them in deadly peril.

They put, however, a bold front on it and on the 18th – a Sunday – took up a defensive position on a ridge near Nouaillé, just above the little hamlet of Maupertius, eight miles from Poitiers.

To the French it seemed certain that the English had tempted fate once too often. All that day two cardinals, sent by the Pope to negotiate a truce, passed backwards and forwards between the armies with surrender terms. The English position was so desperate that the Prince of Wales offered to give up his spoil and prisoners and even, according to one account, not to serve in France for seven years. But the French, who by now outnumbered his little force by something like five to one and were daily growing stronger, refused to let him off so lightly. Nothing but his unconditional surrender and that of a hundred of his best knights would content them.

That night the English commanders held a council of war. Sooner than accept such terms they decided to await the French in the defensive position they had chosen and give battle, and then, if the enemy failed to attack, to slip away by night and make a run for it. The Black Prince had taken the precaution of sending his baggage and plunder across the Nouaillé bridge over the Miosson, and a day's delay would give them a sporting chance to get away. When, therefore, at dawn on 19 September the cardinals arrived in the English camp with the French King's final uncompromising terms, they were told that the sword must decide.

The truce ended at 7.30 a.m. on Monday morning, 19 September 1357. The English held a low ridge facing north-west, crossed by two roads, both from Poitiers, in an undulating, well-wooded countryside of small vine-clad hills. Before them lay a valley with a marsh protecting their left. Along the ridge ran a thick hedge behind which the Prince drew up his dismounted knights and men-at-arms, with Salisbury's division on the right and Warwick's on the left. The archers were posted as at Crécy among vineyards on the flank of each division and protected from cavalry by stakes. A small reserve of mounted knights remained out of sight behind the ridge. On the extreme right, to avoid being enveloped, the Prince had constructed a strong-point of wagons and trenches.

As the horses had to be watered in the valley, several hours elapsed before the whole army was in position – a circumstance which caused French observers to suppose that the English had already started to retreat. When everyone was assembled, the Black Prince rode along the lines, addressing his troops. His words have been handed down by the chroniclers. To the knights and men-at-arms, he said, 'Though we be but a small company, let us not be abashed. If it fortune that the day be ours, we shall be the most honoured of all the world.' To the archers he declared,

> 'You have made it plain that you are worthy sons and kinsmen of those for whom, under the leadership of my father and ancestors, the Kings of England, no labour was too great, no place invincible, no mountain inaccessible, no tower impregnable, no host too formidable . . . If victory shall see us alive we shall always continue in firm friendship together, being of one heart and mind. If envious fortune should decree, which God forbid, that in this present labour we must follow the final path of all flesh, your names will not be sullied with infamy, and I and my comrades will drink the same cup with you.'

It was not till nearly midday that the French vanguard appeared. It came on in two divisions, led by the Constable and two Marshals of France, each following one of the roads from Poitiers. The left-hand column had some initial success, forcing its way through a gap in the hedge, until it was driven back by a counter-attack by the earl of Salisbury. Before it reached the summit the right-hand column was shot to pieces by the archers who, moving down with superb battle-discipline into the swampy ground on the attackers' flank, directed such fierce volleys at the horses' hind-quarters that almost every rider was thrown to the ground and the Marshal in command captured. On both flanks the survivors fell back in confusion. So perfect was the English discipline that not a man moved in pursuit.

The larger part of the French host was now approaching, marching in three successive columns commanded by the Dauphin, the young Duke of Orléans and the King himself. Each division as it appeared seemed as large as the entire English army. At the suggestion of a veteran of the Scottish wars, William Douglas, who was serving in the French host, the knights and men-at-arms had left their horses at Poitiers. But the long march and the weight of their armour had caused them to straggle and, by the time they neared the battlefield, there was a wide gap between the columns.

The Dauphin's division attacked first. Despite the fire of the archers, who were by now running short of arrows, it reached the hedge. But the French knights, who on Douglas's advice had cut down their twenty-foot lances to six foot, were unaccustomed to fighting without their horses and soon began to tire. In the end they, too, fell back in confusion.

At this point, just as the English were beginning to think the battle was over, the last and largest of the French columns, led by King John, appeared on the ridge on the other side of the valley. The effect on the tired defenders of this great host, glittering with steel and banners, was shattering. Almost everyone except their commander gave himself up for lost. The waverers started to leave the field, leading off the wounded, and the rest prepared to sell their lives dearly.

But as the French moved up the hill, the Black Prince showed himself the great commander he was. Instead of waiting to be over-whelmed he decided to attack along the whole front. Ordering the battle-horses to be brought from the rear, he made his exhausted knights and men-at-arms mount and, with a cry of 'Banner, advance in the name of God and St George!' launched them in open line against the foe, himself leading. Simultaneously he sent a small detachment of cavalry which he had kept in reserve round the enemy's left flank under the Gascon, Captal de Buch, one of the founder Knights of the Garter.

The archers, throwing aside their bows, had now joined in the mêlée, striking at the French with their short swords. Suddenly, at the crisis of the fight, Captal's armour charged into the French rear. The result was devastating. Beset on both sides and fight-ing on uneven ground against mounted men, the French broke and fled, pursued by the English knights, hacking and slaughter-ing all the way to the walls of Poitiers. 'Fortune turned her giddy wheel, and the Prince of Wales penetrated the ranks of the enemy and, like a lion with noble wrath, spared the lowly and put down the mighty and took the King of France prisoner. With him were one the latter's sons, an archbishop, thirteen counts, five viscounts, twenty-one barons and nearly two thousand knights. So much potential ransom had never been taken at one time before. Another two thousand five hundred knights and men-at-arms were found dead on the field before the English lines, including two dukes. The oriflamme itself – the most sacred emblem of France – was barely saved.

That night the victor waited at supper on the French King in his tent, serving him on bended knee and saying that 'he was not sufficient to sit at table with so great a prince'. With exquisite courtesy he consoled him with praise of his gallantry. Once during the feast the Prince was called out by those collecting the dead and wounded to say that they had brought in Sir James Audley, one of the heroes of the day, who had been found wounded on the field. The chivalrous prince conferred on him an annuity of five hundred marks and when he learnt that Audley, a Knight of the Garter, had made it over to the four Cheshire squires who had fought so bravely by his side – Dutton of Dutton, Delves of Doddington, Fulleshurst of Barthomley and Hawkstone of Wrinehill – he doubled his award.

*   *   *

When news of Poitiers and the French King's capture reached England anxiety turned to rejoicing. The Black Prince's victory had transcended even that of Crécy. And England was raised to a new pinnacle of glory. Foreigners noted 'the proud mien of Englishmen everywhere'. Having found what seemed an infallible way of winning against almost any odds, they saw before them an endless vista of ransoms, loot and profit. The land of France was their oyster, and the longbow had opened it.

For the wealth won was prodigious. The price put on the King of France was 300,000 crowns. 'I am so great a lord,' the Prince told his officers after Poitiers, 'as to make you all rich.' Even the humblest returned with the sale of battle-horses, swords, jewels, robes and furs. There was hardly a woman in England, it was said, without some ornament, goblet or piece of fine linen brought home by the conquerors. Those fortunate enough to capture some great magnate became themselves lords. Sir Thomas Dagworth was offered £4,900 – an enormous fortune in the money of the time – for the ransom of Charles of Blois. The north country squire who had taken King David prisoner at Neville's Cross received an annuity of £500 – equivalent to an income perhaps of £100,000 today – with the rank of a banneret.

The pageantry which accompanied the bringing home of the French King in the summer of 1357 outshone even that of the year following the capture of Calais, when the Order of the Garter had been founded. Attending him on a small black palfrey, the Prince paraded his prisoner through the London streets on a white charger while bells clanged, fountains spouted wine and thousands of liveried guildsmen marched behind mounted wardens and aldermen through streets hung with tapestry. When the procession reached Westminster Hall, King Edward rose from his throne to embrace his fellow sovereign. Lodged in the duke of Lancaster's new palace of the Savoy, rebuilt from the spoils of Guienne, the fallen monarch took part, with the captive King of Scots, in a succession of feasts and tournaments – the most splendid, it was said, held in England since the legendary days of Arthur. The poor man was under no illusion as to their purport.

For though the Scots were able to ransom their King by selling on his behalf their entire wool export, France was in no condition to meet England's demands. Not only were large parts of Normandy and the north in rebellion against the government of the eighteen-year-old Dauphin, but hordes of professional soldiers, ignoring the two years' truce after Poitiers, refused to return home and, taking service with anyone who would hire them, continued to live at large on the country. One such mercenary band or 'Free Company', led by the Cheshire knight, Robert Knollys, descended on the rich countryside south of Paris and made itself master of forty castles. The charred gables that marked its progress were known as 'Knollys's mitres'. Another band under a Welshman, John Griffith, ravaged the Loire valley, while a Gascon, nicknamed 'the Archdeacon', plundered Provence, making even the Pope pay blackmail.

With all this misery, and her King and so many nobles in

captivity, France dissolved into civil war and anarchy. While the Dauphin and his government were struggling against a bourgeois revolution in Paris, the starving peasantry of the Île-de-France and Picardy rose and avenged themselves on their feudal rulers with massacre, torture and rape. Under the circumstances, all attempts to ransom the King and conclude a peace with England broke down. The only terms Edward would consider were the surrender of all French rights over the whole of the lands he had conquered. And though, in return for the abandonment of his claim to the French throne, King John was now ready to agree to even this, Edward's subjects in Parliament, intoxicated by his victories, insisted on demanding the cession of Poitou, Anjou, Maine, Touraine and Normandy. This was more than any French government would concede, however desperate its plight.

Edward prepared, therefore, to give his enemies a further taste of what he could do. 'He said plainly that his intention was to pass over into the realm of France and not to return again until he had made an end of his war or else a sufficient peace to his great honour and profit.' To bring matters to an issue he proposed to march on Rheims and have himself crowned in its cathedral as King of France. Once more he collected a great army. Not only Englishmen, but Flemings, Hainaulters, Brabançons, Germans and even Frenchmen flocked to his standards to share in the spoils of victory. Eleven hundred ships were assembled at Sandwich and unprecedented quantities of food and stores. There were more than six thousand wagons and carts, mobile workshops for armourers and smiths, handmills and field-ovens, even portable leather coracles from the Severn for supplying the army with fish during Lent from the French rivers, and thirty falconers and sixty couple of greyhounds for the King's sport. For contrary to every rule of medieval war, Edward meant to invade in the autumn and cam-paign through the winter.

At the beginning of October 1359, the advance guard under Lancaster landed at Calais. The King followed at the end of the month. Never before, it was said, 'departed out of England such an army nor so well ordered'. Nearly all the great figures of English chivalry were present – the King's sons, Edward of Woodstock,

John of Gaunt, Lionel of Clarence and Edmund of Langley; the earls of Warwick, Suffolk, Hereford, Northampton, Stafford, Salisbury, March and Oxford; the lords Despenser, Percy, Neville, Mowbray, Grey, Fitzwalter, Hastings, Burghersh, Cobham and the Garter Knights, John Chandos and James Audley. Early in November they set forth, marching out of Calais 'with all their company and carriages in the best order that ever any army issued out of any town; it was a joy', wrote Froissart, 'to behold them.'

It rained all the way. They rode through Artois and past the city of Arras and over the chalky Somme uplands – one day to be the battlefield of another and greater English army. 'The country,' wrote Froissart, 'had been long poor and sore wasted and it was a drear season in the realm of France . . . Day and night it rained without cease so that wine that year was little worth.' Nor, though strict march-discipline was enforced and the army was kept in constant readiness for action, did any enemy appear. The Dauphin had learnt from his father's folly, and his orders were that no one was to challenge the English in open field. When, after four weeks' marching, the latter arrived, wet and dispirited, at the gates of Rheims, they found them barred. Nor, despite repeated summonses, would the archbishop and citizens open.

The English could still destroy any army France could put into the field. But they could not reduce a strongly fortified city except by surprise or starvation, and Rheims was prepared for a long siege. For nearly two months in bitter weather they occupied the surrounding heights while patrolling parties scoured the countryside as far as the walls of Paris, trying to provoke a relieving force to battle. But none came.

In the middle of January, unable to maintain his troops on the frozen Champagne plain any longer, Edward abandoned all idea of being crowned in Rheims and marched south into Burgundy, hoping to find early grazing for his horses. But the winter of 1360 proved the longest of the century. After capturing the wine-town of Tonnerre he remained in the Burgundian uplands for most of Lent, hawking and keeping the fast while he waited in vain for the grass to grow. Finally, having extracted an indemnity of 200,000 florins and a three years' truce from the young duke of Burgundy, he struck north again for Paris, still hoping for the weather to turn and for a chance to force the issue. On the way he learnt that a Norman raiding party had sacked and burnt the royal port of Winchelsea, raping some unfortunate ladies who had taken shelter in St Thomas's church and killing several hundred townsmen before being driven off by the local milita. In his fury, while he halted at Corbeil for Holy Week, the indignant King set fire to every village in sight of the French capital.

But though after Easter he paraded his army in battle array under its walls, the garrison never stirred. The Dauphin was wiser than his years. After waiting for four days, while the heralds issued challenge after challenge, Edward was again forced to retreat. For, with April as cold as March, there was still nothing for his horses to eat and, thanks to the Free Companies, very little for his men. His only resort was to seek the milder country to the south-west and re-provision the army in the Loire valley or Brittany until he was able to resume the siege of Paris in the autumn. Nor, even now, had winter done with him. For on the first day of the retreat, 13 April, long remembered as Black Monday – 'a foul dark day of mist and of hail, so bitter cold that sitting on horseback many died' – an icy storm swept over the army, causing hundreds of vehicles to be abandoned. A fortnight later, when it was moving down to the Loire, a thunderstorm, with hailstones as big as pigeons' eggs, struck it as it traversed the stony heaths beyond Chartres. Helpless in their armour, more knights were said to have been killed that day by lightning than fell in the English ranks at Crécy and Poitiers. It was this storm, according to one chronicler, which caused the English King to 'turn toward the church of our Lady at Chartres and devoutly vow to the Virgin that he would accept terms of peace'.

Even in retreat Edward continued to try to tempt the French to battle. 'Certain knights in the following of the Duke of Lancaster,' wrote Gray of Heton, 'disguising themselves as brigands or pillaging soldiers without lances, rode in pretended disarray in order to give the enemy spirit and courage to tackle them. Some . . . overdid the counterfeit to such an extent . . . that they came to grief and were taken.' It was in such a foray earlier in the year that a young squire named Geoffrey Chaucer, in the service of Prince Lionel of Clarence, had been captured, subsequently having to be ransomed for £16, together with other officers of the Household.

But if Edward had failed to be crowned at Rheims or to tempt the Dauphin to another Crécy, the French on their side could no longer endure the war. Almost anything seemed better than its indefinite continuance, for, so long as the English remained, the country could not rid itself of the Free Companies and the misery and anarchy they caused. Even before Edward had landed in France, Knollys had offered him the services of his Great Company and had been taken back into favour, and all over the land he and his like were continuing their enormities.

At the end of April, therefore, plenipotentiaries arrived at the Black Prince's headquarters at Chartres. This time they were ready to concede the principle for which Edward had contended for a quarter of a century – the complete independence of his French dominions. And thanks to their experiences of that winter and Lancaster's moderating influence, the English were at last ready to be reasonable. 'My liege,' the wise old warrior is reported to have said, 'this war you are waging may be wonderful to all men; it is not so favourable to yourself! If you persist, it will last you a lifetime, and it seems to be doubtful that you will gain your desires. You are wasting your time.'

Negotiations were opened on 1 May 1360 at the village of Brétigny. A week later, 'eight days into the sweet month of May,' as Chandos's herald put it, 'when the birds were no more in dismay', the terms of a provisional treaty were announced. Under these, Edward renounced his claim to the French throne and to the overlordship of Normandy, Anjou, Maine, Touraine, Brittany and Flanders. He also promised to restore any castles and cities held in these provinces. In return he was to receive the unconditional cession, free from the French King's suzerainty, of Calais, Ponthieu and the whole of Aquitaine – nearly a quarter of France. It was to include the Limousin, Agenais, Angoumois, Poitou, Périgord, Quercy and Rouergue and the cities of Limoges, Poitiers, Angoulême, Cahors, Tarbes and La Rochelle, the headquarters of the European salt trade. France also agreed to pay the full 300,000 gold crowns for her King's ransom in six instalments, the first of which was to secure his release on royal hostages being given for the remainder. She was to renounce the Scottish alliance, and England the Flemish. The question of the Breton succession was to be left to discussion. Provision was also made for the subjects of both kingdoms to study once more at each other's universities.

*   *   *

On the morning of 29 May 1360 Edward and the Black Prince returned to Westminster, after galloping through the night from Rye. It was a day of pealing bells, Te Deums and rejoicings. Edward himself announced the good news to his royal prisoner; 'You and I,' he declared, 'are now, thank God, of one accord.' Five weeks later, after three and a half years' imprisonment, King John took leave of him at Eltham palace. But on his arrival at Calais, the poor man was detained for a further three months owing to delays in carrying out the treaty's preliminary terms. Even when on 25 October the two Kings formally ratified it, kneeling together before the altar of St Nicholas church and swearing perpetual friendship, the transfer of territories was still not complete, the people of La Rochelle proving particularly reluctant to change their allegiance. In consequence both Edward's renunciation of the French throne and the French King's of his claim to allegiance were omitted from the treaty and left to letters of ratification to be exchanged later. From this much trouble was to follow, though none seems to have been anticipated, at least by the English. Three of the French King's sons accompanied Edward back to England as hostages, but were subsequently released on parole in return for a promise of 200,000 more crowns.

For Edward felt he could afford to be generous. In his fiftieth year he had obtained all he wanted of France – military glory transcending even his romantic dreams and full dominion over territories far larger than those he had inherited. He was regarded, by foreigners and subjects alike, as the most victorious, chivalrous and magnificent monarch in Christendom – an Arthur, it seemed, reincarnated. Under her 'clement King', too, England had enjoyed a longer period of internal tranquillity than at any time in her history. 'The bringer of peace to his people, was how Edward's epitaph in the abbey was to describe him, and it was thus that his subjects saw him during his life. There had been times when the greatest threat to an English sovereign's authority and his kingdom's peace had come from his own sons; the first Plantagenet had been harried to the grave by them. Edward's were devoted to him. It was an essential part of his policy of national conciliation to marry them to the heiresses of the greater feudal families. Of his four surviving younger sons, the eldest, Lionel of Antwerp, had been betrothed to the only child of the earl of Ulster, William de Burgh, who also represented on the distaff side the great Marcher house of Clare. Shortly after the Treaty of Brétigny the young prince was sent to govern Ireland with the dual object of securing the profits of his wife's vast but largely illusory inheritance and of restoring order to that turbulent country which, since its invasion by the Bruces after Bannockburn, had been in a state of more than usual anarchy. His younger brother, John of Gaunt, had made a still more splendid marriage with his cousin Blanche, daughter and co-heiress of Henry of Lancaster. On the latter's death in 1361 and of his other co-heiress shortly afterwards, he acquired the whole of the vast Lancastrian inheritance, including the earldoms of Lancaster, Derby, Lincoln and Leicester. A year later, to mark his own fiftieth birthday, Edward created him Duke of Lancaster.

'Clement and benign, familiar and gentle to all men', Edward was not, however, an iron man like his grandfather. His supreme object was to please and excel and, being able, courageous and immensely energetic and possessed of wonderful charm, he was at first completely successful. But as difficulties grew he became more and more apt to follow the line of least resistance; to promise, and when promise became impossible of fulfilment, to evade and equivocate. At this time, either through a wish to gain a tactical point or through some unaccountable negligence, he made a fatal blunder. In February 1361, with four sons and the French royal hostages by his side, he had opened the Parliament which ratified the treaty of Brétigny, first marching in procession to the abbey, where Simon of Islip, Archbishop of Canterbury, celebrated High Mass in honour of the Holy Trinity. Yet the one essential condition

279

of the treaty for which England had fought for nearly a quarter of a century was allowed to go unratified, ostensibly on account of French delays in making the promised ransom payments and in handing over certain of the towns and territories agreed under the treaty. The final date fixed for the exchange of mutual renunciations of sovereignty had been 1 November 1361. Yet when, two days before, the French envoys arrived in England they were told that the King was not prepared to abandon his title to the French crown until every detail of the treaty had been complied with. The envoys, therefore, refused to make a unilateral surrender of their master's suzerainty over Aquitaine.

As a result, by far the most important gain of the peace was lost, and the question of ultimate sovereignty was left unsolved to bedevil future Anglo-French relations. Without it, neither the transfers of territory nor the huge ransom instalments were of any permanent use to England, even though, when delays occurred in the time-table for the latter and one of the French royal hostages – temporarily given leave to visit his wife at Boulogne – broke his parole and failed to return, King John most honourably surrendered himself again to his former captors. Returning to England at the beginning of 1364, perhaps not without relief at exchanging his own war-harried and poverty-stricken realm for the luxury and chivalric splendour of the English court, he died there that spring at the age of forty-five.

The French were given another and better excuse for renouncing the terms of the treaty of Brétigny, should they ever wish to do so. For though the disbandment and withdrawal of the Free Companies had been one of its main conditions and when, in Froissart's words, 'their captains departed in courteous manner out of those fortresses they held . . . and gave leave to their men of war to depart', the latter 'thought that to return into their own country was not to them profitable'. After which they continued to behave as they had always done and as though no peace had been made. 'They wasted all the country without any cause and robbed without sparing all that ever they could get and violated and defiled women, old and young without pity, and slew men, women and children without mercy.'

For the English army of which the French had been so anxious to be rid was neither a feudal array bound by social obligations nor a national militia defending its own soil. It was a collection of private war-bands raised by indenture by adventurous nobles and knights for the pursuit of profit. And when, replete with their gains, the larger share-holders withdrew, the smaller took over. Though many of these 'great pillagers' were not English, but Germans, Brabanters, Flemings, Hainaulters, Gascons and even Frenchmen, they had all served England's King, and the blame for their evil doings was laid at his door. One of them, an archer named John Hawkwood – the son of an Essex tanner – after ravaging southern France, led his gang of desperadoes to Avignon 'to see,' as they put it, 'the Pope and cardinals'. Later he transferred himself to Italy where for thirty years he lived by placing his trained and disciplined band – the 'White Company' as it was called – at the disposal of first one warring city or republic, then another. After making an enormous fortune and marrying a natural daughter of Bernabo Visconti, tyrant of Milan, he died in 1394, in the service of Florence, whose grateful government gave him a funeral in the duomo and commissioned as his memorial a magnificent equestrian fresco by Paolo Uccello. [1]

Two years after the end of the war with England the 'brigands' were still strong enough to destroy a French army under a royal duke at Brignais near Lyons. But the accession in 1364 of the twenty-five-year-old Dauphin as Charles V proved the turn of the tide for France. A few weeks later a rough Breton knight with a genius for war, Bertrand du Guesclin, won a victory at Cocherel in Normandy over the forces of the traitor, Charles of Navarre, and an English freelance captain, John Jewel. It was the first decisive French victory for a generation and ended the Norman rebellion. In Brittany, where civil war had again broken out, Sir John Chandos with a few hundred English volunteers again showed that autumn at Auray the unbreakable ascendancy of his countrymen in pitched battle, defeating and killing Charles of Blois and taking du Guesclin

[1] With Robert Knollys and Hugh Calveley he was one of the founders of the English hospital at Rome and, through a daughter who married John Shelley, MP for Rye, an ancestor of the poet.

prisoner. But the new French King turned the defeat to his advantage by recognising the rival claimant, de Montfort, as duke in return for his homage. In doing so he regained Brittany for France and brought the war in that country to an end and, with it, any further pretext for English intervention.

Charles V had none of his father's love of knight-errantry. After his early experience at Poitiers he never took part in another battle. He was a delicate young man, matured by misfortune, with a sharp nose, quizzical look and, under his scholarly appearance, a will of iron. Devout, learned and immensely shrewd, he was a brilliant judge of men; it was he who raised the younger son of a Breton hedge-squire to the command of France's armies. He loved the company of scholars and artists and strove to make his court and Paris once more the centre and arbiter of western civilization, identifying his throne with a stately ceremonial that recalled, in a more luxurious age, his hero and great-great-grandfather, St Louis. Yet, though operating from the library and counting-house rather than the saddle, he proved the most successful director of war of his age, attaining his ends with a minimum expense of life and treasure. Knowing precisely what he wanted, he pursued it with cunning, patience and inflexible resolution. In his sixteen years on the throne he raised France from the depths of defeat and poverty to renewed wealth and grandeur.

Above all, he sought to identify himself with the needs and hopes of the French people. His supreme object was to unite all Frenchmen under a single throne and law. Where the feudal nobility, with their arrogance and selfish separatism, had left France wide open to her enemies, this young King set himself to show that, from the highest to the lowest, safety for life and property could only be won by rallying round the Crown. Little by little he gained his ends, letting Edward leave unratified the renunciation of his claim to the French throne and, with it, his right to untrammelled overlordship over Aquitaine; and, while there was peace with England, driving or bribing out of the country, first one, then another of the plundering Free Companies. All the while, as he restored order and prosperity to France's long tormented countryside, he built up her financial resources and reorganised

282

her armies. The price he had to pay was a heavy one: the *gabelle* or salt monopoly, which he made permanent, and his system of farming the taxes, which led to grave social abuses and oppression. Yet the poor who felt them most saw in him their protector against the English and the lawless soldiery who had so long preyed on them and, when he died at the age of thirty-eight, it was said that the lilies were engraved on every peasant's heart.

*　　　　　*　　　　　*

Though the return of the plague in 1361 had fallen with equal severity on France, striking down no less than eight cardinals in the court of Avignon, it was again the smaller of the two countries which suffered most from its attrition. Yet the area which England with her reduced man-power had to control had been trebled by her conquests. In 1363, faced by the difficulty of finding archers for its foreign garrisons, the government issued a proclamation deploring the nation's degeneracy and enjoining archery practice on saints' days and holidays for all able-bodied men. About this time, too, Edward tried once more to forestall any renewal of a joint attack from France and Scotland by using the latter's poverty and internal anarchy to coax her King and nobles into a union with England. He made generous, if calculated, concessions to her merchants and pilgrims, reopened English universities to Scottish students – for Scotland still had none of her own – and in the autumn of 1363 offered to remit the remaining instalments of King David's ransom and restore Berwick, Roxburgh and Jedburgh and the Stone of Scone in return for the Scots' acknowledging him, or one of his sons, as David's heir should the latter die without children. The Scottish King, who had learnt to love the fleshpots of the Plantagenet court, was ready to agree, as was also, for a time, his chief opponent, the earl of Douglas, who hoped to recover his English estates. But when the treaty was presented to the Scottish Parliament in the spring of 1364, its members proved worthier of the great Bruce and James Douglas than their degenerate successors. Notwithstanding 'the dark and drublie days' through which their country was passing, they declared themselves 'in no way willing to assent' and rejected the terms as 'insufferable'. A few years later, the issue, as Scotsmen saw it, was put by John Barbour, archdeacon of Aberdeen, in the prologue to his epic, *The Brus*, which he wrote round the story of Scotland's liberator.

'Ah, freedom is a noble thing! . . .
Freedom all solace to man gives,
He lives at ease that freely lives!
A noble heart may have none ease
Nor ellés naught that may him please
If freedom fail.'

Edward's hopes, therefore, came to nothing, and Scotland, poverty-stricken, proud and racked by constant civil war, remained the independent nation that Bruce and Wallace had made her and, as a result, a standing threat to England's back door. Meanwhile, beyond the Channel, the latter continued to maintain her vast military empire, the new outlying districts of which, in contra-distinction to a still loyal Gascony, were growing every year more hostile to her arrogant and predatory dominion. In the past the English Kings – descendants of the ancient princes of Anjou and Aquitaine – had behaved as Frenchmen and governed their French provinces through the local nobility and bureaucracy. But with their victories over the Valois kings and the growing identification of England's French-speaking lords with her Anglo-Saxon yeomanry – a union cemented on the battlefield – England's rulers were becoming increasingly insular. Pride in their common Englishry and, with it, contempt for foreigners, were beginning to transcend the unity of class, speech and ideology which had so long identified their French-descended rulers with their ancestral lands across the Channel. In October 1362, the Chief Justice of the King's Bench opened the proceedings of Parliament for the first time in English – a precedent followed at the opening of the next Parliament by the Chancellor. In the same year it was enacted that all pleadings should be in the vernacular on the ground that French was 'too little known in the realm' and that 'people who impleaded or were impeached in the courts knew not what was said for or against them by their serjeants or pleaders'. And though lack of precision in the English language – for so long the despised speech of 'uplandish men' – made this technically impracticable, and for several more centuries lawyers continued in their pleadings to use French to express the exact concepts demanded by their profession, forensic argument in the King's courts was henceforward conducted in English. The old romance tongue of western chivalry was ceasing to be the speech of the ruling class; a generation later Chaucer's high-born prioress spoke French, not after the French of Paris 'which was to her unknowe', but 'after the school of Stratford-atte-Bowe'.

*   *   *

In 1363 the English heir-apparent was sent to govern Aquitaine as a sovereign and independent prince, subject only to his father's overlordship. Here he maintained a splendid court where, in Chandos' herald's words, 'abode all nobleness, all joy and jollity, largesse, gentleness and honour'. Yet, however much the Gascons might admire their new Duke as a model of knightly chivalry and the first warrior of his age, they loved neither the taxation he imposed to maintain his extravagant court nor the horde of English lords and officials he took with him to administer the duchy. Still less did the peoples of the new provinces which had been added to England's French dominion. The new High Seneschal of Aquitaine was a Cheshire knight, Sir Thomas Felton; the Seneschal of Poitou his cousin, Sir William of the same name; of Saintonge Sir Baldwin Treville; of Quercy Sir Thomas Walkfare; of Limousin Lord Ros; of the Agenais Sir Richard Baskerville. Even the chivalry, good sense and moderation of the High Constable of Aquitaine, the universally loved Sir John Chandos, did not remove the sense of shame felt by the proud Gascon nobles that foreigners should hold the highest offices of their ancient dukedom.

The sense of outraged nationality and longing for revenge aroused in Gallic peasants and merchants by a generation of invasion and rapine by English bowmen had spread from France proper into the south-west and had even begun to show itself beyond the Garonne. This growing anti-English, pro-Valois feeling of a countryside which had hitherto preferred the remote rule of its French-speaking English duke to that of Paris was brought to a head by the romantic extravagance and belligerency of the Black Prince. In 1366 the kingdom of Castile became the scene of one of those periodic civil wars that reflect the inability to compromise, impassioned partisanship and fanatic valour of the Spanish temperament. Its King, Don Pedro 'the Cruel', was challenged by his bastard half-brother, Don Erico of Trastamara. Repudiated by a large part of his people, excommunicated by the Pope and opposed, though without open intervention, by the French King who, seeing an opportunity for getting rid of the Free Companies, set off as many of them as possible under Bertrand du Guesclin to help the Bastard, whom he saw as a future ally against England, Pedro was driven from his capital. Taking refuge at Corunna he appealed to the Black Prince for help.

This challenge to his chivalry, as well as to the principle of legitimacy, was more than the Prince could resist. He saw himself as the knight-errant of Christendom leading a righteous war. Obtaining his father's unofficial consent and a promise of help from his younger brother, John of Gaunt, Duke of Lancaster, he assembled an army at Dax and, in the winter of 1366–7, prepared to cross the Pyrenees. Joined by the latter with a thousand archers from the forests of Cheshire and the north, the Prince turned his back on his restless duchy, his debts and the watchful French King beyond his borders, and in February 1367 crossed the Roncesvalles pass, driving his heavily accoutred men, horses and wagons through the wintry gorges of Navarre to the Castilian border.

This chivalric expedition into Spain, ten years after Poitiers and conducted in extremes of winter cold and scorching heat on Castilian mountain and plain, proved the hero Prince's undoing and, ultimately, that of English rule in France. Despite his brilliant victory at Nájera on 3 April 1367, when the flower of the feudal nobility of yet another European kingdom went down under a hail of English steel and goosequill, the Black Prince's last crusade of chivalry ended in disillusionment and disaster. After it, the victors waited all summer under a burning sun for the gold which was to have been paid by King Pedro for their aid, while dysentery, contracted from stagnant pools, continued to diminish their numbers. When in the autumn the Prince sadly led the survivors back across the Pyrenees, they were only a shadow of the splendid host which had crossed them at the beginning of the year. Not one in five, it was said, ever saw England again. All that their leader had to show for his victory was a handful of jewels wrung from Don Pedro in place of the million crowns he had been promised.

At thirty-seven, his giant frame emaciated by dysentery, the Black Prince returned to Bordeaux. His troops were unpaid and his duchy restless under taxation. So troublesome were the survivors of the Free Companies whom he was now forced to quarter on his subjects that, when he summoned the estates of the duchy to meet at the little hill-town of St Emilion, the deputies of Rouergue were forced to turn back by the 'companions' ravaging the Dordogne valley. At the beginning of 1368, disregarding the advice of Chandos, the Prince got the estates to impose a five years' *fouage* or tax on every hearth in the duchy to meet his war debts. It was bitterly opposed by two of the leading magnates of Guienne. When the Prince 'insisted that, right or wrong, his vassals should do his bidding', they refused to allow the tax to be levied in their domains and appealed, first to the King of England, and then, without waiting for an answer, to the King of France.

It was the opportunity for which Charles had been waiting. Yet he proceeded with his usual caution. Privately promising the apellants that he would investigate their case but pledging himself to nothing, he played for time and with the Pope's aid secured the release of the last hostages from the unsuspecting and now ageing Edward in return, it was said, for papal approval of the appointment of the English King's favourite minister, William of Wykeham, to the see of Winchester. Continuing the pretence of non-intervention in Spain, he sent back the now ransomed du Guesclin to restore the Bastard and, through an alliance with Castile, Aragon and Navarre, to circle England's southern dominion with enemies. By getting a French Pope to refuse a dispensation on the grounds of consanguinity, he had already thwarted Edward's hope of marrying his son, Edmund of Langley, to the heiress of Flanders. Now, when English policy had suffered a further set-back through the death in Italy of Prince Lionel of Clarence after his wedding to the niece of Bernabo Visconti of Milan, he brought off a still greater coup by inducing the count of Flanders to give his daughter to his own brother, Philip the Bold of Burgundy, thus bringing Flanders once more into the orbit of royal France. All the while he observed the letter while violating the spirit of the treaty of Brétigny.

By the end of 1368 he was ready. He had already allowed the Gascon appellants to lay their case before the *parlement* of Paris, making a secret pact with them that if it came to war they would stand together. Knowing that hundreds more of the Black Prince's subjects were eager to appeal to him, he now announced that his judges had found that, as Edward had failed to ratify the renunciation of his claim to the French throne, his own father's surrender of the overlordship of Aquitaine had never become effective – and that province was, therefore, still part of France. As its overlord he was entitled, and morally bound, to pronounce judgment on the appeals.

In January 1369 Charles formally summoned the Black Prince as a peer of France to appear in person at Paris. The Prince was taken completely by surprise. When he realised that all that he and his father had fought for had been in vain he swore a mighty oath. 'We shall willingly,' he said, 'attend on the appointed day at Paris since the King of France sends for us. But it will be with helmet on head and with sixty thousand men at our back.'

What the victor of Poitiers threatened and what he could perform, however, were now different things. It was not he who took the offensive, but his discontented vassals and the French King. All round the eight-hundred-mile perimeter of Aquitaine, bands of fighting men poured in to help their compatriots, while the clergy everywhere took the lead in preaching rebellion. Within a few weeks more than nine hundred castles and towns had repudiated allegiance to the English; most of Armagnac, Limousin, Rodez, Quercy and the Agenais was lost without a fight.

Yet Charles still proceeded with caution. In March 1369 his troops helped the Castilians to a decisive victory over Don Pedro, who was taken prisoner and killed. With the Bastard back on the throne, Castile and her fleet, as well as Aragon and Navarre, were now aligned against England. At last, in May 1369, Charles took the decisive step, first declaring the Black Prince contumacious for failing to appear before the *parlement* of Paris, and then informing the English King that, as he had failed to observe the letter of the treaties, his French lands were forfeit. Simultaneously he seized Pontheiu.

Furious, Edward III appealed to Parliament for money and resumed the title, discarded nine years before, of King of France. At this moment the Black Death broke out in England for the third time. Among those who died that summer were the bishops of Norwich, Hereford and Exeter, the earls of Suffolk and Warwick and the young Duchess of Lancaster – the lady Blanche,[1] wife of John of Gaunt. Not till the autumn was it possible to collect even a small force for France, when, to forestall an invasion of the Isle of Wight, Gaunt crossed to Calais with 600 men-at-arms and 1500 bowmen. By striking at Artois and Picardy he was just in time to stop the embarkation of an army in Normandy under the French King's brother. But though he marched to the gates of Harfleur, burning and ravaging, he was unable to tempt the French to battle. For Charles had resolved to give no chance to the English archers to repeat their holocausts of a generation before. By November, unable to supply his troops any longer, John of Gaunt returned to England, to find that he had lost not only his wife but his mother, Queen Philippa having died that month at Windsor.

If 1369 was a disastrous year for England, it saved Scotland. Without enough men to defend both the northern Marches and Aquitaine, a plague-riven England agreed to a fourteen-year truce. But for this, famine, baronial and tribal war and the crushing taxation to pay for her King's ransom would have forced the northern kingdom to accept Edward's terms and acknowledge him as David's successor. As it was, though England still held Berwick, Roxburgh and Annandale, the Scots, freed from danger from the south, were able to put down a rebellion of the Lord of the Isles which had threatened to disintegrate their country. When eighteen months later, in February 1371, King David died, the son of Robert Bruce's daughter, Robert the Steward, succeeded under the

---

[1] 'Who died fair and young, at about the age of twenty-two years. Gay and glad she was, fresh and sportive, sweet, simple and humble semblance, the fair lady whom men called Blanche.' *Froissart.* Daughter of the great warrior Henry of Lancaster, she was the heroine of Chaucer's earliest major poem.

terms of the settlement of half a century before. Without their in-
volvement in a losing war with France the English would never
have recognised him.

The campaign in Guienne fared no better in 1370 than in 1369.
The English could not contend indefinitely against a nation several
times their size. Though they still did not realise it, the door of
opportunity, once wide open, was now bolted against them. They
could no longer finance the war from plunder, which, as they
burnt, ravaged and wasted, brought in diminishing returns. In vain
they called in their Free Companies – Hugh Calveley from Spain
and the 'terrible Robert' Knollys from Burgundy – and enrolled
them to defend the duchy; unpaid and forced to live on the countryside, the companions only made the situation worse, arousing the
hatred of every peasant and burgher. In vain they made *chevauchées*
in the old familiar style to provoke the French to battle. In the
summer of 1370, with fifteen hundred men-at-arms and four
thousand bowmen, Knollys marched from Calais to Troyes and
thence, passing under the walls of Paris, to Brittany. But the only
result was a further growth of French national consciousness, while
the young English lords, humiliated by their lack of success,
grumbled furiously at having to serve under such a low-born
commander; 'the old brigand', they called him.

The French King's strategy was admirably adapted to his
means. It was to avoid pitched battles at all costs, use his superiority
in numbers and the growing French sympathies of the Black
Prince's vassals to liberate first one district, then another, and, by
strengthening the defences of every castle in French hands, to make
it impossible for the English to recover their lost gains. Gone were
the days when a few daring Englishmen could surprise and escalade
supposedly impregnable but weakly guarded strongholds; once
Charles's engineers had put the defences of any fortress or town in
order, nothing but a major army with a siege-train could reduce it.
And this was something far beyond the capacity of the English.

Early in 1370 Sir John Chandos – the most loved figure on
either side – fell in a skirmish near Poitiers. 'Courteous and benign,
amiable, liberal, preux, sage and true in all causes,' Froissart wrote
of him, 'nor was there ever knight better beloved nor praised of

every creature.' His death caused the defection of thousands of Gascons who, as long as he was Constable, adhered to the English cause. With his passing, the Black Prince lost his wisest counsellor and the last hope of an accommodation with the French King.

That summer, Moissac, Agen and even Aiguillon, which twenty years before had defied a French army for months, fell after sieges of only a few days. The count of Armagnac was now less than fifty miles from Bordeaux. At the end of August came the crowning humiliation when the city of Limoges was surrendered to the duke of Berri by its bishop after the townsmen had risen and overpowered the small English garrison under Sir Hugh Calveley. Bitterly resentful – for the bishop had been one of his closest friends – the Black Prince roused himself from his sick bed at Angoulême and, borne in a litter in the midst of his army, marched on the city. Breaching its walls by mining, he stormed it by night. The vengeance taken by his unbridled troops shocked even that unsqueamish age and marred his reputation for chivalry. It did the English cause untold harm.

A month later the French King raised Bertrand du Guesclin to the great office of Constable of France and commander of all her armies. This short, squat, coarse-featured veteran, with his long experience of mercenary war, was exactly the lieutenant Charles needed for his Fabian strategy of wearing down the invaders. In the days of the arrogant feudal nobility that had perished at Crécy and Poitiers, such a promotion would have been unthinkable. Now after a generation of civil war and anarchy it seemed inevitable, for the Breton knight had become the hero of France. But the chief credit for the collapse of the hitherto invincible English belonged to the unmartial, unspectacular sovereign who had seen so clearly, and so cunningly pursued, the means by which they could be defeated.

In November 1370, two months after the sack of Limoges and only three years after his victory at Nájera, the Black Prince, a sick, frustrated man, handed over his command and the lieutenancy of Aquitaine to his brother, John of Gaunt. In January 1371 he sailed for England where he found his father, once the hero of Europe, sunk in a doting dependence on his mistress, Alice Perrers, a former lady-in-waiting of the dead Queen. Withdrawing to Berkhamsted castle and taking no further part in public life, he watched from a bed of sickness the continuing decline of England's fortunes.

His departure made no difference to the course of the war. John of Gaunt, an ambitious, hustling and habitually unlucky man, was no more able to stem the French advance than his brother. In the late summer of 1371, after six months' campaigning, he too relinquished his command and handed over the governance of what remained of England's dominion to the Gascon veteran of Poitiers, Captal de Buch. A few weeks later he married the eldest daughter and co-heiress of the dead Don Pedro and thereafter became increasingly preoccupied with a claim to the Castilian throne.

Yet, though he now called himself a king, the only dowry his wife brought him were 'castles in Spain'. French aid had by now firmly seated the Bastard on that country's throne and aligned him permanently against England. Henceforward Castile's ocean-going fleet became a major factor in the war. In their obsession with military glory the English had omitted to remain strong at sea, and the command which Edward had won at Sluys and which had enabled his armies to ravage France at will had slipped from his hands. Ever since the first Black Death he had overstrained the country's maritime resources by impressing ships and seamen and neglecting to pay for them. He still held both sides of the Dover strait and called himself lord of the seas, but in the Atlantic waters between England and Gascony the great galliasses of Castile were a growing menace to his communications. In the autumn of 1371 Guy de Brian – the standard bearer at Crécy and a founder Knight of the Garter – won an action against French privateers near Roscoff off the coast of Brittany. But on 22 June 1372, a much larger English fleet attempting to relieve La Rochelle under the new Lieutenant of Aquitaine, the earl of Pembroke, was routed by the combined fleets of Castile and France, and with most of his crews, made prisoner. A final attempt by Edward III and the Black Prince to take a new army to Gascony in person failed in a terrible autumn storm which sent thousands to the bottom after six weeks of buffeting at the mouth of the Channel. It was the old King's last appearance in the war.

With La Rochelle in French hands and the Castilian and French navies in control of the Bay of Biscay, the English cause was lost. The Gascon wine trade was ruined and the age-long link between England and the Garonne all but broken. In the summer of 1373 John of Gaunt made an attempt to do by land what could no longer be done by sea, setting out from Calais on 4 August with an army of 15,000 men and crossing eastern France in a *grande chevauchée* which ended at Christmas at Bordeaux after a wintry march across the Auvergne. This feat of endurance, in which vast numbers of horses perished, was regarded as 'most honourable to the English' and probably saved Bordeaux. But as the French avoided battle, it achieved nothing else.

With the fall of La Réole at the beginning of 1374 all that remained of England's overseas empire was Calais and a thin coastal strip between Bordeaux and Bayonne – smaller now even than at Edward's accession. Having awoken the French people to nationhood, her King and princes could no longer retain the willing allegiance of Frenchmen. But the English still could not see this; after so many victories their defeats seemed to them only explicable as a judgment for their rulers' failings. They looked with horror at the spectacle of their King – once the model of Christian chivalry – decking his concubine with the jewels of his dead Queen and enthroning her in the tournament lists as Lady of the Sun. They learnt with pity of the plight of the great warrior, his son, bedridden in his castle at Berkhamsted. And they laid the blame on the King's ministers and, when they were able, through their representatives in Parliament, hounded them from office.

Two years later the victor of Poitiers, England's darling hero – 'the chief flower of chivalry of all the world', as Froissart called him – was laid to rest at Canterbury close to the shrine of St Thomas. His effigy, clad in gilt metal armour, still rests there on its tomb of Purbeck marble, his helmet open, his hands folded in prayer, his dog at his feet and, above the canopy, his crested helm, surcoat and shield, gauntlet and sword. When a year later, on 21 June 1377, his royal father, the victor of Crécy, a dotard with long white beard, deserted by his servants and plundered by his very mistress, followed him to the grave, nothing remained of England's conquests in France but Calais, Brest and a precarious dwindling strip of Gascon coast, while a French army was poised to invade and occupy the Isle of Wight. Before he could be laid in his tomb all the principal English Channel ports – Fowey, Plymouth, Melcombe Regis, Poole, Hastings, Rye – and even Gravesend – had been sacked and burnt by French and Spanish raiders, the mouth of London river was being hastily guarded by booms and chains, and the prior of Lewes, at the head of the posse of East Sussex, called out to resist invasion, had been carried off into captivity.

CHAPTER SIXTEEN

Peasants in Revolt

The Hurling Time

'Englishmen suffer indeed for a season, but
in the end they repay so cruelly that it may stand
as a great warning . . . There is no people under
the sun so perilous in the matter of its common
folk as they are in England.'

Froissart

WITH THE ISLE OF WIGHT OVERRUN by a French army and Castilian
and French fleets riding the Channel, the reign of the ten-year-old
Richard II began in national defeat and humiliation. The Council
of Regency which governed in his name had to face the affronted
patriotism and resentment of the nation's representatives in Parliament. For there was a general belief that the sums voted for the war
had been embezzled or, at best, wasted. The man whom everyone
blamed for England's misfortunes, probably unfairly, was Edward
III's fourth son, John of Gaunt, Duke of Lancaster, whose military
lack of success had been in such sorry contrast to the victories of
his brother, the Black Prince, and his father-in-law, the great
warrior Henry Grosmont, Duke of Lancaster. Gaunt's pride,
arrogance and autocratic ways and his vast wealth, the inheritance
of his dead wife and her sister and co-heiress – whom he was even
popularly suspected of having murdered to secure the whole of his
father-in-law's huge patrimony – made him the most hated man in
the kingdom. Laying claim to a foreign throne through his second
marriage to a Spanish princess while living in open adultery with
his children's governess – the great love of his life and ancestress

of the future British royal line – he seemed to be calling down heaven's wrath on the realm.

Nor was it only the discontent of the politically enfranchised classes that the King's government had to face. There was widespread unrest, too, among the toiling peasant masses outside the constitution. For the most enduring consequence of the Black Death had been a general shortage of labour caused by the death in its first three outbreaks of half the country's population. One result had been a spectacular rise in wages, which the Council and successive Parliaments of landowners had tried vainly to halt by punitive ordinances and legislation. These Statutes of Labourers, as they were called, aroused bitter class feeling.

Yet for a century before the Black Death the position of the English peasant had been slowly improving, whether he was a well-to-do yardlander farming two or three hundred acres or a landless cottar earning his daily bread by wages. Compared with the wretched peasantry of the continent, he was not too badly off except when the harvest failed. For the bowmen of Crécy had not been drawn from an oppressed populace. It was a commonplace to contrast the lot of the English husbandman with that of the French serf, wrapped in sacking and living on apples and bitter rye-bread.

Yet somewhere near half the English peasantry were not legally free, but tied by inheritance to the soil they cultivated. Described as villeins and subject to the discipline of the lord's manorial court or leet – on whose juries and inquests they served – they could not claim a free man's rights under the Common Law, let alone representation in Parliament. Like the feudalism of which it was part, the servile manorial system of the open field villages of central and southern England had long been in decline and was gradually giving way to an economy based on paid labour and rented farms. But it was still the basis of life for nearly a million men and women who were bound by birth to the soil and compelled to perform unpaid menial services for its lord. They could only gain release by a formal grant of manumission or by flight from their homes and fields to some neighbouring chartered borough where servile status had been abolished, and residence for a year and a day gave a man his freedom.

The extent of the services the villein had to perform for his lord varied with the size of his holding and the custom of the manor. But wherever the open-field system operated, as it did in most parts of the country except the pastoral north and west and in Kent, the peasant was confronted by uncertain demands on his time and by galling restrictions on his economic freedom of action. Among these were the obligation to grind his corn, bake his bread and brew his ale at the lord's mill, oven and brewery – 'suit of mill' and 'oven', as they were called – which not only enriched the lord, but offered opportunities for every kind of chicanery and imposition by those to whom the latter leased his rights. An equally resented monopoly was the lord's dovecot and 'free warren', from which hordes of pigeons and rabbits descended on the peasant's crops, while, if he retaliated by trapping such pests, he faced a heavy fine in the manorial court. If he wished to sell a beast, to reside outside the manor, to marry his son or daughter, even if the latter became pregnant – for this depreciated her value – he was fined. And on his death his widow or heir was forced to pay a heriot – the value of the best beast and chattel – and an entry-fine equivalent to a year's rent as the price of taking over the family holding.

All this had come to be intensely resented. Villeinage was seen by the bondsman as an economic imposition and a degrading distinction. It was no longer taken for granted, and every opportunity was seized to escape or evade its burdens. Those who resented them most were the richer villagers who occupied the traditional yardlands – holdings of thirty acres or more in the arable fields, with corresponding rights in the manorial meadowland, waste and woodland. A yardlander had to perform for his holding, in person or by proxy, not only a full half-day's labour on the lord's land for three or four days a week throughout the year but additional services called 'love-boons' – given, in theory, out of love for his feudal protector – at the very seasons, haymaking and harvest, harrowing and sowing times, when he needed all the labour he could command to wrest a living from his own villein soil.

Those who could afford it, therefore, seized every opportunity to commute as many of such services as possible for money payments. In the expanding agricultural economy of the thirteenth and early fourteenth centuries many peasants had been able to free themselves from the more onerous burdens, for progressive land-owners found it paid to hire labour rather than depend on the un-willing services of disgruntled serfs. The halving of the national labour-force by the Black Death halted this gradual emancipation. Labour had suddenly become the most precious commodity in the kingdom. A landowner who had made no composition with or con-cessions to his serfs found himself able to cultivate his depopulated estates far more cheaply than one who had commuted his villeins' services for a cash payment. Bound by agreements to let their serfs enjoy their holdings at rents which now bore no relation to what they themselves had to pay for hired labour, and desperate for lack of workers, many lords, therefore, tried to enforce rights which had lapsed or to stretch those that remained.

If the Black Death made lords more conscious of the value of compulsory services, it made every serf more eager to evade them. Shaking off their ancestral shackles, bondsmen fled from their homes and took service for wages with distant employers who asked no questions. It was the poorer members of the village community with no land to lose who were best able to seize such opportunities – the young and those with no possessions but their tools and skill as husbandmen or craftsmen. The attempts of Parliament and of local justices to keep down wages by branding, imprisonment and the stocks drove them to make common cause with their richer neighbours, who were confronted by demands from their lords for services which they regarded as unjust and oppressive.

It was against the lord's officers and agents that the peasant's indignation was, in particular, directed. From the receivers and bailiffs who wrung from him the services and rents on which the landowner lived, from the steward who presided at his manorial court and the lawyers who made extreme claims on the lord's behalf, he received little mercy. Times were bad, money hard to come by for a luxurious ruling class in need of the income it could no longer obtain from victories abroad. The business of its agents was to exact the uttermost service and payment obtainable. In the process they often took – and even more often were suspected of taking – more than was due or than the lord himself received.

Some of the hardest task-masters were the monasteries who, hit by the economic recession and the plague, had never enjoyed, like the secular lords, the opportunity of making good their losses by the plunder and ransoms of war. Intensely conservative and, like all corporations, impersonal in business relationships, they had the justification that their exactions were for the service of God. More easily than most they were able to prove rights to long-lapsed services by the charters which every religious house pre-served and added to by cultivating the friendship of the great and sometimes, if their critics are to be believed, improved by a little pious and skilled forgery. Nor, conscious of the sanctity of their claims, were they always very tactful with those whose labour they exploited; the abbot of Burton told his tenants that they owned nothing but their bellies.

Of all who enforced the lord's rights the lawyer was the most hated. To the peasant the purpose of the law seemed to be to keep him down and enforce the servile status which deprived him of liberty and opportunity. In the thirty years following the first post-Black Death statute against what Council and Parliament called 'the malice of labourers', nearly nine thousand cases of wage en-forcement were tried by the courts and, in nearly all, judgment was given in the employer's favour. The peasant's indignation at those who put such restraints on him was increased by the spectacle of expanding freedom in the chartered towns which had sprung up in every part of England and to which so many of the younger villagers had fled to better their conditions. Some of these, who had survived the harsh conditions and competition of the medieval town, had themselves grown rich and famous.

*   *   *

Because of this, as well as for other reasons, there was a captious, bitter, disillusioned spirit abroad. The strain and cost of the war, with its latter disasters and humiliations and the successive visita-tions of Black Death had all tended to shake men's faith in society. The pestilence which had driven weak natures to a hectic pursuit of pleasure, elevating the self-indulgence of the moment above duty and morality, had left only half the labour formerly available to do

the nation's work and supply the luxuries of the rich. For a generation the burden of war debts and taxes had fallen with what seemed
insupportable severity on the survivors. The result was a widespread sense of frustration, of loss of familiar standards, of resentment between employer and employed, landowner and husbandman, government and taxpayer. Everyone tended to blame someone else for his sufferings.

Deep down the malaise of England after the Black Death was
spiritual. It was the sickness of soul of a people who felt that justice
was being outraged. The old static feudalism, in which every man
knew and accepted his place, was disintegrating; the more fluid
society that was replacing it was on the make and given to lavish and
ostentatious luxury. The reign of Edward III had witnessed a
steady rise in the standards of comfort, not only of the aristocracy
but of new classes – financiers, merchants, woolmasters, franklins,
master-craftsmen, millers, even farmers. Hearths with chimneys
had taken the place in rich men's houses of sooty open fires;
Flemish glass had appeared in traceried windows; dovecots, fish-
ponds and nut-alleys were laid out in parks and gardens; manor-
houses and fine merchants' dwellings, with private bedrooms and
plastered walls, were rising in place of the old gloomy fortresses
where men and beasts had slept together on filthy, rush-strewn
floors in draughty halls, full of smoke and stink. Yet such signs of
progress struck moralists like the poet William Langland as symptoms of a diseased society; of a selfish decline from the virtues of
austerer days:

> 'Ailing is the hall each day in the week
> Where the lord nor the lady liketh not to sit.
> Now hath each rich man a rule to eaten by himself
> In a privy parlour, for poor men's sake,
> Or in a chamber with a chimney, and leave the chief hall
> That was made for meals and men to eaten in.'

All this was the result of an advance in civilization, arts and
sciences. Exchange of goods and merchandise had thrown the
career open to the talents. In every city a race of men had arisen
who pursued money-making as an end in itself, who bought and
sold not primarily to supply the consumer with goods but to

increase their stock of money and use it for making more. Usury, forestalling, regrating, making a corner in commodities, and artificially lowering market-prices in order to buy and raising them in order to sell – all the practices which the Church had taught were unchristian and unneighbourly – were pursued as a profession by men who made fortunes by doing so and put ordinary folk out of countenance by extravagant living and the grandeur of their ways. Merchants, whose grandfathers or even fathers had been simple craftsmen or serfs, were addressed by their fellow townsmen as worshipful or sire, wore scarlet robes and costly furs as masters and liverymen of monopolistic merchant companies founded originally to protect and foster honest craftsmanship, but since grown into exclusive chartered societies of wealthy entrepreneurs – Mercers, Drapers and Goldsmiths, Grocers, Fishmongers and Vintners, Skinners, Salters, Leathersellers and Ironmongers – famed for their lavish hospitality and elaborate ritual and pageantry. Instead of mixing socially with their employees they hobnobbed with lords and even princes; Sir Henry Pickard, Master of the Vintners Company, on one day in 1364 entertained four kings to dinner in the livery hall.[1] The bitterest hatred of the 'good' Parliament was reserved for another vintner, Richard Lyons, whose memorial brass, as recorded by Stow, depicted him with a 'little beard forked, a gown girt down to his feet of branched damask wrought with the likeness of flowers, a large purse on his right side hanging in a belt from his left shoulder'. With his patron, Lord Latimer, the Treasurer, he was accused of 'buying up all the merchandise that came into England and setting prices at their own pleasure, whereby they made such a scarcity of things saleable that the common sort of people could scarcely live'.

Not all great merchants were crooks; even Lyons was probably maligned. By their own standards most of them were worthy, if self-important, men whose bond could be trusted by their fellows; they could hardly have continued to succeed otherwise. Yet there was a widespread feeling that vintners diluted wine, that woolmongers cheated wool-growers, that grocers and corn-merchants

[1] Of France, Scotland, Denmark and Cyprus – the first two being then prisoners in England.

sold false measure, that those who lent money to the Crown cheated the taxpayer, and that if a man had grown rich by trade he must be a rogue. And some of those who had made money out of the French wars were vulgar upstarts with extravagant standards of display and notorious for jobbery and corruption. 'Soapmongers and their sons for silver,' wrote the indignant Langland, 'are made knights.' 'Covetise hath dominion over all things,' complained his fellow poet, Gower; 'there is no city or good town where Trick does not rob to enrich himself. Trick at Bordeaux, Trick at Seville, Trick at Paris buys and sells; Trick has his ships and servants, and of the noblest riches, Trick has ten times more than other folk.'

Running through society, including the Church, was this sense of division, strife and covetousness. 'Avarice,' a preacher said, 'makes men fight one another like dogs over a bone.' By its side went 'the foul sin of pride'. Both the old ruling class and the new vied in the extravagance of their clothes, feasts and entertainments; 'in such manner they spent and wasted their riches with abuses and ludicrous wantonness that the common voice of the people exclaimed'. The age was marked by absurd fashions in clothes; peaked and curled shoes with toes so long that their wearers were sometimes forced to walk upstairs backwards or hand their shoes to their pages to carry; ladies' fantastic and towering head-dresses; the mincing gait, long hair and trailing sleeves of the young courtiers who often squandered as much on their pampered bodies as would have fed and clothed a whole village. Contrasted with 'the gay robes, the soft sheets, the small shirtes' of the rich was the peasant, with his garment of hodden grey, living on cold cabbage, bacon and penny ale; his wattle-and-log hut full of holes; the poor Norfolk deerstalker whose feet were so putrified by the dungeons of Norwich castle that he could not walk at his trial, and his eight fellow-prisoners who died in Northampton gaol from hunger, thirst and want. 'I have no penny,' declared Langland's Piers Plowman,

'pullets for to buy
Neither geese nor gris but two green cheeses,
A few curds and cream and a cake of oats,
And two loaves of beans and bran to bake for my bairns.'

To him it seemed a denial of Christianity that the honest poor should be defrauded. His heart was stirred and his indignation roused for 'prisoners in pits' and poor folk in cottages 'charged with children and chief lord's rent', and country women 'rising with rue in winter nights to rock the cradle',

'To card and to comb to clout and to wash; . . .
Many the children and nought but a man's hands
to clothe and feed them and few pennies taken.'

Out of the air of fourteenth-century England, with all its glaring inequalities, arose a popular conviction – so strangely contrasted with the assumptions of the warrior and prelate class – that 'the peasant maintained the state of the world' and was receiving less than justice. It was put in its highest form by Langland, the underlying theme of whose poem on the divine mercy and forgiveness of God was that Christ's sacrifice demanded from men in return just living and just dealing – honest work and loving kindness:

'For we are all Christ's creatures and of his coffers rich
And brethren of one blood as well beggars as earls; . . .
Therefore love we as true brethren and each man laugh on
    the other,
And of that each man can spare give aid when it is needed,
And every man help the other, for go hence we all shall.'

He himself examined his conscience on this issue, comparing his idle life as a chantry clerk with that of the peasant folk among whom he had grown up. 'Can you,' Reason asked him,

'cock up haycocks and pitch them in the cart?
Or can you handle a scythe or make a heap of sheaves?
Or keep my corn in my croft from pickers and stealers?
Can you shape a shoe, cut clothes or take care of cattle?
Can you hedge or harrow or herd the hogs or geese?
Or any kind of craft the community needs?'

Langland's poem voiced the recurring English reaction to the contrast between ill-used wealth and undeserved destitution, with its characteristic resolve, not to destroy society, but to redress the balance. Though it never seems to have attained the dignity of an illuminated manuscript – the *imprimatur* of fashionable esteem in that intensely aristocratic age – for a work written before printing by a man without rank or fortune it had an astonishing success. Some sixty copies have survived and, since it circulated among the poor and lowly, many more must have perished. Overlooked by the rich like *A Pilgrim's Progress* of a later age, its readers and copyists were probably parish priests – for it is hardly likely to have appealed much to friars – and it may have been through them and their sermons that the name of its humble peasant hero and his identification with the crucified Christ became so widely known. At the end of the fourteenth and the beginning of the fifteenth century there appeared on the nave walls of parish churches in southern England a number of paintings, crude and almost certainly executed by local hands, of Christ naked, lacerated and bleeding, with a carpenter's tools – mallet, hammer, knife, axe, pincers, horn and wheel – haloed round his head. This figure of 'Christ of the Trades' is to be found in churches as far apart as Pembrokeshire and Suffolk. Many more probably disappeared during the Reformation; among the best preserved are those at Ampney St Mary in the Cotswolds – not far from the hillside on which Langland saw silhouetted the tower of Truth – at Hessett in Suffolk and at Stedham in Sussex. In the first, the labouring Christ faces a painting of the hero of knightly chivalry, St George slaying the dragon; in the last, of the Virgin sheltering the congregation under her cloak.

*   *   *

There was a wide gap between the patient, Christ-like craftsman and peasant of the wall-paintings of Langland's dream, and the angry labourer refusing service for his lord, cursing landlords, monks and lawyers and fingering his bow. It was not hard to inflame uneducated men with a sense of injury, and it was not the selfless side of human nature that was inflamed. The poet himself was well aware of it. 'Then,' he wrote,

> 'would Wastour not work but wandren about . . .
> Labourers, that have no land to live on but their hands,
> Deigned not to dine today on yesterday's cabbage.
> No penny ale may please them nor no piece of bacon,
> But if it be fresh flesh or fish fried or baked.'

He depicted the runagate villein, demanding ever higher wages, who, when refused,

> 'would wail the time that ever he was workman born;
> Then curseth he the King and all his Council with him
> That lay down such laws and labourers to grieve.'

Parliament was being flouted and the Statute of Labourers made a dead letter by surly villeins standing idle in the fields or tramping in angry companies to the nearest town to sell their labour to those who would pay highest for it. Phrases like 'Stand together!' 'Make a good end of what hath been begun!' passed from shire to shire, and wandering agitators preached incendiary sermons on village greens. 'Things will never go well in England,' proclaimed the defrocked hedge-priest and demagogue, John Ball, 'so long as goods be not in common and so long as there be villeins and gentlemen. By what right are they whom we call lords greater than we?' 'We are formed,' he declared, 'in Christ's likeness and they treat us like beasts.'

It was an age of war and violence; war always breeds violence. Resentment amongst the labouring classes against their oppressors was not confined to England. In the middle of the century the Roman mob had risen under the demagogue Cola di Rienzi; a decade later occurred the terrifying *jacquerie* in northern France. Wherever men were brought together in large numbers to serve masters who catered for the luxuries of the rich, the spirit of rebellion was present. In 1378 the oppressed wool-carders of Florence revolted against the merchant oligarchs of the city, stormed the palazzo of the Commune and installed one of their members as Gonfalonier of Justice. A year later the weavers of Ghent and Bruges and the Flemish cloth towns had risen and, under a second van Artevelde, son of Edward III's old ally, were still defying their count and the French King.

In England, unrest had so far mainly taken the form of mass withdrawals of labour-services, particularly in places where the lord was an impersonal ecclesiastical corporation. In 1378, after the jurymen of Harmsworth, Middlesex – the property of a Norman abbey – had defied the lord's steward by returning a false verdict in favour of their fellow villeins who had absented themselves from the previous year's haymaking, the villagers deliberately opened the river sluices to flood the hay. There were mob rescues of fugitive bondsmen as they were being haled back to their 'villein nests', and armed assemblies by night to poach the lord's woods and slay his game. The labour laws, too, help to explain the passion and vehemence of some of these sudden explosions of rustic wrath, often on seemingly trivial pretexts. Englishmen were not prepared to suffer the indignity of being branded on the forehead with an 'F' for 'falsehood' because they took day-hire or demanded more than the inadequate statutory wage allowed by Parliament. As far back as the year before Poitiers, when feeling against this form of class legislation was running particularly high, the peasants from the villages round Oxford joined the townsmen in a murderous attack on the university – later known as St Scholastica's Day – distinguishing themselves by their savagery and furious cries of 'Havak, havoc, smygt faste, gyf good knock!'

During the opening years of Richard's reign such riots had grown ominously in number. They were fomented by the egalitarian sermons of friars and wandering priests like John Ball, who for the past twenty years had been tramping the country preaching, in defiance of the ecclesiastical authorities, against the rich 'possessioners' of Church and State. In the words of the chronicler Walsingham, he preached 'those things which he knew would be pleasing to the common people, speaking evil both of ecclesiastical and temporal lords, and won the good will of the common people rather than merit in the sight of God. For he taught that tithes ought not to be paid unless he who gave them was richer than the parson who received them. He also taught that tithes and oblations should be withheld if the parishioner was known to be a better man than the priest.' Forbidden to preach in church, he continued to do so in streets, villages and fields until he got himself excommunicated. Nothing, however, stopped him and, though he several times suffered imprisonment, as soon as he got out he started again. He also took to circulating inflammatory letters full of dark riddles and rhymes calling on the virtuous poor to prepare for the day when they could fall on their oppressors. 'John Ball, St Mary's priest,' ran one, 'greeteth well all manner of men and biddeth them in the name of the Trinity, Father, Son and Holy Ghost, stand manlike together in truth, and help truth, and truth shall help you.'

*   *   *

On top of this strained situation came the demand for a new and crushing tax. Like all medieval peoples the English tended to regard taxes as a form of robbery and injustice. The evolution of their polity had turned largely on their rulers' recognition that the consent of the taxed to new imposts could only be won by allowing them a share in their imposition. When, Magna Carta having placed limitations on the feudal taxation of land, imposts had been levied on personal wealth and merchandise – moveables, as they were called – the same rule had been adopted.

Superseding the feudal lord's right to tallage at will, the principle that the subject should be party to the fiscal burdens imposed on him had been applied at every stage of the tax-structure. Whenever Parliament agreed that a fifth, tenth or fifteenth should be levied on moveables, justices had been sent into every county to assess the local proportion payable with representative knights from every hundred who, in turn, met the representatives of every vill, where a jury of inquest swore to the number, quantity and value of taxable goods in the township. Shortly before Crécy, as a result of an agreement between Exchequer officials and representatives of the localities, a fixed proportion of the subsidy rate voted by Parliament had been allocated to every county, hundred and township. During Edward III's reign, which lasted fifty years, vast sums were raised by this method for the war with France, which, after the victorious 1340s and 1350s, ceased to finance itself and forced Government and Parliament to seek ever new ways of raising money.

In 1371 the latter adopted the novel device of a tax on every parish in England at a standard rate. Six years later a still more revolutionary innovation was adopted by Edward's last Parliament. This was a poll-tax of fourpence a head on the entire lay adult population except beggers. This 'tallage of groats', as it was called,

307

mulcting the poorest at the same rate as the richest, proved intensely unpopular and very hard to collect. But it appealed to a Parliament of landowners and employers, since for the first time it imposed a direct fiscal burden on the peasant and unpropertied wage-earner.

Three years after Richard II's accession, faced by the Government's now desperate need, a new Parliament, meeting at Northampton in the autumn of 1380, imposed the tax for a third time, trebling the rate per head. For a poor rustic householder with a large family who might have to defray as well the tax of several aged or female relatives, this was a crushing burden. Reflecting the belief of the rich that the labour-shortage caused by the Black Death had placed 'the wealth of the kingdom in the hands of artisans and labourers', it not only showed astonishing ignorance of the circumstances of 'common folk whose occupations standeth in grobbying about the earth'; it ignored the principle for which Parliament had long contended: that there should be no taxation without representation and consent. For the peasantry and town-artisans, on whom the tax bore so hardly, were completely unrepresented in a Parliament of magnates, prelates, landowners, merchants and lawyers.

The consequence of the shilling poll-tax was a wholesale falsification by the villages of southern England of their tax-returns. When these reached the commissioners appointed to collect the money, it seemed as though the population had shrunk by a third since the poll-tax of two years before. The amount brought in fell far below what was expected, and the Government was furious. On 16 March 1381 the Council found that the local collectors had been guilty of gross negligence and favouritism, and appointed a new commission to scrutinize the lists and enforce payment from evaders.

The decision was received with universal execration. It was spoken of as a corrupt job engineered for the private profit of the head of the commission of revision, John Legge, a serjeant-at-law, and of the Treasurer, Sir Robert Hales – 'Hob the robber', as he was called. When news of a further descent of tax assessors reached the villages, the ignorant supposed that a new tax was to be levied on top of that already paid. Everywhere in the populous counties of the south-east, rustic opinion was at boiling point against tax-collectors, escheators, jurymen, lawyers and royal officials in general and against the Chancellor and Treasurer in particular, and, illogically enough, for he was no longer actively engaged in government but absent on a mission in Scotland, the young King's hated uncle, John of Gaunt.

No one in authority treated the dissatisfaction of the peasantry very seriously. But when at the end of May the new poll-tax com-missioner for Essex, Thomas Bampton, appeared at Brentwood with two serjeants-at-arms to open enquiries into the returns for the hundred of Barstaple, he was met by the representatives of the defaulting townships with a sullen refusal to pay. They possessed, they said, their receipt for the subsidy and would not pay a penny more. But it was the fishermen and fowlers of the Thames estuary – the men of the sea and salt-water creeks – who provided the spark which fired the revolution of working-class England. Summoning to their aid their neighbours from Corringham and Stanford-le-Hope, the men of Fobbing-by-Tilbury met Bampton's threats of arrest with open violence, and with sticks and stones drove him and his men out of the town.

*   *   *

This was more than the Government could ignore. On Sunday 2 June, the Chief Justice of the Common Pleas, Sir Robert Belknap, descended on Brentford with a commission of trailbaston and an escort of pikesmen. His business was to punish the rioters and hang the ringleaders. He found the place in a ferment. For by now the rebellious fishermen had prevailed on the entire neighbourhood to rise. Armed with staves, pitchforks and bows, a mob surrounded the judge, seized and burnt his papers and made him swear on his knees never to hold another commission. They then murdered his three clerks and three local tax-assessors or jurymen whose names they had made him reveal. Sticking their heads on poles they bore them in triumph round the villages of south-east Essex, while the terrified Belknap fled back to London.

On the same day trouble began on the other side of the Thames.

At Erith in Kent a band of rioters broke into the monastery of Lesnes and made the abbot swear to support them. The ring-leaders then crossed the river to take counsel of the men of Essex: During the next few days rebellion spread northwards across the county as rioters carried their messages from parish to parish. Everywhere government agents were attacked, their houses plundered and their records and papers thrown into courtyard or street and burnt. The admiral of the Essex coast, Edmund de la Mare of Peldon, and the sheriff, John Sewall of Coggeshall, had their homes sacked, the former's papers being carried on a pitch-fork at the head of the triumphant fishermen. At every manor visited, a bonfire was made of all charters and manorial rolls.

It was as though the whole system of law and government, built up over centuries, was being repudiated by the common people. Yet though damage to property was widespread, there was comparatively little loss of life, most of the local lords managing to escape. The chief escheator of the county was murdered, as well as a number of Flemish merchants in Colchester, where the mob rose at the approach of the peasantry. Had the Treasurer been at his home at Temple Cressing instead of in London, he would certainly have been torn to pieces; as it was, his 'very beautiful and delectable manor', as a chronicler described it, was burnt to the ground after the populace had eaten the fine fare and broached 'the three tuns of good wine' which he had laid in for an impending meeting of the chapter-general of the Order of St John of Jerusalem, of which he was Master.

Meanwhile trouble was growing in Kent. On the day after the assault on the Chief Justice at Brentwood, two serjeants-at-arms acting for Sir Simon Burley, the King's tutor, arrested a respected burgess of Gravesend on the ground that he was a runaway serf. When the townsfolk declined to pay £300 for his manumission – at least £15,000 in today's purchasing-power – the poor man was sent to the dungeons of Rochester castle. Two days later, on Wednesday 5 June, heartened by the arrival of a hundred insur-gents from Essex, the people of all the towns and villages on the south bank of the river between Erith and Gravesend rose in rebellion. They were careful, however, to stress in a proclamation listing the crimes of their young sovereign's ministers that, though there were 'more kings than one in the land', they wished for none but Richard. Patriotically they added that, 'none dwelling within twelve miles of the sea should go with them but should keep the coast of the sea from enemies'.

Next day, 6 June 1381, decided the fate of Kent. At one end of the county the men of Gravesend and Dartford marched on Rochester. At the other end a commission of trailbaston, directed against tax-evaders and accompanied by the hated John Legge, was prevented from entering Canterbury. Rochester castle, though strong enough to withstand a siege for weeks, was surrendered by its Constable that afternoon after several ineffective attempts to storm it. Probably it was under-garrisoned but, like almost everyone else, the defenders were bemused by the fury and turbulence of the mob. For the rustic population of England to behave in such a way seemed something outside nature: it was as though the animals had rebelled.

Certainly the Government seemed unable to grasp the situation. Like the local authorities it remained inert throughout that critical first week of June, helplessly watching the course of events. The Chancellor, its head, was the gentle primate, Simon Thebaud of Sudbury – son of a Suffolk trader whose family had grown rich supplying the local gentry with luxury goods and developing the new rural cloth industry. He was utterly without martial instinct or experience. The King's uncles were far away; John of Gaunt was in Edinburgh negotiating a truce with the Scots, Thomas of Woodstock was in the Welsh Marches, and Edmund of Cambridge had just sailed for Portugal. On news of the outbreak a messenger had been sent to Plymouth to countermand the expedition but arrived too late. Owing to the needs of the English garrisons in France and Brittany, the country was almost denuded of troops except on the remote Scottish and Welsh borders. In the capital and the crucial south-east there were only a few hundred men-at-arms and archers guarding the King, and a small force which the old *condottiere*, Sir Robert Knollys, had started to collect in his London house to reinforce Brittany. Nothing was done to call out the country gentry and their retainers who, in the insurgent counties to the east and north of London, were paralysed with fear.

But if the Government was without an active head, the insurgents had found one. On Friday 7 May, the men of Kent marched up the Medway valley from Rochester to Maidstone, where they were welcomed by the populace who rose and plundered the richer inhabitants, murdering one of them. Here they chose as their captain one Wat Tyler. Little is known of his past, but according to Froissart he had seen service in the French wars and, it subsequently transpired, like many old soldiers, had since been earning a livelihood by highway robbery. He was clearly a mob orator of genius, for he immediately reduced to discipline the motley throng of excited peasants and artisans. And he quickly showed himself a man of action and military talent.

On the day he assumed command Tyler issued a proclamation setting out the insurgents' aims. They would admit, he said, no allegiance except to "King Richard and the true commons' – in other words, themselves – and have no king named John, a reference to the duke of Lancaster. No tax should be levied 'save the fifteenths which their fathers and forbears knew and accepted', and everyone should hold himself in readiness to march, when called upon, to remove the traitors around the King and root out and destroy the lawyers and officials who had corrupted the realm.

The rebels had not only found a military leader. They acquired a spiritual one. Among the prisoners released from Maidstone gaol was John Ball. Only a few weeks before, the long-suffering archbishop had clapped him in again, describing how he had 'slunk back to our diocese like the fox that evaded the hunter, and feared not to preach and argue both in the churches and churchyards and in markets and other profane places, there beguiling the ears of the laity by his invective and putting about such scandals concerning our person and those of other prelates and clergy and – what is worse – using concerning the Holy Father himself language such as shamed the ears of good Christians.' The irrepressible preacher now found himself free again and with a ready-made congregation of twenty thousand ragged enthusiasts after his own heart. According to Froissart who, though often an unreliable witness, visited England soon after the rising and was clearly fascinated by the whole affair, he addressed them in these terms:

'My good friends, matters cannot go well in England until all things be held in common; when there shall be neither vassals nor lords; when the lords shall be no more masters than ourselves. How ill they behave to us! For what reason do they thus hold us in bondage? Are we not all descended from the same parents, Adam and Eve? And what can they show, or what reason can they give, why they should be more masters than ourselves? They are clothed in velvet and rich stuffs, ornamented with ermine and other furs, while we are forced to wear poor clothing. They have wines, spices and fine bread, while we have only rye and the refuse of the straw; and when we drink, it must be water. They have handsome seats and manors, while we must brave the wind and rain in our labours in the field; and it is by our labours that they have wherewith to support their pomp. We are called slaves and, if we do not perform our service we are beaten, and we have no sovereign to whom we can complain or would be willing to hear us. Let us go to the King and remonstrate with him. He is young and from him we may obtain a favourable answer, and, if not, we must ourselves seek to amend our conditions.'

At the same time the preacher sent out to the villages of Kent and Essex more of his inflammatory missives:

'John Ball
Greeteth you all,
And doth you to understand
He hath rung your bell.'

Another, written under a pseudonym and addressed to the men of Essex, was subsequently found in the pocket of a rioter condemned to be hanged:

'John Schep, sometime Saint Mary's priest of York, and now of Colchester, greets well John Nameless and John the Miller and John Carter and bids them that they beware of guile in the town, and stand together in God's name, and bids Piers Plowman go to his work and chastise well Hob the Robber. And take with you John Trueman and all his fellows and more, and look sharp you to your own head and no more.

'John the Miller hath ground small, small, small.
The King's Son of Heaven shall pay for all.'

313

Tyler and Ball – brigand and hedgerow preacher – were the leaders 'the true commons' needed. While Ball addressed himself to his sympathizers, Tyler acted. Sending emissaries to urge the surrounding villages to rise and join him at Maidstone, he set out with several thousand followers for Canterbury. By midday on 10 June he had reached the city, where he was greeted with enthusiasm by the inhabitants, all those, that is, who had nothing to lose. On enquiring whether there were any traitors in the town, he was directed to the houses of the local notables, three of whom he had executed on the spot. Then, having burnt the judicial and financial records of the shire, beaten up the sheriff and sacked the castle, letting out the prisoners from the gaols, he and his followers poured, a vast tumultuous multitude, into the cathedral during Mass. Here with one voice they cried out to the monks to elect a new Archbishop of Canterbury in place of Sudbury whom they declared to be a traitor and 'about to be beheaded for his iniquity'. They also extracted an oath of fealty to the King and true commons from the Mayor and corporation and – for the summer pilgrimage season was at its height – recruited their ranks by a number of pilgrims. At the same time they dispatched agitators to the towns and villages of east Kent.

Early on Tuesday 11 June, having spent less than twenty-four hours in Canterbury and set the eastern weald and coast from Sandwich to Appledore aflame, Tyler set off again. Reinforcements poured in as he marched. By nightfall he was back in Maidstone, having covered eighty miles in two days. Then, pausing only for the night, he marched with his entire host before dawn on the 12th for the capital, sending messengers into Sussex and the western counties to summon the commons to join him and 'close London round about'. Simultaneously on the other side of the Thames the Essex insurgents, who by now had won complete control of the county, began a parallel march under the captaincy of Thomas Farringdon, an aggrieved Londoner.

While the two hosts converged on the capital, terror reigned on either side of their march as village mobs smoked out royal and manorial officials, lawyers and unpopular landlords, breaking into their houses and burning every record they could find. They would have, they declared, 'no bondsmen in England'. Many of the gentry took to the woods, among them the poet John Gower, who afterwards recalled in his long Latin epic, *Vox Clamantis*, the pangs of hunger he suffered while living on acorns and trembling for his life in wet coppices. Others, less fearful or unpopular, made timely contributions to the 'cause' and took the oath of fidelity to the 'King and true commons'. A few, but only a few, were murdered, while others, being persons of distinction who had not done anything to make themselves unpopular, were carried off as hostages to grace Wat Tyler's entourage, including Sir Thomas Cobham and Sir Thomas Tryvet, a hero of the wars.

Meanwhile the authorities had at last resolved to act. On either the Tuesday or Wednesday Tyler's men, pouring towards the capital, were met by messengers from the King at Windsor to ask why they were raising rebellion and what they sought. Their answer was that they were coming to deliver him from traitors. They also presented a petition asking for the heads of the Duke of Lancaster and fourteen other notables, including the Chancellor, Treasurer and every leading member of the Government. On receipt of this the King and his advisers left hastily for London and the Tower to form a focus of resistance round which the forces of order could rally. The King's mother and her ladies, who had been on a summer pilgrimage to the Kentish shrines, also set out for the same place of refuge. On the way they encountered the rebel vanguard. Yet, though greatly frightened, they were subjected to nothing worse than a little ribald jesting and were allowed to continue their journey to the capital. Here the Mayor, William Walworth, after escorting his sovereign to the Tower, was busy putting the city into a state of defence.

That evening the Kentish host encamped on the Blackheath heights, looking down across the Thames to the distant city. On the opposite bank, the Essex men took up their station in the Mile End fields outside the suburb of Whitechapel and about a mile to the east of the walls and the Aldgate. Some of the less exhausted Kentish rebels continued as far as Southwark where, welcomed by the local mob, they burnt a bawdy house rented by some Flemish women from Mayor Walworth and let out the prisoners from the Marshalsea and King's Bench. Finding the drawbridge in the centre of London Bridge raised against them, they went on to Lambeth where they sacked the Archbishop's palace and the house of John Imworth, warden of the Marshalsea.

It was not only the proletariat of Southwark who sympathised with the insurgents. There were thousands of journeymen, apprentices and labourers inside the city walls who did so too. On the Mayor's orders the gates had been closed and entrusted to the aldermen and watch of the adjacent wards. But there were bitter rivalries among the city's rulers. The victualling interests were at daggers drawn with the older merchants, drapers and mercers who, employing labour on a large scale, favoured a policy of free trade and low-priced food in order to keep down wages and feed their journeymen and apprentices cheaply – a matter of vital importance to them since the labour shortage caused by the Black Death. Both were monopolists but, to overthrow their rivals, the victuallers had formed an alliance with the discontented city proletariat – wage-earners and small craftsmen – who regarded their employers and the capitalists who controlled the market for their handiwork in much the same light as the villeins regarded their lords. Among three aldermen whom the Mayor despatched to urge the insurgents to keep the peace was a certain John Horne, a fishmonger who, separating himself from his companions, sought a private interview with Tyler and secretly promised his support. When he returned to London he not only assured the Mayor that the marchers were honest patriots who would do the city no harm but, under cover of darkness, smuggled three agitators across the river to stir up the mob.

Earlier that evening an emissary from the rebel camp had travelled by boat from Greenwich to London to seek an interview with the King and Council. This was the Constable of Rochester castle, Sir John Newton, who for the past week had been a prisoner of the insurgents. Brought into the presence and given leave to speak, he explained that, though his captors would do the King no harm, they were determined to meet him face to face to communicate certain matters of which he had no charge to speak. Since they held his children as hostages and would slay them if he failed to return, he begged for an answer that would appease them and show that he had delivered his message.

To this after some hesitation the Council agreed. Next morning at prime the King and his lords embarked in five barges for Greenwich. Here, on the shore below Blackheath, the Kentish men, after a hungry and sleepless night, were assembled in battle array under two great banners of St George. While they waited, Mass was celebrated, it being Corpus Christi day, and afterwards John Ball preached, taking as his text the old popular rhyme:

> 'When Adam delved and Eve span
> Who was then the gentleman?'

According to the St Albans chronicler, 'he strove to prove that from the beginning all men were created equal by nature, and that servitude had been introduced by the unjust oppression of wicked men against God's will, for, if it had pleased Him to create serfs, surely in the beginning of the world He would have decreed who was to be a serf and who a lord . . . Wherefore they should be prudent men, and, with the love of a good husbandman tilling his fields and uprooting and destroying the tares which choke the grain, they should hasten to do the following things. First, they should kill the great lords of the kingdom; second, they should slay lawyers, judges and jurors; finally they should root out all those whom they knew to be likely to be harmful to the commonwealth in future. Thus they would obtain peace and security, for, when the great ones had been removed, there would be equal liberty and nobility and dignity and power for all.' 'When he had preached this and much other madness,' wrote the disgusted chronicler, 'the commons held him in such high favour that they acclaimed him the future Archbishop and Chancellor of the realm.'

Whether it was this sermon or the presence of the Archbishop in the royal barge or the fact that the Kentishmen had not breakfasted, they greeted the King's arrival with such a tumult of shouting that he was unable to make himself heard. 'Sirs,' he kept calling across the water as the rowers rested on their oars just out of reach of the frantic multitude, 'what do you want? Tell me now that I have come to talk to you.' But as the crowd steadily grew more threatening, fearing lest some of the bowmen might start to shoot, the earl of Salisbury – by far the most experienced soldier present – ordered the boats to put out into midstream and return to the Tower.

At that both the Kentish host and the Essex men, who had been watching from the other shore, set up a great shout of 'Treason' and, with their banners and pennants, moved off towards London. Access to the city's markets and provision shops had by now become essential if they were not to have to disperse through hunger – a fact on which the authorities were counting. Within the city, processions of clergy were marching through the streets praying for peace, while the crowds of sympathisers with the insurgents were gathering in the poorer lanes and alleys. For, though the city gates were still barred against them, the agitators whom Horne had slipped into the city had not been idle. As Wat Tyler's men neared the southern approaches to the bridge they were again met by this liberal-minded fishmonger waving a royal standard which he had procured by a trick from the town clerk. And as, headed by this emblem of loyalty and respectability, they surged on to the bridge, the drawbridge in the midst of its shops and houses was lowered to them by the alderman of the Billingsgate ward. About the same time another alderman of the opposition faction let in the Essex men through the Aldgate.

Once the head of the rebel columns was in possession of the southern and eastern entrances the whole multitude poured in to the city, while the apprentices and journeymen and the labouring poor of the slums flocked into the streets to greet them. For a time the newcomers were too busy eating, drinking and gaping at the city sights to do much harm. But presently, refreshed by several huge barrels of ale which some rash philanthropists had broached in the streets, and incited by the apprentices who had old scores to pay off against John of Gaunt, they set up a cry of 'To the Savoy! To the Savoy!' The Duke might be in Edinburgh, but the superb palace he had furnished from the plunder of France – and, as many supposed, of England – stood a mile outside the western walls where the fields and gardens sloped down to the riverside from the Strand that linked London to Westminster. Thither the men of

Kent, with thousands of excited apprentices – a great company with torches – made their way in an angry tumult, breaking into the Fleet prison on the way and letting out the criminals while the Duke's servants fled as the shouting came nearer.

No time was wasted. In the general desire for justice or revenge even plundering was forbidden. Everything in the great house was hurled out of the windows – tapestry, sheets, coverlets, beds – and hacked or torn to pieces. Then the building was set on fire and burnt to the ground. At the height of the fire there was an explosion caused by three barrels of gunpowder, which were thrown into the flames in the belief that they contained specie. Some of the rioters afterwards continued towards Westminster where they destroyed the house of the under-sheriff of Middlesex and let the prisoners out of the gaol. Others, on their way back to the city, broke into the laywers' home in the Temple, tore the tiles off the roof and took all the books, rolls and remembrances from the students' cupboards to make a bonfire. They also fired some shops and houses which had recently been built in Fleet Street, declaring that never again should any house deface the beauty of that favourite country walk of the Londoners. Those who had gone on to Westminster returned by way of Holborn, setting light to the houses of several 'traitors' pointed out to them by their London comrades and breaking open Newgate still further to enlarge their company. Meanwhile the men of Essex descended on the priory of St John's, Clerkenwell, the headquarters of the Knights Hospitallers just outside the city's northern wall. Here they burnt the priory and hospital and murdered seven Flemings who had taken sanctuary in the church.

That night, while the insurgents camped round the royal fortress in the open spaces of Tower Hill and St Catherine's wharf and while their leaders drew up lists of persons to be liquidated, the King and Council debated long and anxiously what was to be done. Since the morning their position had changed dramatically for the worse; instead of waiting behind London's walls while the rebels starved outside, they themselves were hemmed in the Tower, and the city it was supposed to dominate was in possession of a fanatic, uncontrollable mob. From a garret in one of the turrets into which he climbed, the boy King could see twenty or thirty fires burning in different parts of the town. Beyond, the whole of the home counties to south and east were in revolt, while, unknown as yet to the beleaguered Council, the revolutionary ferment had spread that afternoon into Hertfordshire and Suffolk, where burgesses and bondsmen had risen together against the monks of England's two most famous abbeys, St Albans and Bury.

The key to the situation lay, however, in the capital. If the mob who had taken possession of it could be defeated, the flames of revolt might be put out elsewhere. But, with London lost and the court imprisoned inside it, there was nothing round which the forces of order could rally. Mayor Walworth, a bluff and vigorous man, urged an immediate sally against the insurgents while they were sleeping off the effects of their evening's debauch. There were six hundred armed men-at-arms and archers in the Tower and a hundred or so more in Sir Robert Knollys's house and garden; with a bold front they would probably be joined by all the law-abiding in London. Only a small minority of the insurgents wore armour; if the loyal forces struck at once, thousands might be slain as they slept. But the earl of Salisbury, who had fought at Crécy and Poitiers, thought otherwise. Once fighting began in the narrow streets and lanes, the rebels' immense superiority in numbers would tell and total disaster might ensue. 'If we should begin a thing which we cannot achieve,' he said, 'we should never recover and we and our heirs would be disinherited and England would become a desert.' Instead, he offered the Ulysses-like counsel that an attempt should be made to induce the rebels to disperse by fair words and promises, which could afterwards be repudiated as obtained under duress.

An earlier attempt that evening to persuade them to do so by putting up the King to address them from the ramparts and offer a free pardon to all who should go home had been shouted down in derision. Some more signal mark of royal trust was needed if the populace were to be appeased. It was, therefore, proposed that the King should offer to confer with the rebels in the Mile End fields and to ride out there next morning through their midst with such of his lords as were not expressly marked down for execution. While under cover of this bold move the crowds were drawn away from the Tower, the Archbishop and Treasurer and John of Gaunt's son and heir, young Henry Bolingbroke, earl of Derby, could be smuggled out to safety by water.

The plan depended on the King's readiness to take the risk. But, though he appeared a little pensive, the boy was ready and even eager. He was now fourteen, and it was something to find that at last all the great lords and counsellors around him looked to him for leadership. As soon as it was light a proclamation was made from the walls and soon afterwards, surrounded by an immense multitude of excited country folk, the royal cortège set out along the Brentwood road for Mile End. But many of the Londoners stayed behind to watch the Tower, for the rebels' leaders were not so easily fooled. When the boat by which their intended victims attempted to escape appeared, it was forced to put back as soon as it emerged from the water-gate.

Nor did the royal ride to Mile End prove easy or pleasant. At one moment the Essex leader, Thomas Farringdon, a highly excitable man, seized the King's bridle, demanding to be avenged on that false traitor Prior Hales, the Treasurer, who he said had deprived him of his property by fraud. So threatening was the crowd that the King's half-brothers, the earl of Kent and Sir John Holland, finding themselves at the edge of the throng, seized the opportunity to gallop away and escape into the open country to the north. When, however, the royal party arrived in the Mile End fields, the simple country folk who were waiting there knelt before the King crying, 'Welcome, our lord King Richard, if it pleases you we will have no other King but you.' It was like the scene in the ballads when the sovereign whom Robin Hood and his men had captured revealed his identity and promised to restore to every honest man his own.

It must have seemed to many present that such a golden time had come when their young King – the son of England's dead hero, the Black Prince – announced that he would grant all their demands. He promised the abolition of serfdom, of villein services and seigneurial market monopolies, and that all holders of land in villeinage should henceforth become free tenants at the modest rent of fourpence an acre a year. Nor did he only promise them all free pardons and an amnesty if they would return quietly to their villages, but offered to give a royal banner to the men of every county and place them under his special protection and patronage. His words, as Froissart put it, 'appeased well the common people, such as were simple and good plain men'. They rather took the wind, however, out of their leaders' sails. The latter, therefore, returned to the charge. 'The commons,' Tyler told the King, 'will that you suffer them to take and deal with all the traitors who have sinned against you and the law.' To which young Richard replied that all should have due punishment as could be proved by process of law to be traitors.

This, however, was scarcely what Tyler and his fellow-leaders wanted. While the King, surrounded by the better disposed of his humbler subjects, was helping to set them on their way to their distant villages, the two captains of the Commons of Kent and Essex hurried back with a band of picked followers to the Tower where a large crowd was still waiting outside the gates, clamouring for the Archbishop's and Treasurer's blood. Pushing through them they succeeded in bluffing their way into the fortress itself, either through the treachery of the guards or, more probably, because, with the King and his lords expected back at any moment, the portcullis was up and no one knew what to do. Fraternising with the soldiers, shaking their hands and stroking their beards, the crowd pressed after their leaders into the royal apartments, shouting for the traitors' blood. In their search the King's bed was hacked to pieces and the Princess of Wales subjected to such rude treatment that she was borne off in a dead faint by her pages and put into a boat on the river. John Legge, the serjeant-at-law who had drawn up the poll-tax commission, and three of his clerks, the Duke of Lancaster's physician, a Franciscan friar named Appleton, and several others were found. The Duke's son, Henry Bolingbroke – who eighteen years later was to become King – was more fortunate, being saved by the resource of one of his father's retainers. The Archbishop and Treasurer were taken in the chapel where, expecting death, the former had just received the confession of the latter and administered the last rites. Dragged by the mob into the courtyard and across the cobbles to Tower Hill, they were summarily beheaded across a log of wood. It was the third time in the country's history that an Archbishop of Canterbury had been assaulted at the altar and brutally done to death.

After that, all pretence of moderation and order vanished. While the primate's head, stuck on a pike and crowned with his mitre, was being borne round the city before being set over the gateway to London Bridge – the traditional place for traitors – and the King, shunning the desecrated Tower, made his way with his escort to the royal Wardrobe at Baynard's Castle near St Paul's where his mother had taken refuge, the riff-raff of the capital and the peasants' army ran riot in the streets, forcing passers-by to cry, 'With King Richard and the true commons' and putting everyone to death who refused. By nightfall 'there was hardly a street in the city in which there were not bodies lying of those who had been slain'. The chief victims were the Flemish merchants who were hunted through the streets and killed wherever found; more than a hundred and fifty are said to have perished, including thirty-five who had taken shelter in St Martin-in-the-Vintry and who were dragged from the altar and beheaded outside on a single block. Every disorderly person who had old grudges to pay off or property he coveted seized his opportunity; Alderman Horne, with a mob at his heels, paraded the streets bidding anyone who wanted justice against a neighbour to apply to him. Tyler himself hunted down and cut off the head of the great monopolist, Richard Lyons, whose servant he was at one time said to have been, while his lieutenant, Jack Straw, led a gang to burn the home of the murdered Treasurer, Sir Robert Hales, at Highbury. Far away in Suffolk at about the same hour the head of Sir John Cavendish, Chief Justice of the King's Bench, was being carried on a pike through the rejoicing streets of Bury St Edmunds, while his friend and neighbour, the prior of the great abbey, who had been hunted all day on the Mildenhall heaths, cowered before his captors awaiting the trial that was to lead to his death next morning. Later, on the Saturday, when his head, too, was borne back on a pike to Bury, the crowd carried the heads of the two friends round the town together, making them converse and kiss one another.

Dawn on Saturday 15 June saw the nadir of the once proud

kingdom whose princes a quarter of a century before had led the French King captive through the streets of London. From Lincolnshire, Leicester and Northampton to the coasts of Kent and Sussex its richest and most populous counties were aflame, while, as the news spread of London's capture and the King and Council's humiliation, other shires as far as Cornwall and Yorkshire crackled with rumours of impending rebellion. The greatest officers of state – the Primate and Chancellor, Treasurer, and Chief Justice – had all been brutally done to death, and everywhere magnates and gentry were flying to the woods or, isolated and helpless in their homes, awaiting the sound of mobs and the light of torches. In London riot, plunder, arson and murder had continued all night and, though thousands of law-abiding peasants had returned to their homes on receiving the King's promise, thousands more, including their leaders and all the more violent and criminal elements, were in control both of the capital and what remained of the Government.

The King spent the night at the Wardrobe in Baynard's Castle, comforting his mother. His surrender at Mile End seemed to have achieved nothing, and though thirty royal clerks had been employed all the previous afternoon copying out pardons and charters, the hard core of the insurgents remained both unsatisfied and seemingly unsatiable. Yet, since there was no other way of loosening their stranglehold, Richard resolved, regardless of the risks involved, to try again. Accordingly on the morning of Saturday the 15th he proposed a further meeting with the Commons and their leaders. This time the rendezvous was to be the cattle market at Smithfield, just outside the city's northwestern walls close to the church of St Bartholomew the Great and the smoking ruins of the priory of St John's, Clerkenwell.

Before proceeding there the King rode to Westminster Abbey to pray at the shrine of his ancestor, St Edward the Confessor. Murder and sacrilege had been there that morning before him, a mob having broken into the sanctuary, tearing from the pillars of the shrine to which he had clung in terror the marshal of the Marshalsea – a man hated by the populace as being 'without pity as a torturer'. The monks of Westminster and the canons of

St Stephen's met Richard at the abbey gates, barefooted and carrying their cross. For a while all knelt before the desecrated shrine
while the young King confessed to the abbey's anchorite and
received absolution, afterwards repairing to the little oratory in the
royal closet of St Stephen's chapel to pray before a golden image of
the Virgin which had been a treasured possession of his family since
the days of Henry III and was believed to have special protective
powers. It is possible that it is this deeply moving incident in the
King's life rather than his coronation four years earlier that is
depicted in the Wilton Diptych – the young Plantagenet, robed
and crowned, kneeling before the figures of St Edward, King
Edmund the Martyr and St John the Baptist, whose hand rests on
the boy's shoulder and all three of whom seem to be gazing fixedly
and sternly as at some threatening force, while a winged galaxy of
guardian angels, wearing Richard's badge of the white hart, gather
round the Virgin and her child beneath the banner of St George.[1]

The King and his retainers, about two hundred strong, now
mounted and rode on to Smithfield. Because of their peril they
wore armour under their robes. They were joined at St Bartholomew's church by Mayor Walworth and a small party, while on the
opposite side of the market-place the entire insurgent army
awaited in battle order. It must by now have been about five
o'clock in the afternoon and the weather very hot.

Tyler now felt himself to be master of the kingdom. He was at
the head of a host which outnumbered by many times the little
royal band, and all day news had been coming in from every quarter
of new risings. On the previous evening he had boasted to the rebel
delegates from St Albans that he would shave the beards – by which
he meant slice off the heads – of all who opposed him, including
their abbot, and that in a few days there would be no laws in

---

[1] In discussing the date and occasion of this lovely painting neither Dr
Evans in her volume of the *Oxford History of English Art* nor Margaret Rickert
in her *Painting in Britain in the Middle Ages* seems to have considered this
possibility, both inclining to attribute its occasion either to Richard's coronation at the age of eleven or his re-coronation in St Stephen's chapel after his
assumption of power in 1389 at the age of twenty three. Yet, whenever painted,
the King depicted is neither a child nor a full-grown man, but unmistakably a
boy in his teens.

England save those which proceeded from his mouth. 'He came to the King,' wrote the Anonimalle chronicler, 'in a haughty fashion, mounted on a little horse so that he could be seen by the commons and carrying in his hand a dagger which he had taken from another man. When he had dismounted he half bent his knee and took the King by the hand and shook his arm forcibly and roughly, saying to him, "Brother, be of good comfort and joyful, for you shall have within the next fortnight 40,000 more of the Commons than you have now and we shall be good companions."

'When the King asked Tyler, "Why will you not go back to your own country?" the insurgent chief replied with a great oath that neither he nor his fellows would depart until they had their charter and such points . . . in their charter as they chose to demand . . . The King asked him what were the points that he wanted . . . He asked that there should be no law except the law of Winchester, and that no lord should have any lordship . . . and that the only lordship should be that of the King. That the goods of Holy Church should not remain in the hands of the religious nor of the parsons and vicars and other churchmen; but those who were in possession should have their sustenance from the endowments, and the remainder of their goods should be divided amongst their parishioners; and no bishop should remain in England save one. And that all the lands and tenements now held by them should be confiscated and shared amongst the commons, saving to them a reasonable substance. And he demanded that there should be no more bondsmen in England, no serfdom nor villeinage, but that all should be free and of one condition. And to this the King gave an easy answer, and said that he should have all that could fairly be granted saving to himself the regality of the Crown. And then he commanded him to go back to his home without further delay. And all this time that the King was speaking, no lord nor any other of his Council dared . . . to give any answer to the Commons except the King himself.

'After that Tyler, in the King's presence, called for a flagon of water to rinse his mouth because he was in such a heat, and when it was brought he rinsed his mouth in a very rude and disgusting fashion before the King; and then he made them bring him a flagon of ale of which he drank a great deal, and in the King's presence mounted his horse. At this time a yeoman of Kent, who was among the King's retinue, asked to see the said Wat, the leader of the commons; and when Wat was pointed out to him, he said openly that he was the greatest thief and robber in all Kent. Wat heard these words and commanded him to come out to him, shaking his head at him in sign of malice; but the yeoman refused to go to him for fear of the mob. At last the lords made him go out to Wat to see what he would do in the King's presence; and, when Wat saw him, he ordered one of his followers, who was riding on a horse carrying his banner displayed, to dismount and cut off the yeoman's head. But the yeoman answered that he had done nothing worthy of death, for'what he had said was true and he would not deny it . . . For these words Wat would have run him through with his dagger and killed him in the King's presence, and because of this, the Mayor of London, William Walworth, reasoned with Wat for his violent behaviour and contempt done in the King's presence and arrested him. And because he arrested him, Wat struck the Mayor with his dagger in the stomach with great anger; but as God would have it, the Mayor was wearing armour and took no harm. But like a hardy and vigorous man he drew his cutlass and struck back at Wat and gave him a deep cut on the neck and then a great cut on the head. And in this scuffle a yeoman of the King's household drew his sword and ran Wat two or three times through the body, mortally wounding him. And Wat spurred his horse, crying to the commons to avenge him, and the horse carried him some four score paces, and there he fell to the ground half dead. And when the commons saw him fall and did not know for certain how it was, they began to bend their bows to shoot.'[1]

It was thirty-five years since Crécy and Neville's Cross and a quarter of a century since Poitiers, and even the youngest who had shared in these masterpieces of the bowman's art were now, by the standards of the fourteenth century, old men. Even Nájera was fourteen years away, and few of the English archers who had wrought that Pyrrhic victory can ever have returned to England. Yet there must have been at least several hundred in the insurgent host who

[1] *The Anonimalle Chronicle* (ed. V. H. Galbraith).

327

had served in the French and Breton wars and many thousands more who had learnt to use the long-bow at the butts after church on Sundays and were armed with the terrifying weapon – the most formidable in the world – which the Plantagenet kings had given the yeomanry of England. It seemed, as hundreds of bows were drawn in the rebel ranks, that it was going to cost the last of them his life and throne.

At that moment Richard clapped spurs into his horse and rode straight across the square towards the massed insurgents. 'Sirs,' he cried as he reined in before them, 'will you shoot your King? I am your captain. I will be your leader. Let him who loves me follow me!' The effect was electric; the expected flight of arrows never came. Instead, as the young King slowly wheeled his horse northwards towards the open country, the peasants in ordered companies followed him like the children after the piper of Hamelin.

As they did so, the Mayor galloped back into the city to rouse the loyalists and call them to rescue their sovereign. His chief adversary – Alderman Sibley who had lowered the river drawbridge two days before – arrived just before him, spreading the rumour that the whole royal party had been killed. But Walworth's appearance gave him the lie and, sickened by the plunder, murder and arson of the last forty-eight hours, the shopkeepers and wealthier citizens flocked with their arms into the streets as the sole hope of saving their homes and possessions. Mustered by the aldermen and officers of their wards and led by old Sir Robert Knollys with his archers and men-at-arms, they hurried in thousands out of the Aldersgate in pursuit of the imperilled King and his rabble following. They found them in the Clerkenwell cornfields with the boy, still unharmed, sitting on his horse in their midst, arguing with the insurgents, now leaderless and confused in the absence of Tyler who had been borne dying into St Bartholomew's hospital. While they were so occupied, Knollys quietly deployed his men, outflanking and surrounding the multitude, while a band of heavily armoured knights pushed through the crowd to the King's side.

The threat to the Crown and capital was over. The insurgents made no resistance; it was the end of a long hot day and they must have been parched and exhausted. Encircled by armed men and appeased by the King's promises, even the extremists had no more fight in them and were ready to return home. He refused to listen to the proposal of some of his rescuers that, as his former captors were now at his mercy, he should order them to be massacred; 'three-fourths of them,' he is said to have replied, 'have been brought here by force and threats; I will not let the innocent suffer with the guilty.' Knollys, who was himself of yeoman birth, strongly counselled the course of mercy and helped to organise the march of the Kentish men through London to their homes.

The whole multitude now dispersed. When Richard returned to the Wardrobe amid the rejoicings of the Londoners whose Mayor he had just knighted in the Clerkenwell fields, he said to his anxious mother 'Rejoice and praise God, for today I have recovered my heritage that was lost and the realm of England also.'

*   *   *

Had the King fallen at Mile End or Smithfield there would have been no authority but that of the rebellious peasantry left from Yorkshire to Kent and from Suffolk to Devon. When he and Walworth so unexpectedly, and at the eleventh hour, turned the tables on Tyler, the revolution was on the point of complete success. For on the very afternoon that Richard, preparing for death, confessed and received absolution in the desecrated abbey, the fires of rebellion, fanned by the news of the previous day's massacre in the Tower and the insurgents' triumph, spread to St Albans, Cambridge and Ipswich and into Bedfordshire, the Fens and Norfolk. At St Albans, led by a local tradesman called William Grindcobbe – a brave man with a burning love of freedom – the townsfolk invaded the abbey, seized its charters and burnt them in the market-place, ripping up the confiscated millstones – symbols of the abbey's monopolistic privileges – with which the abbot had paved his chamber, while the countryfolk drained the fish-ponds and trampled down the fences enclosing the monastic woods and pastures. At Cambridge, as during that Saturday village after village rose in the Fenland, the bell of Great St Mary's brought out the mob in a riotous crusade against the university and the adjacent priory of Barnwell. Corpus Christi College, the chief owner of house-property in the town, was gutted, and the university charters, archives and library were burnt next day in the Market Square while an old woman shouted, as she flung parchment after parchment into the flames, 'Away with the learning of the clerks! Away with it!' During the weekend other risings occurred in hundreds of villages in East Anglia, the Fenland and east Midlands. In all of them justices of the peace, tax commissioners, lawyers and unpopular landlords, particularly monastic ones, were attacked, their houses sacked or burnt and their charters and court-rolls destroyed.

The most formidable of all the risings outside the capital occurred in Norfolk, the richest and most populous as well as most independent-minded county in England. In west Norfolk, where it broke out during the weekend of the King's triumph and lasted for ten days, it was without a leader and apparently quite purposeless, the one common denominator being robbery under threats of violence. Many of the victims were persons in humble circumstances, farmers, priests and village tradesmen; in only two of the 153 villages in which felonies were committed did they take the form of attacks on landlords. But in the eastern half of the county, where a leader of Tyler's calibre appeared, rebellion took a political course, though a different one from that of the home counties. Its aim, natural in so remote an area, was not the reform and control of the Government, but the setting up of an independent East Anglia. But though for a week its leader, a dyer named Geoffrey Litster, kept regal state in Norwich, with the King and Council in possession of the capital the revolution collapsed as suddenly as it had begun. By the end of June all resistance was over.

Except for the summary execution of a few ring-leaders like Tyler's lieutenant, Jack Straw, and John Starling – the Essex rioter who had decapitated Archbishop Sudbury and who was taken still carrying the sword that had done the deed – the insurgents were tried and punished by the normal processes of law. Though a large number of persons were charged with treason or crimes of violence, only about a hundred and fifty suffered the death penalty, nearly all of them after being found guilty by a local jury. Most of the ring-leaders perished, including John Ball, who was found hiding at Coventry, and John Wraw, another priest who had led the Suffolk insurgents and who tried to save his life by turning King's evidence. The noblest of all – the leader of the St Albans townsmen against the tyranny of the great abbey that held them in bondage – died with sublime courage, protesting the righteousness of his cause. 'If I die for the liberty we have won,' he said, 'I shall think myself happy to end my life as a martyr for such a cause.'

Before the end of the summer the King put a stop to further arrests and executions, and in December a general amnesty was declared. The peasants' revolt and its repression were over. Only the smouldering ashes of anger and resentment remained; that and fear of its recurrence. But for two circumstances the King would have perished with his ministers. One was his courage, the other the deep-seated loyalty to the throne which transcended the sense of injustice and desire for revenge of the peasant multitude. Fierce as were the passions aroused during 'the hurling time', as it was called, and cruel and atrocious some of the deeds done during it, the majority of those who had marched under the banner of 'King Richard and the true commons' sincerely believed that they were restoring the realm to justice and honest government and rescuing their young sovereign from traitors and extortioners. Unlike their leaders they did not seek to destroy either him or his kingdom and, even at the height of the rebellion, provided for the defence of the country. And, though they released the criminals from the jails and allowed the more savage of their companions to wreak their will on those whom they regarded as oppressors, they made no attempt to massacre their social superiors as in the French Jacquerie of a generation before. When, in their wretchedness after their feudal rulers' defeat in war, the French peasants had risen, they had loosed their vengeance on the entire ruling class, murdering, raping, torturing and mutilating every man, woman and child within their reach. In the contemporary accounts of the English peasants' revolt no instance is recorded of violence to a woman, though for three days the capital and for several weeks the richest parts of England lay at their mercy.

Yet they and their leaders had come very near to overthrowing

331

the government of the country, far nearer than the rebellious peasants of France, Flanders and Italy had ever come. They had done so because their cause was based, not on mere desperation or unthinking anger, but on certain elementary principles of justice on which, when they could free their minds from class prejudice, all Englishmen were agreed. And though they seemed to have been defeated and reduced once more to bondage, they had, in fact, as time was to show, achieved their object. When, a week after the Smithfield meeting, a delegation of peasants waited on the King at Waltham to ask for a ratification of the charters, he replied that his pledges, having been extorted by force, counted for nothing. 'Villeins you are still,' he told them, 'and villeins ye shall remain!' He was wrong. For the present the lords might enforce their rights: they could not do so permanently. The magic of their old invincibility was gone. Given arms by the Statute of Winchester and taught to use them on the battlefields of France, the peasants had tested them on the Crown itself and knew their strength. They would no longer brook servitude.

As an economic means of cultivating the soil for profit, villeinage was doomed. With such surly and mutinous labour and no police to enforce it, it proved impossible to make it pay. Faced by the growing competition of the towns the lord had to make concessions to keep his villeins on the land. And as the population began to rise again after the first annihilating waves of Black Death, the process of commuting services for money payments was resumed and paid labour increasingly took the place of servile. In other places, lords found their demesnes so hard to work that, to maintain their incomes, they were forced to let them to the wealthier and more industrious peasants. Within half a century of the revolt, even in the open-field villages of the Midlands tenant-farming with hired labour had become the norm, and hereditary servile status had ceased to have any practical significance. It was only a question of time, before the Common Law, with its bias in favour of freedom, transformed villein tenure into legally enforceable copyhold. The propertyless bondsman became the copyholder enjoying, by virtue of his copy from the manorial rolls, virtually the same protection from the King's courts and the same right to enjoy or dispose of his hereditary holding as a freeholder.

CHAPTER SEVENTEEN

Dethronement
of an Anointed King

'Such crimson tempest should bedrench
The fresh green lap of fair King Richard's land.'

Shakespeare

'The greatest theme of history still is,
and perhaps always will be, the unending
story of men's efforts to reconcile order
and liberty, the two essential ingredients
of a truly great civilization.'

B. Wilkinson

IN THE SPRING OF 1384, three years after the Peasants' Revolt, the seventeen-year-old King of England, Richard II, presided at Salisbury over a Parliament of his chief subjects and representatives of his lesser ones. As had become customary at the start of such gatherings, petitions from the subject were considered by the assembled Lords and Commons before, in their respective estates, they voted the Crown whatever additional taxes and subsidies it needed to supplement its hereditary revenues. During the debates the earl of Arundel, who was also earl of Surrey, complained in the strongest terms of the misgovernment of the realm. He was supported by the King's youngest uncle, Thomas of Woodstock, earl of Buckingham, and by Thomas Beauchamp, earl of Warwick, after Arundel the richest man in the kingdom not of royal blood.

The young King was furious. Rising from his throne, he told Arundel to go to the devil. 'If you charge me with responsibility

333

for bad governance,' he said, 'you lie in your throat.' Since his accession seven years before, the realm had been governed for him by a succession of elder persons – of whom Arundel was one – who had treated him like a child and directed its affairs regardless of the sacred attributes which it was believed God at their crowning invested Christian sovereigns. Son and grandson of the victors of Crécy and Poitiers, namesake of the crusader, Coeur de Lion, and eighth king of the Plantagenet line, Richard II had grown up with an unshakeable belief in the divine right of anointed princes. In that dreadful summer of 1381, with his capital in the hands of an infuriated peasantry and the great lords who ruled in his name panic-stricken and without resource, he had quelled the multitude solely by the magic of his royalty, riding alone in their midst while his guardians and counsellors cowered behind walls and portcullises. Yet once the rebellion had been suppressed and the peasants dispersed to their homes, instead of allowing him to assume the powers God had granted him for the good of subjects, his guardians and counsellors had continued to keep him in tutelage.

Nor had their stewardship been attended by success. The long dragging and now profitless war with France had continued to go badly. In the year after the Peasants' Revolt the lords of the Council, with Parliament's backing, had authorised the warlike bishop of Norwich, Henry Despenser, to lead an expedition to Flanders in support of the Ghent weavers against their count and his French son-in-law, Philip of Burgundy. Yet before he could arrive, the Flemish pikemen had been routed at Roosebeke by the chivalry of France, and the bishop, after a brief, ignominious campaign, despite the valour of the old Cheshire *condottiere*, Sir Hugh Calveley, had been driven from the continent. This disaster to the chief buyers of England's principal product, wool, had temporarily brought her export trade to a standstill and dried up the Crown's most valuable source of additional revenue. Since then, helped by a band of French knights, the Scots had broken the peace imposed by Richard's grandfather and re-negotiated by his uncle, John of Gaunt, and had harried the English borderland. This had provoked two unavailing and costly invasions of Scotland, the first under

334

Lancaster and a second, in the summer of 1385, when the whole feudal host turned out under the nominal command of the young King, only to return after a few weeks to England, its stores exhausted and its leaders quarrelling violently.

For almost a generation, during the dotage of Edward III and the minority of his grandson, England had been without a ruling King. It was not a deprivation a medieval kingdom could afford. Defeat abroad, division in high places and near-anarchy at home had succeeded the great years of Crécy and Poitiers when the whole nation had been united under a strong and, judging by his success, divinely favoured sovereign. Instead of having one royal ruler capable of enforcing justice and maintaining order, a succession of greedy territorial magnates contended for power, each supported by adherents drawn not only from the lesser feudal barons but from the episcopal bench, the knights of the shire and the rival London trading-guilds.

Chief among the contending lords were the King's uncles, the surviving younger brothers of Richard's father, the Black Prince. Of these by far the most powerful was John of Gaunt, Duke of Lancaster, already in his middle forties – a far more advanced age then than now. Heir through his first wife, the Lady Blanche – herself of royal blood – to the four earldoms and vast domains of her father, the great Edwardian soldier, Henry Grosmont of Derby and Lancaster, he was able to raise more armed men from his estates than the King himself. Having enjoyed untrammelled power during his father's declining years, Gaunt for a time had been the most unpopular man in England, suspected by many, including his royal nephew, of designs on the throne. This was unjust for, while still exercising immense influence through his nominees on the Council, since the young King's accession he had deliberately refrained from monopolising office and had directed his ambitions to a claim through his second wife – a Spanish princess – to the throne of Castile. In pursuit of this phantom he had induced the Council to intervene in the affairs of the Iberian peninsula, where a contingent of English volunteers from his northern estates had been assisting Ferdinand of Portugal to preserve the independence of that country against King Juan of Castile – son of the Black Prince's old enemy, the bastard Don Enrico of Trastamara.

335

Two other of Edward III's seven sons, Edmund of Langley, earl of Cambridge and Thomas of Woodstock, earl of Buckingham, were still alive, while the grandson of their elder brother, Lionel of Clarence – the infant Roger Mortimer, son of the Princess Philippa – stood between all three royal uncles and the succession. All were masters of estates and retinues which constituted a potential challenge to the Crown. For though it had proved successful in uniting a martial nobility for a victorious and, for a time, highly profitable foreign war, Edward III's policy of marrying his sons to the heiresses of the greater feudal earldoms had resulted during his dotage and his grandson's minority in the growth of centrifugal forces beyond the capacity of the throne to contain.

Outside this divided royal family, set apart from the rest of the nation by statute and landed wealth, were the remaining earls and barons. Their right to individual summons by writ to the periodic Parliaments in which the King and his Council met the nation's representatives had, during the past half-century, gradually come to be regarded as automatic, until they by now constituted an hereditary peerage with, at least in their own opinion, an un-challengeable right to share in the royal counsels. For the past fourteen years, during Edward III's dotage and his grandson's minority, this share had grown to be greater than a consecrated King in possession of his full faculties could be expected to allow, and it was inevitable that Richard, as he approached manhood, should mean to challenge it. It was equally inevitable that those who had so long exercised his functions for him should try to retain them.

It was the King's awareness of this reluctance, and the challenge it implied to everything in which he believed, that precipitated a constitutional crisis almost as grave as that which had destroyed his great-grandfather, Edward II, sixty years before. When at the age of fourteen Richard had put his elders to shame and saved the kingdom from anarchy by the courage with which he had confronted the peasants at Mile End and Smithfield, it had seemed as though he might assert his regality before his time and show himself another Edward of Windsor. But he was still too young – and, as the event showed, too neurotic and sensitive – to master the great

336

lords who, as soon as the peasants had been crushed, reasserted their power. Instead of biding his time and giving rein to his resentment only when he had made himself master of the means to do so, he showed his hand too soon and put his constitutional gaolers on their guard.

For Richard had been brought up by his lovely, pleasure-loving mother, who had borne him by her third husband and cousin, the Black Prince, in what by fourteenth-century standards was middle age. Her own father, half-brother to Edward II and, like him, executed by Roger Mortimer, was a son of Edward I by his second wife, Princess Margaret of France, and she herself had been reared in the royal courts of France and of the young Edward III in the highest traditions of hereditary kingshop. Joan was a creature of chivalry, the 'fair Maid of Kent' of courtly legend for whom Arthurian knights had jousted in tournament in the days before Crécy, and her notions of the rights and responsibilities of monarchy derived from a closed society in which a King's word was sacred law. She could not be expected to understand, still less approve, the constitutional changes which had been gradually coming about in England as a result of Edward III's dependence on parliamentary grants for his long war with France and Edward I's creation of representative periodic Parliaments for changing the law. And her spoiled son, born prematurely at Bordeaux just before the Black Prince set out on his ill-omened march into Spain, and left fatherless at the age of nine, had grown up in the firm conviction that lords who opposed him in the Council or parliamentary delegates who criticised his expenditure, his ministers or his friends, were little better than traitors.

Without realising it, young Richard, and the little group of personal favourites and courtiers who surrounded him, were seeking to put back the constitutional clock. They wanted to recover for the monarchy the powers it had exercised at the beginning of the century before confederate lords and even humble shire knights and burgesses had learnt how to use the increasingly frequent meetings of tax-voting Parliaments to call the King's ministers to account. These, by constraining him to give his assent to laws which appeared to encroach on his sacred powers and prerogatives,

337

put into effect Edward I's far-reaching libertarian concept – as yet still in its infancy – of seeking the 'counsel and consent' of the governed for the enactments of the Crown.

Ironically it was thus the very mystique of hereditary kingship which, in the hands of a boy King, had miraculously saved the monarchy in the revolutionary crisis of 1381, in the hands of the same boy grown to manhood was all but to destroy it. For, having seen it effect such magic when his ministers and elders had failed to save the kingdom from otherwise certain destruction, Richard was to spend the rest of his life convinced that he enjoyed a divinely inspired right and capacity to rule. The tall, yellow-haired Plantagenet, with the passionate stammering speech and pale womanly face which flushed when he was crossed, had inherited his warrior grandfather's love of pomp and pageantry and his hero father's passionate temper which, in him, if thwarted, took the form of querulousness. But unlike his grandfather Edward III, who within three years of his accession at sixteen had turned the tables on his usurped father's murderers, Richard was no warrior. Despite his tall stature and splendid Plantagenet looks – 'fair among men as another Absalom' – there was something feminine about him, both in temperament and temper. His tastes were all for the arts of peace – architecture, fine clothes, painting, courtly poetry – instead of the robust pleasures of the chase, tournament and battlefield; his closest friends 'knights of Venus rather than of Bellona'. Quick to resent an injury and seek revenge, he embarked on enterprises with enthusiasm, but quickly tired of them.

His gravest defect was his excitability and imperfect control of his temper; it was this which had caused his outburst in Parliament against his former guardian, Arundel: one account described him as striking him and drawing blood. According to Froissart he aimed a blow, too, at the Archbishop of Canterbury who had rebuked him for 'his insolent life and ill governance'. 'Abrupt and stammering in his speech,' as a contemporary described him, 'prodigal . . . extravagently splendid . . . timid and unsuccessful in foreign war . . . remaining sometimes till morning in drinking and other excesses not to be named', rumour attributed to him the same perverted affections which had sullied the name and ruined the reign of his great-grandfather.

338

Unlike Edward II, however, Richard was neither abnormal nor starved of natural affection. The political loneliness of his position was mitigated by a happy marriage. In January 1382, when he was just fifteen, he had married the Princess Anne of Luxemburg and Bohemia, a year older than himself. After his mother's death she became the central influence of his life and, by her devotion, introduced into his impulsive, wayward temperament a self-confidence and constancy of purpose that made him, so long as she lived, a far more formidable challenger to his warlike nobles' political pretensions than he could otherwise have been.

Already, though still more than a year short of legal age, he had begun to build a party of his own within the royal Council. At its head was a glittering young noble, a few years older than himself, Robert de Vere, ninth earl of Oxford and hereditary Chamberlain, for whom he had conceived a strong affection, lavishing on him every favour. Its moving spirit was the acting Chamberlain of the Household, Sir Simon Burley, the young King's military tutor and a former servant of his father, the Black Prince. A veteran of Nájera, Burley's fidelity to his old master's son was never in doubt, and his unchanging aim, selflessly if injudiciously pursued, was to increase the royal power and reduce that of the great feudal lords who wished to keep the King in perpetual leading-strings. The brain of the royal party was Michael de la Pole, son of a rich Hull merchant who had helped to finance Edward III's first Flemish campaign. A highly conscientious administrator and a first-rate man of business, he had increasingly identified himself with the royal prerogative against aristocratic pretensions. In the summer of 1385, during the abortive invasion of Scotland, Richard had created him earl of Suffolk, simultaneously, to appease their jealousy, conferring the dukedoms of York and Gloucester on his royal uncles, Edmund of Langley and Thomas of Woodstock.

After fifteen years of unsuccessful war against France it was not hard to raise popular indignation against the Crown. Whoever headed it, the royal administration was perpetually short of money and, as a result, repeatedly compelled to ask the nation's representatives in Parliament for new taxes. And as, in those years of defeat and mismanagement, there never seemed anything to show for its expenditure, accusations of corruption and mis-appropriation of public funds were widely believed – especially by the landowning and commercial classes, who were the chief taxpayers. There was a feeling – by no means always unjustified – that the members of the court were feathering their nests and using their influence with an extravagant and generous young sovereign to obtain grants of royal land and other perquisites which, by whittling away the Crown's revenues, increased still further its demands on the taxpayer. In particular, such resentment fastened on Richard's young favourite, de Vere, on whom in 1385 he conferred the marquisate of Dublin – a title new to England, giving him precedence over all the earls.

Despite his share in the government of the country during the past few years Richard Fitzalan, earl of Arundel, was just the man to voice such resentment. He was a magnate of the old school, with the martial accomplishments and temper associated with the victories of an earlier generation of Englishmen. He had served as Admiral of the West and, in the hour of danger after the Chancellor's murder in the Peasants' Revolt, had been temporarily entrusted with the Great Seal. But he was arrogant, rude and tactless – the prototype of the traditional baron who for three centuries had defied the Crown whenever its wearer showed weakness or challenged ancient rights – and the young King had grown to resent and detest him. He was supported by his brother, Thomas Arundel, bishop of Ely – a far more subtle man – by his fellow magnates, the earl of Warwick and, most ominous of all, by Thomas Woodstock, royal Duke of Gloucester. A spoilt, hot-tempered, ambitious magnifico in his early thirties, married to the co-heiress of the great feudal house of Bohun, Edward III's youngest son had grown up too late to share in the chivalric victories of his father's reign and had only known the era of defeats and fruitless marches which had accompanied the decline of English power in France. Because of this, the military glories of the past made an irresistible appeal to him, and he treated with contempt both the unadventurous foreign policy of a government forced to cut its martial coat to its fiscal cloth, and the civilized and pacific tastes of his nephew – a contempt not lessened by the fact that, like so many of the warrior-lords who surrounded the throne, he had owed his life, at a time when his own nerve and everyone else's had failed, to the courage with which the young King had ridden out from the beleaguered Tower to calm the murderous anger of the peasantry.

Only the moderating influence and immense power of John of Gaunt had so far prevented an open breach between his arrogant younger brother, with his aristocratic backers in Council and Parliament, and the impulsive, hypersensitive King. As long as Gaunt remained at the centre of affairs and ignored, as he wisely did, his nephew's boyish tantrums and unjust suspicions of himself, no one in either the aristocratic or the royal party was strong enough to upset the uneasy *status quo*. But during the summer of 1385, as the royal minority drew to a close, Lancaster again became heavily involved in the affairs of Spain. That August at Aljubarrota, two hundred English bowmen from the forests of his northern duchy helped a heavily outnumbered Portuguese army to win a decisive victory at the very moment when his rival, Juan of Castile, seemed about to extinguish Portugal's independence. This almost miraculous defeat of France's principal ally, wrought by English archery and reviving, as it did, memories of the Black Prince's victory at Nájera, caused the Council to approve the despatch to the peninsula of a new expedition, financed partly by Parliament and partly from the revenues of the duchy of Lancaster. It was led by Lancaster himself, who sailed in July 1386 for Galicia with seven thousand archers and men-at-arms, taking with him his daughter, Philippa, as a bride for the victor of Aljubarrota, John I of Portugal.

*   *   *

Lancaster could hardly have left England at a more inopportune moment. During that summer and autumn the French were threatening England with invasion and, though it came to nothing, for many months everyone in authority, national or local, had been engaged in preparing to resist it and in raising money to pay for the country's neglected defences. A year earlier the Commons had petitioned that, in order to be able to 'live of his own', the King should make no further gifts for a year and submit his private accounts to a parliamentary commission. They had been met by an angry rejoinder that he would do whatever he pleased with his own and submit his accounts to no one. When, therefore, in October 1386 – with everyone complaining of intolerable taxes raised to pay for the nation's defence, and with constant requisitions and hungry unpaid soldiers billeting themselves on the country, robbing, raping and murdering – the earl of Suffolk as Chancellor asked the community's representatives for the enormous subsidy of four-fifteenths, a storm burst over the heads of him and his fellow ministers. Charging them with extravagance and corruption, the Commons demanded their immediate dismissal and the banishment of the royal favourite, de Vere. Richard's response, from the seclusion of his luxurious Kentish palace at Eltham, was a refusal to discuss such matters with subjects and a contemptuous message that he would not dismiss a single scullion at their command. A few days later, to underline his defiance, he created his favourite, de Vere, duke of Ireland.

As, however, there seemed no other way of getting the four-fifteenths subsidy voted, in the end the King grudgingly agreed to receive a deputation of forty knights of the shire. But with rumours circulating that the courtiers meant to have them waylaid and murdered, Lords and Commons, acting together, sent to Eltham instead the King's uncle, the Duke of Gloucester, and the earl of Arundel's brother, the bishop of Ely, who were too powerful to be intimidated. A stormy scene ensued, in the course of which Gloucester declared that, by an ancient statute, if the King stayed away from Parliament by his own will 'without infirmity or other needful cause but by his own uncontrolled whim', it was lawful for its members to return to their homes without his permission, leaving his financial needs unmet. When an angry Richard, declaring that his subjects were plotting rebellion, spoke of seeking help from his cousin, the King of France – who was still threatening invasion – Gloucester broke into a tirade, denouncing the French King as the mortal foe of the realm and reminding Richard how his grandfather and father had 'worked untiringly all their lives, in sweat and toil, in heat and cold, for the conquest of the realm of France', which was theirs, and his, by hereditary right.

There remained, Gloucester went on, one thing more to say.

'It is allowed by another ancient law and one put into practice not long ago, that if the King by malignant counsel, foolish contumacy or wanton will . . . should be unwilling to be governed and guided by the laws and statutes and laudable ordinances with the wholesome counsel of the lords and magnates of the realm, but rashly in his insane counsels exercises his own peculiar desire, then it is lawful for them, with the common consent of the people of the realm, to pluck down the King from his royal throne and to raise in his stead some near kinsman of the royal house.'

Faced by this stark reminder of his great-grandfather's dethronement, Richard surrendered. He returned to Westminster, met Parliament and let its members do as they willed. 'All the Commons with one accord,' ran the French record in the rolls of Parliament, 'met in a single body and came before the King, prelates and lords in the Parliament chamber, complaining bitterly about Michael de la Pole, earl of Suffolk and Chancellor of England.' Though, in the face of his spirited defence, they were unable to substantiate their charges of treason, Suffolk was replaced as Chancellor by the bishop of Ely and the Treasurer, John Fordham, bishop of Durham, by the bishop of Hereford. In return for a parliamentary subsidy a wholesale purge of household officials followed. While Suffolk suffered a forfeiture of his property and was sent to the Tower, even such minor functionaries as the favourite court poet, Geoffrey Chaucer – controller of the London Wool Customs – lost their posts. And, as in the days of the Lords Ordainers eighty years before, government was vested in a commission of magnates in continual session – fourteen in all, including Gloucester and his brother the Duke of York, the two Arundels and the Archbishops of Canterbury and York, with four other spiritual and four secular peers. Its purpose was to wean the King from unworthy favourites, reform the administration and, by taking the offensive against France, renew the martial glories of the past. It was to have power to correct all defects in the administration, examine and investigate the King's records and documents, enter his palaces and supervise and dismiss his Household officials. It was even given custody of his jewels and seals.

For, as with Edward II, and his favourites, Gaveston and

343

Despenser, it had been through his private Household and Household servants that the King had been able to increase his power. Just as Edward II had used his Privy Seal to by-pass the Great Seal kept by the Chancellor and his clerks, so, now that the Privy Seal had become an instrument of the permanent administration of the realm and its keeper a national rather than a court official, Richard had used a secret private seal called the Signet to give effect to his will without resort to either Great or Privy Seals. Kept by a courtier known as the Secretary, it had enabled him to disregard the restraints imposed by his constitutional advisers.

*   *   *

The first round of the battle between the nineteen-year-old King and the magnates had now gone to the latter. Richard was once again powerless and at their mercy. He felt the humiliation keenly. Yet his minority was nearing its close and, for all their ingrained distrust of him, Gloucester and Arundel had been unable to prevail with the more moderate elements in the Opposition to prolong his tutelage indefinitely. Their authority, sweeping though it was, had only been entrusted to them for a year; after that the powers inherent in the Crown would automatically revert to it unless King and Parliament together could again be induced to limit them. The future thus still remained uncertain.

No one knew this better than the King. He had only to bide his time and by the next autumn the magnates, if they wished to control him, would have all to do again. Yet, being impulsive and impatient, Richard was not prepared to wait. Even before the end of 1386, he had procured the transfer of Suffolk from the Tower to Windsor, remitted his forfeiture and invited him to join his Christmas feast. A few weeks later, repeating the pattern of his great-grandfather's battles with the Ordainers over Gaveston, he set out on a ten months' progress through the midlands and north, leaving the Council of Fourteen in uneasy control at Westminster.

The royal plan, and that of his favourites, was to meet the magnates' challenge, not merely in the sphere of law and constitutional precedent, but in that in which the latters' true power resided, military force. The private armies which Edward III had authorised them to raise for war abroad and which, despite all enactments to the contrary, they still maintained in their pay and livery, enabled them to threaten the peace of the realm and intimidate the throne. Richard, therefore, proposed to meet theirs with a private royal army in his own pay and livery. All through the spring and summer of 1387, while he moved about the midlands, his officers were enlisting men and distributing royal liveries of red and white, with crowns of gold and badges of the white hart – his personal emblem. Their success was greatest in Cheshire and north Wales, where in his capacity as earl of Chester Richard was the principal landowner and where, from the forest of Macclesfield, his father, the Black Prince, had drawn many of his archers. To preside over his forces there he appointed, as Justiciar of Chester and north Wales, his favourite, the hated duke of Ireland.

While the King strengthened his military position he sought also to strengthen his legal one. In August, first at Shrewsbury and then at Nottingham, he put ten loaded questions to the royal judges under an oath of secrecy. The purport of their answers was that the commission given to the magnates in the previous autumn had impugned the prerogative and that those who had counselled and procured it were therefore guilty of treason. He also obtained from them a declaration that Parliament was under an obligation to discuss any business submitted to it by him before it discussed its own, that he could dissolve it at pleasure, and that those who had urged it to consult the records of his great-grandfather's deposition were traitors and should be punished as such.

Armed with the judges' sealed answers Richard was in a position to bring in a true bill of treason against his enemies. But, his secret betrayed, the latter were too quick for him. Threatened by the terrible penalties of treason – hanging, quartering, disembowelling, forfeiture of property and, for their descendents, attainder of blood – the magnates and the Council of Fourteen did not remain idle. Ignoring Richard's summons to Westminster, to which, leaving de Vere at Chester, he had returned at the end of October, Gloucester, Arundel and Warwick met at Harringay Park, a few miles north of London and on 10 November moved on the capital with their private armies.

345

The King had made a political blunder of the first order. Before he was strong enough, he had declared war *á l'outrance* on his enemies and, to destroy them, had assumed a weapon which struck at the security of every magnate in the land. He and his judges had ignored the statute of 1352 in which, in order to placate his nobles, Edward III had expressly excluded from treason and its penalties the offence of 'accroaching the royal powers'. Not only Gloucester, Warwick and the Arundels were now aligned against him, but almost the entire nobility, threatened as it was by his judges' interpretation of treason. Even the absent John of Gaunt's son, young Henry Bolingbroke, earl of Derby – who, as husband of the co-heiress of the Bohuns, was not normally on friendly terms with his brother-in-law, Gloucester – had now joined the malcontents. Nor had Richard any real support in the country to withstand such a coalition. Except in the western midlands and Wales, and among a small group of royalist merchants in London, there was little sympathy for the court; when de Vere's recruiting officers appeared in East Anglia they were arrested by the local authorities at the orders of the Council of Fourteen. The earl of Arundel was something of a popular hero; in the previous winter, shortly after the Commission had been set up, he had won a spectacular victory off Margate over a French fleet that had been harrying the Thames estuary, subsequently delighting the London mob by releasing on the market at low prices a large quantity of wine captured at sea. And as the Council, which was still the lawfully appointed government of the country, controlled both the Great and Privy Seals, the King's efforts to raise money by the use of his Signet had been only very moderately successful. He had not even sufficient funds to continue to pay his own and de Vere's archers.

Since Richard in his personal capacity had appealed to his courts and lawyers to impugn the authority of the Crown-in-Parliament and the Council set up by it, the magnates now proposed to appeal against his subservient judges and irresponsible advisers in a court of their own. They were the heirs of the great military feudatories who during the past two centuries had called John, Henry III and Edward II to book and at times set limits to the arbitrary power even of such strong monarchs as Edward I and

III. Though trial-by-battle had long been replaced by the assize-at-law, their training and heredity still inclined them to think of justice and the enforcement of rights in ultimate terms of the battlefield, and it was to these they now resorted. Their leader, Gloucester, as Constable of England, was president of the Constable's and Marshal's courts – the supreme chivalric tribunal which settled disputes affecting knightly and martial honour, not by process of Common Law, but by the old Roman Civil Law and, in the last resort, by trial-by-battle. Instead of letting themselves be accused of treason, they meant to strike at the royal minions who were threatening their lives, honour and property, and appeal them of treason under the laws of chivalry in the *Curia Militaris* whose procedure they controlled. Taking up a strategic position at Waltham Cross north of London, where armed sympathisers flocked to them from every part of the country, they confidently awaited their sovereign's surrender and the delivery into their hands of his advisers. The days before Magna Carta seemed to have come again.

Under the circumstances Richard temporised; it was the only thing he could do. He agreed to receive Gloucester and the earls of Arundel and Warwick and let them bring their charges against his ministers and judges. Sitting in the hall of Westminster Palace with the members of the hated Council of Fourteen around him, on 17 November – only two days before their commission expired – he watched the three Lords Appellant, as they now styled themselves, enter the hall in chain mail with an armed throng of followers and abase themselves, almost as though in mockery, three times before him. Then their spokesman, Sir Richard Scrope, declared that there were in the state 'certain traitors, gathered around the King who deserved to be dismissed and punished'. And he named the duke of Ireland, the earl of Suffolk, the Archbishop of York, Chief Justice Tresilian and the London financier, Sir Nicholas Brembre.

The humiliated King accepted the Appeal. He acknowledged the Appellants to be under his protection and designated the Feast of the Purification of the Blessed Virgin – 3 February 1388 – as the date for a meeting of Parliament before whose lords their Appeal was to be judged. But he was still playing for time, and except for

347

Brembre, who continued bravely championing the royal cause in London and allowed himself to be taken prisoner, the accused had gone to ground – hiding, it was believed, in the cellars of the palace. A few days later it became known that the duke of Ireland was in Cheshire raising an army under the secret seal, and about to march to the King's aid. It was neither in Parliament nor in the courts that the issue between the sovereign and his subjects was to be decided but in the field of battle.

Yet it was where the magnates, not the King, were strongest, and they met the challenge as their forbears had done that of Gaveston and Edward II eighty years before. Spreading their forces in an arc from the Severn to Northampton they barred all roads to London, while the King took refuge in the Tower. When five days before Christmas, after a forced march, de Vere and his motley crowd of Cheshire archers and Welsh and Irish clansmen reached the Thames at Radcot bridge near Eynsham, they found the passage barred by Henry Bolingbroke. While they were hesitating, shaken by the spectacle of so many great lords gathered against them, the Duke of Gloucester came up with a force in their rear and surrounded them. The Constable of Chester and two others who showed fight were killed, but the rest yielded without a struggle. Only de Vere, plunging with his horse into the river, reached the far bank and escaped into the fog, subsequently flying to the continent.

The King was now helpless. There was talk of deposing him, but the two latest and younger Appellants, Derby and Nottingham, were opposed to anything so revolutionary, while the earl of Warwick, whose warlike front concealed a somewhat hesitant character, shrank from such an extreme course. Richard was still an anointed king and, even when, with five hundred armed retainers at their back and a vast threatening concourse of angry Londoners waiting outside, the triumphant Appellants waited on him in his last refuge in the Tower, he received them under a canopy of state, enthroned on a chair draped with cloth of gold while they performed the traditional three-fold prostration at his feet. Yet they left the lonely and friendless youth in no doubt that, if he wished to retain the crown, he must amend his ways, surrender the friends who had so misled him, and submit himself utterly to the governance of his rightful lords and advisers. If he did not, Gloucester warned him, there was a successor of full age and royal blood – by which he apparently meant himself – ready to take his place.

Thereafter the Appellants took possession of the palace of Westminster. There, according to the monkish chronicler, they investigated the number of officials in each office of the Household, finding that there were a hundred in the buttery alone. Similarly in the kitchen and all the other offices they found hordes of unnecessary officials. They deprived Sir Simon Burley of the custody of Dover castle, and Sir John Beauchamp, steward of the Household, of his office. And on the first day of January 1388 they held a council at Westminster causing many to be arrested, among them Sir Nicholas Dagworth, Sir William Elmham, Sir James Berners, Sir John Salisbury and Sir Nicholas Brembre, who were all sent for safe custody to various fortresses. By the time they had finished, Richard had not a friend left in the palace.

On 3 February, Parliament met at Westminster to hear the Appellants' appeal of treason. Like all medieval Parliaments it took its colour from the great lords who dominated it, in this case Gloucester and his fellow Appellants. Seated in the white hall of his palace, with the prelates on his right and the secular lords on his left and the new Chancellor, Archbishop Arundel – himself an Appellant's brother – on the woolsack below, the King faced the expectant throng of knights and burgesses who filled the hall, while the five Appellants, in surcoats of gold and with linked arms, made their formal entry and obeisance. Thereafter, for two hours, a clerk of the Crown read aloud at high speed in French the thirty-nine articles setting out the crimes of the five favourites whom the Appellants accused of treason. Throughout, formal blame was laid, not on the King but on his advisers. At its conclusion the hapless Richard, surrounded by his enemies, asked what sentence ought to be passed for such grave and treasonable offences. Proclamation was then made in the hall, and at the door of the palace, that the accused should come to answer the appeal. As none appeared, the Appellants asked for judgment by default.

Yet they did not have everything quite their own way. For all their readiness to resort to the sword when their rights were impugned, the English were a law-loving people accustomed to observe legal processes, and their lawyers were trained to insist on adherence to their letter. When the King and lords of the Council withdrew to consider the Appellants' demand, the question arose, not whether the crimes appealed were treasonable – which no one now questioned – but whether an appeal of treason in Parliament was valid either in Civil or Common Law. When the point was put to the serjeants of the Common Law and the learned doctors of Civil Law, they unanimously agreed that it was not. Nor was this decision that of men who, like the royal judges at Nottingham in the previous summer, were subservient to the King, for they were all lawyers who enjoyed the trust of the Council of Fourteen. But their first and instinctive responsibility was to the law in which they had been bred, and they were not prepared to gainsay it.

The Appellants, however, had little respect for the law, and possessed the power to shape it to their will. They induced their fellow lords, of whom they were the strongest and richest, to declare that, in a matter affecting the estate of the Crown and safety of the realm, Parliament was not, like lower courts, bound by legal rules of precedent and procedure, and was subject to no other law and custom but its own. Having thus proclaimed the untrammelled legal sovereignty of Parliament, they proceeded to sentence the accused unheard and in their absence, adjudging them guilty of treason because they said they were. As this process of condemnation by Parliament in a treason trial would involve the shedding of blood, the prelates, headed by the Chancellor, in accordance with Canon Law, withdrew from the court, leaving the secular peers and commons to pronounce judgment alone. And so, eight days after Parliament's meeting, the Appellants carried their point, and the steward of the court deputising and speaking for the King, pronounced that de Vere, Suffolk and Tresilian should be drawn alive through the city from the Tower of London to Tyburn, there to be hanged on the gallows, their goods confiscated and their successors not to enjoy them. The Archbishop of York escaped the death penalty by virtue of his sacred office, his punishment

350

being referred to the Pope who subsequently translated him to St Andrews in remote poverty-stricken Scotland. The merchant Brembre – the only commoner in their custody – was sentenced separately by judgment of his fellow commoners and, despite an attempt by the King to save him and his own plea to be allowed as a knight to defend himself by battle, was hanged, drawn, and quartered. About the same time Tresilian was found hiding under the table of an attic in the precincts of Westminster Abbey. Clad in an old russet tunic reaching to his shins and looking, with his stiff, thick beard, like a poor pilgrim, the former Chief Justice was dragged from his hiding place with shouts of 'We have him!', bound to a hurdle and, amid the yells of a revengeful crowd which remembered his part in suppressing the Peasants' Revolt, dragged to the gallows.

But the Appellants and their Parliament had only begun, and their thirst for revenge was not yet sated. They now turned to lesser fry. Sir Simon Burley, who was alleged to have helped Suffolk escape, with three other Chamber knights, the royal serjeant-at-law who had drafted the questions to the judges at Nottingham, and the under-sheriff of Middlesex who had angered the anti-victuallers' faction in the city, all perished at their hands. The King's confessor, the bishop of Chichester, and the remaining Nottingham judges were saved by the prelates and suffered only forfeiture and exile to a remote and savage district of Ireland. Two of the Appellants – Derby and Nottingham – pleaded for Burley, who was ill and old and had to be brought from his cell in the Tower to Westminster Hall leaning on the arms of two friends. But Gloucester was adamant, and neither his knighthood of the Garter nor fame as a veteran of Nájera could save him. The Queen went down on her knees before Gloucester to beg for the old courtier's life but was brutally told to spare her prayers for herself and the King.

On 4 June the 'Merciless Parliament', as it became called, was dissolved after a four months' session in which the Commons had showed themselves as eager for blood as the Lords. Before the closing ceremony in the Abbey, at which oaths of allegiance were taken with Richard swearing to be 'a good King and Lord', it voted the five Appellants the enormous sum of £20,000 – the equivalent of millions today – 'for their great expenses in procuring the salvation of the realm and the destruction of traitors'. It also declared that any who should at any time seek to reverse its judgments should be treated as a traitor and enemy of the realm, adding, with a fine disregard for the sovereignty of future parliaments, that its proceedings and the overriding rights it had claimed for itself were not to be regarded as precedents and that Edward III's merciful Treason Act of 1352, which it had flaunted, was henceforth to be observed.

*　　　*　　　*

The Lords Appellant had not only got rid of their enemies and by the most drastic of methods; they had substituted government by an aristocracy for government by a King. And almost at once it was made clear to the country that, even in the sphere which the nobles regarded as peculiarly their own, government by aristocracy alone could not meet England's needs. It was the Scots of the fierce, half-barbaric kingdom beyond the Cheviots who supplied the test. Pitifully poor, almost wholly without native industry and trade – 'things come ready made to them from Flanders,' wrote Froissart, 'and when that fails they have nothing' – and subsisting on the most primitive agriculture, they had been struggling to preserve their independence against their rich and powerful southern neighbour for nearly a hundred years. Broken only by brief, grudging truces and attended since the middle of the century by periodic visitations of plague and famine, the long war had almost completely stripped their rocky, starveacre land of what little wealth it possessed. Even their much-raided, oft-burnt capital had now only about four hundred houses huddled between its castle-crowned rock and the abbey of Holyrood below. Nor was the country welded, like England, by the institutions of a firmly established dynasty. The reigning King, Robert II – son of the great Bruce's daughter by her marriage to the hereditary Steward – was an old tired man of fifty-five when he succeeded to Scotland's precarious throne in 1371, and had now passed the psalmist's span. With a swarm of unruly sons, both legitimate and bastard, to provide for out of a patrimony far smaller than those of the jealous, treacherous, quarrelling nobles who surrounded the Scottish throne, the first of the Stewart line was a figurehead without power or resources.

Yet though the Scots were for ever fighting among themselves, and though the English were quick to exploit their divisions by offering a refuge and plotting-ground to any disaffected Scottish magnate – of whom there was nearly always at least one in England's pay – the Scots' readiness to take up arms against their southern neighbours was instinctive and ineradicable. To harry the valleys of the English March was both a national pastime and a national resource – almost the only way in which a Scotsman could hope to grow rich. It was thus crass negligence on the part of the Appellants, when the existing truce with Scotland expired in June 1388, not to make provision for the defence of the north. Almost at once the Scots began to raid along both sides of the Pennines, and smoking farms and churches and trails of corded prisoners and cattle tramping northwards into slavery were to be seen once more in all the lonely dales between Tyne and Cheviot.

That August the largest Scottish army that had crossed the border since King David's capture at Neville's Cross, forty years before, swept down on Newcastle under James, earl of Douglas – the great-nephew of Bruce's dreaded lieutenant. Though few of his turbulent race had inherited their progenitor's loyalty, and their ambition and treachery had proved a recurrent menace to Scotland's peace and shaky throne, no name was so dreaded in the English Marches. Even the earl of Northumberland shut himself up in his castle at Alnwick, and his fiery son, Harry 'Hotspur' – already at twenty-four one of the most famous knights in Christendom – was forced to withdraw with his brother, Ralph Percy, behind the walls of Newcastle. In the course of a skirmish outside the city gates, Douglas succeeded in capturing Hotspur's personal banner.

Some sort of a challenge for its recovery seems to have passed and, before bearing it off in triumph to his native Dalkeith, Douglas, apparently deliberately, halted his army at Otterburn, thirty miles to the north-west of Newcastle on the Jedburgh road, and laid siege to its little castle. Here on a warm August evening two avenging English columns attempted to surprise the Scottish camp. As so often in medieval warfare, there was a failure in coordination, while a third pursuing column from Newcastle under the bishop of Durham never reached the battlefield at all. In a desperately fought moonlit encounter which continued all night Douglas himself was slain, but the Scots were left in possession of the field and both Percies taken prisoner.

The battle, which was attended by exceptionally heavy casualties, made a deep impression on both sides of the border. Early in the next century it became the subject of a ballad in which, in fulfilment of an old prophesy, Douglas foretold his end:

> 'Last night I dreamed a dreary dream
> Beyond the Isle o' Skye –
> I saw a dead man win a fight,
> And I think that man was I.'

As he lay dying he bade his lieutenants conceal his fall lest it should rob his men of victory. 'Few of my fathers died in their beds,' he cried. 'Raise my banner! Cry Douglas!'

> 'My wound is deep – I fain would sleep –
> Take thou the vanguard of the three,
> And bury me by the bracken bush,
> That grows on yonder lily lea.'[1]

It was not only in chivalric legend and border ballad that Otterburn had repercussions. Even more than Barbour's patriotic epic of *The Brus* – finished a few years before at a dark hour of Scotland's fortunes – it re-animated the national spirit of the hard-pressed, divided northern kingdom. For the first time since the great days of Bruce, Scotland's fighting men had won a victory over an English army in equal fight, exorcising the black memories of Halidon Hill and Neville's Cross. And it gravely discredited the Appellants' claim to be able to restore England's martial glories. Even more than the young King whom they had humiliated they had shown

---

[1] Lines quoted by Walter Scott on his own death-bed and which caused another poet, Philip Sidney – himself to fall in battle – to write, 'I never heard the old song of Percy and Douglas that I found not my heart moved more than with a trumpet.'

themselves incapable of containing the country's enemies. Before the year ended the bishop of Durham was heading an embassy to France to renew a humiliating truce with that kingdom which restored none of England's lost dominions. Meanwhile further Scottish raids kept the border in a state of panic, while a new Parliament, meeting in September in Barnwell priory at Cambridge, was forced to find £3,000 for Hotspur's ransom.

* * *

It was not without significance that the same Parliament made an attempt to restrain the abuses of livery and maintenance – the system under which the great lords who had muzzled the young King retained the private armies that were the source of their excessive and lawless power. It was the first sign of a rift in the parliamentary alliance between the Appellants and the shire-knights of the Commons which had broken the King's party. For, though the Commons complained of royals as well as baronial livery, it was the latter which now constituted the real threat to the country's peace and administration of justice, and the King drove a wedge between the two houses by offering to disband his own retainers if his nobles would do the same. In the end a compromise forbade the wearing of all liveries and badges of later origin than the accession of Edward III. It made little difference to the greater magnates whose rights derived – in most cases through the distaff – from the remote feudal past when retinue by tenure, as distinct from the more modern system of indenture, had been part of the military and constitutional structure of the realm.

Though, after the execution, dismissal and banishment of his friends and advisers, Richard had been left on the throne, he still remained as complete a cipher as when he had inherited it at the age of ten. England had a King living in idleness and luxury in his Surrey palace of Sheen – but a King only in name. His dearest friend and his wisest counsellor were in exile, their lives proscribed; his loyalest servants had been hanged. He presided at the Council table, but the realm was still governed by his uncle, Gloucester, and by the earls of Warwick and Arundel, with the latter's brother – now Archbishop of York – as Chancellor. Yet

355

during the winter of 1388–9 the pendulum began imperceptibly to swing towards the King, whose right to rule was inherent in the law and custom of the realm and who, as was traditionally believed, had been ordained to do so by God. For the very exercise of authority made the Appellants unpopular, and men soon started to murmur against them. The nemesis of all medieval government pursued them, just as it had pursued Richard's favourites. For to rule was to take from men, by taxation or otherwise, some part of their liberty and goods, and whoever suffered loss of either automatically became the ruler's critic and enemy. And as veneration for rank and ancient lineage was in the air of the age, it was to the great man out of power or favour – a de Montfort, a Bigod, a Thomas of Gloucester – to whom subjects instinctively turned for redress of their supposed grievances, so long, that is, as he remained out of power. As men wearied of the rule of Gloucester and his fellow Appellants, they pinned their hopes on that other royal uncle, John of Gaunt who, when he had been ruling the country in his dead father's name a decade earlier, had been the most hated man in the kingdom but who now, having been out of England for three years, seemed to embody all the wisdom and virtue which those in authority should possess but failed to possess.

For, having won, if not the throne of Castile, all he could reasonably expect in the Iberian peninsula, the Duke of Lancaster was now contemplating return to his native land. He had married one daughter to the King of Portugal and the other to the King of Castile, from whom, in return for relinquishing his claim to his crown, he had secured a further addition to his enormous fortune. In 1388, in the hope of keeping him abroad for a further spell, Gloucester and the Council had appointed him Lieutenant of Gascony – an honour traditionally conferred on the King's heir. But Bordeaux was far nearer England than Lisbon, and by the spring of 1389 everyone was aware that the country's greatest magnate and landowner was unlikely to leave his own or the kingdom's affairs in the hands of others much longer.

Already his son, Henry Bolingbroke, earl of Derby, had begun to take sides against his fellow Appellants in the Council. And on 3 May, sure of his support, Richard took a dramatic step. Taking his place in the Council, he asked those who were ruling in his name his age. When they replied, as they could not help doing, that he was twenty-two, he pointed out that the law assured to every heir of full legal age whose father was dead the right to manage his own estate and household. 'Then,' he said, 'I am of full age to govern my house and household and also my kingdom.' Why, he asked, should a right allowed to his meanest subject be denied him? Whereupon – for his foes had no answer – with the assent of a majority of the Council, whose members were tiring of Gloucester's and Arundel's pretensions, he announced that he would now dispense with the services of those who had exercised his functions during his infancy and conduct his own affairs. And, as his first reigning act, he requested the Chancellor, Archbishop Arundel, to surrender the Great Seal. Gathering it under a fold of his dress, he left the Council chamber, returning a few minutes later to confer it on the aged bishop of Winchester, William of Wykeham, who had been his grandfather's Chancellor twenty years before. Next day he appointed a new Treasurer and Keeper of the Privy Seal. A few weeks later the court poet, Geoffrey Chaucer, returned to the payroll as Clerk of the King's Works.

Having freed himself from his former masters, Richard made no immediate attempt to avenge the wrongs and insults he had suffered at their hands. He seemed to have learnt to be politic or, at least, circumspect. Nor did he any longer give the impression of wishing to rule his kingdom without that counsel from its hereditary magnates whose birth, under the long-established custom of the realm, best fitted them to act as constitutional advisers to the throne. In the writs issued to the sheriffs informing them of the King's assumption of full regal authority, stress was laid on his wish 'to promote peace and tranquillity everywhere and firmly to observe the laws and customs of the realm and to administer justice and full right to each of our lieges and subjects, by the advice, assent and counsel of the prelates, peers and magnates of our realm'. The enactments of the Merciless Parliament were confirmed and the balance of the vast sums it had voted to reimburse the senior Appellants for the Radcot Bridge campaign were duly paid. Nor was anything done to recall de Vere, Suffolk and Neville, all of whom were left to die in exile.

357

For that autumn, while Gloucester and the earl of Arundel left the country to crusade with the Teutonic Knights against the pagans of Lithuania, King Richard rode out in person along the Plymouth road to the great Benedictine abbey of Reading to greet the returning John of Gaunt, whom he installed as his most honoured counsellor – a position held till his death a decade later. For the next few years the government of England could be seen to be once more both royal and conciliar without any clash between these two seemingly conflicting conceptions.

During them, Richard made no attempt to avenge the wrongs he had suffered from his former political oppressors. Nor did he show signs of seeking to re-impose the personal rule he had sought during his minority. Perhaps it was because joint royal and conciliar administration was the kind of government most politically conscious Englishmen by now wanted, that the next few years of internal peace and prosperity came to seem in retrospect, in the troubled times to follow, almost a golden age.

*   *   *

Passionately though Richard, now in his middle twenties, wished to excel and unable, as ever, to endure opposition to his imperious will, it was in the rule of his court rather than that of the realm that during the first years of the last decade of his reign and the century the young King found for a time fulfilment. He was an artist, not a man of action; in this he resembled his church-building ancestor, Henry III. So long as, with his Queen by his side, he could dictate his court's personnel, ceremony, pageantry and artistic life, he was for the moment content. For the century into which he had been born had seen the birth of a new and elaborate court culture – one in which the monarch dictated the behaviour, life and fashions of those immediately surrounding the throne. In the closely related French-speaking royal families of western Europe, it had been increasingly taking the place of the rough, masculine and martial baronial and knightly culture which had flourished in feudal castle and hall ever since its emergence, three centuries earlier, under the tutelage of the Roman Church, from the barbarism of the Dark Ages. Brought back by returning crusaders from the Aegean and Levant through contact with the luxurious court of the Byzantine emperors at Constantinople – the last unbroken link with the majestic civilization of the Roman past – it had first taken shape on western Europe's Mediterranean littoral at the beginning of the fourteenth century in the Neapolitan court of King Robert of Anjou. Thence, heralding by a hundred years the Renaissance, it had spread northwards through the Italian city states and princedoms to the Visconti and papal courts at Milan and Avignon and the French capital, and even to remote London, where, in the chivalric circles presided over by the youthful Edward III, it had formed the background to the romantic youth of Richard's future mother.

Nowherè did it flourish more elaborately than in the Hradschin palace at Prague, home of the Bohemian king and of his daughter, Richard's future Queen. Elected Holy Roman Emperor as Charles IV in 1347, he had held that high-sounding but hollow title for more than thirty years and, as such, was the subject of one of Gibbon's most ironical passages in which the great historian contrasted the shadow German, and Holy Roman, Emperor's position as an impecunious ruler of a minor central European state with the unreal grandeur and majesty with which he presided over the periodic meetings of the Diet and Imperial court. 'When a hundred German princes bowed before his throne . . . and, at the royal banquet, the hereditary Electors, who in rank and title were equal to kings, performed before them their solemn and domestic service of the palace.'

It may have been on the elaborate, though meaningless, ceremonial of his father-in-law's imperial court that Richard modelled his own. With its ten thousand retainers and gorgeous heraldic clothes embroidered with gold and jewels, it was famed in an age of splendid royal courts. It gave mankind the handkerchief, which Richard himself is said to have invented, and – for, like all the royal courts, it had a strong feminine bias – the side-saddle. An aesthete with a natural love of beautiful things, especially those which enhanced his personal appearance and gave him that preening vanity of carriage which the age called *superbia*,[1] the young King dressed himself and his court in clothes glittering with jewels. One of his state dresses is believed to have been worth more than a thousand pounds, equivalent of a hundred times that sum today. A royal doublet of white satin, whose description has come down to us, was embroidered with golden orange-trees each bearing a hundred silver-gilt oranges, and its sleeves hung with fifteen silver cockles and thirty mussels and whelks in silver gilt. The fashionable wear set by the King for his courtiers was of huge padded shoulders, vast bell-mouthed sleeves trailing along the ground, skin-tight hose and fantastically long curled and pointed shoes.

Richard's palaces, of which he had seven or eight, were full of treasures – Kentish Eltham with its gardens and vineyards; Sheen, where the royal barges were moored by an island in the Thames; King's Langley; Windsor manor five miles south of the Norman Castle and Round Tower which his grandfather had built for the Knights of the Garter; Leeds castle, hereditary seat of the Queen. Most renowned of all was the palace of Westminster, on the re-building of whose hall – originally dating from Rufus's time and still surviving after six centuries as the central glory, though now only in bare stone and timber, of the parliamentary heart of Britain's government – he employed the greatest architect of the age, the stone-mason Henry Yevele who, during his reign, had refashioned Canterbury's glorious nave. With his fellow craftsman, the master carpenter Hugh Herland, he spanned the new West-minster Hall with a wonderful hammer-beam roof, each beam with pendant angels holding vast heraldic shields. In these palace homes the stately King kept his ivories and alabasters, painted and gilded jewelled chaplets, silver-gilt goblets and ewers, and his own and his Queen's exquisitely painted manuscripts with illuminated capitals and miniatures. For, like her, he was a lover and collector, if not reader, of books. And everywhere were wall paintings in gold and vermillion and brilliant primary colours, adorned with roses and fleur-de-lys and Richard's personal emblem of the white

---

[1] In the nave of a Suffolk church there is a wall-painting, dating from the last decade of the fourteenth century, depicting a young man in Richard's favourite attire, holding in one hand a sceptre and in the other a looking-glass.

hart with its fantastic horns, crowned neck and long golden chain, stamped or embroidered on whatever belonged to him or his retainers.

Richard was not only an aesthete. He was a sensualist, though never a gross one, of a sensibility far in advance of his age. His palaces were equipped with stone-paved or tiled bath-houses, baths with bronze hot and cold taps, for he was a lover of hot baths, and with personal latrines for himself, his Queen and his favourites. He was also a gourmet, famed as 'the best and ryallest vyander of all Christian kings', whose master chef produced the first known English manuscript cookery-book, the *Forme of Curry*.[1] Instead of the customary glutton feasts of roasted oxen, vast loins and haunches of mutton, beef and venison loved by the feudal nobility, he affected small delicately blended and highly spiced dishes of contrasted flavours, with much use of pepper, ginger, cinnamon, cardamon, nutmeg, saffron and mace and other far Eastern spices, and a liberal use of fine and rare wines – white Vernage from northern Italy, Greek, Rhenish and Rochelle, cooked with such foods as shelled oysters and hare's flesh, flavoured with honey and sugar of Cyprus.

*   *   *

In the summer of 1394, when he was twenty-seven, Richard lost his Queen, who since his marriage twelve years earlier had been the sheet anchor of his life. Partner in all his artistic projects and the lodestar of his Court, such was his grief at her death that he ordered their favourite palace, Sheen, to be razed to the ground, so unbearable was the memory of all that they had shared there together. When his old enemy, Arundel, failed to attend the procession which bore her body to the Abbey and, next day, with his habitual lack of tact, interrupted the funeral service with a blunt excuse for absence, the bereaved King was so enraged that he seized a baton from an attendant and struck the earl over the head with such violence that his blood spattered the pavement, and the service had to

[1] It was printed for the Society of Antiquaries in the reign of George III. Gervase Mathew, *The Court of Richard II*, p. 23.

be postponed until the clergy could free the sacred building from pollution.

Henceforward, as in the old days before the Merciless Parliament, it was politics which once more took precedence in Richard's restless mind. That autumn he resumed a project on which his long exiled and now dead favourite, de Vere, had embarked ten years before, of making Ireland, with its turbulent tribes, a recruiting ground, like the Welsh and Cheshire forest borderland, for a private royal army with which to discipline his stiff-necked and constitutional-minded English baronage and gentry. Gathering a strong force of retainers from Wales, he crossed to Ireland, the first English King since Henry II to do so, landing in October at Waterford and marching to Dublin where at Christmas he kept court in great splendour, graciously receiving the homage of the ever-warring chieftains or petty 'kings' of Leinster, Meath, Thomond and Connaught, and conferring on them English knighthoods.

Having thus widened his potential base for recruiting future retinues for reducing England to his will – though whether this was his only motive in spending the winter in Ireland there is no means of knowing,[1] for this loneliest of English rulers had few, if any, confidants – during the rest of 1395, Richard concentrated on further widening his power-base by wooing the French King's six-year-old daughter, Isabella. For her dowry and a promise of Valois' help against disobedient subjects he paid with a twenty eight years' extension of his earlier three years' truce with France and the even more unpopular return to Brittany of the port of Brest – the last, save Calais, of Edward III's conquests. The fact that he could not hope for an heir from his child bride for at least a decade left the problem of a disputed succession, with his royal uncles and their heirs competing for the throne, wide open for both him and his subjects.

By the summer of 1397, at the end of his thirtieth year, Richard felt ready to strike back at his former enemies. For, despite all appearances to the contrary, he had never forgotten or forgiven those who had humiliated him. That February, in a Parliament

[1] Gervase Mathew in his brilliant study of *The Court of Richard II* attributes to him more consistency of purpose and will than do most historians.

packed by sheriffs appointed from his Household, he put up one of his retainers in the commons to denounce the ever-mounting expenses of his Court, and then got a subservient Lords to declare it a treason, punishable by death, to excite the Commons to criticise the royal person, government or regality. So armed, at midsummer he struck at the former Lords Appellant. Holding them guilty, on grounds, real or invented, of secretly conspiring against him, he invited Gloucester, Arundel and Warwick to a banquet at White-hall. Only Warwick was brave or foolish enough to attend and, greeted with fine words, was arrested at the end of it. On the same night, 10 July, with a contingent of City militia led by the young acting Mayor, Richard Whittington – the famous Dick Whitting-ton of popular legend – the King galloped thirty-five miles through the night to Plessey castle in Essex where he arrested the second of his two intended guests and victims, his royal uncle the duke of Gloucester. Him he packed off without a struggle under guard to Calais where, as was widely believed, he had him secretly done to death. His other intended guest, Arundel, who had taken refuge in Reigate castle, was induced to surrender, and then tried for treason and executed on 21 September, his lands being distributed among Richard's followers, while his brother, the archbishop, was sus-pended from the primacy and banished the realm.

Yet it was *superbia* – vain glory – even more than revenge which still animated the King. The amount he expended in personal magnificence, in jewels, in maintaining his private army and the vast swollen departments of his Court, above all in fantastic liberality to all and sundry, was costing the country as much as his grandfather's wars. In successive years he gave away in pensions in Germany and France and, during the festivities for his second marriage, almost as much as the total normal revenue of the Crown. His benefactions in the closing years of his reign included a grant of £2000 – a hundred times as much in present-day money – to a potentate as remotely distant from himself and his realm as the Byzantine Emperor. At this time he seems to have nursed nebulous hopes of himself becoming German – and Holy Roman – Emperor, like his former father-in-law. He even spoke of himself as one, claiming to be '*entier empereur de son royaume*', whose laws, he claimed, resided solely in his own breast.

The strain of all this on his and the kingdom's finances only drove him the faster down the tyrant's perilous path. Having secured an unprecedented grant of the wool and leather duties for life from a Parliament overawed on the day before its meeting by a massive parade of the Cheshire archers of the royal bodyguard, Richard's next step was to raise forced loans, compelling the rich to lend to the spendthrift Crown. It fell with particular severity on civic and merchant corporations like the city of London. This was followed by a far more unjust and onerous tax – for at least it was intended to repay the forced loans – a widespread system of fines called La Plesaunce. Under it those who had ever forfeited the King's pleasure, or opposed him at any time since his accession, were compelled, in order to escape the terrible penalties for treason, to regain his favour by a heavy fine.

At the beginning of 1399, desperate for money to pay for his extravagances, Richard struck still deeper at the property rights, or liberties as they were called, of his subjects. During the previous year a quarrel had broken out between the two younger Lords Appellant, Henry Bolingbroke of Derby and Thomas Mowbray of Nottingham, who ten years before had refused to allow their merciless elders to proceed to extreme measures against the young King and on whom in his policy of enhancing the majesty of the throne by surrounding it with high-titled satellites – *dukettis* as his subjects called them – he had recently conferred the nominal dukedoms of Hereford and Norfolk. Each accused the other (not, it seems, without grounds) of secretly nursing and confiding to the other treasonable fears of the King's good faith towards him. After their charges against one another had been declared insufficient in evidence by a parliamentary committee, the King ordered that they should be judged in trial-by-combat under the rules of chivalry. In arranging that the proceedings should be accompanied by every attendant of dramatic and resplendent pageantry, Richard was in his element, presiding personally over the lists, which were held near Coventry on 16 September 1398.

Just as the combatants, armed *cap-à-pie*, were about to enter the lists, the King threw down his warder. He then proceeded to decree that both should be exiled, Norfolk for life and Hereford –

the former Bolingbroke – for five years. Subsequently, after they had left the realm, he confiscated their estates. But a far more drastic act of confiscation followed. Six months later, on 3 February 1399, Hereford's father, old John of Gaunt, Duke of Lancaster, died, and with him his four ancient earldoms of Lancaster, Derby, Lincoln and Leicester – by far the richest single inheritance in the kingdom.

With Gaunt's son in exile, Richard immediately seized possession of all his vast estates. By doing so he threatened every property owner and heir in England, outraging the most fundamental of all an Englishman's rights – that of inheritance.

The division between Richard and his subjects was now complete. He had alienated the sympathy of every section of the community. It was his misfortune to embody and feel the pageantry and symbolism of his position acutely without being able to understand and realise the national history and spirit which had created it. We see him, through the mists of time, presiding, during the closing months of his reign over his Parliament, in his royal robes before the painted arras in his hall at Westminster, the crown on his head and the sceptre in his hand; his prelates, earls and barons, seated on stools below him, and the knights and burgesses from 'the cities and good towns of the land' on steps below them. There is a contemporary account of him doing so, sitting resplendent and silent from dinner time until Vespers, 'and whenever he looked at any man, that man had to bow the knee'. For by now he was monarch of all he surveyed or supposed himself to be.

At this point Richard 'the Redeless' – the counsel-less, as the author of *Piers Plowman* called him – embarked on a course of action little removed from insanity and which could only have one end. Taking his crown and treasure with him, on 1 June he sailed again for Ireland with most of the private army he had created to overawe his cowed subjects, intending both to put down a rebellion there and gather increased forces to do so in England. In the meantime he left the realm under the regency of his easy-going royal uncle, the Duke of York.

Almost immediately after his arrival in Ireland, while his army, hastily embarked and ill-provisioned, was half starving in the dense forests of the elusive rebel chieftain, Art MacMurrach, Richard's wronged cousin, Henry Bolingbroke – now, by his father's death, Duke of Lancaster – left Paris, where he had been spending his exile, for Boulogne. Sailing with a small band of adherents for Yorkshire and announcing that he had returned to regain his inheritance, he landed at Ravenspur in the Humber on 4 July. An experienced and resolute soldier, he acted with the utmost speed. Marching through Knaresborough to Pontefract and Doncaster and raising an army from his Yorkshire tenants on the way, he was joined by the northern earls of Northumberland and Westmorland with a following of Percies and Nevilles bent, like himself, on saving their possessions from a tyrant King under whom no one could any longer feel secure. Marching together down the London road, at Leicester they swung westward for the Bristol Channel to intercept the King's expected return from Ireland. Here, at Berkeley castle, also hurrying west to meet him and feeling, in that hour of universal repudiation of a failing monarchy, discretion to be the better part of valour and loyalty, the Regent threw in his lot with them. And on 28 July at Bristol, the city having been surrendered to them by its governor, the triumphant invaders seized and executed Richard's Treasurer, William Scrope, earl of Wiltshire, and his hated henchmen, Sir John Bussy and Sir Henry Green of the royal Household, who had also hurried there from an insurgent London to meet their returning sovereign.

Two days later, when the latter, hurrying homewards, landed at Milford Haven with a handful of retainers, he found that his kingdom had already slipped from his grasp. Hurrying north across the Welsh mountains without an army to seek support from his Cheshire stronghold, he found that the invaders had forestalled him there by a forced march up the Severn to Chester, which they reached on 9 August. By the time, after his weary wanderings through the Welsh hills with half a dozen followers, Richard came to rest at Conway castle, joining there his chief remaining armed adherent, the earl of Salisbury, the triumphant Bolingbroke and a powerful army faced him menacingly from Flint.

Here, fluctuating between self-pitying despair and furious defiance, at one moment declaring that Bolingbroke should die a death that would make a noise as far as Turkey, the doomed and forsaken King was prevailed upon by his accommodating and equivocal Regent, the Duke of York, to leave the safety of Conway for Bolingbroke's camp at Flint on 19 August. Thence, next day, he accompanied the latter to Chester. Though his victorious cousin received him with a sovereign's honours, proclaiming that he sought only the restoration of his forfeited estates, to which the defeated King meekly acceded, neither cousin could now for a moment trust the other. During their journey together to London – in the course of which Richard attempted to escape – the royal state changed imperceptibly from that of a monarch returning to his kingdom to that of a state prisoner charged with treason to the realm. On the day after his arrival at Westminster on 1 September, he was consigned to the Tower.

During the next month, while awaiting in that place of tragic memories the meeting of a Parliament called in his name to dethrone him, the state of the captive King's mind is known to us only through the play written two centuries later by Shakespeare who, with his instinctive understanding of human nature in every situation, put into Richard's mouth the words in which he yielded his crown to the man he had wronged. 'Not all the water in the rough rude sea,' he made him declare before his surrender at Conway,

> 'Can wash the balm from an anointed King;
> The breath of wordly men cannot depose
> The deputy elected by the Lord.'

In those secret hours in the Tower, of which history has no record and subject to what unknown pressures, the King, on the day preceding the formal announcement of his abdication on 1 September, was invested by the poet with the words and feelings in which, abject and in despair, he renounced his kingship.

> 'I give this heavy weight from off my head,
> And this unwieldy sceptre from my hand,
> The pride of kingly sway from out my heart;
> With mine own tears I wash away my balm,
> With mine own hands I give away my crown,
> With mine own tongue deny my sacred state'

A fortnight later a new Parliament met, called by Bolingbroke to succeed the one which had accepted Richard's abdication and declared the throne vacant. Claiming the succession 'by right of descent vindicated by conquest', the royal usurper was crowned Henry IV in the Abbey on 13 October 1399 with the ancient and sacred rites used at the crowning of all England's kings. Within six months of the dethronement, imprisoned in turn at Leeds Castle in Kent and at Pickering, Knaresborough and Pontefract in Yorkshire, his broken predecessor, following an unsuccessful rising of his sympathisers in the New Year, was dead, possibly of starvation at his own hand, more probably, like Edward II before him, at that of his merciless gaolers.

Son and grandson of the two greatest heroes of the age, happily married and surrounded by a brilliant Court, at the zenith of his power and fortune, Richard had used time, a private army and not inconsiderable political skill and cunning to destroy his enemies. His reign had seen a flowering of native art and culture which bade fair to anticipate that of fifteenth-century Burgundy and rival that of contemporary Italy. He had Yevele for his architect, John Siferwas for painter, Chaucer for poet. Yet, when he claimed that the laws existed only in his own breast, he made the same mistake as the abbot who told his serfs that they owned nothing legally but their bellies. Because he failed to see that whoever claims absolute power in England will in the end be repudiated by her people, he lost everything and was dethroned by a Parliament of his own subjects. Like his foolish great-grandfather – and others to come – he discovered too late that the English could only be ruled by those who acknowledged the sanctity of their laws and liberties and, when threatened, their right to defend them.

*   *   *

The century and a quarter which ended with the dethronement of Richard II had seen the first evolution of Parliament, the legislative and land reforms of Edward I – 'the English Justinian' – and that great King's attempts to unify Anglo-Saxon and Celtic Britain under a single law and monarchy, successful, after a heroic resistance, in Wales, but in Scotland defeated in an epic war of independence which ensured, happily for mankind, the continued nationhood of the Scottish people. They had been years fraught for England with alternating achievement and disaster. They witnessed her greatest military defeat, Bannockburn, and her first great continental victory, Crécy. On the morrow of that inconceivable triumph she had been struck down by a calamity comparable to that which would today follow a nuclear war. And after further military successes culminating in an even greater victory, Poitiers, and a peace, never ratified, which recognised her King's claim to a quarter of France, during a further two decades of war she lost almost her entire foreign conquests, learning the lesson, not for the last time, that continental conquest can offer an island people nothing but frustration.

Between the accession of Edward I and the tragic fate of his great-great-grandson, England became what, under changing forms, she was to remain, a parliamentary monarchy. By finding a constitutional means to reconcile strong centralised authority with the liberty of the subject and the right to oppose, criticise and reform government, she had made a political contribution of supreme importance to mankind. The creation of England's unique Parliament, with its triple components of Crown, Lords and Commons, makes these years vital to an understanding of all that was to follow. During it, rights were won by trial and error that became the basis of the laws and institutions by which free men still live. In the early part of that struggle the championship of private liberties and of the right to oppose arbitrary power had rested with the greater lords and churchmen; later, as a result of Edward III's French wars, the knights of the shire and the still humbler burgesses of the chartered towns began to share in the process. Out of that conflict between the expanding power of royal central government and the medieval tradition of feudal and religious liberty was wrought the first great English reconciliation between order and freedom. When, twice in a century, a successful revolution ended in the dethronement of a tyrannical hereditary King and the recognition by Parliament of a usurping but still hereditary successor, the victors had the wisdom to preserve the continuity of strong royal government. This combination of respect for central national authority with insistance on individual rights and liberties was to remain the dominating political motive of English, and later British, history.

HOW THEY LIVED

CHAPTER EIGHTEEN

The Medieval Village

THE FOUNDATION OF England's medieval polity was the labour of
some nine thousand scattered agricultural communities. Her
government, law, landed wealth, merchandise, architecture and
art rested on the native clearing in the wild and Piers Plowman in
the 'field full of folk' raising food for all. The owner of the soil, if
not the Crown or an ecclesiastical institution, was usually – at least
until the latter fourteenth century when English became the
language of all classes – a French-speaking lord, resident or absentee, with his manor court or leet to which every villager owed suit.
Its pastor was the parish priest with his church, to which everyone
repaired for communal worship on Sundays and feastdays and for
all the important occasions of life. But its hard core and that of
England's economy was the husbandman. In Kent and the Danelaw and the pastoral west and north he was as often as not a freeman, owning the land he tilled and able to sell it. But until the fifteenth century in the south and midlands the majority of cultivators
were villeins: men tied to the soil. They went with it and could not
leave it without its lord's consent. They were not, legally speaking,
slaves, for they could not be bought or sold as individuals but only
with the land they cultivated. Nor, so long as they paid the feudal
dues and services with which it was charged, could they be deprived
of its fruits. At a time when there was more land in England than
labour to work it, they were indispensable. They held it by hereditary tenure of 'fork and flail'.

Yet a villein, or serf as he was called, was far from free. If he or
his children left the manor they could be brought back to it in
chains on proof of villeinage. Their service was 'in the blood'. The
only legal escape was by public manumission, by entry into the

373

Church – for which the lord's agreement was necessary – or by residence for a year and a day in a chartered borough. There were many types of villein. They ranged from substantial farmers, employing other men's services and commuting for their own by money payments, to humble cottars and bordars holding only a few acres and supplementing their yield by working three or four days a week on their neighbours' land for wages. The average villein-holding was a yardland or virgate of thirty acres. For this a man had to till the lord's land with his own implements for two or three days a week, personally or by deputy perform cartage or carrying duties, give additional 'boon' services at the spring and autumn sowing, harvest-time, hay-making and sheep-shearing, and render on special days a seasonal tribute of farm-produce, like the Easter eggs which still appear on our children's plates. Thus in a survey of Martham at the end of the thirteenth century Thomas Knight held twelve acres in villeinage, paid 16d. for it and 14d. in special aids. 'He shall do,' it was stated, 'sixteen working days in August and for every day he shall have one repast [viz. bread and fish]. He shall hoe ten days without the lord's food – price of a day ½d. He shall cart to Norwich six cartings or shall give 9d., and he shall have for every carting one loaf and one lagena [or gallon] of ale. Also for ditching 1d. He shall make for malt 3½ seams of barley or shall give 6d. Also he shall flail for twelve days or give 12d. He shall plough if he has his own plough, and for every ploughing he shall have three loaves and nine herrings . . . For carting manure he shall give 2d.' These arrangements, which varied from manor to manor, were supervised by the lord's bailiff and by an elected or nominated representative of the villeins called the reeve who directed the common husbandry. The larger the holding, the greater the services demanded. A poor cottar with four or five acres might owe only a single day's labour a week.

Though, like all holders of land, a villein had to pay tallages and aids to his lord, such as the merchet on his daughter's marriage, he enjoyed the usual hereditary rights of feudal tenure. On payment of a heriot of the best beast on his holding, his heir was entitled to succeed to it. Nor were the 'boons' he proffered to his lord wholly one-way. Attached to his services were certain customary privileges,

like the haymaker's right at Borley in Essex to receive for every
load of hay three quarters of wheat, a pat of butter and a piece of
cheese of the second sort from the lord's dairy, the morning milk
from the cows, salt and oatmeal for a stew, and as much hay as
each man could lift on the point of his scythe. A sower was usually
entitled to a basketful of any seed he sowed, a cowherd to the first
seven days' milk of every cow after calving, a shepherd to twelve
nights' dung from the folds at Christmas and a bowl of whey or
buttermilk during the summer.

What distinguished villein service from the higher feudal
tenures was that it was menial and 'servile'. To the extent of the
time for which his service was due, the serf was at the disposal of
the lord and his bailiff. He was not his own master and, as the great
thirteenth-century lawyer Bracton wrote, legally speaking did not
know in the evening what he should do on the morrow. The stigma
in his status was that he was not, in the old English phrase, 'law-
worthy'. He could not defend his person or property in the royal
courts or claim a freeman's right to be tried by his equals, though
gradually, as the power of the Common Law grew, he received from
it protection of life and limb and of the tools of his labour.

Yet though the courts at Westminster in the latter Middle Ages
were often narrow and inflexible, and though, being tied by inherited serfdom to the soil they cultivated, nearly half the English
people could not yet sue in the royal courts in respect of their
'villein' land, livestock or property – all of which in the law's eyes
belonged to their lords – the Common Law operated imperceptibly
to widen the bounds of justice. For its spirit did not favour serfdom.
However strong the class bias and interest of its officers, it leant
instinctively towards liberty. In this it differed from the Civil Law
of the continental kingdoms which derived from Roman imperial
law and a civilization whose economic basis had been slavery.
The English ideal was the 'free and lawful man' – *liber et legalis
homo* – entitled to equal justice, answerable for the acts of others
only if he had commanded or consented to them, and presumed
by the law to be a rational and responsible being and, as such,
expected to play his part in administering justice by representing
the local community before the King's judges and assisting them

375

in the determination of fact. Though vast numbers of once free peasants had become tied to the soil during the feudal anarchy of the Dark Ages, and their liberties had been further eroded under their grasping Norman conquerors, even before the Peasants' Revolt of 1381 the genius of the Common Law was granting to the bondsman rights which it regarded as the heritage of all. It treated him as free in his relation to everyone except his lord, protected him against the latter's crimes and gave him the benefit of the doubt in questions affecting feudal status, holding, for instance, that the illegitimate child of parents, one of whom was free, must be free too, contrary to the practice elsewhere. Though it enforced serfdom where serfdom could be proved, it construed every sign of freedom as a proof of freedom.

Yet the rule of the royal courts was comparatively new. They were not the only source of protection from violence and injustice. There were other and older courts to which a man could resort. The manor-court or moot belonged to the lord; its jurisdiction and fines were among the most valuable of feudal rights. It was presided over by his steward and met once a fortnight in his hall or outhouse, or in summer under the village oak tree. But it was open to the whole village, and the assessors or jurymen, who stated the local customs on which its judgments were based and which formed the law of the manor, were the tenants who owed it suit. Those customs were handed down from father to son and recorded on the court rolls. They expressed the common experience and conscience of the neighbourhood. Nor was it easy for even the most powerful lord to ignore the custom of those on whose labour and skill he depended. Like the great Council of tenants-in-chief, who made the despotic King John promise to observe ancient law and govern with the consent of his chief men, the manor-court was the means by which, little by little, the English peasant community, often in the teeth of tyrannical encroachment, preserved and extended its rights.

In such courts, in thousands of villages up and down England, justice was done between man and man; offences against manorial custom were punished, and the services and rights of the villein-tenant enforced and recorded. On its rolls were entered the exact terms under which he held his land. In time, copies of these entries came to be regarded as title to his holding. It gradually became customary to claim possession of land by 'copyhold', a form of tenure which was later recognised, as the villein acquired full legal rights, by the King's judges.

Service in the manor-courts helped to train Englishmen for a free system of society. It taught them to weigh evidence and distinguish between personal feelings and public needs. 'Richard Smith,' ran the entry of a court leet in 1311, 'beat Alice Hannes twice – Mercy, Order, Poor.' The village jury, that is, found him guilty and recommended him to the mercy of the court, which ordered a fine but remitted part of it because he could not afford it. In his everyday task of helping to administer a little corner of the realm of which he was part, the English peasant learnt to blend legal precision with human give-and-take. The village halimote, which dealt with cases of trespass, neglect of manorial duties and offences against the village peace, and which twice a year became a police-court to try crimes short of felony presented by a jury, had its formal pleadings like a royal court. A thirteenth-century book, written to enable stewards and bailiffs to know their business, gives such examples as,

'Alice, widow of . . . complaineth of . . . her neighbour, that on such a day his pigs entered her garden and rooted up her beans and cabbages, so that she would not willingly have had that damage for 2s. nor that shame for 12d, and she demandeth that amends be made.'[1]

*   *   *

Keeping the King's Peace in the village and enforcing his law and ordinance was a bucolic officer called the petty constable. Appointed by the high constable of the hundred from a rota of householders, he was usually unpaid and served, nominally at least, for a year. By traditional Anglo-Saxon law every able-bodied man between the ages of fifteen and sixty was obliged to take his share in the policing and defence of his native place, and it was the constable's business to see that he did so. An English village was responsible to the sheriff for public order within its boundaries and could be

[1] F. W. Maitland, *The Court Baron* (Selden Society), p. 75.

377

collectively fined for crimes committed in it. It had its stocks, ducking-stool – for scolding wives – and pillory. Its priest, reeve and four 'lawful men' represented it at the sheriff's tourn and hundred court, at coroner's inquests and at the assizes where it had to answer for its corporate offences and present those suspected of felony. It had to keep a nightly 'watch and ward' against suspicious travellers and, when the constable raised the 'hue and cry', to chase and apprehend them. 'If any such passing strangers do not allow themselves to be arrested,' ran an ordinance of Henry III, 'then the watch shall raise the hue upon them on all sides and pursue them with the whole township and neighbouring township with hue and cry from township to township until they are taken!'

The petty constable was not only an amateur policeman but a, soldier. In time of invasion, riot or rebellion he had to see that every man turned out at the sheriff's summons in the shire *fyrd*. England's Norman and Angevin kings used this rude national militia more than once against their turbulent French-speaking nobles. At first it was confined to free men – for to the continental feudal mind there was something shocking in the idea of a bondsman bearing arms – but it was later extended to all classes, including villeins. Edward I's great defining Statute of Winchester of 1285 placed it on a permanent basis. In every county, hundred and township, muster-rolls were prepared from which, in time of war and emergency, Commissioners of Array selected and impressed men to serve as paid soldiers. Armed with daggers, spears, pikes and longbows, clad in quilted jerkins and iron headpieces, and exercised together once a year in the autumn array of muster, this reserve of amateur soldiers formed a second line of defence on which, in days before she had learnt to command the seas, England was able to draw in all her wars. *Fyrd, posse comitatus*, fencibles, militia, by whatever name it was called, it remained a homespun body, affording from the days of Shakespeare's Falstaff to those of Rowlandson much material for humorists. Of its services to the country perhaps the greatest was that, when royal despotism might otherwise have triumphed, it obviated the need for a standing army.

The Statute of Winchester also defined the subject's duties as a policeman and preserver of the peace. Instead of leaving the village community answerable only for felonies committed within its borders, Edward I made it jointly responsible with its neighbour townships for all felonies committed in the hundred. The unit of policing was made to conform to the needs, not merely of the village, but of the nation. As part of this policy the townships along the royal highways were also ordered, on pain of indictment before the justices on *eyre*, to cut back the brushwood on either side of the road to a distance of two hundred feet to reduce the risk of ambush from brigands and outlaws.

In the last resort such a system of delegated self-government depended on the readiness of the local community to identify itself with the assumptions and requirements of the remote royal authority in whose name the law was enforced. When, in the general breakdown of confidence and economic relationships which followed the Black Death and the failure of the French Wars, the peasants of south-eastern England rose against the attempt of their lay and ecclesiastical lords to impose new taxes and enforce anti-quated feudal dues, the system failed completely to stem a revolu-tionary flood that all but destroyed the kingdom. There must have been scores of Kent and Essex constables who marched under Wat Tyler and Jack Straw in their assault on the capital of 1381. Yet once the rebellion collapsed and the young King and his ministers had re-established their authority, the village resumed its tradi-tional method of ruling itself under the supervision of the royal officers of the shire and hundred and the manorial courts.

*　　　　*　　　　*

The manorial system of cultivation was communal, though owner-ship was individual. In the Celtic and pastoral west scattered homesteads and hamlets, small unified holdings and little stone-walled fields were the rule. But in the flat, clay midlands and the south, where corn-growing was the principal activity, the arable land around the village was grouped in two, or, in the better farmed manors, three fields, according as to whether a two- or three-year rotation of crops was followed. These open fields, fenced against the cattle in the summer, were usually several hundred acres in extent. They were divided, without hedges, into narrow, curving strips like elongated Ss, each a furlong or ox-plough-furrow's length. Between the strips were ridges made by the ploughs. As the course of husbandry was the same for all and enforced by the manor court, every villager had so many strips in each field, according to the size of his holding. In some villages the lord's land, called the demesne, and sometimes the parson's glebe land, were enclosed; in others they were scattered about the open fields, where their cultivation, like everyone else's, had to conform to the common rule. The crops were wheat, rye, barley, oats, vetches and peas. They were threshed on barn floors by flails cut from holly or thorn, and winnowed by hand. The wooden ploughs were usually drawn by teams of eight oxen. As few could afford a whole plough-team, they were shared. The normal arrangement was a team to every four yardlands, the hide – approximately 120 acres – being the measure, though it varied widely, of what an eight-ox team could plough in a year.

In addition to the arable there was the meadow lying beside stream or river and tended by the village hayward. Here, too, every peasant had his strip or strips. When the hay had been cut the village cattle were pastured on it and, after the harvest – from Lammas to Candlemas – on the arable stubble, which they helped to dung. They were very small and scraggy, for, under a communal system of grazing, selective breeding was impossible. As there was little winter-feed – root crops were unknown – they were mostly slaughtered and salted at Michaelmas. A few stalled cows and the breeding stock struggled through the winter till the spring.

Beyond the fields and meadow was the waste – forest, moorland, swamp and brackeny common – still covering more than half the country and surrounding the lonely villages like the sea. The lord of the manor might own the soil, but his tenants enjoyed the common use of its rough grasses and herbage for pasture and of its turf and brushwood for fuel. Every holding carried a right or 'stint' to feed so many cattle, horses, geese and swine on the waste, and to take, 'by hook or crook', sticks, fallen timber and loose bracken for litter, sand and clay for building, nuts, berries, rabbits and small birds for the pot. The adjoining woods were full of the villagers' thin, half-wild pigs feeding on beechmast and acorns.

They also abounded in game and, in the wilder parts of the country, with robbers and outlaws, and occasionally wolves.

The life which such a system supported was very simple. There was little scope for initiative or progress, and the pace was that of the least enterprising. The cottages straggling along either side of the unpaved village street and flanked by heaps of manure – the peasant's principal wealth – were mere rectangular-shaped shacks of timber-framing, filled in with wattle, turf and mud and thatched with straw or reeds. They contained usually a single unfloored, hearthless room in which the family slept in verminous squalor with the oxen stalled at the bed's foot, pigs roaming the floor and poultry perched on the beams. The only household goods would be a straw mattress or sack, a few cooking-pots, some home-made tools and, in the homes of the richer villeins, a rude oak chest and perhaps a stool or two. Behind the houses were little closes, growing cabbage, parsley, onions, leek, garlic, herbs, apples and quinces. Their owners' clothes were of coarse, greasy wool and leather, unwashed and unwashable, made from their own beasts. Their diet was cheese, bacon and, in the summer, milk; bean and vegetable broth; oaten cakes and rough, black wholemeal bread; herrings or other salt-fish, honey from their own hives; and small ale or cider. Its staple was cereal; a thirteenth-century English agricultural writer reckoned the labourer's average allowance of corn at thirty-six bushels a year. Butcher's meat was a rare luxury. In Lent everyone fasted, not only because the Church enjoined it, but because, with the harvest so far away, there was no alternative. 'Fridays and fast-days,' wrote the fourteenth-century poet, William Langland, 'a penny's worth of mussels were a feast for such folks.'

Though by the fourteenth century, especially on the large monastic and baronial estates, the village exported much of what it grew for cash-sales to the towns or to feed and finance some distant lord, it still supplied nearly all its own wants except for salt and iron brought by travelling chapmen. It spun and wove wool for clothes from its own sheep, and linen from its own flax. It made shoes from its own wood or skins. It had a miller – a tenant of the lord and usually the richest man in the place, for every villein had to have his corn ground by him – a smith, a wheelwright and a millwright, a tiler and thatcher, a shoemaker and tanner, a carpenter wainwright and carter. Their callings, and those of the parish agricultural officers survive in our names: Shepherd and Foster, Carter and Baker, Parker, Fowler and Hunter; Wolf and Forester; Smith, Cooper and Carpenter. So do the country places, buildings and beasts among which they spent their skilful, laborious lives: Field, Pitt, and Fox, Lane, Bridge and Ford, Stone and Burn, Church and Hill, Brook and Green, Lamb, Bull and Hogg, Sparrow, Crow and Swan. Other men were called after the masters they served – King, Bishop, Abbot, Dean, Prior, Knight, Squire – or after their own appearance – Black, Brown and White, Short, Round and Long.

*   *   *

Book education for the husbandman there was none. Few could read, nor was there opportunity for doing so. There were no printed books – only the priceless, laboriously-copied, jealously-hoarded manuscripts of the monastery libraries and of the very rich. The peasant's hours of labour were long and, when daylight failed, wax candles were far beyond his reach: his sole illumination was a feeble rushlight dipped in fat. There was no travel for him, unless his cart was requisitioned for some baronial or royal service, for the vast majority of villagers never left home.

Yet he was not a wholly uncultivated man. From his father and the fields he learnt a knowledge of nature's laws. He learnt, too, from his earliest years to look after animals and to take pride in his hereditary work as husbandman or craftsman. Nor did he live by plough or adze alone; he was partaker in a faith and a civilization. If he could not read, he could see and he could hear. The brightly coloured and beautifully fashioned images and paintings that covered the walls and, later, windows of his parish church; the legends and parables of the Christian legend linked him with the culture of Catholic Christendom. Its festivals, which were his days of rejoicing, gave him, it has been reckoned, something like six weeks' holiday in a year. Deeper than the servile divisions of class, the harsh bonds of status, the grinding poverty and squalor of the

peasant's lot, the unity and consolation of the Christian faith
sustained him and gave his life meaning.

The cold dark winters in the wild northern landscape must
often have seemed very lonely and comfortless. It is no wonder
that men suffered from superstitious fears and were haunted by
ghosts, witches and demons. They must often, too, have been
hungry. When the harvest failed, famine followed and, in its train,
pestilence, haunting the noisome ditches and insanitary hovels.
Yet at the darkest hour of the long northern night, rich and poor,
old and young celebrated the beginning of things and the mystery
of Christmas. The interminable procession of days in rain-sodden
or frozen fields, with bare trees and grey, colourless skies, and the
nights of shivering in draughty hovels, were broken by the sweet
wintry festival of Christ's birth, with its bright fires, lighted windows and good fare. It came just when it was most needed and
broke the winter into two halves, each bearable for the hope of the
Christian feast which ended the one and the coming of spring
which ended the other. Soon after it the first lambs were born and
the earliest snowdrops appeared in fields made rigid by bitter
winds. When everything was at its bleakest, a light was lit in
darkness.

*   *   *

Every village possessed its priest or parson – the *persona* of the
place – serving an ecclesiastical unit known as a parish, administering the Christian sacraments of baptism, confirmation, communion,
marriage, penance and extreme unction, and entitled by law to an
annual tenth or tithe of the produce of every parishioner. The
system dated from pagan times when the lord's priest or magic man
who served the former's temple had performed magic rites for his
farming neighbours in return for a share in the common fields.
The incumbent was usually a peasant's son, living the same rustic
life as his flock. Taught, at best, in monastic or cathedral grammar
school enough Latin to read the scriptures and declaim the services
in a language his parishioners venerated but could not understand,
and usually the only literate person in the parish, he lived by cultivating the glebe or 'parson's close' – a holding usually of some fifty

or sixty acres in the common fields. He also received dues and offerings from his parishioners for baptisms, weddings, churchings, death-bed visitations and burials. In many of the richer livings the right of presentation or advowson, as it was called, had been given by its patron – a descendant, perhaps, of the church's original donor – to some monastery, college, cathedral or other ecclesiastical foundation which, retaining the bulk of its revenues, paid a deputy to exercise the cure of souls. In other cases the owner of the advowson conferred the living on someone with family claims or on some promising youth marked out for preferment who, by obtaining an episcopal dispensation to reside out of the parish, was allowed to employ a resident vicar or 'perpetual curate' while he completed his education at the Church's universities of Oxford or Cambridge or performed some remunerative ecclesiastical function elsewhere. Usually the absentee rector kept the 'great' tithe on crops, sheep and cattle while allocating to his vicar the farm of the glebe and the 'lesser' tithes on pigs, geese, poultry, eggs, garden-produce, flax, honey and fish.

By the beginning of the fourteenth century nearly a fifth of the country's churches had been appropriated in this way. As only about a third of their income filtered through to the incumbents and, as the holder of a cure was supposed by Canon Law to devote two-thirds of the tithe to the upkeep of the chancel and relief of the parish poor, the latter and the church fabric tended to suffer. Deprived of the 'great' tithes, a vicar was tempted to press his parishioners too strictly for the lesser ones – those which most affected the bondsmen and small-holder – and to spend too much time cultivating his glebe and looking after his live-stock.

Yet there was a compensation. To the average countryman the Church was represented by one of his own class, accustomed from childhood to the same agricultural pursuits and way of life as himself. Though he might not be able to construe the Latin prayers and services he chanted by rote at the altar, he understood the problems of those to whom he ministered. In the market-towns and a few of the richer country parishes the incumbent might be a man of substance like the parson of Trumpington in Chaucer's tale who gave his daughter – he should not, by rights, have had one – a dowry when she married the miller. Usually he was a small free-holder's son or a manumitted villein, for a bondsman could not be admitted to holy orders until he had been freed by his lord.

To a university doctor such a poor rustic priest might seem little better than a 'brute beast' who, immersed in mercenary calculations about crops and beasts, could scarcely expound an article of the faith and was fit only to 'patter up his Matins and Mass'. To his parishioners he was invested with mysterious powers on which rested their hopes and fears of reward or punishment after their hard, brief lives on earth. When, as the sanctus bell sounded, he stood before the altar and officiated at the Mass, bringing about by his priestly office the miraculous transformation of the bread and wine into Christ's body and blood, he seemed a creature of another world. And when death struck and he hastened to the side of the dying, carrying lantern and bell, holy water for sprinkling, oil for anointing and the pyx containing the sacred elements, on him and his power to grant absolution and administer the sacrament of extreme unction depended the lonely, bewildered soul's readiness for its passage to salvation or eternal damnation.

Of what the service of the Church at its best could mean to a country village we have the testimony of Chaucer. For when, in his cavalcade of worldly pilgrims, lay and ecclesiastic, he reached the humble village priest, that cynical, tolerant but scrupulously honest observer of the fourteenth-century scene paused in his amused catalogue of human frailty to draw the portrait of one who came as near to fulfilling the precepts of Christianity as a man can:

> 'This noble example unto his sheep he gave
> That first he wrought and afterwards he taught . . .
> He waited after no pomp or reverence
> Nor made himself no spiced conscience,
> But Christë's lore and his apostles twelve,
> He taught, but first he followed it himself.'

However unsatisfactory many priests may have been, a good priest could make a Christian village.

*   *   *

Every great event of a poor man's life, everything which raised it above that of the beasts and invested it with beauty or significance, centred round the parish church. Here every Sunday and on the more important of the thirty or forty holy days of the year which were his holidays and the occasion of his feasts and fasts, he listened, in awe and with bowed head, to the 'blessed mutter of the Mass' and took part in the ritual dramas and processions which told for an unlettered people the Gospel story – the lighted candles carried round the church by the congregation at Candlemas, the distribution and blessing of the ashes on Ash Wednesday, the hanging of the Lenten veil before the altar, the distribution of branches on Palm Sunday, the dramatic creeping to the Cross in the darkened church on Good Friday, the triumphant procession with vestments and banners on Easter Sunday as the Host and Cross were borne, amid pealing bells and the chanting of the Resurrection anthem, from the Easter Sepulchre, where they had lain since Good Friday, to the High Altar. At Pentecost a dove was loosed from the rafters amid clouds of incense; at the feast of Corpus Christi the entire community knelt in church and village street while the Sacrament was borne in procession through their ranks. At Rogationtide the fields were blessed by the priest, at Lammas the loaf – first-fruit of the harvest – was presented by him at the altar, on New Year's Day he led his parishioners round the apple orchards to bless the fruit of the coming summer.

Except in Lent the village parson seldom preached. Four times a year he was expected to expound in English the Creed, the Gospel precepts and Ten Commandments, and expatiate, like Chaucer's 'poor parson of the town', on the seven deadly sins and their consequences, the seven virtues and the seven sacraments of grace. For the rest he relied, like every parish priest from Calabria to Scandinavia, on the dramatic ritual of the Catholic Church; the rites at the altar, the sonorous Latin prayers and incantations, the statues, images and pictorial representations of Christ crucified or risen in majesty, of saints and martyrs and angels, of the Last Judgment and Harrowing of Hell depicted in brilliant colours and terrifying detail over the chancel arch, of the stories from Bible and Apocalypse which covered even the humblest church.

386

In weaning pagan man from his primitive and bloodstained creeds of terror and human sacrifice, the Church's supreme achievement had been to domesticate and humanise the conception of eternity. Everywhere he was confronted, in church and wayside shrine, with homely and familiar reminders of the Heaven he was enjoined to earn through the virtues of love, faith, compassion, humility, truthfulness, chastity, courtesy – virtues that came so hard and were so much needed by a hot-tempered, ignorant, primitive people. To help them on their way to Paradise and make them shun temptation were the likenesses of men and women who, the Church told them, had struggled and overcome the infirmities of human nature and were now, like the Master whose example they had followed, blessed spirits enthroned in Heaven yet ready to intercede for struggling mortals who called on them for aid. So human were the saints, Christians were taught, that they would help them in their humblest concerns. So St Christopher, who once carred Christ on his shoulders, was the patron and protector of porters; St Bartholomew, who was flayed alive, of tanners; St Apollonia, whose jaw was smashed by his torturers, of those with toothache; St John, who had been plunged into a chaldron of burning oil, of candlemakers. St Giles looked after cripples, St Crispin cobblers, St Katherine little girls, St Eustace and St Hubert huntsmen, St Cecilia the makers of music, St Blaise sufferers from sore throats. And because she had anointed Christ's feet with aromatic oils Mary Magdalene was the protectress of perfumers. If one's oxen were sick one called on St Corneille, if one's pigs on St Anthony, if one's chickens on St Gall. There was even a patron saint, St Osyth, for women who had lost their keys.

Best loved of all who interceded for man was the Virgin. The Gabriel bell rang at evening to call Christians to recite Ave Maria, and the pilgrims flocked to see the replica of her house in the Augustinian priory at Walsingham, believing that the heavenly galaxy, the Milky Way, had been set to guide them there. The events of her life, the Annunciation, Purification, Visitation and Assumption, had taken their place among the great feasts of the Christian year; at the Purification in February, known as Candlemas, everyone walked through the streets carrying candles blessed at the altar in her honour. She was thought of as the embodiment of every womanly virtue; tender, pure and loving and so full of pity that even the most abandoned could hope for forgiveness through her aid.

In no land was Mary more honoured than in England. The number of churches and shrines dedicated to her was past counting; no other name figures so often in the lists of the royal oblations. When William of Wykeham founded his colleges at Winchester and Oxford he placed them under her protection, and at both the bishop still kneels in stone with outstretched hands before her to beg a blessing on his endowments. Nearly every church of import-ance possessed her image in silver, gold or alabaster given by some benefactor, and along the highroads and pilgrim ways were way-side chapels where travellers could tell their beads and say their prayers to the Queen of Heaven. The names on our parish maps, Ladygrove, Ladysmead, Mary's Well and Maryfield, and the flowers that country folk called after her, marigold and ladysmantle, bear witness after four centuries of Protestantism to the homage paid by our Catholic ancestors to Christ's mother.

It was this union of earth and heaven, matter and spirit, the assumption that the other world and this were in continual contact, which made medieval Christianity such a germinating and educa-tive religion. For the ordinary man his parish church was the centre both of his spiritual and terrestrial life. It was the place where the whole community met. Its nave and aisles were the setting not only for prayer and liturgical processions but for proclamations and business transactions. Its porch was used for coroners' inquests and betrothals and for the payment of legacies; its oaken chest for depositing wills, charters and title-deeds. In the churchyard where the village children played and the dead, carried in the parish coffin, were laid in their shrouds to await the reunion of all Chris-tians on Resurrection day, the parishioners met to beat the parish bounds, fairs were held, and miracle plays or 'mysteries' were enacted by bucolic actors in which rustic exuberance and horse-play mingled, incongruously, with the piety of unquestioning faith.

For medieval Christianity was an intensely human religion. It had place for comedy and farce. In the Palm Sunday procession a boy dressed as an angel standing above the west porch threw down cakes for which the congregation scrambled, while a wooden ass was drawn along behind the choir with a man belabouring it with a whip. Even in the deeply impressive Tenebrae services in Passion week when, one after another, the lights on the altar were darkened, the rustic singers in the loft were sustained during their long ordeal by wine and beer provided by the churchwardens, while the resurrection on Easter morning was hailed by the entire congregation banging on clappers.

All the community's corporate life that was not purely economic centred round the church. When a church was rebuilt or added to – and throughout the fourteenth and fifteenth centuries almost every town and village was refashioning and refurbishing its church – the churchwardens raised the money by arranging archery meetings and door-to-door collections. They appointed a village 'Robin Hood' and 'Little John' to lead the way to the butts after Mass on Sundays and holy days and collect the fees of the competitors, and organised the annual Hocktide collection when the young men and wives and maidens went in turn to one another's houses to rope in those of the other sex and make them pay forfeits for the church's benefit – 'the devocyon of the people on Hoke Tuesday', as the churchwardens of St Edmund's, Salisbury, called it. They held, too, the annual church audit when the parishioners, grouped under their respective trades and callings, came in turn to present their gifts and collections – 'comyth in the yonglings and maidens', 'comyth in the weavers', runs the account of the proceedings in one Somerset parish. It was then that the churchwardens received any bequest left to the parish: the keep of a cow for the poor, a swarm of bees to provide wax for candles and honey, a woman's wedding ring, clothing for making into vestments and coverings.

At a time when most men lived in bare, almost unfurnished mud and wattle huts little bigger than those in which a smallholder today keeps his farrowing sows, the wealth lavished on the church by even the poorest village seems little short of miraculous. As the parish inventories of the fifteenth century show, small and remote churches, with no rich benefactors to endow them, possessed chalices, patens, mazers, censers, candlesticks of silver and silver-gilt, panelled and gilded reredoses and altars, jewelled processional crosses and pyxes for the Host, embroidered vestments and altar-cloths of gold. They were furnished with carved rood screens, misericords and bench-ends, stone and alabaster statues, finely cast and engraved bells, and windows blazing with glass bought from the *verriers* of France and Germany. All was paid for and accumulated from generation to generation by the village community, many of whose members – carpenters, masons, smiths – had helped to fashion this great but, after the Reformation, soon to vanish, heritage of rustic corporate life.

CHAPTER NINETEEN

Travellers, Towns and Traders

BRIDGING THE UNCULTIVATED WILD between England's villages
and little towns ran the roads, trodden by growing numbers of men
and horses. The metalled highways with which Rome had spanned
the country had long become a ghostly network overgrown with
grass, their paved surfaces defaced, their causeways broken by
quarrying and their course deflected to serve local needs. The
medieval road did not run straight from city to city. It meandered
round field, park and pale, respecting a thousand local 'liberties'
and quirks of history. It was not surfaced for wheeled traffic or
swift travelling. It was a grassy trackway for horses, carts, cattle
and sheep – a mere way over which travellers had a right to pass.
Where it was a national highway subject to the King's Peace, the
proprietors along its course were under an obligation to keep it
open. No one might raise fences across it or dung-heaps or use it
for quarrying stone or gravel. Towns and villages which permitted
such encroachments were constantly being fined. In winter, in the
clay lowlands, such soft roads became quagmires; in summer a
maze of hard-baked hoof-holes and ruts. But so much of the
countryside was still waste that it was easy to make a detour across
adjoining land. This, however, created a multiplicity of tracks and
made it equally easy to lose the way.

During the Dark Ages travel had been so arduous and dangerous
that the Church in its prayers grouped travellers with prisoners and
captives, sick persons and women labouring with child. The repair
of bridges and the provision of hospitality for wayfarers were
regarded as matters for Christian charity. Crosses were erected by
the wayside in lonely places, lanterns kept burning in church-
towers at night, and bells sounded to guide benighted wayfarers.

391

Rich men left sums to provide rest-houses and *maisons dieu*, and monasteries and incumbents of rectories were enjoined to entertain and relieve travellers.

The lords of the highway, as of everywhere else in that aristocratic age, were the earls, barons and prelates, with their trains of followers, their armour, ceremonial furs and emblazoned mantles and banners, making their way to Council or Parliament or travelling from one estate to another. The greatest of all were the King and his Court. In a single half-year Edward I moved his residence seventy-five times. In days when there no regular posts or means of transmitting news, it was the only way in which a ruler could know and control what was happening in his realm. The grander members of the Court travelled on horseback, the vast army of menials, scullions and poor suitors on foot. Its treasure, plate, pavilions, hangings, beds, cooking-utensils, wine, legal and financial rolls were borne in panniers on pack-horses or in rough, box-like, two-wheeled carts, drawn by oxen, donkeys or dogs, and requisitioned from the countryside. A few great ladies – a queen or some royal invalid – might ride in a litter borne between horses or in a gilded wagon with an arched roof hung with tapestry and suspended on carved, un-sprung beams and huge nailed wheels. But the normal mode of transport was the cavalcade: the long procession of jingling, brightly accoutred, splendidly caparisoned horses, with riders chattering or singing as they wound their way across the fields. To journey in company and make music as one went was the mode of the time. Only the King's messengers, forerunners of the post, travelled alone, and lepers with their bells and clappers, sores and pallid, hooded faces, and adjured felons making their way from sanctuary to the nearest port with bare feet and loose white tunics and carrying wooden crosses as signs of the Church's protection.

The chief interest of the age being religion, there were many clerical travellers. Monastic officers visiting their estates and bishops' commissaries perambulating the diocese, pardoners selling indulgences, summoners with writs for breaches of ecclesiastical law, papal agents collecting money, poor clerks on the way to the universities, and black-gowned Dominican and, even more numerous, grey-gowned Franciscan friars. For every monk on the road there were a dozen friars.

For the mendicants, as they were called, who had first appeared in England in Henry III's reign, had been founded to serve God, not like the monks in the cloister, but in the street and highway. Bound by vows of chastity and poverty, their original mission had been to the very poor. With the spread of civilization and luxury, their mission, though ostensibly the same, had changed. By the fourteenth century they had ceased to be only evangelists to the poor and had become as well confessors to the rich middle class of the merchant towns. Leaving their squalid abodes in the city slums, they had raised great preaching churches – like the famous three-hundred-foot-long Greyfriars church in London – out of the benefactions of merchants who recalled with gratitude the days when they or their forbears had fled from villeinage to the hovels of the nearest town and had been befriended there by the mendicants. They still begged their way wherever they went, but the need to do so had vanished. For more than a century the benefactions and bequests of the rich had flowed into their coffers, and as the confessors of kings, nobles and merchants, their leaders enjoyed vast influence. But they were still to be encountered everywhere, ministering to rich and poor alike, enjoying hospitality wherever they went and employing popular, and even sensational, devices to win converts to their faith and subscribers to their Order. They were particularly popular with the ladies, to whom their gaiety, good humour and here-today, gone-tomorrow approach, and the understanding and ingratiating way with which they heard confessions much endeared them – according to their enemies – far too much.

These were the religious professionals of the road; others were amateurs. Every spring men and women would set out in company, with wallet, staff and scallop shell, broad-brimmed hat and jingling Canterbury bell, to visit some distant or local shrine and return with relics – for the rich a splinter from a saint's staff or a flask of holy water; for ordinary folk, a pewter-badge to be worn on cap or breast as a souvenir. Pilgrimage was one of the penances set by the Church for winning remission of time in purgatory – the place of punishment to which it was believed those not immediately translated to Heaven or Hell were consigned after death until they expiated their sins.

Pilgrimage could be a penance of the most onerous kind, one in which a man left home and family for years, braving immense hardships and perils to visit the Holy Land or Rome or some remote shrine like St James's of Compostella in Spain. But for most people, though seen as a means of acquiring grace, a pilgrimage was an excuse for a holiday, to be taken preferably

'When that Aprillë with his showers sweet
The drought of March hath pierced to the root.'

As soon as the roads dried out after the winter they were thronged with parties making their way to some favourite shrine and beguiling the journey with tales, singing and the playing of bag-pipes. The most popular places of pilgrimage, and there were hundreds, were St Thomas's shrine at Canterbury – the word 'canter' entered the language through it – and Our Lady's statue at Walsingham in Norfolk, 'the most holy name in England' with its famous phial of the Virgin's milk. Both were visited every summer by huge crowds. So were Joseph of Arimathaea's winter-blossoming thorn at Glastonbury, the philtre of Christ's blood at Richard of Cornwall's abbey of Hayles in Gloucestershire, and the Confessor's glittering shrine at Westminster, where the hollows worn by the feet of kneeling pilgrims can still be seen.

The most cautious road-users were those who travelled with merchandise or money, for the woods and thickets were full of thieves. In the early Middle Ages the main roads, especially those to the southern and eastern ports, were much used by foreigners – Flemings and Italians buying Cotswold or Yorkshire wool, Spaniards with steel blades from Toledo, Lombards with silks and spices, Easterlings with furs and tar from the Baltic. But by the end of the thirteenth century much of such trade was beginning to pass to Englishmen. As there were no posts and few facilities for trans-ferring money from one country to another, a merchant had con-stantly to be on the road attending his business. Like the poor man in Chaucer's tale who was deceived by his wife and the young monk, he was always off to Bruges or Bordeaux at break of day.

Humbler traders like pedlars, chapmen and charcoal-sellers went on foot, with their wares on a pack-horse or in a box or sack on their backs. So did a host of poor itinerants, travelling from one village to another: minstrels, buffoons and ballad-singers, some aiming high at the castles and others at gaping rustics on the village greens; bears and bearwards; men with performing monkeys; clowns, jugglers, girls who danced on their hands with swords in their mouths, and herbalists selling panaceas for every disease. There is a picture of one in a thirteenth-century herbal, spreading his wares on his carpet or drugget and haranguing the villagers.

At certain times of the year the roads became crowded with travellers converging on a single spot. Fairs were occasions when a rural neighbourhood did its shopping and caught a glimpse of the outer world. The greatest fair in England was Stourbridge near Cambridge – the property of Barnwell Priory. Here for three weeks every September a town of wooden booths offered for sale everything a rustic community needed. There were streets that sold soap, streets that sold garlic, streets that sold coal. Others vended fish, nails, grindstones, Sussex iron and Worcestershire salt, shovels, brushes and pails, oil and honey, pots and pans, horses and pack-saddles. The centre of the fair was the duddery, where the 'duds' or cloths of East Anglia were displayed. Among those who brought their wares were Spaniards and Moors with Damascus blades and armour, Venetians with gems and velvets, Flemings with linen, Dutchmen with cheeses, Greeks with almonds and spices and Germans or Easterlings with tallow, fur and pitch. A special court of *Pied Poudre* or 'dusty foot' – called by the English 'Pie Powder' – was held to preserve order and enforce the regulations of the fair's owners about weights and measures and the quality of foodstuffs. In the jovial mode of England the fair also provided horse-races, wrestling-matches, tippling, gambling and music booths, rope-dancers and a maypole.

*　　　　*　　　　*

What fairs were temporarily, towns were permanently. During the reigns of the first three Henrys there had been a steady growth in the size and number of towns. The Crown and the great secular and ecclesiastical lords found the sale of free burgess-tenures and the tolls of markets and fairs a valuable supplement to their agricultural revenues. They encouraged commerce by letting the citizens and guild-merchants of favoured towns buy charters of freedom from the tolls and custom-dues which impeded the flow of goods at city gate, port and river crossing. Control of the hours of dealing, of prices, weights and measures, and of the quality of goods sold, was delegated by royal or baronial charter to their corporations and, often, to associations of their traders. These merchant-guilds were empowered to fix wages and prices fair to both buyer and seller, to exclude non-members from trading in the town and to fine and punish for breaches of their rules. They appointed hours, announced by bell, for the opening and closing of markets and levied tolls on goods brought for sale. They also made treaties, interchanging commercial privileges, with the traders of other towns. And in the larger cities, craftsmen and traders associated themselves in livery companies or fraternities, partly commercial and partly religious and social, to regulate the conditions of their trade and afford one another mutual protection.

Like the juries of the villages, these self-governing corporations helped to train Englishmen for political responsibility. They were administered by voluntary officers elected annually, whose duties were borne by the members in turn, and governed by rules reached after mutual and open discussion. Members were punished for selling inferior goods, for sharp or shoddy practice that lowered the name of their craft, for brawling and eavesdropping and breaches of social and professional etiquette. A trader who sold food made from diseased carcasses, who put sand in his bread or water in his wine or otherwise tricked the public, was sentenced by his fellow craftsmen to be drawn through the streets on a hurdle or to sit in penance in the pillory with the offending goods hung round his neck and his crime published on a placard. 'The said John Penrose,' ran the order of one London court, 'shall drink a draught of the same wine which he sold to the common people, and the remainder of such wine shall then be poured on the head of the same John, and he shall forswear the calling of a vintner in the city of London for ever.'

Every English town, with the possible exception of London, had originally grown out of a village. Its institutions had a rustic origin: the borough and ward officers with agricultural names; the moot which had begun as a manorial jurisdiction, and the burgh-mote horn that summoned the burghers to its meetings; the annual perambulation of the bounds when the city fathers, like their village forbears, solemnly beat the young fry over the boundary-stones to make them remember where they stood. The sanitary arrangements of the borough also derived from the village. Such drains as it had, ran down the unpaved or, at best, cobbled roadway. The household refuse and ordure, thrown out of the windows at nightfall, were scavenged by pigs, dogs and kites. Even in London, where the poorer dwellings were totally without privies, there was for long only one public latrine for every ward and a dozen dung-carts for the whole city. The larger the towns grew, the more unwholesome they became, though, after a time their corporations, alarmed at the rising death-rate, began to issue regulations about street-cleansing and water-supply.

Yet, though the towns were dirty, they were also beautiful, with their church towers and spires, their stately gateways and half-timbered houses, and the trees and blossom of their gardens. Their encircling walls were designed more for preventing robberies and controlling suspicious travellers at night than for war. Except on the Welsh and Scottish borders they were seldom the elaborate affairs of the continent, where even the smallest town was heavily fortified. Some of the later boroughs, like Cambridge, never even had walls, but only palisades and ditches crossed by gated bridges. Being in little danger of attack, they were free from the military restrictions that cramped life for European burghers. They did not need governors and garrisons.

For this reason, too, they spread outwards rather than upwards, running to leafy suburbs which, secure in England's immunity from invasion, nestled outside instead of inside the walls. Yet, as no town save London had more than 10,000 inhabitants, and few a third of this number, the fields were never far away. Most of the richer merchants had farms or orchards in the surrounding countryside, as well as gardens, stables and cowstalls round their houses. English urban economy was as much rural as urban. Even the city of Norwich, capital of the clothmaking industry of East Anglia and the third largest town in England, suspended trade during the harvest and sent its weavers into the fields.

*   *   *

One town in England stood alone. With the royal courts of law sitting permanently in the King's palace or hall of Westminster, London had long taken the place of the old Anglo-Saxon capital, Winchester, as the seat of government. One of Henry II's subjects, William FitzStephen, wrote an account of it as it was a century after the Conquest: its clear river bordering it on the south, the royal castle in the east, the high and massive walls with their seven double-gates and towers, the thirteen conventual and hundred and twenty-six parish churches. Most of the houses were still flimsy single or two-storeyed wooden structures; one winter gale flattened more than six hundred, and fires often swept away whole wards. But the richer merchants' and knights' houses were already being built of stone, and red-brick tiles were gradually replacing thatch. Two years before Henry's death in 1189 the Londoners began their first stone bridge; a monument of faith in the country's stability, which took thirty years to complete and lasted for six centuries.

FitzStephen described the merchandise which flowed up the river to the Pool beside the Tower and the little hithes and quays along the north bank – gold and spices from the East, arms from Scythia and purple silk from China; the wine and cook-shops where travellers could buy hot dishes at any hour of the day or night; the market outside the walls in the meadow called Smithfield, where high-stepping palfreys with gleaming coats were put through their paces and country folk brought their goods and livestock for sale. He drew a picture, the first in our history, of the Londoners at play; their summer evening walks among the suburban wells – St Clement's, Holywell, Clerkenwell – and the sparkling streams whose mill-wheels made so cheerful a sound; the hunts in the great Middlesex and Essex forests after stag, fallow deer and wild boar; the apprentices and schoolboys playing

398

football in the fields while 'the fathers and wealthy magnates came on horseback to watch the contests and recover their lost youth'; the archery, running, jumping, wrestling, dancing and stone slinging, rowing and skating, with which the youths and maidens regaled themselves on holy days.

By the fourteenth century, the population of London had risen to about 50,000. Though still much smaller than the great continental cities of Paris, Milan and Florence, with its 'square mile' along the Thames between the Tower and Ludgate it was by far the country's largest town – four or five times the size of York, Bristol, Plymouth, Coventry or Norwich and probably ten times that of Gloucester, Newcastle, Salisbury, Exeter or Winchester. Newcomers were all the time being drawn into it by the commerce of its tidal river and the business of the royal Chancery and the courts of law at Westminster two miles to the west. Already the Strand – the highway between the two places – was lined with nobles' and prelates' palaces whose gardens sloped down to the unembanked Thames. The King himself, unlike his cousin of France, had no palace in his capital – only the Tower on its eastern wall, with its little garrison of knights and men-at-arms, and the Wardrobe or Household clothing store at Baynard's Castle.

For the City was a law to itself. 'Come what may,' ran an old saying, 'the Londoners should have no King but their Mayor.' This functionary, though only a merchant, had taken his place at Runnymede among the great magnates of the realm who imposed Magna Carta. He ruled the capital with the help of two sheriffs, elected annually like himself, and a court of aldermen representing its twenty-five wards. Behind this court's weekly hustings in the Guildhall lay the general body of the corporation – the old folkmoot of the citizens assembled three times a year by bell in the open air outside St Paul's. With the population growing fast, there was a constant tendency on the part of the less privileged to try to gain control of the city's government and oust the older merchant families who monopolised it – a struggle which resulted in frequent faction-fights and rioting. During Edward I's reign the antiquated and unmanageable public assembly was abandoned in favour of an elected Common Council. Through its officers the corporation

399

collected the royal customs on foreign merchandise and levied its own tolls on all goods coming in from the country. It made bye-laws on such matters as building, public order, the use of fountains and precautions against fire. It decided who should have the right to trade in particular districts, where swine should be allowed to wander, when taverns should close and slops and refuse be emptied from the windows. It also fixed the hour of curfew, after which none with swords were allowed in the streets, 'unless some great lord or other substantial person of good reputation'.

London could be a very turbulent city. Behind its bridge and seven portcullised gateways crowded the warlike rabble of apprentices and journeymen who, when roused, became a terrible raging beast. Any infringement of its rights brought it swarming through the narrow streets like a torrent. Once, when some Hoxton residents enclosed a meadow where the Londoners had long taken their Sunday walks, a turner in a fool's coat ran through the streets crying, 'Shovels and spades!', upon which the whole town turned out to level the hedges and ditches. The German merchants of the Cologne Steelyard in Thames Street and the rich Italians of Galley Quay and Mincing Lane barricaded their houses against their English neighbours like fortresses.

Yet the beauty of medieval London impressed travellers even more than its turbulence. It was bordered on the south by a wide, clear river, teeming with fish and with swans on its waters. Beyond it, save for the disorderly little suburb of Southwark, lay unsullied meadows and the wooded Surrey hills. To the north of the walls cornfields and pastures, diversified with streams and water-mills, stretched to the heights of Hampstead and Highgate. To the east lay the great hunting forests of Epping and Hainault. All round were thriving villages supplying the city's needs – Stepney, Bethnal Green, Islington, Hoxton, Holborn, Marylebone and, farther afield, Bow and Bromley, Hackney, Highbury and Stoke Newington, Kilburn, Paddington and Knightsbridge. Though, save for its immense cathedral on the hill and its famous twenty-arch bridge crowned with houses, London lacked imposing buildings, the towers and spires of its churches and monasteries made a wonderful show as they crowded above the walls and river. The sound of their bells was almost continuous. And between the brightly painted wooden houses and red-tiled roofs were countless little gardens or 'herbers' and orchards of waving fruit-trees – mulberry, apple, plum, peach and cherry.

*   *   *

The country of which London was the capital was still predominantly agricultural: a rich primary producing land, with a population only about a third of that of France and Italy, exporting vast quantities of fine wool and, in good years, grain and dairy produce. It also exported hides, leather goods, dried and salted fish, embroideries, metalware, tin, coal and lead; mostly to the overpopulated Low Countries, to Gascony and the Rhineland in exchange for wine, and to the Baltic for timber and shipbuilding stores. Wool was its main source of wealth. The finest – the short wool of the Ryelands sheep and the long of the Lincolns, Leicesters and golden Lion breed of the Cotswolds – came from the Severn valley and the limestone belt between Somerset and Lincolnshire. Yet almost every part of the country, except the far north and extreme south-west, exported wool of some kind. It was reckoned that on an average thirty thousand sacks or eight million fleeces went abroad every year, mostly to northern Italy and the cloth-manufacturing towns of Flanders, Artois, Brabant and Hainault.

Though for most of the Middle Ages England was primarily a supplier of raw wool to others, cloth was always manufactured on a small scale for home consumption in most of the larger towns. Edward III's marriage in 1330 to a Hainault princess brought a new stimulus to native manufacture. Colonies of Flemish weavers, attracted by the cheap and abundant supplies of the raw material of their trade and the social stability of England, established themselves during his reign at Norwich, York and Cranbrook in Kent. Queen Philippa herself made a practice of visiting one of these settlements in Norwich whenever her husband went on progress in East Anglia.

Export of wool and the increased imports which it paid for of spices, wine, silks, furs, timber, pitch, tar, oil, salt, alum, rice and fruits were a great stimulus to native shipping and shipbuilding.

Southampton, Bristol, Plymouth and Falmouth were the chief ports of the west, Lynn, Boston, Newcastle-on-Tyne, Kingston-on-Hull and the Cinque Ports of the east. After London the most important was Southampton, whose deep tidal water, protected by the Isle of Wight from Breton, Gascon and Flemish pirates, rivalled the Thames estuary as the starting-point for the convoys of little sailing-ships, mostly of less than a hundred tons, which carried England's wool to the continent. It was a terminus port, too, for the wine fleets from Bordeaux, Bayonne and La Rochelle, and for the Genoese and Pisan carracks which during the early years of the fourteenth century started to export woolfells from the Solent and Thames to the mills of the Arte della Lana of Florence in return for luxuries from Italy and the Orient. To Southampton came by barge down the Itchen – then navigable as far as Winchester – the wool of the Wiltshire, Berkshire and Gloucestershire downs, while coastwise vessels from Poole, Melcombe Regis, Bridport, Lyme and Exeter brought that of Dorset, Somerset and Devon. Other wool travelled down the Severn and Warwickshire Avon for shipment at Bristol. Carts and packhorses took the canvas-wrapped bales and fells on their journey from the upland pastures to the nearest river.

In days when water provided by far the cheapest form of transport, England's commerce gained from two circumstances. Though her rivers were small compared with those of the continent, the sea was never far away and her coast abounded in estuaries where goods could be shipped either abroad or to her own ports. And at a time when every ruler was trying to fill his coffers by levying tolls on merchandise, England with her strong, unified royal government was the largest free-trading area in Europe. Almost her only internal transportation-tolls were petty portages and viages levied to recoup expenditure where a bridge or road had been provided by private enterprise. Only at the courts of Brabant and Hainault and in the Italian and Flemish cities was the movement of trade as free.

With a coastline longer for her size than that of any western kingdom, England possessed a substantial maritime population living by fishing, coastal trade and voyages to the Baltic, Low Countries, France and Biscay. Though most of her ocean carrying-trade was still in the hands of foreigners and her ships were of much smaller tonnage than those of the Mediterranean trading states – Genoa, Pisa, Venice and Aragon – her seamen, accustomed to the Channel and North Sea tides and storms, were tough, skilful and notorious for their pugnacity. Constantly involved in harbour broils with their Norman, Breton, Flemish and Basque rivals, they fought as often among themselves. Whenever the seamen of the Cinque Ports met the fishermen of Yarmouth, whom they viewed as interlopers, they engaged them in pitched battle 'on lond and strong'. With their seven chartered ports – Winchelsea, Romney, Hythe, Dover, Sandwich, Hastings and Rye, and their outlying 'limbs' – the portmen of the Sussex and Kent lagoons and inlets had long been the aristocrats of the narrow seas, producing their feudal quota of ships for the King in time of war and living in peacetime by a well-tried blend of fishing, piracy and trade with northern France and the Low Countries. But, with the gradual silting up of their harbours and the development of sail, their ascendancy was already beginning to be challenged by the West Country seamen. With the richest fishing grounds in the world at their gates and a Catholic country to feed that lived on fish all Lent and Fridays, coastal Englishmen were learning the business of mastering the watery wastes in which their island was set. Though they seldom yet ventured further than Spain or Norway – Chaucer's shipman knew the coasts from Jutland to Finisterre – the stormy and changeable seas they sailed were well adapted for teaching the finer points of seamanship. A breed apart, transmitting their sea-lore from father to son, they introduced into the make-up of a rustic people an adventurous, carefree strain which was to have far-reaching consequences in the sixteenth century after the discovery of America and the ocean trade-routes round the Cape.

*　　　*　　　*

The merchant town, with its life of freedom and opportunity, was little by little transforming the racially divided society that England had become after the Norman conquest into a fluid one in which every social grade shaded imperceptibly into the next. Many of the leading merchant families, especially in London and the larger

403

ports, traced their descent from foreign traders who had settled in England, like the Bocointes and Buckerells who had come from Italy and the Arraxes who took their name from Arras. Far more were enterprising English countrymen, often of villein blood, who had fled from bondage on their paternal acres to seek their fortunes behind the walls of the self-governing chartered boroughs. Many who did so perished of poverty or disease in their overcrowded slums, defeated by the monopolistic restrictions with which the established burgesses protected themselves and their crafts and trades. Others passed, sometimes in less than a generation, from the harsh, unchanging life of the manor to affluence, the dignity of aldermanic or mayoral status, and even office under the Crown – always in England quick to avail itself of the services of men of business and financial experience. Merchants unknown to the hereditary feudal hierarchy, with rustic names like Dunstable, Haverill and Piggsflesh, served as royal chamberlains, butlers and purveyors, loaned money to the Crown or some great magnate, arranged for the transfer of funds from one part of the Plantagenet Empire to another and offered mortgages to supply their social superiors, lay and ecclesiastic, with the ready cash to cater for their increasingly luxurious tastes. In doing so, though many fell by the way, they made fortunes for themselves, investing their gains in land and founding landed and knightly families.

The prolonged conflicts with Scotland and France of the three Edwards provided an enormous stimulus to the development of the merchant class. Though no English trader could at first offer the Crown the credit facilities of the great banking and cloth-manufacturing houses of Florence and Lombardy, by the end of the thirteenth century there were already native financiers rich enough to play a leading part in equipping the royal armies. It was to those who dealt in wool, 'the sovereign merchandise and jewel of this realm of England', as Parliament put it, that the Crown turned. For alone of England's commodities wool could always be converted into cash; Flanders and Italy could never have enough of it. It was with the help of the great Shropshire woolmonger, Laurence of Ludlow, the builder of Stokesay castle – *'mercator notissimus'* as the royal lawyers described him – that Edward I equipped an expedition to Flanders in 1297. When Laurence was drowned in an over-loaded ship taking the wool to Holland, the monastic chroniclers saw in it the hand of God avenging the lowered prices to the home – and ecclesiastical – producer with which the financier and his fellow monopolists passed on their losses.

The bargaining power which the collection and export of wool gave to the rich subject in his dealings with the Crown played a major part in the development of national taxation and of Parliament. There were three ways in which the Government could raise money from the trade. The first was to requisition part of the season's crop and, treating it as a forced loan from its owners, sell it abroad. The second was to borrow from foreign or English capitalists in return for a temporary monopoly of the wool export. The third – the method finally adopted after much trial and error – was to procure from Parliament a tax on exports and set up a customs-staple in some town or towns, either at home or abroad, through which all exported wool had to pass. The right to levy customs had always been a royal prerogative but, in an age of primitive economy, if the Crown wished to raise money quickly it could do so only with the co-operation of those who dealt in the goods it wished to tax. Sometimes, instead of summoning a Parliament and asking for a subsidy from the entire merchant class as represented by the elected burgesses, the King convened an assembly of leading wool-merchants and negotiated with them a levy on exported wool. But as soon as it became realised that the woolmongers invariably passed on the tax by lowering the prices paid to wool-producers, the latter's representatives in Parliament began to demand that the Crown should negotiate with them instead of with those who paid the tax only in name. In doing so they put forward as a *quid pro quo*, however at first humbly and tentatively, demands not only for redress of grievances but for control over the expenditure of the money raised and of the royal officers who administered it.

The means by which the wool tax was collected was the staple. It was first set up in London and thirteen other English ports at the beginning of Edward I's reign to collect the 'ancient or great custom' or half a mark – 6s. 8d. – per sack, granted to him by Parliament. When in 1297 he forcibly borrowed all the available stocks of English wool to finance an expedition to the Low Countries, a foreign staple had had to be set up, first at Dordrecht and later at Antwerp, to weigh and price the commandeered wool and levy the hated *maltote*, as it was called, on that of the merchants. Here, and in the domestic staple towns in England, the royal officials – collectors, controllers, searchers, surveyors, clerks, weighers and crane-keepers – administered both the ancient and great custom and the so-called petty custom which Edward at the end of his reign imposed on foreign exporters. For though freedom in trade increased both the export of wool and the prices paid to the producer, the Crown could no longer subsist without the revenue of the customs and the credit that could be raised from it. Early in Edward III's reign to finance his wars with France the foreign staple was revived to become a permanent feature of the wool-trade and the national system of taxation. It enabled the King to borrow money on the security of the customs and direct the export of wool to whatever city in the Low Countries suited his foreign policy of the moment. After the capture of Calais in 1347, that town became England's chief staple port and, later, when the export of cloth began to supersede that of wool, the spearhead for its sale to Europe.

The raising of wool was the concern of almost the entire rural community. Not only were the owners of the great feudal and ecclesiastical estates dependent for ready money on their fleeces, but so were knights of the shire, rich franklins and even humble villeins whose communal village flocks helped to swell the flow of wool from the manorial demesnes to the quays and warehouses of the collecting merchants. Travelling with their pack-horses to grange, village and monastery and buying up the year's produce to sell to the exporters who shipped it to Flanders or Italy, the 'wool-men', by offering credit in exchange for low prices, earned a high rate of concealed interest without infringing the Christian rules against usury. Many of the larger landowners, as well as keeping flocks, engaged in this collecting trade, buying the wool of their smaller neighbours who lacked the capital and know-how to dispose of their own produce. The Cistercian abbeys of the northern and western dales were particularly active in such business, drawing

406

from it and their flocks the revenues which enabled them to replace the austere habitations of pioneer days with the magnificent buildings that still, after centuries of desolation and decay, make the ruins of Fountains and Tintern, Rievaulx and Byland places of aesthetic pilgrimage.

Picturing Plantagenet England, one sees the traces of this rural industry everywhere – the open downlands nibbled close by immense flocks of tiny sheep with their shepherds, tinkling bells, sheepcotes and dewponds; the fells and fleeces stacked in great barns of stone and timber; the up-country towns and the market-places of York and Lincoln, Grantham, Louth, Ludlow and Shrewsbury, Winchester and Andover crowded with dealers and factors; the trains of pack-horses and barges moving towards the sea; the London merchants in their furred robes doing business with the King's officers; the English cogs and tall Italian carracks beating out from the Thames estuary and southern ports towards the hungry mills of Flanders and distant Tuscany:

> 'The sward the black-face browses,
> The stapler and the bale,
> The grey Cistercian houses
> That pack the wool for sale.'

The pastoral economy of shepherding and tending 'the silly sheep', of sheep-shearing and dispatching the wool fells to their remote destinations made a lasting impression on the nation's character. It embraced both the solitude and meditation of the shepherd's life, and the journeyings and bargainings involved in selling the wool which the mills of Ghent and Arno transformed into raiment for Europe's rich. The lonely sheepcotes and farms of western and northern England, the epitaph in the downland church –

> 'Faithful lived and Faithful died
> Faithful shepherd on the hillside,
> The hill so high, the field so round,
> In the day of judgement he'll be found' –

are one side of the medal; Chaucer's merchant off to Bruges at break of day and the bustling wife of Bath at her clothier's trade the other. Wool-growing, wool-carrying and wool-mongering all tended to make men more thoughtful and resourceful than the uneventful life of communal arable agriculture by which peasant Christendom lived. They made, too, for a sense of freedom. The man who owned or tended sheep on the uplands felt himself more his own master than the husbandman of the three-field village closely bound by manorial custom and watched by prying neighbours.

*　　　　*　　　　*

During the last half of the fourteenth century the domestic cloth trade started to expand so rapidly that by the middle of the following century – the last of the Middle Ages – it was already absorbing most of the native wool crop. In 1353, two thousand cloths were exported; forty years later, during Richard II's reign, twenty times as many. In 1420 the export of cloth for the first time exceeded that of raw wool, and by the end of the fifteenth century, despite a halt during the Wars of the Roses, was twice as much. The introduction from the East of the fulling-mill and its exploitation by English capitalists created a new industry wherever flowing water was plentiful and good sheep pasture near. It brought an enormous accession of wealth to these localities. In the valleys of the Stroud and the Wiltshire Avon; in the upper reaches of the Aire and the Pennine streams, where the mechanisation of the fulling process laid the foundations of the prosperity of the West Riding towns; and in Suffolk along the Stour and its tributaries there occurred a rural industrial revolution. West Country broadcloths – 'Stroud-waters', 'Cotswolds' and 'Castlecombes' – and the serges and worsteds of East Anglia became as famous on the continent as the products of Ghent and Ypres. In the fifteenth century it was reckoned that nearly 25,000 workers were engaged in the trade. It was an industry based, not on cities but on villages and small towns where, free from the restrictive labour and price regulations of municipality and guild, enterprising clothiers supplied the raw material to cottage weavers from whom they later collected the spun wool, distributing it to the shearers, fullers and dyers before their pack-horses carried the finished product to London or the ports for shipment overseas. Pioneers of what was long to be the country's greatest industry, these rustic capitalists left their mark in the tall-towered churches and stone manor-houses – witnesses to their faith, wealth and enterprise – which they raised among the limestone hills that spanned England from Somerset to Lincolnshire. There, too, can be seen the brasses which preserve their likenesses – the forked beards, hawks and horses, the hall-marks of quality and honest dealing that they stamped on their bales, the fine Flemish beaver hats in which they rode out to bargain for the midsummer clip or autumn fell with Gloucestershire squires and Yorkshire abbots. Such were William Grevil, ancestor of the earls of Warwick, who was buried in 1401 in the beautiful church he built at Chipping Campden – 'late citizen of London and flower of the wool merchants of all England' – Thomas Paycocke of Coggeshall, and John Barton of Holme who had engraved on the windows of his house:

> 'I thank God and ever shall,
> It is the sheep hath paid for all.'

The success of the cloth trade and the fierce and often armed resistance it provoked from foreign competitors – especially the German Hanse in the Baltic – favoured the growth of London. Except for Bristol, with its merchant princes and shipowners like the Canynges – builders of the great Perpendicular church of St Mary Redcliffe, 'the fairest, goodliest and most famous parish church in England' – the burghers of the older provincial towns lacked the capital to finance so costly and speculative a business. The monopoly of the trade with the Low Countries, by far England's most lucrative market, was in the hands of the London Society of Merchant Adventurers. Like the older Merchants of the Staple, they formed the nucleus of a new aristocracy, marrying into the gentry, founding landed estates and playing a part in the luxurious court of Edward IV – a great patron of London merchants and their wives. It was through them and the Mercers' Company that the wealth of the cloth trade flowed into the capital, drawing with it growing numbers of tradesmen, craftsmen and artificers. By the end of the fifteenth century the city's population was nearly

75,000, and its suburbs almost joined the outlying villages of Hoxton, Clerkenwell and Shoreditch whose fields – once the Londoner's playground – were giving way to houses. Its riches were beginning to compare with those of the Lombard and Flemish cities; an Italian traveller counted more than fifty goldsmiths' shops in Cheapside; 'so rich and full of silver vessels is it,' he wrote, 'that in all the shops of Milan, Rome, Venice and Florence put together there would not be found so many of the magnificence that is to be seen in London.' This was an exaggeration, but the Scottish poet, William Dunbar, received much the same impression when he visited it in 1501:

> 'Upon thy lusty bridge of pillars white
> Be merchantïs full royal to behold;
> Upon thy streets goeth many a seemly knight
> In velvet gownës and in chains of gold . . .
> Rich be thy merchantïs in substance that excellïs;
> Fair be thy wives, right lovesome, white and small.
> Clear be thy virgins, lusty under kellis:
> London, thou art the flower of cities all!'

CHAPTER TWENTY

Gothic Glory

'Walk there awhile, before the day is done,
Beneath the banner and the battered casque,
Where graven heraldry is bronze and stone
With lily and with cross and leopard's mask
Spandrils the arch. Thou shalt not walk alone;
There dead men walk again and dead lips ask,
"What of the isles of England and her sea?"
Till whispers fill the tower of memory.'

Muriel Stuart

WHEREVER MAN in the Middle Ages turned his eyes, he was faced
by the majesty of the Catholic Church. A traveller could not
approach a town in any part of western Christendom without seeing the familiar sight of its towers and spires rising above its walls
and houses. For the Church did not depend for its teaching only
on books and sermons or even on the candlelit mystery and drama
of its Latin liturgy. In an age when not one man in a thousand
could read, it drove its lessons home in sculptured stone and vaulted
space, and in the carvings and paintings of artists who employed
their genius to make the Christian story familiar to everyone. The
supreme expression of medieval man's faith was the work of the
'engineers' or architects who, at abbot's or bishop's command,
sketched on deal boards the designs of their vast buildings, and of
the master-masons who carried out their conceptions with teams
of travelling craftsmen. There were hewers trimming the stone
with axes and dressing it with chisels, setters laying the walls and
making mortar-matrixes, turners with stone-lathes shaping column
and shaft; carvers and glaziers, slaters, smiths and plumbers,

wrights and joiners. They fashioned the timber supports from the heart of the tree, graved statues, made ironwork fittings for doors, raised with primitive cranes and pulley-wheels the baskets of stone and rolls of lead to the soaring walls and roofs, and filled the windows with geometrically patterned and brilliantly coloured glass.

During the twelfth and thirteenth centuries nearly every great cathedral and abbey church in the French-speaking lands on either side of the Channel was partly rebuilt or enlarged in the style which later became known as Gothic. The plain rounded vaulting, small windows and heavy columns of the Romanesque and Norman past were superseded by delicately pointed arches, clusters of slender pillars and tiers of long lancet-windows that flooded the vast buildings with light and lit the jewelled shrines, painted walls and stained glass within, in radiant hues. The transformation was the result, partly of revolutionary advances in engineering technique – which rendered unnecessary the unbroken masses of wall space needed to support roof and tower – and partly of new ideas introduced into northern Europe during the Crusades from the Saracen and Byzantine East. The overwhelming impression was one of height, light and energy. With their soaring pinnacles and flying buttresses – built to take the outward thrust of the immense arches and fenestrated walls – these great new buildings, glittering in white stone, looked from a distance like giants on the march.

Inside they were filled with delicate carving, with sculptured shrines, tombs and statues, and with colour and ornamentation that humanised their immense size and made them resemble gigantic jewelled boxes. In England this tendency to fine internal decoration was carried farther than in almost any other western land. Forests of airy shafts of Purbeck marble, exquisitely moulded trefoil arches, flowing leaves and flowers naturalistically carved in stone on capital and arch, elaborate and deeply carved roof-bosses were distinguishing marks of the English school. So were the compound piers that the Anglian masons, stubbornly persisting in an ancient native tradition, evolved to carry the intricate ribbed vaulting – itself partly an English invention – and which reached perfection in the nave of Wells, where dynamics and pure poetry blend and become indistinguishable. So, too were the vast traceried windows and the immense timber trusses and posts of native oak – the hardest in Europe – which, bearing the laminated stone roofs, gave a sense of illimitable height and mystery to the worshippers in choir and aisle below.

These tremendous buildings, so far transcending the apparent economic and technical resources of the time, were not raised like the architectural monuments of the East by slave-labour. They were made by craftsmen able to bargain and of the same faith as those who ordered their making. Though behind them lay the quarrymen and burners of the limestone-hills, the seamen and drovers who brought the materials to the building-sites, and the labour-services and carrying-dues of the local manorial tenants, the main work of building was done by bands of travelling masons who, under their contracting-masters, moved from one great church to another. The name of the lean-to 'lodges' which they erected against the rising walls for shelter still survive in the nomenclature of modern freemasons and trade unions.

Their services were eagerly competed for by prelates whose desire to outbuild one another was as much a stimulus to the craft of building as the later rivalry of eighteenth-century country gentlemen. So were the new fashions of Christian worship which necessitated the erection, at the eastern end of great churches, of chapels to house the shrines of saints, the tombs of benefactors and the relics which the greater religious houses accumulated to attract the offerings of pilgrims. Particularly popular were the Lady Chapels, where men and, still more, women, prayed to the Virgin Mother, whose worship afforded an outlet for a kind of sub-limated chivalry and adoration of the womanly virtues of pity, tenderness and compassion. All this brought about during the first half of the thirteenth century an enlargement of the eastern ends of presbyteries of cathedrals and abbeys, later balanced by the addi-tion of preaching-naves. This made English churches – generally inferior to those of France in height – exceptionally long.

The most complete example extant of thirteenth-century English architecture is the church which rose in the Avon water-meadows at Salisbury. Here, following quarrels between the cathedral clergy and the garrison of Old Sarum castle, Bishop Richard Poore – formerly dean – embarked in 1220 on the prodigious task of rebuilding the cathedral on a new site. Built of freestone from the Chilmark quarries twelve miles away and taking half a century to complete, Salisbury cathedral still stands as its builders designed it – save for its spire and upper tower added a century later – the only medieval cathedral in England which is all of a piece. Inside, it was brilliantly coloured, with scarlet and black scrollwork walls, white-painted vaulting and gilded capitals, across which jewels of ruby and blue in the windows cast glittering reflections with every change of sun and shadow. But, outside, in the close, and in the cloisters – the largest in England with their arches looking on to the quiet garth – one can still feel the faith that prompted men to raise such monuments to their belief in the unity of earth and heaven.

Among those who watched its rising walls was the young king Henry III from his hunting palace of Clarendon a few miles away. From his earliest days he had been brought up to venerate the Anglo-Saxon saints. In 1244, four years after the consecration of St Paul's, he started to rebuild the abbey church of Westminster in honour of its founder, Edward the Confessor, in whose name he had christened his eldest son. In doing so he drew his inspiration from the new cathedrals which, under his brother-in-law, Louis IX of France, were being raised on the other side of the Channel. From Amiens and Rheims – the crowning-place of the French Kings – and, above all, from the exquisite Sainte Chapelle in Paris, he borrowed the lofty eastern chevet and the mosaic-paved ambulatory with its semi-circle of radiating chapels and, to the west of them and St Edward's shrine, he made a raised theatre where the coronation of England's kings could be solemnised. Yet though the abbey's eastern outline was taken from Rheims and the soaring pointed arches, flying buttresses and great circular rose-windows from Amiens, its general plan, with its bold transepts and the exquisite craftsmanship of its interior, was English. The master mason who supervised its building was an Englishman, Henry of Reyns, and so were his successors – for the work took a quarter of a century – John of Gloucester and Robert of Beverley. At one time eight hundred workmen were employed on it. From the Abbey muniments we know the names of many of these craftsmen, who were settled by the Chapter in houses in Westminster: Alexander the carpenter, Odo the goldsmith and Edward his son, Henry the glazier, John of St Albans, the great master-sculptor whose twin angels, once brilliantly coloured, still swing their censers under the vast rose-window of the south transept.

By the end of the thirteenth century the lead in ecclesiastical building had passed from the monks to the canons of the 'secular' cathedrals and the 'courtier' bishops, enriched by their ministerial services to the Crown. Edward I's reign saw the culmination of the rebuilding of Lincoln's glorious cathedral – its towers crowned with three immense spires in an extension of the presbytery to house the shrine of St Hugh. The King himself was present at the translation of the saint's bones to their new resting place. With its huge traceried east window and double-banked lights extending the full width of every bay, the new choir was more brilliantly lit than any building yet erected. Beneath the windows of the clerestory, filling the spandrels of the triforium arches, thirty smiling stone angels looked down, some like those carved a generation earlier in Westminster Abbey, with musical instruments, others holding crowns, scrolls and censers. Some had their feet on monsters, others presented souls at the Judgment seat, one with stern face expelled a crestfallen Adam and disdainful Eve from Paradise. These exquisite figures, saved by their great height from the Protestant iconoclasts of a later age, were painted in vivid colours and patterned with stars.

It was light above everything else that the new architecture sought – the crying need of the sunless north. One after another the great churches of northern England followed the lead of the Angel choir. At Ripon, where every canon contributed a tenth of his prebendary income until the work was done, the east end of the choir was rebuilt during the closing decade of the thirteenth century with a huge window; at York a few years later, a new nave was begun in which, in the search for greater light and space, the upper windows of the clerestory were extended downwards to incorporate the triforium, so that the two storeys, though divided by the

415

concealed roof of the aisle, presented a continuous double bank of light along the church's entire reach. The work took more than half a century to complete, and during that time, like almost every major church in the land, the Minster must have been full of scaffolding and of the sound of hammer and chisel. Yet this great revolution supplemented rather than superseded the country's older ecclesiastical architecture, so that everywhere, in the English mode, new Gothic mingled with old Norman and even, in places, Saxon.

As remarkable, on a smaller scale, were the beautiful polygonal chapter-houses of Salisbury and Wells, completed at the end of the thirteenth and beginning of the fourteenth century. Here, debating the business of the Chapter, the canons sat in a circle, enthroned on stone niches under traceried windows, every one an equal, facing the graceful multi-shafted central pillar which bore the vaulted roof. In the north the new chapter-houses at York and Southwell were vaulted without a central pillar, the former having a free-standing span of nearly sixty feet. At Southwell the naturalistic carving, which had recently taken the place of the more formal stiff-leaf, reached its zenith in the wonderful variegated leaves and flowers carved on the capitals during the years when Edward I was trying to subdue Scotland. Like Pygmalion's Galatea they possess all the qualities of life except movement, though made of stone.

Carved figures as beautiful, wrought in metal and stone, rose at Edward I's behest in his father's rebuilt abbey at Westminster. Soon after his return from his Welsh wars he had commissioned William Torel, the London goldsmith, to make a bronze effigy of his father to lie on his tomb at Westminster above a stone base engraved with royal leopards. Beside it a decade later he placed the effigy of his wife, Eleanor of Castile, recumbent with sceptre in hand and jewelled robe and crown under a canopy of Purbeck marble. Two other noble examples of the sculptor's art were added to the abbey's treasures in his reign – those of his brother, Edmund Crouchback, earl of Lancaster, under an elaborately carved canopy guarded by painted and gilded regal mourners and angels holding candle-sticks, and of his uncle, William de Valence. With his copperplate armour coloured with rich enamels, his mailed hands crossed in prayer and his expression of serene confidence that the aristocratic society he had adorned on earth must be mirrored in Heaven, William's effigy was the forerunner of a whole army of recumbent knights in stone, metal or brass. During the fourteenth century there everywhere appeared in the parish or collegiate church enriched by his benefaction or bequest the likeness of some local worthy, clad in the armour and heraldic trappings of his warrior craft, with his lady in long trailing mantle, kerchief and wimple at his side and his hound or supporting heraldic beast at his feet. Though those which survive constitute only a small fraction of the splendid knightly company that once glittered under the painted roofs and windows of England's churches, owing to Edward I's law of entail they proved more enduring than the statues of saints and holy personages which shared their resting places. For, when the latter were smashed as idols, in later centuries these memorials to bygone benefactors received the protection of those who had inherited their blood or lands.

The brightness of a Gothic cathedral, with its painted walls and jewelled shrines – the gleaming or *nitens* of the monkish chroniclers' phrase – is hard to visualise from the bare, grey stone interiors of today. We see the noble skeleton but not the flesh and blood with which our forefathers clothed it. The walls were frescoed with paintings, telling the Christian story by masters whose names, like their works, have been obliterated by time, though from the few which remain, faint and resuscitated from agelong layers of neglect and defacement, we can dimly apprehend their glory. The paintings on the sedilia in the sanctuary of Westminster Abbey – of the Virgin's blue robe and pink mantle and of Gabriel in mauve and green of a lovely limpidity – executed when the first masterpieces of the Italian artistic renaissance were beginning to appear at Siena, Pisa and Florence; the scenes from the life and Passion of Christ in the little Northamptonshire church of Croughton; the East Anglian figures of saints on the vaulting of the north ambulatory of Norwich cathedral and others recently discovered at Little Missenden in Buckinghamshire and in the beautiful circular room at Longthorpe Tower – once the home of the stewards of Peterborough abbey –

are among the survivors of thousands of pictures that told the Bible story to a people unable to read but able to behold and adore.

As rare today is the coloured glass which filled the windows. These, too, like the frescoes, told in picture the story of Christ and his saints and martyrs. Divided by uprights of stone or lead, each pane – medallion, lozenge, circle or square – formed part of a continuous pattern of colour and light. Most of the glass was imported, either through the Channel ports from Normandy and the Île-de-France, where the French *verriers* had given mankind the splendours of Chartres, Bourges and Rouen, or from Hesse and Lorraine by way of the Rhine and Meuse to England's eastern rivers. Owing to the very richness of this early glass, with its deep reds, blues, greens and golden yellows, some of the quality of light sought by the English Gothic window-builders was lost, and towards the end of the thirteenth century a whitish grey or grisaille glass began to be used.

In all this there was a growing elaboration unknown in western Europe since the days of imperial Rome. As the thirteenth century merged into the fourteenth a richer architectural sumptuousness began to succeed the simplicity of the Early English style, pointed arch and geometrically traceried window giving place to flowing curvilinear lines, fantastic pinnacles, crockets and finials decorated with carved globular buds known as ball-flowers. Pierced balustrades, wave parapets and foliate stone tracery radiated from the mullions of window-heads like the branches of a tree. And everywhere were niches filled with statues of the heavenly family, angels, saints and martyrs, Christian princes and prelates, brilliantly gilded and painted. Such was the passion for carving and ornamentation that the masons, working high above column and clerestory among the roof-trusses and rafters, fashioned whole legions of tiny figures on the bosses – foliage masks of men and monsters, fauns, satyrs and beasts, and the leaves and flowers of their native woods and fields – here the Lamb of God, here St George wrestling with the dragon, here a peasant with toothache or two lovers kissing, here the face of a king or bishop or of a fellow workman, here David with his harp or the Virgin crowned – all carved with a care that must have been born of creation for its own sake since, once the

418

carver's work was done and the platform of scaffolding removed, no eye but that of some unborn craftsman repairing the roof in similar solitude would ever see them again. In Exeter alone, rebuilt between 1301 and 1338, there are more than five hundred carved bosses; in the vast late fourteenth century Bristol church of St Mary Redcliffe over eleven hundred. When the might of the medieval Church was broken and fanatics swept through every place of worship with axe and hammer, smashing and defacing the sculptured masterpieces that to them seemed only painted idols, this invisible host of carved roof-bosses remained, unknown for nearly four hundred years until the telescopic lens of the modern camera revealed their testimony to the genius of English medieval craftsmanship.

The first great cathedral to be rebuilt wholly in the decorated style was Exeter. Between Edward I's accession and that of the early years of his grandson's reign, through the zeal of five great building bishops, the old dark Norman structure was transformed into the broad graceful edifice of today with its multiple-shafted marble pillars, the flowing tracery of its windows, its pinnacled sedilia and bishop's throne, statued screen and reredos and carved roof-bosses representing every kind of man and animal, angel and demon known to the medieval imagination. Another West Country cathedral, Bristol, was rebuilt about the same time, with a feature, unique among English cathedrals, of three aisles of equal height and a vault of lierne ribs of a completely novel pattern.

During the early decades of the fourteenth century almost every great church in England was added to or partly rebuilt in this richly ornamented style. Though the greater Benedictine houses were comparatively little affected by the new style, the Cistercians, with their wealth from wool, had by now abandoned their former austerity and started to build in the grand manner on the sites of their primitive encampments in the wilderness. Fountains had already been rebuilt in Henry III's reign; Tintern, Rievaulx and Byland were refashioned in the enriched architecture of the Edwardian age. Even the friars had left their squalid abodes in the city slums and were raising great churches out of the benefactions of merchants who recalled with gratitude the days when they or their fathers had fled from villeinage to the hovels of the nearest town and were there befriended by the mendicants. As with their evangelical mission the Franciscan and Dominican friars had no need to provide for the elaborate liturgical and processional services of the monastic Orders; their churches were usually built without aisles and with naves larger than the choirs to accommodate the middle-class congregations who flocked to hear their sermons. The most celebrated of all was the vast Greyfriars church in London founded in 1306 by Edward I's second Queen, who was buried in it.

In 1321 the monks of the Benedictine abbey at Ely began to build a Lady Chapel with the largest span of vaulting yet seen in England and, under its traceried roof and wide decorated windows, arcaded niches filled with hundreds of gilded and painted statues, today mutilated and headless, telling the story of the Virgin in sculptured stone. Scarcely had the work begun when the central tower of the abbey church fell, crashing into the choir below and destroying three of its bays. Faced by the problem of revaulting so large a space, the Sacristan, Alan of Walsingham, employed a London mason to build, instead of a new tower, an octagonal lantern of revolutionary design with four traceried windows to flood the centre of the Norman church with light. And, as the seventy-foot span proved too wide to bridge with stone, the monks called in William of Hurley, the King's master-carpenter, to vault it in timber with eight gigantic hammer-posts and hammer-beam trusses. The work took twenty years to complete and, when finished, constituted, as it still does, the only Gothic dome in Europe.

Though the new style was decorative rather than structural, in its seeking for ever greater illumination it continued the trend which had begun with the evolution of the Gothic arch. Even before Edward III's accession in 1327, there were signs that English masons were beginning to feel their way towards a further architectural revolution. There was a sense of ever-growing light and unity in the many-ribbed vaults which broke through the older vaulting system of each separate bay and in the marriage between piers, vaulting and roof. The pillars of the new nave of York were like the trunks and branches of a beech wood, and the lierne vault of the choir at Ely like the stars on a winter's night.

It was the reign of this famous warrior king that saw the first flowering of the Perpendicular style, England's supreme contribution to the art of architecture. Hitherto, with their broad bases and close relationship to the earth, her cathedrals had not sought to emulate the perilous height of the Gothic churches of the Île-de-France. But now, under the leadership of William Ramsey, the King's chief mason, English architects began to evolve a technique which produced the effect of height without sacrificing structural proportion or safety. It was an art not of mass but of line, in which the vertical mullions of vast rectangular windows extended upwards and downwards to form, with the horizontal lines they crossed, continuous rectilinear panels of wall and glass. First used by the London masons in the new chapter-house and cloisters of St Paul's and the royal chapel of St Stephen's, Westminster, its end – a reaction against the excessive ornamentation of the Decorated style – was an all-embracing unity in which the separate parts, arch, pier, vault, window and wall, were subordinated to a single whole.

It is in the West Country abbey which sheltered the murdered body of Edward's father, the hapless Edward II, that the earliest surviving example of the new style can be seen. Aided by the gifts of pilgrims to the dead King's shrine, the monks of Gloucester in the 1340s began to transform the dark Norman south transept by substituting for the end wall an enormous eight-light window crowned with a lierne vault. During the next decade they rebuilt the choir, marrying the massive Norman pillars to delicate vaulting shafts and encasing the walls in a framework designed to flood the interior with light. And at its east end, in place of the Norman apse, they made the largest window in Europe, canting the walls of the last bay outwards to increase its size. This great wall of glass, seventy feet high and nearly forty wide, with over a hundred lights, was glazed, through the munificence of a local lord, with the shields and likenesses of his fellow commanders at Crécy – Edward III and the Black Prince in their midst – and, above, them, Christ, surrounded by apostles, seraphim, saints and martyrs singing the *gloria in excelsis* for the crowning of the Virgin. In the foreground, high above the choir, the masons carved on the bosses of the vault fifteen angels, each with a different musical instrument, to accompany that chant of praise sung by figures poised in painted glass between the glittering interior and the grey Gloucestershire skies.

During the years which saw England's martial triumphs in France one magnificent ecclesiastical building after another was raised by the genius of her craftsmen. The Lady Chapel at Lichfield, the cloisters at Norwich, the retrochoir and St Andrew's arches at Wells, the choir of Bristol, the exquisite decorated nave of Exeter were all completed or partly completed in the same decade as Crécy. So, in the north, was the lovely Percy tomb at Beverley and the west front and nave – finished in the year of Edward's victory – of York Minster. And at Salisbury, Richard of Farleigh crowned the thirteenth-century cathedral with a decorated tower and spire whose proportions have never been surpassed.

Even the Black Death of 1348 and 1349, carrying off probably a third of the country's craftsmen, only temporarily halted the rebuilding of its churches. Almost before the pestilence had ceased, the master-mason of Christ Church, Canterbury was summoned to Windsor to succeed the dead William Ramsey in his task of raising a chapel and college dedicated to St George to accommodate the King's new order of chivalry, the Garter. To build it five hundred masons, carpenters, glass-makers and jewellers were requisitioned by the sheriffs of the southern counties and issued with scarlet caps and liveries to prevent their absconding to rival employment.

It was at Winchester that, in the reign of Edward's grandson, Richard II, the master-mason William Wynford – designer of the western towers of Wells – started to rebuild the Norman nave of the cathedral, making it the longest in England after St Paul's. In the same city he built for its bishop, William of Wykeham, a college for boys and another for the bishop's other scholastic foundation, New College, Oxford, equipping both with Perpendicular chapels dedicated to the Virgin. In the same reign a still greater architect, Henry Yevele – for forty years the King's master-mason – rebuilt the nave of Canterbury and, earlier supervised by the Clerk of the Works, the poet Geoffrey Chaucer, reconstructed William Rufus's hall at Westminster, calling in the royal carpenter, Hugh Herland, to span its 240-foot length and 70-foot width with a hammer-beam roof of Sussex oak – the first of the great hammer-beam roofs which, with the fan-vault and the Perpendicular style, were England's most original architectural achievements.

In the century following Richard II's dethronement, when, after their victories at Agincourt and Verneuil, the English were trying to hold down the French provinces Henry V had conquered, and during the bitter years when the dynastic quarrels of York and Lancaster escalated into civil war and near-anarchy, the work of church building still went on. It was now the turn of the parish churches to be refashioned, many through the munificence of the merchant capitalists, woolmen and clothiers who continued to grow rich while the feudal princes and nobles were destroying one another in their sterile fights of the Wars of the Roses. It was an age of towers which arose everywhere above the western end of rustic churches to become the crowning glory of the English landscape. One of the loveliest was the four-staged tower of St Michael's, Coventry, begun in the reign of Edward III and completed with a soaring three-tiered steeple in that of his great-great grandson, Henry VI. Yet it was only *primus inter pares*. The towers of Lavenham, Boston and Halifax, of Magdalen and Merton Colleges in Oxford, of All Saints', Derby, and Cotswold Cirencester, Chipping Camden and Northleach, and a score of great Norfolk and Somerset churches, have equal claims to perfection of beauty and proportion. Some of the finest were raised by a few hundred parishioners, like the 300-feet steeple of Louth, begun in 1501 and finished in 1515, less than a generation before the English Reformation.

One tower of the time stands in a class by itself, the great 'Bell Harry' of Canterbury, raised during Henry VII's reign by Archbishop Morton's master-mason, John Wastell, and completed in 1497 – the year in which the Portuguese rounded the Cape of Good Hope. It was the same artist who vaulted and roofed the wonderful chapel of King's College, Cambridge, begun by Henry VI as the companion foundation to his school at Eton. By a strange irony the culmination of English Gothic was reached a generation later, in 1517, in the very year of Luther's challenge to the Roman Church, when William Vertue completed the building of Henry VII's Chapel at Westminster, crowning it with the canopy which, in John Harvey's words, is 'one of the wonders of the world'.

CHAPTER TWENTY-ONE

Twilight of Holy Church

' "Holy Church I am," quoth she,
"Thou oughtest to know me,
I was the first to nurse thee,
And taught thee the Faith . . ." '

'Parsons and priests complained to the bishop
That their parishés were poor since the pestilence time,
And asked leave and license in London to dwell,
And sing *requiems* for stipends, for silver is sweet.'

William Langland

ABOVE HIS allegiance to king or lord the medieval Christian had
one loyalty transcending all others. It was to the Christian faith
and the Church which was its repository. Within that Church, set
to guide both rulers and subjects in their spiritual duties, was a vast
hierarchy – cardinals, archbishops and bishops, abbots and priors,
deans and archdeacons, monks vowed to perpetual prayer and
contemplation, parish and chantry priests, confessors and chaplains, learned doctors expounding the lore of the universe of which
the Church was the sole interpreter, wandering friars and solitary
hermits. In England, with a population of not more than four
million before the Black Death and, at most, two and a half
million after it, there were between eight and nine thousand
parishes, each with at least one priest or deacon and many with an
unbeneficed chaplain as well, some seventeen or eighteen thousand
regulars living under corporate vows and rule, and a large, though
uncertain, number of unbeneficed priests and chantry chaplains.
York, with ten thousand inhabitants at the outside, had forty-one

425

parish churches and over five hundred clergy; Norwich, twenty churches and forty-three chapels. Even in the over-crowded capital there was a church for every five hundred people.

In addition to priests and deacons in holy orders who were forbidden to marry and who alone, with their attendant acolytes, officiated in the presbytery or eastern portion of the church shut off from the congregation by the rood-screen, there was a huge army of clerks in minor orders. These had received the Church's initial tonsure – the small round patch cut in the centre of the hair by the officiating bishop as a reminder of Christ's crown of thorns and which, by bringing its wearer under the Church's protection, secured him 'benefit of clergy'. Among them were the acolytes who tended the church-lights and helped the priest at the altar, parish-clerks, readers who read and sang the lessons, exorcists who laid evil spirits, door-keepers who looked after the church and its bells. They included, too, the students of the two universities who numbered at least another two thousand. Probably one in every fifty of the population was a cleric. The poll-tax returns of 1381 listed more than twenty-nine thousand inferior clergy in England, exclusive of friars.

The English Church or *Ecclesia Anglicana* was part of the universal Church of western Christendom. Yet it was also part of the English State. Its bishops and abbots were not only fathers in God but feudal magnates, leaders of the local community and royal advisers. A bishop was a great territorial magnate, enjoying the revenues of numerous manors and knights' fees, who wore princely attire and lived in state. His income of two or three thousand pounds a year was fabulous compared with the yearly wage of forty of fifty shillings earned by a shepherd or ploughman. The bishop of Durham's castle above the Wear was the greatest fortress in the north; the bishop of Exeter had nine residences in Devon alone. The archiepiscopal palace of Bishopthorpe was only one of a score of similar homes owned by the northern metropolitan; the bishop of Lincoln had ten palaces and forty manor-houses including, like every other prelate, a mansion in London from which to perform his duties as a peer of the realm and attend meetings of Parliament and the royal Council. When a bishop travelled it was on horse-back or in a litter with a retinue of thirty or forty mounted clerics and attendants, including knights and men-at-arms drawn from his tenantry to guard him.

For the Church was not, as the saints had sought to make it, above the world; it was part of it. Everywhere was a tacit collusion between Church and State, in which loyalties did not so much clash as merge. Both supported one another; every re-enactment of the great Charter began by guaranteeing the freedom and rights of Holy Church, while anyone who infringed Magna Carta incurred the penalties of excommunication. Clerics administered the Chancery and Exchequer, sat on the judicial bench and headed diplomatic missions and fiscal enquiries. King and community had showered wealth on the Church yet, by doing so, they had made churchmen servants as well as spiritual leaders of the realm, subject, as owners of national land and property, to the same common law as everyone else. England was a country in which the sanctity of canonical doctrine and law was scrupulously respected so long as it did not override the legal rights of Crown and subject. Its very churches were proprietary ones, whose lay owners, having given and endowed them, retained the right to confer their emoluments on any qualified priest who conformed to the spiritual requirements demanded by the Church.

Since every worldly activity was conducted in the Church's name and with the Church's blessing, it followed that official Christianity had grown into a very wordly religion. It was one which had made existence richer and fuller, had fostered artistic and intellectual achievement and, at a time when life was harsh and precarious and death a constant visitant, had given millions a sense of hope and security. Yet many if not most of those who served the Church were very ordinary men who, without any particular sense of calling, had entered it as the only profession offering advancement for anyone not a warrior, land-owner, lawyer or merchant. It was the avenue to wealth, power and dignity and to every learned and intellectual pursuit.

For cleric and layman alike the drama of Christ's life, death and resurrection was seen as a wonderful success-story in whose honour the whole glittering edifice of medieval religion had been raised.

427

The splendid churches and their treasures, the processions, pageants and thrilling rites, the familiar company of tutelary angels and saints ready to help all who propitiated them, and Holy Church itself, watching over man's spiritual fortunes like a wise and far-sighted banker over his client's securities, were all there for his enrichment. And on the principle that to those that have shall more be given, it was the 'possessioners', as the richer clergy were called, to whom the Church offered most.

For though entry to the Church was open to all, and even a bondsman's son, if his lord would free him, could rise, with the necessary parts and patronage, to the glittering top of the profession, there was an unbridgeable gulf between those selected for preferment and the common ruck of poor clerks. Whether the successful aspirant owed his fortune to birth and aristocratic connections, or whether he was a youth of humble antecedents whose talents had brought him to the notice of authority, the pick of the Church's benefices were available to enable him to pay for his education and to support him for the rest of his life in comfort and even affluence. So far as it gave financial independence to men of ability the system had much to commend it and brought outstanding talents to the service of Church and State. But it was subject to grave abuses. Lords and rich landowners with younger sons unfitted for arms or with a taste for clerkhood would present them to livings before they were in their teens; a brother of the earl of Gloucester in Edward I's reign accumulated in the course of his far from edifying career no fewer than twenty-four benefices, in addition to two canonries and three other collegiate and cathedral appointments.

Nor was there any point of contact between the untutored peasant priesthood and the university-trained ecclesiastics who by the end of the fourteenth century all but monopolised the higher ranks of the Church. In their subtle labours of theological and philosophical analysis and classification, expressed in language intelligible only to those trained in dialectic, the regent masters of Oxford and Cambridge were too busy disputing with one another to have time to popularise their learning for the rustic clergy from whom nine Englishmen out of ten derived their religion. The amorphous image conjured up for superstitious parishioners by the Mass magic of bucolic priests bore little resemblance to the highly intellectualised God of the great doctors. Nor did the Church seem concerned by this double standard in its teaching. With reckless disregard of its own Canon Law it continued to dispose of parochial endowments as though the training and competence of the parish clergy were a matter of minor importance. Of the 376 rectors whom one bishop instituted to benefices in lay patronage only 135 were in holy orders; in another diocese, of 193 parishes visited more than a third were held *in absentia*.

This separation of the clerical sheep from the goats was aggravated by the Crown's demand for clerks of parts for the kingdom's growing administrative machine. It was accepted as a necessity of state that the Church should train and support in a condition of dignity its ablest sons to serve the King. One of Edward I's clerks of the Exchequer held twenty-one livings. For such pluralism seemed almost a civic virtue; 'clerks in the King's service,' it was laid down by statute, 'shall be discharged of their residence.' From time immemorial it had been the Church's task to guide and counsel the State and its rulers, and it seemed natural that part of its wealth should be used to maintain those who performed such duty, and that the descendants of the princes and lords who had endowed it should be able to call on churchmen for those administrative services which only churchmen were trained to give. During the fourteenth century more than half the English bishops were employed in offices of state. Many were chosen from the clerical administrators of the royal Household. In 1300 there had been only two civil servants on the episcopal bench; a quarter of a century later there were twelve, most of them Wardrobe or ex-Wardrobe officials. Under Edward III it was the keepers of the Privy Seal who were most favoured; in 1350 six out of the seventeen bishops had held this office. Though there was never in England an aristocratic monopoly of high ecclesiastical office as in some continental countries, about a fifth of the bishops came from the land-owning and warrior families who surrounded the throne –

Beaumont, Cobham, Berkeley, Burghersh, Arundel, Courtenay.[1]

Great nobles too, needed clerical servants, not only for spiritual, but worldly purposes. A fifteenth century earl of Northumberland had ten priests in his service as well as a clerk of the signet, a clerk of the works and a surveyor, a private secretary and a secretary of his privy council. Thanks to the pious bequests of their forefathers such territorial magnates seldom lacked advowsons to provide for them. For centuries the rich and powerful had showered wealth on the Church; and if a rich man, eager for salvation, offered to endow a chantry, a college, a hospital, a perpetual mass for the souls of himself and his relations, to give a stained-glass window, rebuild a church or provide a wayside altar or rest-house for pilgrims, the Church could not do other than accept it. Provided the rich made a show of conforming to its observances and dogma, it reserved for such benefactors a place in the heavenly as in the earthly kingdom, negotiating, as it were, a special relationship between them and the Almighty. With their endowments for obits, masses and private chantries, their benefactions to parish and collegiate churches, their gifts of gems and relics, altar-cloths, statues and painted windows, they were permitted, and encouraged, to buy themselves into Heaven. A rhyme of the time depicts them doing so:

'Thou shall'st kneel before Christ
In compass of gold,
In the wide window westward
Well nigh in the middle;
And Saint Francis himself
Shall folden thee in his cope
And present thee to the Trinity
And pray for thy sins.'

Pride and privilege not only helped to raise and sustain the Church's fabric; they penetrated the very sanctuary. Instead of having to confess to low-born parish priests, nobles were allocated confessors of rank, and the lord of the manor and his lady wor-

---

[1] W. A. Pantin, *The English Church in the Fourteenth Century*, p. 12; R. Highfield, *The English Hierarchy in the Reign of Edward III* (T.R.H.S. 5th series, VI, p. 133).

shipped with the clergy in the chancel instead of with the congregation in the nave. Even at the moment when all Christians, living and dead, were supposed to be united in the sacrament of Christ's sacrifice and when, before Holy Communion, the pax-brede or picture of the crucified Saviour was passed round to be kissed in token of brotherly love, there was jostling and shoving for precedence. Such pomp and vainglory – the sin of *superbia* as theologians called it – was most frequently to be met in the fine new town churches raised by the merchant community and nobility. One indignant preacher spoke of 'great lords and ladies that cometh to holy church in rich and noble apparel of gold and silver, pearls and precious stones and other worldly, worshipful attire before our Lord God Almighty', each fine lady 'stirring up the dust with her train, making the good laymen, the clerks and the priests all drink of it and making it fall upon the altar of the Lord'.

This growing identification of the Church with wealth and power resulted in a grave loss of spiritual influence. Since it had inherited, and insisted on retaining, so large a share of Caesar's goods, it was forced to render unto Caesar the things that were God's. Because its prelates were great landowners and magnates, it had had to concede to the Crown the right of appointing them. They were seen by the laity as servants of the State rather than of the Church and therefore as agents of the State's oppression and injustice. Whatever their gain in worldly dignity, their possession of excessive wealth and the luxurious display which accompanied it lost them the respect of many true Christians. For the values that attached to the pursuit of wealth were not Christian values; by the Church's own tenets they were sometimes diabolical ones. The bishop of Winchester was joint owner of the Southwark stews; even the wonderful new nave of Winchester cathedral and William of Wykeham's scholastic foundations of Winchester and New College, Oxford, were partly and indirectly raised on the profits of prostitution. Such confusion of worldly and spiritual values ran through the Church's structure like an ugly flaw.

The Church's obsession with its wealth – with 'Christ's land', 'Christ's goods', 'Christ's property' – had other consequences. It made it seem obese and conservative. It was no longer, as in the days of St Bernard and St Francis, on the march; it was resting on its endowments. The 'possessioners' who enjoyed its wealth would admit of no change. Religion in their hands had become materialistic and mechanical; it was the quantitative in worship that mattered, not the spirit of the worshipper. Salvation was measured by the number of prayers and masses said – so many *Pater Nosters* an hour, so many *Ave Marias*, so many candles lit, so many benefactions to Holy Church. Great men would hurry into church just before the elevation of the Host and then hurry out again, conscience and public opinion satisfied that they had rendered homage for the day. Outward and visible signs seemed everything, inward and spiritual grace tended to be forgotten.

*   *   *

Among those to be met on the highways in the latter Middle Ages was the pardoner, a sanctified huckster licensed by papal or episcopal letter to sell indulgences at every price-range to anyone prepared to buy. These pardoners, with their wallets 'brimful of pardons come from Rome all hot', not only sold their wares but, though not themselves in holy orders, preached sermons advertising them. Sometimes they sold them on behalf of some chantry or work of piety such as a hospital, the repair of a church or a new painted glass window; sometimes they were complete charlatans, pretending they had the power to absolve from any sin and travelling with a string of forged indulgences round their necks, like the one who was sentenced to ride through Cheapside with his face to his horse's tail and a penitent's paper hat on his head. As a sideline they also peddled faked relics which were supposed to secure for their purchasers remission from punishment or protection from accident. Chaucer's pardoner had a pillow

> 'which he asserted was our Lady's veil.
> He said he had a gobbet of the sail
> St Peter had . . .
> a cross of brasse full of stones.
> and in a glass he haddë piggës' bones.'

The Church did not approve such abuses, but in practice it condoned them. In its need for ever more money to support its huge bureaucracy and magnificent court, the papacy countenanced ways of raising money which amounted to a wholesale sale of indulgences. The ecclesiastical authorities in every country did the same. The theory of an indulgence was that punishment for any venial sin could be partly remitted, with the aid of the Church's intercession, for any genuine penitent who received absolution and did penance. With the advance of civilization the Church had tended to substitute for physical penances, like flogging and fasting, such useful acts of public service and charity as the building and repair of churches, the endowment of almshouses, schools and hospitals and the provision of bridges and wayside chapels. Penance could also take the form of money payments to provide priests to say prayers and masses for an offender, securing for him, provided he had confessed his sins and shown true contrition, remission of so many days in purgatory. Such vicarious intercession by the Church could, it was held, secure earlier release from posthumous suffering. In practice, it proved a step to the tacit assumption by the unrighteous that anyone with a long enough purse to purchase the Church's indulgence could commit sin with impunity.

The sale of indulgences was not the only way of raising money for the Church which aroused criticism. Its finances, the taxation of its vast wealth, the enforcement of its rights and its relations with the temporal power and laity were all regulated by Canon or ecclesiastical Law. And Canon Law was binding, not only on every officer and servant of the Church, but on all Christians. Growing in complexity with the advance of civilization and the multiplication of bureaucratic functions, it operated through an ascending hierarchy of courts that stretched from the humblest rural deanery to the papal *Curia* at Rome or Avignon and with rights of appeal at every level up to the Holy Father himself. It sought to adjudicate between nation and nation – for the Church was traditionally the peace- and truce-maker of Christendom. It investigated and suppressed heresy; it dealt with the moral problems, offences and rights of princes and rulers. It tried – though, as capitalist enterprise grew, with diminishing success – to enforce good faith and equitable dealing in economic matters and to impose the ideal of the just price and wage. Its officers had jurisdiction over every matter that concerned the salvation of souls.

433

In many respects the Canon Law affected the lives of ordinary men and women far more closely than that of the King's courts which normally touched only criminals and men of means. The ecclesiastical courts had cognisance of marriage, bigamy and divorce, intestacy, wills and probate, provision for dower and orphans, libel, perjury and breaches of good faith, as well as sexual offences, including adultery, fornication and brothel-keeping. They dealt with sacrilege, blasphemy, failure to pay tithes and church dues or to attend Mass, and the crime of simony or trading in ecclesiastical preferments. Offences on consecrated ground also came within their jurisdiction. These ranged from poaching and cutting down trees to infringements of the right of sanctuary, for which tremendous penalties could be inflicted. In such cases the Church was both party and judge.

Since the ecclesiastical courts also possessed wide, and in some cases overriding, powers in matters affecting the individual rights of clerics, and since the term cleric included not only those who had been ordained, but anyone who could claim 'benefit of clergy' – by the simple device of translating a verse of Latin psalm known as the 'beck verse' – laymen often suffered what they regarded as gross injustice through the one-sided leniency of the ecclesiastical courts. Among those whom Canon Law protected were university students – a particularly unruly type – schoolmasters, professional men like doctors, and nearly all schoolboys.

It was the inquisitorial methods of the courts Christian and their petty interference in men's daily lives which aroused resentment. Laymen could be convicted for brawling in the churchyard, for failing to attend Mass, for irreverent behaviour in church and disrespect to the clergy, for working on Sundays and holy days. And many of the penances to which they could be subjected were of the most humiliating kind. A man might be sentenced to be whipped at the church door, to appear on consecutive Sundays barefoot in shameful garments, to stand before the high altar holding a candle whilst his crime was proclaimed to the congregation. Thus for mowing a meadow on the feast of St Oswald, two labourers were sentenced to four whippings and to perambulate the village on the next saint's day bearing bundles of hay, while two women who had washed linen on St Mary Magdalene's day were given 'two fustigations with a hank of linen yarn'.

The court which most affected the ordinary man was that of the archdeacon. Nobody much liked archdeacons – 'the bishop's eyes', as they were called – not even their fellow churchmen; it was an old ecclesiastical jest to speculate whether an archdeacon could get to Heaven. He was employed by the bishop to investigate and punish cases of embezzlement and misapplication of church funds, unchastity both of churchmen and laymen, and breaches of the Christian code. The agent, and often instigator, of such petty persecution was the archdeacon's summoner. He was the most hated of all the Church's officials. Usually a clerk in minor orders, he seems all too often to have been a man of the lowest character who kept *agents provocateurs*, including loose women, and made his living by spying and blackmail. The specimen in Chaucer's *Canterbury Tales*, with his drunken bullying ways and fiery face, carbuncles, whelks and pimples, knew the secrets of the entire neighbourhood and would

'allow just for a quart of wine
Any good lad to keep a concubine
A twelvemonth and dispense it altogether',

yet would strip anyone of his possessions who was not prepared to bribe him. 'Purse,' he used to say, was 'the good archdeacon's hell' – by which he meant that any offender could escape penance and punishment provided he paid enough. The customary rate of what was known as 'sin-rent' was £2 p.a.

*   *   *

Medieval man believed that divine justice ruled the universe and that sooner or later every breach of it would be punished. To define justice – *justicia* or righteousness – he looked to the Church. Yet, though the Church existed to teach men how to live righteously, it was all too apparent that this was what so many of its ministers failed to do themselves. Having, like all institutions with a monopoly of power, created an overstaffed profession, it was forced to sacrifice its standards to maintain it. While it admonished men to be virtuous, it virtually allowed them to buy absolution and spare themselves the trouble of trying. Official Christianity had become a gigantic vested interest, living on pardons, indulgences, relics, miracles, shrines, masses for the dead and almost every conceivable device for extracting money out of the faith it taught.

The growing sense of disillusion with the clergy had been intensified by the terrible calamity of the Black Death. The medieval Church, like the medieval agrarian system, never wholly recovered from it. For too often it was those who remained at their posts who died, and those who fled and betrayed their faith who lived. That a priest out of fear for his life could deprive the dying of the last rites and rob them of their hope of salvation was a thing so shattering to the medieval mind that it struck at the roots of belief. Those who suffered most in repute were the friars. A parish priest could only escape the pestilence by openly running away, and most of them, for all their natural fears, probably died at their posts. For a friar, with his vagrant commission, it was temptingly easy to evade his Christian duty; those who performed it were the bravest of all, going out of their way to succour the sick and dying but almost inevitably succumbing. This survival of the worst did the mendicants untold harm. Their very eloquence made their hypocrisy seem the more glaring.

Nor did the damage done to the Church by the Black Death stop there. By demoralising weak natures it drove men, including many of the clergy, to a hectic pursuit of pleasure. 'Where,' asked a preacher, 'will you find the priests of today? . . . Not mourning between the porch and the altar but playing lasciviously around the prostitute and the brothel; not praying in the choir but wandering about the market place; not in the sanctuary but in the tavern and alehouse where sometimes they imbibe so much that they can say neither vespers nor matins properly.' A popular rhyme put it still more forcibly:

> 'At the wrestling and at the wake,
> And chiefe chanters at the ale;
> Market-beaters, and meddling-make,
> Hopping and hooting with heave and hale.

At fairë fresh, and at wine stale;
Dine and drink, and make debate;
The seven sacraments set a' sale;
How keep such the keys of heaven's gate?'

Thus in the half-century which followed the Black Death there grew up a widespread feeling that the Church was failing Christ's people. Bishops too often seemed proud luxurious lords, archdeacons and proctors blackmailers, monks gluttons, friars scroungers and liars.[1] There was no lack of devout Christians in England, a country famed for its orthodoxy. It was the age of the mystic recluse, both clerical and lay, who, withdrawing from the world to a life of religious contemplation, found in the inner experience of the heart a new revelation. It was among such men and women that dissatisfaction with the Church was strongest. The contrast between Christ's life of poverty and the wealth and self-indulgence of so many of its leaders was too great to overlook.

As for the papacy, it was even more fatally damned by its wealth and the shameless rapacity with which its officials and agents pursued it. Its bankers and lawyers, levying toll on every country's ecclesiastical revenues, had become the chief tax-collectors of Europe. To provide for its luxurious court and ever-growing bureaucracy it employed, in Christ's name, the techniques of the lawyer, tax-collector and money-lender. In place of the theological and philosophical ferments of the twelfth and thirteenth centuries the chief canonical controversies of the late Middle Ages centred round papal taxes, fees and subsidies, procurations to meet the expenses of legates and papal emissaries, the sale of pardons and indulgences, fines or *spolia* on the property of dead prelates, and – most resented of all – the *annates*, or first-fruits demanded of all new incumbents for provision to benefices by the

[1] And worse – 'When the good man is from hame
And the friar comes to our dame,
He spares neither for sin nor shame
But that he does his will . . .
Each man that here shall lead his life
That has a fair daughter or a wife
Beware that no friar them shrive.'
Political Poems and Songs (ed. Wright), I, pp. 263–8.

Holy Father, of which the cash to pay was advanced by the papal bankers at crippling interest-rates which were subsequently enforced, in disregard of the Christian prohibition against usury, by threats of excommunication.

The English were devout Catholics and, like all western Christians, believed in the unity of Christendom. But they were growing increasingly insular and did not like to see native benefices and endowments diverted to provide for foreign papal nominees and benefice-hunters. They liked it still less when, during Edward III's wars with France, Pope after Pope was a Frenchman and the papacy itself resided in a French enclave at Avignon. The Holy See seemed to have become the preserve of their enemies, its occupant 'the French King's tame cat'.

So unpopular was the papacy with the English at this time that when, in the last year of Edward III's reign, the city of London put on a pageant 'with great noise of minstrelsy, trumpets, cornets and shawms and many wax torches', the highlight in the procession was a mock Pope accompanied by twenty-four cardinals and 'eight or ten arrayed with black masks like devils, not at all amiable, seeming like legates'. When, following an attempt to re-establish the papacy at Rome, the French cardinals in 1378 challenged the election of a fantastically irascible and autocratic Italian Pope and set up a rival one at Avignon, Christendom was confronted for forty years with the shocking spectacle of two Popes. At one time there were three. Each demanded payment of ecclesiastical taxes, excommunicated the other's supporters and hired 'crusaders' to harry the other's lands.

The 'great schism', as it was called, was the culmination of the scandals which shook men's faith in the Church at the end of the fourteenth century. It was against a background of popular indignation at simony, papal provisions, pluralism, non-residence and the sale of indulgences that the Oxford theologian and philosopher, John Wycliffe, raised his voice of protest. This radical-minded Yorkshireman – at one time Master of the little Oxford college of Balliol and 'holden of many to be the greatest clerk then living' – began by opposing papal claims on native benefices on behalf of Parliament, went on to denounce ecclesiastical wealth, and ended by attacking nearly all the institutional assumptions of the Church. He based his stand on the life and teaching of Christ as revealed by the scriptures, which he maintained were alone necessary for salvation and capable of interpretation by the humblest. 'No man,' he declared, 'was so rude a scholar but that he might learn from the words of the Gospel according to his simplicity.' All that was necessary was that they should be made available in his native tongue. 'To be ignorant of the Bible,' he wrote, 'is to be ignorant of Christ.'

Wycliffe spoke with contempt of the 'possessioners': of monks with 'red and fat cheeks and great bellies' and gowns of superfine cloth big enough to clothe four or five needy men; of the blasphemous sale of papal indulgences, of the worship of relics and images, of excommunication for political and financial ends. The 'dowering of the Church with lordship of the world' had been a heresy, for 'Christ came of poor folk'. Its wealth and power were millstones round its neck, its over-elaborate conventual services 'the religion of fat cows'. Even the Pope himself was only 'a naked servant of God'.

Wycliffe's revolutionary indictment traversed the Church's whole position: that it had been exclusively entrusted with the salvationary powers won for mankind on the cross. Against its claim that God's will could only be known through its sacraments and ordinances, this gaunt, uncompromising North Country puritan set up, not only the right of every man to judge the scriptures for himself, but the direct responsibility of the individual conscience to God. The ministry was requisite for the well-being of the Church but not for its existence; its business, and sole business, was to teach the Gospel. Everything that came between the individual and Christ was evil, and that included most of the ecclesiastical establishment of the day, including episcopacy. Far in advance of his time, Wycliffe foreshadowed an age when family and congregational worship would take the place of the ritual and mystery of the candle-lit altar and what he indignantly called 'the drawing of the people by curiosity of gay windows . . . paintings and babwynerie'.

For a short time Wycliffe was the most popular man in the

439

country. He was supported against the papal charges of heresy by the masters and students of Oxford – at that time, after Paris, the most important university in northern Europe – by the royal Duke of Lancaster and the Princess of Wales, by an anti-clerical Parliament and the London mob. The rising middle class delighted in his defence of national rights and his opposition to foreign ecclesiastical taxation, while many applauded his proposal to confiscate the surplus wealth of the Church and distribute it among deserving noblemen and knights 'that wolden justly govern the people and maintain the land against enemies'. But when he extended his theological arguments and attacks on the institutional side of religion to its central mysteries, repudiating transubstantiation and insisting that the Host remained bread and wine and that it was blasphemy to pretend that Christ's body and blood could be made by the incantations of an ignorant and possibly sinful priest, he lost the support of his patrons. The ordinary Englishman was ready to support an attack on excessive clerical wealth, papal interference and Caesarian bishops but took fright at the idea of challenging hallowed beliefs that were the sacred preserve of the Church. He could see no sense in incurring the risk of excommunication and eternal damnation by abstract speculations which affected neither his personal life nor his purse.

Nor, however much he wanted to see it purged of corruption, did he wish to destroy what was still the most valued and venerable thing in the kingdom's polity – Holy Church. Though riddled with imperfections, its beliefs and practices, including its very superstitions and abuses, were part of the community's continuing life. It had created the society and civilization to which medieval man belonged and, without it, life would have seemed bleak and unthinkable. Owning as it did something like a third of the nation's wealth there can have been few, even of moderate means, who did not have some interest in its survival. This was true even of the monasteries whose widespread financial ramifications, fame and hospitality made them centres of regional social life. Ecclesiastical and lay society were intimately interwoven; many a local knight was proud to act as steward to some neighbouring religious house, and the humble ancestors of Samuel Pepys, by serving the great abbey of Crowland for two and a half centuries as reeves, rent-collectors and granators, raised themselves from servile beginnings to respectability, yeomanry and even gentry.

For this, as well as for other reasons, Wycliffe's attack on clerical abuses failed to make any impression on the Church establishment of his day. It was too sweeping, too academic and too colourless for the ordinary unthinking man. It not only challenged vested interests, it proposed to abolish them altogether. Papacy, episcopacy, endowments, monasteries, friars, images, pilgrimages, gilds and chantries, all were to go and, with them, the outward grace and beauty of religious observance. In stripping Holy Church of its corrupting wealth, Wycliffe and his followers sought to strip it also of its charm. Had they had their way nothing would have remained but the authority of the Bible as interpreted by the individual worshipper, a parish priesthood supported by voluntary offerings, and a presbyterian system of church government under the ultimate authority of the Crown.

Forbidden to lecture in the university and banished to his rustic living at Lutterworth, where he spent his last years supervising the translation of the scriptures, Wycliffe and his heresy passed – for a time – out of the mainstream of English life. For a generation after his death in 1384, his doctrines were preached on village green and highway by the russet-clad evangelists he had trained, and received the support of many younger churchmen and knights of the shire. Even as late as 1414 they precipitated a rising against the government of Henry V on the eve of Agincourt, and the ecclesiastical authorities reacted against the 'mutterers' or Lollards, as they were called, with ruthless repression. In this they were zealously backed by the new Lancastrian dynasty which, seeking to buttress its dubious right to the throne by its orthodoxy, had procured from Parliament a statute – *De Haeretico Comburendo* – that not only forbade unlicensed preaching and the holding of views 'contrary to the faith and blessed determination of Holy Church', but empowered the civil arm to burn, 'in some prominent place', any persistent or relapsed heretic condemned by a spiritual court. In March 1401, rejecting all his persecutors' attempts to make him recant, a London chaplain, William Sawtrey, was burnt at Smithfield, the first martyr of the coming Protestant Reformation. That was still more than a century distant, awaiting the day when the introduction of printing and the growth of a literate laity could bring the forbidden vernacular scriptures to a wider public than existed in Plantagenet and Lancastrian England. Yet, though driven underground by Caesarian bishops, Wycliffe's heretic creed survived, smouldering in secret conventicles and hearth-side readings in the little towns of the Chilterns, east midlands and home counties and in the capital, until, fanned by fresh persecutions, it broke into renewed flame under the early Tudors. Nor did it survive only in England. Carried by the courtiers of Richard II's Bohemian Queen to Prague, it lit in the pyres of the Hussite martyrs a still more prophetic conflagration on the banks of the Elbe, where, a hundred years later, the Saxon monk Martin Luther challenged the Roman Church at Wittenberg.

BOOK LIST

*A short list of the chief documented
and other works on which this book is based*

M. D. Anderson, *Looking for History in English Churches*

G. W. S. Barrow, *Feudal Britain*

H. S. Bennett, *Life on the English Manor*

J. Betjeman, *Collins Guide to English Parish Churches*

H. Braun, *An Introduction to English Medieval Architecture*

A. Bryant, *Makers of the Realm*

——, *The Age of Chivalry*

——, *The Medieval Foundation*

A. H. Burne, *The Crécy War*

——, *The Battlefields of England*

H. M. Cam, *Liberties and Communities in Medieval England*

——, *The Hundred and The Hundred Rolls*

——, *Law-Finders and Law-Makers in Medieval England*

S. C. Carpenter, *The Church in England 597–1688*

C. J. P. Cave, *Roof Bosses in Medieval Churches*

M. V. Clarke, *Medieval Representation and Consent*

R. G. Collingwood and J. N. L. Myres, *Roman Britain and the
English Settlements* (Oxford History of England)

G. G. Coulton, *Medieval Panorama*

——, *The Medieval Village*

——, *Life in the Middle Ages*

——, *Social Life in Britain from the Conquest to the Reformation*

——, *The Black Death*

A. G. Dickens, *The English Reformation*

C. W. Dickinson, *Scotland from the Earliest Times to 1603*

D. C. Douglas, *William the Conqueror*

——, *The Norman Achievement*

D. C. Douglas and G. W. Greenaway (eds.) *English Historical
Documents* Vol. II

D. L. Edwards, *Christian England*

J. Evans, *English Art, 1307–1461* (Oxford History of English Art)

V. H. Galbraith, *The Making of Domesday Book*

V. H. H. Green, *The Later Plantagenets*

John Harvey, *Gothic England*

——, *English Cathedrals*

Jacquetta Hawkes, *A Land*

W. S. Holdsworth, *Makers of Law*

——, *History of English Law, Vols I to III*

W. G. Hoskins, *The Making of the English Landscape*

J. Huizinga, *The Waning of the Middle Ages*

E. F. Jacob, *The Fifteenth Century* (Oxford History of England)

J. J. Jusserand, *English Wayfaring in the Middle Ages*

M. D. Knowles, *The Evolution of Medieval Thought*

——, *The Religious Orders in Medieval England*

W. Langland, *The Vision of Piers Plowman* (ed. W. Skeat)

G. T. Lapsley, *Crown, Community and Parliament in the Later Middle Ages* (ed. H. Cam and G. Barraclough)

E. Lipson, *Introduction to the Economic History of England*

F. W. Maitland, *The Constitutional History of England*

——, *The Court Baron* (Selden Soc.)

——, *Collected Papers* (ed. H. A. L. Fisher)

G. Mathew, *The Court of Richard II*

K. B. McFarlane, *John Wyclif and the Beginnings of English Nonconformity*

M. McKisack, *The Fourteenth Century 1307–1399* (Oxford History of England)

Medieval England, (ed. A. L. Poole) 2 vols

R. J. Mitchell and M. D. R. Leys, *A History of the English People*

S. K. Mitchell, *Taxation in Medieval England* (ed. S. Painter)

J. E. Morris, *The Welsh Wars of Edward I*

J. R. H. Moorman, *Church Life in England in the Thirteenth Century*

A. R. Myers, *England in the Later Middle Ages*

——, (ed.) *English Historical Documents*, Vol. IV

G. R. Owst, *Preaching in Medieval England*

——, *Literature and Pulpit in Medieval England*

W. A. Pantin, *The English Church in the Fourteenth Century*

T. F. T. Plucknett, *A Concise History of the Common Law*
——, *Legislation of Edward I*
A. L. Poole, *From Domesday Book to Magna Carta*
M. M. Postan, *The English Medieval Economy and Society*
Eileen Power, *Medieval People*
——, *The Wool Trade in English Medieval History*
F. M. Powicke, *Henry III and the Lord Edward*
——, *The Thirteenth Century* (Oxford History of England)
——, *Medieval England*
C. W. Previte-Orton, *The Shorter Cambridge Medieval History*
E. Rickert, *Chaucer's England*
J. E. Thorold Rogers, *History of Agriculture and Prices* (Vols I and II)
H. Rothwell (ed.) *English Historical Documents,* Vol. III
L. F. Salzmann, *English Industries of the Middle Ages*
——, *English Life in the Middle Ages*
——, *English Trade in the Middle Ages*
G. O. Sayles, *The Medieval Foundations of England*
——, *Select Cases in the Court of King's Bench under Edward I* (Selden Society)
F. Seebohm, *The English Village Community*
A. L. Smith, *Church and State in the Middle Ages*
J. Maynard Smith, *Pre-Reformation England*
(ed. W. C. Dickinson, C. Donaldson and I. A. Milne) *A Source Book of Scottish History*
T. C. Smout, *A History of the Scottish People 1560–1830.*
F. Stenton, *Anglo-Saxon England* (Oxford History of England)
W. Stubbs, *The Constitutional History of England*
L. Stone, *Sculpture in Britain, The Middle Ages* (Pelican History of Art)
J. Tait, *The English Medieval Borough*
A. Hamilton Thompson, *The English Clergy and Their Organisation in the Later Middle Ages*
S. L. Thrupp, *The Merchant Class of Medieval England*
T. F. Tout, *Chapters in the Administrative History of Medieval England*
S. Toy, *The Castles of Great Britain*

E. W. Tristam, *English Wall Painting of the Fourteenth Century*
W. L. Warren, *King John*
D. Whitelock (ed.) *English Historical Documents*, Vol. I.
B. Wilkinson, *Constitutional History of Medieval England*
——, *Studies in the Constitutional History of the Thirteenth and Fourteenth Centuries*

ACKNOWLEDGEMENTS

In addition to all those who so generously helped me in the research and typing of my earlier books on which this comprehensive and shorter version of so many of them has been based, I have in particular to thank Mrs Judy Airy for her flawless compilation of the present volume's vast Persons and Places Index, and Mrs M. A. Shore who, with others, during the last two years has meticulously and patiently typed every word of the text at least a dozen times.

SUBJECT INDEX
Numbers in italics indicate major references

Administration, 21, 35, 50, *69–70, 76–8,*
85–6, 141–2, 117, 128, 177, 229–30, 309
  Bureaucracy and bureaucrats, *13,* 15,
    60, 103, 182
  Chamber and Chamberlain, 77, 229,
    262, 339
  Chancery and Chancellor, 77, 86, 99,
    107, 108, 110, 140, 154, 164, 168, 229,
    230, 231, 232, 284, 309, 311, 315, 324,
    342, 343, 344, 355, 357, 427
  Constables, High, 377
  Constables, petty, 136, 160, *377–9*
  Corruption and abuses, 165–6, 183, 197,
    295, 298, *301–2,* 308, 311, 340
  Council, Great or Magnum Concilium
    (see also Witan), 63, 68, 69, 77–8, 79,
    86, 87, 99, 132, 133, 139–41, 152, 158,
    181, 221, 226, 239, 295, 299, 308, 316,
    319, 320, 323, 334, 335, 337, 339, 341,
    346, 349, 355, 357, 426
  Exchequer, 78, 82, 85, 86, 87, 107, 120,
    142, 172, 229, 230, 239, 307, 427
  Lower Exchequer, 86
  Household, royal, 77, 111, 229, 230,
    232, 277, 339, 343, 344, 349, 358–60,
    363, 366
  Justiciar, 86, 92, 99, 120, 128, 140, 142
  Local government, 50, 53, 56, 69, 70,
    86, 90, 160–1, 164–5, 373, 378–9
  Pipe-rolls, 86
  Seal, Great, 344, 346, 357
  Seal, Privy, 214, 229, 344, 346, 357, 429
  Secretary, 344
  Sergeant-at-Arms, 310
  Sheriffs, 69, 70, 78, 86, 87, 88, 125, 131,
    142, 150, 151, 156–7, 159, 160, 163,
    164, 165, 196, 222, 227, 314, 357, 377
  Shire and Hundred Courts, 69, 86–7
  Signet, 344, 346
  Treasurer, 85, 86, 140, 230, 231, 309,
    315, 322, 324, 343, 357, 366
  Wardrobe, 229, 399, 429
  Witan, 54, 55, 56
  See also Law, Parliament, Taxation and
  Currency

Agriculture and Rural Life, 3, 4, 6–7,
19–20, 98, 101, 373–90
  Boon services, 374
  Crops, 12, 380
  Cottars and bordars, 374
  Customs, traditional, 26, 51, 395, 399

Dairy products, 98, 101
Dovecots, 297, 300
Famine, occasional, 383
Fishponds and eel-traps, 50, 72, 98,
  300, 309, 329, 400, 403
Gardens, 10, 12, 98, 101, 164, 360, 381,
  390, 397, 400
Livestock, 3, 4, 5, 7, 9, 11, 12, 16, 20,
  42, 70, 96, 98, 101, 255, 303, 380, 382
Meadow, 19, 72, 101, 380, 400
Mills and millers, 51, 72, 300, 313, 329,
  381
Open field system, 19–20, 69, *379–80*
Orchards, 96, 98, 386, 397, 401
Ploughs, plough-teams and yardlands,
  6, 7, 15, 19, 20, 51, 72, 75, 296–7,
  374, 379, 380
Poultry and fowl, 32, 98, 380, 381
Reeves, 69, 160, 165, 374
Sheep and Shepherds, 4–6, 17, 21, 170,
  374, 401, *407–8*
Threshing, 380
Tools, 3, 6, 7, 19, 20, 374, 375
Villeinage, 72–3, 74, 75, 99, 101, 102,
  123–4, 125, 131, 147, 160, 164–5,
  297–9, 302–9, 310, 313, 314, 317, 320,
  321, 324, 326, 329, 332, 368, *373–82,*
  406
Statutes of Labourers, 296, 305
Vineyards, 98, 101, 360
Waste and Common Land, 20, *380–1,*
  383
Water mills, 50, 51
Woodlands, 380
Wool, sale of, 4–6, 17, 21, *101,* 150, 151,
  225, 230, 237, 334, 400–1, 402, 404–9
Yeomen and yeomanry, 221–2, 241,
  250, 284, 328

Army and War, 8, 10, 17, 21, 43, 54, 60,
  61, 73, 74, 113, 177, 209, 210, 212
  Armour, 8, 10, 21, 22, 60, 64, 75, 84,
    129, 239, 245, 252, 271, 276, 293, 320,
    325, 327, 347, 395
  Auxiliaries, 178
  Bannerets, 240, 273
  Castles, 32, 37, 64, 72, 73, 74, 79, 82,
    84, 85, 114, 120, 121, 129, 140, 207,
    208–9, 214, 234, 267, 268, 273, 288,
    300, 314, 360, 363
  Cavalry, 178, 199, 200, 211, 240, 241,
    248, 269, 271

Numbers in italics indicate major references

Commissariat, 178, 179, 207, 222, 235, 241, 244, 245, 246, 247, 268, 269, 274, 276, 365
Commissioners of Array, 131, 161, 178, 239, 378
Feudal Host, 176, 239, 334, 346, 355
Free Companies, 273–4, 276, 277, 280, 281, 282, 285, 287
Fyrd or Militia, 21, 40, 43, 56, 64, 65, 69, 70, 76, 120, 121, 178, 203, 221, 239, 276, 294, 378
Hobelars, 241, 242
House-carls and royal bodyguards, 43, 64, 65–6, 241, 364
Knights and Men-at-arms, 60–3, 64–6, 67, 68–9, 73–4, 76, *83–4*, 199, 211, 239, 245, 246, 247, 249, 250, 260, 261, 264, 266, 267, 269, 270, 271
Livery and maintenance, 355
Mercenaries, 79, 82, 85, 120, 128, 131, 178, 273
Pages, 239, 241
Ransoms, 38, 40, 41, 85, 208, 215, 261, *262*, 264, 267, *272–3*, 286, 287
Retinues raised by Indenture, 239–40, 281, 355
Weapons, 64, 65, 73, 84, 129, 176, 177, 178, 199, 200, 210, 212, 214
  Axes, 20, 36, 36, 56, 64, 65, 199
  Cannon, 217, 319
  Crossbows, 178, 243, 245, 248–9, 260
  Catapults, 85
  Cutlasses, 327
  Daggers, 22, 327, 378
  Flails, 9
  Helmets, 84
  Lances, 60, 61, 222, 249, 271
  Longbow and archers, 145, 177, 178, *221–4*, 228, 235, 237, 238, 239, 240, 240n, 243, 245, 246, 247, 248–9, 250, 260, 261, 262, 264, 266, 269, 270, 271, 286, 290, 296, 304, 311, 318, 320, 327–8, 341, 348, 364, 378
  Pikes, *210–14*, 309, 323, 334, 378
  Spears, 16, 36, 37, 199, 378
  Swords, 9, 21, 22, 33, 65, 113, 222, 223, 250, 261, 271, 293, 327

Art and Literature
Architecture, domestic, 12, 19, 22, 32, 63, 64, 72–3, 84, 111, 273, *300*, 302, 310, 338, 360, 381, 383, 389, 393, 397–8, 409
— ecclesiastical, *see under Church.*
Architects and master masons, 101, 236, 360, 368, 409, 411, 412, 414, 415, 422, 423–4
Alabasters and Ivories, 52, 360, 388, 390
Craftsmen and Artificers, 5, 6, 7, 8, 12, 19, 45, 46, 52, 62, 63, 95, 131, 179,

241, 298, 304, 316, *381–2*, 409, 410, 411–12, 413, 415, 418, 419, 420, 423
Embroidery, 22, 52, 63, 95, 359, 360
Enamels, 8
Glass and glaziers, 95, 96, 102, 412
Goblets, bowls and drinking horns, 52
Illuminated manuscripts 28, 36, 39, 52, 97, 98, 240, 303–4, 360, 382
Literature, 28, 29, 30, 34, 46–7, 63, 87, 126, 133, 152, 158, 284, 289, 295, 300, 302–4, 315, 326–7, 338, 354, 357, 360, 365, 367, 368, 377, 378, 382, 385, 398, 407, 410
Jewellery, 41n, 51, 52, 343, 359, 360, 363, 389, 390
Music, 22, 28, 49, 52, 96, 112, 126, 241, 241n, 366, 392, 394
Painting, 95, 96, 304, 323, 323n, 338, 360, 368, 382, 386
Sculpture and carving, 20, 52, 63, 95–6, 386, 390, 412, 415, 416, 418–19
Silver and gold, articles of, 6, *16*, 21, 22, 52, 63, 98, 170, 360, 389–90
Tapestry, 273, 319, 392
Vestments, stoles and altar cloths, 52, 390

Black Death, *253–9*, 260, 369, 422, 425
consequences of, 258, 260, 262, 292, 296, 298, 299, 300, 316, 379, 422, 425, 436
recurrence of, 283, 289, 299, 352

Chivalry, 61, 182, 252, 259, 260, 262, 264, 272, 278, 286, 293, 337, 340, 347, 358, 359, 364
ideal of, 23, 61, 64, 95, 147, 218, 304
Garter, Order of, and Round Table knights, 188, 189, 219, 236, *252*, 255, 259, 260, 262, 272, 273, 351, 360, 422
heraldry, 73, 75, 99, 127, 165, 226, 240, 246, 250, 276, 292, 293, 323, 346, 359
pageantry, 273, 274–5, 364, 365
tournaments, 61, 85, 189, 219, 228, 236, 240, 252, 273, 293, 337

Christianity, xvii–xx, xxi–xxii, 17
coming of, *24–31*, 51, 197
problems facing, 26, 29, 33, 34, 35, 63
growth of, 28–9, 29–31, 45, 53, 54–5, 60–1

Church, Holy
Appeal to Christian hearts and imaginations, *93–6*, 101, 111, 114–15, 116–17, 303, 385–6, 387
Creator of civilization, xvi–xx, xxiii–xxiv, 97, 382, 427, 446

Numbers in italics indicate major references

Divine Law, belief in, 94
Humanising conception of eternity, *387*, 388–9
Intercessionary function, 95–6, 425
Majesty and power of, *95–101*, 102, 411
Pageantry and ritual, 96, 382, 386, 427–8, 439
Relations with State, 100, 103–5, 106–16, 119–21, 350, *427–8*, 429–31, 435–6, 441–2
Universal quality of, 95, 112, 114, 303, 426
Wealth, 96, 98–9, 326, 389–90, 430–2, 440, 441
Worldliness, growing, *430–2*, 427, 435–7
BUILDINGS, 95–6, 101–2
Abbeys and Cathedrals, xix, 52, 101, 245, 329, 358, 412, 413
Bells, 52, 96, 97, 121, 256, 273, 385, 386, 387, 390, 391, 396, 426
Carvings and sculpture, 20, 52, 63, 95–6, 411, 415, 416, 418–19
Rood screens, 390, 426
Roof bosses, 115, 412, 418–19
Tombs, 412, 416–17, 422
Chantries, 303, 430, 441
Chapels, Lady, 413, 426
Chapter houses, 96, 97, 98, 416, 421
Cloisters, 97, 134, 421
DECORATED STYLE, 418–20, 421, 432
EARLY ENGLISH STYLE, 102, 418
GOTHIC STYLE, 412, 416, 418, 421
NORMAN STYLE, 62–3, 101, 102, 412, 416, 422
PERPENDICULAR STYLE, 409, 423–4
ROMANESQUE STYLE, 412
SAXON STYLE, 38, 52, 63, 101, 416
Hospitals, 93, 135, 136, 433
Monasteries, xvii–xviii, 27, 29, 31, 32, 36, 37, 38, 45, 54, 55, 62, 64, 93, *97–100*, 124, 198, 231, 256, 257, 319, 320, 323, 384, 392, 406–7, 419, 440, 441
Convents, 30, 45, 97
Dormitories, 98
Infirmaries, 98
educative and civilizing work of, 97–100
Frescoes, wall paintings and *nitens*, 115, 414, 417, 439
Parish churches, xxiii, 28, 38, 52, 115, 304, 373, *386–8*, 389–90, 409, 411, 422, *433*
Preaching naves, 393, 413
Refectories, 97
Shrines, 55, 96, 97, 98, 115, 315, 324, 325, 386, 393–4, 412, 413, 415
Towers, 397, 411, 420, 422, *423*
Wheel-head crosses, 27, 28, 38, 43, *52–3*
Windows, 96, 102, 382, 390, 412, 413,
414, 415, 418, 419, 420, 421–2, 430, 439
PERSONNEL
Abbots and Priors, 9, 99, 325, 329, 411, 413, 415, 425
Archbishops, 96, 106–17, 130, 149, 311, 321, 322, 323, 350, 425, 437
Archdeacons, 435
Bishops, 99, 149, 411, 413, 415, 425, *426–7*, 429, 431, 437, 440
Canons, 415, 416
Cardinals, 96, 235, 269, 283, 425, 438
Chantry Chaplains, 303, 425
Deacons, 425, 426, 428
Deans and Deaneries, 433
Hospitallers, Knights, 168, 319
Minor Orders, 96–7, 426, 435
Parish Priests, 63, 258, 304, 373, *383–5*, 425
—— glebe, 383, 384
Popes and Papacy, 32, 33, 34, 60–1, 62, 64, 99, *102–5*, 108, 112, 138, 175, 198, 205, 224, 229, 235, 263, 265, 269, 281, 283, 287, 351, 423, 433, 437–8, 440, 441
Regulars
Monks, 24, 28, 32, 37, 39, 94, 97–100, 198, 256, 257, 258, 314, 320, 421
Augustinian,
Benedictine, 100, 102, 198, 358, 420
Cluniac, 102, 198
Cistercians, *100–101*, 114, 171, 198, 257, 406–7
Nuns, 30, 45, 97
Friars, 134, 136–7, 143, 144, 152, 190, 255, 258, 304, 306, *392–3*, 419–20
Dominicans, 134, 136, 168, 392, 420
Franciscans, *134–8*, 322, 393, 420
Carmelite, 214
Templars, 168
University Students and teachers, 97, 136–8, 168, 193, 232, 283, 306, 329–30, 384, 388, 426, 428, 434, 440
MISCELLANEOUS
Advowson, 384
Baptism, 24, 26, 34, 42, 55, 96, 383, 384
Benefit of Clergy, 103, 105, 107, 108, 115, 426
Candlemas, 380, 386, 387
Canon Law, 97, 105, 109, 350, 384, 427, 429, 433, 434–5
Celibacy, 61, 63
"Christ of the Trades", 303, 304
Christmas, 26, 51, 383
Courtier Bishops, 415
Criminous Clerks, 107, 108, 115
Easter, 26, 386, 387, 389
Excommunication, 104, 107, 109, 111, 112, 113, 117, 176

Numbers in italics indicate major references

Fasts, 381

"Harrowing of Hell". 52, 386

Hedge Priests, 305, 306–7, *312–14*, 317

Hermits, 425

Hocktide collection, 389

Holy Days and holidays, 96, 382, 386

Indulgences, 432, 433, 438, 439

Interdict, 225

Lay Investiture, 104–5

Lent and Lent Veil, 381

Lollards, 441–2

Mariolatry, 98, 102, 115, 304, 325, *387–8*, 394, 413, 420, 422

Marriage, 30, 96, 383, 384

Martyrs, 96, 98, *114–17*, 386

Mass, the, 385, 386, 389, 390, 394, 428, 432

Miracles and Miracle Plays, 94, 114, 388

Missionaries, 24–9, 33, 54

Mystics, 51, 392

Pardoners, 432

Penances, 383, 433, 434–5

Pilgrimages and pilgrims, 32, 39, 55, 106, 115, 116, 127, 170, 314, 315, 385, 387, 393–4, 413, 430

Pluralism, 107, 428, 429, 438

"Possessioners", 428, 432, 439

Provisions, papal, 438

Purgatory, 387, 433

Relics, 96, 98, 386, 393, 430, 432

Ritual, 385, 439

Sacraments, 383, 385, 386

Sacrilege, 104

Saints, 27, 28, 94, 96, 98, 317, 323, *386–7*, 393, 414, 428

Sanctuary, 134, 324, 392, 417, 430

Schism, great, 438

Scholastics, 36–7, 130, 136–8, 425, 428–9

Schools, 45, 93, 97, 383

Scriptures, appeal to, 439, 441

Sermons, 28, 135, 143, 305, 306, 312–13, 317, 386, 420

Simony, 60–1, 63, 94, 434, 438

Stake, burning at, 491–2

Summoners, 392, 435

Superstitions, 29, 94, 96, 104, 383, 429

Tenebrae services, 389

Tithes, 306, 383–4

Tonsure, 103, 426

Transubstantiation, 440

"Truce of God", 61

Wells and waters, holy, 96

CRUSADES, 126, 127, 147, 151, 189, 191n, 237, 253, 266, 266n, 358, 359, 412

Clothes, 8–9, 10–11, 16, 17, 20, 21, 22, 52, 100, 107, 168, 177, 199, 240, 300, 301, 302, 313, 338, 349, 359–60, 381, 392, 409, 410, 431, 439

Cloth Trade, 20, 36, 59, 225, 311, 334, 395, 397, 398, 401, 406, 407, *408–9*

Crusades – *see under Church*

Feudalism. 60–2, 66–9, 70–4, 83–5, 154, 155, 156, 174, 175, 180, 192, 193, 195, 296, 300, 358, 374

fief, the, 84

homage, 74, 192, 194, 195, 225, 229, 263, 282, 359, 363

Food and Drink, 1, 2, 22, 50, 98, 177, 199, 296, 298, 302, 313, 318, 338, 345, 346, *360*, 361, 362, 374–5, *381*, 395

Hospitals – *see under Church*

Language, 6–7, 11, 12, 29, 30, 45, 46, 53, 62, 66, 73, 76, 80, 81, 96, 123, 124, 136, 149, 158, 161, 167, 284–5, 373, 383, 374, 386, 394, 411

Law, xx, 21, 31, 50, 53, 81, 86–9, 131, 150, *152–68*, 169, 232, 375

Using the *Curia Regis*, the inner executive of the Great Council, Henry II, the Conqueror's great-grandson, established a

COMMON LAW, 90, 92, 153–6, 166, 172, 174, 181, 332, 347, 350, 375, 376 for all England, bringing under direct royal control both the despotic and divisive power of the military feudal jurisdictions and the humble village manorial courts their Norman owners had usurped, and the old Anglo-Saxon public courts of

SHIRE AND HUNDRED, 70, 86, 87 To administer and enforce this common system of law he created a body of trained judges whose business it was "to do justice habitually", sending them out to join, and later replace, the royal Sheriffs on annual *Progresses in Eyre*, and

ASSIZES, *86–7*, 131, 157, 160, 161 Others, sitting on the royal Bench in Westminster Hall, formed with them a permanent judicial tribunal which, reinforcing the

COURT OF EXCHEQUER, 85–6, 163, 307 grew into the Courts of

KING'S BENCH, 87, 157, 161, 163, 166, 230, 256, 284, 323, 351 and

COMMON PLEAS, 87, 131, 157, 161, 163, 166, 230, 256 Writs or royal commands issued by these Judges restored possession to any

Numbers in italics indicate major references

freeman forcibly dispossessed of his land and struck at the root of the great lord's power over his feudal tenants dealing a death-blow to trial-by-battle and private law and establishing the most impertant of all English institutions, the RULE OF LAW, 90–2, 121–2, 127. Such WRITS, *88–90*, 157–8, 161–2, 165, 167, 194, though strictly defined, were of many kinds, offering an ever-growing variety of remedies. Among them were – right, 162, praecipe, 88, 162, novel disseisin, 88, 162, mort d'ancestor, 88, 162, replevin, 162, trespass, 162, 164, detinue, 162, debt, 162, account, 162, covenant, 162, assumpsit, 162, case, 162.

Henry's Judges, issuing these Writs, substituted for proof-by-battle an inquest or recognition by "twelve free and lawful men" of the neighbourhood summoned to decide with whom disputed possession lay. Such JURIES, 88–9, 91, 125, 126, 143, 158–9, 160, 163, 164, 165, 166, 378 constituted the conscience of neighbours acquainted with the facts and sworn to speak the truth. Between 1166 and 1176 by the Constitutions of Clarendon and Northampton Henry extended the criminal jurisdiction of the Crown – formerly confined to *lèse majesté* and breaches of the peace on the royal domains and highways – to murder, rape, larceny, arson, forgery and harbouring criminals. Based on precedent and the verdicts of Juries determining question of fact, and of royal Judges expounding and interpreting the Law there grew up a system of CASE LAW, 90–1, 157–8.

This principle of allowing representatives of the neighbourhood to decide questions of fact in criminal, as well as land law, applied to trials, not only of Englishmen, but of Normans, and was governed by the ancient English principle, unknown to Roman law, that every case should be tried in public, as in the presence of the Anglo-Saxon tribe, 91.

The secret tribunal, that instrument of imperial tyranny, was never allowed a lodgment in English Common Law. This participation of the ordinary man in its processes proved a bulwark of both public and private liberties.

OTHER COURTS
Curia Regis, 79, 86, 87
Danelaw, 69, 90, 163, 373
Feudal, 86, 87–8, 89–90, 106, 125, 159–60, 175
Hundred, 51, 69, 86, 90, 123, 125, 126, 160, 163–4
Manor court, leet or moot, 86, 297, 332, 373, 376–7
Marshalsea, 316, 324
Quarter Sessions, 157, 160
Shire, 51, 52, 69, 86, 90, 125, 126, 157, 160, 163–4
Tourn, Sheriff's or halimot, 21, 159, 160, 164–5, 377

LEGAL PROFESSION AND EDUCATION, 150, *166–8*
Apprentices, 166, 167–8, 319
Attorneys, 153, 161, 166
Barristers, narrators and pleaders, 150, 161, 164, 166, 167, 168, 220
Inns of Court, 167–8
Judges, 82, 87, 89, 90–2, 125–6, 127, 128, 149, 150, 152, 153, 154, 155, *157–8*, 159, 160, 161, 163, 165–6, 167–8, 192, 193, 196, 230, 317, 323, 345, 346, 350, 351, 375, 377
Lawyers, unpopularity of, 299, 304, 309, 314, 317, 330
Sergeants-at-law, 153, 158, 161, 166, 167, 168, 220, 322, 350
Year books, 167, 319

MISCELLANEOUS
Civil Law (Roman), 158–9, 166, 347, 350, 375
Compurgation, 163
Copyhold, 332, 376
Coroners, 92, 157, 160, 163, 165, 378
Criminal Jurisdiction, 87, 91, 105, 330
Curia Regis, 79, 86, 87
Corruption, judicial, 165–6, 295, 300–3
De Donis Conditionalibus, 135
Entail, law of, 155–6
Frankpledge, 164
Gaols, 73, 79, 314
Grand Assize, 89
"Hue and cry", 378
Inquests, 89, 92, 125, 157, 158, 163, 296
Justices of the Peace, *156–7*
"King's Peace", 50, 162, 165, 182, 202, 377, 391
Law merchant, 162
Manumission, 373–4
Ordeal of fire and water, 85, 88, 91, 158
Outlaws, 91, 163, 381
Primogeniture, 156
Prisoners, 303, 314, 315–16, 319

Statute law, *148–50*, 167
Tithing, 164–5
Trial by Combat, 85, 88, 89, 151, 161, 163–4, 347, 364
Watch and Ward, 378

Libertarian, Egalitarian and Anti-authoritarian Evolution, 21, 29–30, 53, 90–1, 116, 132, 158–9, 338, 369, 375, 376

Magna Carta, 123, 131–4, 150, 172, 307, 347, 427
events leading to, 127–30
character of, *131–4*
re-confirmed and appeals to, 139, 140, 149, 150, 231, 232, 233

Merchant Guilds and Towns, 125, 126, 127, 131, 144, 150–1, 316, 369, 395–6, 403–4, 407, 423
Livery Companies, 256, 301, 316, 318, 335, 396, 409

Merchants, growing wealth of, *300–2*, 311, 393, 394, 404, 409–10, 431

Monarchy, unifying force of, 31, 35, 47–8, 49, 75, 76, 89, 122, 126, 128, 129, 130, 143, 144, 321, 328, 331, *369–70*
Coronation rites and oath, 31, *49–50*, 130, 170, 232, 325, 368
nationhood, creating sense of, 43–4, 48, 50, 69
prerogative, 89, 153, 339, 405
divine right of kings, 31, 334, 338, 356, 367

Navigation, 2, 3, 12, 16, 18–19, 36, 46, 401–3
feudal service of Cinque Ports, 144, 179, 185, 227, 260, 403
fishermen, 309, 403

Navy, first beginnings of Royal Navy, 40, 43, 179, 227, 242, 244, 251–2, 292, 346, 403

Order and Freedom, reconciliation between, 333, *369–70*, 376–7

Parliament, *139–43*, *145–52*, 154, 169, 176, 181, 203, 218, 219, 220, 224, 226, 232, 233, 234, 239, 243, 256, 262–3, 265, 274, 279, 295, 296, 298, 299, 301, 305, 306, 307, 308, 333, 334, 336, 337, 338, 339, 341, 343, 344, 349, 350, 355, 357, 362–3, 365, 368, *369*, 392, 405, 426
Absolute legal power of, 350
Attainder, 350

Bachelors, Community of, 142, 143
Burgesses, trading, 160, 203, 219, 220, 233, 337, 349, 365, 369
Commons, House of (or representative taxing assembly), 151, 219, 220, 221, 226, 263, 333, 341, 342, 343, 351, 355, 363, 369
Control of Taxation, 226, 339–40
"Counsel and Consent", xx, 139, 146, 152, 153, 217, 218, 219, 226, 231, 307, 308, 357
Knights of the Shire, 157, 160, 203, 219, 220, 231, 232, 233, 337, 342, 349, 365, 369
Lords or Magnates, House of, 220, 226, 232, 233, 333, *336*, 342, 343, 344, 346, 349, 350, 351, 363, 365. 369
Order and Liberty, reconciliation between, 333, 358, *369–70*
Redress of grievances, 140, 405
Representation, idea of, 152, 220, 296, 307, 337
Taxpayers, combination of, against tax imposer, 132, 139
Treason Act, 349, 350, 352, 364, 369

Population, 3, 8, 12, 21, 50, 170, 209, 224, 256, 260, 296, 308, 399, 401, 409–10, 425, 426

Scotland, xvii, 1, 3, 9, 15, 18, 20, 27, 32, 36, 64, 68, 70, 74, 76, 78–9, 125, 184, *189–216*, 221, 222, 224, 228, 231, 233, 234, 235, 236, 246, 251, 257, 273, 311, 333–4, 351
early history of, 70, 74, 78–9, 83, 120, 121, 129, 169, 174, 190, 198, 365–9
Christianity, monastic, 198
civilizing work of David I, 198
failure of royal line, 190–1
France, "auld alliance" with, 195, 234, 251, 278
"great cause" of, 192–4
hardihood, 199
hatred of the English, 199
Highlands, 168, 202–3
national character, *197–9*, *206*, 207, 208, 263, 283–4, 352, 354
poverty, 197, 351
schiltrons, 211–12, 214, 223, 259
"Stone of Destiny", 194, 195, 281
Wars of Independence (1296–1305), 196–200
—— (1306–28), 202–16
—— (1332–69), 234, 235, 236, 251, 257, 263, 265–6, 270, 273, 283–4
Battle of Otterburn (1388), 353–4

Slaves and Slavery, 5, 9, 12, 16, 17, 21, 30, 72, 375

Numbers in italics indicate major references

Taxation, 13, 31, 70, 72, 127, 131, 132,
150–1, 160, 199, 226, 239, 307, 333, 339,
356, 364, 405
Coinage and Currency, 34, 50, 226
Commissioners of Array and Taxes, 157
"Custom, Great and Ancient", 151, 406
Customs, 405
Domesday Book, 70, *72*
Feudal aids, 127, 131, 151, 155, 374
Fines, 78, 128
Inheritance, confiscation of, 365
Loans, forced, 364
Moveables, taxation on, 127, 150–1, 307
'Pleasuance, La', 364
Poll tax, *307–9*
Scutage or shield money, 86, 127, 129,
131, 132
Staple, customs, 224, 252, 405–6, 409
Tallages, 86, 127, 151, 226
Tithing penny, 165
Tonnage on wine imports, 151
Trailbasten, Commission of, 309
Wardships, 128, 131

Transport
Bridges, 35, 101, 391, 433
Cartage, 374, 382
Coaches, 392
Oxen-drawn carts, 102, 392
Pack-horses, 392, 402, 406, 407, 408
Roads, 6, 10, 11, 12, 16, 32, 35, 65, 87,
101, 209, 255, 379, *391–5*
Water, 402
travel, perils of, 391–2

Wales, 1, 9, 16–17, 18, 26–7, 40, 53, 65,
68, 74, 76, 78, 100, 104, 120, 124–5,
169–88, 189–90, 194, 195, 197, 215, 221,
222, 241, 242, 257, 311, 362, 366, 368
early history, 26–7, 83, 143
character of, *181–5*
fighting quality, *177*, 215
eisteddfod, 172
Prince of, 188, 250
Marchers, 74, 76, 118, 141, 143, 146,
170, 171–5, 178, 180, 182, 183, 217n,
218

Way of the World, passing
Ale-houses, 147
Baths, 11, 12, 98, 361
Bawdy-houses, 431
Destitution, 302–3
Fairs, 388, 395
Lepers, 312
Luxury and display, 300–2
May Day rites, 51
Pedlars and chapmen, 381, 395
Sanitation, lack of, 381, 383, 397
Sport
Archery, 221–2, 399
Football, 399
Harvest Home, 51
Hawking, 82, 275
Horse-racing 395
Hunting, 71, 78, 82, 203, 274, 398,
400
Morris dancing, 51
Rowing, 399
Skating, 399
Stone throwing, 399
Wrestling, 395, 399
Trades Unions, 413
Weather-cocks, 52

454

PERSONS AND PLACES INDEX

Abbeville 244, 245, 247
Abbey Dore 100,171
Abbot, name of 382
Abbots Bromley 125
Aberconway 171
   abbey 173n
Aberdeen 197, 207, 284
Aberdeenshire 196
Aberystwyth 180
Achilles 10
Acre 126, 191n
Adams, Henry 63
Adrian IV, pope 99, 117
Aegean, the 6, 9, 359
Aethelred the Redeless
   53–4, 55, 69
Aethelric 70
Agen 291
Agenais 224, 237, 238, 277,
   285, 288
Agincourt 423, 441
Aidan, St., bp. 27, 28, 50,
   100, 135
Aiguillon 238, 239, 242,
   243, 244, 256, 291
Aire, R. 408
Alban, St. 98
Albert the Great 136
Albigensians 144
Alcuin of York 34, 38
Aldhelm, St. 28, 51
Alencon, count of 247, 250
Alexander the carpenter
   415
Alexander the Great 33
Alexander II, k. of Scots
   190, 192, 198
Alexander III, k. of Scots
   190, 198
Alexandria 33
Alfred, k. 32n, 39–48, 41n,
   49, 53, 54, 60, 61, 66, 73,
   76, 122, 129, 198
Aljubarrota 341
Alkimas 10
Almondbury 9
Alnwick castle 121, 353
Alphege, St. abp. 54, 55
Alps 2, 10, 14, 34
Ambion 257
Amboise 268
Amesbury abbey 192

Amiens 145, 225, 244, 265,
   414
Ampney St. Mary 304
Andover 407
Andredsweald 21
Angers 235, 268
Angevin Kings 82, 125,
   126, 169, 182, 267, 378
   see also Henry II,
   Richard I and John
Anglesey 3, 53, 173, 179,
   180, 184, 185, 187, 188
Anglo-Saxons or English
   15–23, 38–48, 49–52, 59,
   60, 61, 65–6, 66–7,
   69–80, 85, 86, 88, 89,
   90–2, 109, 110, 115,
   123–5, 126, 129, 132,
   134–7, 221, 246–7, 284,
   368, 414
Anglo-Saxon Chronicle 47
Angoulême 277, 291
Angoumois 277
Angus, Robert de
   Umfraville, e. of 214
Anjou 64, 79, 81, 247, 274,
   277, 284
   counts of, see Geoffrey
   Plantagenet, Henry II
Annandale 289
Anne of Luxemburg &
   Bohemia, q. of England
   339, 351, 358, 359, 360,
   361, 442
Anonimalle chronicler 326,
   327n
Ansculf, William, son of 70
Anselm, abp. 94
Anthony, St. 387
Antioch 33
Antwerp 225, 226, 406
Apollonia, St. 387
Appledore 45, 314
Appleton, friar 322
Aquae Sulis, see Bath
Aquitaine 80, 81, 169, 224,
   236, 268, 277, 280, 282,
   284, 285, 288–9, 291,
   292
Arabs 33, 136n, 136, 138
Aragon, see Spain
Arbroath 197

"Archdeacon, the" 273
Arden, forest of 21
Ardres 261
Argentan 267
Argyllshire, see Dalriada
Aristotle 136
Armagnac 288
Armagnac, count Jean d'
   264–5, 291
Arno, R. 407
Arran 204
Arras 275, 404
Arraxes, family of 404
Artevelde, James van 225,
   228, 236, 237
Artevelde, Philip van 305
Arthur, k. 17–8, 124, 189,
   192, 195, 219, 236, 278
Arthurian legend 17, 18,
   124, 169–70, 188, 219,
   236, 273, 337
Artois 228, 237, 242, 244,
   265, 275, 289, 401
Artois, Robert of 228,
   234–5
Arundel, earls of, see
   Fitzalan
Arundel, Thomas, b. of
   Ely, abp. of Canterbury
   340, 342, 343, 346, 349,
   355, 357, 363
Aryans 6, 7
Ashdown, battle of 39–40
Ashingdon 54
Asia 6, 7, 16, 253
Asser, bp. 42, 46
Athelney 41, 45
Athelstan, k. 49, 52, 56, 74,
   122
Atlantic 1, 3, 27, 36, 37,
   38, 228, 292
Atlantis 1
Atrebates, the 11
Auberoche, battle of 237,
   241
Audley, Sir James 272, 275
Augustine, St., abp. 24n,
   46
Auray, battle of 281–2
Aurelianus, Amrosius 17
Austria 196

Autemedon 10
Auvergne 80, 293
Avebury 5
Avignon 224, 235, 263, 265, 281, 283, 359, 433, 438
Avon (Ayrshire), R. 204
Avon (Warwickshire), R. 402
Avon (Wiltshire), R. 20, 52, 408, 413
Avranches 119
Axe, R. 51
Ayrshire 204

Babylon 5
Bacon, Sir Roger 138
Badon, Mount 17
Baghdad 34
Baiter, the 256
Baker, name of 382
Baldur 52
Baldwin, family of 69
Balkans 32
Ball, John 305, 306-7, 312-14, 317, 330
Balliol, family of 79, 120, 193
Balliol, Sir John, founder of Balliol college 137, 193n
Balliol, John, k. of Scots 193-5, 202, 205, 206, 214
Baltic 55, 261, 394, 401, 402, 409
Bampton, Thomas 309
Bangor 186
Bannockburn, battle of 210, 211, 212-15, 217, 222, 223, 224, 237, 250, 279, 369
Barbour, John 284, 354
Barcelona 254
Barking 19
Barnack 52
Barnwell priory 330, 355, 395
Barry, Gerald de 124
Barstaple 309
Bartholomew, St. 387
Barthomley 272
Barton, John 409
Baskerville, Sir Richard 285
Basques 403
Bath 11, 407
abbey 49
Battersea 8
Battle abbey 260
Bayeux, bishop of 243

Bayonne 237, 293, 402
Beaker folk 4-5
Beauchamp, family of 69, 241
Beauchamp, Sir John 261, 349
Beauchamp, Thomas, e. of Warwick (1329-69) 246, 261, 269, 275, 289
Beauchamp, Thomas, e. of Warwick (1370-97) 333, 340, 345, 346, 347, 348, 355, 363
Beaumaris 188
Beaumont, family of 69, 120, 430
Beaumont, Henry de 211
Becket, Thomas, St., abp. 106-8, 109-11, 110n, 112-14, 114-17, 118, 119, 120, 121, 137, 231, 293, 394
Beddgelert 173n
Bede, the Venerable 29, 33, 46, 100
Bedfordshire 329
Belgae, the 8
Belknap, Sir Robert, C.J. 309
Belleme, Robert de 84
Bentley, Sir William 261-2
Beowulf 23
Bereford, Sir William, C.J. 155, 167
Bergerac 237, 267
Berkeley castle 218, 366
Berkeley, family of 125, 430
Berkeley, Thomas, lord 241
Berkhamsted 292, 293
Berkshire 39, 101, 402
Bernard, St. 79, 432
Berners, Sir James 349
Bernicia 20
Bernwood forest 21
Berri, Jean, duc de 291
Berry Pomeroy 125
Berwick 193, 194, 195, 197, 200, 201, 203, 214, 215, 222, 223, 265, 283, 289
Bethnal Green 400
Bethune 244
Beverley 422
Bideford 158
Bigod, family of 120, 356
Bigod, Hugh, e. of Norfolk 120
Binnock, farmer 209
Birdlip mirror 8

Biscay, bay of 228, 293, 402
Bishop, name of 382
Bishopstone 256
Bishopthorpe palace 426
Black, name of 382
Blackheath 315, 347
Black Prince, see Edward, Prince of Wales
Black Rood of St. Margaret 251
Black Sea 253
Blaise, St. 387
Blanchetaque 245
Blankenberghe 227
Blind Harry 199, 201-2
Blois, Stephen of, see Stephen, k.
Blois 268
Blois, Louis, count of 250
Blois, Charles, d. of Brittany 234, 235, 261, 273, 281
Boccaccio, Giovanni 254
Bocointes, the 404
Boethius 46
Bohun, family of 56, 68, 69, 74, 120, 170, 178, 241, 340, 346
Bohun, Humphrey de 120
Bohun, Humphrey de, e. of Hereford (1302-22) 211, 214
Bohun, Humphrey de, e. of Hereford (1336-61) 275
Bohun, Sir Humphrey 211
Bohun, William, e. of Northampton 234-5, 236, 243, 246, 249, 275
Bolingbroke, see Henry IV
Bologna 90, 158
Boniface, St. 33, 54
Bordeaux 237, 238, 242, 264, 287, 291, 293, 302, 337, 356, 394, 402
Borestone, the 211
Borley 375
Bosphorus, the 13, 254
Boston 402, 423
Bosworth Field, battle of 257
Bothwell castle 214
Boulogne 280, 366
Bourbon, Louis II, count of 265
Bourchier, Sir Robert 231
Bourges 418
Bow 400
Brabant 224, 225, 229, 274, 281, 401, 402
John III, d. of 224, 228

Brabazon, Roger, C. J. 192, 193
Bracton, Henry de 81, 139, 157–8, 161, 375
Bradford-on-Avon 28, 52
Brander, pass of 207
Brandon 4
Braose, family of 170
Bratton 42
Breamore 52
Brechin castle 195
Brecknock 74
Brecon 178
Brembre, Sir Nicholas 347, 348, 349, 351
Brentford 54
Brentwood 309, 310, 321
Brest 235, 261, 294, 362
Breteuil 266, 267
Bretigny, Treaty of 277–8, 279, 280, 288
Breton, John le, b. of Hereford 161
Bretteville, Richard de 153
Brian, Sir Guy de 246, 292
Bridge, name of 382
Bridgnorth 83, 84
Bridport 402
Brie 224
Brigantes, the 8
Brigham, Treaty of 191, 194, 195
Brignais 281
Bristol 52, 119, 255, 366, 399, 402, 409, 419, 422
St. Mary Redcliffe 409, 419
Bristol Channel 170, 176, 180, 366
British Museum 28
Brittany 27, 64, 75, 83, 120, 224, 225, 234–5, 236, 242, 255, 260, 261–2, 263, 266, 276, 277, 278, 281–2, 290, 292, 311, 328, 362, 402, 403
dukes of, see Charles of Blois. de Montfort
Brixworth 28
Broc, Sir Ranulf de 113, 114
Bromley 400
Bronze Age 5–6, 17, 19, 20
Brook, name of 382
Brown, name of 382
Bruce, family of 79, 120, 191, 193, 279
Bruce, Edward 207, 208–9
Bruce, Robert the competitor 194

Bruce, Robert, e. of Carrick 194
Bruce, Robert, e. of Carrick and k. Robert I of Scotland 189n, 194, 202–16, 217, 222, 223, 234, 236, 266, 283, 284, 289, 354
Bruges 225, 242, 305, 394, 407
Brutus of Troy 189
Brythons, the 8
Buchan, earls of, see Comyn
Buckerells, the 404
Buckinghamshire 70, 417
Builth 173, 185
Bulgars, the 47
Bull, name of 382
Bunyan, John 304
Burgh, William de, e. of Ulster 279
Burghersh, family of 430
Burghersh, lord 275
Burgh-on-Sands 205
Burgundy 275, 290, 368
duke of 275
Burial Barrows 4, 5, 9, 20
Burley, Sir Simon 310, 339, 349, 351
Burn, name of 382
Burnell, Robert, b. of Bath & Wells 149, 154, 175
Burns, Robert 189, 202
Burnt Candlemas 266
Burton, abbot of 299
Bury St. Edmunds 55, 98, 102, 120, 320, 323
Bussy, Sir John 366
Byland abbey 100, 407, 419
Byzantine empire 32, 33, 47, 62, 63, 70, 359, 363, 412 see also Justinian
Byzantium, see Constantinople

Cader Idris 186
Cadiz 191n
Caedmon 30
Caen 101, 243, 244
Caerlaverock 207
Caerleon 11, 12
Caernarvon 187, 188
Caerphilly 173, 188
Caerwent 11
Caesar, Julius 10, 11
Cahors 277
Caistor-next-Norwich 11
Caithness, e. of 207
Calabria 386
Calais 250–2, 253, 259,

261, 263, 265, 273, 274, 275, 277, 278, 289, 290, 293, 294, 362, 406
St. Nicholas church 278
Caldey 27, 53
Caledonia, see Scotland
Calveley, Sir Hugh 218n, 290, 291, 334
Cambria 170
Cambridge 40, 137, 168, 329, 355, 395, 397
University 384, 428
Corpus Christi 330
King's College 423
Cambridgeshire 38
Cambuskenneth abbey 198
Canmore, see Malcolm, k.
Cannock Chase 21
Canossa 104–5
Canterbury 8, 24, 28, 31, 38, 50, 54, 55, 94, 101, 106, 107, 112, 113–4, 115, 116, 119, 121, 134, 293, 311, 314, 360, 394, 422, 423
Christchurch 231, 257, 422
Archbishops of 63, 106, 123, 176, 257, 338, 343
see also Alphege, Anselm, Arundel, Augustine, Becket, Dunstan, Islip, Lanfranc, Langton, Stratford and Sudbury
Canterbury Tales, see Chaucer
Cantii, the 8
Canute, k. 54–5, 56, 63, 66, 74, 129
Canynge, family of 409
Cape of Good Hope 403, 423
Captal de Buch 271, 292
Carcassonne 265
Cardiff 173
Cardigan 74, 172, 185, 188
Cardiganshire 178, 187
Cardross 216
Carlisle 102, 120, 204, 205, 214, 259
Carmarthenshire 187
Carpathians 35
Carpenter, name of 382
Carter, name of 382
Carthaginians 6
Castile, see Spain
Castle Acre 84
Castle Douglas 204

Catuvellauni, the 11
Cavendish, Sir John, C.J. 323, 324
Ceawlin, k. 51
Cecilia, St. 387
Celts or Gaels 7–16, 11, 12, 15–18, 19, 26–7, 32, 50–1, 117, 118, 135, 169, 171, 172, 176, 180, 197, 202, 203, 234, 236, 247, 368, 379
Cerdic, k. 51
Chambertin 101
Champagne 224, 275
Chanctonbury Ring 9
Chandos herald 277, 285
Chandos, Sir John 240, 264, 275, 281, 285, 287, 290–1
Channel, the 6, 8, 10, 18, 64, 74, 78, 228, 255, 259, 260, 263, 284, 292, 295, 403, 412, 414
Charing Cross 191n
Charlemagne, emp. 33–5, 36, 47, 59, 61, 62, 89, 104, 124
Charles II, k. of England 258
Charles IV, k. of France 219
Charles IV of Bohemia, Holy Roman Emperor 359, 363
Charles V, k. of France 270–1, 273, 274, 275–7, 281–3, 286, 287–91, 293, 305
Charles VI, k. of France 342, 362
Charles of Moravia 244, 247
Charles, k. of Navarre 263–4, 265, 281
Chartres 268, 276, 277, 418
Chatellerault 268
Chaucer, Geoffrey 106, 116, 121, 240n, 259, 266n, 277, 285, 289n, 343, 357, 368, 384, 385, 386, 394, 403, 407, 422, 432, 435
Chauvigny 268
Chaworth, family of 170
Cheddar Gorge 2
Chepstow 74
Cheshire 172, 178, 181, 182, 240, 264, 272, 273, 285, 286, 334, 345, 348, 362, 364, 366
Chester 12, 50, 83, 173,

175, 179, 180, 181, 185, 187, 345, 366, 367
earls of 68, 74, 84, 172, 173, 217n, 348
Chevauchee 264, 265, 267, 268, 290, 293
Cheviots 352, 353
Chichester 12, 44, 45
bishop of 351 see also Stratford
Chilmark 414
Chilterns 17, 20, 442
China 3, 253, 398
Chippenham 41, 42
Chipping Camden 409, 423
Christ of the Trades 304
Christopher, St. 387
Church, name of 382
Cinque Ports 144, 179, 185, 227, 260, 402, 403
Cirencester 423
Cîteaux 101
Clanranald 213
Clare, family of 170, 279, 428
Clare, Gilbert de, e. of Gloucester ("red earl") 146, 173, 175, 185, 188
Clare, Gilbert de, e. of Gloucester 205, 211
Clare, Richard de, e. of Gloucester 141
Clare, Richard de, e. of Pembroke (Strongbow) 118
Clare, Roger de 172
Clarendon 87, 109, 414
Clarendon, assize of (1166) 87, 91
Clarendon, Constitutions of 109, 110, 116
Clavell, family of 125
Cleder, St. 27
Cleobury 83
Clerkenwell 168, 323, 329, 398, 410
St. John's 319, 324
Clifford, Robert, lord 211, 212
Clos de Vougeot 101
Clovis, k. of Franks 59
Cluniac reforms 100
Cluny, English monasteries of 100, 102, 198
Clyde, R. 27, 216
Clydesdale 196
Clywd, vale of 74, 185
Cobham, family of 430
Cobham, lord 275
Cobham, Sir Thomas 315
Cocherel 281

Coggeshall 310, 409
Colchester 12, 310, 313
Columba, St. 27
Comyn, family of 193
Comyn, John of Badenoch (the Red) 202, 203, 205
Comyn, John, e. of Buchan 202, 203, 205, 207
Countess of Buchan 203
Conches 267
Connaught 119, 362
Constantine, emp. 190
Constantinople 13, 33, 70, 359
Conway castle 188, 366, 367
Conway, R. 179, 180, 185
Conway, Treaty of 180
Coombe-in-Teignhead 157
Cooper, name of 382
Coquetdale 208
Corbeil 276
Cordoba 191n
Cormac, k. 10
Corneille, St. 387
Cornwall 3, 4, 16, 18, 26, 27, 163, 172, 205, 324
earl of see Gaveston
Coronation, see under Monarchy in Subject Index
Corringham 309
Corunna 286
Cotentin 242, 267
Côte d'Or 101
Cotswolds 11, 101, 304, 394, 401, 423
Council of Fifteen 140–1, 143, 144
Council of Fourteen 344, 345, 346, 347, 350
Courcy, family of 69
Courtenay, family of 480
Courtrai, battle of 225
Coventry 56, 102, 331, 364, 423
bishop of 230
Cow Common 51
Crab's Green 51
Crail 197
Cranbrook 401
Crécy, battle of 245n, 245–50, 253, 265, 269, 272, 276, 277, 291, 292, 293, 295, 307, 320, 327, 334, 335, 337, 369, 421, 422
Crediton 33
Cree, R., battle of 207
Cressingham, Hugh de 199, 200

458

Criccieth 188
Crimea 253, 254
Crispin, St. 387
Crosby 53
Crossthwaite 53
Croughton 417
Crow, name of 382
Crowland abbey 38, 441
Cumberland 52, 83, 215, 259
Cumbria 18
Cuthbert, St. 28, 50
Cynric, k. 51
Cyprus 237, 301n, 361

Dagworth, Sir Nicholas 349
Dagworth, Sir Thomas 261, 264, 273
Dalhousie 234
Dalkeith 353
Dalriada 18, 27
Dalry 203
Dalswinton 207
Damascus 395
Danegeld 40, 41
Danelaw, the 50, 53, 69, 90, 373
Danes, see Vikings
Dartford 311
Dauphin, the, see John II of France & Charles V of France
David I, k. of Scots 198
David II, k. of Scots 234, 251, 263, 265, 273, 283, 289, 301n, 353
David ap Gruffydd 175, 178, 180–1, 183, 185, 186, 190
David, St. 27
Dax 286
Dean, forest of 241
Dean, name of 382
Dee, R. 18, 34, 48, 78, 172, 175, 178
Deheubarth 170
Deira 20
Delves, Sir John 272
Denbigh 185
Denmark 6, 16, 36, 54, 55, 301n
king of 301n, see also Canute
Derby 50, 423
earls of, see Henry of Grosmont, John of Gaunt, Henry IV of Bolingbroke
Derbyshire 40, 68, 178, 264

Dermot, k. of Leinster 118
Despenser, family of 217n, 241, 245n
Despenser, Edward 275
Despenser, Henry, b. of Norwich 334
Despenser, Hugh, the elder, e. of Winchester 217, 218, 232, 344
Despenser, Hugh, the younger, lord 217, 218, 232
Despenser, Hugh, lord 245, 245n
Devon 8, 16, 18, 38, 41, 42, 157, 402, 426
Dialogue of the Exchequer 85
Diarmuid 10
Doddington 272
Dolmens 4, 5
Domesday Book 51, 70, 71–2, 72n
Domfront 268
Dominic, St. 134
Doncaster 366
Doodle Oak 51
Dordogne, R. 237, 268, 287
Dordrecht 406
Dorset 8, 9, 54, 125, 255, 256, 402
Douglas, Sir James (Black Douglas) 204, 205, 206–7, 209, 214, 215, 215n, 234, 283, 353
Douglas, James, e. of 353–4
Douglas, William 270–1
Douglas, William, 1st e. of 265, 266, 283
Douglas, Sir William of Liddesdale 234
Dover 12, 24n, 112, 134, 349, 403
Dover strait 1, 3, 38, 250, 252, 292
Downpatrick 9
Drapers Company 301
Dreux 267
Druids 13
Dublin 118, 119, 362
Trinity College 36
Dumfries 202, 207, 208
Dumfriesshire 204
Dumnonii, the 8, 11
Dunbar 201, 214
Dunbar, William 189, 410
Dundee 199, 200
Dundrennan 198
Dunfermline 193
Dungeness 260

Dunstable, name of 404
Dunstan, St., abp. 49, 51, 52, 198
Durham 28, 71, 102, 191, 208, 215, 241, 251, 426
St. Cuthbert's abbey 100
bishops of 68, 265, 354, 355, see also Fordham
Durotriges, the 8
Dutton, Sir Thomas 272
Dyfor 18
Dyfrig, St. 27

Eadmer of Canterbury 99
Ealing 19
Earl's Barton 52
East Anglia 20, 22, 30, 38, 40, 53, 137, 330, 346, 395, 398, 401, 408, 417
earldom of 56
Easterlings 394, 395
Eastra 26
Ebro, R. 35
Edgar, k. 49, 52, 53, 54, 74
Edinburgh 190, 193, 201, 207, 209, 210, 234, 266, 311, 318
Edington 42, 48
Edmund, St., k. 39, 98, 325
Edmund, e. of Cornwall 163
Edmund, "Crouchback", e. of Lancaster 416
Edmund Ironside, k. 54, 56, 76
Edmund of Langley, e. of Cambridge, d. of York 275, 287, 311, 336, 339, 343, 365, 366, 367
Edmund of Woodstock, e. of Kent 337
Edward I, k. as Prince, 140, 142, 145, 146–7, 149, 152; legal reforms, 147–57, 161, 165–8, 337, 338, 368, 379, 417; conquest of Wales, 169–70, 173–88, 189, 221; dealings with Scotland, 190–4, 195–6, 198, 201–5, 416; death, 205; references to, 218, 225, 239, 279, 337, 346, 369, 392, 399, 404, 405–6, 415, 419, 428, 429
Edward II, k. in infancy, 188, 191, 192; his favourites, 205, 207, 208, 217, 338, 343–4, 348;

Scottish campaign, 208, 209, 210–5, 250; deposition & murder, 218, 345, 368, 369, 421; references to, 155, 219, 231, 336, 337, 339, 346, 404
Edward III, k. character, 218–9; wars with France, 224–5, 226–8, 235–7, 239–50, 251–2, 259, 263, 265, 266, 273–4, 274–80, 287–8, 289, 292, 339, 342, 362, 369, 404; dealings with Scots, 222–4, 234, 251, 263, 265–6, 273, 283–4, 289–90, 334; financial difficulties & parliamentary grants, 224, 226, 229–33, 262–3, 289, 307, 337, 406; order of garter, 252, 255, 360, 422; naval victory, 259–60; old age & death, 283, 291–2, 293–4, 335; references to, 157, 295, 300, 307, 336, 338, 344, 347, 355, 359, 401, 420, 421, 429, 438
Edward IV, k. 409
Edward, Prince of Wales, (the Black Prince), 236, 242, 246, 249–50, 252, 259–60, 264–5, 267–73, 274, 277, 278, 285–8, 290–3, 295, 321, 334, 335, 337, 338, 339, 341, 342, 345, 368, 421
Edward, the Confessor, St., k. 55–6, 60, 63, 66, 69, 77, 255, 324, 325, 394, 414
Edward the Elder, k. 49
Egbert's stone 42
Egypt 5
Eisteddfod 172
Elbe, R. 33, 442
Elboeuf 243
Elderslie 196
Eleanor of Aquitaine, q. of England 80, 81, 82, 83, 120, 169
Eleanor of Castile, q. of England 188, 189, 191n, 191–2, 416
Elham 115
Elizabeth II 51
Elmham, Sir William 349
Eltham palace 252, 278,

342, 360
Ely 38, 50, 79, 101, 236, 420
bishop of 168, see also Arundel, Nigel of Ely
Emma of Normandy, q. 55
Ems, R. 16, 34
Endellion, St. 27
Englesham 52
Don Enrico, see Henry II of Trastamara
Epping forest 20
Erith 310
Escombe 28
Esplechin, truce of 229
Essex 20, 23, 30, 51, 52, 54, 84, 281, 309, 330, 363, 375, 398; peasants revolt, 310, 313, 314–5, 318, 319, 321, 322
Ethandun, see Edington
Ethelbert, k. 24
Ethelwulf, k. 39
Eton college 423
Ettrick forest 210, 234
Eustace, St. 387
Evans, Dr. Joan 325n
Evesham 100, 146, 178, 194
Evreux 266, 267
Exe, R. 28, 51
Exeter 11, 41, 44, 45, 158, 289, 399, 402, 419, 422, 426
Eynsham 348

Fairford 96
Falaise 64
Falkirk 74, 201, 203, 210
Falmouth 402
Farleigh, Richard of 422
Farringdon, Thomas 314, 321
Felton, Sir Thomas 285
Felton, Sir William 285
Fens, the 17, 38, 50, 71, 94, 329, 330
Fenris 53
Ferdinand of Portugal, k. 335
Ferrers, Henry de 68
Fianna, the 9
Field, name of 382
Fife 207
Fife, earl of 203
Finisterre 403
Finn Mac Cool 10
Fishguard 53
Fishermen 309–10, 402–3
Fishmongers Company 301

Fitzalan, family of 170, 241
Fitzalan, Richard, e. of Arundel (1330–76) 233
Fitzalan, Richard, e. of Arundel (1376–97) 333, 334, 338, 340, 343, 344, 345, 346, 347, 355, 357, 358, 361, 363
Fitzneal, Nigel 85
Fitzneal, Richard, bp. 85, 90
Fitzstephen, William 398
Fitzwalter, lord 275
Flanders 120, 274, 281, 403, 410; allied with England, 224–6, 228, 229, 230, 234, 235, 236–7, 243, 244, 250, 260, 263; campaigns in 226–8, 265, 334, 339, 405; loss of English control in, 277, 278, 287–8; rebellions in 225, 237, 305, 332, 242, 334; trade with, 197, 225, 251, 260, 352, 401, 402, 406, 407
Flanders, counts of 305, 334
Louis de Nevers 247, 250
Louis de Male 287
Margaret, heiress of 287–8
Flemings in England 74, 300, 310, 315, 319, 323, 394, 395, 401, 409
Flint 179, 180, 185, 366, 367
Flintshire 187
Florence 254, 281, 305, 399, 402, 404, 410, 417
Arte della Lana 402
Florence of Worcester 99
Fobbing-by-Tilbury 309
Fontenelle 229
Ford, name of 382
Fordham, John, bp. of Durham 343
Forests 2, 3, 4, 5, 7, 8, 10, 12, 16, 19, 20–1, 42, 54, 76, 124, 125, 149, 221, 286, 341, 380
Forest Laws 71
Forester, name of 382
Forfar 207
Forth, Firth of 18, 20, 24, 190, 198, 199, 210, 211, 212, 215
Fosse Way 16
Foster, name of 382

Fountains abbey 79, 100, 178n, 257, 407, 419
Fowey 294
Fowler, name of 382
Fox, name of 382
Framlingham 120
France: under Romans, 10, 14, 24; Frankish empire, 33–4, 40, 41, 50, 59, 60, 61, 64, 104; early French kings, 59, 60, 64, 68, see also Louis VII and Louis IX; relations with Norman England, 66, 68–9, 70, 85, 100, 101, 123, 124–5; Plantagenet inheritance of, 79–81, 83, 84, 119–20, 166, 169, 170, 218, 219, 224, 223, 236, 284, 285, 288; Scottish alliance with, 195, 233–4, 235, 334; Black Death in, 254–5, 259, 283; civil war in, 274, 331–2; wars with England (1337–64), 224–5, 226–9, 234–5, 236–9, 240n, 241, 242–252, 253, 259–60, 260–2, 263–74, 274–78, 279, 280, 281–2; (1369–96), 288–9, 290–4, 295, 311, 334, 339, 340, 341, 342, 346, 362; references to wars, 285, 302, 307, 312, 318, 328, 332, 337, 340, 363, 369, 404, 406, 438; trade with England, 252, 390, 401, 402, 403, 406; other references, 143, 175, 178, 221, 362, 413
Franche Comté 224
Francis of Assisi, St. 134, 430, 432
Franciscans, see Free Companies 273, 276, 277, 280–1, 282, 286–7, 290
Freya 22
Freyr 36
Frisia 16
Froissart, Jean 238, 248, 250, 264, 275, 280, 289n, 290, 293, 295n, 312, 322, 338, 352
Frome, R. 40
Fuller, William 71
Fulleshurst, Sir Robert 272

Gaels, see Celts
Galacia 341
Galahad 188
Galbraith, V. H. 327n
Gall, St. 387
Galloway 27, 120, 196, 204, 205
Garonne, R. 238, 242, 265, 285, 293
Gascony 80, 169, 178, 184, 185, 187, 194, 205, 224, 225, 236, 237, 242, 252, 254, 260, 261, 263, 271, 273, 281, 284, 285, 288, 291, 292, 293, 294, 356, 401, 402
Gaul, see France
Gaveston, Piers, e. of Cornwall 205, 207, 208, 217, 343, 344, 348
Gawain 188
Gelderland 224
Gellinga, family of 19
Genoa 226, 228, 253, 254, 402, 403
Genoese crossbowmen 227, 228, 245, 248–9
George, St. 96, 252, 271, 304, 317, 325, 418
Germans 16, 17, 26, 31, 33, 34, 50, 124, 225, 228, 247, 261, 274, 281, 359, 400
Germany 14, 105, 196, 224, 363, 390
Emperor 78, 104
Gervase of Canterbury 99
Ghent 225, 228, 230, 237, 242, 247, 305, 334, 407, 408
Gibbon, Edward 359
Gibraltar 3
Giffard, family of 69, 170
Giffard, Hugh 152
Giles, St. 387
Gisleham, William of 153
Glamorgan 53
Glanvill, family of 120
Glanvill, Ranulf de 87, 89, 121
Glasgow 196, 201
Glastonbury 31, 51, 189, 394
Glaziers 18, 390, 411, 412, 414, 415, 418, 421, 422, 521, 522, 526, 530–1
Gloucester 12, 41, 68, 75, 101, 102, 255, 399, 421
museum 8
earls of 56, see also Clare
dukes of see Despenser,

Thomas of Woodstock
Gloucester, John of 414
Gloucestershire 9, 96, 394, 402, 409, 422
Godiva, lady 56
Godwin, e. of Wessex 56
Godwinson, Harold, e. of Wessex, see Harold, k.
Goldsmiths company 256, 301
Gosforth cross 52
Govan, St. 27
Gower, John 302, 315
Gower peninsula 2, 53, 74
Graham, Sir John 199
Grainne 10
Granada 237
Grantham 407
Graves, Robert 169
Gravesend 294, 310–1
Gray of Heton, Sir Thomas 276
Great Coxwell 101
Greece 9, 13, 33, 62, 395
Emperors, see Byzantine empire
Green, name of 382
Green, Sir Henry 366
Greenstead 52
Greenwich 316, 317
Gregory I, St., pope 46
Gregory VII, (Hildebrand), pope 102–4, 110
Gresholm 53
Grevil, William 409
Grey, lord 275
Greyfriars, see
Griffith, John 273
Grimes' Graves 4
Grindcobbe, William 329, 331
Grocers company 301
Grosseteste, Robert, bp. 138, 139, 148
Du Guesclin, Bertrand 281–2, 286, 287, 291
Guienne 80, 224, 235, 250, 260, 263, 264, 267, 273, 287, 290
Guinevere, q. 189
Gull Mac Morna 10
Guthrum, k. 41–2
Gwent 18, 74, 177, 222
Gwenwynwyn, ap Gruffydd 181
Gwynedd 18, 172, 173, 176, 177, 179, 180, 183, 184, 186, 187
Gynwell, John, bp. of Lincoln 257

Hackney 400
Haddington 266
Hainault 224, 225, 226, 274, 281, 401, 402
   count of 224
   dowager countess of 229
Hainault forest 400
Hales, Sir Robert 308, 309, 310, 313, 315, 321, 322-3, 324
Halidon Hill, battle of 222-4, 234, 246, 354
Halifax 423
Hamelin 328
Hampshire 135, 203, 239
Hampstead 400
Hannes, Alice 377
Hanseatic League 409
Hapsburgs 196
Harbledown 121
Harbey 191
Harcourt, Godfrey de 249
Harfleur 289
Harlech 188
Harmsworth 305
Harold, k. 49, 56, 64-66
Harold Hardrada, k. of Norway 56, 64-5
Harringay Park 345
Hartlepool 208
Harvey, John 424
Hastings 19, 294, 403
   battle of 63, 65-6, 70, 76, 124, 215, 247
Hastings, family of 241
Hastings, John, e. of Pembroke (1348-76) 238, 242
Hastings, John, e. of Pembroke (1376-89) 292
Hastings, lord 275
Hatfield forest 21
Haverford 53
Haverill, name of 404
Hawarden 180
Hawkes, Jacquetta 6n
Hawkestone, Sir John 272
Hawkwood, John 281
Hayles 394
Hebrews 49
Hebrides, the 36
Hel 23
Helen of Troy 10
Hengham, Ralph de, C. J. 155, 161, 167
Henry I, k. 76-8, 77n, 82, 83, 85, 94, 100, 104, 105, 109, 128, 129, 130, 395
Henry II, k. accession & character, 79, 80, 81-2; fiscal discipline, 83-7,

127, 128, 129; legal reforms, 87-92, 93, 106, 126, 127, 128, 130, 148, 152, 157, 158, 194; relations with Church, 93, 103, 104-5, 106-9, 117, 119, 121, 166, 198; quarrel with Becket, 110-7, 137; conquest of Ireland, 118-9, 362; dealings with Scots, 120, 121-2, 190, 192; other references, 126, 172, 176, 179, 183, 395, 398
Henry III, k. 134, 137, 139n, 139-47, 148, 149, 151, 161, 173, 177, 325, 346, 358, 378, 393, 395, 414, 419
Henry, (the Young King) s. of Henry II 120, 126
Henry IV of Bolingbroke, e. of Derby & Lancaster, d. of Hereford 321, 322, 346, 348, 351, 356, 364-5, 366-7, 368
Henry V, k. 423, 441
Henry VI, k. 423
Henri VII, k. 423
Henry II of Trastamara, k. of Castile 286, 287, 288, 292, 335
Henry the Glazier 415
Henry of Grosmont, e. of Derby & Lancaster, d. of Lancaster 1351 222-3, 226, 234, 236-8, 237n, 239, 242, 250, 252, 261, 264, 266n, 266-8, 273, 274-7, 279, 289n, 295, 335
Henry of Huntingdon 124
Hercules, Pillars of, see Gibraltar
Hereford 50, 146, 289
   bishop of 343
   earls of 56, 68, 74, 178
   see also Bohun
   duke of, see Henry IV of Bolingbroke
Hereward the Wake 71
Herland, Hugh 360, 422-3
Hertfordshire 320
Hesse 418
Hessett 304
Heyham, Justice 167
Highbury 323, 400
Highfield, R. 430n
Highgate 400
Hilda, St. 30
Hildebrand, see Gregory VII

Hill, name of 382
Hogg, name of 382
Hogue, La 242, 266
Holborn 168, 319, 400
Holderness 257
Holland 395, 405
   Florence, count of Holland 193
Holland, Sir John 321
Holland, Thomas, 1st e. of Kent 321
Holme (Notts) 409
Holstein 16
Holy Island 28
Holy Land 147, 189, 394
Holy Roman or German Empire 33-4, 36, 59-60, 61, 78, 104, 244, 247, 359, 363
Holyrood abbey 198, 352
Holywell 398
Homer 9
Horn, Andrew 153
Horn, alderman 323
Horne, John 316, 318
Howard, justice 167
Hoxton 400, 410
Hubert, St. 387
Hugh, St. 415
Hull 339, 402
Humber, R. 8, 20, 24, 34, 38, 100, 257, 366
Hunter, name of 382
Huntingdon, earldom of 56
Huntingdon, justice 167
Hurley, William of 236, 420
Hussites, the 442
Hythe 403
Hywel Dda, Code of 180-2, 184, 187

Iberians, see Spain
Ice Age 2
Iceland 115
Iceni, the 8, 11
Icknield Way 6
Ilchester 138
Ile-de-France 250, 274, 418, 421
Illtyd, St. 27
Imworth, John 316, 324
Inchaffray, abbot of 212
India 2, 6, 33
Ine, k. 34
Inverurie, battle of 207
Iona 27, 36, 197
Ipswich 50, 329
Ireland xvii, 1, 3, 4, 6, 7, 9, 27, 32, 36-7, 40, 52, 53, 117-19, 184, 190, 194,

462

197, 204, 218, 241, 242, 257, 279, 343, 351, *362*, 365–6
Ireland, duke of, see de Vere
Ironmongers company 301
Isabella of France, q. of England, wife of Edward II 207, 218, 231, 245
Isabella of France, q. of England, wife of Richard II 362
Islam, see Moslems
Islington 400
Islip, Simon of, abp. 279
Italy 6, 10, 14, 25, 34, 39, 50, 62, 90, 100, 123, 124, 134, 224, 225, 254, 281, 287, 332, 359, 368, 394, 401, 402, 404, 406, 407, 410

Jacquerie 305, 331
Jaffa 126
Jarrow 29, 31, 33
Jean, princess 254
Jedburgh 198, 283, 353–4
Jerusalem 33, 63, 126, 127, 170
Jervaux abbey 100, 101
Jewel, John 281
Jews 136, 184
Joan of Kent, princess of Wales (the Fair Maid of Kent) 256, 315, 322, 323, 324, 329, 337, 339, 359, 440
John, k. of England (Lackland) 127–34, 139, 143, 172, 176, 238, 242, 267, 268, 346, 376
John, k. of Bohemia 244, 247, 250
John II, k. of France 238–9, 242, 243, 260, 262, 263, 265, 267–74, 277, 278, 280, 301n, 324
John I, k. of Portugal 341, 356
John of Gaunt, d. of Lancaster 228, 260, 266n, 275, 279, 286, 289, 291, 292–3, 295, 309, 311, 312, 315, 318, 319, 321, 322, 334, 335, 341, 346, 356, 358, 365, 440
John the Baptist, St. 212, 325
Johnson, Samuel 191n
Joseph 5
Joseph of Arimathea, St.

51, 394
Juan of Castile, k. 335, 341
Juliers 224
Justinian, emp. 90, 368
Jutland 20, 24, 36, 403

Kaffir wars 8
Katherine, St. 387
Kells, Book of 36
Kenilworth, Dictum of 146–7
Kennet, R. 38
Kent 8, 20, 24, 30, 35, 45, 54, 69, 90, 113, 115, 116, 179, 191n, 297, 342, 360, 368, 373, 401, 403
Peasants revolt 310–19, 322, 324, 327, 329, 379
earl of see Holland
Kilburn 400
Kilsby, William 229, 230, 232, 233
King, name of 382
Kinghorn 190, 197
King's Langley 360
Kipling, Rudyard xi, 15, 49, 59, 123
Kirk Andreas 52
Kirkstall abbey 100
Kite, Robert 164
Knaresborough 366, 368
Knight, name of 382
Knight, Thomas 374
Knightsbridge 301
Knollys, Sir Robert 240, 262, 266, 267, 273, 281n, 290, 311, 320, 328, 329
Knoyle 42

Lacy, family of 69, 120
Ladygrove 388
Ladysmead 388
Lake District 16
Lamb, name of 382
Lamberton, William, b. of St. Andrews 203
Lambeth 55, 316
Lanark 196
Lancashire 121, 178
Lancaster 341
earls and dukes of, see Henry of Grosmont, John of Gaunt & Henry IV of Bolingbroke
Lancaster, Blanche, duchess of 289n, 289, 335
Lane, name of 382
Lanercost priory 204, 251

Langranc, abp. 101
Lang, Andrew 201
Langland, William 168, 300, 302–5, 313, 365, 373, 381, 425
Langton, Stephen, abp. 130–1, 133, 134, 141
Languedoc 238, 264, 265
Lateran Council 159
Latimer, William, lord 301
Lauderdale 210
Lavenham 423
Lea, R. 48
Leathersellers Company 301
Leeds castle 191n, 360, 368
Legge, John 308, 310, 322
Legh, family of 125
Leglen wood 202
Leicester 324, 366
earldom of 143, 279
Leicestershire 40, 257
Leinster 118, 362
Leith 197, 210
Lennox, earl of 200, 207
Leofric, e. of Mercia 56
Lesnes abbey 310
Levant, the 127, 359
Lewes 145, 294
Libourne 237
Lichfield 102, 422
Liddesdale, battle of 18
Liddesdale, knight of, see Douglas
Limoges 265, 277, 291
Limousin 80, 277, 285, 288
Lincoln 12, 50, 102, 407, 426
bishops of 138, 415, see also Grosseteste & Gynwell, John
earldom of 279
Lincolnshire 8, 40, 71, 324, 409
Lindisfarne 28
Lindisfarne Gospel 28
Linlithgow 197
Lionel of Antwerp, d. of Clarence 275, 277, 279, 287, 336
Lisbon 356
Lisieux 243, 267
Lithuania 266, 358
Litster, Geoffrey 330
Littleburn, Martin of 161
Llanbadarn, see Aberystwyth
Llancarfan 171
Llandeillo Fawr 185
Llantwit 171

Llywelyn ap Gruffydd, prince of Wales 143, *173–86*, 187, 190
Llywelyn ap Ioworth (the Great) 172–3, 173n
Lochleven abbey 198
Lochmaben 207, 208
Loire, R. 235, 267, 268, 273, 276
Loki 52
Lollards, the 441
Lombardy 34, 259, 394, 404, 410
London *398–401*, 410; early development of, 11, 21, 38, 44, 48, 50, 55, 73, 102; civic rights of, 69, 90, 131, 146, 399, 400; influence of friars in, 134–5; Inns of Court established in, 167–8; prisoners paraded in, 201, 273, 324, 350; part in constitutional struggles, 232, 345–6, 347, 348, 366; Black Death in, 256, 259; Peasants revolt in, 309, 310, 311, 314–24, 328–9, 334; merchants & trade in, 125, 144, 151, 152, 251, 343, 346, 364, 396, 398, 400, 402, 403, 405, 407, 408, 409, 410; apprentices, 400; craftsmen of, 416, 420; descriptions of, 397, 398, 399–401, 410; other references to, 54, 56, 65, 80, 121
Aldersgate 328
Aldgate 315, 318
Baynard's Castle 323, 324, 329, 399
Billingsgate 318
Bridge 201, 316, 323, 398, 412
Charterhouse 256
Charing Cross 191n
Cheapside 410, 432
Fetter Lane 168
Fleet prison 319
Fleet Street 319
Galley Quay 400
Leadenhall market 11n
Little All Hallows 256
Ludgate 399
Marshalsea, the 316, 324
Mile End fields 315, 320, 321, 324, 329, 336

Mincing Lane 400
Newgate 319
Pardon churchyard 256
Pool of 398
St. Bartholomew the Great 324, 325 hospital 135, 328 priory 168
St. Catherine's Wharf 319
St. Martin-in-the-Vintry 323
St. Paul's cathedral 161, 323, 399, 414, 421, 422
St. Thomas's hospital 135
Savoy, the 273, 318
Smithfield 135, 201, 218, 256, 324, 325, 329, 332, 336, 398, 441
Strand, the 318, 399
Temple, the 319
Thames Street 256, 400
Tower, the 73, 173, 186, 188, 201, 204, 218, 227, 230, 315, 318, 319, 320, 321–3, 329, 341, 343, 344, 348, 350, 351, 367, 398, 399
The White Tower 73n
Tower Hill 319, 322
Whitechapel 315
Long, name of 382
Longfellow, H. W. 46
Longthorpe tower 417
Lorne, John of Argyll, lord of 203, 207
Lorraine 224, 418 duke of 250
Lostwithiel 163
Lothian 120
Loudon, battle of 204
Louis VII, k. of France (1120–80) 79, 80, 81, 84, 99, 112, 120
Louis IX, (St. Louis), k. of France (1215–70) 145, 152, 282, 414
Louth 407
Low Countries 4, 401, 402, 403, 406, 409
Lowther, J. 167
Lucerne 196
Ludlow 407
Lumley, family of 125
Luther, Martin 423, 442
Lutterworth 441
Luttrell Psalter 240
Luxemburg 247

Lyme 402
Lynn 402
Lyonesse 1
Lyonnais 224
Lyons 281
Lyons, Richard 301, 323

Macclesfield forest 178, 221, 345
MacDonald of the Isles, Angus Og 213
MacMurrach, Art 366
Magyars 60
Maiden Castle 9
Maidstone 312, 314
Maine 64, 75, 79, 81, 267, 274, 277
Mainz 33
Maitland, F. W. 377n
Majorca, k. of 247
Malcolm, k. of Scots 74
Maldon, battle of 23
Malkin, John 164
Malmesbury 28, 31, 102
Maltravers, lord 241
Man, Isle of 27, 52
Mandeville, family of 69
Mandeville, Geoffrey de, e. of Essex 79
Manny, Sir Walter 234, 242, 256
March, earls of, see Mortimer
La Marche 80
Mare, Edmund de la, of Peldon 310
Margam abbey 100, 171
Margaret of France, q. of England 337, 420
Margaret, q. of Scotland 74, 198
Margate 346
Marlborough, Statute of 147, 149
Marne, R. 8
Marseilles 254
Marshal, William the 237
Marsh Gibbon 70
Martel, Charles 33, 34
Martham 374
Maryfield 388
Marylebone 400
Mary Magdalene, St. 387, 435
Mary's Well 388
de Massey, family of 120
Matilda, empress 78, 79, 80, 82, 172
Mathew, Gervase 361n, 362n
Maud-atte-Hythe 164

Maupertius 269
Mauron, battle of 261–2, 266
Meath 118, 362
Meaux 257
Medway, R. 312
Mediterranean 3, 6, 10, 12, 18, 32, 33, 62, 254, 265, 359, 403
Melcombe Regis 255, 294, 402
Melibee, the 253n
Melrose abbey 31, 198, 234
Menai Strait 185, 186, 188
Menteith, earl of 207
Mercers Company 301, 409
Merchant Adventurers 409
Mercia 20, 21, 28, 30, 34, 38, 40, 41, 44, 48, 90
Merciless Parliament 349–52, 357, 362
Merioneth 187
Merlin 176
Merovingians, the 33
Merton, Council of 148
Mesopotamia 2
Methven 203
Metyngham, John de, C. J. 166
Meuse, R. 418
Michael, St. archangel 62, 95
Michel, the 227
Middle Carlton 257
Middlesex 305, 319, 351, 398
Milan 281, 287, 359, 399, 410
Mildenhall heath 323
Milford Haven 118, 366
Milton hundred 164
Minster 31
Miosson, R. 269
Mirror of Justices, the 152
Missenden abbey 168
Missenden, Little 417
Moissac 291
Monmouth 74
Monmouth, Geoffrey of 124
Monmouthshire 35
Montague, William, e. of Salisbury 226, 269–70, 275, 318, 320, 366
Montfort de, family of 356
Montfort, Eleanor, de 175–6, 180
Montfort, Joan de, duchess of Brittany 234
Montfort, John de, III, d. of Brittany 234

Montfort, John de, IV, d. of Brittany 234, 235, 236
Montfort, John de, V, d. of Brittany 261, 266, 282
Montfort, Simon de, e. of Leicester 143–7, 151, 173, 175, 177
Montgomery 174
Montgomery, family of 69
Montgomeryshire 74
Montreuil 250
Montrose 197
Moors, the 33, 34, 136, 395
Moray 196, 206
Moray, Andrew de 199
Moray Firth 195
Morbihan, truce of 235
Morgannwy 170
Morlaix, battle of 235, 241
Morris dancing 51
Mortain, Robert de 68
Mortimer, family of 69, 170, 173, 186, 241
Mortimer, Hugh de, lord 83
Mortimer, Roger, e. of March (1328–30) 218, 231, 241, 337
Mortimer, Roger, e. of March (1354–60) 241, 275
Mortimer, Roger, e. of March (1381–98) 336
Mortimer, Roger of Wigmore 186
Morton, abp. 423
Morwenna, St. 27
Moslems 33, 34, 36, 39, 60, 126 see also Arabs, Moors, Saracens
Mowbray, family of 69, 120
Mowbray, John, lord 275
Mowbray, Sir Thomas 209, 210
Mowbray, Thomas, e. of Nottingham d. of Norfolk (1397) 348, 351, 364
Munster 119

Nájera, battle of 286, 291, 327, 339, 341, 351
Nantes 235
Narbonne 265
Navarre, see Spain
Neath abbey 100
Nene, R. 130
Neolithic man 3–6, 19
Nesle, Marshal de 261, 262
Nest, princess 76

Neville, family of 69, 125, 366
Neville, Alexander, abp. of York 343, 347, 350–1, 357
Neville, of Raby, lord 251, 275
Neville's Cross, battle of 251, 273, 327, 353, 354
Nevin 189
Newbattle 198
Newbury 85
Newcastle-upon-Tyne 74, 121, 194, 201, 353, 354, 399, 402
New Forest 76
Newton, Sir John 316–7
Nigel of Ely, bp. 85
Nile, R. 2
Ninian, St. 27
Norfolk 8, 20, 50, 84, 124, 161, 256, 302, 329, 330, 394, 423
earls of, see Bigod, Mowbray
Norham 192
Normandy 61, 62, 63, 64, 66, 67, 75, 76, 79, 81, 100, 101, 112, 119, 120, 238, 242, 255, 263, 266–7, 273, 274, 277, 281, 289, 418
Normans, the, description of, 61–3; conquest of England, 64–6; relations with English, 66–73, 74, 110; insurgent barons & nobles, 76, 79, 121; military strength, 64, 65, 74; assimilation with English, 123–4, 125, 132, 247; seamen raiders, 225, 242–3, 276, 403; references to conquest, 75, 99, 137, 170, 176, 178, 205, 258; other references, 77, 100, 102, 225, 266, 268
Norman Kings 75, 85, 125, 126, 169, 182, 378 see also William I, William II, Henry I & Stephen
Norsemen, see Vikings
North Africa 6, 33
Northallerton 79
Northampton 87, 110, 115, 127, 137, 302, 308, 324, 348
earls of 56. See also Bohun.

Northamptonshire 28, 52, 417
North Cape 46
Northleach 423
North Sea 4, 15, 18, 55, 74, 197, 224, 226, 403
Northumberland 83, 120, 121, 192, 208, 234
  earl of, see Percy
Northumbria 18, 20, 24–6, 27, 28, 30, 35, 38, 40, 41, 50, 53, 100
  earldom of 56
Norton Fitzwarren 125
Norway 36, 55, 64, 191, 403
  Kings of 56, 64, 65, 193
  Queen of 190
Norway, Maid of 190–1, 192
Norwich 50, 102, 115, 157, 289, 302, 330, 399, 417, 422
Nottingham 218, 222, 345, 350, 351
  earl of, see Mowbray
Nottinghamshire 40, 191
Nouaillé 269

Ochils, the 199
Odin cross 52
Odo, the goldsmith 415
  Edward his son 415
Offa, k. 34–5, 38
Offa's Dyke 34
Og, Angus, see MacDonald of the Isles
Old Sarum 102, 414
Orewin Bridge 186
Orkneys 36, 191
Orléans, d. of, see Charles V, k. of France
Ormesby, William de 196
Orne, R. 243
Orosius 46
Orwell 227
Oswald, St. 434
Osyth, St. 387
Otford 54
Othere 46
Otterburn, battle of 353–4
Ouistreham 243
Ouse 65
Ouse, R. 48
Owen ap Gruffydd, prince of Wales 172
Oxford 44, 50, 54, 127, 134, 139, 168, 306
  university 41n, 137, 138, 232, 384, 428, 440
    Balliol college 137,

193n, 438
Magdalen college 423
Merton college 137, 423
New College 388, 422, 431
University college 137
St. Mary's 137
earls of, see Vere
Oxford, Provisions of 140, 142, 143, 144, 147
Oxfordshire 257
Oxus, R. 33

Padarn, St. 27
Paddington 400
Pantin, W. A. 430n
Pardoners 432
Paris 90, 137, 242, 243, 244, 250, 254, 264, 273, 274, 275, 276, 282, 285, 288, 290, 302, 359, 366, 399, 440
  Jacobin convent 136
  Ste. Chapelle 414
Paris, Matthew 99
Parisii, the 8
Parker, name of 382
Parret, R. 42
Parving, Sir Robert 231
Patrick, St. 27, 36, 117
Pattishall, Martin 157
Paul, St. 93, 98
Paulinus, bishop 24–6
Paycocke, Thomas 409
Pedro of Castile, Don, see Peter I
Peldon 310
Pembroke, earls of, see Valence, and Hastings
Pembrokeshire 3, 5, 53, 74, 304
Penmaenmawr 180, 185
Pennines 8, 16, 18, 353, 408
Penrose, John 396
Penselwood 54
Pepin, k. 33, 34
Pepys, Samuel 440
Perceval 188
Percy, family of 69, 366, 422, 430
Percy, Henry, lord of Alnwick, e. of Northumberland (1377) 251, 275, 353, 366
Percy, Henry, lord (Harry Hotspur) 353–4, 355
Percy, Ralph 353–4
Perfeddwlad, Four Cantrefs of 173, 180,

181–3, 185, 187
Perigord 237, 277
Perigueux 237, 268
Perrers, Alice 291–2, 293
Pershore abbey 31, 102
Persia 2, 6
Perth 193, 201, 208
Peter I, the "Cruel", k. of Castile 286–7, 288, 292
Peter, St. 98, 432
Peterborough 37, 38, 94, 102, 417
Petersham 50
Pevensey 65, 260
Peverel, William, of the Peak 83
Philip IV, the "Fair", k. of France (1285–1314) 195, 224
Philip VI, of Valois, k. of France (1328–50) 224, 225, 228, 229, 234, 235, 236, 238, 239, 243, 244, 245, 247, 248, 250, 251, 260
Philip, the "Bold", d. of Burgundy 288, 334
Philippa, princess 336
Philippa of Hainault, q. of England 224, 226, 228, 230, 251, 260, 289, 292, 293, 401
Philippa of Lancaster, q. of Portugal 341, 356
Pickard, Sir Henry 301
Picardy 274, 289
Pickering 368
Picts 15, 27
Piers Plowman, see Langland
Piggsflesh, name of 404
Pillerton Hersey 125
Pisa 402, 403, 417
Pitt, name of 382
Plantagenet, Geoffrey, count of Anjou 78, 79
Plantagenet, Henry, count of Anjou, see Henry II
Plantagenet kings see Henry II, Richard I, John, Henry III, Edward I–III, Richard II, Henry IV & V
Plesaunce, La 364
Pleschey 84
Plessey castle 363
Plymouth 294, 311, 358, 399, 402
Poissy 243
Poitiers 33, 252, 268, 277, 290

battle of 269–72, 273, 276, 282, 286, 288, 291, 292, 293, 306, 320, 327, 334, 335, 369
Poitou 80, 252, 255, 274, 277, 285
Pole, Michael de la, e. of Suffolk 339, 342, 343, 344, 347, 350, 351, 357
Pole, Sir William de la 230
Pont Audemar 266, 267
Pontefract 366, 368
Ponthieu 224, 245, 263, 277, 289
Poole 40, 256, 294, 402
Pools, battle of the, see Bannockburn
Poore, Richard le, bp. of Salisbury 125, 414
Porchester 12
Portsmouth 119, 227, 235
Portugal 311, 341, 423
   kings of, see John I, Ferdinand
Powys 18, 170, 173, 178
Praetorian guard 12
Prague 359, 442
   Hradschin palace 359
Prior, name of 382
Provence 144, 273
Prussia 237
Pulteney, Sir Thomas 230, 256
Purbeck 41, 293, 412, 416
Puttock's End 51
Pyrenees 33, 224, 286

Quercy 277, 285, 288

Radcot bridge, battle of 348, 357
Radnor 178, 241
Ragman roll 195
Ragnar Lothbrok 38
Rahere, founder of St Bartholomew's (hospital) 135
Raleigh, William, bp. 157
Ramsay, Alexander, of Dalhousie 234
Ramsey, William of 421, 422
Ramsey abbey 98
Randolph, Thomas, e. of Moray 209, 215
Rathlin 204
Ravenna 158
Ravenspur 366
Reading 39, 40, 137, 358
Redesdale 208
Regency, Council of 295

Reigate castle 363
Rennes 235, 261, 268
La Reole 238, 239, 242, 265, 293
Reyns, Henry of 414
Rheims 274, 275–6, 277, 414
Rhine, R. 14, 16, 224, 418
Rhineland 401
Rhone, R. 224
Rhuddlan 179, 180, 185, 186, 187
Rhys ap Gruffydd 172
Richard I, Coeur-de-Lion, k. of England 126–7, 177, 192, 235, 334
Richard II, k. of England, minority of, 295, 306, 308, 333–9, 340–1, 342–4, 344–7, 355–6; peasants revolt, 306, 311–17, 320–3, 324–9, 330, 331, 332, 333–4, 336; character & lifestyle of, 337–9, 358–62, 360n, 363; crisis with Appellants, 347–52, 355–6; declares himself of age, 356–7; procures downfall of enemies, 362–5; return from Ireland & deposition, 366–8, 369; other references to, 333, 408, 422, 423
Richard, e. of Cornwall 394
Richborough 12
Richmond (Yorks.) 121
   earls of, see de Montfort
Richert, Margaret 325n
Ridgeway, the 6
Rienzi, Cola di 305
Rievaulx abbey 100, 407, 419
Ripon 415
Robert I, k. of Scots, see Bruce
Robert II, k. of Scots (the Steward) 289–90, 352–3
Robert of Anjou, k. of Naples & Sicily 359
Robert of Beverley 414
Robert of Normandy, see William II
Robin Hood legend 147, 221–2, 222n, 321, 389
La Rochelle 277, 278, 292–3, 402
Rochester 44, 45, 101, 310, 311, 312, 316

Rockingham forest 191
Rodez 288
Roger of Salisbury, bp. 77, 78, 85
Roger of Wendover 99
Roland 34, 124
Roman occupation 10–15, 16, 18, 19, 45, 65, 190, 195, 391
   memories of 33, 34, 169–70, 176, 188, 189–90
Rome 14, 32, 33, 34, 36, 39, 45, 55, 62, 103, 158, 224, 281n, 305, 394, 410, 432, 433, 438
   St. Peter's 34, 55
Romney 403
Romsey abbey 102
Roncesvalles 34, 286
Roosebeke 334
Ros, lord 285
Roscoff 292
Ross 196, 207
Ross, earl of 207
Rouen 242, 243, 418
Rouergue 277, 287
Round, name of 382
Rowlandson, T. 378
Roxburgh 199, 201, 203, 209, 234, 282, 289
Rudolph of Hapsburg, emp. 196
Runnymede 123n, 130, 134, 399
Ruthin 185
Rutland 178
Rye 227, 278, 281n, 294, 401, 403

St. Albans 11, 98, 99, 102, 257, 317, 320, 325, 329, 331
St. Albans, John of 415
St. Andrews 193, 198, 207, 351
   bishop of, see Lamberton
St. Asaph 124
St. Cloud 244
St. Clement's well 398
St. David's 119, 170
St. Denis 243
St. Emilion 287
St. Helens 242
St. James of Compostella 394
St. John of Jerusalem, order of 310, 319
St. Lo 242
St. Neot, rood of 190
St. Ninian's chapel 214

St. Omer 228
St. Scholastica's Day 306
St. Vaast 242
Saintes 261
Saintonge 80, 261, 285
Saladin, sultan of Egypt 127
Salford Priors 125
Salisbury 68, 76, 96, 109, 125, 134, 258, 333, 399, 413–14, 416, 422 St. Edmunds, 389
bishops of, see Poore, Roger
earls of, see Montague
Salisbury, John of 114
Salisbury, Sir John 349
Salisbury Plain 6, 8, 20
Salmonsby 9
Salters Company 301
Saltwood castle 113
Samson of Bury, abbot 124
Samson of Dol, St. 27
Sandwich 112, 235, 260, 274, 314, 403
Sanitation, lack of 93
Saunton, justice 167
Sawtrey, William 441
Scandinavia 36, 52–3, 54, 55, 64, 73, 74, 115, 119, 386
Scheldt, R. 242
Schep, John, see John Ball
Schleswig 16
Scone 194, 195, 196, 203
Scotland, see Subject Index
Scott, Sir Walter 354n
Scotus, John 37
Scrope, Sir Richard 347
Scrope, William, e. of Wiltshire 366
Scythia 398
Seine, R. 8, 61, 243, 244
Selkirk 257
Selwood forest 21, 42
Semetic tribes 5
Senlac, see Hastings
Severn, R. 18, 28, 170, 172, 178, 274, 348, 366, 401, 402
Seville 191n, 302
Sewall, John 310
Shaftesbury 44, 45
Shakespeare, William 262, 333n, 367, 378
Sheen, palace of 355, 360, 361
Shelley, John 281n
Shepherd, name of 382
Shepherd kings, the 5

Sheppey, isle of 37
Sherborne 28, 102
Sherston 54
Sherwood forest 21, 191, 221
Shetlands, the 36
Shoreditch 410
Shrewsbury 172, 173, 175, 186, 345, 407
earls of 68, 74
Short, name of 382
Shropshire 172, 178, 182, 404
Sibley, Alderman 328
Sicily 39, 62, 136
Sidney, Sir Philip 354
Siena 47
Siferwas, John 368
Silchester 11
Silures, the 11
Siward of York 56
Skinners Company 301
Skeldale 100
Skye, Isle of 354n
Sluys, battle of 226–8, 229, 230, 233, 234, 237, 252, 260, 292
Smith, name of 382
Smith, Richard 377
Snowdon 185, 187
Snowdonia 172, 173, 178, 185
Soissons cathedral 59
Solent, the 38, 402
Solway Firth 208
Somerset 41, 54, 138, 389, 401, 402, 409, 423
Somme, R. 65, 244–5, 246, 275
Soundings, the 3
South Africa 8
Southampton 266, 402
Southampton Water 20
Southsea Common 242
Southwark 135, 315, 316, 400, 431
Southwell minster 416
Spain 3, 5, 14, 33, 34, 136, 226, 227, 228, 236, 247, 254, 260, 286, 287, 288, 290, 294, 335, 337, 341, 356, 394, 395, 403
Aragon 287, 288, 403
Castile 134, 191n, 254, 259, 286, 287, 288, 292, 293, 295, 335, 356
King of, see Peter I
Constance of, duchess of Lancaster 292, 295, 335

King of 356, see also Henry II of Trastamara, Juan Navarre 224, 254, 286, 287, 288
King of, see Charles
Sparrow, name of 382
Spartans 197
Spenser, Edmund xi
Spigornel, justice 167
Spottsmuir, battle of 195, 199
Squire, name of 382
Stafford, Ralph, e. of 238, 275
Stamford 137
Stamford Bridge 65
Standard, battle of the 79
Stanford-le-Hope 309
Star, order of the 262
Starling, John 330
Stedham 304
Stenton, Sir Frank 72n
Stephen, k. of England 78–80, 82, 83, 85, 86, 87, 100, 105, 106, 120, 128, 130, 172
Stepney 400
Steppes, the 253
Stevenson, R. L. 1
Stirling 193, 199, 200, 201, 209, 210, 211, 212, 213, 214, 222
bridge 200, 214, 215, 225
castle 210–11, 214,
Stoke Newington 400
Stokesay castle 404
Stone, name of 382
Stonehenge 5
Stone of Destiny 194, 195, 283
Stour, R. 408
Stourbridge Fair 395
Stourmere 23
Stow, John 301
Strata Florida 171
Stratford, John, abp. 227, 229, 230–33, 234, 257
Stratford, Ralph, b. of London 229
Stratford, Robert, b. of Chichester 229, 230
Stratford-upon-Avon 229
Stratford-atte-Bowe 285
Strathclyde 16, 18, 26
Strattondale 182
Straw, Jack 323, 330, 379
Streoneshalh, see Whitby
Stroud 408
Stuart, Muriel 411
Stubbs, William, bp. 217

Sturminster Marshall 125
Sudbury, Simon of, abp. 309, 311, 312, 314, 315, 316, 317, 321, 322–3, 324
Suffolk 20, 120, 138, 229, 304, 311, 320, 323, 329, 330, 331, 360n, 408
earls of, see Pole, Ufford
Suger, abbot 99
Sun worship 5, 6, 9
Superbia 359–60, 363, 431
Surrey 50, 100, 355, 400
earls of, see Warenne
Surt 53
Sussex 9, 20, 30, 56, 65, 145, 179, 294, 304, 314, 324, 395, 403
Sutherland 36, 190
earl of 207
Sutton Hoo 22
Swabia 136, 196
Swan, name of 382
Swansea 53
Swiss Confederation 196
Swynford, Catherine 295–6

Taliesin 169
Tamworth, John de 168
Tancarville, family of 120
Tany, Luke de 185–6
Tarbes 277
Tarrant Crawford 125
Tartars 253
Tay, R. 74, 207
Teilo, St. 27
Temple Cressing 310
Temple Guiting 125
Teutons see Germans
Tewkesbury abbey 102, 245n
Thames, R. 8, 11, 11n, 20, 37, 38, 123, 130, 168, 294, 309, 314, 315, 316, 346, 348, 360, 398, 399, 402, 407
Thanet 38
Thetford 50
Thirty, battle of the 261
Thomas, the 227, 228
Thomas Aquinas, St. 136
Thomas of Woodstock, e. of Buckingham, duke of Gloucester (1385) 274, 311, 333, 336, 339, 340–1, 342–3, 344, 345, 346, 347, 348, 349, 351, 355, 356, 357, 358, 363
Thomond 362
Thorney 55
Thornton, Gilbert of 153

Thunor 22
Thurstan of York, abp. 79
Tiber, R. 12
Tichborne 135
Tilgarsley 257
Tinchebrai 76
Tin Islands 6
Tintern abbey 100, 171, 407, 419
Tiw 22, 22n
Toledo 394
Toller Monachorum 125
Tonnerre 275
Tores, William 416
Torwood 209
Toulouse 83, 238, 252, 264, 265
Touraine 79, 81, 268, 274, 277
Tournai 228, 229
Tours 268
Tramassene, battle of 266, 266n
Treason Act 346, 352
Trent, R. 40
Tresilian, Sir Robert, C. J. 347, 350, 351
Treville, Sir Baldwin 285
Trool, Loch 204
Troyes 290
Trussebut, family of 120
Tryvet, Sir Thomas 315
Tudor, house of 172
Turkey 367
Turnberry castle 204
Tuscany 407
Tweed, R. 195
Twenge, Sir Marmaduke de 215
Tyburn 350
Tyler, Wat 312, 314–5, 316, 318, 322, 325–7, 328, 329, 330, 379
Tylwyth teg 7
Tyne, R. 74, 353
Tynedale 208, 215

Uccello, Paolo 281, 281n
Ufford, Robert de, e. of Suffolk 275, 289
Ultima Thule 197
Uriconium 12

Valence, Aylmer de, e. of Pembroke 204, 215
Valence, William de, e. of Pembroke 416–7
Valhalla 23
Vale Royal abbey 178, 178n

Valle Crucis abbey 100, 171
Vannes 235
Varangian guard 70
Venice 254, 395, 403, 410
de Vere, family of 56, 120, 241
de Vere, John, e. of Oxford 246, 275
de Vere, Robert, e. of Oxford, duke of Ireland (1386) 339, 340, 342, 345, 346, 347, 348, 350, 357, 362
Verneuil 267, 423
Vernon, family of 120
Vertue, William 423–4
Vexin, the 83
Vienne, R. 268
Vikings 29, 36–48, 49, 52, 53–5, 60, 61, 70
Vincennes 152
Vintners Company 301
Vire, R. 267
Visconti, Bernabo 281, 287
Visconti, family of 359
Visigoths 14

Wadicourt 246
Wake, of Liddel, lord 256
Wales, see Subject Index
Walkfare, Sir Thomas 285
Wallace, William 189, 196, 199–201, 202, 203, 204, 206, 225, 284
Walsingham 387, 394
Walsingham, Alan of 420
Walsingham, Thomas 306
Walter, Hubert, J. 87, 92
Waltham 332
Waltham Cross 347
Walton 120, 229
Walworth, Sir William 315–16, 320, 325, 327–9
Wantage 39
Wapentakes 53, 89
Wareham 40
Warenne, family of 69, 241
Warenne, John de, e. of Surrey 185, 195, 199–200, 201
Warenne, John de, e. of Surrey (1307–47) 233
Wark 209
Warminster 42
Warwick, earls of, see Beauchamp
Wars of the Roses 3, 408, 423
Wash, the 20
Wastell, John 423

Waterford 118, 362
Watling Street 16, 48
Waverley abbey 100
Wayland the smith 22
Wear, R. 28, 426
Wearmouth 31
Wedmore, peace of 42
Wednesbury 22n
Weird 23
Wellington, duke of 264
Wells cathedral 410, 416, 422
Wensleydale 101
Weser, R. 16, 34
Wessex 28, 30, 33, 38, 39, 40, 41, 42, 43, 44, 45, 47, 50, 51, 52, 90, 246
House of 39, 49, 53
Western Isles 190
Westminster 75, 142, 173, 175, 180, 191, 191n, 230, 278, 318, 319, 367
abbey 55, 56, 80, 102, 142, 189, 191n, 207, 220, 256, 279, 324–5, 329, 351, 361, 368, 394, 414–5, 416, 417
St. Stephen's chapel 78, 325, 421
Henry VII's chapel 424
hall 55, 77–8, 87, 108, 131, 142, 149, 150–1, 156, 157, 159, 160, 163, 164, 168, 175, 201, 203, 233, 273, 343, 344, 345, 349, 351, 360, 365, 375, 398, 399, 422–3
palace 121, 220, 347, 349, 360, 398
Westminster, Provisions of 143, 147
Westminster, Statutes of 1275 149–50, 153–4
1285 153–4, 155–6
1290 153–4
Westmorland 83
Wexford 119
Weymouth see Melcolmbe Regis
Whitby 30, 30n, 31

Whitchurch Canonicorum 125
White, name of 382
White Company 281
Whitehall 363
White Ladies Aston 125
Whiteway 6
Whittlebury forest 191
Wilkinson, B. 333
Whittington, Richard 363
Wicklow 6
Wight, Isle of 20, 289, 294–5, 402
Wigmore 83
Wilfred, St. 28
William I, the Conqueror, k. of England, as duke of Normandy, 56, 59, 63–6; conquers England, 65–6; reorganises England, 66–74; character & appearance of, 64, 71, 75, 82; death of, 75; references to, 76, 78, 83, 84, 89, 93, 100, 101, 104, 129
William II, "Rufus", k. of England 75–6, 94, 104, 135, 360, 422
William the Lion, k. of Scots 120, 121, 190, 192, 198
William of Durham 137
William of Malmesbury 75, 99, 124
Wilton Diptych 325, 325n
Wiltshire 5, 41, 54, 87, 256, 258, 402
earl of, see Scrope
Winchcombe abbey 100
Winchelsea 227, 260, 276, 403
St. Thomas's 276
Winchester 44, 50, 52, 55, 72, 75, 80, 102, 157, 175, 388, 398, 399, 402, 407, 422, 431
college 422, 431
Winchester, Statutes of 221, 326, 332, 378
Windsor 219, 234, 236, 255, 259, 289, 315, 344,

360, 422
St. George's chapel 255, 259, 422
Winter, Stephen 164
Wisbech 50
Wishart, Robert, b. of Glasgow 202–3
Wittenberg 442
Woden 22, 22n
Wolf, name of 382
Woolard's Ash 51
Worcester 50, 102, 127, 161, 176, 178
Worcestershire 178, 395
Worms, Concordat of 105
Wraw, John 331
Wright, Thomas 437
Wrinehill 272
Wycliffe, John 438–42
Wye, R. 34, 78, 173, 186
Wykeham, William of, bishop of Winchester 287, 357, 388, 422, 431
Wynford, William 422
Wyre Forest 21

Yarmouth 403
Year Books 167, 167n
York 12, 34, 38, 50, 65, 70n, 71, 102, 198, 218, 313, 399, 401, 407, 415–6, 420, 422, 425
St. Mary's abbey 100
archbishops of 79, 112, 198, 343, 347, 350–1, see also Neville, Thurstan, Zouche
duke of, see Edmund of Langley
Yorkshire 8, 9, 26, 40, 71, 79, 100, 121, 257, 324, 329, 366, 368, 394, 408, 409, 438
Ypres 242, 243, 408
Yevele, Henry 360, 368, 422

Zouche, William, abp. of York 251, 255
Zulu wars 8
Zwin, R. 226, 227

403-873-8545 GAUS

Legend:
- ● Towns
- ⚔ Battlefields
- ✱ Castles
- ⌷ Monastic cathed[ral]
- ✝ Secular cathedra[l]
- ▢ Monasteries, colle[ges] churches and nunneries

ROSS

MORAY FIRTH

Urquhart

Inverness
Kinloss
Forres
MORAY
Banff
BUCHAN

Aberdeen

BADENOCH

LORN

ARGYLE

Montrose
Forfar
Dundee
Arbroath

Scone
Perth
St. Andrews
FIRTH OF TAY
Crail
Kinghorn
Dunfermline
L. LEVEN
OCHIL HILLS
Stirling
FIRTH OF FORTH
Bannockburn
Dirleton
Falkirk
Dunbar
Cardross
Glasgow
Leith
Halidon Hill
Dumbarton
CLYDE
Linlithgow
Edinburgh
Newbattle
Berwick
ARRAN
Lanark
TWEED
Dryburgh
Norham
Lindisfarne
Melrose
Kelso
Bamborough
Ayr
Jedburgh
Roxburgh
Alnwick
Turnberry

LOCH TROOL
Dalry
Lochmaben
Wark
Otterburn
CREE
Dumfries
Caerlaverock
Newcastle
GALLOWAY
Castle
TYNE
Tynemouth
Wigtown
Douglas
Lanercost
Hexham
Kirkcudbright
Carlisle
Durham
Hartlepool

Barnard Castle

Richmond
Scarbor[ough]
Jervaulx
Northallerton
ISLE OF MAN
Fountains
Ripon
Rievaulx
Furness
Bridlingto[n]
Lancaster
Boroughbridge
Myton
York
Bever[ley]
Kingston upon [Hull]
Selby
Preston
Pontefract

0   50
Miles

~ARTHUR BANKS~